THE POLITICS OF
ARISTOTLE

THE POLITICS OF
ARISTOTLE

TRANSLATED WITH

AN INTRODUCTION

NOTES AND

APPENDIXES BY

ERNEST BARKER

OXFORD UNIVERSITY PRESS
London   Oxford   New York

Library of Congress Catalogue Card Number: 58-11203
First published by the Clarendon Press, 1946
First issued as an Oxford University Press paperback, 1958

This reprint, 1972

Printed in the United States of America

PREFACE

THE original intention of the translator, when he began work in 1940—on the suggestion, and with the encouragement, of Sir Richard Livingstone—was to produce a simple and possibly shortened version of the *Politics* for the benefit of English readers who were not versed in the classics but were interested in the general history of social and political theory. The original intention has not been abandoned, but it has been partly modified and partly extended.

It has been modified in the sense that any idea of shortening the *Politics* has been dropped. Aristotle is too pithy to be made still pithier. It is expansion, rather than contraction, which the text of the *Politics* demands. Little could profitably have been omitted: a shortened version would have been but little shorter, and yet would have been incomplete; and the translator respected the original too much to sacrifice even its minor details. (Minor details, after all, go to make the character, and to determine the influence, of any great book.) The *Politics* is therefore presented to the reader *in extenso*.

The original intention has also been extended, and that in more than one way. In the first place it seemed desirable to illustrate the argument of the *Politics* by adding a translation of the various passages concerned with matters of politics which are to be found in the other writings of Aristotle—especially the *Ethics*, the *Rhetoric*, and the *Constitution of Athens*. This was the origin of the five appendixes at the end of the book, which attempt to complete and round off the review of political philosophy contained in the *Politics* itself, and thus to present the reader with a general conspectus of the whole body of Aristotle's work in the field of political inquiry. In the second place the translator, who began his study of the *Politics* nearly half a century ago, and dealt with its argument in the first book which he published,[1] was naturally moved, when the translation had been completed and revised, to add an introduction dealing with the life of Aristotle, the place of the *Politics* in his system, the substance of its argument, and some problems of its vocabulary. The introduction runs to some length; but its length may perhaps be excused by the plea that it is the last contribution which the writer can hope to make to the interpretation of the *Politics*.

Was a new translation necessary? The translator asked himself that question before he began his work; and he could only answer

---

[1] *The Political Thought of Plato and Aristotle*, 1906.

(but his answer was inevitably partial) that it was. The *Politics* is
a book which is needed—and needed in modern dress and a
modern English idiom—by the 'general reader' of all the Anglo-
Saxon world. It inspired the political thought of Aquinas: that
in turn inspired Hooker: Hooker in turn helped to inspire Locke;
and the thought of Locke, with all its ancestry, has largely inspired
the general thought both of Britain and America in the realm of
politics. More especially, the study of the *Politics* is a part of the
curriculum in a hundred and more universities, not only in
Britain and the United States, but also in the Dominions and
India. Many—indeed, one may safely say, the great majority—
of the students who attempt its study are students belonging
to the faculties of modern history, or of modern philosophy, or
of economics and politics, who have not been trained in the
classics, and must therefore study the *Politics* in some sort of
modern version. They need a version which is couched in a
modern style (such as a writer would use to-day in treating of
politics) and furnished with appropriate 'helps to study' which
will bring its substance home to their minds. The translator,
who was originally trained in the classics, but has spent most of
his life in teaching students in the faculty of modern history, has
accordingly drawn on his mixed experience in order to make a
translation intended primarily to meet the needs of students of
modern history, philosophy, and economics. This is not to say
that he has not sought to translate the Greek text with as exact
a scholarship as he could command, or that he has failed to remember the needs of the student of classical languages or the student
of ancient history. But he has designed the translation more particularly for the service of the numerous students of social and
political theory, in whatever faculty or department, who simply
desire to study the *Politics* (along with Plato's *Republic*) as the
fountain-head of that theory.

Some technical details should also be added for the guidance
of the reader. (1) The text from which the translation has been
made is that of Newman's edition,[1] but the translator has also
used the Teubner edition of Immisch.[2] He would also add that
he has checked his translation, again and again, with the revised
version of Jowett's translation in vol. x of the *Oxford Translation
of Aristotle*. (2) The reader will find in the text of the translation
a number of passages, marked by square brackets, which have
been added by the translator in order to elucidate the course of
the argument. They may seem numerous, and the frequent recur-
rence of square brackets may confuse the eye of the reader. But

[1] Oxford, 1887–1902. [2] Leipzig, 1909.

no addition has been made to the text unless it seemed to be necessary for a full understanding of the argument; and scholarship demanded that any addition, however small, should be clearly marked. Every addition is simply, and only, designed to bring out clearly the ideas implied in the actual text; and there is no addition which is not based on the words of Aristotle himself or those of his commentators. (3) The titles given to each book (like the divisions and sub-titles within each book) are the work of the translator. But they are based on the authority of Aristotle;· and in many cases they are simply translations of the phrases which he uses in the text of the *Politics*, e.g., in referring back to the contents of a previous book. (The analysis which precedes each chapter is entirely the work of the translator, and has no other authority.) (4) The explanatory footnotes are, of course, the work of the translator. The longer notes have been placed at the end of the relevant chapter, with a heading to indicate their contents, in order not to disturb the page with an excess of annotation. (5) At the top of each left-hand page the reader will find a statement of the book, chapter, and sections translated on the two pages facing him; and at the top of each right-hand page he will find a similar statement of the column (or columns) and the lines of the original Greek text of the same two pages, as that text is printed in the large two-column Berlin edition of the works of Aristotle by Bekker (vol. II, 1831). The beginning of each column of the Greek text of the Berlin edition is marked in thick type at the relevant point in the body of the translation itself. It is the habit of classical scholars to cite passages in Aristotle's works by the Berlin column and lines (as Plato's dialogues are cited by the page and the lettered divisions of the page in the Stephanus edition of 1578); and the translator hopes that the indications given, on the top of each right-hand page and in the body of the text, will form a sufficient guide for the tracing of such citations.

The translation has been a labour of love, and a permanent consolation of such leisure as was left to the writer, from the autumn of 1940 to the spring of 1945, among the anxieties and duties of war. It is a comfort, now that it is finished (*perfectum* in one sense, but in another *imperfectum . . . nec absoluto simile*), because it encourages a hope that something is here presented which may be of use to the students of the coming generation. For the wisdom of Aristotle grows on the mind as one ponders upon it; and the future will be all the better if it continues to digest his wisdom.

Walter Burley, reputed a Fellow of Merton College, is said to have dedicated a translation of the *Politics* (but was it, perhaps, a commentary?) to Richard de Bury, the Bishop of Durham and the author of *Philobiblon*, about the year 1330. History repeats itself in an old country; and six centuries later one who was some time a Fellow of Merton College presents again a work on the *Politics*, but presents it now to the Warden and Fellows of the College. It was Merton College which gave him the opportunity of a scholar's life, when it elected him to a Prize Fellowship in Classics in 1898. ('Surely that day', as Ascham wrote in his *Schoolmaster*, referring to his own election to a fellowship at another college, in another university, over 350 years earlier, 'was . . . *Dies natalis* to me for the whole foundation of the poor learning I have and of all the furtherance that hitherto elsewhere I have obtained.') It was in the College that he learned to know F. H. Bradley, Harold Joachim, John Burnet, and A. E. Taylor: it was during the years which he spent in the College that he was introduced by Harold Joachim to the Aristotelian circle which met round Professor Bywater. *Siquid huic libro insit boni, adscriptum sit*

CUSTODI ET SOCIIS
COLLEGII MERTONENSIS

E. B.

14 December 1945

NOTE

THE translator desires to record, with gratitude, the debt which he owes to Mr. A. E. Quene (sometime one of the principal regional medical officers of the Ministry of Health), who generously checked the references and cross-references in the original edition of 1946, and suggested a number of corrections and improvements which have been incorporated in the present printing.

E. B.

May 1948

CONTENTS

INTRODUCTION

TRANSLATION OF ARISTOTLE'S *POLITICS*

NOTE. *The titles of the different books, the division of each book into parts, and the headings of these parts, are due solely to the translator.*

APPENDIXES

INTRODUCTION

I

THE HISTORICAL BACKGROUND OF THE *POLITICS*

The life of Aristotle in its relation to the Politics, *and the substance of the* Politics *in its relation to contemporary history*

ARISTOTLE was born in the year 384 and died in the year 322. The place of his birth was Stagira, a small Greek colonial town, a little to the east of the modern Salonica, on the borders of the kingdom of Macedonia. The place of his birth and the fact that his father was court physician to a previous king of Macedonia may partly help to explain how he came to be tutor, in his middle age (about 342), to the young prince Alexander. Two facts in his parentage may conceivably have also affected the method and direction of his future studies. In the first place both of his parents were of Ionian origin; and remembering that the tendency of the Ionians was towards the scientific investigation of nature and its physical elements and living types, we are perhaps entitled to fancy—but it is little more than a fancy—that the blood in his veins carried with it a scientific strain, and impelled him towards that preoccupation with nature, or *physis*, which marks so much of his thought. In the second place—and here we are on firmer ground—his father was a doctor, practised in the art of dissection (which Aristotle afterwards pursued), and probably versed in the writings of the school of Hippocrates,[1] with their close observation of the symptoms of diseases, their 'case records', and their suggestions of remedial treatment. This may have helped to turn Aristotle's attention to biological studies, which he certainly began to pursue (as we shall presently see) about 345, and on which he wrote and lectured after 335. It may also help to explain the biological and medical trend in Books IV–VI of the *Politics*, where he classifies constitutions, as a biologist would classify living types, by the structure and arrangement of their parts, and where again, in the spirit of a doctor, he suggests methods of remedial treatment for the infirmities of different constitutions as described in the light of political 'case records'.

The active life of Aristotle naturally falls into three periods. There is the 'apprentice' period, which was spent in Athens and

---

[1] It is perhaps not fanciful to detect some reference to the famous Hippocratean treatise 'On Airs, Waters, and Places' in Book VII of the *Politics*. Chapter VII of that book deals with the relation between climate (or 'places') and character in much the same sense as the treatise; and chapter XI seems clearly indebted to the treatise in its references to the proper siting of cities to suit the prevalent 'airs' and to secure a good supply of 'waters'. Aristotle himself, as well as his father, may well have been versed in the writings of the school of Hippocrates.

lasted for the twenty years from 367 to 347. There is the 'journeyman' period, which was partly spent in the north-western corner of Asia Minor (in the Troad and on the island of Lesbos) and partly in Macedonia, and which lasted for some twelve years, from 347 to 335. Finally there is the period of the 'master', which was spent, like the 'apprentice' period, in Athens, and lasted from 335 to his death in 322.

§ 1. *The period down to 347.* The Athens to which Aristotle came in 367, at the age of seventeen, had begun to renew something of the life and vigour of the Periclean age of the previous century. Sparta, which had defeated and crushed Athens at the end of the Peloponnesian War (404), was already beginning to fail: she had been heavily defeated by Thebes at Leuctra in 371, and the Thebans under Epaminondas were already conducting a third invasion of the Peloponnese in the year in which Aristotle came to Athens. Meanwhile, as early as 377, the Athenians had already formed a second Athenian Confederacy, less wide-spread, indeed, than the old Confederacy of the fifth century, but with a much more generous concession to the autonomy of the confederates (as was shown in its double parliament, partly composed of the Athenian Council and Assembly, but partly also of a synod of representatives drawn from the allied states); and for the next fifty years—down to the battle of Amorgos which destroyed Athenian sea-power in the year of Aristotle's death—Athens was the mistress of the Aegaean. Mistress of the seas, she was also the trade-centre and the money-market of Greece, where Aristotle could study the problems of maritime trade, money, and interest;[1] but above all she was the general culture-centre of the Greek-speaking world— the home of Greek drama; the home of the standard speech which was becoming common to all educated Greeks; the home of the book trade for all Greece; and, above all, the home of a nascent university frequented by the Greek world. If, as the orator Isocrates said, 'Hellas had become a culture', Athens was the heart of Hellas.[2]

The nascent University of Athens was interested in many studies, and not least in the study of politics. Isocrates was the head of a school of political oratory which not only dealt with the

---

[1] The discussions of money and interest in Book I of the *Politics* (cc. IX–XI), and of maritime trade in Book VII (c.VI), have an Athenian background—if they have also, perhaps, the background of Aristotle's intercourse and talk with Hermias, the 'tyrant' and business magnate of Atarneus (see below, p. xv, n. 2).

[2] 'Our city', Isocrates said in his *Panegyricus* of 380, 'has left the rest of mankind so far behind, in thought and expression, that those who are her pupils have become the teachers of others. She has made the name of Greek no longer count as that of a stock, but as that of a type of mind: she has made it designate those who share with us in our culture, rather than those who share in a common physical type' (§ 50).

technique of oratory but also with the substance of statesmanship. But the great and cardinal school of Athens, which also handled politics, but handled it as a part of the general metaphysic of being and the general ethic of life, was the Academy of Plato. It was this Academy which Aristotle joined in 367; and for the next twenty years, from the age of seventeen to that of thirty-seven, he worked with the grey-haired but vigorous Plato (already a man of sixty in the year 367) during the last two decades of his long and active life. We may perhaps best conceive the position of Aristotle in Plato's school as that of a research student, who gradually grew into a research assistant. The researches of the Academy in which he would be concerned were wide and comprehensive. The study of the metaphysic of being involved research into 'ideas', in the Platonic sense of the word which meant the eternal realities or archetypes behind and beyond the world of sense; and here we may note that Plato, at this stage of his development, was tending to something in the nature of a mathematical mysticism, which identified 'ideas' with numbers. The study of the ethic of human life involved an inquiry into natural religion (and here again we may note that this inquiry was also tending to turn in the direction of mathematical astronomy); but it also involved, and it involved more particularly, an inquiry into politics.

That inquiry was twofold: it was practical as well as theoretical. (Politics was always, to the Greeks, an 'art' as well as a 'science'.) On the practical side of politics Plato was deeply concerned—and we may imagine that the members of the Academy would share his concern—in the current politics of Syracuse. Seeking, as he always sought, to make philosophy a pole-star of conduct and 'a way of life', and anxious to guide and instruct by its light the actual rulers of states, he had gone to Syracuse in 367—the very year of Aristotle's coming to the Academy—to advise its tyrant Dionysius II. Little result came of the journey, or of a later journey which he made in 361; but he still continued, as we know from the Platonic *Epistles*, to take a lively interest in the troubled affairs of Syracuse, and especially in the ill-starred fortunes of Dion, his friend and disciple, the would-be liberator who failed to liberate his native city from its factions. This interest lasted steadily down to the year 351; and though it is only a guess, it is a fair and legitimate guess that Aristotle must have watched with a close attention those sixteen years of preoccupation with Syracusan affairs,

> While the lunar beam
> Of Plato's genius, from its lofty sphere,
> Fell round him in the grove of Academe.[1]

[1] Wordsworth's poem on Dion.

Even the theoretical work of the Academy, during the period of Aristotle's student days, had its practical side. The Academy was a school of political training, from which statesmen and legislators issued. It was largely concerned with legal studies; and Plato's great effort, in his last years, was the composition of the twelve books of the *Laws*, which were published in the year after his death (346). The *Laws* had a large inductive basis, alike in the general record of Greek history and in the body of current Greek law; and here again we may fairly guess that Aristotle, with his inductive mind and his natural bent for collecting and cataloguing records,[1] may well have joined in the preparation of this large basis. The influence of the *Laws* may certainly be traced in more than one passage of the *Politics*, and especially in the course of its seventh book. Nor shall we perhaps be wrong in ascribing to this period the development of those views of justice, of equity, and of law, which Aristotle was afterwards to enunciate in the *Ethics* and the *Rhetoric* as well as in the *Politics*.

'Such conversation under Attic shades' ended with Plato's death in 347. The death of Plato was bound, in any case, to mark a break in Aristotle's life; but two events conspired to make the break definite. One was the almost total destruction of Stagira, his birthplace, by the army of Philip of Macedon, which left him without a home; the other, and the more important, was the passing of Plato's mantle and the headship of the Academy to a successor who was not acceptable to Aristotle or to some of his friends. He therefore left Athens with one of these friends, Xenocrates (who was in later days to become the head of the Academy), and moved across the Aegaean to settle in the town of Assus. He carried with him memories of Plato: indeed he went to join friends of Plato. He took with him the spirit of the teaching of Plato's *Laws*; and however far he might depart in future years from the spirit of Plato's philosophy (and perhaps he departed less than critics are apt to think who construct an abstract Plato, and forget the actual Plato, whom Aristotle had actually known, immersed in Syracusan affairs and the practical study of Greek jurisprudence), he retained a deep and lasting veneration for the master, of whom he afterwards wrote, in some memorable elegiac verses, that 'he was a man whom the bad have not even the right to praise—the only man, or the first, to show clearly by his own life, and by the reasonings of his discourses, that to be happy is to be good'.

§ 2. *The period from 347 to 335.* The settlement in Assus in 347, which began the 'journeyman' period of Aristotle's life, was itself

[1] See Appendix V. iii, and section II. 2 of this Introduction.

due to Platonic attraction.[1] When Aristotle and Xenocrates crossed the Aegaean to the Troad, they did not go at random. They went to join two other Platonists, Erastus and Coriscus, who had kept up for some time past a correspondence with the Academy, of which they had once been members. These two Platonists had come to the Academy from the little town of Scepsis, which lay inland, behind the Troad, to the north-east of Mount Ida; and it was to this little town that they had returned (some time before 350) with the lessons they had learned in the Academy, and with memories of their master's lively concern in the affairs of Syracuse and his steady effort to guide and instruct its tyrant Dionysius II. Almost in imitation of their master—or perhaps history simply repeated itself—they had formed a connexion with a neighbouring tyrant, Hermias of Atarneus, a city which lay to the south of Mount Ida and almost exactly opposite to Mytilene in the island of Lesbos. Hermias was a eunuch, who had risen from being a slave (and perhaps a banker's clerk) to become the owner of mining property on Mount Ida;[2] and with his wealth he had bought the title of prince from the Persian king and established his power in Atarneus and the neighbourhood. Erastus and Coriscus attracted him to Platonic studies, and especially to the study of the art of politics. They advised him as Plato had sought to advise Dionysius II: in particular they advised him to make his tyranny milder in order that it might last longer.[3] They were rewarded by him with the gift of Assus: they moved southward to Assus from their own native town of Scepsis; and it was thus to Assus that Aristotle and Xenocrates naturally came to join their fellow Platonists, in the course of the year 347, bringing with them the latest teaching of Plato, and especially the teaching of his latest work, the *Laws*.

The four Platonists made Assus something of a new 'colonial' Academy, which attracted students from the neighbourhood. Aristotle himself entered into close relations of personal friendship with Hermias; he married his niece and adopted daughter;

[1] In this section the writer is largely indebted to Professor Jaeger's *Aristoteles* Part II, c. I.

[2] Perhaps the career of Hermias, and the close connexion formed by Aristotle with this ex-slave who afterwards became a man of business and affairs, may help to explain the chapters on slavery and the economics of 'acquisition' in Book I of the *Politics*. There is a specific reference to mining in I. c. XI, § 5.

[3] Aristotle was later to give similar advice to tyrants in a notable passage of the *Politics* (Book V, c. XI, §§ 17–34). It may be added that the sixth of the Platonic *Epistles* (if we regard it as authentic)—an epistle sent to Hermias and Erastus and Coriscus, perhaps between 350 and 347—suggests to Hermias that 'neither abundance of cavalry or of other military resources, nor the acquisition of gold, could add more to his strength in all directions than would the gaining of steadfast friends of uncorrupted character' (*Thirteen Epistles of Plato*, translated by L. A. Post, p. 128).

and down to the end of his life he cherished his memory. During the three years in which he stayed at Assus (347–344) we may well imagine him discussing politics with a little circle of students (he was already a man of forty, who must have had many memories of political discussions in Plato's Academy): we may even imagine him lecturing on politics; and it is possible that there may be strata in the *Politics*, or at any rate views and ideas, which go back as far as this period. In any case it is a legitimate conjecture that Aristotle added to the knowledge of politics which he brought from the Academy a new body of more empirical knowledge which was due to his intercourse with Hermias. He could not only learn something of business and general 'economics' from Hermias' experience of banking and of the management of mining property: he could also study, at first hand, the nature of personal one-man rule (or 'monarchy'); and as Hermias had foreign connexions as far afield as Macedonia, he would naturally be led to appreciate the importance of foreign relations and foreign policy—a matter to which we find him devoting attention (and criticizing Plato for having omitted to notice) in several passages of the *Politics*.[1]

It is possible that the circle at Assus included Callisthenes, the nephew of Aristotle, who was afterwards to accompany Alexander of Macedon on his Asiatic campaigns: it is possible also that it included Theophrastus, from the neighbouring island of Lesbos— the author of the famous *Characters* which formed a model for a number of English writers in the seventeenth century, but also a natural historian and a botanist, and the successor afterwards of Aristotle as the head of the Lyceum in Athens. It may have been on the suggestion of Theophrastus that Aristotle moved, about 344, to the island of Lesbos and settled at Mytilene: it may also have been under his influence—but the influence was also in Aristotle's own blood—that he now turned for two years to the study of biology, and specially marine biology. The Greek philosophers of the fourth century B.C. took all knowledge to be their province; and the philosopher of politics was equally (at this period of Aristotle's life perhaps even more) the philosopher of nature and 'the things of the sea'.[2]

These two years in the island of Lesbos (344–342) were followed

---

[1] Book II, c. VI, §§ 7–8: ibid. c. VII, § 14 (see also the note): Book IV, c. IV, §§ 10–11; and especially Book VII, c. VI and c. XI.

[2] On Aristotle the biologist see Sir D'Arcy Thompson's chapter on Natural Science in *The Legacy of Greece*. He notes, p. 144, that 'Aristotle spent two years, the happiest perhaps of all his life, . . . by the sea-side in the island . . .: here it was that he learned the great bulk of his natural history, in which, wide and general as it is, the things of the sea have from first to last a notable predominance'.

by a great and sudden change, which carried Aristotle into that association with Alexander the Great on which the imagination of posterity (and especially of the Middle Ages) has more particularly dwelt. He was summoned to Pella, the capital of Macedonia, by Philip of Macedon, and here for some six years (342–336) he acted as the tutor of Philip's son—a boy of 13 when he came; a young man of nineteen when he left. We need not concern ourselves with the cause which led to his summons to Pella—whether it was the old Macedonian connexions of his family, or whether it was the influence of Hermias, who had entered into some sort of connexion with Philip of Macedon, and who may conceivably, in the course of the connexion, have commended Aristotle to his notice.[1] The more serious question—if only there were sufficient material for an answer—is what Aristotle did at Pella, and in what way he taught, and how far he influenced, his pupil. But before we approach that question there is still one fact to be recorded about Hermias which undoubtedly affected Aristotle deeply, and may even have had some effect on his teaching of Alexander. In 341 Hermias was treacherously captured by a Persian general, taken to Susa, and executed. Aristotle celebrated his memory in a lyric poem (as he had celebrated the memory of Plato in elegiac verse), in which he coupled his name with those of Hercules and the great twin brethren as an example of toiling and suffering *Aretē*;[2] and he also testified his affection in an inscription which he wrote for the cenotaph of Hermias at Delphi, recording the treachery of his execution by the Persian king. The effect of the fate of Hermias on his ideas and his teaching may perhaps be traced in passages of the *Politics* which suggest that the 'barbarians' are the natural subjects of the Greeks,[3] and in a fragment of an epistle or exhortation addressed to Alexander, in which he advised him to act as 'leader' of the Greeks but as 'master' of the barbarians.[4] These are lessons which the fortunes of Hermias may have inspired him to teach Alexander (already naturally inclined

---

[1] Professor Jaeger, in the work previously cited, suggests that Philip, already projecting the Eastern expedition which Alexander afterwards achieved, was anxious for a bridge-head on the other side of the Dardanelles; that Hermias, with his territory convenient for this purpose, was thus brought into touch with him; and that Aristotle, as an associate of Hermias and connected with him by marriage, went to Pella to make the touch closer and to forward the Eastern project. The suggestion may have some basis; but it is highly speculative, and it presupposes a Balkan style of diplomacy which belongs more to the twentieth century A.D. than to the fourth century B.C. On the actual facts of the connexion between Hermias and Philip see W. W. Tarn in the *Cambridge Ancient History*, vol. vi, p. 23.

[2] Rose, *Fragmenta*, 675; see Book VII, c. I, § 11, note.

[3] Book I, c. II, § 4, and c. VI, § 6; Book VII, c. VII, §§ 1–3.

[4] See Appendix V. II and IV.

to receive them); but they are also (it must be confessed) lessons which any Greek of the period might have taught him in any case.

We have little evidence about the actual teaching which Aristotle gave to Alexander in the years which he spent at Pella. He was curiously conjoined in his influence on his pupil with Alexander's fierce and stormy mother, the queen Olympias. It was a conjunction of 'a philosopher who taught that moderation alone could hold a state together and . . . a woman to whom any sort of moderation was unknown'.[1] Did the master and his pupil, when they were at work, do more than read the *Iliad* together (in a revised text which Aristotle had prepared, and Alexander kept under his pillow); and was the master's instruction confined to teaching his pupil the example of Achilles and the lesson of ambitious heroism,

> Always to be the best and eminent over all others?[2]

Or was Aristotle perhaps carrying on his own studies, and conducting something of a school, in which Alexander may have been an associate, and where he may have been introduced to ethics, some politics, and even some metaphysics? It is difficult to return any certain answer. It is still more difficult to say whether any parts of the *Politics* were influenced by the association of Aristotle with Alexander: whether, for example, the discussion of absolute kingship, at the end of Book III of the *Politics*, and the figure of the king who is so transcendent in *Aretē* that he is like a god among men, are merely theoretical reminiscences of Platonic discussions in the Academy or actual memories of Alexander at Pella.[3]

Some facts, however, are certain, or at any rate tolerably certain. One is that Aristotle wrote for Alexander two treatises or political pamphlets now lost—a treatise 'on kingship', which may have been sent to Alexander at his accession, and possibly at his request, as something in the nature of a programme for his reign; and a treatise 'concerning colonies', which is also said to have been written at Alexander's request, and which may belong to the period of his foundation of Greek colonial cities in the East.[4] Another fact, which suggests that Aristotle had interested his pupil in scientific investigation as well as in Homer and also, perhaps, in Greek philosophy, is that Alexander assigned a sum of 800 talents from his Eastern spoils for Aristotle's researches. Indeed he had already from the very beginning of his conquests (like Napoleon in Egypt two thousand years afterwards) associated the

---

[1] W. W. Tarn, *C.A.H.*, vol. vi, p. 353.   [2] *Iliad*, vi. 208.
[3] See Book III, c. xv, § 3 and note.
[4] Appendix V, II. On the Greek colonial cities of Alexander's foundation see Tarn, *C.A.H.*, vol. vi, pp. 429–31.

scientist with the soldier; and geography, anthropology, zoology, and botany were all made to profit by the progress of his army. If Aristotle did not himself accompany Alexander to the East, as he is made to do in the medieval French romances of Alexander, he sent his nephew Callisthenes in his stead; and Callisthenes was followed by other philosophers, and by scientists who 'among other things collected information and specimens for Aristotle'.[1]

In the later years of his stay in Macedonia Aristotle can have seen but little of his pupil. In 340, at the age of sixteen, he was governing the kingdom in his father's absence; in 338, at the age of eighteen, he was commanding one of the wings of the Macedonian army at the battle of Chaeronea. It is possible that Aristotle may have been living and working, during some of these later years, near Stagira, where we know that his associate Theophrastus possessed a property; and it is recorded that Alexander, on his accession, had Stagira restored and reconstructed at his desire. But there was no reason which could impel him to make any permanent stay in Macedonia, or at Stagira. Athens was his magnet, and he found Macedonia cold (at any rate a jest attributed to him makes 'the great cold' the cause of his going, as 'the great king' had been the cause of his coming); and to Athens he accordingly returned, somewhere about 335, to begin the third and last period of his life, as the master of a school.

§ 3. *The period after 335.* He came to Athens to found a school of his own, the Lyceum, by the side of the Platonic Academy, now under the headship of his old associate, Xenocrates, with whom he had gone to Assus a dozen years before. The Athens to which he returned was still, in form, a free city; but it was not the old free city which he had left in 347. The battle of Chaeronea, 'fatal to liberty', had made Greece a Macedonian protectorate, with its city-states associated under the protecting power in the League of Corinth. The dominant figure in Greece, for the rest of Aristotle's life, was the Macedonian Antipater, who had been left by Alexander to govern Macedonia and supervise Greek affairs. Antipater has been described as a narrow and unimaginative man,

---

[1] Tarn, *C.A.H.*, vol. vi, pp. 359–60; cf. also p. 353. The medieval romances of Alexander, with their curious pictures of the relations between Alexander and Aristotle, are based on a remarkable flowering of legend which has been examined by M. Paul Meyer and Sir E. Wallis Budge. One of the most curious flowers is the medieval *fabliau* called *Le Lai d'Aristote*, which tells the charming story of Aristotle and the Hindu princess from whom he sought to wean Alexander's affections, and recounts how

Aristotes, qui tout savoit
Quanques droite clergie avoit,

was defeated by her wiles. (The story is carved on the cap of one of the piers of the nave of the church of St. Pierre at Caen.)

who had little liking for his master's policy of treating the Greeks
as free allies, and perhaps no liking at all for the League which was
intended to ensure the fulfilment of that policy, but who was
prepared, as a loyal soldier and a capable administrator, to enforce
the terms of the League on his own interpretation of their meaning.
It was a legal and conservative interpretation: he wished to stand
by the propertied classes against any threat of social upheaval; and
his instincts inclined him to lend support to the cause of oligarchy.[1]
Antipater's ideas and policies have some bearing on Aristotle's life,
and may even have affected the development of his political views
and theories. The two men had already become close friends in
Macedonia: they kept in touch, and in correspondence, during all
the last period of Aristotle's life;[2] and we may almost say that
Antipater, from 335 onwards, took the place once held by Hermias
in his affections. It is curious to find Aristotle once more connected with a representative of the ideas of personal rule and
efficient government, and connected with him in personal friendship and close intimacy. We may well imagine to ourselves that
Aristotle and his Lyceum were regarded in contemporary Athens
as standing under Antipater's protection, and even as committed
to his policy; and we can understand that a modern historian
should describe Aristotle as 'foreign in feeling to the Athenian
democrats' among whom he lived, as having 'nothing in common'
with the contemporary Athenian statesman Lycurgus, who was
seeking to restore the strength and spirit of his city, and as a
'lonely figure' who, 'though in, was not of Athens' and was 'out
of touch with Athenian democracy'.[3]

It is probably true that Antipater and Aristotle had some political views in common: it is even possible that Aristotle's advocacy
of a moderate 'polity' which would do justice to the propertied
classes may reflect the general trend of Antipater's policy.[4] But
we should be doing a grave injustice to the breadth and the balance
of Aristotle's views, and especially to the depth of his understanding of democratic ideas, if we failed to notice some other facts—
facts at least as important as his connexion with Antipater—which
show that he was alive and responsive to the current movement of
Athenian democracy during his last years in Athens. We have not

[1] Tarn, *C.A.H.*, vol. vi, pp. 438–9.
[2] On their correspondence, which is of peculiar interest, see Appendix V.
IV, *ad finem*.
[3] Tarn, *C.A.H.*, vol. vi, pp. 442, 443.
[4] See below, p. xxiv. A curious reference by Aristotle to the 'one man, . . .
of all who have hitherto been in a position of ascendancy, who has allowed himself to be persuaded to agree to the setting up of such a type', may conceivably be
a reference to Antipater: see Book IV, c. XI, § 19 and note.

only to remember that he was writing a work on the constitution and the constitutional history of Athens—a work which shows both sympathy and understanding—at the time when he was teaching politics in the Lyceum. We are also bound to notice that there are references in the *Politics* which show that he was following with a close attention the measures and the reforms of the contemporary Athenian statesman Lycurgus.

Lycurgus was the most prominent of Athenian statesmen from 338 to 326. He was an old pupil of Plato, and a friend of Xenocrates, the friend of Aristotle, who was now at the head of the Platonic Academy. The party which Lycurgus led was, at any rate in theory, a democratic party, composed of the men who had previously followed the orator Demosthenes; and its general aim was to reinvigorate Athens and make her capable of playing once more a leading part in the affairs of Greece. But though he professed to be a democrat, Lycurgus looked with a friendly eye on Spartan ideas and ideals, and he had a regard to the interests of the propertied classes. He has been described as 'a financier with a moral mission';[1] and he certainly seems to have attempted a moral reformation. The walls of Athens were strengthened, with stone instead of brick, and with an 'anti-ram' ditch to cope with the new siege-engines of the day; and the Athenian fleet was equipped with battleships of four and even five banks of oars, in addition to the standard triremes. A new stadium was completed, and the old gymnasium was renovated; and on this material basis Lycurgus introduced a scheme for a two-year course of compulsory military training for the Athenian youth—a scheme half-Spartan in its method, but more than half-Athenian, and very largely Platonic, in its inspiration.[2] An attempt at a religious reformation accompanied this scheme; and a notable law was passed to prohibit Athenian citizens from purchasing as slaves any free men captured in war. These were all measures which Aristotle could not but notice; one of them—the course of compulsory military training—is described in his *Constitution of Athens*; and it is no licence of conjecture to suggest that some of the reforms of Lycurgus may underly a number of the suggestions made in the course of his sketch of an ideal state in Book VII of the *Politics*.[3]

[1] Tarn, *C.A.H.*, vol. vi, p. 440.
[2] For a description of this scheme see Aristotle's own account in the Constitution of Athens, Appendix IV. B. 5.
[3] Some instances may be given. (1) The system of military training of the Athenian youth is assumed in Book VII, c. XII, § 8. (2) The repair of the walls of Athens, and the measures taken against modern siege-engines, are perhaps the basis of Book VII, c. XI, §§ 8–12. (3) The new stadium and the renovation of the old gymnasium may equally be the bases of some of the suggestions made

Lycurgus lost his influence in Athens about 326. Two years before, in distant Asia, an event had happened which, like his policy, was also to affect the political outlook of Aristotle and his colleagues, and to divorce them, if not from Antipater, at any rate from Alexander himself. If, as has just been suggested, it is possible that Aristotle felt some attraction towards the ideas and measures of Lycurgus of Athens, it seems certain that he began to lose sympathy with the ideas and policies of Alexander of Macedon when, in the year 328, his own nephew and pupil Callisthenes was executed by Alexander's orders. Callisthenes, as we have seen, had accompanied Alexander on his Eastern expedition: he had even been his minister of information, and had championed his divinity; but when Alexander sought to introduce a Persian etiquette of humble prostration at the feet of his majesty, Callisthenes revolted. Whether or no he was implicated in a conspiracy formed among Alexander's pages, to whom he is said to have talked about the virtue of tyrannicide, he was treated as an accomplice in it, and put to death accordingly. The effect of his execution was a revulsion of feeling in the Lyceum; and it became the tradition of Aristotle's school—at any rate after his death—to decry the achievement of Alexander and to ascribe his success to chance. Plutarch, centuries afterwards, was to protest against the tradition of the school, and to seek to vindicate Alexander's memory from its 'malice'.[1]

Still the associate of the Macedonian Antipater (and yet an associate who had watched with interest the work of Lycurgus of Athens), but now divorced in feeling from Alexander of Macedon, Aristotle was fated, in the last few years of his life, to sail troubled political seas, vexed by contending cross-currents. In the confused years after 326 Athens was beginning to drift towards a breach with Alexander, now absorbed in far distant affairs by the waters of the Indus and the Euphrates. The drift had already begun when Nicanor, the son-in-law of Aristotle, came to Greece, in the autumn of 324, with decrees from Alexander demanding divine

in Book VII, c. xii. (4) Finally, the law prohibiting the purchase of prisoners of war as slaves may be the basis of Book I, c. vi, § 5 (see the note).

It should be added that if Aristotle was perhaps influenced by the reforms of Lycurgus, those reforms, in their turn, would seem to have been influenced by the teaching of Plato in the *Laws*: for example, the system of compulsory military training may well have been inspired by a passage in Book VI of the *Laws* (760–2). Lycurgus had not attended the Academy in vain.

[1] Tarn, *C.A.H.*, vol. vi, pp. 398–400. But it should be added that the only evidence we possess for any divergence between Aristotle himself and his old pupil is the fact that Alexander acted in the opposite spirit to that of Aristotle's advice that he should deal with the Greeks as 'leader' and with non-Greeks as 'master', preferring to treat both alike in an impartial spirit of equality. See p. lix infra and Appendix V. iv, *ad initium.*

honours for himself and restoration for all the exiles who had been banished in late years from the Greek cities. Athens consented to pay divine honours, though not without opposition: she was more deeply stirred by the demand for the restoration of exiles. Matters were in this pass when news came, in the summer of 323, that Alexander was dead. The current which had been setting for some time past against the Macedonian hegemony at once swept Athens away: the Athenian Assembly declared war; and Athens proclaimed the cause of the general liberty of Greece and the expulsion of the Macedonian garrisons from the cities in which they had been placed. The war was a war against Antipater; and Aristotle, Antipater's friend, fled from Athens, taking refuge in Chalcis, a city in the island of Euboea in which his mother had been born, and which, in earlier times, had itself been the mother-city and founder of Stagira. In his exile he was attacked for his association with Hermias and his loyalty to his memory. It is not clear whether the overt attack on his old association with Hermias was a veil and a pretext for a covert attack on his recent association with Antipater; we only know, from the evidence of Athenaeus and Diogenes Laertius, that he was indicted in Athens for the lyric poem which he had written in memory of Hermias and for the 'impiety' of offering sacrifice to his *manes*.[1] Delphi, too, which had previously paid him honour for his catalogue of the victors in the Pythian games held under its auspices, now revoked the honours—remembering the inscription he had written for the cenotaph of Hermias which stood in its precincts.

Amid these attacks, and during the course of the war which raged in 322, Aristotle died and was buried at Chalcis.[2] The record of his will has been preserved, and some of its details are worthy of mention for their bearing on the character of Aristotle and the teaching of the *Politics*. Antipater was made his executor; and he directed that the remains of his wife, the adopted daughter of Hermias, should be brought and buried at his side. He left instructions for the emancipation of a woman slave and three men slaves, with the children of one of the three; he asked that none of his household slaves should be sold, and he directed that when they had attained a due age they should be emancipated if they so

---

[1] Rose, *Fragmenta*, 645. See also Appendix V, IV, *ad finem*.

[2] Over fifty years ago Sir Charles Walston discovered a tomb, which he believed to be the tomb of Aristotle, on the sacred way between Chalcis and Eretria. The tomb contained, among other things, two styluses, a pen, a signet-ring, and some terra-cottas (one of the figure of a man 'in the attitude of a philosopher'); it also contained a sepulchral stone with the inscription 'Biote the daughter of Aristotle'. The discoverer believed that some fragments of a skull which were found in the tomb were fragments of Aristotle's skull. See the *Corpus Inscriptionum Graecarum*, vol. xii, fasc. ix, s.v. 'Eretria'.

deserved. These dispositions serve as a commentary on the general view of slavery propounded in the first book of the *Politics*; and they may also remind us that Aristotle practised himself what he preached in Book VII, where he recommends that the promise of emancipation should be offered to slaves as a reward for good service.

This sketch of the life of Aristotle, and of its political background, would be imperfect if it did not include some reference to two political developments which came after Aristotle's death. They both show, or at any rate they both suggest, that the influence of his teaching continued to be felt for many years after he was gone; and they may lead us to think that his theory, as it had perhaps been acted upon by Athenian life and experience, was also destined in turn to act upon that life and experience. The first of these developments was the constitutional settlement made by Antipater at Athens in the course of 321, after he had achieved a complete triumph and crippled Athenian sea-power by the victory at Amorgos in the middle of 322. It was a settlement made in the year after Aristotle's death; but the fragments of his correspondence with Antipater show that he had been in touch with him to the end, even while he was living in exile in Chalcis.[1] The nature of the settlement corresponds with views enunciated in the *Politics* and the *Constitution of Athens*; and Antipater's political measures may be said to reflect the political ideas of Aristotle, as they also continue, in some measure, the trend of the policy of Lycurgus of Athens. The franchise was restricted to the possessors of 2,000 drachmas, which meant, in effect, that it was limited to the classes which were liable to infantry service; and the number of Athenian citizens, once upwards of 40,000, was thus reduced to 9,000. This was in the nature of the institution of a 'polity', composed of the middle classes who possessed a moderate property and some military qualification: it may also be called, as it is called by Diodorus Siculus, a restoration of the Solonian constitution, or a return to 'ancestral democracy'.[2] The dikasteries, or popular courts, became a shadow of themselves; and the system of payments by the state

---

[1] Appendix V. IV, *ad finem*.

[2] The effect of this measure was to disfranchise over 20,000 citizens. The whole of the system now introduced naturally brings to the mind a number of passages in the *Politics*, but more especially (1) the general theory of the 'polity', as a constitution of 'the mean', which mixes oligarchy and democracy and is based on the middle classes (Book III, c. VII, §§ 3-4; Book IV, cc. VII-IX and especially c. XI), and (2) the references to Solonian or 'ancestral' democracy (Book II, c. XII, § 2, and Book V, c. V, § 10).

It may be noted that the *Constitution of Athens*, as well as the *Politics*, draws attention to the moderate form of constitution and to Solonian or 'ancestral' democracy: see Appendix IV. A. 4, and notes.

was further reduced by the cessation of the distribution of sur-
pluses from the theoric fund. Possibly the democratic system of
election by lot now ceased; and the general movement of the constitution was towards that mixture of democracy with oligarchy
which Aristotle, always an advocate of the mean, had advocated as
the essence of his conception of the 'polity'.

The second political development, after Aristotle's death, which
shows or suggests the influence of his teaching, is connected with
the name of Demetrius of Phalerum, who governed Athens for
Cassander (the son of Antipater, and the successor to his father's
position in Greece) from 317 to 307. Demetrius was something
of a student, a member of the Aristotelian school, and a friend of
Theophrastus, the friend and associate of Aristotle who succeeded
his master as the head of the school in the Lyceum. 'Under him',
Dr. Tarn writes, 'Aristotle's school was all-powerful: . . . he translated into law many of the ideas of Aristotle and Theophrastus;
the basis of his legislation was the dogma that citizens cannot make
themselves, but must be moulded by the legislator, the source of
all the troubles between the idealist philosophies and the democracy.'[1] He regulated the dress and public deportment of women,
and appointed a board of officers for the supervision of women's
conduct.[2] He vested the supervision of the laws in a body of seven
guardians of the laws, who so controlled the assembly that it
scarcely passed a decree during the ten years of his ascendancy.[3]
He was a philosophic despot, but generally benevolent: he enforced
a general amnesty, and even tolerated the presence of extreme
democrats in the city. But when he was expelled from Athens in
307 by his namesake Demetrius 'the Besieger', a reaction naturally
followed. The officers for the supervision of women and the
guardians of the laws disappeared: a law was passed prohibiting

[1] *C.A.H.*, vol. vi, p. 496. Dr. Tarn's pregnant words deserve the deepest
consideration. They indicate admirably the cleavage between the 'pedanto-
cracy' of the Academy (and even of the Lyceum) and the self-reliant democracy
of the Athenian Assembly and popular courts, with its trust in popular judgement and in the free play of discussion. At the same time it is not clear that
Aristotle himself was a 'pedantocrat', even if Demetrius was. It is true that in
the two books on the ideal state (VII–VIII) he assumes the presence of a moulding
legislator. But it is also true that in Book III, and especially in c. XI of that
book, he shows a profound appreciation of the value of popular judgement;
and even in his ideal state the government is vested in all the citizens when once
they attain the age of maturity.

[2] Such officers are mentioned by Aristotle—but only mentioned, and not
advocated—in two passages of the *Politics* (IV, c. XV, § 3, and VI, c. VIII, §§ 22–3).

[3] 'Guardians of the law' are mentioned by Aristotle in Book III, c. XVI, § 4
(see the note): they are also mentioned, but only incidentally, in Book IV and
Book VI. In the *Laws* of Plato a body of 37 'guardians of the law' forms the
general executive of the state; but this is a different system from the 7 guardians
of the laws in the constitutional scheme of Demetrius.

any philosopher from teaching in Athens without the licence of the assembly and the council; and Theophrastus was driven into exile. If the law had been permanent, and political speculation had been made subject henceforth to political regulation, Athens would have lost her intellectual primacy. It attests the wisdom of the Athenians that the law was repealed within a year (306), as contrary to the legal principle of freedom of associations,[1] and that Theophrastus was simultaneously recalled. The incursion of the Aristotelian school into politics had ended; but the school itself was still left free to speculate as it would, and to teach all comers on all things, human as well as natural.

[1] The legal principle was laid down in a law of Solon, preserved in a fragment of Gaius which is inserted in the *Digest*. It enacted that, among other associations, the associations called *thiasoi* (to which the philosophic schools belonged—see p. xxxii below) should be free to make their own dispositions if they did not clash with the rules of law (Vinogradoff, *Historical Jurisprudence*, vol. ii, p. 120). The special law of 307 was accordingly attacked as 'unconstitutional', or *paranomos*, because it contravened the standing law of Solon; and it was in this way that it was 'repealed' in 306.

II

THE SCIENTIFIC BACKGROUND OF THE *POLITICS*

The personality of Aristotle; the Lyceum and its studies; the character of Aristotle's writings; the composition and structure of the Politics

FROM this sketch of the life of Aristotle, which has here been treated in its relation to politics and the general political background of contemporary history, we may turn to the man himself, the nature of his school and its studies, the scope and style of his writings, and finally, and more especially, the composition and structure of the *Politics*.

§ 1. *The personality of Aristotle and the characteristics of his approach to politics*. The personality of Aristotle is hidden behind his works.[1] Tradition makes him speak with a lisp and pay attention to dress. The busts, which seem to be authentic, show firm lips and intent eyes. He was a man of affairs who knew the ways of courts and the minds of such different statesmen as Alexander, Antipater, and Hermias. He had at its height the invincible curiosity of the Greek mind; and the record of his life also leaves the impression of a generous temper. His will shows him concerned not only for the emancipation of his slaves, but also for the welfare of all his relatives and connexions; and there are passages in his writings which show him struggling upwards from the curiosity of the scientist to the vision of the contemplative.[2]

What were the characteristics which he brought to the study of politics? He had not only a large experience of affairs (added to, or issuing in, a wide humanity which made him think that nothing human, however 'perverse' it might seem, was alien from his studies): he had also an inductive habit of mind, which made him accumulate and catalogue all the available data. The reader of the *Politics* will notice this habit of mind at work throughout—from the eleventh chapter of the First book (with its record of the financial strokes of Thales of Miletus and 'the man of Sicily') and the whole of the Second book (with its exhaustive catalogue of the ideal states of Greek theory and practice) to the series of books, the Fourth, Fifth, and Sixth, which are so abundantly 'documented' that the trees occasionally obscure the wood. Perhaps, as we have already had reason to notice, this inductive habit of mind had already been formed in the Academy and in the collection of data

[1] Here, and in some other passages, the writer has borrowed some sentences from an article on Aristotle which he contributed to the *Encyclopaedia Britannica*.
[2] See Appendix V, *ad finem*, and the passages on the contemplative life in Book VII, cc. XIV–XV.

from Greek history and current Greek law which formed the basis of Plato's *Laws*. What is certain is that the range of induction was largely extended in the Lyceum after 335, when the collection of 158 Greek constitutions was made and the description of the institutions of non-Greek peoples was compiled.[1] What is also certain is that this habit of induction was a general habit of mind, which was far from being peculiar to the study of politics. In the many spheres of reality which he studied he always turned to the observable facts of actual and concrete evidence (the very first words of the *Politics* are 'observation shows us' . . . such-and-such facts about every *polis*). The essence of his procedure was observation and registration of all the relevant data; and the object of his study was, in each case, to discover some general theory which, in the Greek phrase, 'saved'—or, as we may say, explained without doing any violence to them—the observed and registered data of evidence. 'The best course', as he says in his treatise 'on the parts of animals', 'is to begin with the phenomena presented by each group, and, when this is done, proceed afterwards to state the causes of those phenomena and to deal with their evolution'.[2]

This inductive habit of mind was naturally accompanied by what may be termed an historic temper, a respect for tradition, and a readiness to accept the verdict of general opinion. These are features which appear throughout the *Politics*: they appear in his criticism of Plato's novelties, when he pleads that 'we are bound to pay some regard to the long past and the passage of the years': they appear even in his description of his own ideal state, when he turns aside to refer to the antiquity of Egypt, and suggests a law of necessary development (necessary in the sense that it is based on the pressure of necessary wants) which has steadily been the mother of political inventions.[3] But the inductive habit of mind was not only allied with an historic temper: it was also allied, and allied even more closely, with a scientific outlook. Aristotle conducted his study of 'things human', in the fields of politics and ethics (and also of logic, poetry, and oratory), side by side with a study of 'things natural' (physics, medicine, and general biology); and the methods and findings of his study of 'things natural' were naturally linked with the methods and findings of his study of 'things human'. The man of science appears again and again behind the student of politics; and if the one is the cause of the other, and both are not the results of the same general turn of mind,

---

[1] Appendix V. III.
[2] The translation is that of Sir David Ross, *Aristotle Selections*, p. 161.
[3] *Politics*, II, c. v, § 16; VII, c. x, §§ 7–8: see also Appendix V *ad finem*.
On Aristotle's respect for general opinion see also pp. 129, n. 4, 283, n. 2, 389, n. 4.

we may say that the collections and classifications of his scientific works are the cause of the collections and classifications which characterize his work in politics.[1]

The scientific outlook of Aristotle, as we have already had reason to notice,[2] has sometimes been connected with his Ionian parentage. He was certainly inclined towards the Ionian doctrine of 'becoming'—the genetic (or, we may even say, in a loose sense of the term, the 'evolutionary')[3] doctrine of *physis*, according to which the substance of things, and of man himself among other things, is engaged in a process of movement from a primary natural potentiality to the formed and finished completion which is also, and even more, natural. This is a doctrine which he applies, in the course of the *Poetics*, to the development of tragedy: it is a doctrine which he also applies, in the beginning of the *Politics*, to the development of the *polis*.[4] We can readily see that this doctrine of *physis* allies itself with the historic temper: the man who is inspired by the notion of 'becoming' will naturally look back with respect to the historic process, and watch the growth of institutions to discover their trend and end: he will, as Aristotle says, 'begin at the beginning, and consider things in the process of their growth, . . . to attain scientific conclusions'. We may go even further, and say that the man who is inspired by the notion of 'becoming' will study all that is with a deep and close attention, because he sees it all in the light of its ideal possibilities and its immanent power of attaining a high and final completion. There is a passage in his treatise 'on the parts of animals' which has been quoted by more than one scholar:

It remains to treat of the nature of living creatures, omitting nothing (so far as possible) whether of higher or lower dignity. . . . We should approach the study of every form of life without disgust, knowing that in every one there is something of nature [*physis*], and of beauty. For it is in the works of Nature above all that design, in contrast with random chance, is manifest; and the perfect form which anything born or made is designed to realize holds the rank of beauty.[5]

[1] A good example may be found in Book IV, c. IV, § 8, where Aristotle argues from the method of biological classification to the proper method for the classification of constitutions.   [2] *Supra*, p. xi.

[3] In R. G. Collingwood's recently published work on *The Idea of Nature*, the reader will find a brief discussion of the relation between the idea of evolution and Aristotle's idea of *physis* (pp. 82, 83). See also below, p. xlix, n. 1.

[4] Book I, c. II: see the notes to § 1 and § 8. On the general idea of *physis* see below, pp. lxxii–lxxiii.

[5] The translation of the passage (which comes in I, c. v, §§ 3, 6, and 7, of the treatise 'on the parts of animals') is that of the late Professor Cornford, in the *C.A.H.*, vol. vi, p. 350. The whole passage is also translated fully in Sir David Ross, *Selections*, pp. 175–6. It may be noticed that Aristotle often uses the word 'Nature' or *physis* as if it signified a person which did or created things (e.g. he remarks in the *Politics*, Book I, c. II, § 10, that 'Nature makes nothing in

It is easy to understand that the man who wrote these words would be naturally impelled to study in the *Politics*—and to study with attention and even respect—a form of life such as tyranny. It is, after all, a form of life: its study must be approached without disgust; and we should do wrong to imagine that the Aristotle who studies it in Book V is an Aristotle different from, or later than, the Aristotle who studies the ideal state in Books VII–VIII.[1]

It has already been noticed, in the first part of this Introduction, that the scientific trend of Aristotle carried him particularly towards biology and medicine. It is perhaps not fanciful to detect a special medical bias in a number of passages of the *Politics*. This is not merely a matter of the accumulation of 'case records', or of the use of writings of the school of Hippocrates such as the treatise on 'Airs, Waters, and Places'. It is a matter of recurring comparisons between the art of the statesman and the art of the good physician: it is a matter of the deep study of the pathology of constitutions, and of their liability to the fever of sedition, which we find in Book V of the *Politics*; it is a matter of the preoccupation with therapeutics which we also find in the same book—a preoccupation singularly evident in the passage (at the end of chapter XI) which suggests a regimen and cure for the fever of tyranny. The general theme of Aristotle's political therapeutics is the use of moderation and the wisdom of the mean. He preaches avoidance of excess and surfeit: he urges the medical need of proportion and symmetry between the various parts or members of the state:[2] he reiterates the physician's warning *medio tutissimus ibis*. 'Nothing in excess' was an old warning of the Delphic oracle; and the natural emotion of the Greek temper ran readily, by a natural reaction, to a general cult of the golden mean. But it may well be argued that the study of medicine made Aristotle give a new precision, and a fresh emphasis, to an old and general feeling; and it has been well suggested that his general doctrine of the mean is derived from a medical conception of health as a balanced and proportionate state midway between excess and defect.

We have already spoken of Aristotle as a man of an inductive habit of mind, an historic temper, and a scientific outlook. All these characteristics, but especially the last, converge in his philo-

vain'); but this, as Professor Cornford notes, is only a literary device, and 'Nature' is 'merely a collective name for the natures of all natural things' (ibid., p. 337).

[1] On the theory that there are strata of different dates in the *Politics* see below, pp. xlii–xlvi.

[2] The idea of proportion and symmetry between the parts of the body—and, by analogy, between the parts of the state—is developed in Book V, c. III, § 6. Describing the need of a proper proportion for the nose, he notes that the same law of proportion also applies to states (Book V, c. IX, §§ 8–9); and he repeats the observation in the *Rhetoric* (see Appendix I, *ad finem*).

sophy of moderation. He can hardly, perhaps, be called a democrat; but the man who wrote the eleventh chapter of the third book
of the *Politics* cannot be called an anti-democrat. He was not a
believer in the common ownership of property; but he believed in
its common use. He saw that there might be a case for absolutism
(given a people fitted for it, and a person—a god among men—
who was capable of bearing the burden); but he equally saw the
case against tyranny. He inclined to the compromise of the 'polity';
to a limited franchise based on property; to the mixed constitution
which united oligarchy and democracy. Like the Marquis of
Halifax at a later date, he set down what might be called 'the
Trimmer's opinion of the laws and government'; like him, he
thought 'That our climate is a trimmer, between that part of the
world where men are roasted and the other where they are frozen;[1]
... that our laws are trimmers, between the excess of unbounded
power and the extravagance of liberty not enough restrained; that
true virtue hath ever been thought a trimmer, and to have its dwelling
in the middle between the two extremes'.[2] But perhaps Aristotle
was even more of a Whig than of a trimmer—a Whig of the type
of Locke or Burke. Every analogy has its defects and is no sooner
stated than it has to be corrected. But if there is any modern climate
which is the climate of Aristotle's *Politics*, it is the climate of 1688.[3]

§ 2. *The Aristotelian School in the Lyceum.* The school which
Aristotle founded at Athens, side by side with the Platonic
Academy and with the school of oratory which the aged Isocrates
had conducted since the early years of the century, was situated
in a grove on the eastern side of the city, and on the north bank of
the river Ilissus, from which the eye could look upwards to the
Acropolis and the Parthenon[4]. The grove was dedicated to Apollo
Lyceius: it contained a gymnasium, with covered walks (or *peri-
patoi*) which were places of resort and discussion; and this is how
the school of Aristotle came to be known as the Lyceum, and its
students as Peripatetics.[5] Aristotle rented a site in the grove, and

[1] Cf. *Politics*, VII, c. VII, §§ 2-3.
[2] Halifax's *Character of a Trimmer*, ad finem.
[3] See pp. lxi–lxii infra.
[4] A passage in the *Politics* (Book VII, c. VII, § 3) almost seems to suggest this
prospect. Aristotle suggests that the residence of the magistrates in his ideal
city should be associated with the buildings devoted to public worship, 'on an
eminence conspicuous enough for men to look up and see goodness enthroned,
and strong enough to command the adjacent quarters of the city'.
[5] Both the Platonic Academy and the Aristotelian Lyceum were connected
with gymnasia, for the simple reason that gymnasia were places of intellectual
resort, where men congregated to spend their leisure (*scholē*), as well as places
of physical exercise. It is curious how much of our educational vocabulary is
derived from these Greek sources—the word 'school' itself; the French *lycée*;
the German *gymnasium*; and our own 'academy'.

erected or hired a building, with a lecture room and library, and with a shrine dedicated to the Muses (a 'museum') and to the god Apollo. On this semi-religious basis his students were organized as a *thiasos*, a guild or society (we may almost say a 'college') dedicated to the cult of the Muses; and they were thus in some sense analogous to the 'clerks' of the medieval university, which—as its very name indicates—was equally a *thiasos* or 'guild' of students devoted to the sanctities of learning. The guild of Aristotle's scholars had something of a social side, which included monthly gatherings at a common table; and it was regularly organized for morning lectures in more esoteric and philosophic subjects, and for afternoon or evening lectures, of a more public type, on subjects such as politics and rhetoric. The library must have been a cardinal part of the school; and it has even been suggested that Aristotelian treatises such as the *Politics*, whether or no there was some preliminary 'reading' in the lecture room, were mainly intended for the library as text-books which might be consulted and conned by the members of the staff and the students. But the equipment of the school not only included books (or rather manuscript rolls), among which we have to count not only the extant treatises, but also the many lost collections such as the 158 constitutions and the record of institutions among non-Greek peoples: it also contained maps; and it equally contained scientific material, such as the collection called 'the dissections' (*anatomai*), which appears to have been of the nature of an illustrated compendium of anatomy and physiology.

The general work of the school may be expressed in our word 'research', or in the Greek word *historia*, which primarily means inquiry, secondarily information gained by inquiry, and finally the record or written account of the information so gained. The Lyceum was full of 'history' and 'histories' in the Greek sense—a 'history' about animals, a 'history' about constitutions, and 'histories' generally about the whole range of man and nature. It would be irrelevant and otiose even to summarize here the general range of these 'histories', or to describe, however briefly, the collections and catalogues of material in which they issued. But it may be pertinent to describe, as an illustrative example, the collections made in the field of Greek poetry and in that of the religious games and festivals with which the dramatic (and some of the lyric) poetry of Greece was closely connected; and it is certainly pertinent to describe the various collections made in the field of Greek politics.

The collections made in the field of Greek poetry are not only the background of the *Poetics*: they are also forerunners of, and they probably served to instruct and encourage, the Greek critics, grammarians, and antiquaries, who afterwards flourished in Alexandria. One of the Aristotelian collections in this field was the *Didascaliai* or 'dramatic performances', a catalogue of the dramas performed at the Athenian festivals which was based on the original records; and this collection was particularly used by the later scholars of Alexandria. Another collection took the form of a catalogue of the victors in the Pythian games at Delphi, and still another that of a catalogue of the victors in the Olympic games in Elis.[1] In addition to these catalogues, concerned with festivals (and with the dramas, music, and lyrics which were part of the festivals), Aristotle and his school were also concerned with the epics of Homer. We find many references in later writers to a treatise on 'Homeric problems'; and there are also many accounts of a work called the *Peplos*, or 'Robe', which is described as a 'mixed history', and would seem, from the references and surviving fragments, not only to have included a review of all the Greek festivals, but also to have been concerned with matters of the Homeric age, such as the genealogies of the heroes of the Trojan War, the numbers of their ships, and the inscriptions on their tombs.[2]

This illustrative example, drawn from the records of the studies conducted by the Lyceum in the field of Greek culture, will suffice to indicate the wealth of material, the inductive basis, and the general ground of 'history', on which the argument of Aristotle's treatises is based. In the light of this example we may now turn to the record of the studies pursued in the field of Greek politics. The details are given in the third section of the last Appendix; and it is sufficient to notice here that the inductive basis of the *Politics* included not only a record of 158 Greek constitutions, which covered colonial as well as metropolitan Greece, but also a description of the institutions of non-Greek states, from Etruria and Rome to Caria and Libya.[3] It is obvious that the record of

---

[1] These catalogues appear to be the basis of a passage in the *Politics* (Book VIII, c. IV, § 8), as the catalogue called the *Didascaliai* would equally appear to be the basis of another passage (Book VIII, c. VI, § 12): see Appendix V, III, *ad finem*. It has been previously noted, on p. xxiii, that Aristotle was formally honoured by Delphi for his Pythian catalogue.

[2] The work is generally ascribed to Aristotle (i.e. to the Lyceum of Aristotle's time) in the references; but in one of them (Rose, *Fragmenta*, no. 638) it is ascribed to Theophrastus. The title of *Peplos* may be based on the robe of the goddess Athene, embroidered with mythological subjects, which was carried annually in the Panathenaic procession.

[3] Mention should also be made of a compilation of cases in international law, which is briefly described in the third section of the last Appendix, and of a collection of miscellaneous memoranda (ascribed to 'Aristotle or Theophrastus') which dealt—to judge by the fragments—with the habits of different peoples and with matters of geography: see Rose, *Fragmenta*, 631-6.

Greek constitutions and the description of non-Greek states—like
the catalogues, and the other studies, in the field of culture—must
have been the work of students of the Lyceum, or of members of
its staff, working under the general direction of Aristotle himself.
It is possible, however, and it may even be said to be probable,
that the account of one of the 158 Greek constitutions—the *Constitution of Athens*—was actually written by Aristotle. Since 1891
scholars have been able to study the full text of this account, as it
appears on four rolls of papyrus discovered in Egypt. Its composition may be dated, from internal evidence, about the year 330: its
style and substance agree, in the main, with the style and substance
of the *Politics*; and it may well be argued that Aristotle reserved
for himself the description of the most important of all Greek constitutions, which would naturally serve as a model for the rest.[1]

The basis of material for the *Politics* which has just been described is wholly institutional. The question may be raised whether
Aristotle gathered, and if so whether he used, any psychological
material. The *Rhetoric* certainly shows a large measure of psychological insight;[2] but his cardinal works on psychology are the
larger treatise called the *De Anima* and the various smaller treatises
grouped under the general head of the *Parva Naturalia*. In these
works he may be said to have founded the study of psychology—
the study of the *psyche* as the shaping form and inspiring energy
of bodily physique. The interest of this study, in its bearing
on the *Politics*, is that it might conceivably have been used as the
basis for a new approach to political theory, as the study of modern
psychology has been used by scholars in England and France (such
as Graham Wallas and Tarde) during the last half-century. But
it would appear that the study of psychology came at a later date
in Aristotle's development than his study of politics and ethics.
Both in the *Politics* and the *Ethics* he assumes the general conceptions about the nature of mind and emotion which were current
in ordinary Greek thought, or had been developed in the Platonic
Academy; and in neither does he draw upon the stores of observation which were probably first collected in the Lyceum at a later
date than that of their composition.[3]

---

[1] On the *Athenian Constitution* see Dr. E. M. Walker in *New Chapters in Greek
History* (edited by Powell and Barber), First Series, pp. 133–42.

[2] See Appendix I. B, *ad initium*.

[3] Jaeger, on whose *Aristoteles* (pp. 354–7) these observations are based, draws
attention in this connexion to a passage in the *Ethics*, Book I, c. XIII. Here Aristotle argues (1) that the true statesman or *politikos* is essentially concerned with
human goodness and the promoting of such goodness; (2) that human goodness
is goodness of man's *psyche*; and (3) that the true statesman must therefore
possess some sort of knowledge of the facts of the *psyche*, just as the true physician must have some knowledge of the facts of the body—and this all the more

§ 3. *The Aristotelian writings and their different styles.* In point of substance the writings of Aristotle form an encyclopaedia of knowledge, which may be divided into some eight main heads or branches, each covering a separate field of knowledge. These eight heads or branches do not represent Aristotle's own classification, nor does each head correspond to a separate treatise or a separate course of lectures; but they will at any rate serve to give a general idea of the range of his work and to convey some notion of the systematization and classification which he introduced into the field of science. The first branch is logic, or in Aristotle's own terminology 'analytics', which was covered in a number of treatises that came to be designated, some centuries after his time, as the *Organon* or 'instrument' of knowledge. The second branch is physics, in the broad sense of a general study of inorganic nature or the material aspect of *physis*. The third branch is metaphysics or, literally, 'that which comes after physics'—a study of the 'prime philosophy' of being and an inquiry into the first cause and 'prime mover' of the whole world of *physis*. The fourth branch, which we have already had reason to notice, is biology, or the study of organic nature. The fifth, which 'comes after biology' in much the same way as metaphysics comes after physics, is the study of the *psyche*, which we may roughly call by the modern name of psychology.[1] The sixth branch is ethics, or moral philosophy, which appears to have engaged Aristotle's attention enough to be handled in two separate treatises, the *Eudemian Ethics* and the *Nicomachean Ethics*, of which the former may be the earlier and the latter a later version. The seventh branch is politics, which may be said to come after ethics in roughly the same sort of way as metaphysics comes after physics, or psychology after biology. In other words, Aristotle, after he has treated morality in the *Ethics* as a 'disposition' in the individual, proceeds to treat it in the *Politics* as a 'way of life', or organized system of behaviour, operative in a political community which at once produces the 'disposition' by its government, laws, and education, and gives play and scope to its energy by providing a wide circle of persons, engaged in mutual relations, where it can be exercised and breathed.[2] The whole body of

since politics is more important than medicine. But, as Jaeger notes, he proceeds to add that the statesman need only study the *psyche* in connexion with his specific object of knowing and promoting human goodness, and so far as is sufficient for that object: 'further precision is perhaps something more laborious than our purpose requires'; and the study of the *psyche* is thus made subordinate to ethics. (See *Politics*, Book VII, c. xiv, §§ 8–11, and the note on § 11.)

[1] Modern psychology is a study of human emotions, instincts, and behaviour. Aristotle's *De Anima* is concerned with the *psyche* in the whole of animate nature, animal as well as human.

[2] On Aristotle's view of the relation between ethics and politics see Appendix I.

writings, or encyclopaedia, comes full circle in the eighth and last branch, which includes the *Rhetoric* and the *Poetics*; and as it began in the study of logic and ratiocination, so it ends in the study of oratorical persuasion and of the poetic (or tragic) art of 'purifying the emotions by means of pity and fear'.

In point of style, or in method of exposition, the writings of Aristotle have generally been classified by scholars as belonging to three different types or genres. The first, which we only know from fragments, consists of popular or literary writings, mostly in dialogue form (and therefore based on the Platonic tradition), but in some cases taking the form of an exhortation or what may be called, in Quintilian's language, an *oratio suasoria*. Among such exhortations there was, for example, the *Protrepticus*, an early work (which is said to have been imitated by Cicero, and had a great vogue and influence in antiquity down to the days of St. Augustine), addressed to a ruler in the island of Cyprus, and exhorting him to philosophy and philosophic government. We may also rank under the head of exhortations the two treatises—'on kingship' and 'concerning colonies'—which Aristotle is recorded to have written for Alexander. The second type of Aristotelian writings may be called the compilation or catalogue, which must generally have been the work of the school rather than that of the master; but the compilation called the *Constitution of Athens* (the one surviving example, apart from scattered fragments, of the many descriptions of Greek constitutions) may well be, as has already been noticed, the work of Aristotle himself. The third type, to which all the other extant writings of Aristotle belong, is that of the set treatise intended for the use of students. We may imagine that all these treatises were written by Aristotle in connexion with his lectures in the Lyceum—not so much, probably, in the way of 'notes' to be followed in the delivery of lectures (the actual lectures may well have been more discursive, and more of the nature of discussions with the members of the class), but rather in the way of 'memoranda' which may possibly have been written afterwards in order to preserve a record of the results attained in lectures and discussions.

This brief survey of the substance and style of the general body of the Aristotelian writings may enable us to place the *Politics* in its intellectual context, and to see it in its relation to Aristotle's other studies and his general system of thought—just as, in the previous section, an endeavour was made to place it in its historical context, and to see it in its relation to Aristotle's experience of life and his observation of contemporary history. The *Politics*, we can now see, is one of some eight different branches of study, which together form an encyclopaedia of knowledge; and it is, as one of these branches of study, connected peculiarly and particularly with the cognate branch which deals with ethics.[1] It belongs, as we can also now see, to the third type or genre of the Aristotelian writings —that of the set treatise; but it may well include some ideas and conceptions which had already been developed and expressed in writings of the first or literary type (for example in the *Protrepticus*, or in the exhortations addressed to Alexander); and it certainly includes, or at any rate utilizes, a good deal of the matter which had been accumulated and recorded in writings which belong to the second type—that of the compilation or catalogue.

§ 4. *The composition and structure of the* Politics. On this basis we may now turn to consider the composition and structure of the *Politics*. The first thing to be noticed is that it is not a homogeneous or unitary treatise. This is also true of some of Aristotle's other treatises (for instance the *Metaphysics*);[2] but it is perhaps particularly and especially true of the *Politics*. It is a collection or conflation of different essays rather than a single treatise—a collection assembled and arranged by Aristotle (or by some subsequent editor) under a single title, but not welded into a single work. This is a fact which raises problems of order, partly logical and partly chronological: in other words, it raises the two questions (*a*) whether the present order in which the essays are arranged is the proper logical order, and (*b*) whether the different essays represent different chronological strata, and different (and perhaps discrepant) periods in the development of Aristotle's thought. But before we enter upon these two questions it will be well to give a summary account of the different essays (the different sets of notes or 'memoranda') of which the *Politics* is composed.[3]

(*a*) *The different sections or 'methods'*. They are six in number. (A) The first, which is represented by Book I, is concerned with the household, or with 'economy' (which in its Greek sense means

---

[1] The fact that the *Politics* is a part of a general body of interconnected studies will explain to the reader why references are often made, in the course of its argument, to other subjects—not only, as has already been noticed, biology and medicine, but also (to cite another example) the theory of music, which is linked, in Book VIII, with the theory of dramatic poetry expounded in the *Poetics*. It will also explain why the general theory of Aristotle (e.g. the theory of *physis*, or the theory of 'compounds' and 'wholes') is assumed throughout the argument.

[2] 'It must be noted that the longer existing works are not unitary wholes, but collections of essays on connected themes, and that the separate essays are the original units which were connected together sometimes by Aristotle and sometimes (as in the case of the *Metaphysics*) by his editors.' Sir David Ross, *Aristotle*, p. 9.

[3] In the language of Aristotle himself, the essays (as they have here been called) are generally styled by the name of *methodos*—though the term 'discourses' or *logoi* is also used—and that name has accordingly been used in the subsequent course of the argument.

'the management of the household'), as a subject of consideration prior to the *polis* and the government of the *polis*. This section begins by distinguishing the association of the household from other forms of association; and it proceeds to deal with factors in the life of the household such as slavery, property, and the institution of marriage. (B) The second section, which is represented by Book II, is concerned with ideal states both in theory and in practice. It deals first with the theories of Plato's *Republic* and *Laws*, and with those of two other inventors of utopias; and it then proceeds to deal with actual states (in Sparta, Crete, and Carthage) which in one way or another approach the ideal. We might expect this review of ideal states to be succeeded by Aristotle's own sketch of an ideal state: actually it is followed by something different. (C) The third section (or, in Aristotle's own terminology, *methodos*), which is represented by Book III, is concerned with the general theory of political constitutions. It deals with four main themes— the nature of citizenship; the classification of constitutions; the principles of 'distributive justice' followed in different constitutions (especially democracy and oligarchy); and the theory of kingship. (D) The fourth *methodos*, represented by Books IV and V, is entirely realistic, and concerned with the problems of actual politics. It first deals (in Book IV) with the political morphology of the different varieties of democracy and oligarchy; with the 'polity' or mixed constitution, which blends and reconciles oligarchy and democracy; with the 'relativity' of different constitutions to different peoples; and with the methods of organizing the deliberative, the executive, and the judiciary in different constitutions. It then proceeds to deal (in Book V) with what may be called political pathology, or, in other words, with the general causes of revolution in all types of state, and with its particular causes in different types. (E) The fifth *methodos*, represented by Book VI, is concerned with the methods of organizing democracies and oligarchies with a view to ensuring their stability. It thus repeats, in a sense, a theme which has already been handled in the middle of the previous *methodos* (the theme of the proper methods of organizing constitutions); but it does so from a different point of view—that of ensuring constitutional stability—which makes it a new and separate method.[1] (F) Finally, the last *methodos*, which is

---

[1] Some modern editors have altered the order of the books by making Book VI succeed Book IV, on the ground that it proceeds to develop the last of the themes treated in Book IV. They thus intercalate one *methodos* in the middle of another. But (a) the theme actually developed in Book VI is different from that which had been briefly handled at the end of Book IV, in the middle of the previous *methodos*; (b) in the course of developing the theme of Book VI Aristotle more than once refers back to Books IV *and* V as the previous *methodos* (see

represented by Books VII and VIII, deals with the theme of political ideals, and sketches an ideal state. It discusses first the proper population, the territory, the social type and structure, and the physical planning of an ideal *polis*; and it then proceeds to treat of the general principles, and the proper scheme, of education in such a *polis*, with particular reference to the aims and methods of education in music.

(*b*) *The problem of the order of the books.* These six sections have come down to us in the order in which they are here stated— A B C D E F. If a play of fancy may be permitted, the question may be raised and considered, 'How would a modern thinker arrange these six sections, if there were no existing order, and he were given a free hand to create an order?' He might possibly arrange them in three parts. Part I would be entitled 'The General Principles of Social and Political Theory': it would include the social theory of A and the political theory of C. Part II would be entitled 'Political Ideals': it would include the review of ideal states, in theory and practice, which comes in B, and Aristotle's own sketch of an ideal state contained in F. Part III would be entitled 'Political Institutions': it would include the political morphology and pathology of D and the political engineering of E. The order of the books would thus become A C B F D E. But there is an alternative arrangement which a modern thinker might prefer to adopt. He might argue—as Aristotle, or the editor who fixed the present order of the books of the *Politics*, appears to have argued—that 'Political Institutions' should properly come before 'Political Ideals', on the ground that it is best to have studied actual institutions, and to have understood their merits and defects, before one proceeds to construct an ideal scheme of institutions. He might accordingly invert the order of what has been called Part II and what has been called Part III; and the order of the books would then become A C D E B F.

The only point of this play of fancy is that it helps to put in a proper perspective the rearrangements of the order of the books which different editors have actually made in their editions of the *Politics*. The most common of these rearrangements is that which transposes the last method, F (Aristotle's sketch of his ideal state), and places it after method C (on the general theory of political constitutions), but before methods D and E, which are both concerned with the realities of political institutions. The effect of this

p. 259, n. 2); and (*c*) the particular point of view in Book VI, which is that of ensuring constitutional stability, is a logical consequence of Book V (which has dealt with the causes of constitutional instability), and therefore involves the priority of that book.

transposition is to make an order of the 'methods' which is A B C F D E. This order is not, of course, based on any play of fancy: it rests on the scholarly ground of the cross-references which are to be found in the text of the *Politics*, and especially on the reference at the end of the last chapter of C (Book III), which indicates that the next stage of the argument, already reached, must be a treatment of the ideal state.[1] But there are a number of arguments, none the less, against this change of order. It is perhaps only an argument of mere conservatism that it disturbs the sequence in which the books were arranged by Aristotle himself or by an editor of the early days of the Aristotelian school. It is a more serious argument that there are references in method F (Books VII–VIII)—references partly to the catalogue material accumu- lated in the Lyceum, and partly to contemporary political develop- ments—which indicate that it was composed at a late date in Aristotle's career, and thus suggest that it is properly placed as the last method.[2] But perhaps the most serious argument against the transposition of method F is that it does not improve the logic and the general coherence of the argument of the *Politics*. It leaves method B—Aristotle's review of ideal Greek states both in theory and in practice—still divorced from method F. Nor is that all. It also disturbs the logic and the sequence by which, in the existing order of the books, a transition is naturally made from method C, which handles the general theory of political constitutions, to methods D and E, which handle the concrete details of the different constitutions. This is a consideration which is reinforced when we note that there are a number of passages in the early part of D (Book IV) which refer back to C (or Book III) as if it were its immediate precursor, which the reader would have fresh in his mind.[3]

All these arguments may well combine to suggest that it is the course of wisdom to leave the present order of the books of the *Politics* undisturbed. It is possible to imagine a more logical order —for instance an order which connected Aristotle's review of previous ideal states more closely with his own sketch of an ideal state; but as soon as we observe how the books of the *Politics*

[1] See the note at the end of Book III, where it is suggested that the last chapter of Book III raises a number of difficulties, and may be a later addition.
[2] On the references to catalogue material, see above, p. xxxiii, n. 1. On the references to contemporary political developments see above, p. xxi, n. 3.
[3] Some instances may be given. (1) Chapter II of Book IV begins with a reference to the first 'method' on constitutions—i.e. to Book III—and this implies that Aristotle is now writing a second 'method' on constitutions which naturally follows at once on the first. (2) Chapter VII, § 2, refers back to Book III as the 'first discourses' on the subject of constitutions, and this again im- plies that Aristotle is now following on with a second set of discourses on the same subject. (3) Chapter X, § 1, similarly refers back to Book III as 'the first discourses', with the same implication.

actually succeed one another we desist from our imaginations. Aristotle begins, naturally enough, with a 'method' which deals with the social foundations of the state, or, in other words, the household. What he says of marriage and the position of women at the end of that method naturally leads him to consider, in the next method, Plato's views on marriage and the position of women:[1] this leads him to consider Plato's general views: that leads in turn to the views of other inventors of utopias; and from this topic Aristotle is naturally led to consider existing states which approach the ideal. But the theory of the state and its different constitutions —which he had distinguished from that of the household and its institutions early in the first method, but had left for future consideration—has still to be attempted; and a sketch of this theory is therefore given in the next method. A simple logic suggests that the general theory of constitutions should be followed by a detailed study of actual constitutions; and this study is accordingly pursued through the course of the next two methods. It still remains for Aristotle to sketch, on the basis of all the data which he has thus accumulated, his own conception of the ideal state; and that sketch is accordingly attempted, as the culmination and conclusion of the argument—the logical end and the final climax—in the course of Books VII and VIII.

(c) *The problem of the chronology of different sections of the Politics.* But even if we can thus defend the logic of the existing order of the books of the *Politics*, we are left with another problem —the problem of their chronology. What was the order of time in which the different parts of the *Politics* were composed? Can we trace chronological strata? Can we detect divergences and discrepancies of view between earlier and later parts, as Aristotle departed from the Platonic tradition, and as he matured under the experience of the vicissitudes of his life? The story of his life has shown him to us at Assus, at Pella, in Athens, for the period of a quarter of a century, from 347 to 322: it has shown him to us consorting with Hermias, with Alexander, with Antipater: it has suggested that he may well have given lectures, or held discussions, in these different environments, and in contact with these various persons. Did it all leave different deposits in his thought, and in the expression of his thought in his writings; and can we trace, as it were, a geology of the *Politics*, which shows a system of strata belonging to different ages?

---

[1] It will be noticed that Book II begins specifically with Plato's scheme for the community of women and children, which is discussed at length in Chapters II-IV. It is only later in the book that Aristotle proceeds to consider the more general features of Plato's theory.

This is a line of inquiry which was started more than twenty years ago by Professor Jaeger (in a work on Aristotle, published in 1923, which bore the sub-title of 'the foundations for a history of his development'), and was carried on by Professor von Arnim in a study 'on the history of the genesis of Aristotle's *Politics*' which appeared in 1924. It has attracted the attention, and gained the support, of some English scholars, such as Sir David Ross and the late Professor J. L. Stocks.[1] There is indeed some natural propriety in applying to Aristotle himself the genetic method which he suggests in an early passage of the *Politics*—'to begin at the beginning, and consider things in the process of their growth'. But though there may be some natural propriety in the application of a genetic method to the problem (if it be a problem) of the composition and structure of the *Politics*, the results which are gained by its application seem highly dubious; and it is certain that the results attained by one disciple of the method contradict, and contradict flatly, the results attained by another. The fact is that the use of the genetic method is vitiated by subjectivity. The inquirer who uses it becomes the prey of his own interpretation of Aristotle; and he gives or withholds chronological priority—in other words he makes *this* an early stratum, and *that* a later—on the grounds of his own inner feelings about the 'early' and the 'late' Aristotle.

The two books on the ideal state, or what we have called method F, may be used to illustrate the point. To Professor Jaeger they are the 'early' Aristotle. They are close, he feels, to the Platonic tradition; and he therefore assigns them to the period when Aristotle had just left the Academy and was residing at Assus after 347 in close contact with Hermias. Having reached this conclusion, he is prepared to find 'the local atmosphere' of the Troad, and the policies and ideas of Hermias, reflected in the theory of Aristotle's sketch of an ideal state. The argument is ingenious and attractive; but Professor von Arnim has also an argument, no less ingenious and perhaps even more attractive (because it rests on a sounder and deeper knowledge of Aristotle's political philosophy),[2]

---

[1] See Sir David Ross's *Aristotle*, pp. 18–19 and 236, and his introduction to his volume of *Selections from Aristotle*, pp. xxi–xxii; and for the views of Professor Stocks see his articles on 'The Composition of Aristotle's *Politics*' (*Classical Quarterly*, vol. xxi, pp. 177–87) and on *Scholē* (ibid., vol. xxx, pp. 177–87). The present writer was at one time attracted to the view that the *Politics* contained different chronological strata; see his article on 'The Life of Aristotle and the Composition and Structure of the Politics' (*Classical Review*, vol. xlv, pp. 162–72). But five years spent in the constant company of the *Politics* during the preparation of this translation have irresistibly compelled him to change his views.

[2] Professor von Arnim published, as long ago as 1910, a scholarly course of lectures on the political theories of antiquity.

which seeks to prove that the two books on the ideal state are the latest part of the *Politics*, and represent the furthest limit of Aristotle's reaction and departure from the Platonic tradition. Here is a clean contradiction: how is it to be solved?

One way in which it may be solved, if we persist in the attempt to discover chronological strata in the *Politics*, is by giving the verdict in favour of Professor von Arnim, and of his theory of the late composition of the two books on the ideal state. We have already seen, in the course of the present section, that the two books on the ideal state contain references to the 'catalogue' material which was accumulated in the Lyceum after 335, during Aristotle's final residence in Athens;[1] we have already seen, in the course of the previous section—and this is a still stronger argument—that they also seem to contain references to developments at Athens during the period of the ascendancy of the Athenian statesman Lycurgus (336–326), and that 'the local atmosphere' reflected in Aristotle's sketch of an ideal state (if there be any such reflection) is the atmosphere of Athens rather than that of the Troad.[2] We may fairly conclude, on the basis of this double evidence,[3] that Aristotle's sketch of an ideal state belongs to the last stage of his life and the period of the Lyceum. We may also refer to the same stage and the same period the review of the ideal states of Greek theory and practice, which is given in the course of Book II (or 'method' B), and which—though separated from the sketch of the ideal state in the order of the arrangement of the books of the *Politics*—is connected with that sketch both by logic and by chronology.[4]

But there is another way of solving the contradiction between different and rival views about the dates of different parts of the *Politics*. This other way is simple. We can abandon the attempt to apply a genetic method to the composition and structure of the *Politics*, and we can renounce the search for chronological strata. In other words, we can adopt the view that the six 'methods' of

---

[1] *Supra*, p. xxxiii, n. 1.   [2] *Supra*, p. xxi, and note.

[3] There is also a third type of evidence—that of the cross-references in the text of the *Politics*—which may be added. Book VII, in dealing with the ideal state, refers back to the discussion in Book I on the nature of slavery (see VII, c. III, § 2), and to the discussion in Book III on the nature of the different kinds of government (see VII, c. XIV, § 6). It follows that Book VII implies the previous existence both of Book I and Book III.

[4] Jaeger, arguing for the early date of Books VII–VIII, argues equally for the early date of Book II (op. cit., pp. 300 sqq.). But the chronological references contained in Book II imply a *late* date, or at any rate are consistent with a late date: e.g. the reference, in Book II, c. IX, § 20, to 'events at Andros' may refer to the year 333 (Newman, vol. ii, p. 334), and the reference in c. X, § 16 to 'foreign hostilities lately passing over to Crete' may equally refer to the same year (ibid., p. 360).

the *Politics* all belong to the period of the Lyceum, and are all—so far as chronology goes—on exactly the same footing. There is really no valid reason why we should adopt any other view. It is true, of course, that the books on the ideal state deal with political ideals, and are therefore 'idealistic', and that the books of methods D and E (Books IV–VI), which deal with actual states, and with problems of their morphology and pathology, deal with political realities, and are therefore 'realistic'. But this simple fact does not involve the conclusion that the 'idealistic' books belong to an early period of Aristotle's life in which he still felt Platonic ardours, and that the 'realistic' books belong to a later and more wary period of disillusionment. The only conclusion which it involves is that Aristotle—very naturally and very properly—handled different themes in different ways. It would be absurd to expect that the 'method' on political ideals should be the same sort of thing as the 'methods' on actual political institutions. They are *not* the same sort of thing. But neither are they essentially different. The same mind is at work, from the same point of view, in both. The author of the 'method' on the ideal state may be dealing with ideals, but he has a firm grip on realities: he is aware of the problems of foreign relations and of military engineering, the problems of economics and public health, the facts of recent Spartan develop-ment and the latest eccentricities of musical composition. Con-versely, the author of the 'methods' on actual states and their problems may be dealing with realities, but he has still a firm hold on ideals: he may study tyranny closely, but he can also write eloquent words about the reform of the tyrant:[1] he may study, with an equally close attention, the economic bases of sedition (or 'class-war') and revolution, but he can also suggest a notable plan for the institution of social services, both public and private, in aid of the poor.[2] Any translator of the *Politics*, who has lived with the book on his desk day on day, and month after month, is bound to become familiar with his author; and such familiarity breeds in the mind a deep sense of the unity of the author, which is perhaps the strongest argument for the unity of the composition and struc-ture of his book.

The view may therefore be hazarded that the six 'methods' of the *Politics* were all composed in the period between 335 and 322, during the period of Aristotle's teaching in the Lyceum. This view in no way precludes the possibility that he may have put together notes and memoranda on politics during the period of his residence at Assus (347–344) and during the later period of his

---

[1] Book V, c. xi, §§ 17–34, and especially §§ 33–4.
[2] Book VI, c. v, §§ 8–11.

residence at Pella (*circa* 342–336), or that he may later have used, and incorporated in the *Politics*, such notes and memoranda. Nor does it preclude a similar use of material drawn from his own earlier literary writings, such as the *Protrepticus* and the exhortations on kingship and colonies addressed to Alexander. Any writer naturally uses the material which he has accumulated; and there can be no doubt that (apart from all the material of collections and catalogues which was produced by the contemporary research of the Lyceum) the Aristotle of the years from 335 to 322 had earlier material on which he could readily draw. But this material was embedded in the *Politics*, fused with the *Politics*, and cannot now be distinguished as a prior and separate stratum.

We may therefore abandon the subjectivity which would seem to be involved in the genetic method of interpreting the *Politics*, and we may place our reliance on the objective evidence of the actual text—particularly that of the cross-references in the text, which link all the parts together in a unity and suggest that they are all contemporary,[1] and that of the references in the text to contemporary history, which suggest that the different parts were composed in the same period of Aristotle's life, from the year 335 onwards. Using the objective evidence of the actual text, we not only see how the different parts are linked together by a system of cross-reference: we can also detect (as has already been noticed) an inner logic of inter-connexion which may not be the logic that a modern thinker would have chosen, but which *is* a logic, an understandable logic, and the logic which Aristotle himself (or some editor of Aristotle's school) deliberately chose.[2] We are bound to respect that logic, and we are bound to take it as evidence of a work which is generally unitary in composition and structure—composed on a single plan and composed during a single period. No doubt the work, if it was composed during a single period, was composed at different times in that period: no doubt it was composed in different sections or 'methods'; no doubt a number of the sections were left incomplete, with rough edges, and without

---

[1] Some cross references may here be mentioned which show how the parts or 'methods' of the *Politics* are linked in a unity. (*a*) Book I refers forward, in c. XIII, § 15, to a discussion on constitutions; and from the context it seems clear that this is a reference forward to the discussion and review of ideal constitutions which comes in Book II. (*b*) As Book I refers *forward* to Book II, so Book III refers *back*, in c. VI, § 3, to the discussion on household management and slavery in Book I. (*c*) Book IV then proceeds, as has already been noticed on p. xl, n. 3, to refer back to Book III. (*d*) Book VI, at the beginning of c. I (see the note on § 2), refers back to Books IV–V. (*e*) Finally, Book VII, as has already been noticed on p. xliii, n. 3, refers back to Book I and Book III—though it does not (as we should hardly expect it to do, seeing that it is concerned with political ideals) refer back to Books IV–VI which deal with actual politics.

[2] See above, p. xli.

a neat suture to join them with the succeeding section;[1] no doubt, again, some of the sections—because their subject is different— differ in tone and emphasis from others. But even to-day, with all the facilities of the printing-press and proof-sheets, such things are possible; and in the days of manuscript rolls—especially when a busy writer, as Aristotle must have been, was pressing forward hastily to get his life's work done, and was naturally leaving behind him loose threads and imperfect sutures—such things were very easily possible. We shall be wise to practise the gift of sympathetic understanding for conditions of composition very different from our own. In particular we shall be wise to remember that differences of tone and emphasis (even if they exist, and are not the products of our imagination) are not necessarily differences between earlier and later chronological strata, but may well be merely the differences inherent in different contexts. The difference between 'idealism' and 'realism' need not be a difference of early and late: it may be only the difference between a context concerned with political ideals and a context concerned with political institutions; and the same man, at the same period, with the same general substance of ideas, may have written differently in different contexts—now as a prophet of the ideal, and now as an observer and recorder (but also a critic) of the actual.

[1] Several of the 'methods' end in this way. The end of Book I is abrupt (see the note at the end of the last chapter): the end of Book III raises difficulties (see again the note at the end of the last chapter): the 'method' of Books IV–V ends abruptly, almost in the middle of a sentence (see again the note at the end of the last chapter of Book V): Book VI ends in an unfinished state, and its last sentence finishes in the middle (see again the note at the end of the last chapter): and finally the 'method' of Books VII–VIII is left incomplete (see the final note).

III

THE SUBSTANCE AND ARGUMENT OF THE *POLITICS*

§ 1. *The idea of the* Polis. The *Politics*, as its title indicates, is concerned with the *polis*; or to speak more exactly it is concerned with the 160 or so examples of the *polis*, scattered over the Greek mainland and the maritime area of the Greek dispersion, which Aristotle had studied. It presupposes a small Mediterranean world which was a world of 'urbanity' or civic republics (the largest with an area of 1,000 square miles, but many with 100 or less), and which stood, as such, in contrast with the world of 'rurality' in which the nations or *ethnē* lived. There was some notion among the Greeks of a community called 'Hellas', but it was in no sense a political community. Herodotus conceived it as having the four bonds of common blood, common speech, common religious shrines, and common social habits; but he recognized no political bond. Plato, in the argument of his *Republic*, was enough of a Panhellenist to argue for some system of international law, as between *polis* and *polis*, which would mitigate the rigours of their mutual wars; but the very nature of his argument involves the sovereignty of each *polis*. The orator Isocrates preached the unity of Hellenic culture, and advocated a symmachy of autonomous Hellenic cities united in concord and conquest against the nations around, and especially against the Persians; but he left the cities autonomous. Aristotle himself could say that the Greek stock had the capacity for governing every other people, if only it could once achieve political unity;[1] but though he had been the tutor of Alexander, and remained the friend of Antipater, he never sought to investigate the method by which such unity might be achieved.

The assumption of Aristotle, as of Greek thought generally down to the days of Zeno and the Stoic doctrine of the *cosmopolis*, is that of the small state or civic republic whose citizens know one another personally, and which can be addressed by a single herald and persuaded by a single orator when it is assembled in its 'town meeting'. It is a small and intimate society: it is a church as well as a state: it makes no distinction between the province of the state and that of society; it is, in a word, an integrated system of social ethics, which realizes to the full the capacity of its members, and therefore claims their full allegiance. A limit of size is imposed upon it by its very nature and purpose (as, conversely, the limit of its size has helped to produce its nature and purpose): being

[1] Book VII, c. VII, § 3.

a church and a system of social ethics, it cannot be a Babylon.[1]
Small as it is, it is complete in itself: it is 'self-sufficient', in the
sense that it meets from its own resources—its own accumulated
moral tradition and the physical yield of its own soil and waters—
all the moral and material needs of its members; and as it does not
draw upon others, so it is not conceived as giving, or as bound to
give, to others, or as making its own contribution to the general
development of Hellas. Whole and complete, with a rounded life
of its own, the *polis* rises to a still higher dignity than that of self-
sufficiency. It is conceived as 'natural'—as a scheme of life which,
granted the nature of man, is inevitable and indefeasible. In this
conception of 'nature' (*physis*) we touch a cardinal element in the
theory of Aristotle.

§ 2. *The natural character of the* Polis. A distinction between
'nature' and 'convention' (*physis* and *nomos*)—between institutions
existing 'by nature' and those which existed 'by convention'—had
been drawn by popular teachers in Greece for a century before
Aristotle's time. Some of them had regarded the state, in the form
of the civic republic, as merely a conventional thing—a thing that
might or might not be, and only was because men had agreed, by
a contract, that it should be; and some had even argued that it
had better not be at all, because it defeated the good old rule and
simple plan of 'nature', that the strong man armed should dominate
the weak for his own advantage. Such views involved a theory of
'natural rights' and a doctrine of individualism; and a polemic
against that theory and doctrine (a polemic already waged by Plato
in the teaching of the Academy) is implicit in the beginning of the
Politics and recurs in the course of its argument.

It was not only that such a theory and doctrine cut at the roots
of tradition and undermined the *mos maiorum* in the Greek civic
republic, and thus challenged the whole idea of its system of
social ethics, or again that they were allied with a movement of
individualism in contemporary life, which led men to concentrate,
at the best, on the pursuit of private culture, and impelled them,
at the worst, to turn the state into a milch-cow and make it a commercial association for the distribution among its members of
dividends which they had never earned. It was also that this
theory and doctrine, which identified 'nature' with nothing more
than primary instincts and primitive impulses, were entirely
opposed to the general philosophy of 'nature' which Aristotle had

[1] Here, and elsewhere in this section, the writer has used some passages from
his chapter in the *Cambridge Ancient History* (vol. vi, c. xvi) on 'Greek Political
Thought and Theory in the Fourth Century'. He wishes to record his gratitude
to the Syndics of the Cambridge University Press for their permission to use
these passages.

himself developed. Seeing everywhere the growth of an initial
potentiality into a final form or end, and seeing in its form or end
the essential nature of everything, he applied his general philosophy to man and man's long development, as he struggled upward
from the potentiality of primary instincts to the form, or end, or
nature, of a political being—a being intended by his potentialities
for existence in a *polis*, and a being who achieved his 'nature' in
and through such existence. This was the conception which he
opposed to the radical views of popular teachers; and it was a
conception which made the *polis* entirely and perfectly natural,
because it was the natural home of the fully grown and natural
man.[1]

But this conception does not imply that the state is natural
because it has grown. 'It is not growing like a tree . . . that makes
man better be'; and the growth of man into membership of a state,
which makes him better and ensures his moral betterment (and
thereby realizes his nature), is not like the growth of a tree. If
Aristotle uses the language of growth in the beginning of the
Politics, and speaks of the growth of the household into the village
and of villages into the state, he does not rest his belief in the
natural character of political society on the simple fact of such
growth. What makes the State natural, in his view, is the fact that,
however it came into existence, it is as it stands the satisfaction of
an immanent impulse in human nature towards moral perfection—
an immanent impulse which drives men upwards, through various
forms of society, into the final political form. Indeed it would
seem that Aristotle, true to the general Greek conception of politics
as a sphere of conscious creation, in which legislators had always
been active, believed in the conscious construction of the *polis*.
'There is an immanent impulse in all men towards an association
of this order; but the man who first constructed such an association

[1] A brief analysis of the associations of the Greek word *physis* is attempted
below, in the course of section IV 4 of this Introduction. An analysis and
interpretation of Aristotle's use of the term is given in R. G. Collingwood's
posthumous work on *The Idea of Nature*, pp. 80–92. He defines the term, in
the sense in which it is used by Aristotle, as meaning 'the essence of things
which have a source of movement in themselves' (p. 81). He notes that two
notions are here implied. (1) Because there is *movement*, 'nature as such is
process, growth, change: the process is a development, i.e. the changing takes
forms . . . in which each is the potentiality of its successor' (p. 81). (2) Because the things moving have the source of movement *in themselves*, nature as
such is not only change, but self-change: nature is 'characterized not merely by
change, but by effort or nisus or tendency . . . the seed is pushing its way up
through the soil . . . the young animal is working at increasing its size and developing its shape until it reaches the size and shape of an adult' (p. 83).
  Dr. Collingwood notes that modern evolutionary philosophies, such as that
of Whitehead, are frankly accepting 'the ideas of potentiality, nisus, and teleo-
logy' involved in Aristotle's conception of *physis* (p. 83, and later, pp. 167–70).

was the greatest of benefactors.'[1] There is no contradiction in such a sentence; for there is no contradiction between the immanent impulses of human nature and the conscious art which is equally, or even more, a part of the same human nature. Human art may indeed contravene the deepest and best in human nature: it may construct perverted states, based on the pursuit of mere wealth or the lust of mere power; and it may thus defeat the natural human impulse to moral perfection. But equally, and indeed still more, it may help to realize nature.[2] Nature and convention are not in their essence opposites, but rather complements.

§ 3. *The dominance of the* Polis. The State is therefore natural when, or in so far as, it is an institution for that moral perfection of man to which his whole nature moves. All the features of its life—slavery, private property, the family—are equally justified, and also natural, when, or in so far as, they serve that sovereign end. Plato refuses private property and family life to the guardians of the *Republic*, because he believes that they would interfere with the moral life of the guardians, and therefore with the moral life of the state, and therefore with the true order of nature. Aristotle vindicates for every citizen both private property and family life, and regards them both as institutions belonging to all by the order of nature, because he believes that the moral life of every citizen requires the 'equipment' of private property and the discipline of family life. Plato and Aristotle may differ; but for both there is one end—the end of a moral perfection which can only be attained in the *polis*—and that end is the measure of all things. The end can be ruthless; and it shows its hard edge in Plato's theory. It not only deprives the guardians of property and family life; it also deprives the labouring class of citizenship, a high calling which cannot be followed by men engaged in getting and spending. The end is less ruthless in Aristotle's theory. But it serves to justify slavery, which can afford the citizen leisure for the high purposes of the state; and it excludes from real membership of the state all persons other than those who possess that leisure. The end justifies: the end condemns: the end is sovereign. It is easy to glide into the view that the state and its 'well-being' (in the full Greek sense of that term) are thus made into a higher end to which the individual and his personal development are sacrificed. Generally stated, such a view is erroneous: it involves a return, in another form, of that antithesis between political society and the individual which Plato and Aristotle refuse to recognize. The state (they

---

[1] Book I, c. II, § 15.
[2] 'The purpose of education, like that of art generally, is simply to copy nature by making her deficiencies good': see Book VII, c. XVII, § 15 and note.

believe) exists for the moral development and perfection of its individual members: the fulfilment and perfection of the individual means—and is the only thing which means—the perfection of the state; there is no antithesis. But this is true, after all, only for the man who is citizen and the individual who is a member of the body corporate. The rest *are* sacrificed: they lose the development which comes from citizenship, because citizenship is keyed so high. Rich things have a high price. A lower ideal of citizenship, purchasable at a price which the many can afford to pay, is perhaps a more precious thing than the rare riches of the Platonic and Aristotelian ideal.

A state which is meant for the moral perfection of its members will be an educational institution. Its laws will serve 'to make men good': its offices ideally belong to the men of virtue who have moral discernment: its chief activity will be that of training the young and sustaining the mature in the way of righteousness. That is why we may speak of such a state as really a church: like Calvin's Church it exercises a 'holy discipline'. Political philosophy thus becomes a sort of moral theology.[1] Plato in the *Republic* is the critic of the traditional religion of Greece: in the *Laws* he enunciates the canons of a true religion, and even advocates religious persecution: in both he is the censor of art and poetry and music. Aristotle is less drastic: of religion he hardly treats; but he would exercise a moral censorship of plays and tales, and he would subject music to an ethical control. The 'limit of state-interference' never suggested itself to the Greek philosophers as a problem for their consideration. They seek to regulate the family, and the most intimate matters of family life, no less than art and music. Plato's austerities are famous; but even Aristotle can define the age for marriage and the number of permissible children. Whatever has a moral bearing may come under moral regulation. Neither Plato nor Aristotle allows weight to the fundamental consideration that moral action which is done *ad verba magistri* ceases to be moral. The state should indeed promote morality; but the direct promotion of morality by an act of state-command is the destruction of moral autonomy. The good will is the maker of goodness; and the state can only increase goodness by increasing the freedom of the good will. That is why modern thinkers, bred in the tenets of Plato and Aristotle, would nevertheless substitute the formula of 'removal of hindrances' for the formula of 'administration of stimulus' implied in the teaching of their masters. But after all we do an injustice to the theorists of the city-state if we compare them with the theorists of the great modern state. Their state, we have always to remind

[1] On Aristotle's conception of the relation between politics and ethics see Appendix A.

ourselves, was a church as well as a state; and most churches believe in moral guidance and stimulus. Indeed there is a stage of moral growth, when the good will is still in the making, at which it is a great gain to be habituated by precept in right-doing. Any state which undertakes an educational function, like every parent, must recognize the existence of this stage, and must include 'the strengthening of character' in the curriculum of its schools. Yet it is but a stage. The grown man must see and choose his way. Plato and Aristotle perhaps treated their contemporaries too much as if they were 'always children'.

§ 4. *The ideal* Polis *and the criticism of actual states.* If these are the general principles of politics which Aristotle assumes, we can readily see that they will naturally tend to the construction of an ideal state, in which such principles, nowhere purely exhibited in actual life, will find their realization for thought. The building of such ideals, whether on the quasi-antiquarian lines which we find in Xenophon, or on the bolder and freer lines traced by the imagination of Plato, was a staple of Greek political speculation. It accorded with an artistic temper, which loved to shape material into a perfect form, and would even, in the sphere of politics, assume a perfect material (in the sense of a population ideal in disposition, endowed with an ideal territory, and distributed on an ideal social system) in order that it might be the more susceptible of receiving an ideal form. It accorded, too, with the experience of a people accustomed to the formation of new colonial cities, on which the 'oecist' and legislator might freely stamp an abiding mark. Aristotle records, in the second book of the *Politics*, the plans and schemes of previous builders of ideal states: in the seventh and eighth he sketches the plan and scheme of his own ideal. But his ideal state is a torso; and the profundity and the influence of Aristotle's thought are rather to be traced in his enunciation of general principles than in his picture of their realization. He is the master of definition and classification; and it is the terse Aristotelian formula which has always influenced thought.

But ideals will also serve as judges and measuring-rods for the actual. The Greek states of the fourth century came to judgement before the bar of Plato's and Aristotle's ideals. Plato in the *Republic* first constructed his ideal, and then in the later books showed why, and in what degree, actual states were a corruption of that ideal. Aristotle seems to follow a reverse procedure when, early in the *Politics*, he examines actual states in order that their merits and their defects may throw light on the requirements of an ideal state; but he too uses ideal principles to criticize and classify actual states.

Three results seem to follow from the application of the ideal as a touchstone to the actual—first, an elucidation of the principles on which offices should be assigned, and constitutions should therefore be constructed (for 'a constitution is a mode of assignment of offices'); secondly, a classification and a grading of actual constitutions; and, finally, a criticism of that democratic constitution, which in the fourth century had become general, and which, in the populous states of his day, Aristotle regarded as inevitable.

The assignment of office, we are told, must follow the principle of distributive justice. To each the state must assign its awards in proportion to the contribution which each has made to the state; and in estimating the contribution of each we must look to the end of the state, and measure the contribution to that end. Logically, this would seem to mean the enthronement of the virtuous, or an ethical aristocracy: in the last resort, it would involve the enthronement, if he can be found, of the one man of supreme virtue, or an absolute and 'divine' monarchy. Practically, Aristotle recognizes that there are various contributions which, directly or indirectly, tend to the realization of the end. Besides virtue, there is wealth, which is necessary to the end in so far as perfect virtue requires a material equipment; and besides wealth there is 'freedom'—freedom not only in the sense of free birth, but also in the sense of liberty from that dependence on others, and that absorption in mechanical toil, which distract men from the free pursuit of virtue. This is one of the lines along which Aristotle moves to the theory of the mixed constitution, which recognizes various contributions and thus admits various classes to office.

A classification of constitutions readily follows on this line of speculation: its terms, traced already in the speculation of the fifth century, and deepened and broadened by Plato in the *Politicus*, are firmly established by Aristotle in the third book of the *Politics*. The criticism of the democratic constitution follows in its turn. It has abandoned 'proportionate' for 'absolute' equality: it awards the same honour and the same standing to each and every citizen. It is based on recognition of one contribution, and one only—that of 'freedom'; and that contribution is by no means the highest or weightiest. Nor is this all. Not content with the freedom which means a voice for all in the collective control of common affairs, it has added a freedom which means the absence of control, the surrender of moral discipline, and the random life of chance desires. But this is anarchy: it is the negation of the city-state as it was conceived by Plato and Aristotle. It is this fact rather than aristocratic leanings—it is a dislike of what they regard as anarchy, because anarchy is blank negation—which makes them both (but Plato far more than Aristotle) the critics of democracy.

We can understand the rigour of their criticism; but we can hardly admit its justice. Democratic government in the fourth century did not mean anarchy. The Athenian citizens had their defects: they loved the free theatre almost more than the free city; yet the last days of Athenian freedom were not a disgrace either to the city-state or to the democratic constitution, and the career of Demosthenes was an answer to the strictures of Plato and Aristotle. Discipline and order were abroad in the days before and after Chaeronea: neither Eubulus nor Lycurgus was a demagogue; and, indeed, the statesmen of the fourth century in general stand as a proof that the Athenian people had some sense of merit and its desert. Nor can Aristotle's censure upon 'extreme' democracy, that it means the overthrow of established law by temporary decrees of the sovereign people, be justified at the bar of history. It is a misconception of the facts. Apart from this misinterpretation Aristotle is, on the whole, less critical of democracy than Plato. He recognizes, towards the middle of the third book of the *Politics*, that there is, after all, much to be said on behalf of the mass of people. They have a faculty of collective judgement, which hits the mark, alike in questions of art and matters of politics; 'some appreciate one part, some another, and all together appreciate all.'[1] They know again, from their own experience, how government and its actions pinch; and that knowledge has its value, and deserves its field of expression. These things suggest that the people should have their share in the government of the state; and Aristotle would assign to them those functions of electing the magistrates, and of holding the magistrates to account at the end of their term of office, which their faculty of judgement and their experience of the pressure of government both fit them to discharge.

§ 5. *Aristotle's conception of law.* Aristotle's view of law is different from that of Plato. Anxious for a free field for the higher wisdom, Plato will have no laws in the state of the *Republic*. The eternal Ideas matter more than laws; and those who have apprehended these Ideas must be free to stamp them at their discretion on the state. At the most Plato lays down a few fundamental principles—articles of belief rather than laws—to bind and guide the ruler: the state, for example, must never be allowed to exceed its due size, and its citizens must always be kept to the due discharge of specific function. In the *Laws*, as the title indicates, law comes down to earth: philosophy only remains in the shape of 'prefaces' attached to each law for the purpose of explanation and persuasion.

[1] Book III, c. xi, § 3.

It is this admission of law (rather than the surrender of communism, which is by comparison a subsidiary matter) that makes the state of the *Laws* a 'second best'. At the same time, there is a fine philosophy of law in the dialogue; and there is an exact articulation and systematization of law—both criminal and civil—which represents the first real Greek attempt at codification, and influenced the growth both of Hellenistic law and, through it, of the law of Rome. Aristotle rendered less service to law: on the other hand he was, in general and in principle, a steady and consistent advocate of its sovereignty. 'The rule of law is preferable to that of a single citizen: even if it be the better course to have individuals ruling, they should be made law-guardians or ministers of the laws.'[1] The Aristotelian thesis of the sovereignty of law, and the conception of government as limited by law, had a long history, and was a potent influence through the Middle Ages. The law which Aristotle thus enthrones is no code: it is the custom, written and unwritten, which has developed with the development of a state. Aristotle has a sense of historic development, which is as implicit in his general philosophy as the demand for radical reconstruction is embedded in the philosophy of Plato. The growth of potential capacity into actual 'form' or 'end', which is the general formula of his philosophy, leaves room for a large appreciation of history and the value of moving time: the Platonic conception of the impress of a timeless and eternally perfect Idea upon receptive matter, which may take place at any moment when that Idea is apprehended, is inimical to any belief in gradual development. In the same way the Aristotelian formula involves some recognition of progress—though Aristotle believed that progress, alike in poetry and politics, had attained its conclusion and perfection in his time, and he had none of that looking-forward to an unending and unresting progress which is a mark of later thought.

§ 6. *Aristotle's theory of 'economy' and education*. In modern times we distinguish between state and society. The one is the area of politics proper, of obligatory rule and involuntary obedience: the other is the area of voluntary co-operation, conducted in and by a variety of societies, educational, ecclesiastical, economic. It would be difficult to apply any such distinction to ancient Greece. The state was the one organization that embraced and contained its citizens: such groups as there were—small religious societies for the worship of Dionysus or the Orphic mysteries, or trade associations with a common hero or god—were minor things. The *polis* included everything; and in the same way the theory of the *polis* included studies to which we should now give a separate

[1] Book III, c. xvi, §§ 3-4.

existence—in particular the theory of economics, and (we may also add) the theory of education. There is much writing on 'economics' in the fourth century. It dealt partly with household management (the literal meaning of *oikonomia*), and partly with public economy or state finance. There is the *Oeconomicus* of Xenophon, which gave inspiration to Ruskin; there is an *Oeconomica* falsely ascribed to Aristotle; there is a treatise by Xenophon *On the Revenues of Athens*; there is economic theory in the *Republic* and the *Laws*; there is the famous and profoundly influential theory of exchange and of interest in the first book of the *Politics*, which affected so deeply the canonists of the Middle Ages. Such economic theory, subordinated as it is to political theory, which in turn is subordinated to (or, perhaps one should rather say, is the crown of) ethics, admits of no isolation of the economic motive, and of no abstraction of economic facts as a separate branch of inquiry. It is a theory of the ways in which households and cities can properly use the means at their disposal for the better living of a good life. Wealth, on this basis, is a means to a moral end; as such a means, it is necessarily limited by the end, and it must not be greater—as equally it must not be less—than what the end requires. This is not socialism; but it is a line of thought inimical to capitalism (which involves the unlimited accumulation of wealth), and through the influence of Ruskin and others it has, in its measure, tended to foster modern socialism.

There was, however, a certain amount of what we may call quasi-socialistic opinion in Greece in the fourth century. Plato, indeed, was not a socialist: the scheme of his *Republic* is a scheme for the divorce of political power from economic possession, under which the governing class (but not the governed) surrenders private property for the sake of a pure devotion to public concerns. He may have been misinterpreted (as he is by Aristotle in the second book of the *Politics*), and have thus come to be regarded as the advocate of a larger and more drastic policy. Some of the later plays of Aristophanes (the *Ecclesiazusae* and the *Plutus*, produced about 390 B.C.) contain a satire upon plans for the general socialization of private property, which must have been current before the *Republic* appeared (possibly about 387 B.C.), and with which its scheme may have been confused. But socialist schemes remained matters of airy speculation, which never penetrated to the people. The citizen of Athens was more often his own employer than an employee: there was little of a wage-system: if there were rich men, they were relieved by 'liturgies' of part of their wealth: if there were poor, there was the Theoric Fund and the payments made for attending the assembly and law-courts. The system of private property which Aristotle defends, on the ground that virtue needs its 'equipment' and personality its medium of expression, was never in any real danger. It was protected, as it perhaps will always be, by the conservatism of small farmers and small artisans working on their own account. The utmost extremity of the radical politician was a demand for redistribution of land (which is not the same as its socialization) and for cancellation of debts.

Slavery was more of a moot question. It was the enslavement of Greeks by Greeks which first began to raise questionings. What was to be thought of the enslavement of the defeated Athenians at Syracuse in 413 B.C.? Was not Callicratidas right when at the storming of Methymna in 406 B.C. he vowed that no Greek should be enslaved if he could prevent it? An echo of such doubts may be traced in Plato's protest against the enslavement of Greeks in the fifth book of the *Republic*. The question became acute when the Thebans liberated the Messenian serfs of the Spartans at the end of 370 B.C. Was this a theft of the private property of Sparta? Was it the restoration to the Messenians of the liberty which was their due? Isocrates defended the Spartan case: a certain Alcidamas spoke on the other side, and protested that 'God has left all men free, and nature has made no man a slave'. This was perhaps rhetorical exaggeration: Alcidamas may really have meant Greeks rather than men in general. Certainly neither Plato nor Aristotle protests against any and every form of slavery. If Plato objects in the *Republic* to the enslavement of Greeks, in the *Laws* he recognizes slavery and legislates for slaves, whom he couples with children as having imperfectly developed minds. Aristotle, recognizing that there has been much debate, makes no very clear pronouncement on the enslavement of defeated Greeks (Philip of Macedon had enslaved many Greeks since the days when the Thebans liberated the Messenian serfs, and the old rule of war might well seem to have been re-established), but he obviously inclines to regard slavery as only proper for barbarians who are 'by nature' slaves. The natural slave, as Aristotle conceives him, is a man whose chief use is his body, but who possesses mind enough, not indeed to control himself, but to understand and to profit by the control of a superior mind. He is a family slave, who is caught up into and elevated by the life of the family: if he serves its purposes, which after all are moral purposes, he enjoys its benefits, which are also moral benefits. There is no great harshness in Aristotle's view of slavery. From the *Ethics* we learn that the slave—not indeed as a slave, but as a man—may be his master's friend; at the end of the *Politics* we are promised (but not given) an explanation of the reason why 'it is wise to offer all slaves the eventual

reward of emancipation'. We may not be convinced by his argument for 'natural' slavery; but we must admit that, by treating
slavery as a moral institution, he lent it the best sanction which it
could receive. To defend slavery on the ground of its potential
moral benefits is better than defence (or even attack) based merely
on an economic calculus.

Another problem of family life debated in the fourth century
was the position of women. The tragedies of Euripides show a
certain feminism: the *Ecclesiazusae* of Aristophanes is a satire upon
women's suffrage: Plato would have women emancipated from
household drudgery for political service in his ideal state. In
speculation of this order the emancipation of women was connected with community of wives, and it was assumed that women
could only be free if the institution of marriage and the mono-
gamous family were abolished. It was the negative assumption,
rather than the positive proposal, which attracted attention and
criticism; and Aristotle, for example, in his criticism of Plato's
proposal, discusses only the question whether wives and children
should be common to all citizens. Upon this line of argument he
defends the private family as vigorously as he defends private
property, and on the same ground: the family is justified by the
moral development which it makes possible. This is very true;
but the problem of the position of women is not solved by the
justification of the family.

It has already been noted that the state which is intended for
the moral perfection of its members is by its very nature an
educational institution. Aristotle's theory of education is thus an
integral and essential part of his theory of the *polis*. He holds that
education should be conducted by the state (and not by individuals
or voluntary associations), and should be directed to the making
of character; and he holds in consequence—the consequence was
readily apparent to Greeks living in a great age of art, and sensitive
to its influence—that the curriculum of education (apart from its
higher and scientific ranges) should be in the domain of aesthetics,
and especially of noble music, such as might insensibly infect the
mind and mould the character by its own nobility. No actual
system of education in Greece was after this pattern. If Spartan
education was conducted by the state, it was merely a military
training: if Athenian education had its aesthetic side, it was neither
conducted nor controlled by the state. Here, as in so many respects,
the theory of Plato and Aristotle departs from contemporary facts.
This is a consideration we have always to bear in mind. We must
be very cautious in using the writings of Plato and Aristotle to
illustrate or to explain contemporary political conditions, or the

actual political thought of their time. Their philosophy is mainly ideal, because it is ethical, and because an ethical philosophy must deal with the ideal. Even when they deal with the actual, and criticize the actual—when, for instance, they are concerned with democracy—they deal with the actual as they saw it rather than as it actually was. The actual as they see it has already been brought into contact with the ideal: it has been, as it were, singed and blackened by the fire of the ideal. This is not to deny that they both started from the ground of the actual to attain their ideals. Nor is it to deny—least of all to Aristotle, who has a large capacity for analysis and appreciation of the given—that they understood the actual which they saw. It is only to say that they understood it in the light of their own philosophy, and condemned it because it was dark in that light.

§ 7. *The later history of Aristotle's political theory.* The Aristotelian theory of man's natural citizenship of the *polis*, and of the moral training and habituation required by such citizenship, was a theory which, as was noted at the beginning of this section, was peculiar to an inner Mediterranean world of 'urbanity', and in no way designed for the outer world of the nations, or *ethnē*, immersed in the 'rurality' of barbarism. Aristotle would have preserved the distinction of the two worlds: he advised Alexander, in the exhortation 'On Colonies', to distinguish between Greeks and barbarians, dealing with the former as a leader or *hēgemōn*, and with the latter as a master or *despotēs*. Alexander did the opposite. He preferred to act in the spirit of the policy afterwards enunciated by Eratosthenes (an Alexandrian scholar of the next century), who 'refused to agree with men who divided mankind into Greeks and barbarians and advised Alexander to treat the former as foes and the latter as friends, declaring that it was better to divide men simply into the good and bad'. By 330, while Aristotle was still teaching the theory of the *polis* in the Lyceum, Alexander was already planning an empire in which he should be equally lord of Greeks and Persians, and both should be equally knit together by intermarriage and common military service. This meant a great revolution. It meant the appearance of the *cosmopolis* in place and instead of the *polis*. It meant the appearance of the idea of the equality of all men—urban or rural, Greek or barbarian—in that *cosmopolis*. Alexander anticipates in action, as Plutarch long afterwards wrote, what Zeno and the Stoics were soon to be teaching in theory: 'men should not live their lives in so many civic republics, separated from one another by different systems of justice; they should reckon *all* as their fellow-citizens, and there should be one life and one order (*cosmos*), as it were of one flock on a common pasture feeding in common under one joint law'.[1] This conception of the *cosmopolis*, and the cognate conception of the equality and fraternity of all men within its general embrace, are the two fundamental conceptions which inaugurate a new epoch—an epoch which succeeds to that of the *polis*, as it precedes that of the national state; an epoch which covers the eighteen centuries (300 B.C.–A.D. 1500) between Aristotle and Alexander at one end and Luther and Machiavelli at the other, and which embraces in its scope the three empires of Macedon, Rome, and Charlemagne. First Stoicism and then Christianity (inheriting and transfiguring the teaching of the Stoics) was the vehicle of these conceptions. St. Paul believed in one church of all Christians which should cover the world, and he held that in that church there was 'neither Greek nor Jew, ... Barbarian, Scythian, bond nor free'.

In the realm of political theory there was for centuries no great book which expressed these conceptions, or explained the revolution which they entailed in men's ideas of the nature of community. Perhaps we may say that such a great book first appeared when St. Augustine wrote, at the beginning of the fifth century of our era, his work on *The City of God*. Here is the first great treatise on the theory of human community since Plato's *Republic* and Aristotle's *Politics*.[2] It was a treatise which was in turn to be succeeded, after the lapse of many centuries, by a system of social and political theory which is still the text and the staple for many thinkers to-day. This was the system of St. Thomas Aquinas, the great Dominican Schoolman of the thirteenth century—a system which is not, indeed, compact in a single book, but scattered through the *Summa Theologica*, the authentic parts of the *De Regimine Principum*, and the political sections of his various commentaries.[3] It is here, and in this system, that the *Politics* of Aristotle is brought once more, after a long interval of oblivion, into the general current of European political thought, of which it has always since been an ingredient.

St. Thomas was furnished by some of his brother Dominicans with a close and literal translation of the *Politics* into Latin. We may say that he fused the teaching of Aristotle's *Politics* with the teaching of St. Augustine's *City of God* in an amalgam which still

---

[1] There is a double play on words in this passage. The Greek 'Cosmos' has the double sense of order and universe; and the Greek 'Nomos' has the double sense of pasture and law (see below, p. lxx).

[2] The translator ventures to refer to his introduction to Healey's translation of *The City of God*, now published in Everyman's Library.

[3] Besides his commentaries on epistles of St. Paul and on the *Sentences* of Peter the Lombard (they too contain some statements of his views on social and political theory), St. Thomas also wrote a commentary on the *Politics*.

remains, after the lapse of seven centuries, the essence of Catholic theory of society and the state. This was one of the great fusions of history—a fusion which united Aristotle not only to St. Augustine, but also to the theory of the canonists, the doctrines of the early Fathers, and the teaching of St. Paul; a fusion, too, which also united some of his essential doctrines of the *polis* with the doctrine and practice of the *cosmopolis*. It was through this fusion that there passed into the general thought of the later Middle Ages some of the essential doctrines of the *Politics*—the doctrine that law is the true sovereign, and that governments are servants of the law; the doctrine that there is a fundamental difference between the lawful monarch and the tyrant who governs by his arbitrary will: the doctrine that there is a right inherent in the people, by virtue of their collective capacity of judgement, to elect their rulers and to call them to account. It is through this fusion that Aristotle's political theory still survives and speaks in the political theory of Jacques Maritain, and that echoes of it may even be traced in the doctrine of associations propounded in the Papal encyclical *Quadragesimo Anno*.[1]

If we ask ourselves, at the end of this summary review of the substance and argument of the *Politics*, 'What has been, and still is, the nature of the legacy which it bequeathed to the common thought of Europe?', the answer may almost be compressed in a single word. The word is 'constitutionalism'. That is the fundamental nature of the legacy derived from the *Politics*, and especially from its third book on 'the theory of citizenship and constitutions'.[2] A famous saying of Dr. Johnson, reported by Boswell, is that 'the first Whig was the devil'. Lord Acton suggested an emendation: not the devil, but St. Thomas Aquinas, was the first Whig. But St. Thomas drew his Whig principles in no small measure from Aristotle; or at any rate, as it is perhaps juster to say, he used Aristotle to corroborate a medieval trend towards constitutionalism already expressed in the purpose of Magna Carta—the purpose 'that the king is, and shall be, below the law'.[3] We may therefore

[1] There is a brief statement of Maritain's theory in his little book on *The Rights of Man* (1944), with references back to Aristotle through the commentaries of St. Thomas (see Appendix III to the present work, *ad initium*). The doctrine of associations, and the general theory of *vita socialis per diversi generis consociationes composite evoluta*, are stated in Part II, section 5, of *Quadragesimo Anno*.

[2] When Laud was impeached for having 'endeavoured to subvert the fundamental laws and government . . and instead thereof to introduce an arbitrary and tyrannical government against law', he answered: 'I could not endeavour this: my knowledge and judgement going ever against an arbitrary government in comparison of that which is settled by law. I learned so much long ago out of Aristotle; and his reasons are too good to be gone against.' Quoted by W. C. Costin, lecture on *William Laud*, p. 18.

[3] Pollock and Maitland, *History of English Law*, vol. i, p. 173.

suggest an emendation of Lord Acton's emendation of Dr. Johnson: not St. Thomas Aquinas, but Aristotle, was the first Whig. Aristotle taught St. Thomas: through St. Thomas he taught Catholic Europe: through St. Thomas he also taught Richard Hooker, who drew from this origin the theory of law and government enunciated in the first book of the *Ecclesiastical Polity*. The 'judicious Hooker' (the term is Locke's own) was in turn one of the masters of Locke, and one of the great sources of the two *Treatises on Civil Government*. The theory of Locke descended in turn to Burke, but Burke also drew from his own studies, and from his reading at Trinity College, Dublin, a direct acquaintance with the general theory of St. Thomas and the general views of Aristotle.[1] There is thus a long line of transmission which runs from Aristotle to St. Thomas, from St. Thomas to Hooker, from Hooker to Locke, and so eventually to Burke. There is not only an analogy, as we have already had reason to suggest,[2] between the climate of Aristotle's *Politics* and the climate of English political thought in the seventeenth and eighteenth centuries. There is also some measure of affiliation.

[1] See the translator's *Essays on Government*, in the essay on 'Burke on the French Revolution', pp. 223, 227.
[2] *Supra*, p. xxxi.

THE VOCABULARY OF THE *POLITICS*

MANY words in every language have associations, echoes, and overtones, which no translation can convey. This is a fact which makes
the translation of poetry especially difficult, if not impossible; for
the poet uses overtones and evokes echoes, by the very nature of
poetic diction, in an especial degree. But it is also a fact which makes
the translation of a work on political theory difficult, and especially
difficult when it is a translation from the Greek. There are overtones, echoes, and associations in the political vocabulary of the
ancient Greeks which we can hardly recapture. Their political
terms were charged with the significance of their own political
environment and their own political experience; and neither the
environment nor the experience is ours. They are terms belonging
to a vanished Mediterranean world of 'urbanity', which is not our
world; and only those who lived in that vanished world could hear
and understand the fullness of their music. It is easy to translate
the Greek word *polis* by our word 'state'; but the essence vanishes
in the translation. The sunshine, the common life, and the civic
ardour of some 'little town'[1] on a land-locked bay of the Mediterranean has passed into something larger, more sombre, and far
more distant. The word 'state' comes to us from the Latin *status*,
in its sense of standing or position: it meant, when we adopted it
in the sixteenth century, the standing or position of the person (or
persons) in authority, so that Louis XIV was etymologically justified in saying *L'État, c'est moi!*; and though it has widened in the
course of time to designate also the whole political community, it
is still used to-day in its old sense (as when we speak of 'state
interference'), and its overtones are still the overtones of authority. How different are the suggestions of the word *polis*—the city:
our city; the violet-crowned city of the Virgin Goddess, with its
citizens

> Ever delicately walking
> Through the most pellucid air.[2]

This difference between *polis* and 'state' may serve to remind
us of a general feature in our English vocabulary of politics. It is
true that we use the word 'politics' (and even the word 'politician'
—though that has a very different significance from the *politikos*

---

[1] . . . Little town, by river or sea shore,
  Or mountain-built with peaceful citadel.
                    (Keats: *Ode on a Grecian Urn*.)
[2] Euripides, *Medea*, the chorus beginning in line 824.

of Plato and Aristotle); but the bulk of our English vocabulary of politics is drawn from the Latin. We speak not only of the 'state', but also of 'constitution', 'government', 'administration', 'sovereignty', 'statute', 'justice'—and every word is derived from the Latin. The bulk of our political vocabulary is a Latin vocabulary.[1] It is a useful, and indeed a majestic vocabulary: Latin has not only sonority, but it has also the gift of solemnity; and it adds precision to both. But the precision of Latin cannot do proper justice to the flexibility and the nuances of the Greek. This is a point which has been admirably emphasized by Sir John Myres, in the concluding pages of his work on *The Political Ideas of the Greeks*. 'With the necessary translation of Greek philosophical nomenclatures into Latin', he writes, 'grave disaster happened.' Perhaps there was hardly disaster,[2] but there certainly was confusion; and the history of the term 'Law of Nature'—a Latin term used to express an idea which comes from the Greek, but fated to alter the original idea it was used to express—is a testimony to the confusion.[3]

In the light of these observations it may be useful to elucidate briefly the ideas implicit in some of the cardinal terms of Aristotle's political vocabulary. Five sets of terms deserve a particular examination. The first set of terms, which may be briefly expressed under the rubric of 'the state', includes the term *polis*, with its derivatives, and a number of cognate terms. The second set, which comes under the rubric of 'government', includes the term *archē* and some allied terms. A third set, of peculiar importance, which comes under the head of 'law and justice', includes the two terms *nomos* and *dikē* and their derivatives. A fourth may be added, which is less political than philosophic—the term *physis* or nature, with its peculiar Greek associations and its special connotation in Aristotle's system of thought. Finally there is a set of terms— terms descriptive of social life and moral conduct—which is so closely connected with the terms of Aristotle's political vocabulary that it equally demands some notice and examination.

§ 1. *The vocabulary of the conception of state.* The word *polis*, as has already been noticed at the beginning of the previous section, means a civic republic, or, more particularly and especially, the city which is its heart. But this is a general statement; and it

----

[1] This, of course, is not peculiar. A little more than half of our ordinary vocabulary consists of Latin words.

[2] It is only just to say that the Latin translations of Aristotle's philosophical terminology (substance and attribute, quality and quantity, and many others) have given to French and English thinkers a clarity denied to German philosophers, who have used native Teutonic forms. But see the Note on p. lxxvi.

[3] Myres, op. cit., pp. 237–40. The writer would add that he is indebted to Sir John Myres in several passages of this section.

instantly needs qualification. We must therefore add, speaking more precisely, that the Greeks had a special word for the city as a place of residence—the word *asty*—and that the word *polis* originally meant the citadel (or acropolis, as it was called at Athens) at the foot of which lay the *asty*. But if this was its original sense, the word *polis* came in time to mean the whole organized political community, including both the residents in the *asty* (with, of course, any magistrates or others resident in the citadel) and the country-dwellers around the *asty* who frequented it for business and politics. This transference and extension of the sense of the word *polis* is easy to understand. The citadel, to which alone the appellation of *polis* was originally given, was the natural centre of gravity and the focus of authority; and it was an easy matter to use the term which originally denoted the centre in order to denote the whole circle and its content.

A further refinement may be added. It has been noted by scholars that the word *polis* was specially applied in Athenian documents to denote the circle of the organized community when it was acting externally (in the way of treaties or otherwise), and was thus engaged in relations with other organized communities. In other words, it was used as a term of the language of diplomacy; and it signified a 'power' engaged in relation with other 'powers'. Another term was employed, in the usage of Athenian documents, to designate the organized community when it was acting internally, and was thus engaged in the conduct of its own domestic affairs. This was the term *demos*, the ancestor of the word 'democracy'. Here again we have to record a growth and a transference of the original sense of the term. The word *demos* was originally used to denote the countryside and the country dwellers (the people of the *agros*, as distinct from the people of the *asty*); and we accordingly find the units of the countryside called, in general Athenian usage, by the name of *demoi*, and their inhabitants by the name of *demotai*. But by the fifth century a new use had supervened. The term *demos*, used in the singular as a general collective noun, had come to signify more particularly the whole Athenian community when assembled for its domestic affairs in an 'assembly of the summoned' or 'meeting of those called out for attendance'—which is the literal meaning of the word *ecclesia*. We may connect the rise of this new use of the term *demos* with the reforms of Cleisthenes (509 B.C.), who organized the Athenian community in a new system of tribes based on the demes of the country-side. 'The result', it has been said, 'was literally "demokratia", government by the country-side population of Attica';[1] but *demos* was

[1] Myres, op. cit., p. 214; cf. also pp. 38–40.

an engulfing term, and it included, of course, the people of the *asty* as well as the people of the country-side.[1]

From this refinement (which, it will be noticed, relates specifically to Athens—but Attic speech and Athenian terminology set the general tone for all Greece) we may now return to the word *polis*. It had a large number of derivatives. There is the derivative *politēs*, or, as we translate it by a Latin word, 'citizen'. There is the derivative *politikos*, which is better translated (though, even so, it is translated imperfectly) by the Latin word 'statesman' than by the word 'politician'. There is the derivative *politikē*, which signifies the theory (or rather the art) of the common life of the *polis* and the betterment of that life, and which is thus something different from 'political theory' or 'the theory of the state'. There is the derivative *politeia*, which we translate by the Latin terms 'constitution' or 'form of government', but which again is something different from either; for it means, as Aristotle explains, a way of life, or a system of social ethics, as well as a way of assigning political offices. Finally, there is the derivative *politeuma*, which is used by Aristotle to signify the concrete or personal side of the *politeia*, or, in other words, to mean the body of persons enjoying full civic rights under the *politeia*.[2]

This abundant wealth of derivatives from the one word *polis* creates two difficulties for the translator. The first is that he is bound to use different words (citizen, statesman, political theory, constitution, civic body) for a set of words which are all verbally interconnected and all chime verbally together in the original Greek. He therefore loses inevitably the consonance and concordance, drawn from the common associations and overtones of the common life of the *polis*, which the words originally carried. The second, and added, difficulty is that most of the words which he is compelled to use in translating the derivatives of *polis* are words derived from the Latin. They are good

---

[1] It may be added here that Aristotle uses a number of other words which are cognate with *demos*—a term which has been translated, according to the nature of the context, either by the word 'people' or the word 'populace'. One of these other words is *plēthos* (with its two companions *hoi polloi* and *hoi pleiones*—the many and the more), which has been generally translated as 'the masses', but might be rendered more truly, if also more pedantically, as 'the *plenum*' or 'the plurality'. ('The masses' has an overtone of depreciation, which the Greek word, with its suggestion of 'fullness', does not carry.) Another word is *ochlos* (the crowd or mob), which Aristotle applies to the crowds in the market-square, or to the mob of oarsmen in the Athenian triremes, but sometimes uses more simply to designate mere multitude.

[2] In the translation the term *politeuma* is generally rendered as 'the civic body'. In one passage (III, VI, § 1) Aristotle identifies the *politeuma* with the *politeia*, enunciating the principle that 'the civic body is the constitution itself' (cf. III, VII, § 2).

words, but they are words of a more rigid and static quality. They are more legal and (if that word may be used) less social. A 'constitution', in our sense of the word, is not a way of life. The *politeia* was; and it was thus something more—if also, in legal precision, something less—than a constitution.

§ 2. *The vocabulary of the conception of government.* Turning from the notion of the state to that of government, we may now proceed to examine the significance and the associations of some of the current Greek terms connected with the latter notion. We have already seen that the term *polis* supplied two derivatives—the *politikos* or statesman, and the *politeuma* or civic governing body— which are both connected with the notion of government. But there are also two other terms—the term *archē* and the term *kyrios* —which deserve investigation. The term *archē* is the general term for rule or government, as the term *archōn* is the general term for a ruler, governor, or magistrate. The word originally signifies 'beginning' or 'initiative'; and we may imagine that the reason why it was extended, by an easy transference, to mean authority or rule was that the Greeks regarded those in authority as beginning, or starting, or initiating a course of political action.[1] If the essence of authority is thus initiative, the question will naturally arise whether the initiative needs confirmation, or some process of validation, before it can proceed on the way to achievement and consummation—in other words, to the *telos* or end which follows the *archē* or beginning. It is perhaps no licence of conjecture to answer this natural question by turning to the term *kyrios*. It is a term familiar in the Christian liturgy in the sense of 'Lord'; but the essential sense of the Greek root from which it comes is con- firmation, ratification, and the general process of giving validity. The word *kyrios* often occurs in the *Politics*, sometimes as a neuter noun and in the form of *to kyrion*, and sometimes as an adjective. It is most readily translated (but, as we shall see, imperfectly trans- lated) by the word 'sovereign'. What, then, is the 'sovereign', or *to kyrion*, which gives validity to the initiative of magistrates—or, it may be, of persons other than magistrates who, in the phrase of

---

[1] The point is fully developed by Myres, op. cit., pp. 80–97. It may be noted that Attic usage described those who were in authority not only by the name of 'those in the *archē*' (or at the beginning of action), but also by that of 'those in the *telos*' (or at the end and achievement of action). The magistrate begins, or initiates; but he must also end, or achieve, the initiative which he has started. Aristotle, however, does not appear to follow this usage. He needs the term *telos* for his philosophical doctrine of final causes; and he uses it in that sense throughout the *Politics*. The one passage in which there is an approach to a political use of the term *telos* is in Book VI, c. VIII, § 17, where he speaks of an office possessing the double power 'of introducing [i.e. initiating] matters and bringing them to completion' (*telos*).

Aristotle, 'introduce matters'?[1] The answer of Aristotle is simple. Again and again he speaks of the deliberative body as being *to kyrion*. It is therefore the deliberative body which is the validity-giving organ, or sovereign, in any constitution. That organ will vary, of course, in size and in breadth of composition from one constitution to another. In democratic Athens it would include the thousands of citizens who attended the *ecclesia*. In an oligarchy it might be restricted to a council, or even to an inner council. But whatever may be its size or the breadth of its composition, the deliberative is *to kyrion*, and it exercises what we call sovereignty.[2]

The system of government implied in the genius of the Greek language and the terminology of Aristotle is thus a system in which the 'initiative' of civic magistrates is combined with 'validation' by the civic organ of deliberation. These are the terms in which we must think of the government of the Greek *polis*. They are also the terms in which we may think of the government of the Roman *civitas* in the early days of the Republic. But the Roman Republic passed into an empire; and the Latin terminology acquired an imperial tincture. Government became a matter of *principatus* —of 'the first place' or 'pre-eminence' rather than of 'initiative': it came to be surrounded by the idea of *maiestas*—of a 'superiority' of grandeur resident in the *princeps*. This *maiestas* passed, or was changed, during the later Middle Ages, but more especially during the sixteenth century, into the cognate word 'sovereignty', which was derived, through the popular Latin *superanus*, from the Latin preposition *super*. We thus enter upon the days of a high and transcendent 'sovereignty', naturally allied with an idea of the 'state' (which also came on the scene, as we have already had reason to notice at the beginning of this section, during the course of the sixteenth century) by virtue of which a 'state' was regarded as the 'standing' or position of the person (or persons) in the enjoyment of superior authority. All of this issues, and is expressed, in the Benthamite and Austinian notion of the sovereignty of a determinate person or body of persons in receipt of habitual obedience from the bulk of a given society; and much of this is still implied in our use of the word 'sovereignty' to-day. But little, if anything, of this is germane to the ancient world of the *polis*, with its initiating magistrates and its validating deliberative body. If, therefore, we use the word 'sovereign' in translating any of Aristotle's Greek, we are importing something in the act, and we are bound to give warning of the importation.

[1] In Athenian use by the end of the fifth century, demagogues who were not magistrates exercised initiative in the assembly: see Book IV, c. IV, § 25 and note.

[2] But only an *immediate* sovereignty, subject to the *ultimate* law (see Index, under Sovereignty).

§ 3. *The vocabulary of the conceptions of law and justice.* We may now proceed to the terms connected with the notions of law and justice. Early in the course of the *Politics*, at the end of the second chapter of the first book, Aristotle, in a striking passage, introduces the Greek terms for these notions. 'Man, when perfected, is the best of the animals; but if he be isolated from "Nomos" and "Dikē" he is the worst of all.' He adds—and these words are also striking—' "Dikē" belongs to the *polis*; for "Dikē", which is the determination of what is just (*to dikaion*), is an ordering of the political association.'

The greater of these two words is the word *dikē*. What does it signify, and what are its associations? Literally it means a showing or 'indication', and it is perhaps derived from the same root as the word *digitus* or finger. On this basis it comes to mean a showing or indication—in the form of a pronouncement—about the 'right' or 'straight' thing to do, or about the proper 'correction' of something which has been done askew or amiss; and it may thus be said to connect itself with the Latin *rectum* and with modern derivatives of that word (through the compound *directum*) such as the French *droit* and the Italian *diritto*, as well as with our own word 'right'. But we shall not understand the full implication of the word *dikē* unless we trace it in its derivatives (for it too, like the word *polis*, was fruitful in derivatives), and particularly in the two derivatives *dikaiosynē* and *dikastērion*.

Dikaiosynē is the quality of going straight or doing right. But it means something more than, or at any rate something different from, the Latin *iustitia* and our English 'justice'. These are specifically legal words—except when they are used with religious connotations derived from the Vulgate and the Latin Fathers or from our English Bible. The Greek term *dikaiosynē* is not specific-ally legal. If *dikē*, as Aristotle says, 'is an ordering of the political association', we have to remember that the association of the *polis* was a system of social ethics. *Dikaiosynē* is the quality of a man belonging to such a system; and it is therefore ethical as well as legal. It has the overtones and suggestions of our own word 'righteousness'. Whenever we meet the word 'justice' in a transla-tion from the Greek—particularly from the Greek of Plato's *Republic*, but also from the Greek of Aristotle's *Politics*—we have to remember that what we are meeting is something more than our 'justice'. We are meeting a moral virtue as well as a legal quality; and though the legal quality may be often in the foreground, and may seem to occupy the whole stage, the moral virtue is always in the background. The strict sense of law as law was not a mark of the *polis*. From some points of view this may be counted a defect;

but at any rate it was a fact. *Dikaiosynē* was one of the virtues: indeed it could be counted as the compendium and consummation of the virtues, in which the whole of goodness stood compact.[1]

Dikastērion is an institutional word: it denotes a court in which *dikē* is administered and the right and straight course is shown or indicated. But such a court is hardly a law court in our sense of the word; nor were its members (the *dikastai*), properly speaking, judges. The Athenian dikasteries were popular courts of hundreds of members which expressed the people's sense of *dikē* and the demands of *dikaiosynē*. They are thus the organ, in the judicial sphere, which corresponds to the deliberative in the other spheres of the State: they are in that sphere (we may almost say) *to kyrion*. They are the final force beyond the 'initiative' of any magistrate or college of magistrates which may administer justice: they are in some sense sovereign: at any rate they are the validation and confirmation of *to dikaion*. From any strict legal point of view this system is of course defective: it remits what ought to be strict and impartial justice to the emotional pleadings of litigants and the fluid popular sense of justice. But it would be an error to adopt a strict legal point of view. The Athenian dikasteries were not administering a strict legal system of justice. They were seeking to express, as samples and representatives of the civic community, an idea of what was 'right', or 'straight', or (we may even say) 'fair'. They were seeking, in other words, to express a public opinion of what was generally *equitable*. They were, if we like to say so, transcending legal justice, and running into the subjective; but the historian of jurisprudence may none the less pass a verdict on their action which is not unfavourable.[2]

We may now turn to the word *nomos*, and to the relation between *nomos* and *dikē*. *Nomos* comes from a root *nem* which grew into many trunks—not only law, but also pasture: not only law and pasture, but also currency (*nomisma*), and also nemesis or (as it is defined in the dictionary) 'the righteous assignment of anger at anything unjust or unfitting'. The fundamental notion of the root is assigning or apportioning; and the suggestion which it conveys is that of assigning a place or position and fixing its bounds. That is how the notion of law can go with the notion of pasture (*in loco pascuae me collocavit*—He stationed me by his assignment in a place of pasture): that is why it is congenial with the notion of nemesis (in the Greek sense of the word); and that is why it is connected with

---

[1] See Appendix II, *ad initium*.

[2] See Vinogradoff, *Historical Jurisprudence*, vol. ii, pp. 63–9 and pp. 143 sqq., and on the conception of fairness or the equitable (*to epieikes*) see Appendix II. A, *ad finem*, and B (especially n. 3 on p. 371).

the notion of currency as a thing assigned and apportioned.[1] The *nomos* of a political association is thus the assignment or apportionment of places and their bounds; and the *nomoi*, in the plural, are the several rules of this assignment. *Nomos* is thus close to *dikē*, which, as we saw, is a showing or indication of the right and straight thing to do; and conversely *dikē* (defined by Aristotle as 'an ordering of the political association') is close to the *nomos* which assigns and apportions places and bounds. The relation of *nomos* to *dikē* is therefore one of close congruity; but it is at the same time a relation of difference. *Dikē* is a showing of what is right in actual and particular cases: *nomos* is a general formulation or assignment of positions. *Dikē* moves and bends to the case, 'like the flexible rule of lead used in the Lesbian style of building':[2] *nomos* has the rigidity of a general rule. *Dikē* speaks by the *dikastērion*: *nomos* speaks either by some ancient written formulation or by some old and unwritten customary rule of the same general scope and validity.

It will be seen that *nomos* is not legislation in our sense of the word; and it may be noted here that a legislature, sitting in constant session and regularly making laws, was in no way an institution of the Greek *polis*.[3] *Nomos* is an old formulation rather than a contemporary legislative act; and it is a formulation which transcends strict law and may enter the domain of social ethics. (That is why Aristotle can connect education with the spirit of the laws, and why he can speak of the laws as intended 'to make the citizens good and just'.) In both of these ways *nomos* is different from *lex*, which specifically means an enactment or contemporary legislative act, and which is specifically legal in its intention and scope. There is a passage in one of the speeches of Demosthenes, addressed to an Athenian *dikastērion*, which has been more than once quoted by scholars,[4] but may be quoted here once more for the light which it throws on the current Greek conception of *nomos*, as an Athenian orator and statesman presented it to his fellow citizens:

Be the *polis* in which they have their abode great, or be it small, men's lives are all controlled by nature (*physis*) and by *nomos*. Nature is something unordered, something uneven, something peculiar to each man; *nomoi* are something common, something ordered, something identical for all men. Nature, if it be evil, often wishes for evil things;

---

[1] On the connexion between *nomos* and *nomisma* see Book I, c. IX, § 8 and note.

[2] See Appendix II. A, *ad finem*.

[3] See the notes on the nature of Greek law in Book III, c. XI, § 19, and in Appendix II. B, *ad finem*, p. 371, n. 3.

[4] See Vinogradoff, *Historical Jurisprudence*, vol. ii, c. ii, § 1, and Sir John Myres, *The Political Ideas of the Greeks*, pp. 189–94.

and you will therefore find men of that type doing wrong. *Nomoi* wish for the just, the good, and the beneficial: this is what they seek; and this is what, when once it was found, was shown[1] to men as a common injunction, equal for all and alike for all. This is *nomos*, to which it is proper that all men should render obedience. There are many reasons why they should do so; but the chief of them are—first, that law is an invention and gift of the gods [and has thus a religious origin]; next, that it represents the opinion of sensible men [and is thus based on the best of public opinion]; next, that it is a correction of wrongdoings, whether voluntary or involuntary [and it thus sets matters 'right' or 'straight']; and, finally, that it is the general covenant of a *polis*, in accordance with which it is proper that all the members of the *polis* should live.

The last of the reasons which Demosthenes gives for obedience to *nomos* is the only one of the four which introduces the specific notion of volition (though that notion has already been implied in the use of the term 'injunction'); and we may notice that it introduces volition, or 'enactment', in the particular form of a covenant, or agreement, made between the members of a *polis*. That is a homage to liberty; but it is a homage which Aristotle, in the third book of the *Politics*,[2] is unwilling to pay. Regarding the *polis* as something more than an alliance, he equally regards its *nomos* as something more than a covenant (he uses the same word as Demosthenes) or 'a guarantor of men's rights against one another'. Law is to him something higher: it is 'a rule of life such as will make the members of a polis good and just'. It is the sister of *dikaiosynē*; and *dikaiosynē* is a righteousness which transcends any terms of contract.

§ 4. *Philosophical terms.* The vocabulary of the *Politics* not only raises questions of political nomenclature. It also raises questions of philosophical terminology. Aristotle assumes that students and readers will be familiar with the general 'terms of art' which belong to his philosophy. He assumes, for instance, that they will understand the sense in which he uses the word *physis* and its derivatives; he assumes that they will know what he means by saying that 'the *polis* is by *physis*', or that 'man is by *physis* an animal intended for life in the *polis*'. Something has already been said, in the previous sections, about the origin and the significance of his general conception of *physis*. Here it can only be noticed that an English translator is bound to render *physis* and *physikos* by the Latin words 'nature' and 'natural', and that he is equally bound to alter the exact significance of the Greek by using those Latin terms. The

---

[1] Two things may be noted in this verb—first, that it is in the past tense (which suggests the antiquity of law), and secondly that it is the same verb of 'showing' which is the root of *dikē*.

[2] III, c. IX, § 8.

Latin *natura*, connected with a verb which indicates the idea of birth, suggests the primitive: the Greek *physis*, connected with a verb which indicates the idea of growing (and which may be used, in the transitive sense, of 'growing' a family, or teeth, or an understanding), suggests the whole process that leads from the first inception of 'growing', through all the stages of 'growth', to the completion of the 'grown' man. That is all implied in the saying that 'the *polis* is by *physis*'. It is hardly implied in the rendering that 'the state exists by nature', which rather carries the mind towards the notion of primitive origin. To get a true conception of Aristotle's doctrine of the natural state—and of his doctrine of natural justice and natural law as expressed in the *Ethics* and the *Rhetoric*[1]—it is necessary always to remember that the word 'natural' is here raised to a power which is higher than it possesses in our ordinary speech. We have, as it were, to unhook the word from the Latin *natura*, and to hitch it to the Greek *physis*, in order to become aware of its associations and echoes, and to see that it includes the process of 'growth' and the condition of being 'grown' as well as the beginnings of 'growing'.

§ 5. *Social and moral terms.* There are many other 'terms of art' in Aristotle's philosophical vocabulary which the translator has sought, wherever it seemed to him necessary, to explain in his notes to the text.[2] But there are also some terms which are not Aristotelian 'terms of art', but common terms of ordinary usage in the general vocabulary of the Greeks, about which some final words may be said. They are terms of everyday life, common to all civilized peoples; but they are terms which were used by the Greeks, and are regularly used in the *Politics*, with something of a peculiar flavour. There are two main sets of such terms. The first set may be called social. It includes the various terms which were used to denote social grading and the difference between social classes. Greek life, like the life of most peoples and states, was based on a distinction of social strata. Apart from the depressed class of household slaves (*douloi*) and that of the serfs or dependants tied to the soil (who went by various names in different Greek states, but may be generally designated as *perioikoi*), there were two main strata. The upper is called by various names in the course of the *Politics*: numerically, it is 'the few' (*oligoi*): economically, it is 'the wealthy' (*plousioi*) or 'the possessing' class: in point of culture and prestige, it is 'the better' or 'the best' (*beltiones*

[1] See Appendix II. A. 4, and B, *ad initium*.
[2] The reader, for instance, will find explanatory notes on the term 'association' (or *koinōniā*) in Book I, c. 1, § 1: on the terms 'whole' and 'compound' (*holon* and *syntheton*), as applied to the state, in Book III, c. 1, § 2: on the term 'leisure' (*scholē*), and cognate terms, in Book VII, c. xv, § 2.

or *aristoi*), or again it is 'the notables' (*gnōrimoi*), or it is 'the reasonable and fair' (*epieikeis*) who make up the better sort, or it is 'the men who are reasonable and fair and able to enjoy leisure'. The other class has also a variety of names. Numerically, as we have already noticed, it is called the 'people' or 'populace' (*demos*),[1] or the 'masses' (*plēthos*), or sometimes the 'mob' (*ochlos*). Economically, it is 'the poor' (*penētes*), or, if we look at its subdivisions, it is 'the manual labourers' (*chernētes*), 'the workers for hire' (*thētes*), and 'the artisans' (*technītai*). In point of culture and manners, it is 'the mechanics' or 'the vulgar' (*banausoi*),[2] who fill their lives

> By mere mechanic operation;

who must say to themselves

> My nature is subdued
> To what it works in, like the dyer's hand;

who are by their nature 'the unleisured' (*ascholoi*), spending their days in a cycle of 'toil' and 'relaxation' (*ponos* and *anapausis*), and having no 'opportunity of leisure'.

The connotations and associations of this set of social terms, as it appears in the *Politics*, were by no means entirely true to the actual facts of Athenian life, where the workman—the mason, or the tanner—had his honour, could play his part in the general system of the State, and could enjoy its treasures of culture on the Acropolis or in the theatre. It would rather appear that the whole set of terms belonged to the vocabulary of the higher society in which Aristotle and his students would more particularly move, and that they reflect the prejudices of that society.[3] Something the same may be said of the second main set of terms, which may be called by the name of moral. The general moral terminology of the *Politics* assumes a system of ethics which is based on the rational principle of a trained and discerning mind. Virtue is defined in the *Ethics* as 'a state of character, concerned with choice, which consists in a mean . . . determined by a rational principle' (or *logos*)

---

[1] In a broader sense, as was noted above, *demos* denotes *all* the members of the state assembled in the *ecclesia* for the conduct of domestic affairs.

[2] The word *banausos* is said to be derived from the Greek word for a furnace, and to denote originally the man who works by the forge or in the smithy. It may therefore be apposite to refer to Ecclesiasticus, xxxviii. 24–34, and especially to verse 28, which denies wisdom to 'the smith sitting by the anvil', whose flesh 'the vapour of the fire will waste'. The whole passage, written under Greek influence (perhaps between 200 and 180 B.C.), gives a striking account of general Greek ideas of social structure. See the note on Book VII, c. IX, § 4.

[3] Aristotle himself, when he escapes from the current vocabulary of a circle, and pauses to examine impartially the capacity of the many, defends that capacity alike in the sphere of politics and in that of aesthetics; see Book III, c. XI, §§ 2–3 and note.

'such as the man of practical wisdom (the *phronimos*) would use'·
It is also noted in the *Ethics*, and equally in the *Politics*,[1] that virtue
needs an 'equipment' (or *chorēgia*) of necessary instruments; it
needs, for instance, the means for the practice of liberality. *Aretē*—
the Greek word which we translate by 'virtue', or 'goodness', or
'excellence'—has thus for Aristotle a double association: it is
associated with intellect, and it may also be said to be associated
with social position. The word in itself, apart from its Aristotelian
associations, has a shade of meaning in general Greek usage which
makes it at once something more and something less than our word
'virtue'. It is something more, because it can mean excellence in
any field: there is an *aretē* of the good citizen as well as an *aretē*
of the good man, and the two may be different;[2] there is an *aretē*
of the soldier, or martial virtue, as well as an *aretē* of the civilian,
or civic virtue. Again, the word *aretē* is something less than our
'virtue': it has, in itself, no necessary moral implication; and we
must add the adjective ethical, and speak of *ēthikē aretē*, to make
sure that that implication is present. We may thus say that *aretē*
has suggestions of *virtù* (in the Italian sense of a taste for fine art)
as well as suggestions of virtue; and we may even say that those
who possess the gift of *aretē* are *virtuosi* as well as 'virtuous'. We
may be guilty of an extravagance in so saying; and we have to
remember that our own word 'virtue' can be applied to the qualities
of precious stones and plants as well as to man's moral nature. But
the extravagance will be justified, at any rate in some measure, if
it helps the reader to remember that the *aretē* of which Aristotle
so often speaks is a word of many associations—intellectual, social,
and general—which differentiate it from our 'virtue'.

This theory or speculation (as it might be called by Aristotle)
on the vocabulary of the *Politics* may end with one last observation.
It has been noted, more than once, that the Latin element in our
English speech is not always a good conductor of the sense with
which Greek words are charged. But there are times when Latin
may stand us in good and happy stead. The Greek word *eudaimonia* may furnish us with an instance. It is generally translated
by our word 'happiness'. But happiness carries with it the material
association of pleasure; and *eudaimonia* is a word of different and
higher associations. Literally it means the condition of being
under a good genius; and it is defined in the *Politics*[3] as a state of
activity (and not of enjoyment), which consists in the energy and
practice of goodness. It is thus a conquest rather than a happening

---

[1] See Book VII, c. XIII, § 3 and § 7: see also pp. 180, n. 2, 282, n. 2, 290, n. 1.
[2] This question engages Aristotle in Book III, cc. IV–V.
[3] Book VII, c. XIII, § 5.

or good hap; and it may be better expressed by the Latin word 'felicity' than by any other word. 'Bliss' and 'blessedness' might perhaps serve; but they raise philological difficulties,[1] and they import the religious associations of Christianity. 'Felicity' has the felicity of matching most nearly the shade of meaning in the original Greek.

[1] 'Bliss' and 'blessedness', as the *Oxford English Dictionary* notes, are separate words, from separate roots, which crossed and blended in the process of time. (The one meant blitheness: the other meant being marked with blood and so consecrated.) The crossing and blending of senses grew greater still when, after the conversion of England to Christianity, 'blessedness' began to be coloured by the Latin word 'benediction'.

NOTE TO p. lxiv.

A member of the staff of the University Press has made the apposite and felicitous suggestion that a reference should be added to the passage of the *De Rerum Natura* (I 136–9) in which Lucretius notes the difficulty of explaining the thought of Greece in the language of Rome.

> nec me animi fallit Graiorum obscura reperta
> difficile inlustrare Latinis uersibus esse,
> multa nouis uerbis praesertim cum sit agendum
> propter egestatem linguae et rerum nouitatem.

It would hardly be just to apply the words *obscura reperta* to the argument of the *Politics*. But when a translator seeks to express the argument of the original Greek in English terms of politics drawn from the Latin language, it is certainly true that he finds himself confronted by an *egestas linguae*; and there is also a *rerum nouitas* in the ideas and institutions presupposed in the Greek—a novelty of men's outlook, and a novelty in the life and ways of the streets of their 'little towns'—which baffles the translator, as the Grecian Urn baffled Keats.

Thou, silent form, dost tease us out of thought.

THE POLITICS OF
ARISTOTLE

BOOK I

THE THEORY OF THE HOUSEHOLD

A

THE POLITICAL ASSOCIATION AND ITS RELATION TO OTHER ASSOCIATIONS (CC. I–II)

CHAPTER I

All associations have ends: the political association has the highest; but the principle of association expresses itself in different forms, and through different modes of government.

1252 a § 1. Observation shows us, first, that every polis (or state) is a species of association, and, secondly, that all associations are instituted for the purpose of attaining some good—for all men do all their acts with a view to achieving something which is, in their view, a good. We may therefore hold [on the basis of what we actually observe] that all associations aim at some good; and we may also hold that the particular association which is the most sovereign of all, and includes all the rest, will pursue this aim most, and will thus be directed to the most sovereign of all goods.[1] This most sovereign and inclusive association is the polis, as it is called, or the political association.

§ 2. It is a mistake to believe[2] that the 'statesman' [the *politikos*, who handles the affairs of a political association] is the same as the monarch of a kingdom, or the manager of a household, or the master of a number of slaves.[3] Those who hold this view consider that each of these persons differs from the others not with a difference of kind, but [merely with a difference of degree, and] according to the number, or the paucity, of the persons with whom he deals. On this view a man who is concerned with few persons is a master: one who is concerned with more is the manager of a household: one who is concerned with still more is a 'statesman', or a monarch. This view abolishes any real difference between a large household and a small polis; and it also reduces the difference between the 'statesman' and the monarch to the one fact that the latter has an uncontrolled and sole authority, while the former exercises his authority in conformity with the rules imposed by

---

[1] See Note A, p. 2.

[2] This belief is, in Aristotle's view, that of Plato. The immediate reference is to the *Politicus* of Plato, 258 E–259 D.

[3] The political association, as appears later in Book III (see e.g. c. VI, § 9), is an association of 'equal and like' members; and the *politikos* who handles its affairs will therefore be only *primus inter pares*. That is why he differs essentially from the ruler of a kingdom, or of a household, or of a body of slaves.

the art of statesmanship and as one who rules and is ruled in turn. But this is a view which cannot be accepted as correct. [There is an *essential* difference between these persons, and between the associations with which they are concerned.]

§ 3. Our point will be made clear if we proceed to consider the matter according to our normal method of analysis. Just as, in all other fields, a compound[1] should be analysed until we reach its simple and uncompounded elements (or, in other words, the smallest atoms of the whole which it constitutes), so we must also consider analytically the elements of which a polis is composed. We shall then gain a better insight into the difference from one another of the persons and associations just mentioned; and we shall also be in a position to discover whether it is possible to attain a systematic view of the general issues involved.[2]

NOTE A (p. 1): *The nature of associations*

Two passages from the *Ethics* may be cited in illustration and explanation. They both come from the part of the *Ethics* (Books VIII–IX) which deals with the nature of friendship, or what may be called 'social sympathy'.

(*a*) '*Every* form of friendship involves association. But kinship and comradeship may be distinguished as peculiar forms [because they depend peculiarly on natural feeling and innate sympathy]. The form of friendship which unites fellow citizens—or fellow tribesmen, or fellow voyagers —is more in the nature of pure association, since it seems to rest on a sort of compact' (*Ethics*, VIII, c. XII, § 1). Association, it will be noticed, is here connected with compact and 'construction': see below, c. II, § 15, and note.

(*b*) 'All associations are in the nature of parts of the political association. Men journey together with a view to some particular advantage, and by way of providing some particular thing needed for the purposes of life; and similarly the political association seems to have come together originally, and to continue in existence, for the sake of the *general* advantage which it brings' (ibid., c. IX, § 4).

On the part played by associations in the life of Greek states see Vinogradoff, *Historical Jurisprudence*, vol. ii, c. VI, § 4, on 'Societies and Unions'.

CHAPTER II

To distinguish the different forms of association we must use an analytic or genetic method, tracing successively the association of the household, that of the village, and that of the polis. The polis, or political association, is the crown: it completes and fulfils the nature of man: it is thus natural to him, and he is himself 'naturally a polis-animal'; it is also prior to him, in the sense that it is the presupposition of his true and full life.

[1] On the sense which Aristotle attached to the technical term 'compound' see below, Book III, c. I, § 2, and note.
[2] These general issues, as they emerge later, turn on the nature of authority over slaves, the nature of marital and parental authority, and the nature of household management in general.

§ 1. If, accordingly, we begin at the beginning, and consider things in the process of their growth, we shall best be able, in this as in other fields, to attain scientific conclusions by the method we employ.¹ § 2. First of all, there must necessarily be a union or pairing of those who cannot exist without one another. Male and female must unite for the reproduction of the species—not from deliberate intention, but from the natural impulse, which exists in animals generally as it also exists in plants, to leave behind them something of the same nature as themselves. Next, there must necessarily be a union of the naturally ruling element with the element which is naturally ruled, for the preservation of both. The element which is able, by virtue of its intelligence, to exercise forethought, is naturally a ruling and master. element; the element which is able, by virtue of its bodily power, to do what the other element plans, is a ruled element, which is naturally in a state of slavery; and master and slave have accordingly [as they thus complete one another] a common interest. . . . **1252 b** § 3. The female and the slave [we may pause to note] are naturally distinguished from one another. Nature makes nothing in a spirit of stint,² as smiths do when they make the Delphic knife to serve a number of purposes: she makes each separate thing for a separate end; and she does so because each instrument has the finest finish when it serves a single purpose and not a variety of purposes. § 4. Among the barbarians, however [contrary to the order of nature], the female and the slave occupy the same position—the reason being that no naturally ruling element exists among them, and conjugal union thus comes to be a union of a female who is a slave with a male who is also a slave.³ This is why our poets have said,

> Meet it is that barbarous peoples should be governed
>   by the Greeks

—the assumption being that barbarian and slave are by nature one and the same. . . .

¹ The analytic method of the previous chapter is, in effect, identical with the genetic method here suggested (the method of 'considering things in the process of their growth'), since the genetic method begins with the simple elements, and thus implies the use of analysis.

² i.e. the spirit which makes the female serve the purpose of a slave as well as that of a mate.

³ The argument is that among the barbarians the female is slave (as well as mate) for the simple reason that all alike are slaves, men as well as women, and the emergence of a true *consortium* of marriage, distinct from the nexus of slavery, is thus impossible. The cause of this uniform condition of slavery is the absence of a free class, capable of holding office and practising the art of 'ruling and being ruled in turn'—the sort of class which was the essence of the Greek political association and the cause of its freedom. On the other hand, a people, such as the Greeks, which possesses such a class, may naturally aspire (Aristotle incidentally reflects) to rule the general slave world of the barbarian peoples.

§ 5. The first result of these two elementary associations [of male and female, and of master and slave] is the household or family. Hesiod spoke truly in the verse,

> First house, and wife, and ox to draw the plough,

for oxen serve the poor in lieu of household slaves. The first form of association naturally instituted for the satisfaction of daily recurrent needs is thus the family; and the members of the family are accordingly termed by Charondas 'associates of the bread-chest', as they are also termed by Epimenides the Cretan 'associates of the manger'. The next form of association—which is also the *first* to be formed from more households than one, and for the satisfaction of something more than daily recurrent needs—is the village. § 6. The most natural form of the village appears to be that of a colony or offshoot from a family; and some have thus called the members of the village by the name of 'sucklings of the same milk', or, again, of 'sons and the sons of sons'[1]. . . . This, it may be noted, is the reason why each Greek polis was originally ruled—as the peoples of the barbarian world still are—by kings. They were formed of persons who were already monarchically governed [i.e. they were formed from households and villages, and] households are always monarchically governed by the eldest of the kin, just as villages, when they are offshoots from the household, are similarly governed in virtue of the kinship between their members. § 7. This primitive kinship is what Homer describes, [in speaking of the Cyclopes]:

> Each of them ruleth
> Over his children and wives,

a passage which shows that they lived in scattered groups, as indeed men generally did in ancient times. The fact that men generally were governed by kings in ancient times, and that some still continue to be governed in that way, is the reason that leads us all to assert that the gods are also governed by a king. We make the lives of the gods in the likeness of our own—as we also make their shapes. . . .

§ 8. When we come to the final and perfect association, formed from a number of villages, we have already reached the polis—an association which may be said to have reached the height of full self-sufficiency; or rather [to speak more exactly] we may say that

---

[1] The latter phrase comes from Plato's *Laws*. The general argument of Aristotle at this point is clearly stated by Newman in his note: 'He has proved that the household is necessary and natural, and if he can prove that the village is an outgrowth of the household, and the polis of the village, then the polis will be shown to be natural.' The analytic-genetic method which he is using thus ends by providing a proof of the 'natural' character of the polis.

while it *grows* for the sake of mere life [and is so far, and at that
stage, still short of full self-sufficiency], it *exists* [when once it is fully
grown] for the sake of a good life [and is therefore fully self-
sufficient].[1]

Because it is the completion of associations existing by nature,
every polis exists by nature, having itself the same quality as the
earlier associations from which it grew. It is the end or consummation to which those associations move, and the 'nature' of things
consists in their end or consummation; for what each thing is
when its growth is completed we call the nature of that thing,
whether it be a man or a horse or a family.[2] **1253 a** § 9. Again
[and this is a second reason for regarding the state as natural] the
end, or final cause, is the best. Now self-sufficiency [which it is
the object of the state to bring about] is the end, and so the best;
[and on this it follows that the state brings about the best, and is
therefore natural, since nature always aims at bringing about the
best].[3]

From these considerations it is evident that the polis belongs to
the class of things that exist by nature, and that man is by nature
an animal intended to live in a polis.[4] He who is without a polis,
by reason of his own nature and not of some accident, is either a
poor sort of being, or a being higher than man: he is like the man
of whom Homer wrote in denunciation:

'Clanless and lawless and heartless is he.'

§ 10. The man who is such by nature [i.e. unable to join in the
society of a polis] at once plunges into a passion for war; he is in
the position of a solitary advanced piece in a game of draughts.

The reason why man is a being meant for political association, in a higher degree than bees or other gregarious animals
can ever associate, is evident. Nature, according to our theory,

[1] See Note B, p. 7.
[2] The state is natural because it develops from natural associations. But it
would be wrong to think it is only natural because *they* are natural and because
it grows from *them*. It is natural *in itself*, as the completion, end, or consummation of man and man's development—the essentially natural condition of anything being its final, or complete, or perfect condition. If we could imagine a
state coming into existence directly and immediately, without the preceding
stages of the household and the village, it would still be natural, in virtue of
completing and perfecting man and his development.
[3] The explanatory passage is borrowed from Newman's note.
[4] 'It would be a strange thing to make the happy man a solitary: no one would
choose to have all the good things of the world in solitude: man is a being meant
for political association, and whose nature it is to live with others' (*Ethics*, IX,
c. IX, § 3); cf. also *Ethics* I, c. VII, § 6—'a man is a being meant for political
association'. But see also *Ethics* VIII, c. XII, § 7—'man by his nature is even more
meant for marriage than he is for political association, in proportion as the
family is earlier and more necessary than the polis.'

makes nothing in vain; and man alone of the animals is furnished with the faculty of language. § 11. The mere making of sounds serves to indicate pleasure and pain, and is thus a faculty that belongs to animals in general: their nature enables them to attain the point at which they have perceptions of pleasure and pain, and can signify those perceptions to one another. But language serves to declare what is advantageous and what is the reverse, and it therefore serves to declare what is just and what is unjust. § 12. It is the peculiarity of man, in comparison with the rest of the animal world, that he alone possesses a perception of good and evil, of the just and the unjust, and of other similar qualities; and it is association in [a common perception of] these things which makes a family and a polis.

We may now proceed to add that [though the individual and the family are prior in the order of time] the polis is prior in the order of nature to the family and the individual. § 13. The reason for this is that the whole is necessarily prior [in nature] to the part.[1] If the whole body be destroyed, there will not be a foot or a hand, except in that ambiguous sense in which one uses the same word to indicate a different thing, as when one speaks of a 'hand' made of stone; for a hand, when destroyed [by the destruction of the whole body], will be no better than a stone 'hand'. All things derive their essential character from their function and their capacity; and it follows that if they are no longer fit to discharge their function, we ought not to say that they are still the same things, but only that, by an ambiguity, they still have the same names.

§ 14. We thus see that the polis exists by nature and that it is prior to the individual.[2] [The proof of both propositions is the fact that the polis is a whole, and that individuals are simply its parts.] Not being self-sufficient when they are isolated, all individuals are so many parts all equally depending on the whole [which alone can bring about self-sufficiency]. The man who is isolated—who is unable to share in the benefits of political association, or has no need to share because he is already self-sufficient— is no part of the polis, and must therefore be either a beast or a god. § 15. [Man is thus intended by nature to be a part of a

---

[1] The whole is prior to the part in the sense that the part presupposes it; the idea of the whole must first be there before the part can be understood, and the whole itself must first be there before the part can have or exercise a function.

[2] These two points are interconnected. The polis exists by nature in the sense that it is the whole to which man naturally moves in order to develop his innate capacity, and in which he is thus included as a part. Because it is the whole, of which the individual is necessarily a part, it is prior to the individuals who are its parts, as wholes generally are prior to their parts.

political whole, and] there is therefore an immanent impulse in all men towards an association of this order. But the man who first *constructed* such an association was none the less the greatest of benefactors.[1] Man, when perfected, is the best of animals; but if he be isolated from law and justice he is the worst of all. § 16. Injustice is all the graver when it is armed injustice; and man is furnished from birth with arms [such as, for instance, language] which are intended to serve the purposes of moral prudence and virtue, but which may be used in preference for opposite ends. That is why, if he be without virtue, he is a most unholy and savage being, and worse than all others in the indulgence of lust and gluttony. Justice [which is his salvation] belongs to the polis; for justice, which is the determination of what is just, is an ordering of the political association.[2]

NOTE B (p. 5): *The development of the* polis *in Aristotle's view and in Greek history*

The elementary associations of husband and wife, and of master and slave, have first been attributed to the natural necessities of reproduction and self-preservation; and the family generally, as the first form of developed association, has then been attributed to the satisfaction of daily recurrent needs. The village, as the second form, has next been attributed to the satisfaction of 'something more than daily recurrent needs'—e.g. (one may guess) the satisfaction of such higher and more spiritual needs, above the daily round of material necessities, as the village tribunal for justice, or the village festival in honour of the gods. The polis, as the third and final form, is now attributed to the satisfaction of still higher and still more spiritual needs. Its origin, indeed, may be ascribed to the bare necessities of life (such as the necessity of defence from external enemies by means of greater numbers and from a more central and commanding position). But its essence is essentially and fundamentally due to moral or spiritual causes—causes already operative in the village, but now operative upon a far larger scale; causes, as Aristotle proceeds to explain, such as the establishment of a complete and common system of justice; causes which may be generally comprehended under the head of 'the attainment of a good quality of life'. (The general gist of this argument recurs in Book III, c. VI, §§ 3–4.) The polis thus fulfils the whole nature of man, and especially the higher part of his nature; and that is why it has 'reached the height of full self-sufficiency', containing as it does in itself (and not needing to draw from any other association outside or above itself) all the resources necessary for full and complete human development. Thus fulfilling the whole nature of man, the polis is particularly

[1] Aristotle here concedes, and indeed argues, that in saying that the state is natural he does not mean that it 'grows' naturally, without human volition and action. There is art as well as nature, and art co-operates with nature: the volition and action of human agents 'construct' the state in co-operation with a natural immanent impulse.

[2] The conception of the nature of politics suggested in the first two chapters of Book I may be compared with the conceptions stated at the beginning and end of the *Ethics*, and with that which is stated at the beginning of the *Rhetoric*. (See Appendix I. A and B.)

and specially 'natural', in that sense of the word which means the final and perfect condition of ultimate development—not the *terminus a quo*, but the *terminus ad quem*.

The actual and historical development of the Greek polis is described by Professor Adcock in the *Cambridge Ancient History*, vol. iii, c. xxvi. The causes of the development, as they are there sketched, may be classified under three heads. (1) The geographical and economic: a place with a good water-supply, a good harbour, and other conveniences for population and trade naturally expanded, upon this basis, into a polis (Aristotle assumes these conditions for his ideal *polis* in Book VII, c. vi and c. xi, §§ 1–5). (2) The military: a place with a stronghold, which could serve as a citadel or acropolis, naturally offered facilities which encouraged the growth of a polis (Aristotle again assumes these military conditions in Book VII, c. xi, §§ 5–12). (3) The socio-political: a place which could offer a common system of impersonal and impartial justice naturally attracted a large population and grew to the dimension of a polis (Aristotle particularly notes this condition in § 12 of this chapter).

It may be added that the term 'self-sufficiency' (in Greek *autarkeia*, or as we now say 'autarky') is defined in the *Ethics*, Book I, c. vii, § 7, as 'that which by and of itself makes life desirable and lacking in nothing'. This may be understood to mean the possession of such material resources, and such moral incentives and impulses, as make a full human development possible, without any dependence on external help, material or moral.

B
THE ASSOCIATION OF THE HOUSEHOLD AND ITS DIFFERENT FACTORS (cc. iii–xiii)

CHAPTER III

1. The constituent elements of the household. *The three relations of master and slave, husband and wife, and parent and child. The fourth element of 'acquisition'.*

1253 b § 1. Having ascertained, from the previous analysis, what are the elements of which the polis is constituted, we must first consider the management of the household; for every state is [primarily] composed of households. The parts of household management will correspond to the parts of which the household itself is constituted. A complete household consists of slaves and freemen. But every subject of inquiry should first be examined in its simplest elements; and the primary and simplest elements of the household are the connexion of master and slave, that of the husband and wife, and that of parents and children. We must accordingly consider each of these connexions, examining the nature of each and the qualities it ought to possess. § 2. The factors to be examined are therefore three—first, the association of master and slave; next, what may be called the marital association (for there is no word in our language which exactly describes the union of husband and wife); and lastly, what may be called the parental association, which again has no single word in our language peculiar to itself. § 3. But besides the three factors which thus present themselves for examination there is also a fourth, which some regard as identical with the whole of household management, and others as its principal part. This is the element called 'the art of acquisition' (*chrematistic*); and we shall have to consider its nature.

We may first speak of master and slave, partly [for reasons of utility] in order to gather lessons bearing on the necessities of practical life, and partly [for reasons of theory] in order to discover whether we can attain any view, superior to those now generally held, which is likely to promote a scientific knowledge of the subject. § 4. There are some who hold that the exercise of authority over slaves is a form of science. They believe (as we said in the beginning) that the management of a household, the control of slaves, the authority of the statesman, and the rule of the monarch, are all the same. There are others, however, who regard the control of slaves by a master as contrary to nature. In their view the distinction of master and slave is due to law or convention; there is no natural difference between them: the relation of master and slave is based on force, and being so based has no warrant in justice.

Chapter IV

2. Slavery. *The instruments of the household form its stock of property: they are animate and inanimate: the slave is an animate instrument, intended (like all the instruments of the household) for action, and not for production.*

§ 1. We may make the assumption that property is part of the household, and that the art of acquiring property is a part of household-management; and we may do so because it is impossible to live well, or indeed to live at all, unless the necessary conditions are present. We may further assume that, just as each art which has a definite sphere must necessarily be furnished with the appropriate instruments if its function is to be discharged, so the same holds good in the sphere of household management. § 2. Finally, we may also assume that instruments are partly inanimate and partly animate: the pilot, for instance, has an inanimate instrument in the rudder, and an animate instrument (for all subordinates, in every art, are of the nature of instruments) in the look-out man. On the basis of these assumptions we may conclude that each article of property is an instrument for the purpose of life; that property in general is the sum of such instruments; that the slave is an animate article of property; and that subordinates, or servants, in general may be described as instruments which are prior to other instruments [i.e. animate instruments which must first be present before other, and inanimate, instruments can be used[1]]. § 3. There is only one condition on which we can imagine managers not needing subordinates, and masters not needing slaves. This condition would be that each [inanimate] instrument could do its own work, at the word of command or by intelligent anticipation, like the statues of Daedalus or the tripods made by Hephaestus, of which Homer relates that

> Of their own motion they entered the conclave of Gods on Olympus,

as if a shuttle should weave of itself, and a plectrum should do its own harp-playing. **1254 a** § 4. [Here, however, we must draw another distinction.] The instruments of which we have just been speaking [e.g. the shuttle] are instruments of *production*; but articles of household property [such as the slave or other chattels] are instruments of *action*.[2] From the shuttle there issues something which is different, and exists apart, from the immediate act of its use; but from [articles of household property, e.g.] garments or beds, there only comes the one fact of their use. We may add that, since production and action are different in kind, and both of them need their own proper instruments, those instruments must also show a corresponding difference. § 5. Life is action and not production; and therefore the slave [being an instrument for the purpose of life] is a servant in the sphere of action.[3]

There is a further consideration [which is necessary to explain fully the nature of the slave]. An 'article of property' is a term that is used in the same sense in which the term 'part' is also used. Now a part is not only a part of something other than itself: it also belongs entirely to that other thing [and has no life or being other than that of so belonging]. It is the same with an article of property as it is with a part. Accordingly, while the master is merely the master of the slave, and does not belong to him, [having a life and being of his own beyond that of a master], the slave is not only

---

[1] Thus the look-out man is necessary to the pilot as an animate instrument, before he can properly use the inanimate instrument, the rudder.

[2] This distinction between production (or *poiēsis*) and action (or *praxis*) is based on the idea that 'production' aims at a result beyond the immediate doing, which remains when the doing is over, but 'action', such as the rendering of a service, is complete in itself, and aims at no result beyond the immediate doing. The distinction is explained in the *Ethics*, Book VI, c. iv: cf. also c. v, § 4 'production has an end other than itself: action cannot have; for good action is itself its own end.'

[3] See Note C, p. 11.

the slave of his master; he also belongs entirely to him, [and has no life or being other than that of so belonging].

§ 6. From these considerations we can see clearly what is the nature of the slave and what is his capacity. We attain these definitions—first, that 'anybody who by his nature is not his own man, but another's, is by his nature a slave'; secondly, that 'anybody who, being a man, is an article of property, is another's man'; and thirdly, that 'an article of property is an instrument intended for the purpose of action and separable from its possessor'.

NOTE C (p. 10): *Slaves and other 'instruments' of life*

The argument of § 4 and the first sentence of § 5 is subtle; and, as stated by Aristotle, it is so logically stated that the simple meaning is almost hidden. We may explain it as follows. At the end of § 3 Aristotle had seemed to imply that slaves would not be necessary if, e.g., shuttles could do their own work of producing a web by themselves. He reflects, in § 4, that this is not really the case. The slave is not, after all, concerned with producing things; and he would still be necessary even if machines could produce things by themselves without any attendants. (Aristotle is thus not thinking of factory-slavery or plantation-slavery, but of the household slave.) The slave is concerned with the *life* of the household and its activity, rather than with production: he does not help in the making of things, but in living and all its activities. This is the simple argument of § 4 and the first sentence of § 5; but the simplicity gets complicated by the fact that Aristotle (always ready for refinements) introduces the idea that inanimate household goods or articles, such as clothes and beds, also differ from inanimate articles which are used in production. This is true enough, and it teaches us that not only the slave, but also the things which he tends, belong to the area of living and the activities of living rather than to those of production. But we are tempted to lose sight of the slave himself when we are diverted to the consideration of other household goods.

CHAPTER V

There is a principle of rule and subordination in nature at large: it appears especially in the realm of animate creation. By virtue of that principle, the soul rules the body; and by virtue of it the master, who possesses the rational faculty of the soul, rules the slave, who possesses only bodily powers and the faculty of understanding the directions given by another's reason. But nature, though she intends, does not always succeed in achieving a clear distinction between men born to be masters and men born to be slaves.

§ 1. We have next to consider whether there are, or are not, persons who are by nature such as are here defined; whether, in other words, there are persons for whom slavery is the better and just condition, or whether the reverse is the case and all slavery is contrary to nature. The issue is not difficult, whether we study it philosophically in the light of reason, or consider it empirically on the basis of the actual facts.[1]   § 2. Ruling and being ruled [which is the relation of master and slave] not only belongs to the category of things necessary, but also to that of things expedient; and there are species in which a distinction is already marked, immediately at birth, between those of its members who are intended for being ruled and those who are intended to rule. . . .   There are also many kinds both of ruling and ruled elements. This being the case, the rule which is exercised over the better sort of ruled elements is a better sort of rule—as, for example, rule exercised over a man is better than rule over an animal.   § 3. The reason is that a function is a higher and better function when the elements which go to its discharge are higher and better elements; and where one element rules and another is ruled, we may speak of those elements as going together to discharge a function. . . . In *all* cases where there is a compound, constituted of more than one part but forming one common entity—whether the parts be continuous [as in the body of a man] or discrete [as in the relation of master and slave]—a ruling element and a ruled can always be traced.[2]   § 4. This characteristic [i.e. the presence of ruled and ruling elements] is present in animate beings by virtue of the whole constitution of nature, inanimate as well as animate; for even in things which are inanimate there is a sort of ruling principle, such as is to be found, for example, in a musical harmony. But such considerations [of the inanimate part of nature] perhaps belong to a more popular method of inquiry; and we may content ourselves here with saying that animate beings are the first [in the ascending scale of nature] to be composed of soul and body, with the former naturally ruling and the latter naturally ruled.   § 5. Dealing with such animate beings, we must fix our attention, in order to discover what nature intends, not on those which are in a corrupt, but on those which are in a natural condition. It follows that we must consider the man who is in the best state both of body and soul, and in whom the rule of soul over body is accordingly evident; for in those who are [permanently] bad, or who [for the time being] are in a bad condition, the reverse would often appear to be true **1254 b**—the body ruling the soul as the result of their evil and unnatural condition.

[1] The two different methods, as Newman remarks, are not actually distinguished in the subsequent argument; but on the whole Aristotle follows the first.

[2] The fact that a ruling element and a ruled can be traced in *all* cases of compounds goes to prove that, as Aristotle has said previously, there are many kinds both of ruling and ruled elements. Compounds, as they range through the whole scale of nature, from inanimate objects to animate beings and ultimately to man, differ greatly from one another. The ruling and ruled elements which they contain must therefore differ greatly. On Aristotle's conception of 'compounds' see below, Book III, c. 1, § 2, and note.

§ 6. Whatever may be said of inanimate things, it is certainly possible, as we have said, to observe in animate beings—and to observe there first [with any certainty]—the presence of a ruling authority, both of the sort exercised by a master over slaves and of the sort exercised by a statesman over fellow citizens. The soul rules the body with the sort of authority of a master: mind rules the appetite with the sort of authority of a statesman or a monarch. In this sphere [i.e. in the sphere of man's inner life] it is clearly natural and beneficial to the body that it should be ruled by the soul, and again it is natural and beneficial to the affective part of the soul that it should be ruled by the mind and the rational part; whereas the equality of the two elements, or their reverse relation, is always detrimental. § 7. What holds good in man's inner life also holds good outside it; and the same principle is true of the relation of man to animals as is true of the relation of his soul to his body. Tame animals have a better nature than wild, and it is better for all such animals that they should be ruled by man because they then get the benefit of preservation. Again, the relation of male to female is naturally that of the superior to the inferior—of the ruling to the ruled. This general principle must similarly hold good of all human beings generally [and therefore of the relation of masters and slaves].

§ 8. We may thus conclude that all men who differ from others as much as the body differs from the soul, or an animal from a man (and this is the case with all whose function is bodily service, and who produce their best when they supply such service)—all such are by nature slaves, and it is better for them, on the very same principle as in the other cases just mentioned, to be ruled by a master. § 9. A man is thus by nature a slave if he is capable of becoming (and this is the reason why he also actually becomes) the property of another, and if he participates in reason to the extent of apprehending it in another, though destitute of it himself. Herein he differs from animals, which do not apprehend reason, but simply obey their instincts. But the use which is made of the slave diverges but little from the use made of tame animals; both he and they supply their owner with bodily help in meeting his daily requirements.

§ 10. [We have hitherto been speaking of mental differences.] But it is nature's intention also to erect a physical difference between the body of the freeman and that of the slave, giving the latter strength for the menial duties of life, but making the former upright in carriage and (though useless for physical labour) useful for the various purposes of civic life—a life which tends, as it develops, to be divided into military service and the occupations of peace. The contrary of nature's intention, however, often happens: there are some slaves who have the bodies of freemen—as there are others who have a freeman's soul.[1] But if nature's intention were realized—if men differed from one another in bodily form as much as the statues of the gods [differ from the human figure]—it is obvious that we should all agree that the inferior class ought to be the slaves of the superior. §11. And if this principle is true when the difference is one of the body, it may be affirmed with still greater justice when the difference is one of the soul; though it is not as easy to see the beauty of the soul as it is to see that of the body.

1255 a It is thus clear that, just as some are by nature free, so others are by nature slaves, and for these latter the condition of slavery is both beneficial and just.

CHAPTER VI

Legal or conventional slavery: the divergence of views about its justice, and the reason for this divergence. In spite of the divergence, there is a general consensus—though it is not clearly formulated—that superiority in goodness justifies the owning and controlling of slaves. Granted such superiority in the master, slavery is a beneficial and just system.

§ 1. But it is easy to see that those who hold an opposite view are also in a way correct. 'Slavery' and 'slave' are terms which are used in two different senses. [There is, as we have seen, a kind of slavery which exists by nature; but] there is also a kind of slave, and of slavery, which exists [only] by law or (to speak more exactly) convention. (The law in virtue of which those vanquished in war are held to belong to the victor is in effect a sort of convention.) § 2. That slavery can be justified by such a convention is a principle against which a number of jurists bring what may be called an 'indictment of illegality'.[2] [They think that the principle violates the nature of law; and] they regard it as a detestable notion that anyone who is subjugated by superior power should become the slave and subject of the person who has the power to subjugate him, and who is his superior [merely] in power. Some, however, support, if some oppose, [the principle]; and even men of judgement differ. § 3. The cause of this divergence of view, and the reason

[1] Newman would translate: 'it often comes to pass that [the body does not match the soul, and] slaves have the bodies of freemen, but freemen have only the souls'.

[2] The 'indictment of illegality' might be brought against any one who proposed a measure in the assembly which could be held to contravene the established law (*nomos*). By analogy, the convention in favour of the victor enslaving the vanquished might be held to be in the nature of a measure which contravened *nomos*.

why the opposing contentions overlap one another, is to be found in the following consideration.[1] There is a sense in which goodness, when it is furnished with an equipment [of material resources],[2] has the greatest power to subjugate; and [conversely] a victor is always pre-eminent in respect of *some* sort of good. This connexion of power with goodness or some sort of good leads to the idea that 'power goes with goodness'; and [as this idea is shared by both sides in the dispute about slavery] the dispute between the two sides thus comes to turn exclusively on the point of justice. § 4. On this point, one side holds that justice is a relation of mutual goodwill [and is therefore incompatible with slavery imposed by convention]; the other side holds that the rule of a superior is in itself, and by itself, justice [and is therefore a justification of such slavery. But the ambiguity of the idea which is common ground for both sides obscures the whole issue.] If the divergent views are pitted separately against one another [i.e. deprived of their common ground], neither view has any cogency, or even plausibility, against the view that the superior *in goodness* ought to rule over, and be the master of, his inferiors.[3]

§ 5. [The same general result—that superior goodness is really the ground of owning and controlling slaves—may be attained in another way.] There are some who, clinging, as they think, to a sort of justice (for law is a sort of justice), assume that slavery in war is always and everywhere just [because it is warranted by law]. Simultaneously, however, they contradict that assumption; for in the first place it is possible that the original cause of a war may not be just [in which case, in spite of the warrant of law, slavery so caused will not be just], and in the second place no one would ever say

[1] Newman analyses clearly the argument at this point. There is a divergence of views, arising from the fact that two contentions overlap in the area of a common principle, accepted by the holders of either contention, but interpreted differently by either. The common principle is that 'power goes with goodness'. One side interprets this to mean that power of itself implies goodness, and therefore confers a right (based on the goodness which it implies) to enslave any captive. The other side interprets it to mean that power must be accompanied by goodness—i.e. must have goodness added to it (and thereby the goodwill which goodness conciliates)—before there can be a rightful relation of master and slave which is attended, as such a relation should be, by goodwill.

[2] On Aristotle's conception of equipment, or *choregia*, and of the relation in which it stands to goodness or excellence, see below, Book VII, c. 1, § 13, note.

[3] Stated 'separately', one view is that the convention in favour of the victor enslaving the vanquished is always unjust, and the other is that the convention is always just. So stated, neither view can be maintained against a third or intermediate view which Aristotle suggests. This is the view that superiority in goodness alone justifies its possessor in being a master of slaves. On this view it follows that a victor may justly enslave the vanquished *if he possesses such superiority*—but only on that condition. The convention will accordingly sometimes be just, and sometimes unjust; it cannot be always either the one or the other.

that a person who does not deserve to be in a condition of slavery
is really a slave. If such a view were accepted, the result would
be that men reputed to be of the highest rank would be turned into
slaves or the children of slaves, if it happened to them or their
parents to be captured and sold into slavery.[1] § 6. This is the
reason why Greeks [though ready to defend the enslavement of
prisoners of war] do not like to call such persons slaves, but prefer
to confine the term to barbarians. But by this use of terms [they
contradict their own view, and] they are, in reality, only seeking
to express that same idea of the natural slave which we began by
mentioning. They are driven, in effect, to admit that there are
some [i.e. the barbarians] who are everywhere and inherently
slaves, and others [i.e. the Greeks] who are everywhere and inherently free. § 7. The same line of thought is followed in regard
to nobility, as well as slavery. Greeks regard themselves as noble
not only in their own country, but absolutely and in all places;
but they regard barbarians as noble only in their own country—
thus assuming that there is one sort of nobility and freedom which
is absolute, and another which is only relative. We are reminded
of what Helen says in the play of Theodectes:

> 'Scion of Gods, by both descents alike,
> Who would presume to call me serving-maid?'

§ 8. When they use such terms as these, men are using the one
criterion of the presence, or absence, of goodness for the purpose
of distinguishing between slave and freeman, or, again, between
noble and low-born. **1255 b** They are claiming that just as man
is born of man, and animal of animal, so a good man is born of
good men. It is often the case, however, that nature wishes but
fails to achieve this result.

§ 9. It is thus clear that there is some reason for the divergence
of view which has been discussed, and that not all those who
are actually slaves, or actually freemen, are natural slaves or natural
freemen. It is also clear that there are cases where such a distinction [of the natural slave and the natural freeman] exists, and that
here it is beneficial and just that the former should actually be a
slave and the latter a master—the one being ruled, and the other
exercising the kind of rule for which he is naturally intended and
therefore acting as master. § 10. But a wrong exercise of his rule
by a master is a thing which is disadvantageous for both master
and slave. The part and the whole, like the body and the soul,

---

[1] A law promoted by the Athenian statesman Lycurgus, about 330 B.C.,
prohibited Athenians from purchasing as slaves any free men taken in war.
Aristotle may have had this law in his mind.

have an identical interest; and the slave is a part of the master, in the sense of being a living but separate part of his body. There is thus a community of interest, and a relation of friendship, between master and slave, when both of them naturally merit the position in which they stand.[1] But the reverse is true [and there is a conflict of interest and enmity], when matters are otherwise and slavery rests merely on legal sanction and superior *power*.

CHAPTER VII

The training of slaves, and the art of using them properly. How they may be justly acquired.

§ 1. The argument makes it clear that the authority of the master and that of the statesman are different from one another, and that it is *not* the case that all kinds of authority are, as some thinkers hold, identical.[2] The authority of the statesman is exercised over men who are naturally free; that of the master over men who are [naturally] slaves; and again the authority generally exercised over a household by its head is that of a monarch[3] (for all households are monarchically governed), while the authority of the statesman is an authority over freemen and equals. § 2. Now [the definition of the master being that given at the end of the previous chapter— i.e. that he is a man naturally endowed with a gift for controlling natural slaves] masters are not so termed in virtue of any science which they have acquired, but in virtue of their own endowment; and the same is true of slaves and freemen generally. But there *may be* a science [of ruling] which belongs to masters, and another [of serving] which belongs to slaves; and the latter would be of the nature of the science taught by the man of Syracuse, who instructed servants for pay in the discharge of their ordinary duties. § 3. In-

[1] The idea that friendship is possible between master and slave also occurs in the *Ethics*, VIII, c. XI, §§ 6–7: 'With the slave as a slave one cannot be friends: with the slave as man, one can; for there seems to be a relation of justice as between any person whatever and any other person, whoever he be, who can share in a system of law or be a party to an agreement; and therefore there can also be a relation of friendship with a slave in so far as he is a man.' We cannot but note that if the slave can be regarded as sharing in a system of law, he becomes a *subject* of rights, and ceases to be a mere *object* or 'inanimate instrument'.

[2] Here Aristotle returns to a view which he had already challenged in the beginning of the *Politics*, c. I, § 2. The theme running through the early chapters of the *Politics* (though it sometimes seems to be lost in the ramifications of the argument) is the theme of the peculiar character of the Greek polis, and therefore of the peculiar character of the political authority (an authority of freemen over freemen) which is exercised in the polis.

[3] Such authority includes that of the master over his slaves, but it also includes that of a parent over his children and that of a husband over his wife. Aristotle thus extends the scope of the argument, in the latter half of the sentence, to cover *all* forms of household authority.

struction in such subjects might be extended further: it might include, for example, the art of cookery and other similar forms of skilled domestic service. The reason why this might be done is that some duties [i.e. the skilled] are of a higher standing, even if others [i.e. the ordinary and menial] are needed more: as the proverb says:

'Slave may go before slave, and master may go before master.'

§ 4. All such forms of science are necessarily of a servile character. But there is also a form of science belonging to the master, which consists in the *use* of slaves: a master is such in virtue not of owning, but of using slaves. This science belonging to the master is something which has no great or majestic character: the master must simply know how to command what the slave must know how to do. § 5. This is why those who are in a position to escape from being troubled by it delegate the management of slaves to a steward, and spend on politics or philosophy the time they are thus able to save. The art of *acquiring* slaves for ownership differs both from the art of being a master and from that of being a slave—that is to say, when it is justly practised; for in that case it is, in a way, part of the art of war, or of the art of hunting.[1]

This may serve to suffice for the distinction, and the definition, of master and slave.

CHAPTER VIII

3. Property and the art of acquisition. *The art of household management is distinct from that of acquisition. It has to provide a stock of requisites for the household; and the different methods by which this is done produce different ways of life—the hunting, the pastoral, the agricultural, and so forth. Nature intends and provides the requisites for household use; and the acquisition of such requisites is a natural mode of acquisition. Property in them is limited to the amount required by household needs; and it is the nature of all true wealth to be so limited.*

1256 a § 1. We may now study[2] generally all forms of property and the art of acquiring it,[3] following our normal method [the analytical and genetic method, which proceeds from the parts to the whole and from the first beginnings to the developed result]; for we have already seen that the slave is an article of property, [and this leads us to consider the whole institution of which he is part]. The first problem which may be raised is whether the art

---

[1] Aristotle thus implies the justice of the slave-trade when the slaves handled are barbarians either captured in war or seized in the course of slave-raids.
[2] See Note D, p. 22.   [3] See Note E, p. 22.

of acquiring property is identical with that of household management, or is a part of it, or is ancillary to it;[1] and whether, if it be ancillary, it is so in the sense in which the art of making shuttles is ancillary to the art of weaving, or in the sense in which the art of casting bronze is ancillary to the art of sculpture. . . . Either of these ancillary arts serves its master-art in a different way; the one provides it with an instrument, and the other with material. § 2. (By 'material' we mean the substance from which a product is made: wool, for instance, serves the weaver as the substance from which he produces cloth; and bronze serves the sculptor in the same way.) . . . That the art of household management is not identical with the art of acquiring property is obvious. It is the function of the latter simply to *provide* [either instruments or materials, as the case may be], but it is the function of the former to *use* what has been provided; for what art can there be, other than that of household management, which will deal with the use of the resources of the household? But the question whether the art of acquisition [if not identical with that of household management] is a part of it, or a separate art altogether, is one which admits of a divergence of views. [Indeed it is a question which raises a number of issues.] § 3. If a man who is engaged in acquisition has to consider from what different sources he can get goods and property, and if property and wealth include many different parts [drawn from many different sources], we shall first have to consider [these parts before we can consider acquisition as a whole; we shall have to ask] whether farming is a part of the art of acquisition, or a separate art: indeed we shall have to ask that question generally, in regard to *all* modes of occupation and gain which are concerned with the provision of subsistence. § 4. This leads to a further observation. There are a number of different modes of subsistence; and the result is a number of different ways of life, both in the animal world and the human. It is impossible to live without means of subsistence; and in the animal world we may notice that differences in the means of subsistence have produced consequent differences in ways of life. § 5. Some animals live in herds, and others are scattered in isolation, according as they find it convenient for the purpose of getting subsistence—some of them being carnivorous, some herbivorous, and some, again, omnivorous.[2] Nature has thus distinguished their ways of life, with a view to their greater comfort and their better attainment of what they need: indeed, as the same sort of food is not naturally agreeable

[1] The problem has already been indicated, in c. III, § 3.
[2] The implication appears to be that carnivorous animals are solitary and herbivorous live together.

to all the members of a class, and as different sorts suit different species, we also find different ways of life even inside the class of carnivorous animals—and equally in that of the herbivorous—distinguishing species from species. § 6. What is true of animals is also true of men. Their ways of life also differ considerably. The most indolent are the pastoral nomads. They acquire a subsistence from domestic animals, at their leisure, and without any trouble; and as it is necessary for their flocks to move for the sake of pasturage, they also are forced to follow in their tracks and to cultivate what may be called a living and moving farm. § 7. There are others who live by hunting; and of these, again, there are different kinds, according to their different modes of hunting. Some live by being freebooters:[1] some, who live near lakes and marshes and rivers, or by a sea which is suitable for the purpose, gain a livelihood by fishing; others live by hunting birds or wild animals. Most men, however, derive their livelihood from the soil, and from cultivated plants.

§ 8. The different ways of life (at any rate if we take into account only those who follow an occupation dependent on their own labours, and do not provide themselves with subsistence [at the expense of others] by exchange and petty trade) may be roughly classified as five **1256 b**—the pastoral, the farming, the freebooting, the fishing, and the life of the chase. But there are some who live comfortably by means of a combination of different methods, and who eke out the shortcomings of one way of life, when it tends to fall short of being sufficient in itself, by adding some other way. For example, some combine the pastoral way of life with the freebooting: others combine farming with the life of the chase; and similar combinations may similarly be made of other ways of life, as needs and tastes impel men to shape their lives.

§ 9. Property of this order [that is to say, for the purpose of subsistence] is evidently given by nature to all living beings, from the instant of their first birth to the days when their growth is finished. § 10. There are animals which, when their offspring is born, bring forth along with it food enough to support it until it can provide for itself: this is the case with insects which reproduce themselves by grubs, and with animals which do so by eggs. Animals which are viviparous have food for their offspring in themselves, for a certain time, of the nature of what is called milk.

---

[1] It is curious to find freebooting or piracy regarded as on the same footing with a pastoral or farming life, and as a mode of acquisition dependent on the freebooter's own labour. But piracy was a tolerated pursuit in the eastern Mediterranean (on something like the same footing as trade) down to Aristotle's time, and indeed later. Pompey had to deal with the pirates of the Levant as late as 67 B.C.

§ 11. [If it is evident that there is thus a natural provision for food at birth, and during growth,] it is equally evident that we must believe that similar provision is also made for adults. Plants exist to give subsistence to animals, and animals to give it to men. Animals, when they are domesticated, serve for use as well as for food; wild animals, too, in most cases if not in all, serve to furnish man not only with food, but also with other comforts, such as the provision of clothing and similar aids to life. § 12. Accordingly, as nature makes nothing purposeless or in vain, all animals must have been made by nature for the sake of men. It also follows that the art of war is in some sense [that is to say, so far as it is directed to gaining the means of subsistence from animals] a natural mode of acquisition. Hunting is a part of that art; and hunting ought to be practised—not only against wild animals, but also against human beings who are intended by nature to be ruled by others and refuse to obey that intention—because war of this order is naturally just.

§ 13. It follows that one form of acquisition [i.e. what may be called the 'hunting' form] is naturally a part of the art of household management. It is a form of acquisition which the manager of a household must either find ready to hand, or himself provide and arrange, because it ensures a supply of objects, necessary for life and useful to the association of the polis or the household, which are capable of being stored.[1] § 14. These are the objects which may be regarded as constituting true wealth. [True wealth has a limit of size, determined by the purpose of the association it serves]; and the amount of household property which suffices for a good life is not unlimited, nor of the nature described by Solon in the verse,

'There is no bound to wealth stands fixed for men.'

§ 15. There *is* a bound fixed [for the property needed by the art of household management], as is also the case in the means required by the other arts. All the instruments needed by all the arts are limited, both in number and size, by the requirements of the art they serve; and wealth may be defined as a number of instruments used in a household or state [and needed for their respective 'arts'].

It is thus clear that there is a natural art of acquisition which has to be practised by managers of households and statesmen; and the reason for its existence is also clear [the reason being that it is

[1] We may note that though he is speaking of the household only in the be-ginning of the sentence, Aristotle also includes the polis at the end. 'Economy', as we have noticed, though it literally means only household management, is treated by him in its political as well as its domestic aspect; cf. note E at the end of this chapter.

natural for man to acquire what is naturally provided for his use].

NOTE D (p. 18): *The sequence of argument in* CC. VIII–XII

We might have expected that Aristotle, after having considered that part of the household which is constituted by the relation of master and slave, would have proceeded to consider the two other parts which are constituted by the relations of husband and wife and of parent and child. We might further have expected that he would then have proceeded to the village, as the next stage after the household, and that he would thus have finally reached the polis. But his consideration of the slave, who has been treated in connexion with property (c. IV, §§ 1–2) and defined as an animate article of property, leads Aristotle to pass from this species of property to a consideration of the general subject of property; and in treating property he is led to consider the whole subject of acquisition ('chrematistic'), which he had already stated (in c. III, § 3) to be at any rate an element—and, in the view of some, a principal part, or even the whole—of household management. . . . He reverts to the relations of husband and wife and parent and child at the end of Book I (cc. XII–XIII).

NOTE E (p. 18): *The different senses of 'chrematistic'*

The art of acquisition, or 'chrematistic', is treated by Aristotle, in the next four chapters (cc. VIII–XI), not only in connexion with the household, but also in connexion with the polis. Under this head he may be said to attempt to state the elements of 'economics', and to deal both with 'domestic' and with 'political' economy. In his technical use of the term 'chrematistic', we may note, as Newman does, that he varies. (1) Sometimes the term is used to indicate the art of acquisition generally, and as if it covered all forms—sound or unsound—of the acquisition of property. (2) Generally—and this is its most common use—it is used to indicate only those forms of acquisition which are perverted or unsound, in the sense that they are directed merely to selfish monetary gain. (3) Sometimes—but more rarely—it is used to indicate only the sound or natural forms of acquisition, which are necessary for the life of the household or state.

CHAPTER IX

The 'art of acquisition', as a way of acquiring property distinct from the natural way of the household. It originates in exchange, when exchange is conducted through the medium of currency and for profit. The view thus arises that the art of acquisition is specially concerned with accumulating a fund of currency. But there is a contrary view that currency is a mere convention, and not the true object of the art of acquisition. This contrary view has its truth. There is a natural form of the art of acquisition, which is not distinct from, but a part of, the art of household management. This natural form of acquisition aims at the accumulation not of currency, but of true wealth—and therefore not at the infinite, but at the finite.

§ 1. But there is a second form of the general art of getting property, which is particularly called, and which it is just to call, 'the art of acquisition'. It is the characteristics of **1257 a** this second form which lead to the opinion that there is no limit to wealth and property. There are many who hold this second form of the art of getting property to be identical with the other form previously mentioned, because it has affinities with it. In fact it is not identical, and yet it is not far removed. The other form previously mentioned is natural: this second form is not natural, but is rather the product of a certain sort of experience and skill.

§ 2. We may start our discussion of this form from the following point of view. All articles of property have two possible uses. Both of these uses belong to the article as such, but they do not belong to it in the same manner, or to the same extent. The one use is proper and peculiar to the article concerned; the other is not. We may take a shoe as an example. It can be used both for wearing and for exchange. Both of these uses are uses of the shoe as such. § 3. Even the man who exchanges a shoe, in return for money or food, with a person who needs the article, is using the shoe as a shoe; but since the shoe has not been made for the purpose of being exchanged, the use which he is making of it is not its proper and peculiar use. The same is true of all other articles of property. § 4. Exchange is possible in regard to them all: it arises from the natural facts of the case, and is due to some men having more, and others less, than suffices for their needs. We can thus see that retail trade [which buys from others to sell at a profit] is not naturally a part of the art of acquisition. If that were the case, it would only be necessary to practise exchange to the extent that sufficed for the needs of both parties [and not to the extent of the making of profit by one of the parties at the expense of the other].

§ 5. In the first form of association, which is the household, it is obvious that there is no purpose to be served by the art of exchange. Such a purpose only emerged when the scope of association had already been extended [until it issued in the village]. The members of the household had shared all things in common: the members of the village, separated from one another [in a number of different households], had at their disposal a number of different things, which they had to exchange with one another, as need arose, by way of barter—much as many uncivilized tribes still do to this day. § 6. On this basis things which are useful are exchanged themselves, and directly, for similar useful things, but the transaction does not go any further [that is to say, no money is involved]; wine, for instance, is given, or taken, in return for wheat, and other similar commodities are similarly bartered for one another. When used in this way, the art of exchange is not contrary to nature, nor in any way a form of the art of acquisition [in the second sense of that term defined at the beginning of this chapter]. Exchange simply served [in its first beginnings] to satisfy the natural requirements of sufficiency. § 7. None the less it was from exchange, as thus practised, that the art of acquisition [in its second sense] developed, in the sort of way we might reasonably expect. [Distant transactions were the cause.] The supply of men's needs came to depend on more foreign sources, as men began to import for themselves what they lacked, and to export what they had in superabundance; and in this way the use of a money currency was inevitably instituted. § 8. The reason for this institution of a currency was that all the naturally necessary commodities were not easily portable; and men therefore agreed, for the purpose of their exchanges, to give and receive some commodity [i.e. some form of more or less precious metal] which itself belonged to the category of useful things and possessed the advantage of being easily handled for the purpose of getting the necessities of life. Such commodities were iron, silver, and other similar metals. At first their value was simply determined by their size and weight; but finally a stamp was imposed on the metal which, serving as a definite indication of the quantity, would save men the trouble of determining the value on each occasion.[1]

1257 b   § 9. When, in this way, a currency had once been instituted, there next arose, from the necessary process of exchange [i.e. exchange between commodities, with money serving merely as a measure], the other form of the art of acquisition, which consists in retail trade [conducted for profit].[2] At first, we may allow, it was perhaps practised in a simple way [that is to say, money was still regarded as a measure, and not treated as a source of profit]: but in process of time, and as the result of experience, it was practised with a more studied technique, which sought to discover the sources from which, and the methods by which, the greatest profit could be made. § 10. The result has been the emergence of the view that the art of acquisition is specially concerned with currency, and that its function consists in an ability to discover the sources from which a fund of *money* can be derived.

---

[1] The account of money or currency here given may be compared with that in the *Ethics*, Book V, c. v: 'All goods must be measured by some *one* thing. Now this unit is really demand, which brings and holds all goods together . . . but money has become, by virtue of convention, a sort of representative of demand. That is why it has the name it bears ("numismatic"): it exists by law or convention (*nomos*), and not by nature; and we have the power of changing or cancelling its value' (§§ 10–11). . . . 'Money suffers the same vicissitudes as goods: its value is not always constant; but it is steadier than the values of goods. That is why all goods must be priced in money; for then there will always be the possibility of exchange and with it of association between man and man' (§ 14).   [2] See Note F, p. 27.

In support of this view it is urged that the art is one which produces wealth and money; indeed those who hold the view often assume that wealth is simply a fund of currency, on the ground that the art of acquisition (in the form of retail trade for profit) is concerned with currency. § 11. In opposition to this view there is another which is sometimes held. On this view currency is regarded as a sham, and entirely a convention. Naturally and inherently (the supporters of the view argue) a currency is a nonentity; for if those who use a currency give it up in favour of another, that currency is worthless, and useless for any of the necessary purposes of life. A man rich in currency (they proceed to urge) will often be at a loss to procure the necessities of subsistence; and surely it is absurd that a thing should be counted as wealth which a man may possess in abundance, and yet none the less die of starvation—like Midas in the fable, when everything set before him was turned at once into gold through the granting of his own avaricious prayer.

§ 12. Basing themselves on these arguments, those who hold this latter view try to find a different conception of wealth [from that which identifies it with a fund of currency] and a different conception of the art of acquisition [from that which makes it specially concerned with currency]. They are right in making the attempt. The [natural] art of acquisition, and natural wealth, *are* different. The [natural] form of the art of acquisition is connected with the management of the household [which in turn is connected with the *general* acquisition of *all* the resources needed for its life]; but the other form is a matter only of retail trade, and it is concerned only with getting a fund of money, and that only by the method of conducting the exchange of commodities. This latter form may be held to turn on the power of currency; for currency is the starting-point, as it is also the goal, of exchange. § 13. It is a further point of difference that the wealth produced by this latter form of the art of acquisition is unlimited.[1] [In this respect the art of acquisition, in its retail form, is analogous to other professional arts.] The art of medicine recognizes no limit in respect of the production of health, and the arts generally admit no limit in respect of the production of their ends (each seeking to produce its end to the greatest possible extent)—though medicine, and the arts generally, recognize and practise a limit to the means they use to attain their ends, since the end itself constitutes a limit.

---

[1] Wealth produced by the natural form of acquisition, which is part of the art of household management, is limited in amount, because it has only to serve the actual needs of the household. Wealth produced by the other and unnatural form of acquisition is not limited by any object which it serves.

The same is true of the retail form of the art of acquisition. There is no limit to the end it seeks; and the end it seeks is wealth of the sort we have mentioned [i.e. wealth in the form of currency] and the mere acquisition of money.   § 14. But the acquisition of wealth by the art of household management (as contrasted with the art of acquisition in its retail form) *has* a limit; and the object of that art is not an unlimited amount of wealth. It would thus appear, if we look at the matter in this light,[1] that all wealth must have a limit. In actual experience, however, we see the opposite happening; and all who are engaged in acquisition increase their fund of currency without any limit or pause.

§ 15. The cause of this contradiction lies in the close connexion between the two different modes of acquisition [that of the house-holder, and that of the retail trader]. They overlap because they are both handling the same objects and acting in the same field of acquisition; but they move along different lines—the object of the one being simply accumulation, and that of the other something quite different. This overlap of the two modes explains[2] why some men believe that mere accumulation is the object of household management; and in the strength of that belief they stick to the idea that they must keep their wealth in currency untouched, or increase it indefinitely.   § 16. But the fundamental cause of this state of mind is men's anxiety about livelihood, rather than about well-being; **1258 a** and since their desire for that is unlimited, their desire for the things that produce it is equally unlimited. Even those who do aim at well-being seek the means of obtaining physical enjoyments; and, as what they seek appears to depend on the activity of acquisition, they are thus led to occupy themselves wholly in the making of money. This is the real reason why the other and lower form of the art of acquisition has come into vogue. § 17. Because enjoyment depends on [the possession of] a super-fluity, men address themselves to the art which produces the superfluity necessary to enjoyment; and if they cannot get what they want by the use of that art—i.e. the art of acquisition—they attempt to do so by other means, using each and every capacity[3] in a way not consonant with its nature. The proper function of

[1] i.e., in the light of the fact that true wealth is the sum of what is needed for the subsistence and the general needs of the household, and is limited by those needs. (Newman's note.)

[2] But, as Newman notes, Aristotle argues a little later (in the next section, § 16) that the explanation is not so much this overlap of two modes as a deeper cause—that is to say, a misconception of the purpose of life and of the nature of well-being.

[3] 'Capacity', as the next sentence makes clear, includes both moral qualities, such as courage, and professional abilities such as those of the soldier or doctor.

courage, for example, is not to produce money but to give confidence. The same is true of military and medical ability: neither has the function of producing money: the one has the function of producing victory, and the other that of producing health. § 18. But those of whom we are speaking turn all such capacities into forms of the art of acquisition, as though to make money were the one aim and everything else must contribute to that aim.

We have thus discussed the unnecessary form of the art of acquisition: we have described its nature, and we have explained why men need [or think that they need] its services. We have also discussed the necessary form: we have shown that it is different from the other, and is naturally a branch of the art of household management, concerned with the provision of [a due amount] of subsistence, and *not*, therefore, unlimited in its scope, as the other form is, but subject to definite bounds.

NOTE F (p. 24): *'Chrematistic' in the sense of money-making*

'Chrematistic', or the art of acquisition, is a term used by Aristotle in various senses: see note E above on p. 22. Here 'the other form', which he proceeds to discuss, is money-making proper, where *monetary* gain is the object. It is distinguished from the form (where no actual money-making is involved, but a gain is none the less made) in which the object is simply the exchange of commodities. This latter form is sound or natural 'chrematistic': 'the other form' is perverted or unsound. It should be noted that, in the Greek, 'chrematistic' means not the making of money, but the acquisition of things (*chrēmata*). At the same time it should also be noted that *chrēmata* is a term which, though it primarily means things, tends to imply the notion of money ('an ambiguous word, often meaning money and always suggestive of it', Newman, ii, p. 187).

CHAPTER X

Household management is concerned with the use, and not (except in the way of general supervision) with the acquisition, of property; generally the householder should be able to count on nature supplying the means he needs. Acquisition for acquisition's sake shows its worst side in usury, which makes barren metal breed.

§ 1. The argument of the last chapter provides a clear solution to the problem which we originally raised:[1] 'Does the art of acquisition belong to the province of the manager of the household and the statesman [and is it thus a part of, or otherwise

---

[1] See § 1 of chapter VIII, where the question was raised whether the art of 'chrematistic' was identical with, or a part of, or ancillary to, the art of household management. Aristotle here introduces the art of the statesman, as well as that of household management, in connexion with 'chrematistic'; but as has already been noticed (in note 1 on p. 21 and note E on p. 22) his treatment of 'economy' tends to be political as well as domestic.

connected with, their art]? Or is it outside that province, and should property be regarded as something on which they can simply count [and with the acquisition of which they need not concern themselves]?' It may be urged, in favour of the second alternative, that just as the art of the statesman does not produce human stock, but counts on its being supplied by nature and proceeds to use her supply, so nature must also provide the physical means of subsistence—the land, or sea, or whatever it be. Then, and upon that basis, it is the province of the householder to manage properly the means which are ready to his hand.   § 2. It is not the business of the art of weaving to produce wool, but to use it, and to distinguish the sorts of wool which are good and suitable from those which are poor and unsuitable. [The same principle applies to the art of household management.] If this were not the case, and if the art of acquisition were held to be a part of the art of household management, the question might be raised why the art of medicine should not equally be held to be a part; and it might be argued that the members of a household must needs have health, in the same way as they must needs have life or any of the other necessaries.   § 3. The reasonable view of the issue thus raised is that there is a sense [that of general supervision] in which the manager of a household or a ruler is bound to see to the health of the members of his household or state; but there is another sense [that of actual treatment] in which they have no obligation, and doctors alone are concerned. Similarly, in the matter of property, there is a sense in which it is the business of the manager of a household to see to its acquisition; but in another sense that is not his business, and acquisition belongs to an ancillary art.

On a general view, as we have already noticed, a supply of property should be ready to hand [as a provision of nature]. It is the business of nature to furnish subsistence for each being brought into the world; and this is shown by the fact that the offspring of animals always gets nourishment from the residuum of the matter that gives it its birth.[1]   § 4. The natural form, therefore, of the art of acquisition is always, and in all cases, acquisition from fruits and animals. That art, as we have said, has two forms: one which is connected with retail trade, and another which is connected with the management of the household. Of these two forms, the latter is necessary and laudable; the former is a method of exchange which is justly censured, because **1258 b** the gain in which it results is not naturally made [from plants and animals], but is made at the expense of other men. The trade of the petty usurer [the extreme example of that form of the art of acquisition which

---

[1] This is a point already made in c. VIII, § 10.

is connected with retail trade] is hated most, and with most reason:
it makes a profit from currency itself, instead of making it from
the process [i.e. of exchange] which currency was meant to serve.
§ 5. Currency came into existence merely as a means of exchange;
usury tries to make it increase [as though it were an end in itself].
This is the reason why usury is called by the word we commonly
use [the word *tokos*, which in Greek also means 'breed' or 'offspring'[1]]; for as the offspring resembles its parent, so the interest
bred by money is like the principal which breeds it, and [as a son
is styled by his father's name, so] it may be called 'currency the
son of currency'. Hence we can understand why, of all modes of
acquisition, usury is the most unnatural.[2]

CHAPTER XI[3]

*A practical consideration of the art of acquisition. The divisions of
that art which may be made on practical grounds. Instances of the
successful practice of the art, especially by the creation of monopolies.*

§ 1. We have now discussed sufficiently that part of our subject
[i.e. the art of acquisition] which is related to pure knowledge: it
remains to consider the part which is related to actual use. All
subjects of this nature may be treated liberally in theory, but have
to be handled in practice as circumstances demand. The parts of
the art of acquisition which are of actual use are the following.
The first is an experience of farm-stock. We have to know which
are the most profitable breeds, and on what soil, and with what
treatment, they will give us the greatest profit: we have to know,
for example, the right way of stocking horses, or cattle, or sheep,
or any other kind of farm-stock. § 2. (Only experience can tell us

[1] Shakespeare thus speaks of interest as a 'breed for barren metal', when he
makes Antonio ask Shylock

When did friendship take
A breed for barren metal of his friend?

[2] Aristotle's condemnation of 'chrematistic', and his attitude to the lending
of money at interest, may be connected with the economic development of
Athens during the fourth century. Deposit banks, which made loans to merchants from their funds, were coming into existence; and the Athenian banks
were making Athens the principal money-market of Greece. The creation of
new capital particularly fostered shipping, and made Athens 'a mart of the
world' (see Book VII, c. VI, § 4). On this general development see the *Cambridge
Ancient History*, vol. vi, pp. 72–4.

[3] This chapter, as Newman notes, differs in some respects from those preceding it, and its argument cannot be altogether squared with that of the previous chapters. It differs, for example, from the three previous chapters (cc.
VIII–X) in the account given of 'chrematistic'. Some of it may possibly be an
addition, which has not altogether been reduced to harmony with its context.
The whole chapter—alike in its practical trend and in its collection of instances—
is more akin to the *Oeconomica* (which is *not* an Aristotelian treatise) than it is
to the *Politics*.

how different breeds compare with one another in point of profit, or what breeds are most paying on what sorts of soil: for some breeds thrive on one sort of soil, and some on another sort.) Other useful parts of the art of acquisition are experience in cultivation, not only of cornland but also of land planted with vines and olives; experience in bee-keeping; and experience in the rearing of such fish and fowl as may help to provide subsistence. § 3. These are the parts and the original elements of the art of acquisition in its soundest and properest form [which consists in production]. We now come to exchange [as a second part or form of the art of acquisition]. This includes, first and foremost, commerce (which is divided into the three operations of the provision of a ship, the carriage of freight, and offering for sale—operations which differ from one another in the sense that some have a greater margin of safety, and others a greater margin of profit); it includes, in the second place, investment at interest; and it also includes, in the third place, service for hire. § 4. This last part of exchange [service for hire] is partly a matter of skilled craftsmen in the mechanical arts, and partly of unskilled workers who can render only the service of bodily labour. A third form of the art of acquisition[1] is a form intermediate between the first and second; for it possesses elements both of the first, or natural, form, and of the form which consists in exchange. It is concerned with things extracted from the earth [metals] or with products of the earth which bear no fruit but are still of use [trees used for timber]; and we may thus cite, as examples, the industries of lumbering and mining. § 5. Mining, in its turn, has many forms, because there are many species of metals extracted from the earth.

A general account has now been given of the various forms of acquisition: to consider them minutely, and in detail, might be useful for practical purposes; but to dwell long upon them would be in poor taste. § 6. Suffice it to say that the occupations which require most skill are those in which there is least room for chance: the meanest are those in which most damage is done to physique: the most servile are those in which most use is made of physical strength: the least noble are those in which there is least need for the exercise of goodness.

§ 7. There are books on these subjects by several writers: **1259 a** Charetides of Paros and Apollodorus of Lemnos have written on the cultivation of cornland and land planted with vines and olives: others have written on other themes; anyone who is interested should study these subjects with the aid of these writings. A collection ought also to be made of the scattered stories about the

[1] See Note G, p. 32.

ways in which different people have succeeded in making a fortune.[1]
§ 8. They are all useful to those who value the art of acquisition.
There is, for example, the story which is told of Thales of Miletus.
It is a story about a scheme for making money, which is fathered
on Thales owing to his reputation for wisdom; but it involves a
principle of general application. § 9. He was reproached for his
poverty, which was supposed to show the uselessness of philosophy; but observing from his knowledge of meteorology (so the
story goes) that there was likely to be a heavy crop of olives [next
summer], and having a small sum at his command, he paid down
earnest-money, early in the year, for the hire of all the olive-presses
in Miletus and Chios; and he managed, in the absence of any
higher offer, to secure them at a low rate. When the season came,
and there was a sudden and simultaneous demand for a number
of presses, he let out the stock he had collected at any rate he chose
to fix; and making a considerable fortune he succeeded in proving
that it is easy for philosophers to become rich if they so desire,
though it is not the business which they are really about. § 10. The
story is told as showing that Thales proved his own wisdom; but,
as we have said, the plan he adopted—which was, in effect, the
creation of a monopoly—involves a principle which can be generally
applied in the art of acquisition. Some states, therefore, as well as
individuals, adopt this resource when in need of money: they
establish, for instance, a monopoly in provisions. § 11. [But state
monopolies may clash with private.] In Sicily a man with whom
a sum of money had been deposited bought up all the iron from
the ironworks; and afterwards, when retailers came from their
shops to get a supply, he was the only seller from whom they could
buy. He did not raise the price to any great extent; but he gained,
none the less, a profit of a hundred talents on an outlay of fifty.
§ 12. This speculation came to the notice of Dionysius, the ruler
of Syracuse, and he ordered the man to leave the city, though he
allowed him to take his gains: the reason was his discovery of a way
of making profit which was injurious to the interests of Dionysius
himself. Yet his idea was simply the same as that of Thales; and
what both of them did was merely to establish a private monopoly.
§ 13. But a knowledge of these methods is useful to statesmen as
well [as private persons]: states—like households, but to an even
greater extent—are often in want of financial resources and in
need of more ways of gaining them. This is the reason why some
of those who adopt a political career confine their political activity
to matters of finance.

[1] Aristotle and his pupils were interested in making collections of all sorts of
data: see Introduction, II, § 2 and Appendix V. III.

NOTE G (p. 30): *A different account of the senses of 'chrematistic'*

It has been already noticed, in the first note to this chapter, that Aristotle gives in it a somewhat different account of 'chrematistic' and its divisions. The classification of the different divisions of 'chrematistic' which appears in the previous chapters (VIII–X) has already been explained in note E on p. 22. In the present chapter the classification of the different divisions is: (1) 'the soundest and properest form', which consists in dealing with farm-stock, arable cultivation, bee-keeping, and the like; (2) 'the form which consists in exchange'—a form here made to include even usury, which in c. X, § 4 was distinguished from exchange; (3) a third form 'intermediate between the first and the second', which consists, somewhat curiously, in lumbering and mining—industries which certainly have some elements of the first form of the art of acquisition, but in which it is difficult to see any elements of the second or 'exchange' form (unless one assumes that these industries produce for exchange, and not for immediate use).

CHAPTER XII

4. Marriage, Parenthood, and the general management of the household. *The nature of marital authority, which is like that exercised by a statesman over his fellow citizens. The nature of parental authority, which is like that of a king over his subjects.*

§ 1. We said, in a previous passage,[1] that there were three parts of the art of household management—the first, of which we have already spoken, being the art of controlling slaves: the second, the art of exercising paternal authority; and the third, that of exercising marital authority. [The last two remain to be discussed, and to be discussed separately; for] while the head of the household rules over both wife and children, and rules over both as free members of the household, he exercises a different sort of rule in either case. **1259 b** His rule over his wife is like that of a statesman over fellow citizens; his rule over his children is like that of a monarch over subjects. The male is naturally fitter to command than the female, except where there is some departure from nature; and age and maturity are similarly fitter to command than youth and immaturity. § 2. In most cases where rule of the statesman's sort is exercised there is an interchange of ruling and being ruled [which does not occur in regard to husband and wife]: the members of a political association aim by their very nature at being equal and differing in nothing. Even so, and in spite of this aim, it is none the less true that when one body of citizens is ruling, and the other is being ruled, the former desires to establish a difference

[1] This previous passage comes in c. III, § 1. Aristotle here reverts (after a long passage on property and profit-making, which includes the four chapters VIII–XI) to the consideration of the three integral elements of the household which he had begun to discuss in the chapters on slavery, IV–VII; see note D on p. 22.

—in outward forms, in modes of address, and in titles of respect—
which may remind us of the saying of Amasis about his foot-pan.[1]
The relation of the male to the female is permanently that in which
the statesman [temporarily] stands to his fellow-citizens. § 3.
Paternal rule over children, on the other hand, is like that of a
king over his subjects. The male parent is in a position of authority
both in virtue of the affection to which he is entitled and by right
of his seniority; and his position is thus in the nature of royal
authority. Homer, therefore, was right and proper in using the
invocation

Father of Gods and of men

to address Zeus, who is king of them all. A king ought to be
naturally superior to his subjects, and yet of the same stock as they
are; and this is the case with the relation of age to youth, and of
parent to child.

CHAPTER XIII

*The art of household management is a moral art, aiming at the moral
goodness of the members of the household; and this is true in regard
to slaves as well as to other members. The goodness of the head of the
household has a quality of its own: the different classes of members
have also different qualities of goodness. This is part of a general law
that goodness is relative to function, and that it is the function of some
to guide, and of others to be guided—and guided, too, in different ways.
The master's duty of guiding the slaves of the household. The subjects
of marriage and parenthood (only briefly mentioned in the previous
chapter) are to be reserved for future treatment, in connexion with the
polis and the proper mode of its government (Book VII, cc. XVI–XVII).*

§ 1. It is clear from the previous argument that the business of
household management is concerned more with human beings
than it is with inanimate property;[2] that it is concerned more with

---

[1] Amasis, who from being a subject had become a ruler, had a golden foot-
pan made from the image of a god, which the Egyptians proceeded to reverence
greatly. He seized on the analogy, in an address to his subjects. He had fared
himself, he told them, like this foot-pan; as it had been merely a utensil, and
then had become an object of reverence, so he had been merely a subject, and
now had become a king, entitled to honour and respect (Herodotus II. 172).

[2] Aristotle has, it is true, dealt largely with inanimate property, under
the head of the art of acquisition, in the four chapters VIII–XI. But the main
conclusions still remain: (1) that the art of acquisition is not a part of household
management (or what the Greeks termed 'economy') in the same sense as the personal exercise of authority over the persons of the slave, the wife, and the child;
(2) that the essential parts of the household, which are the material of the house-
holder's art of management, are the three personal relations of master and slave,
husband and wife, and parent and child; and (3) that the essence of the art of
household management is to make these three relations as good as possible, and
is thus, in the last resort, moral, and not 'economic', in the modern sense of
that word.

the good condition of human beings than with a good condition of property (which is what we call wealth); and, finally, that it is concerned more with the goodness of the free members of the household than with that of slaves. § 2. Here a preliminary question may be raised in regard to the slave. Has he any 'goodness' beyond that of discharging his function as an instrument and performing his menial service—any goodness of a higher value, such as belongs to temperance, fortitude, justice, and the rest of such moral qualities?[1] Or has he no 'goodness' outside the area of the bodily services he renders? § 3. Either alternative presents difficulties. If slaves have a 'goodness' of the higher sort, in what respect will they differ from freemen? If they have not, it is a surprising thing: they are human beings, with a share in reason [and we should naturally expect them to have the higher goodness of reasoning beings]. But the question thus raised in regard to the slave may be asked almost equally in regard to the wife and the child. Can *they* have 'goodness' [of the higher sort]? Must a wife be 'good', in the sense of temperate, and brave, and just? Should a child be called licentious or temperate? Is the answer Yes, or must it be No?

§ 4. [Before we can give any answer, we must carry the argument further:] we must raise the question [not in particular cases, but] in a general form. Is the goodness of those who naturally rule the same as the goodness of those who are naturally ruled, or does it differ? If we say that both of them ought to share in the nobility of goodness,[2] why should one of them permanently rule, and the other be permanently ruled? The difference between them cannot be simply a difference of degree [which would admit of their both sharing in that nobility, though to a different extent]: the difference between ruler and ruled is one of kind, and degree has nothing to do with the matter. § 5. If, on the other hand, we say that one of them ought, and the other ought not, to share, we commit ourselves to a strange view. How can the ruler rule properly, or the subject be properly ruled, unless they are both temperate and just? Anyone who is licentious or cowardly will utterly fail to do his duty. **1260 a** The conclusion which clearly emerges is that both classes [the ruled as well as the ruler] must share in goodness, but that

[1] Aristotle enumerates three of the four cardinal Greek virtues, but instead of enumerating the fourth (Wisdom) he contents himself with an 'etcetera'. It would be difficult to predicate wisdom of the slave, since he 'participates in reason to the extent of apprehending it in another, though destitute of it himself' (c. v, § 9).

[2] The Greek word—*Kalokagathia*—means literally the quality of one who is both handsome and good, and was originally applied to the character of the 'complete gentleman'.

there must be different kinds of goodness [one for the ruler and one for the ruled]—just as there are also different kinds of goodness among different classes of the ruled.

§ 6. The view here suggested [that the ruler and the ruled have separate kinds of goodness] takes us straight to the nature of the soul. The soul has naturally two elements, a ruling and a ruled; and each has its different goodness, one belonging to the rational and ruling element, and the other to the irrational and ruled. What is true of the soul is evidently also true of the other cases [i.e. those of the household and the state]; and we may thus conclude that it is a general law that there should be naturally ruling elements and elements naturally ruled.[1] § 7. [Just because there is a general law, operative in many spheres, there are different modes of its operation, according to the sphere in which it operates.] The rule of the freeman over the slave is one kind of rule; that of the male over the female another; that of the grown man over the child another still. It is true that all these persons [freeman and slave, male and female, the grown man and the child] possess in common the different parts of the soul;[2] but they possess them in different ways.[3] The slave is entirely without the faculty of deliberation; the female indeed possesses it, but in a form which remains inconclusive; and if children also possess it, it is only in an immature form. § 8. What is true [of their possessing the different parts of the soul] must similarly be held to be true of their possessing moral goodness: they must all share in it, but not in the same way—each sharing only to the extent required for the discharge of his or her function. The ruler, accordingly, must possess moral goodness in its full and perfect form [i.e. the form based on rational deliberation], because his function, regarded absolutely and in its full nature, demands a master-artificer, and reason is such a master-artificer;[4] but all other persons need only

---

[1] Aristotle here appears to argue in a circle—first from the relations of persons to the relation of the elements in the soul, and then back from the relation of the elements in the soul to the relations of persons. But the centre of the circle is the general principle of rule and subordination; cf. c. v of this book, §§. 1-7.

[2] A full account of the different 'parts' of the soul is given later in the *Politics* (Book VII, c. xiv). The 'parts' with which Aristotle is here concerned are simply the rational and ruling element, and the irrational and ruled element, which are mentioned in the previous section.

[3] A difficulty here arises in Aristotle's argument. If the slave has in him *both* of the different parts of the soul, the rational as well as the irrational, why should he be treated as if he had only the irrational part? The answer which Aristotle gives (cf. c. v, § 9) is that the rational element in the slave, while inadequate for his own deliberation about alternative courses of action, enables him to understand the rational character of his master's commands to follow a given course of action. But in spite of the answer, some discrepancy remains.

[4] The argument may be elucidated from an analogy cited by Newman in his note. The function of healing is regarded 'absolutely and in its full nature'

possess moral goodness to the extent required of them [by their particular position].   § 9. It is thus clear that while moral goodness is a quality of all the persons mentioned, the fact still remains that temperance—and similarly fortitude and justice—are not, as Socrates held,[1] the same in a woman as they are in a man. Fortitude in the one, for example, is shown in connexion with ruling; in the other, it is shown in connexion with serving; and the same is true of the other forms of goodness.

§ 10. This conclusion also emerges clearly when we examine the subject more in detail, and in its different divisions [i.e. if we consider the nature of goodness separately in women, children, and slaves]. To speak in general terms, and to maintain that goodness consists in 'a good condition of the soul', or in 'right action', or in anything of the kind, is to be guilty of self-deception. Far better than such general definitions is the method of simple enumeration of the different forms of goodness, as followed by Gorgias.   § 11. We must therefore hold that what the poet Sophocles said of woman

A modest silence is a woman's crown

[a saying which implies that there is a special form of goodness for women] contains a general truth—but a truth which does not apply to men. [Children, again, have their own special form of goodness]; a child is immature, and his goodness is therefore obviously not a matter of his relation to his present self, but of his relation to the end [which he will attain when mature] and to the guiding authority [of the parent, which prepares him for that end]. § 12. Similarly, too, the goodness of the slave is a matter of his relation to his master.

We laid it down, in treating of slaves, that they were useful for the necessary purposes of life.[2] It is clear, on that basis, that they need but little goodness; only so much, in fact, as will prevent them from falling short of their duties through intemperance or cowardice. If this be true [i.e. if the slave should have goodness to this extent], the question may be raised whether artisans too ought not to have goodness, seeing that they often fall short of their duties through intemperance.   § 13. But does not the case of

when it is ascribed to the physician who directs and superintends healing as a master-artificer; it is regarded 'only in a qualified way' when it is ascribed to a subordinate who executes his directions. When we consider the ruler's function in the light of this analogy we see that it requires (1) the full power of reason, which includes the deliberative faculty, and (2) the full form of moral goodness which that supplies.

[1] The reference is to the argument of Plato's dialogue, the *Meno*, 72-3.

[2] Cf. c. v, § 9, 'they supply their owner with bodily help in meeting daily requirements'.

the artisan differ greatly from that of the slave? The slave is a partner in his master's life: the artisan is less closely attached to a master. The extent of the goodness incumbent on him is proportionate to the extent of the servitude to which he is subject; [and this is less than that of the slave,] since the mechanical type of artisan is subject only to what may be called a limited servitude.[1] Again [and this is another difference] **1260 b** the slave belongs to the class of those who are naturally what they are; but no shoemaker, or any other artisan, belongs to that class.[2] § 14. It is therefore clear [whatever may be said of artisans and their employers] that the master of a household must produce in the slave the sort of goodness we have been discussing,[3] and he must do so [as master and moral guardian, and] not as a manager giving instructions about particular duties.[4] This is the reason why we may disagree with those who are in favour of withholding reason [i.e. rational instruction and admonition] from slaves, and who argue that only command should be employed. Admonition ought to be applied to slaves even more than it is to children.

§ 15. This may serve as a sufficient discussion of these topics. There remain for discussion a number of questions—the relation of husband and wife, and that of parent and child; the nature of the goodness proper to each partner in these relations; the character of the mutual association of the partners, with its qualities and defects and the methods of attaining those qualities and escaping those defects. All these are questions which must be treated later in the discourses which deal with forms of government.[5] [The reason for postponing them is this.] Every household is a part of a polis. The society of husband and wife, and that of parents and children, are parts of the household. The goodness of every part must be considered with reference to the goodness of the whole. We must therefore consider the government [of the whole polis] before we proceed to deal with the training of children and women—at any rate if we hold that the goodness of children and women makes any difference to the goodness of the polis. § 16. And it *must*

[1] That is to say, he is under a servitude for the one purpose of his particular task, and not (like the genuine slave) for all purposes.

[2] They are not born in their occupation, but voluntarily enter it. They are not therefore intended by their birth and character for a particular form of goodness (as slaves are): they are on their own account, except when they are acting in the field of their 'limited servitude', and they must achieve their own goodness accordingly.

[3] Goodness, that is to say, over and above technical goodness in the discharge of physical duties; or, in other words, goodness of the moral order.

[4] Management, as we have seen, can be delegated: cf. the beginning of c. VII, and especially § 5. But the master cannot delegate his inherent duty of the moral guidance of slaves.

[5] See Note H, p. 38.

make a difference. Women are a half of the free population: children grow up to be partners in the government of the state.

As we have already discussed some aspects of the household [i.e. slavery and the art of acquisition], and as we are to discuss the rest [i.e. marriage and parenthood] at a later stage, we may dismiss our present inquiry as finished, and make a new start. Let us first examine the theories of those who have expressed opinions about an ideal form of government.[1]

NOTE H (p. 37): *The incompleteness of Book I*

This passage is puzzling. Naturally these questions, which are concerned with the household, would be treated in Book I, which is a book about the household. Not only so; but the beginning of c. XIII seems definitely to promise a treatment of the relations of husband and wife, and of parent and child, as an integral part of the book. Why these relations should be postponed from the 'economic' to the 'political' part is not really clear, in spite of Aristotle's attempt to make it so. Meanwhile the village, which we should expect to be treated somewhere, after what has been said in c. II, has disappeared from view. (Yet the local villages, or *demes*, were an important part of Athenian life.) On the whole it would seem that this course on the household, which is a separate course or *methodos*, was left incomplete. *Desinit in harenam.*

---

[1] This paragraph seeks to make a transition between the incomplete Book I, which treats of 'economics', and the remaining books, which deal with 'politics' in its various forms. The paragraph as it stands may be the work of a later editor. In any case there is not an easy transition from Book I to Book II.

As regards the promise here made, that marriage and parenthood will be discussed later, it can only be said that some remarks are made on these themes in the last two books of the *Politics*, in which Aristotle sketches his own picture of an ideal form of government. But the remarks are only made incidentally, and the themes are not treated as independent themes.

BOOK II

REVIEW OF IDEAL STATES

A

IDEAL STATES IN THEORY (cc. i–viii)

Chapter I

1. Plato's Republic. *Political association is a sharing: how much should be shared? Plato's scheme of communism.*

1260 b 27 § 1. Our purpose is to consider what form of political association is the ideal for those who can count upon the material conditions of their life being, as nearly as possible, just what they would themselves wish.[1] We must begin by investigating ideal forms of government other than our own [i.e. other than that depicted in Books VII and VIII]; and we must investigate not only forms which are actually practised by states that are accounted to be well governed, but also forms of a different order which have been designed by theorists and are held in good repute. The gain of such a discussion will be twofold. In the first place, we shall discover what is right, and what is useful, in our field of inquiry. In the second place, when we proceed to seek for something different from the forms of government we have investigated, we shall not be thought to belong to the class of thinkers who desire at all costs to show their own ingenuity, but rather to have adopted our method in consequence of the defects we have found in existing forms.

§ 2. Our beginning must start from the point which is the natural starting-point of such a discussion [i.e. from the question, 'What are the things in which the members of a political association are associated, and what is the extent of their association?'] One of three alternatives must be adopted. All the citizens must have all things in common; or they must have nothing in common; or they must have some things in common, and others not. The second alternative—that they should have nothing in common—is clearly impossible: the constitution of a polis involves in itself some sort of association, and its members must initially be associated

---

[1] We may have (1) a form of association which is the best possible under actual conditions, and which is therefore the best relatively to those conditions, or (2) a form of association which is the best possible under ideal conditions, and which is therefore the best absolutely. Aristotle discusses the first form in Books IV–VI, and especially in the latter half of Book IV. He discusses the second form in Books VII–VIII. Here, in the first half of Book II, he only discusses the views of others about the second form.

in a common place of residence. **1261 a** To be fellow-citizens
is to be sharers in one state, and to have one state is also to
have one place of residence. [There must therefore always be
sharing in a common neighbourhood.]   § 3. But we have still to
choose between the first and the third alternative. Is it better that
a state which is to be well conducted should share in all the things
in which it is possible for it to share, or that it should share in
some things and not in others? It is certainly possible [to adopt the
first alternative, i.e.] that the citizens should share children and
wives and property with one another. This is the plan proposed
in the *Republic* of Plato, where Socrates argues for the necessity
of community of wives and children and community of property.
We are thus faced by the question whether it is better to remain
in our present condition [of separate families and private pro-
perty] or to follow the rule of life laid down in the *Republic*.

CHAPTER II

Community of wives and children. *Criticisms of the end or object—
unity—which Plato proposes to attain by it: (a) carried to its logical
extreme, that object would produce a one-man state; (b) it neglects the
social differentiation necessary in a state (a differentiation which, even
in a state of 'equals and likes', produces the distinction of governors
and governed); (c) it thus makes self-sufficiency impossible, because
self-sufficiency involves different elements making different contributions.*

§ 1. The establishment of a system of community of wives
involves, among many others, two major difficulties. The *object*
for which Socrates states that it ought to be instituted is evidently
not established by the arguments which he uses. Considered as
a *means* to the end which he states as necessary for the polis, his
scheme as set out is impracticable; and yet he gives no account
of the lines on which it ought to be interpreted.[1]   § 2. The
object which Socrates assumes as his premiss is contained in the
principle that 'the greatest possible unity of the whole polis is
the supreme good'. Yet it is obvious that a polis which goes on and
on, and becomes more and more of a unit, will eventually cease to
be a polis at all. A polis by its nature is some sort of aggregation:
[i.e. it has the quality of including a large number of members].

---

[1] Two fundamental criticisms are here raised—first, that the end of the
Platonic scheme (unity) is not proved by Plato to be the right end for a political
association; secondly, that the means proposed for the attainment of that end
are not capable of realizing it, nor indeed, as Aristotle's argument goes on to
suggest, practicable in themselves. The first line of criticism is developed in
§§ 2–8 of this chapter: the second is developed in c. III.

If it becomes more of a unit, it will first become a household instead of a polis, and then an individual instead of a household; for we should all call the household more of a unit than the polis, and the individual more of a unit than the household. It follows that, even if we could, we ought not to achieve this object: it would be the destruction of the polis.

§ 3. There is a further objection. Not only is the polis composed of a *number* of men: it is also composed of different *kinds* of men, for similars cannot bring it into existence. There is a difference between a polis and a military alliance. A military alliance, formed by its very nature for the sake of the mutual help which its members can render to one another, possesses utility purely in virtue of its quantity; and a great alliance, even if there is no difference of kind among its members, is like a weight which depresses the scales more heavily in the balance. [A polis is essentially different: it necessarily requires a difference of capacities among its members, which enables them to serve as complements to one another, and to attain a higher and better life by the mutual exchange of their different services.][1] In this respect a polis will also differ from a tribe: [a tribe, like a military alliance, may be the stronger merely by virtue of being larger], provided, however, that it does not allow its members to be scattered in separate villages, but unites them in a confederacy like that of Arcadia. [Unlike a mere aggregate, such as a tribe or alliance,] a real unity, such as a polis, must be made up of elements which differ in kind.

§ 4. A consequence follows [from this conception that the polis is composed of different elements, mutually exchanging different services in virtue of different capacities]. It is that the well-being of every polis depends on each of its elements rendering to the others an amount equivalent to what it receives from them. This is a principle already laid down in the *Ethics*.[2] It is a principle which has to be observed even among free and equal citizens [in spite of the fact that, as such, they appear to be identical in kind].[3] They

[1] This passage is inserted in order to make explicit what is implied in Aristotle's argument—the idea that the polis, being an *association*, must be composed, like all associations, of different elements which can exchange services, and can thus attain, in virtue of their different capacities, a higher standard of life.

[2] *Ethics* V, c. v, § 4: see Appendix II. A.

[3] The argument of this passage is excellently stated in Newman's note. 'This is true even of free and equal citizens, among whom one would least expect any difference in kind to exist, for though here there is no intrinsic difference, yet the impossibility of all ruling at the same time leads to an "imitation" of, or approximation to, such difference, and breaks them into rulers and ruled, two classes different in kind, even though they interchange their positions from time to time. Hence here too "the rendering to others of an amount equivalent to what has been received" is in place.'

cannot all rule simultaneously; they must therefore each have office for a year—or by some other order of succession and for some other period.   § 5. In this way it comes about that all are rulers [in turn], just as [all would be shoemakers and carpenters in turn] if shoemakers and carpenters changed their occupations, and the same men were not always shoemakers and carpenters.   § 6. It would be better indeed if the principle followed in the arts and crafts [that 'the cobbler should stick to his last'] were also applied to the affairs of the political association; and from this point of view it is better for the same men always to be rulers wherever possible. But where this ideal is impossible, **1261 b** through the natural equality of all the citizens—and also, it may be argued too, because justice requires the participation of all in office (whether office be a good thing or a bad)—there is yet an imitation of it, or an approximation to it, if equals retire from office in turn and are all, apart from their period of office, in the same position.[1]   § 7. This means that some rule, and others are ruled, in turn, as if they had become, for the time being, different sorts of persons. We may add that even those who are rulers for the time being differ from one another, some holding one kind of office and some another [which again proves that difference of kinds is essential to the constitution of a polis].

These considerations are sufficient to show, first, that it is not the nature of the polis to be a unit in the sense in which some thinkers say that it is, and secondly, that what is said to be the supreme good of a polis is really its ruin. But surely the 'good' of each thing is what preserves it in being.   § 8. There is still another[2] consideration which may be used to prove that the policy of attempting an extreme unification of the polis is not a good policy. A household is an institution which attains a greater degree of self-sufficiency than an individual can; and a polis, in turn, is an institution which attains self-sufficiency to a greater degree than a household. But it only attains that goal, and becomes fully a polis, when the association which forms it is large enough [and diversified enough] to be self-sufficing.[3] On the assumption, therefore, that the higher degree of self-sufficiency is the more desirable thing, the lesser degree of unity is more desirable than the greater.

---

[1] The original text is uncertain. The translation is based on emendations in the text proposed by scholars.

[2] The first consideration is that urged in § 2—that when unity is made the end, the end defeats itself. The second is that urged in §§ 3-7—that unity contravenes the essential differentiation of the different elements of the polis. (Aristotle inverts the order of these two considerations in his *résumé* at the end of § 7.) The third, urged here, is that self-sufficiency is a more desirable end than unity.

[3] See Book I, c. ii, § 8, and note B to that chapter.

CHAPTER III

Community of wives and children (continued). Criticisms of such community considered as a means for producing the end of unity: (a) as all collectively, and not each individually, are parents, there will be no real feeling, but rather a general apathy; (b) kinship will be fractional kinship (when 1,000 are father to the same child, each father is only 1/1,000 father); (c) nature will 'recur', and spoil the scheme.

§ 1. [We now turn from criticism of the end to criticism of the means.] Even if it were the supreme good of a political association that it should have the greatest possible unity, this unity does not appear to follow from [i.e. to be achieved by] the formula of 'All men saying "Mine" and "Not mine" at the same time [and of the same object'],[1] which, in the view of Socrates, is the index of the perfect unity of a polis. § 2. The word 'all' has a double sense: [it may mean 'each separately', or 'all collectively']. If it be understood in the first sense, the object which Socrates desires to realize may perhaps be realized in a greater degree [than if it be understood in the second]: each and all separately will then say 'My wife' (or 'My son') of one and the same person; and each and all separately will speak in the same way of property, and of every other concern. But it is not in the sense of 'each separately' that all who have children and wives in common will actually speak of them. They will all call them 'Mine'; but they will do so collectively, and not individually. § 3. The same is true of property also: all will call it 'Mine'; but they will do so in the sense of 'all collectively', and not in the sense of 'each separately'. It is therefore clear that there is a certain fallacy in the use of the term 'all'. It is a term which, like the similar terms 'both' and 'odd' and 'even',[2] is liable by its ambiguity [to produce quarrels in actual life, and] equally to breed captious arguments in reasoning. We may therefore conclude that the formula of 'all men saying "Mine" of the same object' is in one sense [the sense of 'each separately']

[1] The formula is that used in Plato's *Republic*, 462 c. We may note, in regard to the whole of this chapter (and also the next), that the means criticized in it by Aristotle is only one sort of means—community of wives and children, or the abolition of the family. The criticism of the other sort of means (community of property) is postponed to c. v. Some of the considerations adduced apply, indeed, equally to both sorts of means (e.g. the consideration in §§ 2-3, and again that in § 4); but on the whole Aristotle follows two distinct lines of criticism for the two different means.

[2] 'Both' may mean 'both together' or 'either separately': the quality of being 'even' may exist in a whole (when all the parts collectively are 'even' with something else) without existing in the parts, of which 'each separately' may be odd; and the same is true of the quality of being 'odd'.

something fine but impracticable, and in another sense [that of 'all collectively'] in no wise conducive to harmony.[1]

§ 4. Not only does it not conduce to harmony: the formula also involves an actual loss. What is common to the greatest number gets the least amount of care. Men pay most attention to what is their own: they care less for what is common; or, at any rate, they care for it only to the extent to which each is individually concerned. Even where there is no other cause for inattention, men are more prone to neglect their duty when they think that another is attending to it: this is exactly what happens in domestic service, where many attendants are sometimes of less assistance than a few. § 5. The scheme of Plato means that each citizen will have a thousand sons: they will not be the sons of each citizen individually: any and every son will be equally the son of any and every father; and the result will be that every son will be equally neglected by every father.

1262 a There is still a further objection [which arises from what has just been said about each citizen having a thousand sons]. Each citizen, when he says 'Mine' of any child who is prosperous or the reverse, is speaking fractionally. He does not mean that the child is wholly 'Mine', but only that he is 'Mine' to the extent of a fraction determined by the total number of citizens. When he says 'He is mine' or 'He is so-and-so's', the term 'Mine' or 'So-and-so's' is used with reference to the whole body concerned —the whole thousand, or whatever may be the total number of citizens.[2] Even so he cannot be sure [i.e. he cannot even be sure that he is as much as the thousandth part of a father]; for there is no evidence who had a child born to him, or whether, if one was born, it managed to survive.[3] § 6. Which is the better system— that each of two thousand, or ten thousand, persons should say 'Mine' of a child in this fractional sense, or that each should say 'Mine' in the [total] sense in which the word is now used in ordinary states? § 7. As things are, A calls by the name of '*My*

---

[1] Why should the formula, in the second or collective interpretation of 'all', be in no wise conducive to harmony? The answer comes later, when Aristotle argues that discord rather than harmony (or at any rate a 'watery friendship') is produced by community of wives and children (*infra*, § 7).

[2] We may illustrate Aristotle's argument from a phrase of Edmond About— 'the Frenchman looks with pride at his face in the glass as he shaves in the morning, remembering that he is the forty-millionth part of a tyrant, and forgetting that he is the whole of a slave'. This might be inverted to run—'the Platonic citizen looks at himself with pride in the mirror, thinking that he is the father of a thousand sons, but forgetting that he is only the thousandth part of a father'.

[3] In the scheme of the *Republic* (459–60), the working of the system of temporary marriages is 'a secret which only the rulers know'. The offspring of these marriages is taken by the proper officers; if good, it is reared: if bad, it is 'put away'.

son' the same person whom B calls by the name of 'My brother':
C calls him 'My cousin': D, E, and so forth call him 'My relative',
because he is somehow connected with them, either closely or dis-
tantly, and whether by blood or by marriage; while besides these
different modes of address X and Y may use still another, and call
him 'My clansman' or 'My tribesman'.[1] It is better to be own
cousin to a man than to be his son after the Platonic fashion. § 8.
Even on Plato's system it is impossible to avoid the chance that
some of the citizens may guess who are their brothers, or children,
or fathers, or mothers. The resemblances between children and
parents must inevitably lead to their drawing conclusions about
one another's identity. § 9. That this actually happens in real life
is stated as a fact by some of the writers on descriptive geography.
They tell us that some of the inhabitants of upper Libya have their
wives in common; but the children born of such unions can still
be distinguished by their resemblance to their fathers. Indeed
there are some women, and some females in the animal world
(mares, for instance, and cows), that show a strong natural tendency
to produce offspring resembling the male parent: the Pharsalian
mare which was called the Just Return is a good example.[2]

Chapter IV

*Community of wives and children (continued). Problems arise when
parents do not know their children, or children their parents. At best
such a community produces a watery sort of fraternity. Plato's addition
to it of a scheme of transposition of ranks raises further difficulties.*

§ 1. There are also other difficulties in a system of community
of wives and children, which its advocates will not find it easy to
meet by any precautions. We may take as examples cases of
assault, unintentional (and, we may also add, intentional) homicide,
fighting, and slander. All these offences, when they are committed against father or mother or a near relative, differ from
offences against persons who are not so related, in being breaches
of natural piety. Such offences must happen more frequently

[1] The argument implied by Aristotle is that the ordinary system of the family
and of family relationship (1) enables A, B, and the rest to feel to a man, in their
different ways and from different angles, 'that keen sense of something *idion*
[i.e. of personal interest] which . . . the change proposed by Plato would take
away or seriously diminish' (Newman's note), and (2) enriches the man himself,
who is placed in these different and individual relations to A, B, and the rest, by
giving him, as it were, a number of facets, which would be absent on the Platonic
plan, and the absence of which would leave him one plain, dull, and unrelieved
surface.
[2] So called because she returned, in her offspring, exactly what had been
given by its sire.

when men are ignorant of their relatives than when they know who they are; and when they do happen, the customary penance can be made if men know their relatives, but none can be made if they are ignorant of them.   § 2. It is also surprising that Plato, after having made all the young men of his state the common sons of the older citizens, should content himself with debarring older men who are 'lovers' of the young from carnal intercourse with them, and should not debar them from behaving as 'lovers' or practising other familiarities.   Such familiarities, if practised between son and father, or brother and brother [as might easily happen if relationship were unknown], are the very height of indecency, all the more as the mere cherishing of this form of love, without giving it actual expression, is in itself indecent.   § 3. It is surprising, too, that Plato should debar male lovers from carnal intercourse on the one ground of the excessive violence of the pleasure, and that he should think it a matter of indifference that the 'lovers' may be father and son, or again that they may be brothers.[1]

§ 4.   Community of wives and children would seem to be more calculated to serve Plato's object if it were practised among the governed class of the farmers rather than among the governing guardians.   **1262 b** The spirit of fraternity is likely to exist to a less degree where wives and children are common; and the governed class ought to have little of that spirit if it is to obey and not to attempt revolution.   § 5. Generally, a system such as Plato suggests must produce results directly opposed to those which a system of properly constituted laws should produce, and equally opposed to the very object for which, in his view, this community of wives and children ought to be instituted.   § 6. Fraternity is generally held to be the chief good of states, because it is the best safeguard against the danger of civil dissensions. Plato himself particularly commends the ideal of the unity of the state; and that unity is commonly held, and expressly stated by Plato, to be the result of fraternity.   We may cite the argument of the *Symposium*, where, in the discourse on love, Aristophanes is made, as we all know, to speak of two lovers desiring in the excess of their 'fraternity' to grow together into a unity, and to be one instead of two.   § 7. Now in the case of two lovers, the result of an excessive desire for unity must be either the disappearance of both of them into a new being, or the disappearance of one of them into the other.   But in the case of the political association

---

[1] The two objections to the Platonic system in this paragraph depend on contemporary Greek notions and practices—the notion of what constitutes 'holiness' or natural piety among kinsfolk, and the practice of homosexuality between older and younger men.

the result of an excessive desire for unity would be different: it would be merely a watery sort of fraternity [and therefore less unity, instead of more]: a father would be very little disposed to say 'Mine' of a son, and a son would be as little disposed to say 'Mine' of a father.[1] § 8. Just as a little sweet wine, mixed with a great deal of water, produces a tasteless mixture, so family feeling is diluted and tasteless when family names have so little meaning as they have in a constitution of the Platonic order, and when there is so little reason for a father treating his sons as sons, or a son treating his father as a father, or brothers one another as brothers. § 9. There are two things which particularly move men to care for an object and to feel affection for that object. One of them is that the object should belong to yourself: the other is that you should like it. Neither of these motives can exist among men who live under a constitution such as the Platonic.

There is still a further difficulty. It concerns that part of Plato's scheme which may be called the transposition of ranks, under which children born to parents in the inferior rank of farmers and craftsmen are to be transferred [if they prove to be superior in endowment] to the superior rank of the guardians, and vice versa children born to parents in the superior rank are to be transferred [if they prove inferior] to the inferior. How such transposition is actually to be effected is a matter of great perplexity; and in any case those who transfer such children, and assign them their new place, will be bound to know who are the children so placed and with whom they are being placed.[2] § 10. In addition, those problems of assault, unnatural affection, and homicide, which have already been mentioned [as generally raised by the whole of Plato's scheme], will be raised even more by this part of his scheme. Transposition of ranks will mean that those transferred from the rank of guardian to an inferior rank will cease for the future to address the guardians as brothers, or children, or fathers, or mothers, as the case may be [though they will still be actually related to them in those ways]; and it will have the same effect for those who have been transferred to a superior rank. Such persons will thus lose entirely any deterrent which kinship provides against the commission of these offences.[3]

[1] Because, in either case, he is only the thousandth part, and he is removed by that whole distance from full fatherhood or full sonship.

[2] The difficulty arising from such knowledge (which may leak out and spread) will be, as Welldon suggests, that 'a child cannot be absolutely separated from the class to which he belongs [by birth]'. He will still trail the cloud of his previous origin in his new position.

[3] In § 1 of this chapter Aristotle had argued that offences against kinsfolk, which involved a breach of natural piety, were more likely to occur under Plato's system of diluted kinship than they were under the ordinary system of

This may serve as a determination of the issues raised by the idea of community of wives and children.

CHAPTER V

Community of property. *Three possible systems of property. The difficulties of a system under which ownership and use are both common: the merits of a system under which ownership is private and use is common—it gives more pleasure, and it encourages goodness more. Communism cannot remedy evils which really spring from the defects of human nature: it is also based on a false conception of unity, and neglects the true unity which comes from education; finally, it is contradicted by experience. Plato's particular scheme of community of property leaves the position of the farming class obscure. The system of government which he connects with his scheme is too absolute, and is likely to cause discontent: it also deprives the ruling class of any happiness.*

§ 1. The next subject for consideration is property. What is the proper system of property for citizens who are to live under an ideal constitution? Is it a system of communism, or one of private property? § 2. This is an issue which may be considered in itself, and apart from any proposals for community of wives and children. **1263 a** Even if wives and children are in severalty [and the family system is preserved], as is now universally the case, questions relating to property still remain for discussion. Should use and ownership both be common? [Or should one be common and the other private?] We may note three possible alternatives. First, we may have a system under which plots of land are owned in severalty, but the crops (as actually happens among some uncivilized tribes) are brought into a common stock for the purpose of consumption. Secondly, and conversely, the land may be held in common ownership, and may also be cultivated in common, but the crops may be divided among individuals for their private use: some of the uncivilized peoples are also said to practise this second method of sharing. Thirdly, the plots and the crops [i.e. ownership and use] may both be common.[1]

§ 3. When the cultivators of the soil are a different body from the citizens who own it [as will be the case if they are serfs or slaves], the position will be different and easier to handle; but when the citizens who own the soil are also its cultivators, the problems of

kinship. The argument of this section adds a further refinement. Transferred children, it is argued, have lost even the safeguard of diluted kinship, by losing connexion with the members of the class in which they were actually born.
[1] See Note I, p. 55.

property will cause a good deal of trouble. If they do not share equally in work and recompense, those who do more work and get less recompense will be bound to raise complaints against those who get a large recompense and do little work.[1] § 4. Indeed it is generally true that it is a difficult business for men to live together and to be partners in any form of human activity, but it is specially difficult to do so when property is involved. Fellow-travellers who are merely partners in a journey furnish an illustration: they generally quarrel about ordinary matters and take offence on petty occasions. So, again, the servants with whom we are most prone to take offence are those who are particularly employed in ordinary everyday services.

§ 5. Difficulties such as these, and many others, are involved in a system of community of property. The present system [of private property] would be far preferable, if it were adorned[2] by customs [in the social sphere] and by the enactment of proper laws [in the political]. It would possess the advantages of both systems, and would combine the merits of a system of community of property with those of the system of private property. [It would be the ideal]; for property *ought* to be generally and in the main private, but common in one respect [i.e. in use].[3] § 6. When everyone has his own separate sphere of interest, there will not be the same ground for quarrels; and the amount of interest will increase, because each man will feel that he is applying himself to what is his own. And on such a scheme, too, moral goodness [and not, as in Plato's scheme, legal compulsion] will ensure that the property of each is made to serve the use of all, in the spirit of the proverb which says 'Friends' goods are goods in common'. Even now there are some states in which the outlines of such a scheme are so far apparent, as to suggest that it is not impossible; in well-ordered states, more particularly, there are some elements of it already existing, and others which might be added. § 7. In these states each citizen has his own property; but when it comes to the use of this property, each makes a part of it available to his friends, and each devotes still another part to the common enjoyment of all fellow-citizens. In Sparta, for example, men use one another's slaves, and one another's horses and dogs, as if they were their own; and they take provisions on a journey, if they happen to be in need, from the farms in the country-side belonging to other

[1] See Note J, p. 55.
[2] The Greek word is the same as that which comes in the proverb 'Sparta has fallen to your lot: adorn it' (*Spartam nactus es: hanc adorna*). The 'adorning' of common property which Aristotle has in mind consists in its common use— partly under the influence of social habit, and partly under that of legal rule.
[3] Aristotle thus arrives at his formula, which may be stated in a sort of jingle (cf. § 8 below)—*idia ktesis, koine chresis*, or 'property several; use of it communal'.

citizens. § 8. It is clear from what has been said that the better system is that under which property is privately owned but is put to common use; and the function proper to the legislator is to make men so disposed that they will treat property in this way.

There is a further consideration which must be taken into account. This is the consideration of pleasure. Here too [as well as in the matter of goodness] to think of a thing as your own makes an inexpressible difference. [The satisfaction of a natural feeling brings pleasure]; and it may well be that regard **1263 b** for oneself [and, by extension, for what is one's own] is a feeling implanted by nature, and not a mere random impulse. § 9. Self-love is rightly censured, but what is really censured is not so much love of oneself as love of oneself in excess[1]—just as we also blame the lover of money [not so much for loving money as for loving it in excess]; the simple feeling of love for any of these things [self, or property, or money] is more or less universal. We may add that a very great pleasure is to be found in doing a kindness and giving some help to friends, or guests, or comrades; and such kindness and help become possible only when property is privately owned. § 10. But not only are these pleasures [that arising from the satisfaction of a natural feeling of self-love, and that arising from the satisfaction of our impulse to help others] impossible under a system of excessive unification of the state. The activities of two forms of goodness are also obviously destroyed. The first of these is temperance in the matter of sexual relations (it is an act of moral value to refrain from loving the wife of another in the strength of temperance): the second is liberality in the use of property.[2] In a state which is excessively unified no man can show himself liberal, or indeed do a liberal act; for the function of liberality consists in the proper use which is made of property.

§ 11. Legislation such as Plato proposes may appear to wear an attractive face and to argue benevolence. The hearer receives it gladly, thinking that everybody will feel towards everybody else some marvellous sense of fraternity—all the more as the evils now existing under ordinary forms of government (lawsuits about contracts, convictions for perjury, and obsequious flatteries of the rich) are denounced as due to the absence of a system of common

---

[1]   Self-love, my liege, is not so vile a thing
                          As self-neglecting.
The regard which a man has for himself is, on a higher plane, a moral necessity: it is the basis of a sense of moral responsibility.

[2] In referring to the first of these activities, Aristotle introduces again, in a chapter which is otherwise concerned with community of property, the idea of community of wives and children. It may also be noticed that in this section (§ 10) he leaves the consideration of pleasure, begun in § 8, and returns to the consideration of goodness.

property. § 12. None of these evils, however, is due to the absence of communism. They all arise from the wickedness of human nature. Indeed it is a fact of observation that those who own common property, and share in its management, are far more often at variance with one another than those who have property in severalty—though [we tend to be misled by the fact that] those who are at variance in consequence of sharing in property look to us few in number when we compare them with the mass of those who own their property privately.

§ 13. Another consideration must also be pressed. Justice demands that we should take into account not only the evils from which men will be liberated when once they have turned their property into a common stock, but also the benefits of which they will be deprived. The life which they are to live appears to be utterly impossible.[1] The cause of the fallacy into which Plato falls must be held to be the wrong character of the premiss [about the nature of unity] on which he bases his argument. § 14. It is true that unity is to some extent necessary, alike in a household and a polis; but total unity is not.[2] There is a point at which a polis, by advancing in unity, will cease to be a polis: there is another point, short of that, at which it may still remain a polis, but will none the less come near to losing its essence, and will thus be a worse polis. It is as if you were to turn harmony into mere unison, or to reduce a theme to a single beat. § 15. The truth is that the polis, as has already been said,[3] is an aggregate of many members; and education is therefore *the* means of making it a community and giving it unity. [This is the sense in which unity is necessary, and the extent to which it is necessary.] It is therefore surprising that one who intends to introduce a system of education, and who believes that his ideal polis will achieve goodness by means of this system, should none the less think that he is setting it on the right track by such methods as he actually proposes, rather than by the method of social customs, of mental culture, and of legislation [intended to promote a proper spirit in the use of property].[4] An

On Aristotle's argument, a system of common property injures life by (1) diminishing the area of goodness, §§ 6 and 10 (2) starving men of natural and proper pleasures, §§ 8–9, and (3) increasing instead of diminishing discord, § 12.

[2] The argument here returns to the point which was made (in regard to community of wives) in c. II, § 2.   [3] c. II, § 2.

[4] The precise meaning of 'legislation' is to be gathered from § 8 of this chapter, where Aristotle argues that the proper function of the legislator is to create a disposition or mental habit of putting private property to common use. The statement that a conjunction of social customs, mental culture, and legislation is the proper method of making a community and giving it unity is a repetition and amplification of the point made in § 5 of the chapter, where Aristotle argues that the present system of private property would be preferable, 'if adorned by customs and by the enactment of proper laws'.

example of such legislation may be found in Sparta and Crete, where the law has made the institution of property serve a common use by the system of common meals.

1264 a § 16. There is another matter which must not be ignored —the teaching of actual experience. We are bound to pay some regard to the long past and the passage of the years, in which these things [advocated by Plato as new discoveries] would not have gone unnoticed if they had been really good. Almost everything has been discovered already; though some of the things discovered have not been co-ordinated,[1] and some, though known, are not put into practice. § 17. It would shed a great deal of light on the value of Plato's ideas, if we could watch the actual construction of a constitution such as he proposes. The foundation of any state will always involve the division and distribution of its members into classes—partly in the form of associations for common meals, and partly in that of clans and tribes. [Plato's system of classes being therefore a matter of common form,] it follows that the only peculiar feature of the legislation proposed by Plato is the rule that the guardians are not to farm the land; and even that is a rule which the Spartans already attempt to follow.[2]

§ 18. [But it is not only the position of the guardians which may be challenged]; the scheme of the whole constitution is open to criticism.[3] Plato has not explained, nor indeed is it easy to explain, the position of the different members under that scheme. The mass of the citizens who are not guardians—in other words, the farmers—will be, in effect, nearly the whole of the citizen body. But their position is left undefined. We are not told whether these farmers, as well as the guardians, are to have property in common, or to own it individually; nor do we learn whether their wives and children are to be common to them all, or to belong to each separately.[4] § 19. [We may take three possible alternatives, and examine each in turn.] The first alternative is that all things [wives and

---

[1] The Greek word used by Aristotle implies the drawing of a logical conclusion from all the relevant data. Newman suggests the translation, 'gathered together for scientific use'.

[2] The Spartan 'peers' (who are analogous to Plato's guardians) owned the land, but left the farming to 'helots'. This, however, is not the Platonic system. Plato's guardians do not own the land; and his farmers, who are owners as well as farmers, are not helots.

[3] Aristotle has just mentioned, at the end of § 17, the guardians and the guardians only. But he passes on naturally here to the other class of the farmers, and to the general problem of the relations of farmers and guardians.

[4] Aristotle here forgets, or at any rate neglects, the actual argument of the *Republic*. Plato makes it clear that the farmers own private property, and live in private or separate families. We may also notice that here again, as in § 10 (and in §§ 19–20 below), Aristotle introduces the subject of community of wives in a chapter otherwise concerned with community of property.

children as well as property] should belong to them all in common. In that case, what will be the difference between them and the guardians? What advantage will they gain by accepting the government of the guardians? What is to make them actually accept it?— unless it be some shift of policy such as is used in Crete, where the serfs are allowed to enjoy the same general privileges as their masters, and are excluded only from athletic exercises and the possession of arms. § 20. The second alternative is that the institutions of property and of marriage should be the same for the farmers as they actually are in most states to-day, [and that there should thus be a system of separate families and private property]. In that case, we may inquire, what will be the scheme on which the whole community is based? There will inevitably be two states in one, and those two states will be opposed to one another—the guardians being made into something of the nature of an army of occupation, and the farmers, artisans, and others being given the position of ordinary civilians.[1] § 21. Again, [upon the assumption that the farmers have a system of separate families and private property], legal complaints, and actions at law, and all the other evils which Plato describes as existing in actual states, will equally exist among them. It is true, indeed, that he says that the farmers, in virtue of their education, will not need a number of regulations (such as rules of city police, market bylaws, and other similar regulations); but it is also true that he provides education only for the guardians. § 22. It is a further difficulty in Plato's scheme that he attaches a condition to the farmers' control of their holdings—the condition that they shall pay a quota of their produce to the guardians. This is likely to make them far more difficult to handle, and much more filled with high ideas of their own importance, than the helots of Sparta, or the serfs of Thessaly, or the farm-slaves of other states. § 23. In any case Plato's scheme, as it stands, fails to indicate whether the farmers should live under a system of communism equally with the guardians, or should live under a different system. It also fails to throw any light on other questions connected with this—such as the position of the farmers in the political system, the nature of their education, and the character of the laws they are to observe. We thus find it difficult to discover—and yet this is a matter of the highest importance— how the farming class is to be constituted if the common life of

---

[1] We should have expected that the opposition of the 'two states in one' would have consisted in the fact that one proceeded on the system of community of wives and property, and the other on the opposite system. Actually, the opposition is here described as consisting in the fact that the guardians are like a garrison placed in a dependent city, and the farmers are like the citizens of such a city.

the guardians is to be preserved. **1264 b** § 24. The third and last alternative is that the farmers should have a system of community of wives, combined with a system of private property. In that case, who will see to the house while the men are seeing to the business of the fields? . . . And, for that matter, who will see to the house on the first alternative, when property is common as well as wives? . . . It is strange, too, that Plato should draw an analogy from the animal world in order to prove that women should follow the same pursuits as men. Animals, unlike women, have no domestic duties.

§ 25. There is also an element of danger in the method of government which Plato proposes to institute.[1] He makes one body of persons the permanent rulers of his state [thus rejecting the principle of 'ruling and being ruled in turn']. This is a system which must breed discontent and dissension even among the elements which have no particular standing, and all the more, therefore, among the high-spirited and martial elements.[2] § 26. The reason which makes it necessary for him to make one body of persons permanent rulers is obvious. [They alone have the natural endowment for ruling]: 'the divine gold which is mixed in the soul' cannot reside at one time in one body of men and at another time in another; it must reside permanently in one body. This is why he says that 'the god who fashioned you mixed gold in the composition' of some, silver in that of others, and brass and iron in that of the rest, who were to be craftsmen and farmers.[3] § 27. It is a further objection [to Plato's general scheme for his ruling class] that he deprives his guardians even of happiness,[4] maintaining that it is the happiness of the whole state which should be the object of legislation. It is impossible for the whole of a state to be happy unless most of its parts, or all, or at any rate some, are happy. The quality of being happy is not of the same order as the quality of being even. The quality of being even may exist in a whole without existing in either of its parts: the quality of being happy

---

[1] In this section, and in the remaining sections of the chapter, Aristotle passes from a criticism of the Platonic scheme of communism of property to a criticism of the Platonic system of government. The two things are of course connected; but the passage, as it stands, is of the nature of an appendix to the rest of the argument of the chapter.

[2] The 'elements of no particular standing' may indicate the class of farmers. The 'high-spirited and martial elements' naturally suggests the class of auxiliaries, who serve as soldiers in the Platonic state, and whose particular quality is that of high spirit.

[3] Aristotle here criticizes, by implication, the doctrine of a particular endowment of classes, and suggests, as more applicable to the conditions of the Greek city and its practice of 'ruling and being ruled', the doctrine of a general endowment of all citizens, by virtue of which they are able to turn from other occupations to the occupation of ruling, and vice versa.

[4] They lose the natural pleasures, arising from private property, which Aristotle has discussed in §§ 8-10 of this chapter.

cannot. § 28. A further point may be raised. If the guardians are not happy, what are the other elements of the state which are? There is certainly no happiness for the craftsmen, or for the mass of the common people.

We may thus conclude that the Republic which Plato has described raises all the difficulties we have mentioned, and others which are no less serious.[1]

Note I (p. 48): *The course of the argument of* c. v.

Aristotle does not mention a fourth alternative—that ownership and use may both be private. Nor does he proceed, after stating his three alternatives, to examine each in turn. What he actually does is (1) to examine, in §§ 3–4, some difficulties of the Platonic scheme of communism, apparently on the assumption that it corresponds to the last of his three possibilities; (2) to discuss, in §§ 5–10, the advantages of a system of private property combined with common use—a system which, more or less, corresponds to the first of his three alternatives; and (3) to return, in the rest of the chapter, to a detailed criticism of the Platonic scheme—a criticism which sometimes fails to do justice to its real character. The second of the three alternatives is thus left unexamined—except in so far as Aristotle's own preference for the first alternative (which is the opposite of the second) implies its rejection.

It may be added that Aristotle's outlook is purely agrarian. He deals exclusively with the problem of the ownership and use of land. Under the small-scale system of industrial production no problem arose (at any rate in his view) about the ownership and use of other forms of capital.

Note J (p. 49): *Common property and its cultivation*

Aristotle is here assuming, though he does not make the assumption explicit, that there is a system of common ownership of land. On that assumption, two alternatives are possible in regard to the cultivation of the land so owned. (1) The cultivation may be done by a class separate from and subordinate to the citizens who own the land; or (2) it may be done by the citizens themselves who own the land. The second alternative, in Aristotle's view, leads to the troubles mentioned in the text: the first would produce a different and easier position, 'for as the citizens would not work themselves, individual citizens would not be in a position to compare their own hard work and small recompense with the easy work and large recompense of others, and thus one more source of disagreement among the citizens would be removed' (Newman's note).

We may note, as Newman does, that neither alternative is proposed in the *Republic*, because the assumption on which both are based—that of common ownership of the land—is *not* an assumption made in the *Republic*. On Plato's scheme the land is owned in severalty by the farming class, and the one element of communism is that the class of the

---

[1] Aristotle's criticisms of the *Republic*, in the first five chapters of Book II, are very justly described in Newman's note on this sentence. 'The object . . . is, we see from this sentence, in the main to point out difficulties enough . . . to show that there is still room for another attempt to depict a "best constitution" (cf. c. 1, § 1). The same may be said to be true of the somewhat grumbling criticism of the *Laws* which follows.'

guardians make a common 'use' of that part of the produce raised from the land which is paid to them by the members of the farming class in return for their discharge of political and military duties. There is thus no common ownership in the Platonic system; there is only common consumption, and that only among the class of the guardians. The members of the farming class own, cultivate, and consume in severalty— subject only to two conditions, first that they pay a quota of their produce to the guardians, for *their* common use, and secondly that the amount of land which each may own is restricted. There is thus a sense in which it may be said that Aristotle's own formula of 'property several, use of it communal' is observed in the *Republic*.

CHAPTER VI

2. Plato's Laws. *The scheme of the* Laws *is not greatly different from that of the* Republic. *It postulates too large a territory, but fails to pay proper attention to the problem of foreign relations. It does not sufficiently define the amount of property required, or the object for which it is required; nor does it make proper provision for a balance between property and population. The system of government is a sort of 'polity', but it is not properly balanced: the method of electing the magistrates and councillors is too oligarchical.*

§ 1. The same, or nearly the same, is true of Plato's later work, the *Laws* [i.e. it raises difficulties which show that there is room for another attempt to depict an ideal constitution]; and this makes it advisable for us to examine briefly the constitution there de- scribed. A further reason for doing so is that [the argument of the *Laws* is fuller, while] in the *Republic* Plato has only attempted to solve a very small number of issues—mainly the proper method for ensuring community of wives and children and community of property, and the proper way of distributing power under the con- stitutional system. § 2. He contents himself in the *Republic* with dividing the population into two parts: one consists of the farmers, the other of the military class; and from this last there is recruited, to form still another part, the deliberative and sovereign class of the perfect guardians.[1] § 3. But so far as the first part—the farmers and artisans—are concerned, the scheme of the *Republic* leaves it unsettled whether or no they are to have some share in office, and whether or no they too are to bear arms and join in military service. It is stated, indeed, that the women [i.e. those in the military class of the ordinary guardians] should join in military service and enjoy the same education as the male guardians; but otherwise Plato has

---

[1] Later, in Book IV, c. XIV, § 16, Aristotle ascribes sovereignty (*to kyrion*) to the deliberative element in the state. This is the reason why, in this passage, he combines the terms 'deliberative' and 'sovereign' in his description of the 'perfect guardians' who form the government.

filled up the dialogue with digressions extraneous to the main theme, and with a discussion of the proper nature of the education of his guardians.

1265 a § 4. The great bulk of the *Laws* is concerned with legislation. Plato says little about the constitution; and in what he does say [he is inconsistent, for] though he speaks of desiring to institute a form of government which will be more in the reach of existing states, he gradually brings the form he proposes round again to the other type [i.e. that described in the *Republic*]. § 5. In all matters other than community of wives and of property, he provides identical institutions for both of his states. Education is the same in both: the members of both are to live a life free from menial duties: there is the same arrangement for common meals in both. The only differences are that in the *Laws* women as well as men are to be included in the arrangements for common meals, and the number of citizens who bear arms—which in the *Republic* is only 1,000—is to be fixed at a total of 5,000.

§ 6. All the writings of Plato are original: they show ingenuity, novelty of view, and a spirit of inquiry. But perfection in everything is perhaps a difficult thing. Take, for example, the number of citizens which has just been mentioned. We cannot overlook the fact that such a number will require a territory of the size of Babylon or some such space which is similarly unlimited in extent. It will need all that to support 5,000 persons in idleness, especially when we reflect that they will be augmented by a crowd of women and attendants many times as great as themselves. § 7. We may admit that it is right to make assumptions freely; but it cannot be right to make any assumption which is plainly impossible.[1]

It is stated in the *Laws* that there are two factors to which the legislator should pay regard in enacting laws: the territory of the state, and the inhabitants of that territory. But there is also a third factor. If a polis is to live a political life [involving intercourse with other states], and not a life of isolation, it is a good thing that its legislator should also pay regard to neighbouring countries. For example, a state should not only employ such instruments of war as are serviceable in its own territory: it should also employ the instruments which are serviceable for use abroad. § 8. Even if such a life [i.e. a life of activity rather than contemplation, and of military activity at that] is not accepted as an ideal, either for the individual's own way of life or for the state's common way, the

---

[1] Aristotle is thinking in terms of a Greek polis, with a limited territory surrounded by arms of the sea or ranges of hills. Athens was exceptional in having a territory of 1,000 square miles: Corinth had 350: the general average was perhaps about 70 (*Cambridge Ancient History*, vol. iii, p. 698).

fact remains, none the less, that men should be formidable to their
enemies when they are in retreat, as well as when they are invading.[1]

The amount of property [as well as the amount of military
preparation] should also be considered; and we have to ask whether
it is not better to determine it in a different—that is to say, a more
definite—way than that of Plato.[2] He states in the *Laws* that the
amount should be 'sufficient for a life of temperance'. § 9. [This
is vague]: it is much the same as saying, 'sufficient for a good life';
indeed [if you aim at generality] that expression has the advantage
of being more general; and besides [if you stop at Plato's definition]
there is the further difficulty that 'a life of temperance' may also
be a life of misery. A better definition than Plato's [because fuller
and more inclusive] would be, 'sufficient for a life of temperance
and liberality'. These two objects—which should always be combined, for if they are parted liberality will be accompanied by
luxury, and temperance by penury—represent the only qualities
to be desired in the use of wealth. A man cannot use his wealth
either in a meek or in a manly spirit [i.e. in a spirit which involves
the quality of fortitude]; but he can use it both in a temperate and
in a liberal spirit. The two qualities of temperance and liberality
must therefore be the qualities involved in the use of wealth.

§ 10. [Another point arises in connexion with Plato's view of the
amount of property required by his citizens.] It is strange that he
should distribute landed property in [a fixed number of] equal
lots, without making any corresponding arrangements to secure a
[fixed] number of citizens.[3] He imposes no restriction on the
number of children who may be brought into the world: he believes
that, however many children may be born [in some families], the
absence of children [in others] will mean that the rate of reproduction will just suffice to maintain the level of the population;
and he bases his belief on the fact that this is what actually appears
to happen in existing states. **1265 b** § 11. But a stationary popula-

---

[1] The importance of what may be called 'foreign policy', and of military pre-
paredness as the necessary basis of foreign policy, is more than once emphasized
by Aristotle: see c. VII of this book, § 14, and note, and the Introduction, p. xvi.

[2] In discussing the amount of military equipment required, Aristotle has
argued that the objects for which it is intended should first be clearly and fully
defined. They must be made, for example, to include the object of resistance
to foreign invasion, as well as that of domestic defence. Similarly, he now argues,
a clear and full definition of the objects for which it is intended is necessary in
order to determine the amount of property required. We must not stop short
at the single object of a life of temperance: we must include the further object
of a life of liberality, which by its nature involves relations to others—just as
we have also included, in dealing with the amount of military equipment
required, the further object of resistance to aggression, which equally involves
relations to others.

[3] Here Aristotle is unjust to Plato, who does seek to face the problem (*Laws*,
740).

tion will need to be maintained with far more accuracy in the state of the *Laws* than it is in existing states. In existing states, properties can be freely divided to cover the whole population, however large it may be, and nobody need be destitute: in Plato's state, the properties are indivisible, and any surplus population which may arise, whether it be large or small, will have no property at all. § 12. One would have thought that it was even more necessary to limit population, and to prevent reproduction from exceeding a certain level, than to limit property [by instituting a fixed number of equal lots]. If population is limited, the rate of reproduction should be fixed to allow for the incidence of infant mortality and for the amount of infertility among married couples. § 13. If no restriction is imposed on the rate of reproduction (and this is the case in most of our existing states), poverty is the inevitable result; and poverty produces, in its turn, civic dissension and wrongdoing. Pheidon of Corinth, one of the earliest legislators, held that the number of family plots and the number of citizens should be kept equal to one another, even if the citizens had all started originally with plots of unequal size; but what we find in the *Laws* is the opposite of Pheidon's policy.[1]

§ 14. We must leave to a later occasion any discussion of the improvements which might be suggested in this part of Plato's scheme.[2] Here we must notice another omission of which Plato is also guilty. He has not explained how the rulers are to differ from the ruled. He simply uses a simile: the relation of ruler and ruled, he suggests, should be like that of warp and woof, which are made out of different wools. § 15. It is a further omission that while he allows a man's whole property to be increased fivefold, he does not explain why his plot of land should not also be allowed to increase up to some given point. The distribution of the farm-houses is another subject which needs further consideration: it hardly seems to conduce to efficiency of household management. Plato assigns to each of his citizens two separate houses, situated in different parts [of his plot]. It is difficult to live in two houses [without loss of efficiency].[3] § 16. [But there is more to be said about the form

[1] Pheidon was willing to leave the plots themselves unequal, but insisted on preserving equality between the total number of the plots and the total number of the citizens. Plato, in the *Laws*, insists on having the plots equal, but takes no measures (so Aristotle argues) to secure equality between the number of the plots and the number of the citizens.

[2] The promise is partly redeemed in Aristotle's own sketch of an ideal state, Book VII, c. x, § 11, and c. xvi, § 15.

[3] Plato's object, as Newman says in his note, seems to have been that of providing a separate house and quarters for a married son. The curious thing is that Aristotle himself, in his sketch of an ideal state, gives each of his citizens two separate plots and (by implication) two separate houses, one near the city and one on the frontier (Book VII, c. x, § 11).

of government proposed in the *Laws*.] The whole system tends to be one neither of democracy nor of oligarchy, but rather an intermediate form, of the sort which is usually called 'polity':[1] the citizens, for example, are drawn only from those who bear arms. If Plato's view in constructing this constitution is that it represents the form which is most readily attainable by most states, he may very well be right; but if he regards it as the form which comes next in merit to his first, or ideal, form of constitution [i.e. that in the *Republic*], he is mistaken: one might commend more highly the constitution of Sparta, or some other form of a more aristocratic character [than that depicted in the *Laws*]. § 17. There are, indeed, some thinkers who hold that the ideal constitution itself should be a mixture of all constitutions; and they commend, for this reason, the constitution of Sparta. These thinkers are all agreed that the Spartan constitution is composed of all the three elements—monarchy, oligarchy, and democracy—but [they differ in their interpretation of these elements]. According to some of them, monarchy is represented by the two kings: oligarchy by the Council of Elders; and democracy by the Ephors, who are drawn from the ranks of the people. Others, however, regard the Ephoralty as representing tyranny; and these consider that the element of democracy appears in the Spartan system of common meals, and in the general habit of daily life at Sparta. **1266 a** § 18. [Whatever may be thought of this line of opinion, and of these different interpretations of the Spartan constitution], the argument of the *Laws* is to the effect that the best constitution should be composed of democracy and tyranny [only][2]—forms which one would classify as either not constitutions at all or the worst of all constitutions. One comes nearer the truth in seeking to combine more forms [than two]; for a constitution is better when it is composed of more numerous elements.[3] It is a further objection to Plato that the

---

[1] The 'polity', as described by Aristotle himself later, in Book IV, cc. VIII–IX and XI–XIII, is a constitution which may be described as a mixture of, or a 'mean' between, democracy and oligarchy. It rests on the middle class, and the franchise is therefore vested in those who can afford to bear arms (cf. Book III, c. VII, § 4). In Book IV Aristotle describes the 'polity' as the best possible constitution for average states; and he treats the Spartan constitution as an example of this mixed form (c. IX, §§ 7–9). Here, as will be seen, he seems to take a different line, distinguishing the Spartan constitution from the 'polity', and including even Plato's scheme of a 'polity' in his general 'grumbling' criticism of the *Laws*.

[2] This statement seems doubly unjust to Plato. In the first place, he is not dealing in the *Laws* with the ideal constitution, but (as Aristotle himself has just implied) with the form which comes nearest to the ideal. In the second place, the forms which he proposes to mix are not tyranny and the sort of democracy which is 'either not a constitution at all or the worst of constitutions', but a constitutional form of monarchy and a tempered form of democracy.

[3] This seems to be inconsistent with Aristotle's view, in Book IV, that a

constitution depicted in the *Laws* has really no element of monarchy, but only the elements of oligarchy and democracy, with a particular inclination towards oligarchy.[1] § 19. This appears clearly in the method proposed for appointing magistrates. There is, indeed, one feature which combines democracy with oligarchy. This is the use of the lot for the purpose of finally choosing magistrates from a panel of persons who have been previously elected. But there are two other features which are definitely oligarchical. In the first place, the richer citizens are compelled to attend the assembly, to vote in elections of magistrates, and to discharge other forms of political duty, while the other citizens are allowed to abstain. Secondly, an attempt is made to secure a greater number of magistrates from the wealthier class, and to fill the highest offices from the ranks of those whose assessments are highest.   § 20. The method of electing councillors is also oligarchical.[2] All the citizens, it is true, are compelled to take part in the election. But this general compulsion extends only to the preliminary election of a number of candidates from the first assessment class, and of an equal number from the second: when it comes to the preliminary election of candidates from the third and fourth classes, the system of general compulsion stops; indeed in the preliminary election from the fourth class only the members of the first and second classes are compelled to vote.[3] § 21. [All this relates to the process of pre-election.] Then, from the whole list of pre-elected persons, there must next be elected, says Plato, an equal number of persons for each assessment class. The result will be that the electors who have the largest assessments and belong to the higher orders will form the majority, because many of the common people, not being compelled to do so, will not vote.[4]

'polity' composed of the two elements of democracy and oligarchy is the best possible form for average states. On the other hand he also urges in Book IV (c. VIII, § 9) that it is better to combine more elements than are combined in the 'polity'.

[1] The previous objection (urged in §§ 16 and 17, and in the first half of § 18) is that the constitution depicted in the *Laws*, even if it were a combination of monarchy and democracy, would not be the next best to the ideal constitution—being only a 'polity' which mixes two elements, and being thus inferior to the more 'aristocratical' form, such as the Spartan, which combines three elements. The objection now urged is that Plato is not true to his own conception of the 'next best' constitution, and does not actually mix monarchy and democracy.

[2] See Note K, p. 62.

[3] Plato's scheme (*Laws* 756) is that (1) the members of all the four classes must join in the pre-election of representatives of the first two classes, (2) only those of the first three classes need join in the pre-election of representatives of the third class, and (3) only those of the first two classes need join in the pre-election of representatives of the fourth class.

[4] This statement is strictly true only of the first, or preliminary, stage of pre-election. It is not strictly true of the second stage of final election, in which *all* are compelled to vote. But it must be admitted that if the wealthy have an

§ 22. These considerations, and others which will be mentioned when the time comes for us to examine the nature of the best constitution, are sufficient to prove that it should not be formed by combining democracy and monarchy.[1] We may add that there is also a danger in the method of electing the magistrates by the double process of pre-election and a final election. If a knot of people, even of moderate size, decide to act in combination [at both stages], they will always decide the way in which the elections will go. . . . These are the considerations which are raised by the constitution described in the *Laws*.

NOTE K (p. 61): *The method of electing councillors in the Laws*

We must note, in order that Aristotle's brief references may become clear, that Plato's scheme for the appointment of the 360 members of the council involves three successive stages. (1) The first stage is concerned with *pre-election*. At this stage preliminary elections are made—on four successive days—of representatives of each of the four assessment grades or classes. No definite number is suggested by Plato for the number thus elected to represent each class in this stage of pre-election; but he does suggest the 'class' method of voting described by Aristotle in § 20. (2) The second stage is concerned with the definite *election* of representatives. The whole list of all the representatives pre-elected in the first stage is now published; and all the citizens, of all the four assessment classes, must now join *together* in electing an equal number of representatives (180) for each assessment class. (3) Even now the process is not finished. The second period may be that of the definite election; but election itself is not final. The *lot* has still to be used. The third and last stage in Plato's scheme is accordingly the stage in which the lot is used to cut down by half the number of representatives of each assessment class (i.e. from 180 to 90). We thus get at last the 90 representatives of each of the four classes who constitute the final Council of 360. It will be noticed that Aristotle is not quite accurate in suggesting that an *equal* number of candidates is pre-elected for each class in the first stage.

CHAPTER VII

3. Phaleas of Chalcedon. *His proposal for the equalization of property in land. It would involve regulation of the population: it would also involve determination of the exact standard on which*

advantage in the first stage, they will have some consequent advantage in the second.

[1] It has already been remarked, in the note to § 18 above, that Plato is not dealing in the *Laws* with the *best* constitution, but only with the *next best*.

The 'somewhat grumbling criticism of the *Laws*' contained in this chapter of the *Politics* is no doubt due, as Newman suggests, to the fact that Aristotle wishes to show that there is room for another treatment, such as he eventually attempts in Books VII and VIII. But it is curious, none the less, that this treatment, when it comes, shows many parallels with the *Laws*, and is at many points based on Plato (see the writer's *Greek Political Theory*, 'Plato and his Predecessors', pp. 380–2). When Aristotle criticizes, he criticizes. When he seeks to construct, he is ready to borrow suggestions from the predecessor whom he has criticized.

equality was to be achieved. Generally, equality matters more in the moral, or educational, sphere than in the material: disorder and crime are due to moral defects as well as to economic causes. The amount and distribution of property in a state are affected by considerations of foreign as well as domestic policy; but the essential criticism of Phaleas is that he lays too much emphasis on material factors.

§ 1. There are also a number of other schemes for new constitutions, some of them proposed by amateurs, and others by men who were versed in philosophy or statesmanship. They all come nearer to the existing constitutions, under which men are now actually living, than does either of the schemes proposed by Plato. No other thinker·has proposed such novelties as community of wives and children or common meals for women: on the contrary, thinkers have rather started from the immediate necessities of life. § 2. Thus there are some who hold that the proper regulation of property is more important than any other object, because this is the issue on which civil discords always arise. Phaleas of Chalcedon was the first to suggest regulation of property for the purpose of preventing discord; and he proposed accordingly that all the citizens should have equal amounts of property [i.e. in land]. **1266 b** § 3. He thought that in new colonies this could be achieved, without any difficulty, at the moment of their foundation. States which were already established would present a greater problem; but even here equality could be introduced—and that in the shortest possible time—if the rich gave dowries [in land] but did not receive them, and the poor, conversely, received but did not give them. § 4. Plato, when he was writing the *Laws*, was of the opinion that the amount of property should be left unrestricted up to a given point; beyond that point, he was in favour of restriction, proposing, as has already been said,[1] that no citizen should be allowed to accumulate to an extent which would make his property more than five times as large as the smallest property owned by any other citizen.

§ 5. Those who propose such legislation ought not to forget, as they continually do, that regulation of the amount of property ought to be accompanied by regulation of the number of children in the family. If the number of children exceeds what the amount of the property will support, the abrogation of the law [establishing a system of equal properties] must necessarily follow; and, apart from that consequence, it is a sorry thing that a large number of

---

[1] See c. VI, § 15. But it appears from that section that Plato was thinking of the accumulation of the *total* property of each citizen, while Phaleas was concerned with *landed* property only. Phaleas, we may note, was a contemporary of Plato.

persons should be reduced from comfort to penury. It is difficult
for men who have suffered that fate not to be revolutionaries.
§ 6. We must admit, indeed, that [there are arguments in favour
of equality of property, and that] there were some, in times past,
who clearly recognized that such equality had an influence on the
character of a political association. We may cite the example of
Solon's legislation at Athens; and in other states too there are
laws to be found which prevent men from acquiring land to any
extent they desire. Similarly there are laws to be found which
prevent the *sale* of property: among the Locrians, for instance,
there is a law to the effect that men cannot sell their property
unless they can prove that an evident misfortune has befallen them.
§ 7. There are also laws to be found which provide that the original
lots [of landed property] must be maintained intact: it was the
neglect of such a law at Leucas, to mention one instance, which
made the constitution excessively democratic; men came into
office, as a result, who no longer possessed the necessary legal
qualification.[1] But [in spite of the arguments in favour of equality
of property derived from these facts] it is possible that equality of
property may exist, and yet [be a defective system, because] the
amount possessed by each individual may be either unduly large,
which leads to luxury, or unduly small, which results in penury.
It is therefore clear that it is not enough merely to establish the
general principle of equality of property: it is [also] necessary to
aim at [a definite system of equality based on] a fixed and moderate
amount. § 8. But even if one were to fix the same moderate
amount for each, there would still be no real gain. It is more
necessary to equalize men's desires than their properties; and that
is a result which cannot be achieved unless men are adequately
trained by the influence of laws.[2] Phaleas, however, might possibly
retort that this is just the view which he himself propounds; for it
is his opinion that equality should be doubly pursued in states, and
should mean equality of education as well as of property. § 9. But
in that case we ought to be told what is to be the character of the
education [which all are equally to receive]. There would be no
real gain if it were merely one and the same for all; for it is possible
for education to be one and the same for all, and yet to be of a

[1] In consequence of the failure to maintain the original lots intact, men who
had only part of a lot had to be admitted to office, in spite of legal requirements
which (we may gather) demanded the possession of a whole lot as the necessary
qualification.
[2] This argument is like the argument previously advanced against the
Platonic system of common property; cf. c. v, §§ 5, 15. Aristotle prefers to trust
neither to a system of common *ownership* nor to a system of equal *ownership*
(both, in his view, material in their nature), but to a system of moral training
which affects the moral disposition and secures the right *use* of property.

character which will produce a disposition to covet wealth, or to
covet office, or to covet both. § 10. This raises a further point.
[It is necessary to deal with office, or political power, as well as
with property]: civil discord arises not only from inequality of
property, but also from inequality of the offices which men hold.
But here we must note a difference. The distribution of property
works in the opposite way from the distribution of office. The
masses become revolutionary when the distribution of property is
unequal. Men of education become revolutionary when the distribution of office is *equal*.[1] **1267 a** This is the point of the verse
in Homer:

> Office and honour are one and the same for the good and
> the bad man.

§ 11. [There is also a further point which has to be taken into
account. We have to consider not only the causes of civil discord,
but also the causes of ordinary crime.] There are some crimes
which are due to lack of necessities; and here, Phaleas thinks,
equality of property will be a remedy, and will serve to prevent
men from stealing simply through cold or hunger. But want is not
the only cause of crimes. Men also commit them simply for the
pleasure it gives them, and just to get rid of an unsatisfied desire.
Vexed by a desire which goes beyond the simple necessities of life,
they will turn criminals to cure their vexation. § 12. [There is
still a third factor to be considered.] Men may not only commit
crime to cure a desire they already feel: they may start some desire
[and then commit crime to satisfy that desire] just in order to enjoy
the sort of pleasure which is unaccompanied by pain.

What is the remedy for these three kinds of crime?[2] For the
first kind, we may answer, some modicum of property and some
sort of work: for the second, a temperate disposition; as for the

---

[1] Aristotle's own principle, stated later in Book III (c. ix, §§ 1–6), is that
office should be awarded in proportion to desert, and therefore on a principle
of 'proportionate equality', which gives men office in equal proportion to the
different contributions which they make to the well-being of the state. Now
'men of education' contribute something additional, which (on the principle of
'proportionate equality') should receive an additional recognition in the distribution of office.

[2] 'The three are', as Newman explains in his note, '(1) wrongdoing for the
sake of absolute necessaries; (2) wrongdoing for the sake of superfluities with a
view to curing painful desire and obtaining pleasure; (3) wrongdoing for the
sake of superfluities with a view to obtaining painless pleasure'.
The distinction between (2) and (3) is subtle. Under (2), the criminal seeks
to cure a painful desire, from which he *already* suffers, by attaining release from
pain and enjoying the pleasure of such release. Here there is a mixture of
pleasure and pain. Under (3), the criminal seeks to enjoy a pleasure altogether
unmixed with pain by *immediately* indulging in desire and proceeding to gratify
it at once without any interval of suffering.

third kind, we can only say that if there are men who want to get unmixed pleasure purely by their own independent effort, they will find no satisfaction except in the aid of philosophy; for all pleasures other than that of philosophy need the assistance of others. § 13. [Other remedies are therefore necessary besides the remedy of Phaleas, which touches only the kind of crime committed from want of necessities.] The greatest crimes are committed not for the sake of necessities, but for the sake of superfluities. Men do not become tyrants in order to avoid exposure to cold. This is the reason why[, the crime of the tyrant being great,] the honours paid to the man who assassinates a tyrant—and not a mere thief—are also great.[1] We thus see that the general scheme of the constitution proposed by Phaleas avails only against the lesser crimes.

§ 14. There is a further criticism to be made of Phaleas. He seeks to arrange most of the details of his scheme with a view to the proper working of the constitution internally. But [external affairs have also to be considered; and] arrangements should also be made to meet the problem of defence against all neighbouring and foreign states.[2] It is therefore necessary that the constitution should be constructed with a view to military strength; and of this Phaleas has nothing to say. § 15. What applies to the constitution also applies to property. It should be adequate not only as a basis for the political activities of the citizens internally, but also as a resource for meeting external dangers. This latter consideration suggests the proper amount. On the one hand, it should not be so large that neighbouring and more powerful states will covet it, while its owners are unable to repel an attack: on the other hand, it should not be so small that those who own it are unable to sustain the burden of a war even with states otherwise equal and similar to their own. § 16. Phaleas has given us no indication; but we must not forget that *some* amount of property is an advantage, and

---

[1] The question whether tyrannicide was justifiable was much debated in the Middle Ages and in the sixteenth century. Aristotle does not discuss the general question of tyrannicide: he simply remarks—perhaps remembering the honours paid in Athens to Harmodius and Aristogeiton, who assassinated the tyrant Hipparchus—that tyrannicides are actually honoured.

[2] The problem of external relations—of foreign policy and defence—is one which is always present to Aristotle. He has already raised it (c. VI, §§ 7-8) in criticizing Plato's *Laws*; and when he comes to construct his own ideal constitution he pays special attention to the problem (Book VII, c. VI, and especially c. XI). There is also a reference to the problem of defence in Book IV, c. IV, §§ 10-11. We may also refer to the *Rhetoric*, Book I, c. IV, § 9, where it is stated that the orator dealing with political affairs should be conversant with matters of war and peace; should understand the actual and potential strength of his state, and know its military history; and should also have a similar understanding and knowledge about neighbour states.

we may perhaps suggest, as the best criterion of that amount, that stronger states shall find no advantage in going to war with a state because its wealth is excessive, but will go to war with it only in circumstances in which they would do so even if its wealth were less than it is. § 17. There is an historical incident which illustrates our argument. When the Persian Autophradates was planning to besiege the town of Atarneus, Eubulus, the ruler of the town, asked him to consider the length of time which it would take to capture it, and to calculate the expense which a siege of that duration would mean.[1] He was willing, he said, to surrender the town immediately for less than that amount. This had the effect of causing Autophradates, after a little reflection, to abandon the siege of the town.

§ 18. [Returning to the theme of the *internal* effects of the distribution of property] we must admit that a system which gives equal properties to all the citizens has a certain advantage, in that it helps to prevent mutual discord; but the advantage, on the whole, is inconsiderable. Men of education would be aggrieved by the system, feeling that they deserved something more than mere equality; indeed, as a matter of actual observation, they often rise in revolt and cause civic discord for this very reason. § 19. [Indeed there would be a general revolt against pure equality]: **1267 b** the naughtiness of men is a cup that can never be filled: there was once a time when two obols were a sufficient allowance,[2] but now that this has become the tradition men are always wanting something more, and are never contented until they get to infinity. It is the nature of desire to be infinite; and the mass of men live for the satisfaction of desire. § 20. The source from which a remedy for such evils may be expected is not the equalization of property, but rather a method of training which makes the better sort of natures unwilling, and the poorer sort unable, to indulge in covetousness.[3] The latter object will be attained if men of a poorer nature are put in an inferior position without being subjected to injustice.

§ 21. [It is a final argument against the scheme of Phaleas that] even in regard to his proposal for equality of property he has expressed himself imperfectly. He would equalize property only in land; but wealth may also consist in slaves, cattle, and money,

[1] Eubulus was at one time ruler of two towns, Atarneus and Assus, in the north-west of Asia Minor, somewhere about 350 B.C. Aristotle would naturally be interested in his fortunes, because he stayed in Assus, for some years after 347, as the guest of Hermias (the successor of Eubulus) whose niece he married.

[2] The daily allowance made in the fifth century to each Athenian citizen, during festivals, to pay for seats in the theatre.

[3] Aristotle repeats his constant theme (see the note on § 8, above) that a system of moral training, which affects the moral disposition, and secures the right attitude to property, is the method to be followed.

and in addition there will be a considerable stock of what are called movables. The proper course is either to deal with all these forms of wealth by an equal distribution or the fixing of a moderate maximum, or to leave all alike unregulated. § 22. It is also evident, from the legislation proposed by Phaleas, that he proposes to institute only a small body of citizens: the artisans are all to be public slaves, and are not to furnish any addition to the citizen body. § 23. It may be the case that one class of artisans—those who are employed on public property—should be made public slaves.[1] If so, it ought to be done on the lines which are followed at Epidamnus, or on the scheme which Diophantus once sought to introduce at Athens.

The observations which we have made on the constitution proposed by Phaleas will enable the student to judge whether his suggestions are good or bad.

CHAPTER VIII

4. Hippodamus of Miletus: *a planner of towns, who also sought to plan states on new lines. His advocacy of 'triads'—three social classes; three divisions of the territory; three sorts of laws. Criticism of his three classes and three divisions of territory. Criticism of his legal novelties, and especially of his proposal to reward the inventors of reforms. Tradition has its claims; and the value of a law-abiding habit may be greater than that of legal reforms.*

§ 1. Hippodamus the son of Euryphon, a citizen of Miletus, was the first man without practical experience of politics who attempted to handle the theme of the best form of constitution. He was a man who invented the planning of towns in separate quarters, and laid out the Peiraeus with regular roads.[2] In his general life, too, [apart from these innovations] he was led into some eccentricity by a desire to attract attention; and this made a number of people feel that he lived in too studied and artificial a manner. He wore his hair long and expensively adorned: he had flowing robes, expensively decorated, made from a cheap but warm material, which he wore in summer time as well as in winter; and he aspired to be learned about nature generally [as well as about town-

---

[1] Aristotle, apparently rejecting the proposal that *all* artisans should be public slaves, limits himself to considering the possibility that only those artisans who are employed on public property should be public slaves. Even this limited possibility, he suggests, can only be realized in a particular way—which he does not, however, explain, except by reference to two examples of which we know nothing.

[2] Miletus, his native city, had been laid out on a fine scale, and on geometrical lines, soon after 480 B.C. He perhaps learned his methods in Miletus and carried them to Athens, where he may have written a work on town-planning to which Aristotle is here referring (*Cambridge Ancient History*, vol. v, p. 463).

planning].   § 2. The state which he planned to construct was one
of 10,000 citizens, divided into three classes: the first of artisans,
the second of farmers, and the third a defence force equipped with
arms.   § 3. The territory was to be similarly divided into three
parts. One was intended for religious purposes; the second for
public use; and the third was to be private property. The first part
was to meet the expenses of the regular worship of the civic
deities; the second part—that devoted to public use—was to support the defence force; and the third was to be the private property
of the farming class.   § 4. Hippodamus also believed that there
should be only three classes of laws, corresponding to the three
main issues—wanton assault, damage, and homicide—on which
he held that all lawsuits arise. He proposed, too, that there should
be a single supreme court, to which all cases that appeared to have
been improperly decided should be referred; and this court, on his
plan, was to be constituted of elders selected for the purpose.
1268 a   § 5. He also held that judgements should not be given in
the courts by the method of dropping a pebble into the voting urn:
each judge should deposit a tablet. If he gave an absolute verdict
of condemnation against the defendant, he would write that verdict
on the tablet: if he gave an absolute verdict of acquittal, he would
leave the tablet blank; if he wished to record a qualified verdict—
partly of condemnation, and partly of acquittal—he would specify
the nature of his verdict. Hippodamus objected to the ordinary
method of voting as a bad sort of arrangement: it compelled a
judge [in a border-line case] to violate his judicial oath by giving a
verdict of absolute acquittal or condemnation.   § 6. He also proposed a law for conferring honours on any who should make an
invention of benefit to the state; and he further suggested, as a
novelty not hitherto included in the legislation of any state, that
the children of those who had been killed in action should be supported at the public expense. . . . Actually, such a law is already in
existence at Athens, and also in other states. . . . § 7. Finally, the
magistrates, on his scheme, were all to be elected by the people:
the people was to be constituted of the three classes already mentioned; and the magistrates whom they elected were to devote
themselves to three subjects—public matters, matters relating to
aliens, and matter relating to orphans.

These are the main and most notable features in the political
arrangements proposed by Hippodamus. The first criticism which
we may raise concerns the division of the citizen-body. § 8. The
artisans, the farmers, and the military class all share in the constitution, in the sense of possessing the *active* franchise; but the farmers
share without possessing arms, and the artisans share without

possessing either land or arms, which makes them both, in effect, the slaves of the class in possession of arms. § 9. It is thus impossible that these two classes should share in all the offices of the state; for the members of the class which possesses arms must necessarily be appointed generals and police magistrates, and must thus hold, in the main, the highest offices. But if the members of these two classes do not share in the constitution [i.e. in the sense of being eligible for office and thus possessing the *passive* franchise], how can they be friendly disposed to the constitution? It may be rejoined that the class which possesses arms ought to be superior to both of the other classes. We may answer that rejoinder by the argument, that it will be difficult for this class to be superior unless it is also numerous. § 10. But, in that case, is there any need for the other two classes to share in the constitution [in the sense of exercising the *active* franchise], or to control the appointment of magistrates? We may also raise the larger question whether the farmers are really of any service to the state. We may admit that artisans are necessary (they are necessary in every state), and that they can earn a subsistence from their crafts in the state proposed by Hippodamus as they do in all other states. But the case of the farmers is different. If they had provided the means of existence for the military class, they might reasonably have been counted as an integral part of the State [for by contributing to the support of an essential class they would have made an essential contribution to the state]; but on the scheme of Hippodamus they own their land as private property, and they will farm it for their private benefit. § 11. A further difficulty arises with regard to the third part of the territory which is to be common property, and from which the members of the defence force are to draw their subsistence. If the members of the defence force farm this common land themselves, there will be no distinction, such as Hippodamus wishes to establish, between the military and the farming class. If, on the other hand, those who farm this common land are to be distinct both from the class of farmers on private estates and from the military class, we shall have a fourth class in the state; and this class will have no share in anything whatsoever and will be extraneous to the constitution. § 12. There is, indeed, another and third alternative—that the same persons who farm their own private estates should also farm the common land. In that case, however, it will be difficult for each cultivator to produce enough to maintain two households [his own, and that of a member of the military class]; and the question may also be fairly asked, **1268 b** ['Why begin by dividing public from private land?] Why not start at once with a system by which the farmers—using all the land,

and each cultivating his share as a single plot—will at one and the same time get subsistence for themselves and provide it for the military class?' There is a sad confusion in the ideas of Hippodamus on all these matters.

§ 13. We may also disagree with the law he proposes in regard to the method of giving judicial decisions. He prescribes that a judge should, [if he thinks fit,] give a qualified verdict, even though the plaint on which he gives his decision is stated in absolute terms. This is, in effect, to prescribe that the judge should become an arbitrator. A qualified verdict is possible in a court of arbitration, even when there are several arbitrators (for they can confer with one another in order to determine their verdict); but in a court of law such a verdict is impossible, since, far from permitting any conference, the majority of legal codes contain specific measures for securing that the judges shall *not* communicate.[1]
§ 14. The perplexity to which decisions will thus be reduced [if the method of the qualified verdict is introduced into courts of law] can easily be seen. Let us suppose that any given judge is of the opinion that damages should be given—but not to the amount for which the plaintiff sues. A plaintiff, for example, may sue for 20 minae but a judge will give a verdict for 10 (or a plaintiff may sue for a still larger sum and a judge will give a verdict for something still less); but [as there are a number of judges] another will give a verdict for 5, and still another a verdict for 4. In this way, it is obvious, the various judges who give a qualified verdict will each award a different proportion of the amount claimed. But [this is not all: we have also to consider the judges who give a plain and unqualified verdict; and of these] some will award the whole sum claimed, while the rest will award nothing at all. § 15. What is the method of estimating [the total effect of] the different decisions thus given? . . . Turning to another point [also made by Hippodamus—that the giving of a plain verdict compels a judge to violate his oath], we must notice that a plain verdict of pure acquittal or pure condemnation never compels a judge to violate his oath, provided that the plaint itself has been duly laid in a plain and unqualified form. If, for instance, the plaint laid against the defendant is for 20 minae, the judge who gives a verdict for his acquittal does not decide that the defendant owes nothing; he only decides that he does not owe 20 minae. We

---

[1] Aristotle is assuming the existence of popular courts of law, each containing a large number of judges or 'dicasts'—it may be several hundreds. He is also assuming that each of these judges votes separately, and is debarred from communicating with other judges. In these circumstances there cannot be any conference, such as is necessary to a qualified verdict; and there cannot, therefore, be a qualified verdict.

only arrive at a judge who really violates his oath when we find one who gives a verdict *against* the defendant although he does not believe that he owes the 20 minae claimed by the plaintiff.

§ 16. In regard to the further question raised by Hippodamus—whether some honour ought not to be conferred on those who suggest an improvement which is of benefit to the state—we may argue that legislation in such a sense cannot be safely enacted, and has only a specious sound. It might encourage false accusations [of revolutionary plans] against the reformers, and perhaps lead, in this way, to political disturbances. But the proposal also involves another problem, and suggests a further argument. There are some thinkers who raise a doubt whether states lose or gain by changing their traditional laws when some other and better law is possible. § 17. If, on this issue, we take the line that change is *not* a gain, it is difficult to agree readily with the proposal made by Hippodamus; for changes which are really subversive of the laws, or of the constitution, may be proposed on the plea that they tend to the common good. However, as the issue has now been mentioned, it will be as well to define our views about it a little further. § 18. It is, as we have said, an issue which is in debate; and a case may be made for the view that change is the better policy. Certainly in other branches of knowledge change has proved beneficial. We may cite in evidence the changes from traditional practice which have been made in medicine, in physical training, and generally in all the arts and forms of human skill; and since politics has to be counted as an art or form of skill, it can be argued logically that the same must also be true of politics. § 19. It can also be argued that the actual facts [of history] provide an indication [of the benefits of change]. The usages of old times were exceedingly simple and uncivilized: Greeks went about armed, and bought their brides from each other. § 20. Indeed the relics of ancient customs which are still in existence, here and there, are utterly absurd: **1269 a** there is, for instance, a law at Cyme, relating to homicide, that if an accuser can produce a definite number of witnesses from his own kinsmen, the person accused shall be liable to the charge of murder.[1] § 21. All men, as a rule, seek to follow, not the line of tradition, but some idea of the good; and the earliest known human beings, whether

---

[1] The law at Cyme is not so 'utterly absurd': it has its analogies, as Newman notes, in the old Germanic custom of compurgation. Aristotle, and the Greeks generally, had naturally less of the historic sense, and of the spirit of historical understanding and sympathy, than we may properly be expected to possess after centuries of historical scholarship. On the other hand Aristotle has a deep respect for the general wisdom of the ages (cf. c. v, § 16); and though he may criticize ancient usages (*nomima*), as he does here, he also made a collection of the *nomima* of uncivilized peoples, in addition to his collection of the 'polities' of Greek states.

they were 'earth-born', or the survivors of some cataclysm, were in all probability similar to ordinary or even foolish people to-day. (Indeed that is actually the tale that is told of the 'earth-born' men.) It would therefore be an absurdity to remain constant to their notions. But besides these considerations [which relate to *un-written* custom], it may also be urged that to leave *written* laws unchanged is not a good policy. § 22. The reason is that in matters of political organization, as in the arts generally, it is impossible for every rule to be written down precisely: rules must be expressed in general terms, but actions are concerned with particulars. [The first form of a law will thus be inexact; and it will need to be changed in the light of further experience of men's actions in detail.]

But while these arguments go to show that in *some* cases, and at *some* times, law ought to be changed, there is another point of view from which it would appear that change is a matter which needs great caution. § 23. When we reflect that the improvement likely to be effected may be small, and that it is a bad thing to accustom men to abrogate laws light-heartedly, it becomes clear that there are some defects, both in legislation and in government, which had better be left untouched. The benefit of change will be less than the loss which is likely to result if men fall into the habit of disobeying the government. § 24. We must also notice that the analogy drawn from the arts is false. To change the practice of an art is not the same as to change the operation of a law. It is from habit, and only from habit, that law derives the validity which secures obedience. But habit can be created only by the passage of time; and a readiness to change from existing to new and different laws will accordingly tend to weaken the general power of law. § 25. Further questions may also be raised. Even if we admit that it is allowable to make a change, does this hold true, or not, of all laws and in all constitutions? And again, should change be attempted by any person whatsoever, or only by certain persons? It makes a great difference which of these different alternatives is adopted. . . . We may therefore dismiss this question for the present. It belongs to a different occasion.

B

ACTUAL STATES WHICH APPROACH THE IDEAL (CC. IX–XII)

CHAPTER IX

1. The Spartan Constitution. *The problem of finding a leisured class for the purposes of government: serfdom as a solution: the Spartan Helots. The undue influence of women at Sparta: the bad*

distribution of property, and its bad effects on the army. The defects of the Ephorate, the Council of Elders, and the dual kingship: defects of the Spartan system of common meals. The bad results of Spartan militarism, and the bad state of the public finances at Sparta.

§ 1. When we consider the constitutions of Sparta and Crete—or indeed, for that matter, of any other state—two questions emerge.[1] The first is whether any of their provisions is good or bad when it is judged by the standard of an *ideal* system: the second is whether any provision runs contrary to the principles and character of their constitutions *as actually established.* § 2. It is generally agreed that leisure, or in other words freedom from the necessity of labour, should be present in any well-ordered state; but it is difficult to see by what mode of organization this leisure is to be secured. The serfdom of the Penestae in Thessaly is one sort of mode, but the serfs there have often revolted against their masters; and the helots have similarly revolted against the Spartans, for whose misfortunes they are always on the watch, just as if they lay in an ambush. § 3. Nothing similar, it is true, has hitherto happened in Crete. Perhaps **1269 b** the reason is that the neighbouring cities of the island, although engaged in mutual hostilities, never enter into any alliance with revolting serfs: it is not to the interest of any, as each has serfs of its own. But all the neighbours of Sparta—Argos, Messenia, and Arcadia—have been her enemies; and this is the cause of the frequent revolts of the helots. [The example of Thessaly proves the same point]: the early revolts of their serfs against the Thessalians were due to the fact that they were still engaged in hostilities with the peoples on their borders—the Achaeans, the Perrhaebians, and the Magnesians. . . . § 4. Even if there were no added trouble, the handling of serfs is, in itself, an irksome business. It is not easy to determine on what footing one should associate with them: if they are driven with a loose rein, they become insolent, and proceed to claim equality with their masters: if they have a hard life, they fall into conspiracy and rancour. The moral is plain. States which suffer in this way from having a system of serfdom have not discovered the best mode of organization [for the purpose of securing leisure].

---

[1] In the preceding eight chapters Aristotle has considered, according to the plan laid down in c. 1, § 1, 'forms of government designed by theorists and held in good repute'. He now turns to 'forms actually practised by states that are accounted to be well-governed'. In either case his method is critical: he seeks to discover the defects which are to be avoided, in order to avoid those defects in constructing his own ideal state. His account of the Spartan constitution—like his account of Plato's proposals and his accounts of the schemes of Phaleas and Hippodamus—is therefore critical. It does not necessarily represent his considered view of the general value of the Spartan constitution.

§ 5.   Another criticism of the Spartan constitution turns on the indulgence permitted to women.   This hinders Sparta from attaining either the purpose of its own constitution or the happiness of its citizen body.   Just as husband and wife are alike essential parts of the family, so a state should also be considered as almost equally composed of men and women members.   In all constitutions, therefore, where the position of women is poorly regulated, one-half of the citizen body must be considered as left untouched by the laws.   § 6.   This is what has actually happened at Sparta.   The legislator who made the Spartan code intended to make the whole citizen body hardy; but if he fulfilled that intention, as he obviously did, in regard to the men, he has wholly neglected to achieve it in regard to the women, who indulge in all sorts of licence and live a luxurious life.   § 7.   The inevitable result, in such a constitution, is the worship of wealth, especially if—as happens with most military and martial stocks—the citizens are dominated by their wives.   (But the Celts are an exception to this general rule: so, too, are such peoples as openly approve of homosexual attachments.) § 8.   There was wisdom in the earliest author of myths when he paired Ares and Aphrodite: the facts show that all martial races are prone to passionate attachments either to men or to women. It was attachments of the latter sort which were common in Sparta; and the result was that, in the days of her hegemony, affairs largely fell into the hands of women.   § 9.   But what is the difference between governors being governed by women and women being actually governors?   The results are the same.   [We may take one example of those results.]   Even in the matter of courage, which is useless in all life's ordinary affairs and only of use, if it has a use, in time of war, the women of Sparta have had a most mischievous influence.   § 10.   They showed this during the Theban invasions; unlike the women of other states, they were of no use whatever, and caused more confusion than the enemy.   We may admit that the licence enjoyed by women seems to have come about originally at Sparta in a way which it is easy to understand. **1270 a**   § 11.   The men were absent on expeditions for long periods: there was war with the Argives, and with the Messenians and Arcadians.   Living a military life (which develops a number of good qualities) they were provided with some preparation [for a system of state-training], and on the return of peace and leisure they were thus ready to place themselves at the disposal of the legislator.   [It was different with the women, who had been living their own life at home.]   Lycurgus indeed attempted, according to tradition, to bring the women too within the range of his laws; but they opposed him, and he had to abandon the attempt.   § 12.   But while we can thus explain what actually happened, and so account for the origin of this defect in the Spartan system, we have to remember that we are not concerned with what can, or cannot, be excused [historically], but with what is actually right or wrong.

§ 13. The defects in the position of women at Sparta, as we have already suggested, seem not only calculated to produce some lack of harmony in the constitution, if we take that by itself, but also likely to foster the growth of avarice. It is natural, therefore, to pass from the observations just made to some criticism of the unequal distribution of property at Sparta. § 14. While some of the Spartans have come to possess an excessively large amount of property, others have been reduced to the merest fraction; and in this way the land has mostly passed into the hands of a very few persons. This matter has been badly handled by the legislation of Sparta. The legislator, very rightly, made it improper to buy or sell any land belonging to a Spartan citizen; but he also allowed any person who so desired to give or bequeath his property—though the same results must necessarily follow in the one case as in the other. § 15. Actually, about two-fifths of the whole country belongs to [a few owners, and those few] women; this is due to the number of heiresses and the practice of giving dowries. It would have been better to have had no dowries at all, or to have fixed them at a small, or at any rate a moderate, amount. As it is, a citizen may give the daughter who inherits his property to any man whom he likes (rich or poor); and if he dies intestate before he has done so, the man who is left in the position of guardian gives her in marriage at *his* discretion. § 16. The result has been that while the territory would have supported 1,500 horse and 30,000 foot, the number had dwindled [by the time of the Theban invasions of 369-362 B.C.] to less than 1,000. History itself has clearly shown the defects of the Spartan methods of dealing with property. Sparta was unable to weather a single defeat in the field; and she was ruined by want of men. § 17. It is stated that, under the early kings, the Spartans were in the habit of giving citizenship to strangers, and that, as a result, they suffered from no want of men, in spite of the long wars they were fighting: indeed they are said to have numbered, at one time, as many as 10,000 citizens. Whether this statement is true or false, Sparta would have done better to keep her ranks filled by maintaining an equal distribution of property. § 18. Such a reform is, however, impeded by the very law which the Spartans have adopted for the encouragement of the birth-rate. Anxious for **1270 b** the Spartans to be as numerous as possible, and seeking accordingly to induce his fellow-citizens to have as many children as possible, the legislator has

enacted a law that the father of three sons should be exempt from
military service, and the father of four entirely free from all taxes.
§ 19. Yet it is obvious that, if families are large, and the land is
divided accordingly [among a number of children], a large number
of the citizens must necessarily be reduced to poverty.

This leads to a further criticism, which turns on the defects of
the institution called the Ephorate.[1] The Ephors at Sparta have
a sovereign authority in matters of the highest importance; but
they are all drawn from the people at large, and it often happens
that very poor men, whose lack of means renders them open to
bribery, attain this office. § 20. This weakness has often been
shown in the past; and there is a recent instance in the affair at
Andros, when some of the Ephors, by taking bribes, did their best
to involve the whole state in ruin. It is a further defect of this
institution that it is so important, and so much in the nature of a
dictatorship, that even the kings have been compelled to court the
favour of the Ephors. The result has been that—apart from their
venality—the whole constitution has suffered, in common with the
monarchy, from their overgrown power; and from being an aristocracy it has tended to turn into a democracy. § 21. But it must be
admitted that the Ephorate is a force which holds the constitution
together. The right of sharing in the most important office of the
state makes the people at large contented; and this result, whether
it be due to the influence of legislation or to the working of chance,
has a beneficial effect on the affairs of Sparta. § 22. If a constitution is to survive, all the elements of the state must join in willing
its existence and its continuance.[2] [Such a will exists in each of
the elements at Sparta]: it exists in the two kings, who are content
with the honour paid to their persons: it exists among the upper
classes, who are content with their access to the Senate (for a seat
in the Senate is given as a reward for excellence); and it also exists
in the people at large, who are made contented by the Ephorate
and by all being eligible alike for that office. § 23. But [though the
Ephorate has this advantage, it still suffers from defects]. It is
right and proper that all should be eligible for the office, but not
that the election should be conducted on the present method,
which is far too childish.[3] Again, the Ephors are just ordinary men,

---

[1] The five Spartan Ephors, or 'overseers', had a general superintendence of
the Spartan constitution. A number of modern thinkers, from Calvin and
Althusius to Fichte, have sought to advocate an imitation of the Spartan
Ephorate, in the form of some ultimate supreme council, or supreme court,
finally controlling the action of the state.   [2] See Note L, p. 80.

[3] We do not know what this 'childish' method was—whether it was real
election of any sort (by acclamation or otherwise), or election mixed with some
element of chance (such as the use of the lot or the taking of auspices), or pure
reliance on chance.

but they have power to decide important cases; and it would be better, therefore, that they should not decide at discretion [as they now do], but on the basis of written rules set down in legal form. § 24. Finally, their mode of life is not in agreement with the aim of the state. It permits too much indulgence. This contradicts the discipline imposed on the other citizens, which inclines so much to the opposite extreme of severity that men cannot endure its rigour, and escape from it into the secret enjoyment of sensual pleasures.

The institution of the Council of Elders has also its defects. § 25. If the members of the council were men of probity, and adequately trained in manly virtues, it might be argued that the institution was of benefit to the state. . . . Even so, it would be dubious whether councillors should be life-judges in important cases, [as they now are]: the mind, as well as the body, is subject to old age. . . . But when, as a matter of fact, **1271 a** the training of the councillors is such that even the legislator distrusts their character, the council cannot be regarded as a safe institution. § 26. It is evident from experience that those who have held the office of councillor have often been influenced by bribery and favouritism in dealing with public affairs. This is a reason why they should not, as they now are, be free from any scrutiny of their conduct. It is true that the Ephors would appear to have the right to scrutinize the conduct of every magistrate; but this is too sweeping a prerogative for them to possess, nor is it the way in which, in our view, the councillors should be subjected to scrutiny. § 27. The method of electing councillors is also defective. The final election is made in a childish way [by a peculiar form of acclamation]; and there is an impropriety in requiring that, to be eligible, a man should openly seek election. The man who deserves the office should have it whether he wants it or no.   § 28. In requiring candidates to seek election, the legislator is plainly acting in the spirit which he seeks to infuse into the whole of the constitution. He has imposed the requirement because he wants to make his citizens generally ambitious of honours and office; for no one would seek election as councillor unless he had such an ambition. Yet ambition and avarice are exactly the motives which lead men to commit nearly all intentional crimes.

§ 29. The general theme of kingship, and the question whether it is good or bad for states to have kings, may be left to another occasion. But if there are to be kings, they had better not come to the throne on the principle now followed in Sparta, and each new king should be appointed for his personal conduct and character.[1]

_____

[1] The monarchy at Sparta (which was a dual monarchy, with two kings ruling simultaneously) was an hereditary office confined to the family of the Heraclidae,

§ 30. On the present system it is clear that even the legislator him-self must be of the opinion that he cannot make the kings behave well and honourably. At any rate he shows a distrust of their being sufficiently good for his purpose; and this distrust has appeared in the practice of joining opponents with the kings on embassies, and in the general opinion that divisions between them served as a political safeguard.

The legal arrangements made, at the time of its introduction, for regulating the system of common meals (or, as the Spartans call them, *phiditia*), may also be criticized. § 31. The cost of such gatherings ought to be defrayed from public funds, as it is in Crete; but the rule at Sparta is for each man to bring his own contribution, in spite of the fact that some of the citizens are extremely poor and unable to bear the expense. The natural result is the very opposite of the legislator's intention. § 32. The system of common meals was meant to be democratic, but the rule which is followed at Sparta makes it almost the reverse. Citizens who are extremely poor find it difficult to share in the common meals; and yet it is the traditional rule of the Spartan constitution that those who cannot contribute their quota are debarred from sharing in constitutional rights.

§ 33. Other writers have also censured, not without justice, the law relating to the office of admiral. It is a cause of civil discord. The office of admiral is a sort of second kingship, set up as a counterpoise to the kings, who hold the position of generalissimos for life.

§ 34. There is another respect in which the purpose and inten-tion of Spartan legislation may be censured; **1271 b** and the censure has already been passed by Plato in his *Laws*. The whole system of legislation is directed to fostering only one part or element of goodness—goodness in war—because that sort of goodness is useful for gaining power. The inevitable result has followed. The Spartans remained secure as long as they were at war; but they collapsed as soon as they acquired an empire. They did not know how to use the leisure which peace brought; and they had never accustomed themselves to any discipline other and better than that of war. § 35. There is another defect at Sparta which is equally grave. The Spartans hold that the 'goods' for which men strive [happiness, honour, and the like] are to be attained by being good, and not by being bad. They are right in thinking that goodness is

and descending by right of seniority. According to Plutarch, Lysander had sug-gested (early in the fourth century B.C.) that the office of king should be turned into something in the nature of a presidency, and should be open to merit irre-spective of descent. Aristotle, as Newman notes, appears to agree with this suggestion.

the way to the 'goods' of life; but they are wrong in believing that these 'goods' are greater than goodness.

§ 36. Another defect at Sparta is the state of the public finances. The treasury is empty, while the state is compelled to wage major wars; and the taxes are not properly paid. Most of the land is in the hands of citizens, and [as the taxes fall on land] none of them looks at all closely at another man's payments. § 37. The effect of the Spartan system is here the reverse of beneficial: it has reduced the state to penury while encouraging private avarice. This may serve as an account of the Spartan constitution, and these are the defects which are particularly open to censure.

NOTE L (p. 77): *Aristotle on will or consent in politics*

This important Aristotelian idea—that 'will is the basis of the state'—is implied in the whole conception of 'association'; and it is constantly repeated by Aristotle. It appears in Book IV, c. IX, § 10 (where the mixed constitution is said to be dependent on the will of every part); in IV, c. XII, § 1 (where it is stated, as a principle common to all constitutions, that the part which wills the continuance of the constitution should be stronger than the part which does not); and in V, c. IX, § 5 (where the same principle is laid down in the same words). It will be noted that Aristotle sometimes assumes the consent of *all* the parts (e.g. in the present context, where he is primarily thinking of Sparta, and again in the passage in which he is speaking of the mixed constitution), and sometimes only assumes the consent of the *major* part. Perhaps we may say that he assumes the consent of the major part for all constitutions, and only assumes that of all the parts for constitutions of the mixed type.

CHAPTER X

2. The Cretan type of constitution. *Crete possibly the model of Sparta: similarities between the two. The Cretan system of common meals is superior to the Spartan; but the Cretan Cosmoi, who correspond to the Spartan Ephors, are inferior to them. Cretan 'feudalism': confederations of nobles: feuds and factions: Crete hitherto saved from their evil effects by its geographical isolation.*

§ 1. The Cretan type of constitution is allied to the Spartan; but it is, on the whole, inferior in finish, though equal at one or two points. It may well have been the model on which the constitution of Sparta was generally based: indeed, this is said to be the case; and institutions of an older origin are generally less elaborate than the more modern. § 2. Tradition records that Lycurgus, when he relinquished the office of guardian to King Charillus and went abroad, spent most of his time in Crete, to which he was drawn by ties of connexion—the people of Lyctus [one of the cities of Crete]

being a colony from Sparta. . . . These Spartan settlers adopted
the form of law which they found existing among the inhabitants
at the time of their settlement.   § 3. The adoption of these ancient
laws by the Spartan colonists in Crete may help us to understand
why they are still in vogue among the serfs of the island, as a body
of law supposed to go back as far as the times of Minos. . . .

[The mention of Minos may remind us that] the island seems
to be naturally designed, and admirably situated, for holding an
empire in the Greek world. It commands the whole of the sea [the
eastern Mediterranean] on whose shores nearly all of the Greeks
are settled: it is not far from the Peloponnese on the west, and close
to the corner of Asia round Cape Krio and Rhodes on the east.
§ 4. This explains the success of Minos in establishing a maritime
empire. He subdued some of the neighbouring islands, and
colonized others; and finally he carried his attacks as far as Sicily,
where he died near Camicus. . . .

The general body of Cretan institutions resembles the Spartan.
§ 5. The helots who cultivate the land for the Spartans correspond
to the Perioeci, or serfs, in Crete; and both **1272 a** states have a
system of common meals, which the Spartans, in former times,
used to call *andreia* (and not, as they now do, *phiditia*)—a term still
used by the Cretans, and a proof that the Spartans derived their
system from Crete.   § 6. There is also a resemblance between the
constitutional system of Crete and that of Sparta. The Spartan
Ephors have the same position as the Cretan *Cosmoi*: the only
difference is that the Ephors are five in number, and the *Cosmoi*
ten. Similarly the Spartan elders correspond to the Cretan; but
the latter are called the *Boulē* [while the Spartan elders are called
the *Gerousia*]. Like Sparta, Crete had formerly a monarchy; but
it was afterwards abolished, and the *Cosmoi* are now in command
of the army.   § 7. All Cretan citizens [like the Spartans] have the
right of attending the general assembly; but its only power is that
of ratifying the decisions of the elders and the *Cosmoi*.

The arrangements for common meals in Crete are better than
they are at Sparta. At Sparta each citizen contributes individually
the quota allotted to him, and if he fails to do so he is legally
debarred, as has already been noted, from a share in constitutional
rights.   § 8. In Crete the common meals are placed on a more
public footing. The whole of the agricultural produce and live
stock raised on the public land, and all the rents paid in kind by the
Perioeci, form a common fund, of which one moiety is devoted to
the cult of the gods and the discharge of public services, and the
other to the provision of common meals. This makes it possible
for all alike—men, women, and children—to be fed at the public

cost.[1] § 9. The legislation of Crete contains a number of ingenious
devices intended to encourage an abstemious form of diet in the
interest of the state; it also includes a provision for the segregation
of women, to prevent them from having too many children, and
it sanctions homosexual connexions. (Whether that is right or
wrong is a question which may be left for a later occasion.)

What we have said will show that the arrangements for common
meals in Crete are superior to those at Sparta. On the other hand,
the *Cosmoi* are an institution which is inferior even to the Ephoralty.
§ 10. They share the defect of the Ephors—that of being casually
appointed [through the absence of any proper qualification]—without presenting the constitutional advantage which the Ephors
present. In the Spartan system, under which every citizen is eligible
for the Ephoralty, the people at large can share in the enjoyment
of this highest of offices, and the popular will is therefore enlisted
in support of the constitution. In Crete, however, the *Cosmoi* are
drawn from a limited number of families, and not from the people
at large; while the members of the council of elders are drawn,
in their turn, from the limited circle of those who have served as
Cosmoi. § 11. This Cretan council of elders may be criticized on
the same grounds as the Spartan. Their immunity from the
rendering of any account, and their life-tenure, are both prerogatives beyond their desert; and their power of acting at their own
discretion—and not on the basis of written rules—is a positive
danger. § 12. As for the institution of the *Cosmoi*, we must add that
it is no proof of its being properly organized that the people should
remain contented in spite of their exclusion from it. The *Cosmoi*,
unlike the Ephors, have no opportunity of using their powers for
their own profit: they live on an island, remote from the danger of
corruption.

1272 b § 13. The remedy which the Cretans provide for the
defects of this institution is curious, and belongs to an arbitrary
oligarchy rather than a constitutional state. Again and again a
confederation[2] is formed—either by some of their own colleagues,
or by a group of private persons—which proceeds to eject the *Cosmoi*
from office; and they are also allowed to resign their office before
their term has expired. Surely it is better that all such matters
should be regulated by law, and not settled by the mere will of men,
which is a dangerous standard for action. § 14. Still worse, how-

---

[1] Aristotle follows the Cretan plan in his own ideal state (Book VII, c. x, § 11).
[2] This practice of a right of confederation may remind us of the 'Confederations' formed by Polish nobles against the government under the old Polish
constitution. The practice of declaring an abeyance of the office of *Cosmoi*,
which is mentioned below, may also remind us, as Newman notes, of the *liberum
veto* of unreformed Poland.

ever, is the practice of declaring an abeyance of office of the *Cosmoi*, to which powerful nobles often resort when they are unwilling to submit to justice. This proves that the Cretan system, if it has some of the elements of a constitution, is not really a constitution at all, but an arbitrary form of oligarchy.[1] It is a habit [of the Cretan nobles] to break up the people and their own followers into many factions; to set up, on that basis, as many monarchies; and then to quarrel and fight. § 15. In effect, and as long as it lasts, such a state of things simply means the disappearance of the state and the dissolution of political society. A state which is brought to this pass is in danger: those who wish to attack it will now have also the power. But Crete itself, as has already been noted, is saved from this danger by its geographical position; and distance has here the same effect which is achieved elsewhere by laws for the expulsion of aliens. § 16. The isolation of Crete will also explain why the Perioeci there stay quiet, while the helots of Sparta are often in revolt. The Cretans have no foreign dominions;[2] and it is only lately that foreign forces have penetrated into the island—with results which have gone to show the frailty of Cretan institutions.

So much of the Cretan type of constitution. We may now turn to the Carthaginian.

CHAPTER XI

3. The Carthaginian constitution. *Similarities of Carthage and Sparta, with the balance, in some respects, in favour of Carthage. The constitution of Carthage is generally based on the principle of aristocracy; but it deviates from that principle, partly towards democracy and partly towards oligarchy. Its main defect is that it attaches too much importance to wealth, and is thus, in effect, a moneyed oligarchy. Another defect is the habit of pluralism. Carthage has sought to correct her defects by a policy of encouraging the emigration of the poor; but while this policy has been fortunate in its results, it is not an adequate remedy.*

§ 1. The constitution of Carthage[3] is generally accounted a good

---

[1] The word used by Aristotle is *dynasteia*, which designates an oligarchical government, in the hands of a clique of powerful nobles (*dynatoi*), acting by arbitrary discretion—and not by constitutional rules—in the style and spirit of a 'tyrant'. A *dynasteia* is thus a plural form of tyranny; and the use of the word naturally leads Aristotle in the next sentence, to speak of monarchy (in its 'tyrannical' form) as characteristic of Crete.

[2] The suggestion is that if they had such dominions, the dominions might become discontented, and then stimulate the Perioeci into a sympathetic revolt.

[3] It seems curious that Aristotle should give an account of a non-Hellenic constitution as one of the three 'actually practised by states that are accounted to be well governed'. It seems the more curious when we reflect that Carthage

constitution, and one which is peculiar in many respects; but the chief thing about it is its likeness, at a number of points, to the Spartan. Indeed the three constitutions with which we are here concerned—the Cretan, the Spartan, and the Carthaginian—are all closely related to one another, and they all differ greatly from other constitutions. Many of the institutions at Carthage are certainly good. § 2. It is a proof of a well-ordered constitution that Carthage, with her large populace, should steadily keep to the same political system: she has had no civil dissensions worth mentioning, nor any attempt at a tyranny. § 3. There are a number of similarities between the Carthaginian and the Spartan constitution. The common meals shared by the 'messes' at Carthage are similar to the Spartan *phiditia*. The office of the Hundred and Four is similar to the Ephoralty—but with the difference (which is to the credit of Carthage) that the elections to the office are made on the basis of merit, while the Ephoralty is recruited at haphazard. Finally, the kings and the Council of Elders at Carthage are analogous to the Spartan kings and Council of Elders. § 4. But here again it is to the credit of Carthage that her kings are not, as they are at Sparta, always drawn from a single family of no more than ordinary merit. They are drawn from any family which is outstanding at the time, and they are drawn from it by election, and not by seniority. Kings, after all, have considerable powers: **1273 a** and if they are insignificant persons, they can do a great deal of harm—as, indeed, they have actually done at Sparta.

§ 5. Most of the features which may be criticized at Carthage, as deviations from its principle, are features common to all of the constitutions with which we are here concerned. But it is a feature peculiar to the Carthaginian constitution that while it is generally based on the principle of aristocracy, or 'polity',[1] it sometimes deviates from it in the direction of democracy, and sometimes in that of oligarchy. It is a deviation in the direction of democracy that while the kings[2] and the Elders, if they are both agreed, can freely decide whether or no they will submit any issue to the assembly, the assembly is equally free to deal with an issue if they

was challenging the Greek hold on Sicily at the time at which he wrote. But Carthage, along with Sparta and Crete, had a constitution of that mixed type to which Aristotle himself inclined as 'the best possible under actual conditions' (see note 1 to c. 1 of this book); and it is probably for this reason that he gives an account of Carthage. It is on the same ground that he refers again to the Carthaginian constitution in Book IV, c. VII, § 4, where it is mentioned as paying regard to wealth, merit, and numbers, and thus mixing oligarchy, aristocracy, and democracy.

[1] See Note M, p. 87.

[2] Aristotle is referring to the Carthaginian Suffetes, who seem, like the Spartan kings and the Roman consuls, to have been two in number.

are *not* agreed about its submission. §6. Again, when the kings and the Elders submit a proposal by agreement, the assembly is not confined to hearing and approving the decision of the government: it has the power of final judgement, and any of its members who so desire may oppose the proposal. These are rights which the assembly does not enjoy under the Spartan and Cretan constitutions. § 7. On the other hand, there are a number of deviations in the direction of oligarchy. First, there is the rule that the quinquevirates, or colleges of five, which are in control of many important matters, should be recruited by co-optation. Next, there is the rule that these colleges, thus recruited, should choose the Hundred [and Four], who are the highest authority in the state. Lastly, there is the rule that the members of these colleges should hold office longer than other magistrates: they are virtually in office both before and after the period of regular tenure . . . . On the other hand, again, we must count as aristocratic features, [and therefore as in accordance with the principle of the constitution], the rule that the magistrates are not paid or appointed by lot,[1] and other similar rules; and we must equally count as aristocratic the rule that *all* lawsuits may be decided by any body of magistrates, and not some by one and some by another, as is the case at Sparta.[2]

§ 8. We have still to notice the great and main feature in the Carthaginian system which shows a deviation from aristocracy in the direction of oligarchy. This consists in a trend of opinion which is current [not only at Carthage, but also] generally—a trend in favour of the election of magistrates on the ground of means as well as the ground of merit, because poor men make poor magistrates and have no leisure for their duties. § 9. If election on the ground of means is characteristic of oligarchy and election by merit of aristocracy, the system on which the Carthaginian constitution is formed would seem to be something different from either. Both grounds are taken into consideration in the elections of magistrates at Carthage, especially in those of the highest—the kings and the generals. § 10. This deviation from the pure principle of aristocracy must be regarded as an error of the original

---

[1] If the magistrates *were* paid, and appointed by lot, that would be a deviation towards democracy.

[2] It is not clear why the Carthaginian rule, that any body of magistrates could try any lawsuit, is more suitable to an aristocracy than the Spartan practice of assigning different kinds of lawsuits to different bodies. Equally it is not clear whether the Spartan practice—which, it seems to be implied, is a deviation— is a deviation towards oligarchy or towards democracy. It may be regarded as a deviation towards oligarchy, if we regard it as meaning that very few persons will try *any particular kind* of lawsuit; it may also be regarded as a deviation towards democracy, if we regard it as meaning that more judges may be employed in deciding *all kinds* of lawsuits in the aggregate.

law-giver. It is one of his initial and greatest duties to see to it that the most meritorious are in a position to enjoy leisure time—not only when they are in office, but even when they are not—and to refrain from occupations which are unworthy of their gifts. In any case—and even admitting that it may be right to take means too into consideration, in order to secure men of leisure—we may still criticize the Carthaginian practice of making the highest of offices (those of the kings and the generals) open to simple purchase. § 11. A rule of this nature puts riches in a more honourable position than merit, and imbues the whole of the state with a spirit of avarice. The values attached to things by the heads of the state will necessarily determine the opinion of the rest of the citizens; and a constitution in which merit does not receive the highest place of honour is one in which aristocracy cannot have a secure existence. § 12. Besides, **1273 b** when money has been spent to get office, the purchasers may naturally be expected to fall into the habit of trying to make a profit on the transaction. If men who are poor but honest are likely to want to make profit, how can we expect the worse sort to refrain, when they are already out of pocket? We may therefore conclude that those who can govern best [i.e. those of the highest merit] should be enabled to govern; and even if legislators abandon any attempt at a permanent endowment of the better sort of citizens, they ought at any rate to provide for their having leisure during the period for which they hold office.

§ 13. It would also appear to be a defect that one person should hold a number of offices, which is a practice in vogue at Carthage. Each job is done best when it is done by one man;[1] and the law-giver should see that this rule is followed, and not set the same man to be (as it were) both flute-player and cobbler. § 14. Accordingly, where the state is large, it is at once more statesmanlike and more democratic to distribute its offices among a number of persons. It is more democratic because, as we have already argued,[2] it is the fairer to all concerned: it is more statesmanlike because it means that each particular job is done better and quicker. The advantage of distributing offices widely is clearly evident in military and naval matters. In both, the habit of exercising—and of obeying—authority may be said to extend through the whole of the service and all its members.[3]

---

[1] See Book I, c. II, § 3.   [2] See above, c. II, § 6.

[3] We might have expected Aristotle simply to say that 'in both of these spheres the exercise of authority is spread over a large number of persons, each with his own special job'. But his mind runs forward to a further point; he reflects that ruling and *being ruled* are both spread over the whole of these two services; and he therefore remarks, as Newman puts it in his note, that 'in fleets and armies almost every one may be said both to rule and to be ruled, for each has a superior at the same time as he commands inferiors'.

§ 15. The Carthaginians have a constitution which [though based on the principle of aristocracy] is in practice oligarchical; but they avoid the dangers of oligarchy by encouraging the diffusion· of wealth. From time to time a section of the populace is planted out among the dependent cities—a policy which remedies the defects of the constitution and serves to give it stability. But this may be said to be the effect of chance; and legislation, not chance, is the true means for preventing the risk of civil discord. § 16. In the present position of affairs the law provides no way of ensuring· internal peace if chance should begin to turn adverse and the masses revolt against their rulers.

Such is the character of the three constitutions—the Spartan, the Cretan, and the Carthaginian—which are justly held in high regard.

NOTE M (p. 84): *Aristotle's use of the words* polity *and* aristocracy

'Polity' is a word which has two senses in the *Politics*—the general sense of a constitution, and the particular sense of a mixed constitution. The word is here used in the latter sense. The reader may be puzzled by the fact that Aristotle here uses the words aristocracy and 'polity' as if they were equivalent—the more as he often speaks of aristocracy as one of the elements (but only *one* of the elements) included in a mixed constitution. But he sometimes uses the term aristocracy to denote a mixed constitution—apparently on the ground that the principle of recognition of merit (which is the essential element of aristocracy) is also essential in a good 'polity'. There may, however, be 'polities' which do not recognize the claims of merit, but only those of wealth and numbers (thus mixing only the features of oligarchy and democracy); and such 'polities', containing no aristocratic element, cannot be called aristocracies.

CHAPTER XII[1]

4. Postscript on other legislators. *Solon and the constitution of Athens. The earliest legislators. Various notes (e.g. on the severity of Draco's laws, and on the legislation of Pittacus about the offences of drunken persons).*

§ 1. Those who have left any record of their views on questions of government may be divided into two classes. Some have been men who took no part in political affairs of any kind or description, but lived for the whole of their lives in a private capacity; we have already mentioned practically everything worthy of note which has come from men of this class. Others, again, have been men who actively served as law-givers—some in their own and others in foreign states—and who were thus personally concerned in government. [We may subdivide this second class]: some of its members

[1] See Note N, p. 91.

were only concerned with codes of laws: others were authors of
constitutions as well as codes. Lycurgus and Solon are both in
the latter category: they not only framed codes of law, but also
made constitutions. § 2. The constitution of Sparta has already
been described. Solon is held, by one school of thought, to have
been a good lawgiver, who may be credited with a triple achievement. He swept away an oligarchy which was far too absolute;
he emancipated the people from serfdom; and he instituted that
'ancestral democracy' under which the constitution was so admirably tempered[1]—with the Council of the Areopagus standing for
oligarchy, the method of electing the executive magistrates for
aristocracy, and the system of popular law courts for democracy.
§ 3. In actual fact, **1274 a** however, it would appear that two of
these elements—the council and the method of electing the executive magistrates—existed before his time and were simply continued by him. But he certainly introduced the principle of
democracy by making membership of the law-courts open to every
citizen; and that is the reason why he is blamed by some of his
critics, who argue that he really destroyed the other elements by
making these popular law-courts, with their members appointed by
lot,[2] supreme in every case. § 4. Later, as these courts grew in
strength, the successors of Solon, seeking to flatter the people in
the way that men flatter a tyrant,[3] transformed the constitution
into its present form of extreme democracy. Ephialtes and Pericles
curtailed the Council of the Areopagus; Pericles introduced the
system of paying the members of the law-courts; and thus each
demagogue, in his turn, increased the power of the people until the
constitution assumed its present form. § 5. This development,
however, appears to be due to accident rather than to any deliberate design on the part of Solon. The people, who had been
the cause of the acquisition of a maritime empire during the
course of the Persian wars, acquired a conceit of themselves; and
in spite of the opposition of the better citizens they found
worthless demagogues to support their cause. Solon himself
would seem to have given the people only the necessary minimum

---

[1] The more conservative classes at Athens, after the Peloponnesian War and
the shock which it brought to advanced democracy, advocated a programme of
reversion to the 'ancestral constitution' of earlier days. It is perhaps the view
of these classes which Aristotle is here describing. See Appendix IV, A. 4.

[2] The appointment of members by lot, which threw the office of judge open
to all indiscriminately, accentuated the popular character of the 'dicasteries'.

[3] Aristotle, in later passages of the *Politics*, compares 'extreme' or 'final' democracy with tyranny. It is, he argues, a collective version of tyranny: the people,
in such a form of democracy, impose the arbitrary fiat of mass-will in the same
way that the tyrant imposes the arbitrary fiat of his single will. (Book IV, c. IV,
§ 26, and Book V, c. V, § 10.)

of power.[1] He gave them simply the rights of electing the magistrates and calling them to account;[2] and if the people do not enjoy
these elementary rights, they must be a people of slaves, and thus
enemies to the government.   § 6. [Even in giving these rights, he
instituted a check]: only the notable and the well-to-do were made
eligible for any office; and the magistrates were exclusively drawn
from the Pentecosiomedimni [the class with an income, from
landed property, of 500 measures of produce], the Zeugitae [the
class with an income of 200], and the Hippeis [the class with an
income of 300]—while the lowest class, that of the Thetes [with
an income of less than 200], was ineligible for any office.

Other legislators, besides Lycurgus and Solon, were Zaleucus,
who framed laws for the Epizephyrian Locrians [in the south of
Italy], and Charondas of Catana, who legislated for his own and
for other cities in Italy and Sicily which had been settled from
Chalcis [in Euboea].   § 7. There are some writers, however, who
would go farther back, and argue that Onomacritus was the earliest
expert in legislation. They make him a Locrian, who was trained
in Crete during a visit paid there in the course of his vocation as
prophet: they make Thales of Crete his colleague: finally, they
make Lycurgus and Zaleucus the disciples of this Thales, and
Charondas the disciple of Zaleucus. § 8. This is a view which
pays too little regard to chronology; but we may certainly include
in our list of legislators Philolaus of Corinth, who framed laws for
Thebes. He belonged by birth to the Bacchiad family in his native
city; but he was the friend and lover of Diocles, an Olympian
victor who quitted Corinth in disgust at his mother Halcyone's
incestuous passion for himself, and he accompanied Diocles to
Thebes, where they lived and died together. . . . § 9. Their tombs
are still shown to-day: they stand in full view of one another, but
one of them looks towards the soil of Corinth, and the other in a
different direction; and the story goes that the two friends deliberately arranged to be buried in this way—Diocles remembering
his past with horror, and anxious that Corinth should not be
visible from the mound under which he lay, but Philolaus desiring
that it should be from his. . . . § 10. This was the **1274 b** reason of
their settling at Thebes; and this was how Philolaus came to make
laws for that city. Among his laws there are some which deal with
membership of the family. They are called the laws of adoption;

[1] In his own phrase, 'I gave the people so much authority as was sufficient
for it; and I did not permit either side to carry the day unfairly.'
With the general view of the development of Athenian democracy here stated
compare the view expressed in the *Constitution of Athens* (Appendix IV. A. 3).
[2] These are the rights assigned to the masses by Aristotle himself in Book III,
C. XI.

and they are a peculiar feature of the legislation of Philolaus,
intended to keep the number of family plots constant and undisturbed.[1] § 11. The only peculiar feature of the legislation of
Charondas is that relating to suits brought against persons guilty
of perjury (he was the first to institute the practice of denunciation
for false witness); but in the general precision of his laws he showed
himself a still better draftsman than our modern legislators.
[§ 12. The peculiar feature of the legislation proposed by Phaleas
is the equalization of property; the peculiar features of Plato's
legislation are many—community of property and of wives and
children; a system of common meals for women; the rule about
drinking, which provides that the sober must be in the chair at a
drinking-party; and the rule about military training, which provides that soldiers must practise themselves in ambidexterity,
because both hands ought to be equally useful.][2]

§ 13. Draco made a number of laws; but they involved no change
in the existing constitution. They have no peculiar feature worth
mentioning, except the severity which they show in fixing the amount
of punishments. Pittacus, like Draco, was the author only of laws,
and not of a constitution. One of the laws peculiar to him is the law
that a drunken man should be punished more heavily for an offence
than a sober person. He noted that drunken men commit offences
of violence more frequently than sober persons; but instead of holding that this entitled them to greater consideration, he preferred to
take his stand on the ground of public policy. § 14. Androdamas of
Rhegium was another legislator, who made laws for the Chalcidian
settlements in Thrace. Some of them are concerned with homicide, and with the succession of women to property; but his
legislation has no peculiar feature that need be mentioned.

This may conclude our inquiry into matters connected with
both types of constitutions—those which are actually in force, and
those planned by political theorists.[3]

---

[1] Philolaus, in seeking to adjust the membership of the family to the distribution of property, was remembering what Aristotle criticizes Phaleas for forgetting (c. VII, § 5)—'that regulation of the amount of property ought to be
accompanied by regulation of the number of children in the family'.

[2] This section is bracketed in Newman's text, as a repetition, and as also
irrelevant in its context.

[3] It may seem curious that the account of actual and theoretical 'best constitutions', which is given in Book II, is not immediately followed by Aristotle's
sketch of his own 'best constitution'. That sketch is not given until we reach
the last two books of the *Politics* (VII–VIII). This raises the question—discussed
in the Introduction—of the proper order of the different sections of the *Politics*
and the date of their composition. But whatever answer we give to that question,
it is obvious that the general questions raised in the book which next follows—
perhaps the most important of all the books of the *Politics*—had first to be
treated before any sketch of a best constitution could be attempted.

NOTE N (p. 87): *The character of Book II, c. XII*

This chapter, as Newman notes, hardly squares with the plan laid down at the beginning of Book II. That plan envisaged (1) an account of 'constitutions constructed by theorists and held to be well constructed', which is given in cc. II–VIII, and (2) an account 'of states that are accounted to be well governed', which is given in cc. IX–XI. In this chapter Aristotle turns to a new theme—that of lawgivers who had played a part in politics. In a sense this theme has already been treated, at any rate partially, in the account of Sparta, and of the Spartan legislation attributed to Lycurgus. It may have occurred to Aristotle that he had still to treat of Athens and of the legislation of Solon at Athens. If that be so, we can only say, first, that the account of Solon's legislation is very brief, and secondly, that it is followed by jottings about other legislators which have no particular relevance and are only in the nature of scraps. The account of Solon's legislation, as Newman suggests, may be Aristotelian in composition, but tacked on here by some later hand: the other jottings, as he also suggests, may be based on rough notes of Aristotle, which were afterwards completed by some member of his school.

BOOK III

THE THEORY OF CITIZENSHIP AND CONSTITUTIONS

A

CITIZENSHIP (cc. i–v)

CHAPTER I

To understand constitutions (or polities), we must inquire into the nature of the state (polis); and to understand that—since the state is a body of citizens (politai)—we must examine the nature of citizenship. Citizenship is not determined by residence, or by rights at private law, but by constitutional rights under the system of public law: 'a citizen is one who permanently *shares in the administration of justice and the holding of office.' This definition is more especially true in a democracy: to make it generally applicable, we must modify it to run, 'a citizen is one who shares* for any period of time *in judicial and deliberative office'.*

1274 b 32 § 1. When we are dealing with the subject of polity [i.e. constitutions or forms of government], and seeking to discover the essence and the attributes of each form, our first investigation may well be directed to the polis itself; and we may begin by asking, 'What is the nature of the polis?' [There are three reasons for so doing.] In the first place, the nature of the 'polis', or state, is at present a disputed question; and while some affirm, 'It was the *state* that did such and such an act', others reply, 'It was not the state, but the *government*—the governing oligarchy or tyrant.' In the second place, all the activity of the statesman and the law-giver is obviously concerned with the state; [and we must therefore understand the state in order to understand that activity]. Finally, a polity or constitution is a scheme established [in order to regulate the distribution of political power] among the inhabitants of a polis; [and we must first understand the polis in order to understand that scheme].

§ 2. [But as we have gone back beyond the polity to the polis, so we have to go back beyond the polis to the politēs or citizen.] A polis or state belongs to the order of 'compounds', in the same way as all other things which form a single 'whole', but a 'whole' composed, none the less, of a number of different parts.[1] This being the case, it clearly follows that we must inquire into **1275 a** the nature of the citizen [i.e. the part] before inquiring into the

---

[1] See Note O, p. 95.

nature of the state [i.e. the whole composed of such parts].[1] In other words, a state is a compound made up of citizens; and this compels us to consider who should properly be called a citizen and what a citizen really is. The nature of citizenship, like that of the state, is a question which is often disputed: there is no general agreement on a single definition: the man who is a citizen in a democracy is often not one in an oligarchy. § 3. We may leave out of consideration those who enjoy the name and title of citizen in some other than the strict sense—for example, naturalized citizens. A citizen proper is not one by virtue of residence in a given place: resident aliens and slaves share a common place of residence [with citizens, but they are not citizens]. § 4. Nor can the name of citizen be given to those who share in civic rights only to the extent of being entitled to sue and be sued in the courts. This is a right which belongs also to aliens who share its enjoyment by virtue of a treaty; though it is to be noted that there are many places where resident aliens do not enjoy even this limited right to the full—being obliged to choose a legal protector [to sue and be sued on their behalf], so that they only share to a limited extent in the common enjoyment of the right. § 5. [We may thus dismiss those who have only the right to sue and be sued from our consideration,] just as we may also dismiss children who are still too young to be entered on the roll of citizens, or men who are old enough to have been excused from civic duties. There is a sense in which the young and the old may both be called citizens, but it is not altogether an unqualified sense: we must add the reservation that the young are undeveloped, and the old superannuated citizens, or we must use some other qualification; the exact term we apply does not matter, for the meaning is clear.

What we have to define is the citizen in the strict and unqualified sense, who has no defect that has to be made good before he can bear the name—no defect such as youth or age, or such as those attaching to disfranchised or exiled citizens (about whom similar questions have also to be raised and answered). § 6. The citizen in this strict sense is best defined by the one criterion, 'a man who shares in the administration of justice and in the holding of office.' Offices

---

[1] The argument at this point may remind us of the argument at the beginning of Book I, c. 1, § 3 (see also c. 11, § 1, and the note on that section). There is, however, a difference. There, the argument was genetic as well as analytic: the polis was considered not only in the light of an analysis of its parts, but also in the light of an account of its genesis, as one part developed into another (marriage into the family: the family into the village: the village into the polis). Here, the argument is purely analytic. Again, and in consequence of this difference, there is also a further difference. There, the parts were contained societies (the society of marriage, the society of the family, and so forth): here, the parts are the individual citizens.

may be divided into two kinds. Some are discontinuous in point of time: in other words, they are of the sort that either cannot be held at all for more than a single term or can only be held for a second term after some definite interval. Others, however, have no limit of time—for example, the office of judge in the popular courts, or the office of a member of the popular assembly. § 7. It may possibly be contended that judges in the courts and members of the assembly are not holders of 'office', and do not share in 'office' by virtue of their position. But it would be ridiculous to exclude from the category of holders of office those who actually hold the most sovereign position in the state; and we may dismiss the contention as trivial, since the argument turns on a word [or rather the absence of one]. The point is that we have no one word to denote the factor common to the judge and the member of the assembly, or to describe the position held by both. Let us, in the interest of a clear analysis, call it 'indeterminate office' [i.e. office held for an indeterminate period]. § 8. On that basis we may lay it down that citizens are those who share in the holding of office as so defined.

Such is the general nature of the definition of citizen which will most satisfactorily cover the position of all who bear the name. [But it still leaves us confronted by difficulties.] Citizenship belongs to a particular class of things where (1) there are different bases on which the thing may depend, (2) these bases are of different kinds and different qualities—one of them standing first, another second, and so on down the series. Things belonging to this particular class, when considered purely as so belonging, have no common denominator whatever—or, if they have one, they have it only to a meagre extent.[1] § 9. [The different bases of citizenship are different constitutions]; constitutions obviously differ from one another in kind, and some of them are obviously inferior **1275 b** and some superior in quality; for constitutions which are defective and perverted (we shall explain later in what sense we are using the term 'perverted') are necessarily inferior to those which are free from defects. It follows that [as constitutions differ, so] the citizen under each different kind of constitution must also necessarily be different. § 10. We may thus conclude that the

[1] Applying these general considerations to citizenship, we may say (1) that the 'basis' of citizenship is the constitution; (2) that constitutions are of different 'kinds', with the different kinds of constitutions having different 'qualities'; and (3) that citizenship has therefore differences of quality, so that a common denominator or definition can hardly exist. Considered purely as members of the class of citizens, the citizen under an extreme oligarchy and the citizen under an extreme democracy have little or nothing in common; though if we consider them not as citizens, but as human beings, we may find that they have a common, if meagre, denominator in *that* capacity.

citizen of our definition [one holding the indeterminate office of judge in a court and member of an assembly] is particularly and especially the citizen of a democracy. Citizens living under other kinds of constitution *may* possibly, but do not necessarily, correspond to the definition. There are some states, for example, in which there is no popular element: such states have no regular meetings of the assembly, but only meetings specially summoned;[1] and [so far as membership of the courts is concerned] they remit the decision of cases to special bodies. In Sparta, for example, the Ephors take cases of contracts (not as a body, but each sitting separately); the Council of Elders take cases of homicide; and some other authority may take other cases. § 11. Much the same is also true of Carthage, where a number of bodies of magistrates have each the right to decide all cases.[2]

But our definition of citizenship [may still be maintained, in spite of these difficulties, since it] can be amended. We have to note that in constitutions other than the democratic, members of the assembly and the courts do not hold that office for an indeterminate period. They hold it for a limited term; and it is to persons with such a tenure (whether they be many or few) that the citizen's function of deliberating and judging (whether on all issues or only a few) is assigned in these constitutions. § 12. The nature of citizenship in general emerges clearly from these considerations; and our final definitions will accordingly be: (1) 'he who enjoys the right of sharing in deliberative or judicial office [for any period, fixed or unfixed] attains thereby the status of a citizen of his state', and (2) ' a state, in its simplest terms, is a body of such persons adequate in number for achieving a self-sufficient existence'.[3]

NOTE O (p. 92): *'Compounds' and 'wholes'*

The terms 'compound' (*syntheton*) and 'whole' (*holon*) are both technical terms of Aristotle's philosophy. The 'compound' is the genus:

[1] These 'specially summoned' meetings may also have been attended only by persons specially summoned; but Aristotle appears to refer here to the *time* of the meeting, and not to the *persons* attending the meeting. Democracies had regular meetings: states of a different type had only irregular meetings. The point of time here taken is in general agreement with Aristotle's emphasis on the argument of time in his definition of citizenship as the holding of deliberative and judicial office for *an indeterminate period*.

[2] See Book II, c. XI, § 7.

[3] On the meaning of self-sufficiency, see Book I, c. II, § 8, and the note on that passage. On the general implications of Aristotle's definition of citizenship, see the Introduction, IV, 2, and what is there said in regard to the conception of *to kyrion* (and also IV, 3, and what is there said about the term *dikastērion*). Sir John Myres speaks of Aristotle's definition, which assigns to the citizen even *archē* itself, as giving room for the expression of 'the voice of human reason, facing facts, opinions, and traditions . . . open-minded'. (*Political Ideas of the Greeks*, pp. 229–30.)

the 'whole' is a species of that genus. 'Compounds', as defined by Grote in a passage quoted in Newman's note, 'are of two sorts—aggregates like a heap (mechanical), and aggregates like a syllable (organic)'. 'Wholes' are aggregates of the second or organic kind: they have a Form which gives them an organic unity, and an End or Final Cause which gives them a single purpose. The polis is such a 'whole'.

There is a further point to be noted in regard to the idea of 'compound' (including that of 'whole'). The idea involves a distinction between the ruling element or elements and those which are subject to rule: in other words it involves a hierarchy of rule and subordination (see Book I, c. v, § 3 and note). Aristotle accordingly notes in the *Ethics*, Book IX, c. viii, § 6, that 'a polis, or any other systematic whole, may be identified particularly with the most sovereign element in it'.

CHAPTER II

A popular and pragmatic view of citizenship makes it depend on birth, i.e. descent from a citizen parent or two citizen parents. This does not carry us far, and in any case it only relates to old established citizens. A more serious question is raised when we consider new citizens, who have been given constitutional rights in the course of a revolution. Are they actually citizens? On the criterion of sharing in judicial and deliberative office (which is a functional criterion), they are actually citizens when once they possess that function.

§ 1. For practical purposes, it is usual to define a citizen as 'one born of citizen parents on both sides', and not on the father's or mother's side only; but sometimes this requirement is carried still farther back, to the length of two, three, or more stages of ancestry. This popular and facile definition has induced some thinkers to raise the question, 'How did the citizen of the third or fourth stage of ancestry himself come to be a citizen?' § 2. Gorgias of Leontini—perhaps partly from a sense of this difficulty and partly in irony—said, 'As mortars are things which are made by the craftsmen who are mortar-makers, so Larissaeans are persons who are made by the "craftsmen" who are Larissaean-makers'.[1] § 3. But [there is no reason to raise any difficulty about the title of the earlier citizens:] the matter is really simple. If, in their day, they enjoyed constitutional rights in the sense of our own definition [i.e. the right of sharing in judicial or deliberative office], they were certainly citizens. It is obviously impossible to apply

[1] Gorgias was punning on the Greek word *demiourgoi*, which has the general significance of craftsmen, but was also used, in some states, as the regular designation of the magistrates. But he was also defining citizenship seriously, by making its *origin* depend not on birth, but on the act of the state. Aristotle, however, is not interested in the question of origin: here, as elsewhere, he is concerned with *function*. 'All things derive their essential character from their function' (Book I, c. ii, § 13). It follows that on his view we must look to function, and not to origin, if we wish to define the essential character of the citizen.

the requirement of descent from a citizen father or a citizen mother to those who were the first inhabitants or original founders of a state.

A more serious difficulty is perhaps raised by the case of those who have acquired constitutional rights as the result of a revolutionary change in the constitution. We may take as an example the action of Cleisthenes at Athens, when after the expulsion of the tyrants he enrolled in the tribes a number of foreigners and a number of resident aliens belonging to the slave class. §4. The question raised by such an addition to the civic body is not the question of fact, 'Who is actually a citizen?' It is the question of justice, 'Are men [who are actually citizens] rightly or wrongly such?' It must be admitted, however, that the further question may well be raised, **1276 a** 'Can a man who is not justly a citizen be really a citizen, and is not the unjust the same thing as the unreal?' §5. [This further question may be easily answered.] Obviously there are holders of office who have no just title to their office; but we none the less call them office-holders, though we do not say they are justly such. [The same is true of citizens also:] they, too, are defined by the fact of holding a sort of office (for the definition we have given of the citizen involves his sharing in office of the deliberative and judicial kind); and it follows, therefore, that those who have received this sort of office after a change in the constitution must, in practice, be called citizens.

Chapter III

This still leaves us faced by the question, 'Are they justly citizens?' It may be argued that it was not the state, but only a revolutionary government, which gave them the position of citizens, and that they have accordingly no just title. This argument raises the general question of the identity of the state. Is the state identical with the government for the time being? Generally, what are the factors which constitute its identity? The identity of a state does not depend on its being surrounded by one set of walls, or on its consisting of one stock of inhabitants. The state is a compound; and its identity, like that of all compounds, is determined by the scheme of its composition—i.e. by its constitution.

§1. The question whether, in justice, they are citizens or not is a different matter, which is closely connected with a larger question already mentioned [at the beginning of the first chapter].[1] The problem raised by this larger question is that of deciding when a given act can, and when it cannot, be considered to be the act

[1] See Note P, p. 100.

of the state. We may take as an example the case of an oligarchy
or tyranny which changes into a democracy. § 2. In such a
case there are some who are reluctant to fulfil public contracts—
arguing that such contracts were made by the governing tyrant,
and not by the state—and unwilling to meet other obligations
of a similar nature.[1] They hold the view that some constitutions
exist [only] by virtue of force, and not for the sake of the common
good: [on which it follows that acts done under such constitutions
cannot be acts of the state, which must always, by its nature, act
for the common good]. This argument, however, [cuts both ways;
for it] leads us to the conclusion that when we find a democracy
which exists by virtue of force we have to admit that acts done
under the government of such a democracy are no more acts of
the state concerned than were acts done under the oligarchy or
tyranny [which previously existed]. § 3. But the question here
raised would seem to be closely allied to a question which takes us
still further—'On what principles ought we to say that a state has
retained its identity, or, conversely, that it has lost its identity and
become a different state?'

The most obvious mode of dealing with this question is to
consider simply territory and population [i.e. to treat the issue of
identity merely in *physical* terms]. On this basis we may note that
the territory and population of a state may be divided into two
(or more) sections, with some of the population residing in one
block of territory, and some of it in another. [Does such a division
destroy the identity of a polis?] § 4. This difficulty need not be
regarded as serious: the issue which it raises can easily be met
if we remember that the word 'polis' or state is used in different
senses.[2] If we now proceed to take the case in which the whole
population of a state resides in a single territory, the question
still remains, 'When, or on what conditions, should this state be
considered as possessing a real [in addition to its physical]
identity?' § 5. The identity of a polis is not constituted by its
walls. It would be possible to surround the whole of the Peloponnese by a single wall: [but would that make it a single polis?].
Babylon (which, it is said, had been captured for three whole days
before some of its inhabitants knew of the fact) may perhaps be
counted a polis of this dubious nature: so, too, might any polis
which had the dimensions of a people [*ethnos*] rather than those of

[1] This was the general issue raised when the Communist government succeeded the government of the Tsars in 1917.
[2] The settlement of the problem of identity will go one way, and the verdict
will be that the polis has not a single identity, if we are using 'polis' in the sense
of a city or place. The settlement will go another way, and the verdict will be
in favour of identity, if we are using 'polis' in the sense of a political community.

a city. § 6. But it will be better to reserve the consideration of
this question [i.e. how large a polis can be and yet remain a single
polis] for some other occasion. To determine the size of a polis—
to settle how large it can properly be, and whether it ought to
consist of the members of one people or of several—is a duty incumbent on the statesman. [It is, therefore, a matter to be
considered in connexion with the art of statesmanship, rather than
in connexion with the theory of the identity of the polis.][1]

[We may now turn from considerations of size to considerations
of stock.] Still assuming a single population inhabiting a single
territory, shall we say that the state retains its identity as long as
the stock of its inhabitants continues to be the same (although the
old members are always dying and new members are always being
born), and shall we thus apply to the state the analogy of rivers
and fountains, to which we ascribe a constant identity in spite of
the fact that part of their water is always flowing in and part
always flowing out? Or must we take a different view, and say that
while the population remains the same, for the reason already
mentioned [i.e. that the stock of the inhabitants continues to be
the same], the *state* may none the less change?

1276 b § 7. [The latter view carries the day.] If a polis is a
form of association, and if this form of association is an association
of citizens in a polity or constitution, it would seem to follow
inevitably that when the constitution suffers a change in kind,
and becomes a different constitution, the polis also will cease to
be the same polis, and will also change its identity. We may cite
an analogy from the drama. We say that a chorus which appears
at one time as a comic and at another as a tragic chorus is not
continuously the same, but alters its identity—and this in spite
of the fact that the members often remain the same. § 8. What
is true of a chorus is also true of every other form of association,
and of all other compounds generally. If the scheme of composition
is different, the compound becomes a different compound. A
harmony composed of the same notes will be a different harmony
according as the 'mode' [or scheme of its composition] is Dorian
or Phrygian. § 9. If this is the case, it is obvious that the criterion
to which we must chiefly look in determining the identity of the
state is the criterion of the constitution. [The criterion of stock
is irrelevant]: whether the same group of persons inhabits a

---

[1] Aristotle accordingly considers the size of the polis as a *practical* question
for statesmanship when he comes to construct an ideal state (Book VII, c. iv).
He thus leaves unsolved, in this passage, the problem of the connection of the
size of the polis with the *theoretical* question of the identity of the state—though
he seems to incline to the view that a very large polis cannot possess a real
identity.

polis, or a totally different group, we are free to call it the same polis, or a different polis [in the light of the other and final criterion]. . . . It is a different question, and another matter, whether it is right or wrong for a state to repudiate public obligations when it changes its constitution into another form.[1]

NOTE P (p. 97): *The problem of the identity of the state*

The essence of this larger question is concerned with the nature and identity of the state. Is the nature of the state such that we may identify it with the constitution in force, and therefore with the government in power, at any given time? Or is the nature of the state such that we must distinguish it from the particular constitution which may be in force, and the particular government which may be in power, at any given time? On the first alternative any action of a government in power (e.g. the action of making new citizens, or the action of making public contracts) will (1) be the action of the state, (2) as such, be valid, and (3) continue to be binding even when the form of government is changed. On the second alternative the action of a government in power—at any rate in the case of a government which has attained power after a revolutionary change in the constitution—will (1) not necessarily be the action of the state, (2) not necessarily be valid, and (3) not necessarily continue to be binding when the form of government is changed.

NOTE Q: *Public contracts after a revolution*

Aristotle thus leaves unsolved the problem raised at the beginning of the chapter, whether public contracts should still be kept when the constitution is changed and (for instance) a tyranny or oligarchy is turned into a democracy. Two different conclusions may be drawn from the arguments which he uses in the course of the chapter. (1) The first is that, if the identity of the state depends on the constitution, a state with a new constitution is a new state, not necessarily bound by the acts of the old state. (2) The second is that if contracts made for the common good are always binding (which is the argument implied in § 2), then any such contract will be binding in spite of a change of constitution; and thus a contract made for the public good under an oligarchy will still be binding under a democracy. It is perhaps this latter consideration which leads Aristotle to say that the question of the validity of public contracts is a different question from that of the identity of the state.

A passage in Appendix IV. A. 4 (p. 381, n. 2) shows how the question of the validity of public contracts, after a change of constitution, was actually solved at Athens in 404 B.C. and afterwards. The restored Athenian democracy honoured even the contracts made with Sparta by their predecessors, the Thirty Tyrants: 'in spite of financial difficulties . . . the debts contracted at Sparta by the Thirty were honoured by their successors and gradually repaid.' (*Cambridge Ancient History*, vol. vi, p. 35.)

The general problem of the identity, or corporate personality, of the Greek state is discussed in Vinogradoff's *Historical Jurisprudence*, vol. ii, c. VI, § 1 ('The city as a juridical person').

---

[1] See Note Q.

Chapter IV

*The idea of the constitution thus provides an answer to the question,
'What is the identity of the State?' It also provides an answer to the
question, 'What is the relation of the excellence of the good citizen to
the excellence of the good man?' If we look at constitutions generally,
we must note that different constitutions require different types of good
citizen, while the good man is always the same. If we look at the ideal
constitution, we may argue that even here there must be different types
of good citizen, because there are different sorts of civic function; and
thus here too the good citizen cannot be identified with the good man.
On the whole, therefore, the good citizen and the good man cannot be
identified. But there is one case in which they can be. This is the case
of the good citizen under an ideal constitution who possesses the quality
of moral wisdom required for being a good ruler as well as the other
qualities required for being a good subject. The quality of moral
wisdom which he possesses is the essential quality of the good man;
and in his case the excellence of the good citizen is identical with that
of the good man.*

§ 1. A question connected with those which have just been
discussed is the question whether the excellence of a good man
and that of a good citizen are identical or different.[1] If this question is to be properly investigated, we must first describe the excellence of the citizen in some sort of outline. Just as a sailor is a
member of an association [i.e. the ship's company, with its various
members and their different duties], so too is a citizen. § 2. Sailors
differ from one another in virtue of the different capacities in
which they act: one is a rower, another a pilot, another a look-out
man; and others again will have other names in the same sort of
way [i.e. according to their capacities]. This being the case [i.e. the
ship's company being composed of men acting in different capaci-
ties], it is clear that the most accurate definition of the excellence
of each sailor will be special to the man concerned; but it is also
clear that a common definition of excellence will apply to all,
inasmuch as safety in navigation is the common end which all
must serve and the object at which each must aim. § 3. What is
true of sailors is also true of citizens. Though they differ [in the
capacities in which they act, they all have a common object]; the
end which they all serve is safety in the working of their association; and this association consists in the constitution. The conclusion to which we are thus led is that the excellence of the citizen
must be an excellence relative to the constitution. It follows on

[1] See Note R, p. 106.

this that if there are several different kinds of constitution [the excellence of the citizen must also be of several different kinds, and] there cannot be a single absolute excellence of the good citizen. But the good man is a man so called in virtue of a single absolute excellence.

§ 4. It is thus clear that it is possible to be a good citizen without possessing the excellence which is the quality of the good man. But we may reach the same conclusion in another way, by discussing the question [not, as we have hitherto done, in relation to constitutions generally, but] with particular reference to the best or ideal constitution.[1]   § 5. If it is impossible for a polis to be composed entirely and only of good men; if, none the less, each citizen of a polis must discharge *well* the function belonging to him; if his good discharge of his function involves, as it must, his excellence—then, as it is impossible for all the citizens to be alike [differing, as they must, in their functions and their capacities], the excellence of a good citizen cannot be identical with that of a good man. 1277 a [In other words, there cannot be a single excellence common to both]: the excellence of being a good citizen must belong to all citizens indifferently, because that is the condition necessary for the state being the best state; but the excellence of being a good man cannot possibly belong to all—unless, indeed, we hold that every citizen of a good state [by virtue of belonging to it] must also be a good man. ... § 6. There is a further point to be made.[2] The polis is composed of unlike elements. Just as a living being is composed of [the different elements of] soul and body, or the soul of the different elements of reason and appetite, or the household of man and wife, or property of master and slave, so the polis too is composed of different and unlike elements—among them not only the various elements already mentioned [e.g. man and wife, and master and slave], but also others in addition [e.g. ruler and ruled, or soldier and civilian]. It follows upon this difference between the elements of which the polis is composed that there cannot be a single excellence common to all the citizens,

---

[1] The argument of the preceding section has proved that in constitutions generally, with all their variety, there cannot be a single excellence of the citizen which can match, and be identified with, the single excellence of the good man. The argument of this and the following section proves that, even if we isolate the ideal constitution, the excellence of *its* citizen cannot invariably match, or be identified with, the excellence of the good man.

[2] It has been shown in §§ 4-5 that, though all the citizens of the best state have the excellence of the good citizen, that excellence is none the less different from that of the good man. The additional point made in this section is that while all the citizens of such a state have the excellence of the citizen, they have that excellence *in different ways*—with the result that there are different kinds of the excellence of the citizen, which is not the case with the excellence of the good man

any more than there can be a single excellence common to the leader of a dramatic chorus and his assistants.

§ 7. It is clear from these considerations that the excellence of the good citizen and that of the good man are not in *all* cases identical. But the question may still be raised whether there are not *some* cases in which there is identity. [The cases we have to consider are those of the ruler and statesman.[1]] We call a good ruler a 'good' and 'prudent' man, and we say of the statesman that 'he ought to be 'prudent'.[2] § 8. [This is to differentiate the ruler, and to make *his* excellence identical with that of the good man.] Indeed there are some who hold that the very training of the ruler should be, from the first, of a different kind; and it is a matter of observation that the sons of kings are specially trained in riding and the art of war. Thus Euripides makes a king say [of the education of his sons]

> No subtleties for me,
> But what the state most needs,

which implies a special training for the ruler. § 9. We may thus assume that, in the case of the ruler, the excellence of the good citizen is identical with that of the good man. But we have to remember that subjects too are citizens, [and *their* case is different]. It therefore follows that the excellence of the good citizen cannot be identical with that of the good man in all cases, though it may be so in a particular case [i.e. where the citizen is acting as a ruler]. The excellence of the ordinary citizen [which requires the virtues of obedience as well as those of command] is different from that of the ruler; and this may well be the reason why Jason, the tyrant of Pherae, said that 'he was a hungry man except when he was tyrant', meaning that he did not know how to live in a private station.

§ 10. [So far, the argument favours the ruler who is purely a ruler, because it makes his excellence identical with that of the good man.] On the other hand, men hold in esteem the double capacity which consists in knowing both how to rule and how to obey, and they regard the excellence of a worthy citizen as consisting in a good exercise of this double capacity. Now if the excellence of the good man is in the one order of ruling,[3] while

---

[1] The ruler is the *genus*: the statesman is the *species*, i.e. that particular sort of ruler who holds office in a free polis composed of free associates.

[2] 'Prudent' is a word which fails to give the exact sense of the Greek *phronimos*. The man who is *phronimos* is the man who possesses that quality of 'moral wisdom', or *phronesis*, which is the ultimate goal of moral development—succeeding and crowning the prior stage of 'habituation', by social environment and education, through which we all pass in our earlier years. He is 'the good man'.

[3] The good man, possessing the quality of 'moral wisdom', is able to rule his appetites; and, generally, he meets moral difficulties with the quality of deliberate choice which should characterize the ruler.

that of the good citizen is in both orders [i.e. both ruling and obeying], these two excellences cannot be held in the same esteem.   § 11. The position thus being that we find men holding (1) that ruler and ruled should have different sorts of knowledge, and not one identical sort, and (2) that the citizen should have both sorts of knowledge, and share in both, we can now see the next step which our argument has to take.[1] [There is a conflict of views, which needs and admits of reconciliation; and in order to attain that reconciliation, we must proceed to distinguish the different sorts of ruling and being ruled, and to show that there are *some* sorts of being ruled which the citizen need not learn.]

There is rule of the sort which is exercised by a master [over slaves]; and by this we mean the sort of rule connected with menial duties. Here it is not necessary for the ruler to know how to do [what he requires the ruled to do], but only to know how to use [the capacities of the ruled]: indeed the former kind of knowledge (by which we mean an ability to do menial services personally) has a servile character.   § 12. [We may go on to note that menial services are not confined to those who are actually slaves, but have a wider scope.] There are a number of forms of servile position, because there are a number of forms of menial service which have to be rendered. One of these forms of service is that which is rendered by manual labourers. These, as their very name signifies, are men who live by the work of their hands; and the menial craftsman, or mechanic, belongs to this class. This is the reason why in some **1277 b** states the working classes were once upon a time excluded from office, in the days before the institution of the extreme form of democracy.   § 13. The occupations pursued by men who are subject to rule of the sort just mentioned [i.e. the rule of a master or an employer over persons in a servile position] need never be studied by the good man, or by the statesman, or by the good citizen—except occasionally and in order to satisfy some personal need, in which case there ceases to be any question of the relation of master and servant.

But [besides rule of the sort exercised by their ruler over persons in a servile position] there is also rule of the sort which is exercised

---

[1] Newman's note admirably illustrates the argument. 'One view is that the ruler and the ruled should learn different things; the other is that the citizen, who is in part a ruler, should learn both how to rule and how to be ruled, or in other words should learn the same things as the ruled. Both of these views are partly true. Those who hold that the ruler and the ruled should learn different things are so far correct that the citizen-ruler over citizens, and therefore the citizen, should not learn the work of unfreely ruled persons. Those who hold that the ruler and the ruled should learn the same things are so far correct that the citizen-ruler over citizens should learn to be ruled as a freeman is ruled. Thus the truth lies midway . . between the two opinions.'

over persons who are similar in birth to the ruler, and are similarly free. § 14. Rule of this sort is what we call political[1] rule; and this is the sort of rule which [unlike rule of the first sort] the ruler must begin to learn by being ruled and by obeying—just as one learns to be a commander of cavalry by serving under another commander, or to be a general of infantry by serving under another general and by acting first as colonel and, even before that, as captain. This is why it is a good saying that 'you cannot be a ruler unless you have first been ruled'. § 15. Ruler and ruled [under this system of political rule] have indeed different excellences; but the fact remains that the good citizen must possess the knowledge and the capacity requisite for ruling as well as for being ruled, and the excellence of a citizen may be defined as consisting in 'a knowledge of rule over free men from both points of view' [i.e. that of the ruler as well as that of the ruled].

§ 16. [In the light of these considerations about political rule, and about the nature of the excellence of a good citizen under a system of such rule, we may now return to the question whether the excellence of a good citizen is identical with that of a good man.] A good man, like a good citizen, will need knowledge from both points of view. Accordingly, on the assumption that the temperance and justice[2] required for ruling have a special quality, and equally that the temperance and justice required for being a subject in a free state have *their* special quality, the excellence of the good man (e.g. his justice) will not be one sort of excellence. It will include different sorts—one sort which fits him to act as a ruler, and one which fits him to act as a subject.[3] . . . We may note that the temperance and the courage of a man differ from those of a woman in much the same sort of way [as the temperance and courage of a person acting as ruler differ from those of a person acting as subject]. § 17. A man would be thought to be cowardly if his courage were only the same as that of a courageous woman; and conversely a woman would be thought to be forward if her modesty were no greater than that which becomes a good man. The function of the man in the household is different from that of the woman [as the function of ruling persons in the state is

---

[1] See Note S, p. 106.
[2] The excellence of the good man and citizen (*aretē*, or general goodness) embraced, in the current view of the Greeks, four particular forms of goodness—temperance, justice, courage, and wisdom. Aristotle here selects some of these particular forms in order to elucidate his argument.
[3] Previously, in § 3 of this chapter, Aristotle had assumed that the good man was such in virtue of a single excellence. He now discovers that the excellence of the good man is, after all, a double excellence, because, in order to be excellent, he must be able, according to the position in which he is placed, either to command or to obey as a good man should.

different from that of subjects]: it is the function of the one to acquire, and of the other to keep and store. . . .

'Prudence' is the only form of goodness which is peculiar to the ruler. The other forms [temperance, justice, and courage] must, it would seem, belong equally to rulers and subjects [though their *quality* in the ruler differs from their *quality* in the subject]. § 18. The form of goodness peculiar to subjects cannot be 'prudence', and may be defined as 'right opinion' [or a proper state of *feeling*]. The ruled may be compared to flute-makers: rulers are like flute-players who use what the flute-makers make.[1]

These considerations will suffice to show whether the excellence of the good man and that of the good citizen are identical or different—or [rather] in what sense they are identical and in what sense they are different.[2]

NOTE R (p. 101): *The unity or variety of virtue*

The general considerations which lie behind the question here raised are well summarized in Newman's note. 'Socrates had taught the unity of virtue, claiming that virtue is one and the same in all who possess it. Aristotle holds, on the contrary, that virtue varies with the work a person has to do, and that, as a citizen's work is relative to the constitution, his virtue varies with the constitution. To identify the virtue of a good citizen with that of a good man is therefore to ignore the difference between one constitution and another.'

The connexion between the new question now raised and the question previously discussed is thus that both are determined by the fact of the constitution. It is that fact which determines the identity of the state. It is also that fact which determines the relation of the good man's excellence to that of the good citizen.

NOTE S (p. 105): *The word* polis *and its derivatives*

'Political', in the sense that it is exercised in a free polis, over the free *politēs* or citizen, by the *politikos* or statesman. It is one of the difficulties of translating the *Politics* that Aristotle uses five connected and associated words—*polis*, *politēs*, *politeia*, *politeuma*, and *politicos*—which the translator is forced to render by separate and dissociated words. *Polis* must often become 'state': *politēs* has to become 'citizen': *politeia* must be translated as 'constitution': *politeuma* must be rendered as 'the civic body', or in other words the body of persons established as sovereign by the constitution: *politicos* cannot be rendered by 'politician' (which has its own peculiar connotation in English), and has to be translated as 'statesman'. In Greek each term, connected with the rest, carries its own associations clearly. See the Introduction, IV. I.

[1] It is easy to see the analogy between the flute-player and the ruler. It is less easy to see in what sense the ruled are like flute-makers (they would seem to be more like flutes)—unless it be that they have to supply the material in the use of which the ruler may show his moral wisdom or 'prudence'.
[2] See Note T, p. 107.

NOTE T (p. 106): *The course of the argument of* C. IV

The argument of this chapter, which pursues the 'aporetic' method of raising and discussing various difficulties, is difficult. It may be said to fall into two parts. (1) The first part, in §§ 1–4, deals with the problem of the identity or difference of the excellence of the good man and that of the good citizen *in reference to all types of state.* Here the conclusion is that there is not identity, but difference—for the simple reason that there are many types of state, some good and some bad, and that the bad type demands a kind of excellence from its good citizen which is very different from that of the good man. (2) The second part, in §§ 5–18, deals with the problem *in reference to the ideal state.* This second part falls itself into two subdivisions. (*a*) The conclusion of the first subdivision, in §§ 5–7, is that the excellence of the good citizen of the ideal state is not *in all cases* identical with that of the good man. (*b*) The conclusion of the second subdivision, in §§ 8–18, is that the excellence of the good citizen of the ideal state is *in one case* identical with that of the good man. The case in which identity exists is that of the excellence of the good citizen of an ideal state who possesses the quality of wisdom required for ruling in addition to possessing the qualities required for being ruled.

It may be added that in the course of the argument Aristotle shifts his ground (as has already been observed in a previous note on § 16) about the unity of the excellence of the good man, considered in itself. Having said, in § 3, that the excellence of the good man is a 'single absolute excellence', he argues, in § 16, that his excellence (e.g. his justice) 'has different qualities'—one which fits him to act as ruler and one which fits him to act as subject. But though there is a shifting of ground, there is no contradiction.

CHAPTER V

There is a further question relating to citizenship, 'Can mechanics and labourers be citizens, and if they cannot be citizens, how are they to be described?' They should not be citizens, because they cannot achieve the excellence of the good citizen; they may be described as necessary conditions of the state. But the answer varies from one kind of constitution to another: in an aristocratic constitution, mechanics and labourers cannot be citizens; in an oligarchy, a rich mechanic may.

§ 1. There is still a question which remains to be considered in regard to citizenship. Is citizenship in the true sense to be limited to those who have the right of sharing in office, or must mechanics be also included in the ranks of citizens? If we hold that mechanics, who have no share in the offices of the state,[1] are

---

[1] Aristotle here seems to vary his view. Previously he has made only a share in judicial and deliberative office a requisite for citizenship: and this is a requisite which a mechanic might satisfy. Now he makes a share in the 'offices of the state', which would seem to mean the executive offices, a requisite; and this is a requisite which a mechanic, for want of time as well as capacity, cannot satisfy. Perhaps the cause of this change of view is the argument of the previous chapter, with its emphasis on knowledge of ruling as a part of good citizenship.

also to be included, we shall have some citizens who can never achieve the excellence of the good citizen [which requires an experience of ruling as well as of being ruled]. If, on the other hand, mechanics should not be called citizens, in what class are they to be placed? They are not resident aliens, neither are they foreigners: what is their class? § 2. It is difficult to say; but may we not hold **1278 a** that the difficulty does not involve us in any absurdity? [If mechanics cannot be placed in any of the classes mentioned] neither can slaves, nor freedmen. The truth is that we cannot include as citizens all who are 'necessary conditions' [without being 'integral parts'] of the state's existence.[1] Similarly, too, children [though they come nearer to being citizens] are not citizens in the same sense as adults. Adults are citizens absolutely; children are citizens only in a qualified sense and with a reservation—the reservation that they are undeveloped.[2] § 3. There were some states, in ancient times, where the class of mechanics was actually composed of slaves or foreigners only, and this explains why a great number of mechanics are slaves or foreigners even to-day. The best form of state [will not go so far, but at the same time it] will not make the mechanic a citizen. In states where mechanics *are* admitted to citizenship we shall have to say that the citizen excellence of which we have spoken [that of the good citizen who has experience of ruling as well as of being ruled] cannot be attained by every citizen, or by all who are simply free men, but can only be achieved by those who are free from menial duties. . . . § 4. Those who do menial duties may be divided into two classes—slaves, who do them for individuals, and mechanics and labourers, who do them for the community. . . .

If we start from this basis, and carry our inquiry a little further, the position of these mechanics and labourers will soon become evident; in fact, enough has already been said to make it clear, once the bearing of the argument is grasped.[3] § 5. Constitutions are various: there must thus be various kinds of citizens; more

[1] Aristotle here draws, by implication, a distinction between (1) those members of a polis who are 'integral parts' and actively share in its life, thus enjoying the status of *politēs* or citizen, and (2) those members of the polis who are 'necessary conditions' or *sine quibus non*, and whose share in its life is not that of active participation in its political activity, but only that of providing the material basis (of housing, food, commodities, and services) which is a condition of that activity. See below, Book VII, c. VIII.

[2] The argument here repeats that of c. I, § 5, of this book.

[3] 'Enough has already been said' is a reference to c. I, § 9 of this book, where it was noticed that constitutions differed and were of different qualities. It follows naturally from these differences that citizenship differs from constitution to constitution, and that under some constitutions the position of mechanics and hired labourers may be that of citizens, though it will not be such under other constitutions.

especially, there must be various kinds of citizens who are subjects. In one variety of constitution it will be necessary that mechanics and labourers should be citizens: in other varieties it will be impossible. It will be impossible, for example, where there is a constitution of the type termed 'aristocratic', with offices distributed on the basis of worth and excellence; for a man who lives the life of a mechanic or labourer cannot pursue the things which belong to excellence. § 6. The case is different in oligarchies. Even there, it is true, a labourer cannot be a citizen (participation in office depending on a high property qualification); but a mechanic may, for the simple reason that craftsmen often become rich men. § 7. Yet in Thebes [even when it was an oligarchy] there was a law that no man could share in office who had not abstained from selling in the market for a period of ten years. On the other hand there are many constitutions where the law goes to the length of admitting aliens to citizenship. There are, for example, some democracies where a man who has only a citizen-mother is admitted; and there are many states where the same privilege is given to persons of illegitimate birth. § 8. But the policy of extending citizenship so widely is [generally a temporary policy] due to a dearth of genuine citizens; and it is only a decrease of numbers which produces such legislation. When the population increases again [a different policy is gradually followed]: first sons of a slave-father or slave-mother are disqualified; then those who are born of a citizen-mother but an alien father; and finally citizenship is confined to those who are of citizen parentage on both sides.

§ 9. These considerations prove two things—that there are several different kinds of citizens, and that the name of citizen is particularly applicable to those who share in the offices and honours of the state. Homer accordingly speaks in the *Iliad* of a man being treated

like an alien man, *without honour*;

and it is true that those who do not share in the offices and honours of the state are just like resident aliens.[1] To deny men a share [may sometimes be justified, but] when it is done by subterfuge its only object is merely that of hoodwinking others.[2] § 10. Two conclusions also emerge from our discussion of the question, 'Is

[1] The Greek word *timē* which is here used means, like the Latin *honos*, both 'office' and 'honour'. The passage in the *Iliad* refers to honour in the latter sense: Aristotle himself is using it in the former; but it is natural to slide from the one into the other.

[2] This section of summary, § 9, is intended to recapitulate the fifth chapter. The section which follows, § 10, seems intended to recapitulate the fourth; but it does not do that very exactly. It may be an interpolation.

the excellence **1278 b** of the good man identical with that of the good citizen, or different from it?' The first is that there are some states in which the good man and the good citizen are identical, and some in which they are different. The second is that, in states of the former type, it is not all good citizens who are also good men, but only those among them who hold the position of statesmen—in other words those who direct or are capable of directing, either alone or in conjunction with others, the conduct of public affairs.

B

CONSTITUTIONS AND THEIR CLASSIFICATION (cc. vi–viii)

CHAPTER VI

The definition of a constitution. The classification of constitutions depends on (1) the ends pursued by states, and (2) the kind of authority exercised by their governments. The true end of a state is a good life, and this is the common interest: the right kind of authority is authority exercised in the common interest. We may thus distinguish 'right' constitutions, which are directed to the common interest, and 'wrong' or 'perverted' constitutions directed to the selfish interest of the ruling authority.

§ 1. Citizenship has now been defined and determined. We have next to consider the subject of constitutions. Is there a single type, or are there a number of types? If there are a number of types, what are these types; how many of them are there; and how do they differ?[1] A constitution (or polity) may be defined as 'the organization of a polis, in respect of its offices generally, but especially in respect of that particular office which is sovereign in all issues'.[2] The civic body [the *politeuma*,[3] or body of persons established in power by the polity] is everywhere the sovereign of the state; in fact the civic body is the polity (or constitution) itself.   § 2. In democratic states, for example, the people [or *dēmos*] is sovereign: in oligarchies, on the other hand, the few [or *oligoi*] have that position; and this difference of the sovereign bodies is the reason why we say that the two types of constitution differ—as we may equally apply the same reasoning to other types besides these.

[1] See Note U, p. 113.
[2] Another and similar, but fuller, definition is given in Book IV, c. 1, § 10.
[3] On the sense of the word *politeuma* or supreme civic authority see the previous note S on p. 106. Aristotle, as Newman remarks in his note, 'proves that the constitution is especially an ordering of the supreme authority by showing that the supreme authority is decisive of the character of the constitution, from which it follows that the main business of the constitution is to fix the supreme authority'.

[It is thus evident that there are a number of types of constitution, but before we discuss their nature] we must first ascertain two things—the nature of the end for which the state exists, and the various kinds of authority to which men and their associations are subject. § 3. So far as the first of these things is concerned, it has already been stated, in our first book (where we were concerned with the management of the household and the control of slaves), that 'man is an animal impelled by his nature to live in a polis'. A *natural impulse* is thus one reason why men desire to live a social life even when they stand in no need of mutual succour; but they are also drawn together by a *common interest*, in proportion as each attains a share in good life [through the union of all in a form of political association].[1] § 4. The good life is the chief end, both for the community as a whole and for each of us individually. But men also come together, and form and maintain political associations, merely for the sake of life;[2] for perhaps there is some element of the good even in the simple act of living, so long as the evils of existence do not preponderate too heavily. § 5. It is an evident fact that most men cling hard enough to life to be willing to endure a good deal of suffering, which implies that life has in it a sort of healthy happiness and a natural quality of pleasure.

[So far of the end for which the state exists. As regards the second question], it is easy enough to distinguish the various kinds of rule or authority of which men commonly speak; and indeed we have often had occasion to define them ourselves in works intended for the general public.[3] § 6. The rule of a master is one kind; and here, though there is really a common interest which unites the natural master and the natural slave, the fact remains that the rule is primarily exercised with a view to the master's

[1] Aristotle here suggests two ends for which the state, as an association, exists—(1) the end of providing satisfaction for a natural impulse, which exists and acts even apart from interest, and (2) the end of providing satisfaction for a common interest. This common interest, it should be noted, is not only or mainly economic: it is an interest in the attainment of a *good* (rather than a comfortable) life: and it requires for its satisfaction those institutions, such as a system of justice, which are necessary to such a life. It is this common interest in the attainment of a good life which is the chief end served by the state.

[2] In the previous section Aristotle has distinguished 'social life' and 'good life'. Here he introduces a third factor—the factor of 'life' itself, independently of its being 'social' or 'good'. The state or polis is connected with all three factors: it satisfies men's impulse towards a social life (which may exist apart from any need of mutual succour); it gives men a share in the good life which is their common interest; but it also helps men simply to live—and life itself is a thing of value. Compare Book I, c. II, § 8.

[3] Literally 'in exoteric discourses', as contrasted with the 'esoteric discourses' (such as the discourses or *logoi* on politics here translated) which were intended for the students of the Lyceum.

interest, and only incidentally with a view to that of the slave, who must be preserved in existence if the rule itself is to remain. § 7. Rule over wife and children, and over the household generally, is a second kind of rule, which we have called by the name of household management. Here the rule is either exercised in the interest of the ruled or for the attainment of some advantage common to both ruler and ruled. Essentially it is exercised in the interest of the ruled, as is also plainly the case with other arts besides that of ruling, such as medicine **1279 a** and gymnastics— though an art may incidentally be exercised for the benefit of its practitioner, and there is nothing to prevent (say) a trainer from becoming occasionally a member of the class he instructs, in the same sort of way as a steersman is always one of the crew. § 8. Thus a trainer or steersman primarily considers the good of those who are subject to his authority; but when he becomes one of them personally, he incidentally shares in the benefit of that good— the steersman thus being also a member of the crew, and the trainer (though still a trainer) becoming also a member of the class which he instructs.

§ 9. This principle also applies to a third kind of rule—that exercised by the holders of political office. When the constitution of a state is constructed on the principle that its members are equals and peers, the citizens think it proper that they should hold office by turns [which implies that the office of ruler is primarily intended for the benefit of the ruled and is therefore a duty to be undertaken by each in turn, though incidentally the ruler shares in the general benefit by virtue of being himself a member of the citizen body]. At any rate this is the natural system, and the system which used to be followed in the days when men believed that they ought to serve by turns, and each assumed that others would take over the duty of considering his benefit, just as he had himself, during his term of office, considered the interest of others. § 10. To-day the case is altered. Moved by the profits to be derived from office and the handling of public property, men want to hold office continuously. It is as if the holders of office were sick men, who got the benefit of permanent health [by being permanently in office]: at any rate their ardour for office is just what it would be if that were the case. § 11. The conclusion which follows is clear. Those constitutions which consider the common interest are *right* constitutions, judged by the standard of absolute justice. Those constitutions which consider only the personal interest of the rulers are all *wrong* constitutions, or *perversions* of the right forms. Such perverted forms are despotic [i.e. calculated on the model of the rule of a master, or 'despotēs', over slaves]; whereas the polis is an association of freemen.[1]

NOTE U (p. 110): *The course of the argument in* c. VI

In the first two sections of c. I of this book Aristotle had begun by raising the question 'What is a polis?' In order to answer that question, he found it first necessary to ask (following his analytic method of resolving a compound into its elements), 'What is the member of a polis, or, in other words, the citizen?' The first five chapters have fully discussed that question. We might now expect him to return to the previous question, 'What is a polis?' But that question has already been answered in the course of the discussion of the other question (cf. the definition of the polis in c. I, § 12); and Aristotle now turns to a different question, 'What is a *politeia*, or constitution?' This is a question which logically follows on the discussion of citizenship. Since citizenship is participation in office, and since participation in office is regulated by the constitution, a discussion of the *politēs* necessarily leads to a discussion of the *politeia*.

NOTE V: *The basis of the classification of constitutions*

This preliminary classification of constitutions into the two *genera* of right and wrong, or normal and perverted, is based on the principle that political rule, by virtue of its specific nature, is essentially for the benefit of the ruled. That is the principle of absolute justice in regard to the proper use of political power; and it is a principle which squares with what has been said above, in § 4, about the main end of the polis—that it is a *common* interest, which, as such, is for the benefit not of a section, but of each and all. Aristotle has thus concluded in this chapter (partly from what has been said in §§ 2-5 about the end of the polis, and partly from what has been said in §§ 5-10 about the specific nature of political rule, or rule over a political association of freemen, as contrasted with other forms of rule) that the fundamental principle to be followed in a polis, and therefore in its *politeia* or constitution, is the principle of the holding of office for the common interest of all the members, and particularly for the interest of the ruled, who are nearly the whole of the members. That principle separates the right constitutions which follow it from the wrong which contravene it.

CHAPTER VII

These two types of constitution each fall into three subdivisions on the basis of number, i.e. according as the One, or the Few, or the Many, are the ruling authority in each type. We have thus, as the three subdivisions of the 'right' type, Kingship, Aristocracy, and 'Polity': as the three subdivisions of the 'wrong' type, Tyranny, Oligarchy, and Democracy.

§ 1. Now that these matters have been determined, the next subject for consideration is the number and nature of the different constitutions. We may first examine the class of right constitutions [and consider its different species]; the different perversions will at

---

[1] See Note V.

once be apparent when the right constitutions have been determined. § 2. The term 'constitution' [*politeia*] signifies the same
thing as the term 'civic body' [*politeuma*]. The civic body in every
polis is the sovereign (*to kȳrion*); and the sovereign must necessarily be either One, or Few, or Many. On this basis we may say
that when the One, or the Few, or the Many, rule with a view to
the common interest, the constitutions under which they do so
must necessarily be right constitutions. On the other hand the
constitutions directed to the personal interest of the One, or the
Few, or the Masses, must necessarily be perversions. [They deviate
from the true standard by not regarding the interest of all, and
are thus involved in a dilemma]: either the name of citizen cannot
be given to persons who share in the constitution [but whose
interests are not regarded], or, if the name is to be given, they must
have their share of the benefits.[1] § 3. Among forms of government
by a single person Kingship, in the general use of language, denotes
the species which looks to the common interest. Among forms
of government by a few persons (but more than one) Aristocracy
denotes the species [which similarly looks to that interest]—that
name being given to this species either because the best [*aristoi*]
are the rulers, or because its object is what is best [*ariston*] for the
state and its members. Finally, when the masses govern the state
with a view to the common interest, the name used for this species
is the generic name common to all constitutions (or polities)—the
name of 'Polity'. § 4. There is a good reason for the usage [which
gives to this form the generic name, and not a special name which
connotes, as the name 'Aristocracy' does, a special excellence]. It
is possible for one man, or a few, to be of outstanding excellence;
but when it comes to a large number, we can hardly expect a fine
edge of all the varieties of excellence. What we can expect
particularly is the military kind **1279 b** of excellence, which is the
kind that shows itself in a mass. This is the reason why the
defence forces are the most sovereign body under this constitution, and those who possess arms are the persons who enjoy
constitutional rights.

§ 5. [These are the three subdivisions of the class of right
constitutions.] Three perversions correspond to them. Tyranny

---

[1] It follows from what has been said, as Aristotle proceeds to argue, (1) that
the criterion of the end of the polis and the true nature of political rule gives
us the two genera of right and wrong constitutions; and (2) that the criterion of
number gives us three species of each genus—the three species of monarchy,
aristocracy, and 'polity' (in a peculiar sense of that word) in the genus of right
constitutions; and the three species of tyranny, oligarchy, and 'democracy'
(again, as we shall see, in a somewhat peculiar sense of the word) in the genus
of wrong constitutions. But the criterion of number, as the argument proceeds
turns into a criterion of class, as it does in the course of the next chapter.

is the perversion of Kingship; Oligarchy of Aristocracy; and Democracy of Polity. Tyranny is a government by a single person directed to the interest of that person; Oligarchy is directed to the interest of the well-to-do;[1] Democracy is directed to the interest of the poorer classes. None of the three is directed to the advantage of the whole body of citizens.

CHAPTER VIII

The basis of number is not, however, adequate. The real basis, at any rate so far as oligarchy and democracy are concerned, is social class: what makes an oligarchy is the rule of the rich (rather than the few), and what makes a democracy is the rule of the poor (rather than the many). Number is an accidental, and not an essential attribute; but the accidental generally accompanies the essential.

§ 1. We must treat at somewhat greater length of the nature of each of these last constitutions. There are certain difficulties involved; and when one is pursuing a philosophical method of inquiry in any branch of study, and not merely looking to practical considerations, the proper course is to set out the truth about every particular with no neglect or omission. § 2. Tyranny, as has just been said, is single-person government of the political association on the lines of despotism [i.e. treating the citizens as a master treats slaves]: oligarchy exists where those who have property are the sovereign authority of the constitution; and conversely democracy exists where the sovereign authority is composed of the poorer classes, and not of the owners of property. § 3. The first difficulty which arises concerns the definition just given [of democracy and oligarchy]. We have defined democracy as the sovereignty of numbers; but we can conceive a case in which the majority who hold the sovereignty in a state are the well-to-do. Similarly oligarchy is generally stated to be the sovereignty of a small number; but it might conceivably happen that the poorer classes were fewer in number than the well-to-do, and yet—in virtue of superior vigour—were the sovereign authority of the constitution. In neither case could the definition previously given of these constitutions be regarded as true. § 4. We might attempt to overcome the difficulty by combining both of the factors— wealth with paucity of numbers, and poverty with mass. On this basis oligarchy might be defined as the constitution under

---

[1] It will be noticed that Aristotle is here introducing, in lieu of the criterion of number, that of class; and he proceeds in the next chapter further along that line. What makes an oligarchy is not so much the fact that a few men rule for their own advantage: it is rather the fact that a wealthy class rules; and oligarchy is thus really plutocracy.

which the rich, being also few in number, hold the offices of the state; and similarly democracy might be defined as the constitution under which the poor, being also many in number, are in control. But this involves us in another difficulty.   § 5. If our new definition is exhaustive, and there are no forms of oligarchy and democracy other than those enumerated in that definition, what names are we to give to the constitutions just suggested as conceivable—those where the wealthy form a majority and the poor a minority, and where the wealthy majority in the one case, and the poor minority in the other, are the sovereign authority of the constitution?   § 6. The course of the argument thus appears to show that the factor of number—the small number of the sovereign body in oligarchies, or the large number in democracies—is an accidental attribute, due to the simple fact that the wealthy are generally few and the poor are generally numerous. Therefore the causes originally mentioned [i.e. small and large numbers] are not in fact the real causes of the difference between oligarchies and democracies.   § 7. The real ground of the difference between oligarchy and democracy is poverty and riches. It is inevitable that any constitution 1280 a should be an oligarchy if the rulers under it are rulers in virtue of riches, whether they are few or many; and it is equally inevitable that a constitution under which the poor rule should be a democracy.

§ 8. It happens, however, as we have just remarked, [and this is why number becomes an accidental attribute of both of these constitutions], that the rich are few and the poor are numerous. It is only a few who have riches, but all alike share in free status; and these are the real grounds on which the two parties [the oligarchical and the democratic] dispute the control of the constitution.[1]

C

THE PRINCIPLES OF OLIGARCHY AND DEMOCRACY, AND THE NATURE OF DISTRIBUTIVE JUSTICE (CC. IX–XIII)

CHAPTER IX

The principle of a constitution is its conception of justice; and this is the fundamental ground of difference between oligarchy and democracy. Democrats hold that if men are equal by birth, they should in justice have equal rights: oligarchs hold that if they are unequal in wealth, they should in justice have unequal rights. True justice means that those who have contributed to the end of the state should have rights

---

[1] Aristotle's general account of the classification of constitutions in cc. VI–VIII of this book may be compared with the accounts given in the *Ethics* and the *Rhetoric* (see Appendix III. A and B).

*in proportion to their contribution to that end. The end of the state
is not mere life, nor an alliance for mutual defence; it is the common
promotion of a good quality of life. We must distinguish between the
necessary conditions of the state's existence (contiguity, consanguinity,
and economic co-operation) and its operative aim. The operative aim
is always the promotion of a good quality of life; and those who contribute most to the realization of that aim should in justice have most
rights.*

§ 1. We must next ascertain [now that we have discovered the
social ground on which they rest] what are the distinctive principles attributed by their advocates to oligarchy and democracy,
and what are the oligarchical and the democratic conceptions of
justice.[1] Both oligarchs and democrats have a hold on a sort of
conception of justice; but they both fail to carry it far enough, and
neither of them expresses the true conception of justice in the
whole of its range. In democracies, for example, justice is considered to mean equality [in the distribution of office]. It does
mean equality—but equality for those who are equal, and not for
all. § 2. In oligarchies, again, inequality in the distribution of
office is considered to be just; and indeed it is—but only for those
who are unequal, and not for all. The advocates of oligarchy and
democracy both refuse to consider this factor—who are the persons
to whom their principles properly apply—and they both make
erroneous judgements. The reason is that they are judging *in their
own case*; and most men, as a rule, are bad judges where their own
interests are involved. § 3. Justice is relative to persons; and a
just distribution is one in which the relative values of the things
given correspond to those of the persons receiving—a point which
has already been made in the *Ethics*. [It follows that a just distribution of offices among a number of different persons will involve
a consideration of the personal values, or merits, of each of those
persons.] But the advocates of oligarchy and democracy, while
they agree about what constitutes equality in the *thing*, disagree
about what constitutes it in *persons*.[2] The main reason for this is
the reason just stated—they are judging, and judging erroneously,
in their own case; but there is also another reason—they are misled
by the fact that they are professing a sort of conception of justice,
and professing it up to a point, into thinking that they profess one

[1] The fact that democracy and oligarchy, as perversions of right constitutions,
rest on a social class, is essentially connected with the 'distinctive principle' of
each, which leads them to *justify* the predominance of that class. This 'distinctive principle' is thus, in effect, a conception of justice—that is to say, of *distributive* justice, or, in other words, of the justice which distributes the offices of
the state among its members on a plan or principle.

[2] See Note W, p. 120.

which is absolute and complete.   § 4. The oligarchs think that superiority on one point—in their case wealth—means superiority on all: the democrats believe that equality in one respect—for instance, that of free birth—means equality all round.

§ 5. Both sides, however, fail to mention the really cardinal factor [i.e. the nature of the end for which the state exists]. If property were the end for which men came together and formed an association, men's share [in the offices and honours] of the state would be proportionate to their share of property; and in that case the argument of the oligarchical side—that it is not just for a man who has contributed one pound to share equally in a sum of a hundred pounds (or, for that matter, in the interest accruing upon that sum) with the man who has contributed all the rest—would appear to be a strong argument.   § 6. But the end of the state is not mere life; it is, rather, a good quality of life. [If mere life were the end], there might be a state of slaves, or even a state of animals; but in the world as we know it any such state is impossible, because slaves and animals do not share in true felicity[1] and free choice [i.e. the attributes of a good quality of life]. Similarly, it is not the end of the state to provide an alliance for mutual defence against all injury, or to ease exchange and promote economic inter-course. If that had been the end, the Etruscans and the Cartha-ginians [who are united by such bonds] would be in the position of belonging to a single state; and the same would be true of all peoples who have commercial treaties with one another.   § 7. It is true that such peoples have agreements about imports and exports; treaties to ensure just conduct [in the course of trade]; and written terms of alliance for mutual defence. On the other hand they have no common offices of state to deal with these matters: each, on the contrary, **1280 b** has its own offices, confined to itself. Neither of the parties concerns itself to ensure a proper quality of character among the members of the other;[2] neither of them seeks to ensure that all who are included in the scope of the treaties shall be free from injustice[3] and from any form of vice; and neither of them goes beyond the aim of preventing its own mem-bers from committing injustice [in the course of trade] against the members of the other.   § 8. But it is the cardinal issue of goodness

---

[1] The Greek word is *eudaimonia*, which means something higher than the mere happiness of pleasure (*hēdonē*), and involves an 'energy of the spirit' impossible to slaves and animals. In Book VII, c. XIII, § 5, Aristotle defines *eudaimonia* as 'the energy and practice of goodness'. See the Introduction lxxv–lxxvi.

[2] Aristotle here implies (what he proceeds to make explicit) that a true state does concern itself to secure *excellence* of character and conduct among its members; that its end is essentially a *good* quality of life; and that its laws are intended to make the citizens *good* and just men.

[3] I.e. unrighteousness.

or badness in the life of the polis which always engages the attention of any state that concerns itself to secure a system of good laws well obeyed [*eunomia*]. The conclusion which clearly follows is that any polis which is truly so called, and is not merely one in name, must devote itself to the end of encouraging goodness. Otherwise, a political association sinks into a mere alliance, which only differs in space [i.e. in the contiguity of its members] from other forms of alliance where the members live at a distance from one another. Otherwise, too, law becomes a mere covenant—or (in the phrase of the Sophist Lycophron) 'a guarantor of men's rights against one another'—instead of being, as it should be, a rule of life such as will make the members of a polis good and just.[1]

§ 9. That this is the case [i.e. that a polis is truly a polis only when it makes the encouragement of goodness its end] may be readily proved.[2] If two different sites could be united in one, so that the polis of Megara and that of Corinth were embraced by a single wall, that would not make a single polis. If the citizens of two cities intermarried with one another, that would not make a single polis—even though intermarriage is one of the forms of social life which are characteristic of a polis. § 10. Nor would it make a polis if a number of persons—living at a distance from one another, but not at so great a distance but that they could still associate—had a common system of laws to prevent their injuring one another in the course of exchange. We can imagine, for instance, one being a carpenter, another a farmer, a third a shoemaker, and others producing other goods; and we can imagine a total number of as many as 10,000. But if these people were associated in nothing further than matters such as exchange and alliance, they would still have failed to reach the stage of a polis. § 11. Why should this be the case? It cannot be ascribed to any lack of contiguity in such an association. The members of a group so constituted might come together on a single site; but if that were all—if each still treated his private house as if it were a state, and all of them still confined their mutual assistance to action against aggressors (as if it were only a question of a defensive alliance)—if, in a word, the spirit of their intercourse were still the same after their coming together as it had been when they were living apart—their association, even on its new basis, could not be deemed by any accurate thinker to be a polis. § 12. It is clear, therefore, that a polis is not an association for residence on a common site, or for the sake of preventing mutual injustice and easing exchange. These are indeed conditions which must be present

---

[1] On the general Greek notion of law (or *nomos*) see the Introduction, IV. § 3, and the references there given.   [2] See Note X, p. 121.

before a polis can exist; but the presence of all these conditions is not enough, in itself, to constitute a polis. What constitutes a polis is an association of households and clans in a good life, for the sake of attaining a perfect and self-sufficing existence.[1]   § 13. This consummation, however, will not be reached unless the members inhabit one and the self-same place and practise intermarriage.[2] It was for this reason [i.e. to provide these necessary conditions] that the various institutions of a common social life—marriage-connexions, kin-groups, religious gatherings, and social pastimes generally—arose in cities. But these institutions are the business of friendship [and not the purpose of the polis]. It is friendship [and not a polis] which consists in the pursuit of a common social life. The end and purpose of a polis is the good life, and the institutions of social life are means to that end. § 14. A polis is constituted **1281 a** by the association of families and villages in a perfect and self-sufficing existence; and such an existence, on our definition, consists in a life of true felicity and goodness.

It is therefore for the sake of good actions, and not for the sake of social life, that political associations must be considered to exist. § 15. [This conclusion enables us to attain a proper conception of justice.] Those who contribute most to an association of this character [i.e. who contribute most to good action] have a greater share in the polis [and should therefore, in justice, receive a larger recognition from it] than those who are equal to them (or even greater) in free birth and descent, but unequal in civic excellence, or than those who surpass them in wealth but are surpassed by them in excellence.[3] From what has been said it is plain that both sides to the dispute about constitutions [i.e. both the democratic and the oligarchical side] profess only a partial conception of justice.

NOTE W (p. 117): *The theory of distributive justice*

Aristotle is here enunciating a theory of distributive justice which goes on the basis of proportionate equality. As A and B have given to the state,

[1] See Book I, c. II, § 8 (and note B on p. 7), for the implications of this definition.

[2] In other words, contiguity and consanguinity are necessary conditions, or *sine quibus non*; but the essence, and the *causa causans*, is co-operation in a common scheme of good life. Social life (*to suzēn*), arising from the ties of contiguity and consanguinity, is a necessary basis; but the essential structure which arises on this basis is a good life (*to eu zēn*).

[3] The conception of distributive justice here enunciated is that the criterion of contribution to the specific and essential end of the state—the performance of good actions—is greater than either the democratic criterion of free birth or the oligarchical criterion of wealth. Those who contribute more to the performance of good actions in and by the association, and who thus show a greater 'civic excellence' (i.e. a higher quality of membership of the association), deserve more from the polis—even if, on the ground of free birth, they are only equal or even inferior, and even if, on the ground of wealth, they are actually inferior.

in the way of personal merit and personal contribution to its well-being, so A and B should receive from the state, in the way of office and honour. If the personal merit and personal contribution of both are equal, they will receive equal amounts : if they are unequal, they will receive unequal amounts : but in either case the basis of proportionate equality will be observed, and the proportion between the thing A receives and A's personal merit will be the same as that between the thing B receives and *his* personal merit. The reference to the *Ethics* is to Book V, c. III, §§ 4 and following (1131 a 14 onwards). We may notice especially the phrase in the *Ethics*, 'The same equality will exist between the persons and the things concerned' ; . . . 'if they are not equal, they will not have what is equal—but this is the origin of quarrels and complaints'. (See Appendix II. A. 2, p. 363.)

NOTE X (p. 119): *Aristotle's method of determining the state's purpose*

The method of proof which follows is a method of exhaustion of possibilities. Aristotle takes various possibilities—(1) contiguity of place, (2) a common scheme of intermarriage, (3) a common scheme for the prevention of mutual injuries—and proves that none of them is sufficient to constitute a polis. It is only a common scheme for the encouragement of a good quality of life which can be the basis of a polis. . . . The same method of exhaustion of possibilities has been followed in the definition of the citizen (c. I, §§ 4–5), and in the discussion of the identity of the state (c. III, §§ 1–9).

We may also note that the same problem which is here discussed—the problem of the true end of the state, which 'constitutes' it and makes it a state—has already been discussed in c. VI, §§ 3–5. In that passage the problem was discussed as a preliminary to a classification of states. Here it is again discussed, but now as a preliminary to a proper notion of distributive justice. We can only determine properly the principle on which offices and honours should be distributed after we have ascertained the true purpose of the state. It will be contributions to that purpose which must justly be rewarded in the distribution of offices and honours ; and that purpose will thus be the standard of distributive justice.

CHAPTER X

What person or body of persons should be sovereign in a state—the people, the rich, the better sort of citizens, the one best, or the tyrant? All these alternatives present difficulties; and there is a difficulty even in a further alternative—that no person or body of persons, but law, should be sovereign.

§ 1. A difficulty arises when we turn to consider what body of persons should be sovereign in the polis.[1] [We can imagine five

[1] Hitherto, in c. IX, Aristotle has been considering what persons, on the ground of distributive justice, should have a superior recognition in the award of office and honours. He now turns to consider what persons, or body of persons, should receive supreme recognition, and thus be vested with supreme authority or sovereignty. It is still a question of distributive justice; but that question now advances from a consideration of who should have more, and on what grounds they should have more, to a consideration of who should have most, and on what grounds they should have most.

alternatives]: the people at large (*to plēthos*); the wealthy; the better sort of men; the one man who is best of all; the tyrant. But all these alternatives appear to involve unpleasant results: indeed, how can it be otherwise? [Take, for example, the first alternative.] What if the poor, on the ground of their being a majority, proceed to divide among themselves the possessions of the wealthy—will not this be unjust? 'No, by heaven' (a democrat may reply); 'it has been justly decreed so by the sovereign.' § 2. 'But if this is not the extreme of injustice' (we may reply in turn), 'what *is*?' Whenever a majority of any sort, irrespective of wealth or poverty, divides among its members the possessions of a minority, that majority is obviously ruining the state. But goodness can never ruin anything that has goodness, nor can justice, in its nature, be ruinous to a state. It is therefore clear that a law of this kind [i.e. a law of spoliation passed by a majority of any sort] cannot possibly be just. § 3. [To treat such a law as just is really to justify tyranny.] The tyrant's acts too [on the principle alleged by the democrats that any decree of the sovereign is just] must necessarily be just; for he too uses coercion by virtue of superior power in just the same sort of way as the people coerce the wealthy. [We may now take the alternative that the wealthy are sovereign.] Is it just that a minority composed of the wealthy should rule? If they too behave like the others—if they plunder and confiscate the property of the people—can their action be called just? If it can, the action of the people, in the converse case, must equally be termed just. § 4. It is clear that all these acts of oppression [whether by the people, the tyrant, or the wealthy] are mean and unjust. [But what of the next alternative?] Should the better sort of men have authority and be sovereign in all matters? In that case, the rest of the citizens will necessarily be debarred from honours, since they will not enjoy the honour of holding civic office. We speak of offices as honours; and when a single set of persons hold office permanently, the rest of the community must necessarily be debarred from all honours. § 5. [We come to a last alternative.] Is it better than any of the other alternatives that the one best man should rule? This is still more oligarchical [than the rule of the wealthy few or the few of the better sort], because the number of those debarred from honours is even greater. It may perhaps be urged that there is still another alternative; that it is a poor sort of policy to vest sovereignty in any person [or body of persons], subject as persons are to the passions that beset men's souls; and that it is better to vest it in law. [But this does not solve the difficulty.] The law itself may incline either towards oligarchy or towards democracy; and what difference will the sovereignty

of law then make in the problems which have just been raised?
The consequences already stated will follow just the same.

CHAPTER XI

*It is possible, however, to defend the alternative that the people should
be sovereign. The people, when they are assembled, have a combination
of qualities which enables them to deliberate wisely and to judge
soundly. This suggests that they have a claim to be the sovereign body;
it also suggests the scope of affairs in which they should be sovereign, or
the powers which they should exercise. They should exercise deliberative and judicial functions; in particular, they should elect the magistrates and examine their conduct at the end of their tenure. Two
objections may be raised. (1) It may be argued that experts are better
judges than the non-expert; but this objection may be met by reference
to (a) the combination of qualities in the assembled people (which
makes them collectively better judges than the expert), and (b) their
knowing 'how the shoe pinches' (which enables them to pass judgement
on the behaviour of magistrates). (2) It may be urged that the people,
if they have such powers, have more authority than the better sort of
citizens who hold office as magistrates—though they are not of so
good a quality; but we may answer to this that the people as a whole
may well be of a high quality. We have always, however, to remember
that rightly constituted laws should be the final sovereign, and that
personal authority of any sort should only act in the particular cases
which cannot be covered by a general law.*

§ 1. The other alternatives may be reserved for a later inquiry;
but the first of the alternatives suggested—that the people at large
should be sovereign rather than the few best—would appear to be
defensible, and while it presents some difficulty it perhaps also
contains some truth. § 2. There is this to be said for the Many.
Each of them by himself may not be of a good **1281 b** quality; but
when they all come together it is possible that they may surpass—
collectively and as a body, although not individually—the quality
of the few best. Feasts to which many contribute may excel those
provided at one man's expense. In the same way, when there are
many [who contribute to the process of deliberation], each can
bring his share of goodness and moral prudence; and when all
meet together the people may thus become something in the nature
of a single person, who—as he has many feet, many hands, and
many senses—may also have many qualities of character and intelligence. § 3. This is the reason why the Many are also better judges
[than the few] of music and the writings of poets: some appreciate one part, some another, and all together appreciate all.[1]

[1] See Note Y, p. 127.

§ 4. [We may note that this combination of qualities, which gives the Many their merit, can also be traced in cases of *individual* merit.] The thing which makes a good man differ from a unit in the crowd—as it is also the thing which is generally said to make a beautiful person differ from one who is not beautiful, or an artistic representation differ from ordinary reality—is that elements which are elsewhere scattered and separate are here combined in a unity. [It is this unity which counts]; for if you take the elements separately, you may say of an artistic representation that it is surpassed by the eye of this person or by some other feature of that.[1]

§ 5. It is not clear, however, that this combination of qualities, which we have made the ground of distinction between the many and the few best, is true of all popular bodies and all large masses of men. Perhaps it may be said, 'By heaven, it is clear that there are some bodies of which it cannot possibly be true; for if you included them, you would, by the same token, be bound to include a herd of beasts. That would be absurd; and yet what difference is there between these bodies and a herd of beasts?' All the same, and in spite of this objection, there is nothing to prevent the view we have stated from being true of *some* popular bodies.

§ 6. It would thus seem possible to solve, by the considerations we have advanced, both the problem raised in the previous chapter 'What body of *persons* should be sovereign?' and the further problem which follows upon it, 'What are the *matters* over which freemen, or the general body of citizens—men of the sort who neither have wealth nor can make any claim on the ground of goodness—should properly exercise sovereignty?'[2] § 7. It may be argued, from one point of view, that it is dangerous for men of this sort to share in the highest offices, as injustice may lead them into wrongdoing, and thoughtlessness into error. But it may also be argued, from another point of view, that there is serious risk in not letting them have *some* share in the enjoyment of power; for a state with a body of disfranchised citizens who are

[1] Aristotle here follows a subtle line of argument, in drawing an analogy between the composite quality of the Many and the composite quality which may also be traced in the individual good man, or in a beautiful individual, or in an individual work of art. But his fundamental contention is simple. In each case there is a general system of unity: in each case this system of unity issues in something which *as a whole* is the best—though in each case any particular constituent of the whole may not be the best.

[2] Aristotle states two questions; but he assumes that the first has already been answered, and that 'the body of persons which should be sovereign' is the general body of free citizens, who have no individual claims based on wealth or goodness, but a common claim based on common freedom. On this basis he addresses himself, in the rest of the chapter, to the second problem, 'What is the scope of the sovereignty of this body, and over what matters should it be exercised?'

numerous and poor must necessarily be a state which is full of enemies.   § 8. The alternative left is to let them share in the deliberative and judicial functions;[1] and we thus find Solon, and some of the other legislators, giving the people the two general functions of electing the magistrates to office and of calling them to account at the end of their tenure of office, but *not* the right of holding office themselves in their individual capacity.   § 9. [There is wisdom in such a policy.] When they all meet together, the people display a good enough gift of perception, and combined with the better class they are of service to the state (just as impure food, when it is mixed with pure, makes the whole concoction more nutritious than a small amount of the pure would be); but each of them is imperfect in the judgements he forms by himself.

§ 10. But this arrangement of the constitution [which gives the people deliberative and judicial functions] presents some difficulties. The first difficulty is that it may well be held that the function of judging when medical attendance has been properly given [a function analogous to that of the people in judging the conduct of magistrates] should belong to those whose profession it is to attend patients and cure the complaints from which they suffer— in a word, to members of the medical profession. The same may be held to be true of all other professions and arts; **1282 a** and just as doctors should have their conduct examined before a body of doctors, so, too, should those who follow other professions have theirs examined before a body of members of their own profession. § 11. [We may note, however, that] the term 'doctor' is used in three different senses. It is applied to the ordinary practitioner: it is applied to the specialist who directs the course of treatment; and it is also applied to the man who has some general knowledge of the art of medicine. (There are men of this last type to be found in connexion with nearly all the arts; and we credit them with the power of judging as much as we do the experts—i.e. the practitioners and specialists.)[2]   § 12. When we turn to consider the matter of election [as distinct from examination], the same principles would appear to apply. To make a proper election, it may

---

[1] These are the rights assigned to the citizen, as such, in c. 1, § 11 of this book. In the rest of the sentence, 'electing the magistrates' may be regarded as an exercise of the deliberative power, and 'calling them to account' as an exercise of the judicial.

[2] Aristotle has here suggested a distinction which may prove, after all, to justify the right of the people (as possessed, collectively, of general knowledge) to *examine* the conduct of magistrates. Instead, however, of pursuing this train of thought immediately to its conclusion, he turns aside in § 12 from the right of examining to that of *electing*, and here he begins by pressing the idea of the right of the expert to elect. Eventually, however, in § 14, he returns to the idea of the rights belonging to men of general knowledge—alike in respect of election and in respect of examination.

be argued, is equally the work of experts. It is the work of those who are versed in geometry to choose a geometrician, or, again, of those who are acquainted with steering to choose a steersman; and even if, in some occupations and arts, there are some non-experts who also share in the ability to choose, they do not share in a higher degree than the experts. § 13. It would thus appear, on this line of argument, that the people should not be made sovereign, either in the matter of the election of magistrates or in that of their examination. § 14. It may be, however, that these arguments are not altogether well founded. In the first place we have to remember our own previous argument of the combination of qualities which is to be found in the people—provided, that is to say, that they are not debased in character. Each individual may indeed, be a worse judge than the experts; but all, when they meet together,[1] are either better than experts or at any rate no worse. In the second place, there are a number of arts in which the creative artist is not the only, or even the best, judge. These are the arts whose products can be understood and judged even by those who do not possess any skill in the art. A house, for instance, is something which can be understood by others besides the builder: indeed the user of a house—or in other words the house-holder—will judge it even better than he does. In the same way a pilot will judge a rudder better than a shipwright does; and the diner—not the cook—will be the best judge of a feast.

§ 15. The first difficulty which confronts our argument about the rights of the people would appear to be answered sufficiently by these considerations. But there is a second difficulty still to be faced, which is connected with the first. It would seem to be absurd that persons of a poor quality should be sovereign on issues which are more important than those assigned to the better sort of citizens. The election of magistrates, and their examination at the end of their tenure, are the most important of issues; and yet there are constitutions, as we have seen, under which these issues are assigned to popular bodies, and where a popular body is sovereign in all such matters. § 16. To add to the difficulty, membership of the assembly, which carries deliberative and judicial functions, is vested in persons of little property and of any age; but a high property qualification is demanded from those who serve

---

[1] This qualification, 'when they meet together', is a qualification which recurs (cf. *supra*, §§ 2, 9). The people at large have the merit of a good collective judgement not as a static mass, but when they are dynamic—in other words when they assemble, and when the process of debate begins. It is thus not an unfair gloss to suggest that Aristotle by implication assumes that the dialectic of debate is the final foundation of the principle of popular government, so far as he accepts that principle. In other words, democracy is based upon discussion.

as treasurers or generals, or hold any of the highest offices. This difficulty too may, however, be met in the same way as the first; and the practice followed in these constitutions is perhaps, after all, correct. § 17. It is not the individual member of the judicial court, or the council,[1] or the assembly, who is vested with office: it is the court as a whole, the council as a whole, the popular assembly as a whole, which is vested; and each individual member —whether of the council, the assembly, or the court—is simply a part of the whole. § 18. It is therefore just and proper that the people, from which the assembly, the council, and the court are constituted, should be sovereign on issues more important than those assigned to the better sort of citizens. It may be added that the collective property of the members of all these bodies is greater than that of the persons who either as individuals or as members of small bodies hold the highest [executive] offices.

§ 19. This may serve as a settlement of the difficulties which have been **1282 b** discussed. But the discussion of the first of these difficulties [whether expert skill or general knowledge should be the sovereign authority] leads to one conclusion above all others. Rightly constituted laws should be the final sovereign; and personal rule, whether it be exercised by a single person or a body of persons, should be sovereign only in those matters on which law is unable, owing to the difficulty of framing general rules for all contingencies, to make an exact pronouncement.[2] § 20. But what rightly constituted laws ought to be is a matter that is not yet clear; and here we are still confronted by the difficulty stated at the end of the previous chapter—that law itself may have a bias in favour of one class or another. Equally with the constitutions to which they belong [and *according to* the constitutions to which they belong] laws must be good or bad, just or unjust. § 21. The one clear fact is that laws must be constituted in accordance with constitutions; and if this is the case, it follows that laws which are in accordance with right constitutions must necessarily be just, and laws which are in accordance with wrong or perverted constitutions must be unjust.

NOTE Y (p. 123): *The democratic argument in politics and aesthetics*

It is to be noticed that Aristotle here applies the same 'democratic'

---

[1] Aristotle here includes the council (*boulē*) along with the assembly (*ecclēsia*) in his discussion of the rights of the people. Strictly speaking the council—at Athens a small body of 500 members which prepared the business for the assembly (see p. 383 *infra*)—was a body of a different type from the popular courts and the assembly. But election to the council was by lot, from all classes of citizens over the age of 30; and Aristotle thus naturally includes membership of the council in his discussion of popular rights.

[2] See Note Z, p. 128.

argument (if it may so be called) both to politics and aesthetics. The two go together in his view—just as, in Athenian practice, the people at large were asked not only to pronounce on politics in the assembly, but also to vote on architectural plans and (through judges drawn by lot from a large panel) to award the dramatic prizes in the theatre. Plato also applied the same line of argument to politics and aesthetics—but in an opposite direction. He condemned 'theatrocracy' in matters of art along with democracy in politics. Speaking primarily of music (*Laws* 700 E–701 A) he notes: 'Our once silent audiences have found a voice, in the persuasion that they understand what is good and bad in art: the old "sovereignty of the best" in that sphere has given way to an evil "sovereignty of the audience" ['theatrocratia']: . . . no great harm would have been done, so long as the democracy was confined to art, . . . but as things are with us, music has given occasion to a general conceit of knowledge and contempt for law, and liberty [i.e. political democracy] has followed in their train' (A. E. Taylor's translation).

It may be added that later Athenian practice, as described in Aristotle's treatise on the *Constitution of Athens* (c. XLIX, § 3), assigned to a popular law-court the right of deciding on architectural and other designs, which had once belonged to the council. The council was held to have shown favouritism: the popular law-court was substituted as a more unbiased body. See Appendix IV. B. 4, p. 384, n. 1.

Finally, and in regard to Aristotle's general argument in favour of the capacity and the efficiency of the general civic body when its members 'meet together' (see § 14 of this chapter, and the note), we may note that it squares (*a*) with his own definition of citizenship in c. I (see § 12 of that chapter, and the note), and (*b*) with the common Greek idea that the general civic body is *to kyrion* in matters of deliberation, and is entitled to express its public opinion through the *dikastēria* in matters of justice (see the Introduction, IV. 2 and 3, and—on the action of the *dikastēria*— p. 371, n. 3).

NOTE Z (p. 127): *Aristotle's conception of the sovereignty of law*

To understand Aristotle's conception of the sovereignty of law and the subordination of magistrates to its rule we must remember the nature of Athenian law and the position of the Athenian magistrates. (1) Athenian law was an ancient body of standing rules which was seldom changed. Legislative changes were not a matter for the assembly, which was a deliberative body, and not a legislature: they were, indeed, initiated and proposed in the assembly, but they were then referred to the judicial side of the constitution and to a judicial commission, and it was there that changes were considered and enacted. It may thus be said that there was little legislation, and no separate and specific legislature, in the Athenian system; and when the people in the assembly sought to act as a legislature, by passing decrees or *psephismata* which had the force of law or overrode law, such action was regarded—at any rate by Aristotle— as a usurpation. (See Book IV, c. IV, § 25 and note.) (2) The Athenian magistrates were kept in subordination to law by the exercise of the right, vested in every citizen, to arraign a magistrate who had broken the law; and this was viewed as one of the great safeguards against abuses. The *graphē paranomōn*, or indictment for illegality, was a weapon which never rusted from disuse. (See Vinogradoff, *Historical Jurisprudence*, vol. ii, c. VI, § 2 (on the Rule of Law) and c. VII, §§ 1–2.)

CHAPTER XII[1]

Justice is the political good. It involves equality, or the distribution of equal amounts to equal persons. But who are equals, and by what criterion are persons to be reckoned as equals? Many criteria can be applied; but the only proper criterion, in a political society, is that of contribution to the function of that society. Those who are equal in that respect should receive equal amounts: those who are superior or inferior should receive superior or inferior amounts, in proportion to the degree of their superiority or inferiority. If all are thus treated proportionately to the contribution they make, all are really receiving equal treatment; for the proportion between contribution and reward is the same in every case. The sort of equality which justice involves is thus proportionate equality; and this is the essence of distributive justice.

§ 1. In all arts and sciences the end in view is some good. In the most sovereign of all the arts and sciences—and this is the art and science of politics—the end in view is the greatest good and the good which is most pursued.[2] The good in the sphere of politics is justice; and justice consists in what tends to promote the common interest. General opinion makes it consist in some sort of equality.[3] Up to a point this general opinion agrees with the philosophical inquiries which contain our conclusions on ethics. In other words, it holds that justice involves two factors—things, and the persons to whom things are assigned—and it considers that persons who are equal should have assigned to them equal things. § 2. But here there arises a question which must not be overlooked. Equals and unequals—yes; but equals and unequals *in what*? This is a question which raises difficulties, and involves us in philosophical speculation on politics.[4] It is possible

---

[1] The last three chapters—IX, X, and XI—have all been concerned, in different ways, with the general problem of distributive justice, or, in other words, with an attempt to determine what persons, in view of their contribution to the state, should be specially recognized by it in its distribution of office and honour. The argument of c. XI has appeared to go in favour of the special recognition of the people at large. The argument of the present chapter goes along a somewhat different line, and in favour of the view that all contributions, by all different persons and bodies of persons, should alike be recognized.

[2] The argument is the same as that of the first section of the first chapter of the first book.

[3] Here the argument repeats that of c. IX, §§ 1–3 of this book, where Aristotle has already raised the issue of equality in reference to justice, and has already referred to the *Ethics*, as he does again here. The relevant passages of the *Ethics* are noted in Appendix II. A. 2.

[4] In all this passage a contrast is implied between 'general opinion' (*doxa*, or the current views of the ordinary man), and 'philosophic inquiry', which does not despise, but is none the less bound to analyse (and by analysing to correct and to elevate) the implications of 'general opinion'. Aristotle has a fundamental

to argue that offices and honours ought to be distributed unequally [i.e. that superior amounts should be assigned to superior persons] on the basis of superiority *in any respect whatsoever*—even though there were similarity, and no shadow of any difference, in every other respect; and it may be urged, in favour of this argument, that where people differ from one another there must be a difference in what is just and proportionate to their merits.   § 3. If this argument were accepted, the mere fact of a better complexion, or greater height, or any other such advantage, would establish a claim for a greater share of political rights to be given to its possessor.   § 4. But is not the argument obviously wrong?   To be clear that it is, we have only to study the analogy of the other arts and sciences.   If you were dealing with a number of flute-players who were equal in their art, you would not assign them flutes on the principle that the better born should have a greater amount. Nobody will play the better for being better born; and it is to those who are better at the job that the better supply of tools should be given.   If our point is not yet plain, it can be made so if we push it still further.   § 5. Let us suppose a man who is superior to others in flute-playing, but far inferior in birth and beauty.   Birth and beauty may be greater goods than ability to play the flute, and those who possess them may, upon balance, surpass the flute-player more in these qualities than he surpasses them in his flute-playing; but the fact remains that *he* is the man who ought to get the better supply of flutes. [If it is to be recognized in connexion with a given function], **1283 a** superiority in a quality such as birth—or for that matter wealth—ought to contribute something to the performance of that function; and here these qualities contribute nothing to such performance.

§ 6. There is a further objection.   If we accept this argument [that offices and honours should be assigned on the basis of excellence in *any* respect], every quality will have to be commensurable with every other.   You will begin by reckoning a given degree of (say) height as superior to a given degree of some other quality, and you will thus be driven to pit height in general against (say) wealth and birth in general.   But on this basis— i.e. that, *in a given case*, A is counted as excelling in height to a greater degree than B does in goodness, and that, *in general*, height is counted as excelling to a greater degree than goodness does—qualities are made commensurable. [We are involved in

respect for general opinion, and indeed he states, in the *Ethics*, that a general opinion which is universally held is, in ethical matters, the truth—'that which everyone thinks *is* so' (*Ethics*, X, c. ii, § 4). But he also believes that general opinion must be analysed, corrected, and elevated by philosophic analysis.

mere arithmetic]; for if amount X of some quality is 'better' than amount Y of some other, some amount which is other than X must clearly be equal to it [i.e. must be *equally* good].¹ § 7. This is impossible [because things that differ in quality cannot be treated in terms of quantity, or regarded as commensurable]. It is therefore clear that in matters political [just as in matters belonging to other arts and sciences] there is no good reason for basing a claim to the exercise of authority on any and every kind of superiority. Some may be swift and others slow; but this is no reason why the one should have more [political rights], and the other less. It is in athletic contests that the superiority of the swift receives its reward. § 8. Claims to political rights must be based on the ground of contribution to the elements which constitute the being of the state.² There is thus good ground for the claims to honour and office which are made by persons of good descent, free birth, or wealth. Those who hold office must necessarily be free men and taxpayers: a state could not be composed entirely of men without means, any more than it could be composed entirely of slaves. § 9. But we must add that if wealth and free birth are necessary elements, the temper of justice and a martial habit are also necessary. These too are elements which must be present if men are to live together in a state. The one difference is that the first two elements are necessary to the simple existence of a state, and the last two for its good life.

CHAPTER XIII

This raises the question, What constitutes a contribution to the purpose of a political society? Wealth, birth, goodness, and the aggregate quality of numbers, may all claim to be contributors. How are these rival claims to be reconciled when they all coexist in the same society? A case may be made in favour of the aggregate quality of numbers; but a case may also be made in favour of the single man of exceptional and outstanding goodness. Such a man must either be made a king or sent into exile. The democratic policy of ostracism means a choice of the latter alternative; and the proportion, or balance, needed in a constitution is certainly disturbed if any one element is outstandingly

¹ The argument is that if you say that $\frac{6}{8}$ of a perfect stature is 'better' than $\frac{7}{8}$ of perfect goodness, you are also bound to say that $\frac{1}{2}$ of a perfect stature is equal to $\frac{1}{2}$ of perfect goodness. But in that case you make stature and goodness commensurable: i.e. you treat either of them as a quantitative mass, without any difference of quality, and on that basis you assume that some fraction of the one is as good as some fraction of the other.

² The elements which constitute the life of the polis are defined later, in Book IV, c. XII, § 1 as 'free birth, wealth, culture, and good descent'. Culture may be held to imply, or to be linked with, goodness, as appears in the first section of the next chapter of this book. The Greek word for it is *paideia*, the general 'training' of the human faculties.

eminent. On the other hand it cannot be just, in a good constitution, to refuse the recognition which is due to a man of outstanding goodness; and such a man should not be banished, but should rather be made a king. We are thus brought to the subject of kingship.

§ 1. If we are thinking in terms of contribution to the state's existence, all of the elements mentioned, or at any rate several of them, may properly claim to be recognized in the award of honours and office; but if we are thinking in terms of contribution to its good life, then culture and goodness, as we have noted already,[1] may be regarded as having the justest claim. On the other hand—and following our principle that it is not right for men who are equal in one respect, and only in one, to have an equal share of all things [as the democrats claim], or for men who are superior in one respect to have a superior share of everything [as the oligarchs claim]—we are bound to consider all constitutions which recognize such claims as perverted forms. § 2. We have noted already[2] that there is a certain sense in which all the contributors of the different elements are justified in the claims they advance, though none of them is absolutely justified. (*a*) The rich are so far justified that they have a larger share of the land, which is a matter of public interest: they are also, as a rule, more reliable in matters of contract. (*b*) The free and the nobly born [who both contribute the element of birth] may claim recognition together as being closely connected. The better-born are citizens to a greater extent than the low-born; and good birth has always honour in its own country. § 3. In addition [and apart from any honour paid them] the descendants of better men are likely to be intrinsically better; good birth means goodness of the whole stock. (*c*) Similarly we may also allow that goodness of character has a just claim; for in our view the virtue of justice, which is necessarily accompanied by all the other virtues [and which may thus be identified with *general* virtue or goodness] is a virtue which acts in social relations [and is therefore one of the elements essential to the existence of political society].[3] § 4. (*d*) But there is a further claim that may also be urged. [Besides the claims of individuals, based on their having the particular attribute of wealth or birth or goodness, there is the claim of the people at large, based on its having, collectively, still more of all these attributes.] The many may urge their claims against the few: taken together and compared with the few they are stronger, richer, and better.

[1] *Supra*, c. IX, §§ 14–15.
[2] *Supra*, c. IX, § 1, where Aristotle allows that both oligarchs and democrats 'have a hold on a sort of conception of justice'.
[3] See Note AA, p. 137, and Appendix II, p. 362, (1) (*a*), and n. 2.

1283 b Let us suppose these rival claimants—for example, the good, the wealthy and well-born, and some sort of general body of citizens—all living together in a single state. Will they fall to disputing which of them is to govern, or will they agree? § 5. This issue is not a matter of dispute in any of the constitutions mentioned in our previous classification.[1] These constitutions differ in virtue of different groups being sovereign: one of them [oligarchy] is distinguished by sovereignty being vested in the wealthy; another [aristocracy] by its being vested in the good; and so with each of the rest. But the question we are discussing is different. It is a question of determining who is to govern when the claims of different groups are simultaneously present. § 6. Suppose, for example, that the good are exceedingly few in number: how are we to settle their claim? Must we only have regard to the fact that they are few for the function they have to discharge; and must we therefore inquire whether they will be able to manage a state, or numerous enough to compose one? Here there arises a difficulty which applies not only to the good, but to all the different claimants for political office and honour.[2] § 7. It may equally be held that there is no justice in the claim of a few to rule on the ground of their greater wealth, or on that of their better birth; and there is an obvious reason for holding this view. If there is any *one* man who in turn is richer than all the rest, this one man must rule over all on the very same ground of justice [which the few rich plead for *their* right to rule]; and similarly any one man who is preeminent in point of good birth must carry the day over those who claim on the ground of birth. § 8. In aristocracies, too, the same logic may be applied in the matter of merit or goodness.[3] If some one man be a better man than all the other good men who belong to the civic body, this one man should be sovereign on the very same ground of justice [which the other men plead in defence of *their* right to govern. . . . Even the claims of the Many may be challenged by this line of argument]. If the reason why they should be sovereign is their being stronger than the Few, we are logically

---

[1] In c. VII of this book.

[2] If you defend the good on the ground of their quality, in spite of the paucity of their numbers, you are faced with the difficulty, 'May not the one best be defended on the ground of *his* quality, in spite of the fact that he is only one in number?' The same difficulty may also be raised in regard to the wealthy or the well-born: the one wealthiest, or the one best-born, in spite of being only one, may claim the reward of his eminence. It may even be raised in regard to the Many: the one strongest may claim a preference over the collective strength of the Many.

[3] In our modern usage of the term we connect aristocracy with birth. In Aristotle's use it is not connected with birth (birth, in his view, goes generally with wealth, and the two together form the basis of oligarchy): it is connected with merit or goodness, and it means the government of the best (*aristoi*).

driven to conclude that where one man is stronger than all the rest—
or a group of more than one, but fewer than the Many, is stronger—
that one man or group must be sovereign instead of the Many.

§ 9. All these considerations would seem to prove that none of
the principles [wealth, birth, goodness, and the strength of num-
bers], in virtue of which men claim to rule and to have all others
subject to their rule, is a proper principle.   § 10. Take, for example,
those who claim to be sovereign over the citizen body on the
ground of goodness; or take, again, those who base their claim on
the ground of wealth. The claims of both may be justly challenged
by the masses; for there is nothing whatever to prevent the Many
—collectively if not individually—from being better, or richer,
than the Few.   § 11. This last reflection enables us to take another
step, and to meet a difficulty which is sometimes raised and discussed. The difficulty is this. Suppose that the Many are actually
better, taken as a whole, than the Few: what, in that case, is the
proper policy for a lawgiver who wishes to enact right laws to
the best of his power? Should he direct his legislation to the
benefit of the better sort, or should he direct it to that of the
majority? § 12. We may reply [that the benefit of neither ought to
be considered exclusively]; that what is 'right' should be understood as what is 'equally right'; and what is 'equally right' is what
is for the benefit of the whole state and for the common good of its
citizens. . . . Citizens, in the common sense of that term, are *all*
who share in the civic life of ruling and being ruled in turn. In the
particular **1284 a** sense of the term, they vary from constitution
to constitution; and under an ideal constitution they must be
those who are able and willing to rule and be ruled with a view to
attaining a way of life according to goodness.[1]

§ 13. [We have just been considering the case in which the
Many are collectively superior to the Few. We may now take the
opposite case.] If there is one person (or several persons, but yet
not enough to form the full measure of a state) so pre-eminently
superior in goodness that there can be no comparison between
the goodness and political capacity which he shows (or several
show, when there is more than one) and what is shown by the rest,
such a person, or such persons, can no longer be treated as part of
a state. Being so greatly superior to others in goodness and political
capacity, they will suffer injustice if they are treated as worthy only
of an equal share; for a person of this order may very well be like

---

[1] These last sentences are in the nature of an additional gloss. What is the
general conclusion at which Aristotle has arrived, before he adds this gloss, in
regard to the proper object of legislation? Briefly—that legislation should not
be directed either to the benefit of the better sort or to that of the majority, but
to the benefit of both and all.

a god among men. § 14. This being the case, it is clear that law generally [as well as any particular rule of equality in the distribution of office] is necessarily limited to those who are equal in birth and capacity. There can be no law which runs against men who are utterly superior to others. They are a law in themselves. It would be a folly to attempt to legislate for them: they might reply to such an attempt with the words used by the lions, in the fable of Antisthenes, when the hares were making orations and claiming that all the animals had equal rights, ['Where are your claws and teeth?'] § 15. Reasons of this nature will serve to explain why democratic states institute the rule of ostracism. Such states are held to aim at equality above anything else; and with that aim in view they used to pass a sentence of ostracism [banishment from the state for some fixed period] on those whom they regarded as having too much influence owing to their wealth or the number of their connexions or any other form of political strength. § 16. We may also cite the evidence of legend: the Argonauts left Heracles behind for this sort of reason; and the *Argo* itself [the ship that talked] refused to have him among the crew because he was so greatly superior to all the others. From this point of view we cannot altogether regard as just the strictures passed by the critics of tyranny on the advice once given by the tyrant Periander to his fellow-tyrant Thrasybulus. § 17. Thrasybulus, according to the tale that is told, sent an envoy to ask for advice. Periander gave no verbal answer; he simply switched off the outstanding ears, in the corn-field where he was standing, until he had levelled the surface. The envoy did not understand the meaning of his action, and merely reported the incident; but Thrasybulus guessed that he had been advised to cut off the outstanding men in the state. § 18. It is not only tyrants who may derive some benefit from this policy; nor is it only tyrants who put it into practice. Oligarchies and democracies are both in the same position; and ostracism has, in its way, the same effect of pulling down and banishing men of outstanding influence. § 19. States which have gained an ascendancy apply the same sort of policy to other states and peoples. Athens, for instance, acted in this way to Samos, Chios, and Lesbos: once she had gained a firm grip of her empire, she humbled them all, in violation of her former treaties. Similarly the King of **1284 b** Persia repeatedly curtailed the power of Media, Babylonia, and other parts of his realm which were made presumptuous by memories of having once had an empire themselves.

§ 20. The difficulty which we are discussing is one which is common to all forms of government, the right as well as the wrong;

and if wrong or perverted forms adopt this policy of levelling with a view to their own particular interest, something the same is also true of forms which look to the common good.   § 21. This rule of proportion may also be observed in the arts and sciences generally. A painter would not permit a foot which exceeded the bounds of symmetry, however beautiful it might be, to appear in a figure on his canvas. A shipwright would not tolerate a stern, or any other part of a ship, which was out of proportion. A choir-master would not admit to a choir a singer with a greater compass and a finer voice than any of the other members.   § 22. In view of this general rule, a policy of levelling need not prevent a monarch who practises it from being in harmony with his state—provided that his government is otherwise beneficial; and thus the argument in favour of ostracism possesses a kind of political justice in relation to any of the recognized forms of pre-eminence. § 23. It is true that it would be better if the legislator could so frame a constitution initially that it would never need any such remedy; but the next best course, should the need arise, is to endeavour to apply this sort of correction. Actually, states have not applied the policy in this spirit; and each, instead of considering what was required by the interest of its own particular constitution, has resorted to acts of ostracism in a spirit of mere faction.

§ 24. So far as perverted forms are concerned, it is clear that the practice of banishing the eminent is expedient and just from their own point of view—though perhaps it is also clear that it is not absolutely just. But a serious difficulty arises about the use of any such practice in the ideal constitution. The difficulty does not arise in regard to pre-eminence in qualities such as political strength, or wealth, or an abundance of connexions. The real question is rather, 'What is to be done when we meet with a man of outstanding eminence in goodness?'   § 25. Nobody, we may assume, would say that such a man ought to be banished and sent into exile. But neither would any man say that he ought to be subject to others. That would be much as if human beings should claim to rule over Zeus, on some system of rotation of office between themselves and *him*. The only alternative left—and this would also appear to be the natural course—is for all others to pay a willing obedience to the man of outstanding goodness. Such men will accordingly be the permanent kings in their states.[1]

---

[1] Newman cites, most appositely, Milton's defence of the position of Cromwell, in his *Second defence of the people of England*: 'we all willingly yield the palm of sovereignty to your unrivalled ability and virtue, except the few among us who . . . do not know that nothing in the world is . . . more agreeable to reason . . . than that the supreme power should be vested in the best and wisest of men.' Milton's *Prose Works*, Bohn's edition, vol. i, p. 288.

NOTE AA (p. 132): *The conception of justice in* c. XIII

There are two ideas involved in this succinct sentence. The first is
that the form of goodness called justice (in the sense of the temper and
disposition of the just man) is really total goodness, because it embraces
or involves all other forms: as one of the Greek poets expressed it, 'in
justice doth all goodness dwell compact'. The second idea is that justice,
being essentially operative in social relations, is necessarily a contribution
(as much as, or even more than, wealth or birth) to the existence of a
political society: indeed we may say, in the language of § 1 of this chapter,
that it is a contribution to its good life, and not merely to its existence.
For the second of these ideas cf. Book, I, c. 11, § 12 and § 16: 'it is association in a common perception of the just and unjust that makes a polis'.

D

KINGSHIP AND ITS FORMS (cc. XIV–XVIII)

CHAPTER XIV

There are five forms of kingship: (1) *the Spartan form;* (2) *kingship
among uncivilized peoples;* (3) *the dictatorship or* elective *form of
tyranny;* (4) *the kingship of the Heroic Age;* (5) *absolute kingship,
with the king exercising a plenary power in the nature of* patria
potestas.

§ 1. It will perhaps be well, after the previous discussion, to
make a transition, and to proceed to consider kingship.[1] Government by a king is, in our view, one of the right constitutions. The
question we have to consider is whether this form of government
is expedient for states or territories which are to be properly
governed; or whether this is not so and some other form is more
expedient—or, at any rate, more expedient in *some* cases, even if
it is not in others. § 2. We must begin by determining whether
there is only one kind of kingship, or whether it has several
varieties. **1285 a** It is easy to see that it includes a number of
different kinds, and that the system of government followed is not
the same in all these kinds.

§ 3. In the first place, there is the kind of kingship to be found
in the constitution of Sparta. This is regarded as the strongest
form of constitutional kingship. That is hardly the case. The
Spartan kings are not vested with any general sovereignty: they
have simply the power of commanding in war when they are
outside Spartan territory, and the right of dealing with matters
of religious observance. § 4. Kings of the Spartan kind are thus
of the nature of generals, with an independent command and a
permanent tenure. Such kings do not possess the power of life
and death, or, if they do, it is only in some particular variety of this

[1] See Note BB, p. 140.

type of kingship—for instance that of the Heroic Age, when kings could put men to death on military expeditions, by right of superior force. Homer may be cited in proof: he represents Agamemnon, in the *Iliad*, as patient under abuse in the presence of the assembly, but as exercising the power of life and death on the field of battle. § 5. At any rate he puts this speech in his mouth:

Whomso I find apart from the fight . . .
> he shall have no hope of escaping:
Dogs and vultures shall rend him; for mine is the power to command death.

We may thus say that one type of kingship is a military command held for life; and we may add that this type of kingship has two different species, the one hereditary and the other elective.

§ 6. Another type of kingship is the sort which is to be found among some uncivilized [i.e. non-Hellenic] peoples. Kingships of this sort all possess an authority similar to that of tyrannies; but they are, none the less, constitutional, and they descend from father to son. The reason is that these uncivilized peoples are more servile in character than Greeks (as the peoples of Asia, in turn, are more servile than those of Europe); and they will therefore tolerate despotic rule without any complaint. § 7. Kingships among uncivilized peoples are thus of the nature of tyrannies; but, being constitutional and hereditary, they are at the same time stable. We may also note that the bodyguards used in such states are such as suit kings, and not tyrants. Kings are guarded by the arms of their subjects; tyrants by a foreign force. Ruling constitutionally, and with the consent of their subjects, kings have bodyguards drawn from their subjects: the tyrant, who rules contrary to the will of his subjects, has a [foreign] bodyguard to protect him against them.

§ 8. These are two types of monarchy; but there is also a third, which used to exist among the ancient Greeks, and which goes by the name of dictatorship [*Aisumnēteia*]. This may be roughly described as an elective form of tyranny. It differs from the type of kingship among uncivilized peoples, but only in being non-hereditary, and not in being non-constitutional. § 9. Some of the dictators held their office for life: others for a fixed period, or for the discharge of a definite duty.[1] Pittacus, for instance, was elected

---

[1] Some of the Greek *aisumnētai* were ordinary magistrates; but Aristotle is dealing with the term only in its application to extraordinary magistrates. The extraordinary *aesumnētēs* was generally analogous to the Roman dictator. We may note (1) that the Roman dictator was appointed by one of the consuls on the strength of a regular decree duly passed by the Senate; (2) that his term was six months or less; and (3) that he was always appointed for the discharge of a definite duty—either *rei gerundae causa* (to do some difficult job, generally in

at Mitylene to deal with the attacks of the exiles commanded by
Antimenides and the lyric poet Alcaeus. § 10. The fact of the
election of Pittacus is attested by Alcaeus, in one of his drinking-
songs, where he bitterly says:

> Meanly born Pittacus over their gall-less and heaven-doomed
>   city
> **1285 b** Was enthroned by them for their tyrant, with
>   clamour of praise, in the throng of the hustings.

§ 11. These dictatorships were, and still are, of a double
character: they were tyrannies in their despotic power, but kingships in being elective and in resting on the assent of their subjects.
But there is a fourth type of kingship, [which is less ambiguous].
This is the type of the kingships of the Heroic Age, which were
constitutional, rested on consent, and descended from father to
son. § 12. The founders of royal lines had been benefactors of
their people in the arts or in war: they had drawn them together
in a city, or provided them with territory; and they had thus
become kings by general consent, and had established kingships
which descended to their successors. Such kings had three
sovereign functions: they were commanders in war; they had the
religious function of offering such sacrifices as did not require
a priest; and they were also judges in legal actions. Sometimes
they judged upon oath, and sometimes without oath: the form of
the oath, when they took one, was the lifting up of their sceptre.
§ 13. In ancient times they enjoyed a permanent authority, which
included urban, rural, and foreign affairs: at a later date this was
altered. Some of their prerogatives were voluntarily relinquished:
others were taken away by the masses; in the issue the only
prerogative left to the kings, in the majority of cases, was the
management of the traditional sacrifices. Even in cases where it
could be said that a real kingship still existed, the only effective
power of the king was that of military command in foreign
expeditions.

§ 14. There are thus four types of kingship—(1) the kingship
of the Heroic Age, based on general consent but limited to a
number of definite functions, with the king acting as general and
judge and the head of religious observances; (2) the type of kingship among uncivilized peoples, with the king exercising, by right
of descent, a despotic authority which is none the less constitutional; (3) kingship of the type which is termed dictatorship, and
which is an elective form of tyranny; and (4) the Spartan type of

the sphere of foreign policy and military defence) or *seditionis sedandae causa* (to
allay some internal discontent).

kingship, which may be roughly defined as a permanent command of the army exercised by right of descent.   § 15. These four types differ from one another in the ways just mentioned; but there is still a fifth type of kingship [which differs from all the four]. This is the absolute type, where a single person is sovereign on every issue, with the same sort of power that a tribe or a polis exercises over its public concerns. It is a type which corresponds to paternal rule over a household.[1] Just as paternal rule is kingship over a family, so conversely this type of kingship may be regarded as paternal rule over a polis, or a tribe, or a collection of tribes.

NOTE BB (p. 137): *The course of the argument in* c. XIV

The previous discussion (in cc. IX–XIII) has been concerned with the problem of the proper distribution of political power, or, in other words, with the problem of distributive justice. Various claims have been canvassed—the claims of the various *qualities* (birth, wealth, and goodness) which contribute to the being and the working of the state, and what may be called the *quantitative* claims of the Many, the Few, and the One. Sometimes the argument has swayed in favour of the Many: at the end of c. XIII it has swayed in favour of the One. At that point, and for the rest of Book III, Aristotle turns to consider kingship—at first on the ground of expediency rather than that of justice, but ultimately on both grounds. In a previous part of Book III (cc. VI–VIII), in which he was concerned with the classification of states, he had suggested that the various constitutions had to be considered in turn—and first the right constitutions (c. VII, § 1). It is in pursuance of this suggestion that, having concluded the exhaustive argument of cc. IX–XIII on the general principles of the distribution of political power, he now proceeds to consider kingship as one of the right constitutions.

CHAPTER XV

Only the last of the five forms of kingship mentioned in the last chapter needs special examination. It raises the problem of personal rule versus *the rule of law. There are arguments on either side: personal rule has the quality of initiative; the rule of law has that of impartiality. The rule of law is of major importance, and should be the main factor in all constitutions, including kingship, which should therefore be a constitutional kingship limited by law. There are, however, matters of detail which cannot be settled by law. Even so, the question arises whether such matters are best settled by one person, or by a body of persons. The balance is in favour of a body of persons. Where government by a single person exists, in the form of kingship,*

---

[1] Being 'sovereign on every issue', a king of this sort may be called the all-king [or, in Greek, *pambasileus*], as he is afterwards called at the beginning of the next chapter. His total power means that his position may be compared (1) to the position of a whole community governing itself by a similar power, or (2) to the position of the patriarch exercising a similar power over all his family. From the second point of view, the *pambasileus* is analogous to the patriarchal sovereign of Bodin's and Filmer's theory.

it raises two special problems: should it be hereditary, and should it be backed by a guard or standing army?

§ 1. For practical purposes there are only two of these five types of kingship which we need consider—the type just mentioned, and the Spartan type. Most of the instances of the other three types are intermediate between these two: their kings are sovereign to a less extent than they are in the absolute type, or *pambasileia*, but to a greater extent than they are in the Spartan type. § 2. [The intermediate forms may be understood from a study of the two extremes; and] our inquiry is practically reduced to two issues. The first is the issue whether the existence of a permanent general (either on a hereditary basis, or on some scheme of rotation) is, or is not, an expedient system of government. The second is the issue whether it is expedient **1286 a** or not that one man should be sovereign in all matters.

The first of these issues belongs more to the scope of legal enactment than to that of constitutional form. A permanent general may exist under any form of constitution; and we may therefore dismiss this issue for the present. § 3. The absolute type of kingship is a different matter. It is a form of constitution; and we are therefore bound to study it philosophically, and to examine briefly the difficulties which it involves.

Our inquiry will naturally start from the general problem, 'Is it more expedient to be ruled by the one best man, or by the best laws?'[1] § 4. Those who hold that kingship is expedient argue that law can only lay down general rules; it cannot issue commands to deal with various different conjunctures; and the rule of the letter of law is therefore a folly in any and every art [whether the art of politics, or that of medicine, or any other art]. In Egypt it is permissible for doctors to alter the rules of treatment after the first four days, though a doctor who alters them earlier does so at his own risk. If we follow this line, it is clear that a constitution based on the letter and rules of law is not the best constitution, in the same way and for the same reason [as medical treatment by strict rule is not the best treatment]. § 5. [This is an argument in favour of personal initiative.] But we have to remember that general principle must also be present in the ruler's mind. [We have also to remember a further point.] That from which the element of passion is wholly absent is better than that to which such an element clings. Law contains no element of passion; but such an element must always be present in the human mind. The rejoinder may, however, be made that the individual mind, if it

[1] See Note CC, p. 144.

loses in this way, gains something in return: it can deliberate better, and decide better, on particular issues. § 6. These considerations lead us to conclude that the one best man must be a law-giver, and there must be a body of laws [even in a state which is governed by such a man], but these laws must not be sovereign where they fail to hit the mark—though they must be so in all other cases.[1] There is, however, a whole class of matters which cannot be decided at all, or cannot be decided properly, by rules of law. [They must thus be decided by personal initiative;[2] but] the question arises whether this authority should be vested in the one best man or in the whole of the people. [We are thus brought back to our previous problem of the rights of the people.]

§ 7. In the actual practice of our own day the people in their gatherings have both a judicial and a deliberative capacity, and in both capacities they make decisions which are all concerned with particular matters [i.e. the matters that cannot be decided, or properly decided, by law]. Any individual member of these assemblies is probably inferior to the one best man. But the state is composed of many individuals; and just as a feast to which many contribute is better than one provided by a single person,[3] so, and for the same reason, the masses can come to a better decision, in many matters, than any one individual. § 8. Again, a numerous body is less likely to be corrupted. A large volume of water is not so liable to contamination as a small; and the people is not so liable to corruption as the few. The judgement of a single man is bound to be corrupted when he is overpowered by anger, or by any other similar emotion; but it is not easy for all to get angry and go wrong simultaneously. § 9. We may assume that the people are all freemen, do nothing contrary to law, and only act outside it in matters which law, by its nature, is obliged to omit. It may be objected that these limitations will not be easily observed in a large body. But if we have a body of persons who are both good men and good citizens, which will be the more likely to be free from corruption—the one man, or the body of persons who are all good men? Is not the balance clearly in favour of the latter? **1286 b** Another objection may, however, be urged—that a body of men will be subject to faction, from which the one man will be free. § 10. It is perhaps an answer to this objection that the

---

[1] Law may deviate, or miss the mark, owing to its generality, which may prevent it from meeting the requirement of some particular conjuncture. Here, it is suggested, the one best man may dispense with law, and use his discretion to apply considerations of equity. See Appendix II, pp. 368, 370–1.

[2] It is perhaps worth noting that the Greek word *archē* had the general sense of 'initiative'. See Introduction, IV. 2.

[3] This repeats the argument of c. XI, § 2.

body may be of good character [and therefore free from faction] equally with the one man. [We thus reach the following conclusion.] If we call by the name of aristocracy a government vested in a number of persons who are all good men, and by the name of kingship a government vested in a single person, we may say that aristocracy is better for states than kingship (whether or no the rule of a king is supported by the force of a bodyguard)—provided only that a body of men who are all equally good can be actually found.[1]

§ 11. Perhaps the reason why kingship was formerly common was because it was rare to find a number of men of outstanding goodness—all the more as states were then thinly populated. A further reason why kings were appointed was that they were benefactors—which it is the duty of all good men to be [but only one man was then able to be]. Later there arose a number of persons of equal goodness; and they, refusing to tolerate the rule of a single person, desired to have something they could share in common, and so established a constitution. § 12. Later still, they deteriorated in character: they enriched themselves from the public property; and it is to some such origin—the honour in which wealth now began to be held—that we may reasonably ascribe the rise of oligarchy. At a still later stage, there was a change from oligarchies to tyrannies, and then from tyrannies to democracy. The reason was that the members of the government, greedy for the gains which office conferred, limited it to a narrower and narrower circle; and by this policy they strengthened the masses until they rose in rebellion and established democracies. § 13. Nowadays, when states have become still larger, we may almost say that it is hardly even possible for any other form of constitution to exist.[2]

[Returning to our consideration of the relative merits of monarchy and aristocracy, we may raise two further questions. The

[1] The ground of the argument would seem to be shifted at this point. Previously, from the end of § 6 onwards, Aristotle has been discussing the rights of numbers in the sense of *all*, or the whole people—i.e. on a democratic basis. Here, beginning in § 9 and reaching his conclusion in the present section, he discusses the rights of numbers in the sense of *some*, or the class of good citizens —i.e. on an aristocratic basis.

[2] This digression, which arises from the final sentence at the end of § 10, gives an account of the historical succession of constitutions in Greece (based partly on considerations of population, and partly on considerations of social development) which does not square with the subsequent account given in Book IV, c. XIII, §§ 10–11, which is based on considerations of changes in the art of war. Neither account, in turn, squares with the ideas expressed in the criticism of Plato's views on the historical succession of constitutions (Book V, c. XII, §§ 7–18). We can only say, first that Aristotle naturally expresses different views in different contexts, and secondly that the views expressed in the present context are introduced by the saving word 'perhaps'.

first is this.] If kingship be accepted as the best form of government for states, what is to be the position of the issue of a king? Are we to say that the kingship is vested in the family, and that his descendants should also be kings? If they turn out to be ordinary persons, the result will be mischievous. § 14. It may be argued that a king, even if he has the power to do so, will not transmit the crown to his children. But it is hardly to be believed that a king will act in this way: it is a difficult thing to do, and it needs a greater degree of goodness than human nature warrants us in expecting. The other question, which also raises difficulties, is that of the king's bodyguard. Should the man who is to be king have a force about his person which will enable him to coerce those who are unwilling to obey? If not, how can he possibly manage to govern? § 15. Even if he were a sovereign who ruled according to law, and who never acted at his own discretion and went outside the law, he must necessarily have a bodyguard in order to guard the law. § 16. In the case of a king of this sort, who rules according to law, it is perhaps easy to settle the question. He ought to have some amount of force—less, indeed, than what his people commands, but greater than that commanded by any one individual or any group of individuals. This was the nature of the bodyguard assigned in ancient times, when a man was made head of the state under the title of dictator or tyrant.[1] It was also the size of the force which a counsellor at Syracuse advised the people to give to Dionysius when he asked for a bodyguard.

NOTE CC (p. 141): *Aristotle's attitude to absolute monarchy*

This general question had been raised by Plato, particularly in the *Republic*, but also in the *Politicus* and, to a less extent, in the *Laws*. The general answer of Plato had been in favour of the free philosophic intelligence of the individual ruler (or rulers) properly trained for the work of government: it had been adverse to the rule of a fixed and dead body of law. The answer of Aristotle, as it develops, is more balanced, and, on the whole, more favourable to the rule of law; but he admits, and indeed he urges, that there are cases in which the free intelligence of the one best man should be sovereign. It may be noticed, however, that Plato was less concerned with the problem of the *one* man, or sole monarch, than Aristotle appears to be. His interest is in the rule of free intelligence, whether of one or more than one (cf. the famous passage on the rule of 'philosopher kings'—in the plural—in the *Republic* 473 C–D); while Aristotle's interest is an interest in monarchy as such, or the rule of a single person. Was Aristotle affected by his residence in Macedonia (after 343 B.C.) and his education of the young Alexander, for whom he is recorded to have written a work *On Monarchy*?

[1] Strictly speaking, a 'tyrant', in the Greek sense of the word, is not 'made' head of the State: he makes himself head, generally by a *coup d'état*, and proceeds to rule, for an indeterminate period, without respect for law and without any regard to popular assent.

Chapter XVI

The general considerations of the previous chapter, so far as they favour
kingship at all, are in favour of a constitutional and limited kingship.
But the question still remains whether a case can be made in favour of
an absolute kingship. It may be objected to such a form of kingship
that it is contrary to the idea of a free society of equals, and adverse to
the rule of law. True, the rule of an absolute king may be defended on
the ground of his expert knowledge; and the analogy of science and the
arts may be invoked in his favour. But the analogy does not really
hold; and in any case expert knowledge is more likely to reside in a
number of men than in one. So far, therefore, the conclusion would seem
to be adverse to absolute monarchy—at any rate on general grounds.

1287 a § 1. [We have just been speaking of the king who acts
according to law, and does nothing at his own discretion.] But the
argument which now confronts us, and the inquiry we have still
to attempt, is concerned with the king who does everything at his
own discretion.[1] . . . A kingship which acts according to law, as has
already been noted [in § 2 of the previous chapter], is not in itself
a form of constitution. A permanent military command [which is
what such kingship generally means] may exist in any form of
constitution—for example, in a democracy or an aristocracy; and
in the sphere of civil administration too there are a number of states
with different forms of constitution which make a single person
sovereign [subject to his acting according to law]: there is a magistrate of this order at Epidamnus, for instance, and another, though
with somewhat more limited powers, at Opus.[2] . . . § 2. But an
absolute kingship, or, as it is called, a *pambasileia*, is a form of
constitution in which a king governs at his own discretion and
in all affairs. Now there are some who take the view that the
sovereignty of one man over all the other members of a state is
not even natural [far less expedient] in any case where a state is
composed of equals. On this view those who are naturally equal
must naturally have the same rights and worth; and therefore the
assignment of unequal amounts to equals (or, conversely, the
assignment of equal amounts to unequals) is a method of dealing
with the distribution of honours and offices which is as bad [for
men's minds] as it would be for their bodies if you followed that
method in distributing food and clothing. § 3. The conclusion
drawn is that justice for equals means their being ruled as well as
their ruling [*not* their always ruling, as absolute kings do], and
therefore involves rotation of office. But when we come to that, we
already come to law; for the arrangement [which regulates rotation

[1] See Note DD, p. 148.   [2] Both of these states were oligarchies.

of office] *is* law. The rule of law is therefore preferable, according to the view we are stating, to that of a single citizen. § 4. In pursuance of the same view it is argued that, even if it be the better course to have individuals[1] ruling, they should be made 'law-guardians'[2] or ministers of the law. There must, it is admitted, be offices of state; but these, it is urged, cannot be vested in one man, consistently with justice, when all are equals and peers.

[Further considerations may be added in favour of the rule of law.][3] If there are a number of cases which law seems unable to determine, it is also true that a person would be equally unable to find an answer to these cases. § 5. Law [does the best it can: it] trains the holders of office expressly in its own spirit, and then sets them to decide and settle those residuary issues which it cannot regulate, 'as justly as in them lies'.[4] It also allows them to introduce any improvements which may seem to them, as the result of experience, to be better than the existing laws.[5] He who commands that law should rule may thus be regarded as commanding that God and reason alone should rule; he who commands that a man should rule adds the character of the beast. Appetite has that character; and high spirit, too, perverts the holders of office, even when they are the best of men.[6] Law [as the pure voice of God and reason] may thus be defined as 'Reason free from all passion'.[7]

---

[1] The plural words here used show that the argument has slipped away from the one man. It began by pressing the claims of the impersonal rule of law in preference to any personal rule. It now suggests the idea that even if there is personal rule (and *so far as* there is personal rule) it should be plural rather than singular.

[2] 'Law-guardians' (*nomophylakes*) was a term used at Athens for a board of 7 members who sat by the side of the presidents, in the council and the assembly, to guard against hasty legislation or the passing of measures which injured the state or the constitution. But there seems to be no evidence that they were an active body (Vinogradoff, *Historical Jurisprudence*, vol. ii, p. 137); and Aristotle may be using the term in a purely general sense, to signify that the magistrates should guard or observe the law, as he had suggested before in c. XI, § 19. (But see also the Introduction, p. xxv.)

[3] See Note EE, p. 149.

[4] Newman notes that this phrase is taken from the oath of the Athenian jurors, who swore 'to vote according to the laws where there are laws, and where there are not, to vote as justly as in us lies'. The passage generally implies the idea of 'equity', or *to epieikes*: see Appendix II. A, *ad finem*, and B (with the note on p. 371).

[5] See Note FF, p. 149.

[6] The terms here used (*epithymia* and *thymos*) are reminiscent of the psychology of Plato's *Republic*. Appetite, or *epithymia*, is the physical appetite for material satisfaction: high spirit, or *thymos*, is something less physical, and less set on material objects, but still self-centred, and still of the nature of the beast. It is the spirit expressed in Shakespeare's lines,

> But if it be a sin to covet honour
> I am the most offending soul alive.

[7] On Aristotle's general conception of *nomos* or law see the Introduction, IV. 3, and Appendix II. A. 5, pp. 366–7.

§ 6. The parallel of the arts [e.g. that of medicine, already mentioned[1]] is false. It may be true that medical treatment according to the rules of a text-book is a poor sort of thing, and that it is very much better to use the services of those who possess professional skill. [But we have to remember that there is a vital distinction between the physician and the politician.]   § 7. Physicians never act in defiance of reason from motives of partiality: they cure their patients and earn their fee. Politicians in office have a habit of doing a number of things in order to spite their enemies or favour their friends. If patients suspected physicians of conspiring with their enemies to destroy them for their own profit, they would be more inclined to seek for treatment by the rules of a text-book.   § 8. Again, physicians, when they are **1287 b** ill, call in other physicians to attend them; and trainers, when they are in training, use the services of other trainers. [They turn to a neutral authority], feeling that they cannot judge truly themselves because they are judging in their own case under the influence of their own feelings. This shows that to seek for justice is to seek for a neutral authority; and law is a neutral authority. § 9. [We have been speaking hitherto of written rules of law.] But laws resting on unwritten custom are even more sovereign, and concerned with issues of still more sovereign importance, than written laws; and this suggests that, even if the rule of a man be safer than the rule of written law, it need not therefore be safer than the rule of unwritten law.

It is a further objection to the rule of a single man that [apart from the danger of partiality] he cannot even keep his eye readily on a number of things at once. He will thus find it necessary to appoint a number of officers to give him assistance. But is there any real difference between having these officers [at the start] and having them appointed afterwards by the choice of a single man? § 10. We may add, to clinch the argument, a point which has already been made.[2] If the good man has a just title to authority because he is better than others, then two good men are better than one [and have therefore a still juster title]. This is what Homer suggests in the line,

> Two men going together, one sees in advance of the other,

or again in the prayer which he puts into Agamemnon's mouth,

> Would that I had ten men for my counsellors like unto Nestor.

In our own day, too, we find a number of officers—such as judges,

---

[1] See c. XV, § 4, and also c. XI, §§ 10–11.
[2] In the previous chapter, c. XV, §§ 10–11.

for example—who are vested with a power of decision on certain issues on which the law is not competent to pronounce, but only on such issues; for no one disputes the fact that law will be the best ruler and judge on the issues on which it is competent. § 11. It is because law cannot cover the whole of the ground, and there are subjects which cannot be included in its scope, that difficulties arise and the question comes to be debated, 'Is the rule of the best law preferable to that of the best man?' Matters of detail, which belong to the sphere of deliberation, are obviously matters on which it is not possible to lay down a law. The advocates of the rule of law do not deny that such matters ought to be judged by men; they only claim that they ought to be judged by many men rather than one. § 12. *All* persons in office who have been trained by the law will have a good judgement; and it may well be regarded as an absurdity that a single man should do better in seeing with two eyes, judging with two ears, or acting with two hands and feet, than many could do with many. Indeed, it is actually the practice of monarchs to take to themselves, as it were, many eyes and ears and hands and feet, and to use as colleagues those who are friends of their rule and their person. § 13. The colleagues of a monarch must be his friends: otherwise they will not act in accordance with his policy. But if they are friends of his person and rule, they will also be—as a man's friends always are—his equals and peers;[1] and in believing that his friends should have office he is also committed to the belief that his equals and peers should have office.

These are the main arguments pressed by those who argue against the cause of kingship.

NOTE DD (p. 145): *The course of the argument in* c. XVI

Aristotle had started the previous chapter by an examination of the antithesis, *Aut rex aut lex*. But by the end of § 6 of that chapter he had abandoned the antithesis: he had assumed the general principle of the sovereignty of *lex*; and on that assumption he had started an inquiry into a different antithesis—the antithesis between the claims of one man and those of a number of men to the right of deciding particular cases which lie outside the general rules of *lex*. He had settled the inquiry into this new antithesis by a decision in favour of the claims of a number of men. Now, however, at the beginning of c. XVI, he returns to the old antithesis, *Aut rex aut lex*. In spite of the general presumption in favour of the sovereignty of law, there *may* (he feels) be a case, or cases, in which one man is so eminent, and so good, that his free discretion may be a better mode of sovereignty than the rule of law. It is this question that he now examines.

---

[1] 'The friendships aforesaid are in the sphere of *equality*: *both* get the same things from one another, and wish them for one another' (*Ethics*, VIII, c. VI, § 7).

NOTE EE (p. 146): *The logic of the argument in c.* XVI

It may be noted that there is something in Aristotle that holds him
back—even when he has returned once more to the idea of absolute
monarchy after the preliminary conclusion of c. XV in favour of the rule
of law—from admitting that such a form of monarchy can be accepted.
The new discussion in this chapter, which we might expect to state the
case in its favour, rapidly turns into a second statement of the case in
favour of the rule of law. It needs still another chapter (XVII) before a
defence of absolute monarchy, *in some cases*, is at last attempted. It may
be added that up to this point Aristotle has been speaking in this chapter
as if he were stating the views of others, and he has accordingly expressed
himself in *oratio obliqua*. From this point onwards, and for the rest of
the chapter, he speaks in *oratio recta*, and may therefore be held to be
stating his own views—which are, in effect, the same as those hitherto
ascribed to others. On the other hand, it may also be noted that when he
summarizes the whole argument at the end of the chapter (§ 13), he
ascribes the views developed in it to 'those who argue against the cause
of kingship'.

NOTE FF (p. 146): *The process of amendment of law at Athens*

This passage also would seem to be a reference to Athenian practice.
Under the reforms of Pericles provision was made for annual consideration and amendment of existing law by a balanced combination of different
authorities, which included two special bodies as well as the popular
assembly, and was so constructed as to give something of the forms and
the guarantees of judicial procedure to the making and changing of law.
The effect was (1) that six officials called the *thesmothetai* were charged
with the duty of annually reviewing the laws, reporting on imperfections,
and drafting any new laws which were necessary; (2) that the popular
assembly then considered the state of the laws, on the basis of the report
of the *thesmothetai*; and (3) that, if new laws were proposed, a body of
nomothetai was next appointed, taken from the members of the *dikastēria*,
before which the case for new legislation had to be argued. In this way
the executive, the deliberative, and the judicial organs were all combined
for the process of reviewing and amending the laws—the executive
through the *thesmothetai* (the six junior 'archons', who all belonged to the
sphere of *archē*); the deliberative through the popular assembly; and the
judicial through the *nomothetai* taken from the members of the law-courts.

CHAPTER XVII

*There may, however, be a particular sort of society in which absolute
kingship ought to be instituted. This is the sort of society in which
one family, or one person, is of merit so outstanding as to surpass all
the other members. Here justice and propriety may be argued to
require that there should be absolute kingship, with plenary power and
no limit of tenure.*

§ 1. These arguments, however, may only be partly true—true
when applied to some societies, but not when applied to others.
There is one sort of society which is meant by its nature for rule

of the despotic type [i.e. rule of the type exercised by a master over his slaves], another for rule by a king, and another still for rule of a constitutional type; and it is just and expedient that each of these societies should be ruled accordingly. (But there is no society which is meant by its nature for rule of the tyrannical type, or for rule of the other types found in wrong or perverted constitutions: the societies that are under such types of rule have fallen into an unnatural condition.) § 2. What has just been said is sufficient to show that in a group whose **1288 a** members are equal and peers it is neither expedient nor just that one man should be sovereign over all others. This is equally true whether laws are absent, with the one man ruling as a law in himself, or are present; it is true whether the one man is a good man ruling over the good, or a bad man ruling over the bad; it is even true when the one man is superior [to others] in goodness . . . unless his superiority be of a special character. § 3. We have now to see what that character is—though as a matter of fact it has already been in some sense explained in an earlier passage.[1]

[[We must first determine what sorts of group are appropriate to kingship, to aristocracy, and to government of the constitutional type. § 4. The society appropriate to kingship is one of the sort which naturally tends to produce some particular stock, or family, pre-eminent in its capacity for political leadership. The society appropriate to aristocracy is one which naturally tends to produce a body of persons capable of being ruled, in a manner suitable to free men, by those who are men of leading in their capacity for political rule. The society appropriate to government of the constitutional type [i.e. the 'polity'] is one in which there naturally exists a body of persons possessing military capacity, who can rule and be ruled under a system of law which distributes offices among the wealthy in proportion to merit.]][2]

§ 5. [The special character of the superiority which may entitle one man to rule, in spite of the general presumption to the contrary, is this.] When it happens that the whole of a family, or even a single person, is of merit so outstanding as to surpass that of all the rest, it is only just that this family should be vested with kingship and absolute sovereignty, or that this single person

[1] The earlier passage is in c. XIII, § 13, and again §§ 24-5. It may be noticed that the sentences (bracketed in the text) which immediately follow in the present chapter seem to be in the nature of an interruption or interpolation. Their position in the text may be defended; but they interrupt the argument, and the connexion suggested between constitutional government and military organization (though it agrees with the views expressed later in Book IV, c. XIII, §§ 10-11) does not agree with the general view about the succession of forms of government previously expressed in c. XV, § 11. The final words, too, present a difficulty.
[2] See Note GG, p. 151.

should become king [and absolute sovereign]. § 6. But it is not only a question of what is just. Justice is a ground which is usually pleaded in establishing any form of constitution—be it aristocracy or oligarchy, or be it, again, democracy. In all forms alike the claim is made that justice demands the recognition of some sort of superiority, though the sort for which the claim is made varies from one form to another. Here, however, there is a special ground which we have already had reason to mention[1]—the ground of what is proper. § 7. It would be surely improper to execute a man of outstanding superiority, or to banish him permanently, or to ostracize him for a period. It would be no less improper to require him to take his turn at being a subject under a system of rotation. A whole is never intended by nature to be inferior to a part; and a man so greatly superior to others stands to them in the relation of a whole to its parts. § 8. The only course which remains is that he should receive obedience, and should have sovereign power without any limit of tenure—not turn by turn with others.[2]

These may serve as our conclusions in regard to kingship, and as our answers to the three questions—what are its different forms? is it, or is it not, advantageous to states? and, if it be so, to what states, and under what conditions, is it advantageous?

Note GG (p. 150): *The interpretation of the 'Polity'*

These words 'among the wealthy in proportion to merit' are curious and difficult. In the first place, they seem self-contradictory. If offices are distributed among the wealthy, will they be also distributed in proportion to merit? And vice versa, if they are distributed in proportion to merit, will they be distributed only among the wealthy? In the second place, the words are contrary to what we should expect, which is that offices should be distributed among *all* the citizens, but with a preference for the more meritorious. It may be, however, that 'the wealthy' here means only 'those wealthy enough to provide themselves with armour for military service'; and it may be urged in favour of this view that Aristotle has already presupposed that the civic body possesses military capacity. In that case offices will be open to, and will rotate among, *all* members of the civic body possessing that amount of wealth, but a preference will be given to merit. We may then compare c. VII, § 4 of this book, where it is stated that in the 'polity', or government of the constitutional type, 'those who possess arms are the persons who enjoy constitutional rights'. We may also compare Book IV, c. XIII, § 10, where the succession of constitutions is connected with changes in the art of war, and the 'polity' is connected with the development of a heavy-armed infantry.

[1] See above, c. XIII, § 25.
[2] This paragraph contains the utmost that Aristotle can say on behalf of absolute monarchy. It turns out to be rather a logical necessity (which is left in vague and general terms) than a practical proposition.

CHAPTER XVIII

We may now turn to inquire by what means a good constitution—be it an aristocracy or a kingship—should be brought into existence. The same means must be used to make a good constitution as are used to make a good man. We are thus led to inquire into the nature of the good life, which is the aim of both the good man and the good constitution.

§ 1. [We may now turn to inquire how a good constitution can be brought into being.] We have laid it down that there are three types of right constitution, and that the best of these must be the one which is administered by the best. This is the type in which there is a single man, or a whole family, or a number of persons, surpassing all others in goodness [and therefore entitled to rule], but where ruled as well as rulers are fitted to play their part in the attainment of the most desirable mode of life. We have also shown, at the beginning of our inquiry,[1] that the goodness of the good man, and that of the good citizen of the best state, must be one and the same. It clearly follows that just the same method, and just the same **1288 b** means, by which a man achieves goodness, should also be used to achieve the creation of a state on the pattern of aristocracy or kingship [i.e. on a pattern which makes the goodness of the good citizen coincide with that of the good man]; and thus the training and habits of action which make a good man will be generally the same as the training and habits of action which make a good statesman[2] or a good king.

§ 2. These issues determined, we must next attempt to treat of the best form of constitution, asking ourselves, 'Under what conditions does it tend to arise, and how can it be established?' In order to make a proper inquiry into this subject it is necessary[3] . . . [to begin by determining the nature of the most desirable mode of life].

NOTE HH: *The problem of the end of Book III*

The words at the close of this chapter, which ends in this abrupt manner, are repeated exactly at the beginning of Book VII. (The words added here in square brackets do not occur in the original text at the end of Book III, where the sentence ends in the middle: they are the words used when the sentence is completed at the beginning of Book VII.) It is an old question among scholars whether the order of the books of

---

[1] See c. IV of this book, especially from § 11 onwards.

[2] The statesman or *politikos* may be generally defined as a person who exercises authority, in his turn, over a society of equals and peers: cf. *supra*, c. IV, § 14, note. Here he is the statesman in an ideal aristocracy, in which all are equals and peers in goodness.

[3] See Note HH.

the *Politics* should be changed, and Book VII should be made to follow
immediately on Book III. (See the Introduction, III, pp. xxxix–xli.)
Meanwhile it is sufficient to say that the end of this chapter, or even
possibly the whole, may well be a later addition. It is by no means clear;
and the assumption that the best state, or best type of constitution, will
be an aristocracy or kingship does not agree with the argument of
Books VII and VIII, where nothing is said of kingship, and little if
anything of aristocracy. On the other hand it *does* agree with what is said
about the classification of constitutions in c. VII of this book.

BOOK IV

ACTUAL CONSTITUTIONS AND THEIR VARIETIES

A

INTRODUCTORY (cc. i–ii)

CHAPTER I

Politics, like other arts and sciences, must consider not only the ideal, but also the various problems of the actual—e.g. which is the best constitution practicable in the given circumstances; what are the best means of preserving actual constitutions; which is the best average constitution for the majority of states; what are the different varieties of the main types of constitution, and especially of democracy and oligarchy. Politics, too, must consider not only constitutions, but also laws, and the proper relation of laws to constitutions.

1288 b 10 § 1. There is a rule which applies to all the practical arts and sciences, when they have come to cover the whole of a subject, and are no longer engaged in investigating it bit by bit. Each of them severally has to consider the different methods appropriate to the different categories of its subject. For instance, the art of physical training has to consider (1) which type of training is appropriate to which type of physique; (2) which is the ideal type of training—i.e. the training best for a physique of the best endowment and the best equipment (for the ideal type of training must be one which is suitable for such a physique); and (3) which is the type of training that can be generally applied to the majority of physiques—for that too is one of the problems to be solved by the art of physical training. § 2. Nor is this all. (4) There may be men who want to have physical training, but do not want to attain the standard of skill and condition which is needed for competitions; and here the trainer and the gymnastic master have still another duty—to impart the degree of capacity which is all that such men want.[1] . . . What is true of the art of physical training is obviously no less true of medicine, or of shipbuilding, tailoring, and all the other arts.

[1] If we apply this analogy to the art and science of politics, it will have four functions: (1) to discover which sort of constitution is appropriate to which sort of civic body; (2) to discover the best constitution which is appropriate to the best sort of civic body; (3) to discover the sort of constitution (e.g. the 'polity') which is generally appropriate to most sorts of civic bodies; (4) to discover the constitution, or constitutions, which—without being either ideally best or generally appropriate—will suit a civic body that is content with a lower degree of civic life (and will accordingly put up with an oligarchy, or an inferior type of democracy, or even a tyranny).

§ 3. It follows that the study of politics [which belongs to the practical arts and sciences] must be equally comprehensive. First, it has to consider which is the best constitution, and what qualities a constitution must have to come closest to the ideal when there are no external factors [e.g. want of means, or unequal distribution of means] to hinder its doing so. Secondly, politics has to consider which sort of constitution suits which sort of civic body. The attainment of the best constitution is likely to be impossible for the general run of states; and the good law-giver and the true statesman must therefore have their eyes open not only to what is the absolute best, but also to what is the best in relation to actual conditions. § 4. Thirdly, politics has also to consider the sort of constitution which depends upon an assumption.[1] In other words, the student of politics must also be able to study a *given* constitution, just as it stands and simply with a view to explaining how it may have arisen and how it may be made to enjoy the longest possible life. The sort of case which we have in mind is one where a state has neither the ideally best constitution (or even the elementary conditions needed for it) nor the best constitution possible under the actual conditions, but has only a constitution of an inferior type. § 5. Fourthly,[2] and in addition to all these functions, politics has also to provide a knowledge of the type of constitution which is best suited to states in general. Most of the writers who treat of politics—good as they may be in other repects—fail when they come to deal with matters of practical *utility*.[3] § 6. We have not only to study the ideally best constitution. We have also to study the type of constitution which is practicable [i.e. the best for a state under actual conditions]—and with it, and equally, the type which is easiest to work and most suitable to states generally. As things are, writers fall into two different classes. Some confine their investigations to the extreme of perfection, which requires a large equipment [of initial advantages]. The

---

[1] i.e. the assumption of a lower standard of civic attainment than the absolute or even the relative best. It is an assumption which, in the sphere of politics, corresponds to that made in the sphere of training by the man who 'does not want to attain the standard . . . needed for competitions'.

[2] It will be noticed that the order in which Aristotle arranges the functions of the science of politics differs from that in which he arranges the functions of the science of physical training. The first function enumerated for the science of physical training corresponds to the second enumerated for the science of politics: the second to the first; the third to the fourth; and the fourth to the third.

[3] This phrase (*ta chrēsima*) strikes the general keynote of Books IV, V, and VI, which are all occupied with matters of practical utility—in the first instance, with what is useful for the preservation of actual constitutions as they stand, and, in the second, with what is useful in the way of a practical reform of actual constitutions such as can be generally adopted.

rest, addressing themselves rather to an attainable form, still banish from view the general range of existing constitutions, and simply extol the Spartan or some other *one* constitution. **1289 a** § 7. The sort of constitutional system which ought to be proposed is one which men can be easily induced, and will be readily able, to graft onto the system they already have. It is as difficult a matter to reform an old constitution as it is to construct a new one; as hard to unlearn a lesson as it was to learn it initially. The true statesman, therefore, must not confine himself to the matters we have just mentioned [the study of the ideally best constitution, or that of some one particular form such as the Spartan]: he must also be able, as we said previously, to help *any* existing constitution [along the path of reform].[1] § 8. He cannot do so unless he knows how many different kinds of constitutions there are. As things are, we find people believing that there is only one sort of democracy or oligarchy. This is an error. To avoid that error, we must keep in mind the different varieties of each constitution; we must be aware of their number, and of the number of different ways in which they are constituted.[2]

§ 9. Making the same effort of discrimination, the student of politics should also learn to distinguish the laws which are absolutely best from those which are appropriate to each constitution. We use the phrase, 'appropriate to each constitution', because laws ought to be made to suit constitutions (as indeed in practice they always are), and not constitutions made to suit laws. § 10. The reason is this. A constitution may be defined as 'an organization of offices in a state, by which the method of their distribution is fixed, the sovereign authority is determined, and the nature of the end to be pursued by the association and all its members is prescribed.'[3] Laws, as distinct from the frame of the constitution, are the rules by which the magistrates should exercise their powers, and should watch and check transgressors. § 11. It follows on this conception of the relation between laws and constitutions that we must always bear in mind the varieties of each constitution, and the number of those varieties, [not only in order to be able to reform each by the appropriate constitutional amend-

---

[1] In other words, which are the words of an old Greek proverb, he must say to himself, '*This* has fallen to thy lot: make the best of it.'

[2] The different varieties of democracy, for example, are constituted in a number of ways—one variety by having a greater amount of the features of democracy, another by having a smaller amount, and a third by having them all (VI. c. 1, § 9).

[3] Compare with this definition of 'constitution' the definition already given in Book III, c. VI, § 1: 'the organization of a polis, in respect of its offices generally, but especially in respect of that particular office which is sovereign in all issues'

ments, but] also in order to be able to enact the laws appropriate to each. If we assume [as we must] that there is not a single
form of democracy, or a single form of oligarchy, but a number of
varieties of either, the same laws cannot possibly be equally beneficial to *all* oligarchies or to *all* democracies.

CHAPTER II

*On this basis, after the general considerations of the previous book and
the account of kingship and aristocracy there given, it remains to
discuss the 'right' form of constitution called 'polity', and the three
'perverted' forms called democracy, oligarchy, and tyranny. These
three perversions may be graded in an ascending order—tyranny the
worst; oligarchy the next worst; and democracy the least bad. The
general programme of future inquiry may be stated under five heads:*

1. *The varieties of the main types of constitutions (especially democracy and oligarchy);*
2. *The type of constitution which is most generally practicable;*
3. *Which sort of constitution is desirable for which sort of civic body;*
4. *The methods of establishing constitutions;*
5. *The causes of the destruction, and the methods of the preservation,
   of different constitutions.*

§ 1. In our first discussion of constitutions[1] we distinguished
three varieties of right constitution (kingship, aristocracy, and the
'polity'), and three corresponding perversions of those varieties
(tyranny being the perversion of kingship, oligarchy of aristocracy,
and democracy of the 'polity'). Aristocracy and kingship have
already been treated. To consider the ideal constitution is, in
effect, to consider the two constitutions so named;[2] for they both
aim, like the ideal constitution, at a society whose basis is goodness
duly equipped with the necessary means for its exercise. We have
also defined, in a previous passage, the nature of the difference
between aristocracy and kingship, and we have explained when
and where a kingship should be established.[3] It only remains,
therefore, to discuss (1) [under the head of right constitutions] the

[1] See Note II, p. 159.
[2] This is a puzzling statement, especially when we remember that monarchy
and aristocracy are actual constitutions, and that the ideal constitution is something which, by its nature, transcends the actual—as Books VII and VIII
subsequently show. But Aristotle would seem to be referring here to the end of
Book III (c. XVIII, § 1), where the ideal constitution is stated—not, it is true,
very clearly—to be aristocratic or monarchical. We have to recognize, however,
that Aristotle, in different contexts, says different things, which cannot be easily
reconciled with one another.
[3] The difference between aristocracy and kingship is defined in Book III,
c. VII, § 3, c. XV, § 10, and c. XVII, § 4: the proper time and place for establishing
a kingship is explained in Book III, c. XVII, §§ 5–8.

'polity', which is called by the generic name common to all constitutions or polities, and (2) [under the head of perversions] oligarchy, democracy, and tyranny.

§ 2. [We may pause to note that, just as the order of merit of the right constitutions is obvious, so] it is also obvious which of these perversions is the worst, and which of them is the next worst. The perversion of the first and the most nearly divine of the right constitutions must necessarily be the worst. Kingship [is the first and most nearly divine of the right constitutions; for it] **1289 b** must either be merely a name, without any substance, or be based on the fact of a king's great personal superiority. Tyranny, therefore, is the worst, and at the farthest remove of all the perversions from a true constitution: oligarchy, being as it is far removed from aristocracy, is the next worst: democracy is the most moderate [and so the least bad]. § 3. One of our predecessors [Plato, in his dialogue the *Politicus*] has already advanced the same view; but he used a different principle. On his principle all constitutions could have a good as well as a bad form: oligarchy, for example, could be good as well as bad; and going on this principle he ranked the good form of democracy as the worst of all the good forms of constitution, and the bad form of it as the best of all the bad. In our opinion these two constitutions, in any of their forms, are wholly on the side of error. It cannot properly be said that one form of oligarchy is better than another; it can only be said that one is not so bad as another.[1]

§ 4. But we may dismiss for the present this issue of the grading of constitutions in an order of merit [and return to our programme of matters which still remain for discussion]. We have, first, to distinguish and enumerate the varieties of each type of constitution, on the assumption that democracy and oligarchy [not to speak of other types] have each several different forms. Secondly, we have to examine what type of constitution—short of the ideal— is the most generally acceptable, and the most to be preferred; and here we must also examine whether, besides this general type, there is any other constitution to be found, of a more aristocratic and well-constructed character but suitable, none the less, for adoption in most states. § 5. Thirdly, and in regard to constitutions generally, we have to inquire which constitution is desirable for which sort of civic body. It is possible, for instance, that democracy rather than oligarchy may be necessary for one sort of civic body, and oligarchy rather than democracy for another.

---

[1] The difference between Plato and Aristotle is only a difference of nomenclature. And even in the matter of nomenclature, as Newman notes, Plato had not spoken of 'a good form of oligarchy': he had used the term 'aristocracy'.

Fourthly, we have to consider how those who wish to do so should set to work to establish these various constitutions—i.e. the different varieties both of democracy and oligarchy. § 6. Fifthly, when we have given a concise account of all these subjects, to the best of our power, we must attempt to handle a final theme. How are constitutions generally, and each constitution severally, liable to be destroyed; how can they be preserved; and what are the causes which particularly tend to produce these results?[1]

NOTE II (p. 157): *The course of the argument in* c. II

We might have expected, after the statement of the four functions of the science of politics in §§ 3–5 of the previous chapter, that Aristotle would inquire into each of the functions in order. Actually he goes back— perhaps under the influence of what has been said at the end of c. I about the importance of distinguishing the varieties of each constitution, and of discovering the number of those varieties—to the classification of constitutions already sketched in Book III, c. VII; and on the basis of that classification he proceeds to state a new programme of inquiry.

When he uses the phrase, 'the first discussion of constitutions', Aristotle is apparently referring to Books II and III, and especially III. From this point of view Book IV may be said to begin 'the second discussion of constitutions', which is continued in Books V and VI. It is never made clear how Books VII and VIII (on the ideal constitution) fit into the scheme of the *Politics*—and, in particular, how they are related either to Book II (with its sketch of previous ideal constitutions, theoretical and actual) or to Book III (which ends with a promise of the immediate treatment of the ideal constitution). But see the Introduction, pp. xl–xli.

NOTE JJ: *Aristotle's programme of inquiry*

The five headings of this programme are, in effect, a recapitulation of the four functions assigned to politics in §§ 3–5 of the previous chapter; but there are some differences. First, the order is different; secondly, the first function assigned to politics—that of investigating the ideal constitution—disappears in the recapitulation, on the ground that the ideal constitution has already been discussed, and need not enter into the programme of future inquiry; thirdly, some questions which were only incidentally mentioned in the previous statement (e.g. the number of the varieties of actual constitutions, the methods of establishing each variety, and the ways in which each variety may be destroyed and can be preserved) now become separate and main headings of inquiry. Roughly we may say (1) that the first function of politics is here eliminated; (2) that the second function corresponds to the third heading of the new programme; (3) that the third function corresponds to the fourth and fifth headings of the new programme; (4) that the fourth function corresponds to the second heading of the new programme, while a matter only incidentally mentioned in connexion with it before (c. I, § 8) now becomes the first heading. It remains to be added that the headings of the new programme are not altogether followed, as we shall see later, in the subsequent course of the argument. Aristotle sketches plans in advance; but he lets the argument develop afterwards in its own way.

[1] See Note JJ.

B

THE VARIETIES OF THE MAIN TYPES OF CONSTITUTION
ESPECIALLY DEMOCRACY, OLIGARCHY, AND 'POLITY'. (cc. iii–x)

Chapter III

*The reason for the variety of constitutions is the varieties to be found
in the 'parts' or social elements of the state—especially among the
populace and the notables. A constitution is an arrangement of offices;
and there will be as many constitutions as there are methods of distributing offices among the different parts of the state. There is a
general opinion that there are only two sorts of constitutions, just as
there are only two sorts of winds and two sorts of musical modes; but
this is a simplification which cannot be accepted.*

§ 1. The reason why there are a number of different constitutions is to be found in the fact that every state has a number of
different parts.[1] In the first place, every state is obviously composed of families. Secondly, this aggregate of families is bound to
be divided into classes—the rich, the poor, and the middle class,
with the rich possessing and the poor being without the equipment
of the heavy-armed soldier. § 2. Thirdly, the common people
(or *dēmos*) are engaged in different occupations—partly agriculture,
partly trade, and partly the mechanical arts. Fourthly, there are
also differences among the notables—differences based on their
wealth and the amount of their property; and these differences
appear, for example, in the matter of keeping horses, which can
only be done by the very wealthy. § 3. (Incidentally, this is the
reason why states whose strength lay in cavalry were in former
times the homes of oligarchies. These oligarchies used their
cavalry in wars with adjoining states: we may cite the examples of
Eretria and Chalcis in the island of Euboea, and of Magnesia on
the Maeander and many other cities in Asia Minor.) § 4. There
are also other differences, besides that of wealth, among the notables. There is difference of birth: there is difference of merit;
1290 a and there are other differences based on other factors of
the same order—factors already described as being parts of a state
in our discussion of aristocracy, where we distinguished and
enumerated the factors which are necessary to the life of all states.[2]

---

[1] See Note KK, p. 162.

[2] It will be noticed that the word 'part', as it is here used, sometimes denotes
a quantity or body of persons, and sometimes a quality or attribute possessed by
a body of persons. The variation of meaning is natural; for generally the body
of persons is united and constituted by the fact of possessing a common attribute
or quality, and, conversely, the attribute or quality marks off some body of
persons who possess it as a separate body. We may thus speak either of the
wealthy or of wealth as a 'part' of the state. The previous 'discussion of aristocracy' is probably the discussion which comes in Book III, c. XII, §§ 8–9. The

These are the parts of which states are composed. Sometimes all these parts share in the control of the constitution; sometimes only a few of them share; sometimes a number of them share. § 5. It thus follows clearly that there must be a number of constitutions, which differ from one another in kind. The parts that share in their control differ from one another in kind; and *they* must differ accordingly. A constitution is an arrangement in regard to the offices of the state. By this arrangement the citizen body distributes office, either on the basis of the *power* of those who receive it, or on the basis of some sort of *equality* existing among all who receive it (i.e. the power of the rich *or* the poor, or—if equality be the basis—an equality existing among both rich *and* poor). § 6. There must therefore be as many constitutions as there are modes of arranging the distribution of office according to the superiorities and the differences of the parts of the state.[1]

There is indeed a prevalent opinion that there are only two constitutions. Just as winds, in ordinary speech, are simply described as north or south, and all other winds are treated as varieties of these two, so constitutions are also described as democratic or oligarchical. § 7. On this basis aristocracy is classified, as being a sort of oligarchy, under the heading of oligarchical, and similarly the constitution called 'polity' is classified under the heading of democratic—much as westerly winds are classified under the head of northerly, and easterly winds under that of southerly.[2] The same division into two main kinds is also true, some thinkers believe, of modes in music, which are accordingly described as being Dorian or Phrygian—other arrangements then being called by one or other of these two names. § 8. But though this is the prevalent view about constitutions in current opinion, we shall do better, and we shall come nearer the truth, if we classify them on a different basis, as has already been suggested.[3]

'other similar factors' there described as parts which are necessary to the life of the state are 'a temper of justice and a martial habit'.

[1] The meaning of this, as Newman notes, is that constitutions vary (1) according to the 'superiorities' (in wealth, or birth, or merit) possessed by parts such as the notables, (2) according to the 'differences' (in occupation—agricultural, commercial, or artisan) exhibited by a part such as the common people or *dēmos*.

[2] In England we should naturally reverse this order, and associate west winds with the south and east winds with the north. But the Greek east wind (*euros*) was really an east-*south*-east wind; and similarly the Greek west wind was *north*-west, and accordingly associated by Homer (as a rainy and stormy wind) with the north.

[3] The previous suggestion came in c. II of this book, §§ 2–3. But neither that passage nor the present passage quite squares with the classification of constitutions given in Book III, c. VII, where there are three 'right' constitutions (not 'one or two', as is here suggested); and the parallel drawn between constitutions and musical modes has the curious result of making restricted oligarchies 'hypo-Dorian' and advanced democracies 'hypo-Phrygian'.

On that basis we shall have one or two constitutions which are 'right' or properly formed constitutions; all the others will be perversions of the best (just as in music we may have perversions of the properly tempered modes); and these perversions will be oligarchical when [like perversions of the Dorian mode] they are more than ordinarily severe and dominant, and democratic when [like perversions of the Phrygian mode] they are soft and relaxed.

NOTE KK (p. 160): *The course of the argument in* c. iii–c. iv

We should expect this chapter, if it followed the headings of the programme stated at the end of the previous chapter, to begin with a discussion of the question, 'How many are the varieties of each constitution, and especially of democracy and oligarchy?' Instead of this, the chapter (like the chapter by which it is followed) is actually concerned with the question, 'Why are there a number of constitutions, and not one constitution only?' This is obviously a different question; and the change of front presents us with something of a difficulty. Again, in discussing this new question, Aristotle is led to inquire into the parts of the state, because he regards the plurality of constitutions as due to the variety of those parts—each different part issuing, when it is dominant, in a different constitution. Here our difficulty is increased by the fact that c. III gives one account of the parts of the state and c. IV proceeds to give another and discrepant account. There is thus a double difficulty: (1) that of the relevance of the whole argument of both chapters to the programme previously sketched, and (2) that of the discrepancy between the two chapters. The first difficulty may be dismissed: Aristotle, as we have already noted, does not bind himself down to follow exactly the plans he sketches. The second difficulty is more serious. We may try to solve it by the suggestion that Aristotle left two different drafts, which are both reproduced in our text (possibly with some connecting links which were added by a later editor); or we may cut the knot by bracketing as an interpolation the whole of c. III and the first 20 sections of c. IV.

CHAPTER IV

Democracy does not mean only the rule of number: it also means the rule of a social class. Both criteria must be used to define democracy, as both number and social class must also be used to define oligarchy. On this basis we may now study the different varieties of democracy and oligarchy, which (as stated in the previous chapter) will depend on the varieties to be found in the 'parts' of different states—i.e. on the different natures of their social composition. We shall accordingly classify the varieties of constitutions as we should classify the various species of animals—by the varieties of their parts and of the composition of those parts. We therefore proceed to enumerate the ten or so parts which go to the composition of a state, contrasting our enumeration with the different enumeration of Plato. We must also take note of the different forms assumed by the dēmos, or populace—and also by the upper class—according as one or another part predominates

in its make-up. This enables us to distinguish five varieties of demo-
cracy, in a descending scale which ends in 'extreme democracy'—a
variety of democracy, analogous to tyranny, where law has ceased to be
sovereign and the notion of a constitution has practically disappeared.

§ 1. It ought not to be assumed, as some thinkers are nowadays
in the habit of doing, that democracy can be defined off-hand,
without any qualification, as a form of constitution in which the
greater number are sovereign. Even in oligarchies—and indeed
in all constitutions—the majority [i.e. the majority of those who
enjoy constitutional rights] is sovereign. Similarly, oligarchy cannot be simply defined as a form in which a few persons are the
constitutional sovereign. § 2. Assume a total population of 1,300:
assume that 1,000 of the 1,300 are wealthy; assume that these 1,000
assign no share in office to the remaining 300 poor, although they
are men of free birth and their peers in other respects. Nobody
will say that here there is a democracy. § 3. Or assume, again,
that there are only a few poor men, but that they are stronger than
the rich men who form the majority [and are therefore sovereign].
Nobody would term such a constitution an oligarchy, when no
share in honours and office is given to the majority who possess
riches. It is better, therefore, to say that democracy exists where-
ever the **1290 b** free-born are sovereign, and oligarchy wherever
the rich are in control. § 4. As things go, the former are many,
and the latter few: there are many who are free-born, but few who
are rich. [The essence, however, in either case is not the factor
of number, but the factor of social position.]¹ Otherwise [i.e.
if number alone were the essence] we should have an oligarchy if
offices were distributed on the basis of stature (as they are said to
be in Ethiopia), or on the basis of looks; for the number of tall or
good-looking men must always be small. § 5. Yet it is not sufficient to distinguish democracy and oligarchy merely by the criterion
of poverty and wealth, any more than it is to do so merely by that
of number. We have to remember that the democratic and the
oligarchical state both contain a *number* of parts; and we must
therefore use additional criteria to distinguish them properly. We
cannot, for example, apply the term democracy to a constitution
under which a few free-born persons rule a majority who are not
free-born [as if birth were the one and only criterion]. (A system
of this sort once existed at Apollonia, on the Ionian Gulf, and at

¹ The argument at this point largely repeats the argument already advanced
in Book III, c. VIII, §§ 3–7; but, as Newman notes, the previous argument
differs—and differs for the better—in taking fuller account of the difficulties of
the question, and in arriving, in consequence, at a fuller definition of democracy
and oligarchy.

Thera. In both of these states honours and offices were reserved for those who were of the best birth—in the sense of being the descendants of the original settlers—though they were only a handful of the whole population.) Nor can we apply the term oligarchy to a constitution under which the rich are sovereign simply because they are more numerous than the poor [as if number were the one criterion]. (An example of such a constitution formerly existed at Colophon, where before the war with Lydia a majority of the citizens were the owners of large properties.) § 6. The proper application of the term 'democracy' is to a constitution in which the free-born and poor control the government—being at the same time a majority; and similarly the term 'oligarchy' is properly applied to a constitution in which the rich and better-born control the government—being at the same time a minority.

§ 7. The general fact that there are a number of constitutions, and the cause of that fact, have been established. It remains to explain why there are more constitutions than the two just mentioned [i.e. democracy and oligarchy]; to indicate what they are; and to suggest the reasons for their existence. In doing so we may start from the principle which was previously stated, and which can now be assumed, that every state consists, not of one, but of many parts.[1] § 8. [Here we may use a biological analogy.] If we aimed at a classification of the different kinds of animals, we should begin by enumerating the parts, or organs, which are necessary to every animal. These will include, for example, some of the sensory organs: they will also include the organs for getting and digesting food, such as the mouth and the stomach; they will further include the organs of locomotion which are used by the different animals. We shall then assume that our enumeration of the necessary organs is exhaustive; and we shall proceed to the further assumption that there are varieties of these organs—or, in other words, different species of mouths, stomachs, sensory organs, and organs of locomotion. We shall thus reach the conclusion that the number of possible combinations of these varieties will inevitably produce several different kinds of animals (for the same kind of animal cannot exhibit several varieties of mouth, or of ears); and thus the whole of the possible combinations of varieties will account for the different kinds of animals, or [to put the same

---

[1] These sentences may be an editorial addition, intended to introduce a new account of the parts of the state, which (as has already been noted) is discrepant from the previous account. This new account, which extends from § 7 to § 19, is followed at the beginning of § 20 by a repetition of the first sentence of § 7. We can only regard this new account as a second and alternative treatment of the same theme, added in a somewhat baffling manner, with an introductory explanation which does not succeed in explaining the addition.

point in another way] the number of kinds of animals will be equal to the number of the possible combinations of the necessary organs.

§ 9. It is just the same with the constitutions which have been mentioned.[1] [There are as many kinds of *them* as there are possible combinations of the necessary parts of the state.] States too, as we have repeatedly noticed, are composed not of one but of many parts. One of these parts is the group of persons concerned with the production of food, or, as it is called, the farming class. A second, which is called the mechanical class, is the group of persons **1291 a** occupied in the various arts and crafts without which a city cannot be inhabited—some of them being necessities, and others contributing to luxury or to the living of a good life. § 10. A third part is what may be termed the marketing class; it includes all those who are occupied in buying and selling, either as merchants or as retailers. A fourth part is the serf class composed of agricultural labourers; and a fifth element is the defence force, which is no less necessary than the other four, if a state is not to become the slave of invaders. § 11. How is it possible, with any propriety, to call by the name of state a society which is naturally servile? It is the essence of a state to be independent and self-sufficing; and it is the absence of independence which is the mark of the slave.

We may pause to note that this is the reason why Plato's account of the parts of the state, in his *Republic*, is inadequate, though ingenious. § 12. He begins by stating that the four most necessary elements for the constitution of a state are weavers, farmers, shoemakers, and builders. He then proceeds, on the ground that these four are not self-sufficient, to add other parts—smiths; herdsmen to tend the necessary cattle; merchants and retail dealers. These are the parts which form the whole complement of the 'first state' which he sketches—as though a state merely existed for the supply of necessities, and not rather to achieve the Good, and as though it needed the shoemaker as much as it needs the farmer. § 13. The part which serves as a defence force is not introduced till a later stage, when the growth of the city's territory, and its contact with the territory of its neighbours, result in its being plunged into war. [Nor is this all that Plato has omitted in his 'first city'.] The four original parts—or whatever may be the number of the elements forming the association—will require some authority to dispense justice, and to determine what is just. § 14. If the mind is to be

---

[1] The reference here would seem to be, not to democracy and oligarchy (as in § 7 above), but to all the six kinds of constitution mentioned in Book III, c. VII—and not only to these six kinds, but also to the species into which some of the kinds (and especially oligarchy and democracy) can be subdivided.

reckoned as more essentially a part of a living being than the body, parts of a similar order to the mind must equally be reckoned as more essentially parts of the state than those which serve its bodily needs; and by parts of a similar order to the mind we mean the military part, the part concerned in the legal organization of justice, and (we may also add) the part engaged in deliberation, which is a function that needs the gift of political understanding. § 15. Whether these three functions—war, justice, and deliberation —belong to separate groups, or to a single group, is a matter which makes no difference to the argument. It often falls to the same persons both to serve in the army and to till the fields; [and the same may be true of these three functions]. The general conclusion which we thus reach is that if those who discharge these functions are equally parts of the state with those who supply its bodily needs, they, or at least the armed forces, are *necessary* parts. . . .

The seventh part[1] is the group composed of the rich, who serve the state with their property. § 16. The eighth part is the magistrates, who serve the state in its offices. No state can exist without a government; and there must therefore be persons capable of discharging the duties of office and rendering the state that service, permanently or in rotation. § 17. There only remain the two parts which have just been mentioned in passing—the deliberative part, and the part which decides on the rights of litigants. These are parts which ought to exist in all states, and to exist on a good and just basis; and this demands persons **1291 b** of a good quality in matters political. § 18. [Here we begin to confront a difficulty.] The different capacities belonging to the other parts may, it is generally held, be shown by one and the same group of persons. The same persons, for example, may serve as soldiers, farmers, and craftsmen; the same persons, again, may act both as a deliberative council and a judicial court. Political ability, too, is a quality to which all men pretend; and everybody thinks himself capable of filling most offices. There is one thing which is impossible: the same persons cannot be both rich and poor. § 19. This will explain why these two classes—the rich and the poor—are regarded as parts of the state in a special and peculiar sense. Nor is this all. One of these classes being small, and the other large, they also appear to be *opposite* parts. This is why they both form constitutions to suit their own interest [that of wealth in the one case, and

---

[1] It will be noticed that no sixth part has been enumerated by Aristotle. We may perhaps assume, from his mention of a judicial part in the criticism of the *Republic*, that the judicial part is intended to be the sixth in his own enumeration. The difficulty of this assumption is, however, that Aristotle afterwards proceeds to mention the judicial part explicitly (§ 17); and perhaps it is best to assume a lacuna.

that of numbers in the other]. It is also the reason why men think that there are only two constitutions—democracy and oligarchy.

§ 20. The fact that there are a number of constitutions, and the causes of that fact, have already been established. We may now go on to say that there are also a number of varieties of two of these constitutions—democracy and oligarchy.[1] This is already clear from what has been previously said [at the beginning of the previous chapter]. § 21. These constitutions vary because the people (*dēmos*) and the class called the notables vary. So far as the people are concerned, one sort is engaged in farming; a second is engaged in the arts and crafts; a third is the marketing sort, which is engaged in buying and selling; a fourth is the maritime sort, which in turn is partly naval, partly mercantile, partly employed on ferries, and partly engaged in fisheries. (We may note that there are many places where one of these subdivisions forms a considerable body; as the fishermen do at Tarentum and Byzantium, the naval crews at Athens, the merchant seamen in Aegina and Chios, and the ferrymen at Tenedos.) A fifth sort is composed of unskilled labourers and persons whose means are too small to enable them to enjoy any leisure; a sixth consists of those who are not of free birth by two citizen parents; and there may also be other sorts of a similar character. § 22. The notables fall into different sorts according to wealth, birth, merit, culture, and other qualities of the same order.

The first variety of democracy is the variety which is said to follow the principle of equality closest. In this variety the law declares equality to mean that the poor are to count no more than the rich: neither is to be sovereign, and both are to be on a level. § 23. [We may approve this law]; for if we hold, as some thinkers do, that liberty and equality are chiefly to be found in democracy, it will be along these lines—with all sharing alike, as far as possible, in constitutional rights—that they will most likely be found. A constitution of this order is bound to be a democracy; for [while all share alike] the people are the majority, and the will of the majority is sovereign. § 24. A second variety of democracy is that in which offices are assigned on the basis of a property qualification, but the qualification is low: those who attain it have to be admitted to a share in office, and those who lose it are excluded. A third **1292 a** variety is one in which every citizen of unimpeach-

---

[1] Aristotle here touches, at last, the question which was stated, at the end of c. II, to be the first heading of his programme of inquiry. The fact that this question is here first faced explains why some commentators have bracketed, as an interpolation, the whole of c. III and the first 20 sections of this chapter. But as Aristotle now proceeds to use the argument developed in c. III the remedy seems too drastic. It is simpler to believe that he has made a digression (as he often does, and as most lecturers do), and that he now returns to his theme.

able descent can share in office, but the law is the final sovereign. § 25. A fourth variety is one in which every person [irrespective of descent, and] provided only that he is a citizen, can share in office, but the law is still the final sovereign. A fifth variety of democracy is like the fourth in admitting to office every person who has the status of citizen; but here the people, and not the law, is the final sovereign. This is what happens when popular decrees are sove-reign instead of the law;[1] and that is a result which is brought about by leaders of the demagogue type.[2] § 26. In democracies which obey the law there are no demagogues; it is the better class of citizens who preside over affairs. Demagogues arise in states where the laws are not sovereign. The people then becomes an auto-crat—a single composite autocrat made up of many members, with the many playing the sovereign, not as individuals, but collectively.[3] § 27. It is not clear what Homer means when he says that 'it is not good to have the rule of many masters': whether he has in mind the collective rule of the many, or the rule of a number of magistrates acting as individuals. However that may be, a democracy of this order, being in the nature of an autocrat and not being governed by law, begins to attempt an autocracy. It grows despotic; flatterers come to be held in honour; it becomes analogous to the tyrannical form of single-person government. § 28. Both show a similar temper; both behave like despots to the better class of citizens; the decrees of the one are like the edicts of the other; the popular leader in the one is the same as, or at any rate like, the flatterer in the other; and in either case the influence of favourites predomin-ates—that of the flatterer in tyrannies, and that of the popular leader in democracies of this variety. § 29. It is popular leaders who, by referring all issues to the decision of the people, are re-sponsible for substituting the sovereignty of decrees for that of the laws. Once the people are sovereign in all matters, *they* are sove-reign themselves over its decisions; the multitude follows their guidance; and this is the source of their great position. § 30. But the critics of the magistrates are also responsible. Their argument is, 'The *people* ought to decide': the people accept that invitation readily; and thus the authority of all the magistrates is under-

---

[1] Aristotle is here drawing a distinction (based on Athenian constitutional history) between (1) a régime in which laws (*nomoi*) are distinguished from decrees (*psephismata*), are superior to decrees, and cannot be overridden by decrees, and (2) a régime in which the distinction has practically disappeared, decrees are as good as laws, and decrees may override laws. See Vinogradoff, *Historical Jurisprudence*, vol. ii, pp. 129-31, and the note on Book III, c. XI, § 19.

[2] See Note LL, p. 169.

[3] We may repeat the saying (quoted before, p. 44, n. 2) about the modern democrat, 'who looks with pride at his face . . . remembering that he is the forty-millionth part of a tyrant, and forgetting that he is the whole of a slave'.

mined. There would appear to be solid substance in the view that a democracy of this type is not a true constitution. Where the laws are not sovereign, there is no constitution. § 31. Law should be sovereign on every issue, and the magistrates and the citizen body should only decide about details. The conclusion which emerges is clear. Democracy may be a form of constitution; but this particular system, under which everything is managed merely by decrees, is not even a democracy, in any real sense of the word. Decrees can never be general rules [and any real constitution must be based on general rules]. . . . So far, then, as concerns the different forms of democracy, and the definition of those forms.

Note LL (p. 168): *The demagogue at Athens*

The rise of the demagogue at Athens (it is Athens which Aristotle has in mind) may be dated from the death of Pericles in 429 B.C. It was connected with a social revolution—the growth of industry and commerce, and the consequent growth of the importance of the urban population in Athens itself, in comparison with that of the 'demes' of the country-side. Cleon, the first notable demagogue, and the successors of Cleon, were town-bred men, unlike the previous statesmen of Athens (such as Aristides and Pericles) who had belonged to good families in the country-side.

But the rise of the demagogue was also connected with a political or constitutional change, as well as with a social revolution. The previous 'leaders of the people' (see Appendix IV, p. 378, n. 1) had generally held some official position—for instance, that of general—along with their *de facto* position of leadership. The 'demagogue' proper had no official position: he simply exercised, in a peculiar degree and with a permanent influence, the right of the private member of the assembly to take the initiative and propose a policy. The assembly thus became the paradise of the influential private member, playing the part of an un-official leader; and such a leader—having no official executive position—could exercise initiative and determine policy without incurring political responsibility, since it was not his duty to execute the policy which he had induced the assembly to accept. (See Dr. E. M. Walker, in the *Cambridge Ancient History*, vol. v, pp. 106–10.)

It may be added that it was this political irresponsibility of the dema-gogue, rather than his flattery of the people or his inducing the people to act by decree in the teeth of law, which was the fatal defect of his position.

Chapter V

We may similarly classify four varieties of oligarchy. But constitu-tions which are formally and legally democratic, or formally and legally oligarchical, may in their actual working be of a different character. Legal form and actual working are two different things, and this is particularly liable to be the case after a revolution.

§ 1. Among oligarchies one of the varieties is that in which the holding of office depends on a property-qualification, high enough to exclude the poor—although they form the majority—from a share in constitutional rights, but still giving a share to all who can satisfy its requirements. A second variety is that in which the property-qualification **1292 b** is high, and elections to vacant offices are made only *by* those who possess this high qualification. (Where they are also made *from* the whole body of qualified persons, the constitution may be held to incline in the direction of aristocracy: where they are made only from a privileged section, it may be held to be oligarchical.) § 2. A third variety is the hereditary, in which sons succeed to their fathers. The fourth variety is like the third in being hereditary; but here, instead of the rule of law, there is a system of personal rule. This variety is the parallel, among oligarchies, to what tyranny is among monarchies or the variety of democracy last mentioned among democracies. An oligarchy of this sort is called a junto or 'dynasty'.[1]

§ 3. These are the several varieties of oligarchy and democracy. It should be noted, however, that in actual life it is often the case that constitutions which are not legally democratic are made to work democratically by the habits and training of the people. Conversely, there are other cases where the legal constitution inclines towards democracy, but is made by training and habits to work in a way which inclines more towards oligarchy. § 4. This happens particularly after a revolution. The citizens do not change their temper immediately; and in the first stages the triumphant party is content to leave things largely alone, without seeking to take any great advantage of its opponents. The result is that the old laws remain in force, even though the party of revolution is actually in power.

CHAPTER VI

[A second or alternative account of the varieties of democracy and oligarchy, based less on their political structure—which has been, after all, the basis mainly adopted in the account just given in cc. IV–V—and more on their social composition.] *Classifying once more the varieties of democracy, we may distinguish an agricultural or 'peasant' form from three other forms—the main criterion being the degree of leisure which its social conditions enable a people to devote to politics. In the same way, and on the same general social-economic basis, we may also distinguish four varieties of oligarchy, according to the distribution of property and the relative degree of importance attached to its ownership.*

§ 1. What we have already said [about the various groups to be

[1] A 'dynasty' in our English use is a single family possessing an hereditary power which may be (though it is not necessarily) an absolute power. Aristotle means by a 'dynasty' a group of families possessing an hereditary power which is always an absolute power.

found in the people and among the notables][1] is sufficient of itself to prove that there must be all these varieties of democracy and oligarchy. One of two things must happen: either *all* the various groups of the people previously mentioned must share in constitutional rights, or some must share and others not. § 2. When the farming class and the class possessed of moderate means are the sovereign power in the constitution, they conduct the government under the rule of law. Able to live by their work, but unable to enjoy any leisure, they make the law supreme, and confine the meetings of the assembly to a minimum; while the rest of the population is allowed to share in constitutional rights as soon as its members attain the property-qualification determined by the law. § 3. We may lay it down generally that a system which does not allow every citizen to share is oligarchical, and that one which does so is democratic. Here, accordingly, every citizen who possesses the necessary qualification is allowed to share; but the want of sufficient means prevents the enjoyment of leisure [which is needed for political activity]. This is one form of democracy; and these are the causes which produce its character. A second form is based on the criterion which comes logically next—the criterion of birth. Here all who possess irreproachable descent are legally allowed to share, but only share in practice when they are able to find the necessary leisure. § 4. In a democracy of this order the laws are accordingly sovereign, simply because there are not the revenues [to provide the leisure needed for personal political activity]. A third form is that in which all are allowed to share in constitutional rights, on the one condition of free birth, but the rights are not actually exercised for the reason already given [i.e. want of means]; and here, once more, the rule of law is the necessary consequence. § 5. A fourth form **1293 a** of democracy is the one which comes chronologically last in the actual development of states. Here, under the influence of two causes— the large increase in the population of states, compared with their original size, and the accruing of a considerable revenue—all alike share in constitutional rights, owing to the numerical superiority of the masses, and all alike join in political activity, owing to the facilities for leisure which are provided even for the poor by the system of state-payment [for attendance in the assembly and the courts]. § 6. A populace provided with such facilities may indeed be said to have more leisure than any other section. They are not hindered in any way by the duty of attending to private affairs; the well-to-do are, with the result that they often absent themselves from the assembly and the courts. Under these conditions the

[1] The reference is to c. IV, §§ 9–11, §§ 21–2.

mass of the poor become the sovereign power in the constitution, instead of the laws.

§ 7. Such, and so many, are the forms of democracy; and such are their causes. Turning to the forms of oligarchy, we may rank first the form in which a majority of the citizens have property, but the amount they possess is moderate and not excessively large, while all who acquire this moderate amount are allowed to share in constitutional rights. § 8. Since the generality are thus included in the enjoyment of constitutional rights, it follows that sovereignty, under this form, will be vested in the law, and not in persons. A moderate oligarchy of this type is totally different from the personal rule of a monarch; and as its members have neither so much property that they are able to enjoy a leisure free from all business cares, nor so little that they depend on the state for support, they will be bound to ask that the law should rule for them, and they will not claim to rule themselves. § 9. The second form of oligarchy arises when the owners of property are fewer, and the property they own is larger. Under these conditions they have greater power; and they demand a greater share in constitutional rights. They thus assume the right of selecting themselves the members of the other classes who are to be admitted to the civic body; and— not being powerful enough, as yet, to rule without law—they enact a law to this effect. § 10. A further advance is made, and a third form of oligarchy arises, when matters are strained still further and still fewer persons become the owners of still larger properties. The members of the governing oligarchy now keep the offices entirely in their own hands; but they still act in terms of law—if only of a law which provides that sons shall succeed to their fathers. § 11. The fourth and last form of oligarchy arises when matters are strained to the last degree, alike in the size of properties and the influence of connexions. A junto or 'dynasty' of the type which now emerges is closely akin to the personal rule of a monarch; and it is persons, and not the law, who are now the sovereign. This fourth form of oligarchy is analogous to the last [or 'extreme'] form of democracy.

CHAPTER VII[1]

Having classified the varieties of democracy and oligarchy, we may now classify the varieties of the other forms. Aristocracy—apart from

---

[1] Aristotle might be expected, after having treated fully of the first item of the programme sketched at the end of c. II (the various forms of oligarchy and democracy), to proceed to the second item ('which is the most generally accept- able constitution?'); but he postpones that item until c. XI, in order to deal first with forms of constitution other than oligarchy and democracy. It may be noted that Aristotle proceeds to speak of four constitutions, while in Book III, c. VII, he had enumerated six (the three 'right' constitutions, or kingship, aristocracy, and

the true aristocracy which is really the government of the Best—has
three varieties, which are all, more or less, of the nature of mixed
constitutions, and thus approximate to the 'polity'.

§ 1. There are still two forms of constitution left, besides democracy and oligarchy. One of these [kingship] is usually reckoned,
and has indeed already been mentioned, as one of the four main
forms of constitution, which are counted as being kingship,
oligarchy, democracy, and the form called aristocracy. . . . There
is, however, a fifth form, in addition to these four. It is called by
the generic name common to all the forms—the name of 'constitution' or 'polity'—but being of rare occurrence it has not been
noticed by the writers who attempt to classify the different forms
of constitution; and they usually limit themselves, as Plato does in
the *Republic*, to an enumeration of only four forms. . . . **1293 b** § 2.
The name 'aristocracy' should properly be applied to the form of
constitution which has already been treated in our first part.[1] The
only constitution which can with strict justice be called an aristocracy is one where the members are not merely 'good' in relation
to some standard or other, but are absolutely 'the best' (*aristoi*) in
point of moral quality.[2] Only in such a constitution can the good
man and the good citizen be absolutely identified; in all others
goodness is only goodness relatively to the particular constitution
and its particular standard. § 3. But we have to admit that there
are some further forms of constitution, which differ enough both
from oligarchies and from the so-called 'polity' to be also called
aristocracies [even though they do not attain the true standard of
aristocracy]. This is the case when elections to office are based not
only on wealth but also on moral desert. Constitutions of this
type differ from both of the forms just mentioned [i.e. oligarchy
and 'polity']; and they thus come to be called aristocracies. § 4.
This usage is just, because even in states which do not make the
encouragement of goodness a matter of public policy, there may
still be found individuals who are of good repute and esteemed to
be of high quality. Accordingly a constitution which pays regard
to all the three factors—wealth, goodness, and numbers—as the
Carthaginian does, may be called an aristocratic constitution; and

'polity', and the three perversions of these, or tyranny, oligarchy, and democracy).
But it may also be noted that Aristotle immediately adds the 'polity' to the four
constitutions here mentioned, and the sixth form, tyranny, is readily understood.

[1] The reference would appear to be to various passages in Book III, which is
thus regarded as 'the first part' of a course 'on constitutions' of which Books
IV–VI form 'the second part'.

[2] Two considerations are here involved: (1) that in an aristocracy the *members*
must be not merely 'good', but the 'best', and (2) that in it the *standard* by which
they are so reckoned must not be a variable standard ('some standard or other'),
but the one absolute standard of moral quality.

the same may also be said of constitutions, such as the Spartan, which pay regard only to the two factors of goodness and numbers, and where there is thus a mixture of the democratic and the aristocratic principle. § 5. We may therefore hold that there are these two forms of aristocracy in addition to the first or best form of that constitution; and we may also include, besides them, the form presented by those varieties of the so-called 'polity' which incline particularly to oligarchy.[1]

<h2 style="text-align:center">CHAPTER VIII</h2>

We now come to the 'polity' and its varieties. Generally, a 'polity' is a mixture of democracy and oligarchy; but in common usage the term 'polity' is reserved for mixtures which incline more towards democracy, and the mixtures which incline more towards oligarchy are called aristocracies. This leads us into a digression on the uses of the term 'aristocracy' and the reasons why that term—through being associated in men's minds partly with the rule of gentlefolk, and partly with the rule of law—is somewhat vaguely and widely applied. The proper use of terms depends on a recognition of the fact that there are three elements to be considered in a state—the free-born poor, the wealthy, and the men of merit—and not only the two elements of the poor and the wealthy. On this basis we shall confine the term 'aristocracy' to constitutions which recognize merit in some way or other; and we shall use the term 'polity'—and only that term—for constitutions which recognize only the two elements of free birth and wealth.

§ 1. It remains to treat of the form of constitution called 'polity' and of tyranny. Here we are associating 'polity' with a perverted constitution, although it is not in itself a perversion, any more than are the forms of aristocracy which we have just mentioned. But we may plead in excuse that all these constitutions ['polity' and the connected forms of aristocracy] really fall short of the best form of right constitution, and are therefore to be reckoned among perversions; and we may add that, as has already been mentioned in our first part, the perversions among which they are reckoned are those to which they themselves give rise.[2]   § 2. It is natural and

---

[1] It emerges from this somewhat crabbed passage that there are four different forms of aristocracy—(1) the first and best form, where regard is paid only to goodness; (2) the Carthaginian form, where regard is paid to wealth and numbers as well; (3) the Spartan form, where regard is paid to numbers as well as to goodness; and (4) the form presented by those mixed constitutions or 'polities' which pay less regard to numbers than the Spartan constitution does, and thus incline more towards oligarchy.

[2] The reference appears to be to Book III, c. VII, § 5. But the reference is not accurate, because in that passage oligarchy—the perversion here mainly in question—is stated to be a corruption of the true or pure aristocracy, whereas here it is stated, by implication, to be a corruption of the less pure (or mixed) aristocracy and of 'polity'.

proper to mention tyranny last, because we are engaged in an inquiry into constitutions; and tyranny, of all others, has least the character of a constitution.

We have thus explained the reason for the order we propose to follow; and we must now proceed to treat of the 'polity'. Its character will emerge the more clearly now that we have already defined the nature of oligarchy and democracy. § 3. The 'polity' may be described, in general terms, as a mixture of these two constitutions; but in common usage the name is confined to those mixtures which incline to democracy, and those which incline more to oligarchy are called aristocracies, and not 'polities'—the reason being that culture and breeding [the attributes of aristo-cracy] are more associated with the wealthier classes [who form the basis of oligarchy]. § 4. We may also note [as explaining this common usage of the term 'aristocracy'] that the wealthy are generally supposed to possess already the advantages for want of which wrongdoers fall into crime; and this is the reason why they are called 'gentlemen' or 'notables'. Now as aristocracy aims at giving pre-eminence to the best, men are led in this way to extend the term and to describe oligarchies too as states governed by gentlemen [i.e., in effect, as aristocracies].

§ 5. [Another reason for the extension of the term 'aristocracy' is a general tendency to suppose that any law-abiding state must be an aristocracy.] **1294 a** Men regard it as impossible that the rule of law should exist in a state which is governed by the poorer sort, and not by the best of its citizens; and, conversely, they regard it as equally impossible that aristocracy should exist in a state which is not under the rule of law. But you do not secure the rule of law by having a good set of laws which are not actually obeyed. § 6. We have to distinguish two senses of the rule of law— one which means obedience to such laws as have been enacted, and another which means that the laws obeyed have also been well enacted. (Obedience can also be paid to laws which have been enacted badly.) The latter sense admits, in its turn, of two sub-divisions: men may render obedience to laws which are the best that are possible for *them*, or they may render obedience to laws which are absolutely the best. [It follows that aristocracy, if it is to be associated with the rule of law, should only be associated with the better form of such rule.]

§ 7. It is a general opinion that the essential criterion of aristo-cracy is the distribution of office according to merit: merit is its criterion, as wealth is the criterion of oligarchy, and free birth of democracy. The principle of the rule of majority-decision is [not peculiar to aristocracy, but is] present in all constitutions. Alike in oligarchies, in aristocracies, and in democracies, the decision of the majority of those who share in constitutional rights is final and sovereign.[1] § 8. The form of constitution called 'polity' is embellished, in most states, by a higher title. The mixture attempted in it seeks only to blend the rich and the poor, or wealth and free birth; but the rich are regarded by common opinion as holding the position of gentlemen [and a 'polity' in which they are included thus comes to be embellished by the higher title of aristocracy]. § 9. In reality there are *three* elements which may claim an equal share in the mixed form of constitution—free birth, wealth, and merit. (Nobility of birth, which is sometimes reckoned a fourth, is only a corollary of the two latter, and simply consists in an inherited mixture of wealth and merit.) Obviously, therefore, we ought always to use the term 'polity' for a mixture of only two elements, where these elements are the rich and the poor; and we ought to confine the name 'aristocracy' to a mixture of three, which is really more of an aristocracy than any other form so called—except the first and true form.[2] § 10. We have now shown that there are other forms of constitution besides monarchy, democracy, and oligarchy; what the nature of these other forms is; how aristocracies differ from one another, and 'polities' differ from aristocracy; and, finally, that aristocracies and 'polities' are not far removed from one another.

Chapter IX

We may now consider finally the various forms which 'polity' proper may take. There are three possible ways of combining the free-born poor and the rich—or, in other words, of mixing democracy and oligarchy. The first is to mix democracy as a whole with oligarchy as a whole. The second is to take the mean between the two. The third is to take some elements from democracy and some from oligarchy. It is a good criterion of a proper mixture of democracy and oligarchy that you should be able to describe a mixed constitution indifferently as either. Sparta may be cited as an example of such a mixture.

§ 1. We have now to discuss, in continuation of our argument, how the constitution called 'polity' comes into existence by the side of democracy and oligarchy, and in what way it ought to be

---

[1] Aristotle seems, in §§ 4–7, to have digressed from 'polity' into aristocracy. But what he has really in mind, all along, is the shading off of 'polity' into aristocracy; and he is inquiring into the reasons why mixed constitutions, of the type of the 'polity', are often termed aristocracies. Recognition of gentle birth (§ 4), and the presence of the rule of law (§§ 5–6), are two of these reasons. Neither of these, in his view, is a valid reason. The only valid reason for using the term 'aristocracy', as he proceeds to argue in § 7, is recognition of merit at any rate as *one* among other standards, if not as the only standard.

[2] i.e. the form in which regard is paid *only* to merit or moral quality.

organized. In the course of that discussion it will also be evident
what are the distinguishing marks of democracy and oligarchy; for
[to create a 'polity'] we have first to ascertain the difference between
these two forms, and then to form a combination between them by
taking from both their complements or 'tallies'.¹ § 2. There are
three different principles on which men may act in making such a
combination or mixture. The first is to take and use simultaneously
both democratic and oligarchical rules. We may take as an example
the rules for a seat in the law courts.² In oligarchies the rich are
fined if they do not sit in the courts, and the poor receive no pay
for sitting. In democracies, on the other hand, the poor are given
pay for sitting, and the rich are not fined if they fail to sit. § 3. To
combine both of these rules is to adopt a common or middle term
between either; and for that reason such a method is characteristic
of a 'polity', **1294 b** which is a mixture of the two constitutions.
This is, accordingly, one of the possible ways of combination. A
second is to strike an average, or take a mean, between the two
different rules. One constitution, for example, requires no property qualification at all, or only a very low qualification, for the
right to attend the assembly: the other requires a high qualification.
Here both of the rules cannot be used to provide a common term;
and we have to take the mean between the two. § 4. The third
way of combination is [neither to take the whole of both rules, nor
to strike an average between them, but] to combine elements from
both, and to mix part of the oligarchical rule with a part of the
democratic. In the appointment of magistrates, for example, the
use of the lot is regarded as democratic, and the use of the vote
as oligarchical. Again, it is considered to be democratic that a
property qualification should not be required, and oligarchical that
it should be. § 5. Here, accordingly, the mode appropriate to an
aristocracy [of the mixed sort] or a 'polity' is to take one element
from one form of constitution and another from the other—that is
to say, to take from oligarchy the rule that magistrates should be
appointed by vote, and from democracy the rule that no property
qualification should be required.

§ 6. We have now dealt with the general method of mixture.
We may add that it is a good criterion of a proper mixture of
democracy and oligarchy that a mixed constitution should be able
to be described indifferently as either. When this can be said, it
must obviously be due to the excellence of the mixture. It is a

¹ The word used in the Greek refers to a coin 'which two contracting parties
broke between them' in symbol of their contract.
² It has to be remembered that in ancient Greece the law courts or 'dikasteries'
were composed of citizens rather than of professional judges.

thing which can generally be said of the mean between two extremes: both of the extremes can be traced in the mean, [and it
can thus be described by the name of either]. § 7. The constitution
of Sparta is an example. There are many who would describe it
as a democracy, on the ground that its organization has a number
of democratic features. In the first place, and so far as concerns
the bringing up of the young, the children of the rich have the
same fare as the children of the poor, and they are educated on a
standard which the children of the poor can also attain. § 8. The
same policy is followed for adolescence; and it is equally followed
in adult years. No difference is made between the rich and the
poor: the food at the common mess is the same for all, and the
dress of the rich is such as any of the poor could also provide
for themselves. § 9. A second ground for describing Sparta as a
democracy is the right of the people to elect to one of the two
great institutions, the Senate, and to be eligible themselves for the
other, the Ephorate. On the other hand there are some who
describe the Spartan constitution as an oligarchy, on the ground
that it has many oligarchical factors. For example, the magistrates
are all appointed by vote, and none by lot; again, the power of
inflicting the penalty of death or banishment rests in the hands
of a few persons; and there are many other similar features.
§ 10. A properly mixed 'polity' should look as if it contained both
democratic and oligarchical elements—and as if it contained
neither. It should owe its stability to its own intrinsic strength,
and not to external support; and its intrinsic strength should be
derived from the fact, not that a majority are in favour of its
continuance (that might well be the case even with a poor constitution), but rather that there is no single section in all the state which
would favour a change to a different constitution.

We have now described the way in which a 'polity', and the
other forms [of mixed constitution] called aristocracies, ought to
be organized.

CHAPTER X

*It now remains to consider, in conclusion, the varieties of tyranny.
Two of its varieties, as we have already incidentally noticed (in
Book III, c. XIV), are kingships rather than tyrannies—i.e. the kingships found among uncivilized peoples, and the dictatorships, or 'elective'
tyrannies, of the early Greeks. The third variety is tyranny proper—
the irresponsible rule of an autocrat acting for his own advantage.*

1295 a § 1. Tyranny remains to be treated.[1] There is not

[1] See c. VIII, § 1, where tyranny is reserved for treatment in connexion with
'polity'.

much to be said about it; but as it has been included in our
classification of constitutions, it must have a place in our inquiry.
Kingship [of which, as we saw, it is the corruption] has already
been discussed in our first part.[1] In the course of discussing it
we there dealt with kingship in the most usual sense of the term;
we inquired whether it was beneficial or prejudicial to states, what
sort of person should be king, from what source he should be
drawn, and how he should be established. § 2. In the course of the
discussion we also distinguished two forms of tyranny,[2] which we
treated in that connexion because—being both of them forms of
government conducted in obedience to law—their nature in some
sense overlaps with that of kingship. These two forms were (1) the
elective monarchs, with absolute power, to be found among some
uncivilized peoples, and (2) the monarchs of the same type, termed
aisumnetai (or dictators), who once existed among the early Greeks.
§ 3. There are some differences between these two forms; but
they may both be called half royal and half tyrannical—royal
because government rests on consent, and is conducted on a legal
basis; tyrannical because it is conducted in the temper of a master
of slaves, and according to the ruler's will. But there is also a third
form of tyranny, which is what is most commonly understood by
the term. This is the converse of absolute kingship, or *pambasileia*.[3]
§ 4. This third form of tyranny is bound to exist where a single
person governs men, who are all his peers or superiors, without
any form of responsibility, and with a view to his own advantage
rather than that of his subjects. It is thus a rule of force; and no
freeman will voluntarily endure such a system.

These, for the reasons that have just been given, are the forms
of tyranny; and this is their number.

C

THE TYPE OF CONSTITUTION WHICH IS MOST GENERALLY
PRACTICABLE (c. xi)

Chapter XI

*We are here concerned with the best constitution and way of life for
the majority of men and states. Goodness itself consists in a mean;
and in any state the middle class is a mean between the rich and the
poor. The middle class is free from the ambition of the rich and the
pettiness of the poor: it is a natural link which helps to ensure political
cohesion. We may thus conclude that a constitution based on this
class—i.e. a 'polity'—is most likely to be generally beneficial. It will
be free from faction, and will be likely to be stable. But 'polities' have*

[1] Book III, cc. xiv–xvii.   [2] Book III, c. xiv, §§ 6–10.
[2] See Book III, c. xiv, *ad finem* (and note), and also c. xvi, § 2.

*been historically rare—partly for internal reasons, and partly because
the policy of the Athenian and the Spartan empires has encouraged
extremes in preference to a middle way. Still, the 'polity' may serve
as a standard in judging the merits of actual constitutions.*

§ 1. We have now to consider what is the best constitution and
the best way of life for the *majority* of states and men.[1] In doing so
we shall not employ, [for the purpose of measuring 'the best'], a
standard of excellence above the reach of ordinary men, or a
standard of education requiring exceptional endowments and
equipment, or the standard of a constitution which attains an
ideal height. We shall only be concerned with the sort of life
which most men are able to share and the sort of constitution
which it is possible for most states to enjoy.   § 2. The 'aristocracies', so called, of which we have just been treating, [will not
serve us for this purpose: they] either lie, at one extreme, beyond
the reach of most states, or they approach, at the other, so closely
to the constitution called 'polity' that they need not be considered
separately and must be treated as identical with it. The issues we
have just raised can all be decided in the light of one body of fundamental principles.   § 3. If we adopt as true the statements made
in the *Ethics*—(1) that a truly happy life is a life of goodness lived
in freedom from impediments,[2] and (2) that goodness consists in
a mean—it follows that the best way of life [for the *majority* of
men] is one which consists in a mean, and a mean of the kind attainable by every individual.[3] Further, the same criteria which determine whether the citizen-body [i.e. all its members, considered as
individuals] have a good or bad way of life must also apply to the
constitution; for a constitution is the way of life of a citizen-body.
1295 b § 4. In all states there may be distinguished three parts, or
classes, of the citizen-body[4]—the very rich; the very poor; and the

[1] Aristotle here begins to discuss the second question in the programme
sketched at the end of c. II; 'What constitution is the most acceptable, and the
most to be preferred, short of the ideal constitution?' It will be noticed that he
connects a constitution with 'a way of life'. It is not merely an 'arrangement of
offices' (IV. III, § 5); it is also 'a scheme of life, directed to attaining a particular
quality of life' (III. IX, §§ 7–14).
[2] 'Freedom from impediments', if we interpret it positively, means the
possession of an adequate 'equipment' of wealth, health, and material resources.
[3] On the theory of Aristotle, goodness in general, and each of the separate
virtues, consists in a regulated 'mean' between the extreme of 'excess' and
the other extreme of 'defect' to which human affections are prone. In the sphere,
for example, of those affections which are stirred by the presence of danger,
there is the excess of foolhardiness and the defect of cowardice, and the virtue
of courage is a mean between the two.
[4] Here Aristotle follows a line of thought similar to one which he has previously
followed in c. VI. There, after a previous discussion of the varieties of oligarchy
and democracy (in cc. IV–V), which is mainly based on their political structure,
he proceeds to a new discussion which is based on their social composition.

middle class which forms the mean. Now it is admitted, as a general principle, that moderation and the mean are always best. We may therefore conclude that in the ownership of all gifts of fortune a middle condition will be the best. § 5. Men who are in this condition are the most ready to listen to reason. Those who belong to either extreme—the over-handsome, the over-strong, the over-noble, the over-wealthy; or at the opposite end the over-poor, the over-weak, the utterly ignoble—find it hard to follow the lead of reason. Men in the first class tend more to violence and serious crime: men in the second tend too much to roguery and petty offences; and most wrongdoing arises either from violence or roguery. It is a further merit of the middle class that its members suffer least from ambition, which both in the military and the civil sphere is dangerous to states. § 6. It must also be added that those who enjoy too many advantages—strength, wealth, connexions, and so forth—are both unwilling to obey and ignorant how to obey. This is a defect which appears in them from the first, during childhood and in home-life: nurtured in luxury, they never acquire a habit of discipline, even in the matter of lessons. But there are also defects in those who suffer from the opposite extreme of a lack of advantages: they are far too mean and poor-spirited. § 7. We have thus, on the one hand, people who are ignorant how to rule and only know how to obey, as if they were so many slaves, and, on the other hand, people who are ignorant how to obey any sort of authority and only know how to rule as if they were masters of slaves. The result is a state, not of freemen, but only of slaves and masters: a state of envy on the one side and on the other contempt. Nothing could be further removed from the spirit of friendship or the temper of a political community. Community depends on friendship; and when there is enmity instead of friendship, men will not even share the same path. § 8. A state aims at being, as far as it can be, a society composed of equals and peers [who, as such, can be friends and associates]; and the middle class, more than any other, has this sort of composition. It follows that a state which is based on the middle class is bound to be the best constituted in respect of the elements [i.e. equals and peers] of which, on our view, a state is naturally composed. The middle classes [besides contributing, in this way, to the security of the

Similarly here, after a previous discussion of 'polity' (in cc. VII–IX) which is based on its political structure as a mixture of oligarchy and democracy, he proceeds to a new discussion which is based on its social composition. We now find that 'polity' is the best constitution for the majority of states because it mixes the different classes in, or under, a common and dominant middle class. This is really a new view, or at any rate an extension of the previous view; for a constitution which mixes elements of oligarchy with elements of democracy is not, *per se*, a constitution dominated by the middle class.

state] enjoy a greater security themselves than any other class. § 9. They do not, like the poor, covet the goods of others; nor do others covet their possessions, as the poor covet those of the rich. Neither plotting against others, not plotted against themselves, they live in freedom from danger; and we may well approve the prayer of Phocylides

> Many things are best for the middling:
> Fain would I be of the state's middle class.

§ 10. It is clear from our argument, first, that the best form of political society is one where power is vested in the middle class, and, secondly, that good government is attainable in those states where there is a large middle class—large enough, if possible, to be stronger than both of the other classes, but at any rate large enough to be stronger than either of them singly; for in that case its addition to either will suffice to turn the scale, and will prevent either of the opposing extremes from becoming dominant. § 11. It is therefore the greatest of blessings for a state that its members should possess a moderate and adequate property. Where **1296 a** some have great possessions, and others have nothing at all, the result is either an extreme democracy or an unmixed oligarchy; or it may even be—indirectly, and as a reaction against both of these extremes—a tyranny. Tyranny is a form of government which may grow out of the headiest type of democracy, or out of oligarchy; but it is much less likely to grow out of constitutions of the middle order, or those which approximate to them [e.g. moderate oligarchies]. § 12. We shall explain the reason later, when we come to treat of revolutions and constitutional change.

Meanwhile, it is clear that the middle type of constitution is best [for the *majority* of states]. It is the one type free from faction; where the middle class is large, there is least likelihood of faction and dissension among the citizens. § 13. Large states are generally more free from faction just because they have a large middle class. In small states, on the other hand, it is easy for the whole population to be divided into only two classes; nothing is left in the middle, and all—or almost all—are either poor or rich. § 14. The reason why democracies are generally more secure and more permanent than oligarchies is the character of their middle class, which is more numerous, and is allowed a larger share in the government, than it is in oligarchies. Where democracies have no middle class, and the poor are greatly superior in number, trouble ensues, and they are speedily ruined. § 15. It must also be considered a proof of its value that the best legislators have come from the middle class. Solon was one, as his own poems prove: Lycurgus was another (and not, as is sometimes said, a member of the royal family); and the same is true of Charondas and most of the other legislators.

§ 16. What has just been said also serves to explain why ['polities' are rare, and] most constitutions are either democratic or oligarchical. In the first place, the middle class is in most states generally small; and the result is that as soon as one or other of the two main classes—the owners of property and the masses—gains the advantage, it oversteps the mean, and drawing the constitution in its own direction it institutes, as the case may be, either a democracy or an oligarchy. § 17. In the second place, factious disputes and struggles readily arise between the masses and the rich; and no matter which side may win the day, it refuses to establish a constitution based on the common interest and the principle of equality, but, preferring to exact as the prize of victory a greater share of constitutional rights, it institutes, according to its principles, a democracy or an oligarchy. § 18. Thirdly, the policy of the two states which have held the ascendancy in Greece [i.e. Athens and Sparta] has also been to blame. Each has paid an exclusive regard to its own type of constitution; the one has instituted democracies in the states under its control, and the other has set up oligarchies: each has looked to its own advantage, and neither to that of the states it controlled. § 19. These three reasons explain why a middle or mixed type of constitution has never been established—or, at the most, has only been established on a few occasions and in a few states. . . . One man, and one only, of all who have hitherto been in a position of ascendancy, has allowed himself to be persuaded to agree to the setting up of such a type.[1] And now it has also become **1296 b** the habit in each individual state [as it was of Athens and Sparta when they stood at the head of a group of states] not even to want a system of equality, but, instead of that, either to try to dominate or, if beaten, just to submit to the victor.

§ 20. It is clear, from the argument, which is the best constitution [for the *majority* of states], and what are the reasons why it is so. Once we have thus settled which is the best, it becomes easy to take all the others (including the different varieties, both of democracy and of oligarchy, which we have already distinguished), and to arrange them in an order of merit—first, second, and so on in turn—according as their quality is a better or a worse quality. § 21. The nearest to the best must always be better than all the rest, and the one which is farthest removed from the mean [and therefore from the best] must always be worse, if we are judging [on

[1] See Note, MM, p. 184.

general grounds, and] not in relation to particular circumstances.
I use the words 'in relation to particular circumstances' for this
reason: one sort of constitution may be intrinsically preferable, but
there is nothing to prevent another sort from being more suitable
in the given case; and indeed this may often happen.

NOTE MM (p. 183): *The one man who favoured a mixed constitution*

Newman suggests that the one man was Theramenes, a moderate
leader at Athens in 411 B.C., and the chief promoter of a moderate constitution which vested power in the 5,000 citizens who could furnish
themselves with arms (see Appendix IV. A, 4). It is true that Thucydides
refers to this constitution as a moderate mixture of oligarchy and democracy (viii, c. 97); but it is also true (1) that Theramenes was never 'in a
position of ascendancy' in Greek affairs, and (2) that he can hardly be
said to have 'allowed himself to be persuaded to agree to the setting up of
a type of constitution'—a phrase which implies co-operation with others
in setting up a general system of 'polities' in Greek states generally.

Was it Antipater that Aristotle had in mind—the regent for Alexander,
who exercised an 'ascendancy' on his behalf during his absence in the
East? The suggestion raises chronological difficulties; for though Antipater
did establish a moderate constitution at Athens (under which power was
vested in a body of 9,000 citizens), he did not do so till 321, the year after
Aristotle's death. Had Aristotle discussed Greek politics with Antipater
at an early date, and endeavoured to persuade him to favour a system of
'polities' in Greece? (This might explain the phrase 'allowed himself to
be persuaded to agree'.) Or is this sentence a later insertion? It must be
admitted that it is grammatically difficult—unless the sentence is a later
insertion—to include Antipater among those 'who have *hitherto* been in
a position of ascendancy'. He held that position just at the time when
Aristotle was lecturing at Athens.

On the general policy of Antipater and his relations to Aristotle see the
Introduction, I, pp. xix-xxiii.

D

WHAT SORT OF CONSTITUTION IS DESIRABLE FOR WHAT
SORT OF CIVIC BODY ? (CC. XII–XIII)

CHAPTER XII

*In constitutions quantity and quality have to be balanced against
one another. When the weight of numbers among the poor more than
balances the quality of the other elements, a democracy is desirable.
When the quality of the other elements more than balances the weight
of numbers among the poor, an oligarchy is desirable. When the middle
class more than balances both the others—or even one of the others—
a 'polity' is desirable. Considerations on the value of 'polities', and
on the folly of devices intended to trick men into believing that they
have rights when they have none.*

§ 1. The next subject to consider, according to our programme,
is the question, 'What and what sort of constitution is suited to

what and what sort of persons?'[1] In order to answer this question, we must first assume a general axiom which is true of all constitutions—that the part of a state which wishes a constitution to continue must be stronger than the part which does not. Here we have to remember that quality and quantity both go to the making of every state. By 'quality' we mean free birth, wealth, culture, and nobility of descent; by 'quantity' we mean superiority in numbers. § 2. Now quality may belong to one of the parts which compose a state, and quantity to another. For example, those who are low-born may be more numerous than the high-born, or the poor than the rich; but the superiority in quantity on the one side may not be sufficient to balance the superiority of quality on the other. Quantity and quality must thus be placed in the balance against one another. § 3. [On that basis we may lay down three propositions.] First, where the number of the poor is more than enough to counterbalance the higher quality of the other side, there will naturally be a democracy; and the particular variety of democracy will depend on the particular form of superiority which is shown, in each case, by the mass of the people. If, for example, the mass of the people are predominantly farmers, we shall have the first—or 'peasant'—form of democracy:[2] if they are mechanics and day-labourers, we shall have the 'extreme' form;[3] and the same will also be true of the intermediate forms between 'peasant' and 'extreme' democracy. Secondly, where the superiority of the rich and the notables in point of quality is greater than their inferiority in point of quantity, there will be an oligarchy; and the particular variety of oligarchy will similarly depend on the particular form of superiority which is shown by the oligarchical body. § 4. (It may be noted, in passing, that a legislator should always make the members of the middle class partners in any constitution which he establishes. If the laws he makes are oligarchical, he should aim at including the middle class in their benefits: if they are democratic, he should seek to attach that class to his democratic laws.) Thirdly, where the number of the members of the middle class outweighs that of both the other classes—and even where it only outweighs that of one of the others—a 'polity' can be permanently established. § 5. There is no risk, in such a case, of the rich uniting with the poor to oppose **1297 a** the middle class: neither will ever be willing to be subject to the other; and if they try to find a constitution which is more in their common interest than the 'polity' is, they will fail to find one. Neither class would

---

[1] Aristotle here proceeds to the third item of the programme previously laid down in c. II, §§ 4–6.

[2] See above, c. VI, § 2.   [3] c. VI, § 5.

tolerate a system under which either ruled in its turn: they have
too little confidence in one another. A neutral arbitrator always
gives the best ground for confidence; and 'the man in the middle'
is such an arbitrator. § 6. The better, and the more equitable, the
mixture in a 'polity', the more durable will it be. It is here that
an error is often made by those who desire to establish aristocratic
constitutions. [Forgetting the claims of equity], they not only give
more power to the well-to-do, but they also deceive the people [by
fobbing them off with sham rights]. Illusory benefits must always
produce real evils in the long run; and the encroachments made
by the rich [under cover of such devices] are more destructive to a
constitution than those of the people.

CHAPTER XIII

*This mention of devices leads us to consider the various devices used by
oligarchies, and to mention the counter-devices used in democracies.
The better policy is to pursue a* via media, *and to aim at an honest
compromise rather than to use devices. This policy may be illustrated
from a study of the proper nature of a civic army and the methods by
which it can be honestly recruited without recourse to any devices.
This leads us to consider the effects of the nature and composition of
the army on Greek constitutional development.*

§ 1. The devices adopted in constitutions[1] for fobbing the
masses off with sham rights are five in number. They relate to the
assembly; the magistracies; the law courts; the possession of arms;
and the practice of athletics. As regards the assembly, all alike are
allowed to attend; but fines for non-attendance are either imposed
on the rich alone, or imposed on the rich at a far higher rate.
§ 2. As regards the magistracies, those who possess a property
qualification are not allowed to decline office on oath,[2] but the poor
are allowed to do so. As regards the law courts, the rich are fined
for non-attendance, but the poor may absent themselves with
impunity; or, alternatively, the rich are heavily fined and the poor
are only fined lightly—as is the rule under the laws of Charondas.
§ 3. In some states a different device is adopted in regard to attendance at the assembly and the law courts. All who have registered
themselves may attend; those who fail to attend after registration
are heavily fined. Here the intention is to stop men from register-
ing, through fear of the fines they may thus incur, and ultimately

    [1] 'Constitutions' here, as Newman suggests, may mean only 'polities', or
mixed constitutions; but it may also include 'aristocracies' of the mixed type
described in c. VII.
    [2] i.e. an oath that their wealth (or health) is inadequate for the performance
of the duties of an office.

to stop them from attending the courts and assembly as a result of their failure to register. § 4. Similar measures are also employed in regard to the possession of arms and the practice of athletics. The poor are allowed not to have any arms, and the rich are fined for not having them. The poor are not fined if they absent themselves from physical training: the rich are; and so while the latter are induced to attend by the sanction of a fine, the former are left free to abstain in the absence of any deterrent.

§ 5. The legal devices just mentioned are of an oligarchical character. Democracies have their counter-devices: the poor receive payment for attendance at the assembly and the law courts; the rich are not fined if they fail to attend. § 6. If we want to secure an equitable mixture of the two sides, we must combine elements drawn from both: in other words, we must both pay the poor for attendance and fine the rich for non-attendance. On this plan all would share in a common constitution: on the other, the constitution belongs to one side only. **1297 b** § 7. It is true that the constitution of a 'polity' or mixed state must be based on a citizen-body composed only of those who have arms, [and that this involves a property qualification]. But it is not possible to define this qualification absolutely, or to say that it must consist of a fixed amount in all cases. We must seek to discover in each given case, and to fix for each, the highest amount which it is possible to require without sacrificing the principle that those who enjoy political rights should be in a majority over those who do not. § 8. [This will involve no difficulty with the poor]: even when they do not enjoy political privileges, the poor are ready enough to keep quiet, provided that they are not violently handled or deprived of any of their property. But moderation does not come readily; and those who enjoy political rights are not always humane to inferiors. § 9. There may, for example, be a difficulty in time of war. The poor are usually reluctant to serve, if they are given no subsistence allowance, and are thus left without any means. But if they are provided with subsistence they are willing enough to fight.

There are some constitutions in which the citizen-body includes not only those who are actually serving, but also those who have previously served.[1] The Malian constitution, for example, in the south of Thessaly, gave the franchise to both; but it restricted eligibility to office to those who were actually on service. § 10. The

---

[1] Aristotle is here led into a digression on the connexion between political forms and military organization. The digression becomes an historical disquisition, in the course of which he shows that the development of political forms is connected with the development of the art of war. It is obvious, especially when we reflect on recent development in modern Europe, that Aristotle here touches on a theme of cardinal importance.

first form of constitution which succeeded to monarchy in ancient Greece was one in which the soldiery formed the citizen-body. At first it consisted only of cavalry. Military strength and superiority were then the prerogative of that arm; infantry is useless without a system of tactics; and as the experience and the rules required for such a system did not exist in early times, the strength of armies lay in their cavalry. When, however, states began to increase in size, and infantry forces acquired a greater degree of strength, more persons were admitted to the enjoyment of political rights. § 11. For this reason [i.e. because there was then a notable exten-tion of the franchise] the name 'democracy' was given at that time to constitutions which we now call 'polities'. It is not surprising that the old constitutions should have been oligarchical and, earlier still, monarchical. With their populations still small, states had no large middle class; and the body of the people, still few in number, and insignificant in organization, were more ready to tolerate government from above.

§ 12. [We have now considered three of the five subjects men-tioned in our programme of study.] (1) We have explained why there is a variety of constitutions, and why there are other forms than those commonly enumerated. (Democracy has more than one form; and the same is true of other constitutions.) We have also explained the differences between the various forms, and the causes of the character of each. (2) We have explained which is the best constitution in the majority of cases. (3) We have ex-plained, so far as other constitutions are concerned, which sort of constitution suits which sort of civic body.[1]

E

THE METHODS OF ESTABLISHING CONSTITUTIONS, IN RELA-TION TO THE THREE POWERS—DELIBERATIVE, EXECUTIVE, AND JUDICIAL (cc. xiv–xvi)

CHAPTER XIV

There are three elements or powers in the government of a state. The first is the deliberative; and that may be arranged on three different systems. The first system assigns all matters of deliberation to all: it is

---

[1] The programme of study is that stated at the end of c. ii, §§ 4–5. The first subject has been considered in cc. iii–x. The second subject has been considered in c. xi; but there is a preliminary consideration of it in cc. viii–ix, and the consideration is continued incidentally in c. xii, §§ 4–6. The third subject is considered in c. xii, and incidentally in c. xiii, §§ 10–11. There have been some digressions in the course of the argument (e.g. c. xiii is largely a digression on political devices in oligarchies and the counter-devices of democracies); but on the whole the programme stated at the end of c. ii has been steadily followed. The two remaining subjects of the programme are now duly treated, at the end of Book IV and in the course of Book V.

the system of democracy, and it may be carried into effect in four different ways. The second system assigns all matters to some: it is the system of oligarchy, and it may be carried into effect in three ways. A third system assigns some matters to all the citizens, and others to some of them: this system is characteristic of an aristocracy and of 'polities'. How the deliberative element may best be arranged, as a matter of policy, in democracies and in oligarchies.

§ 1. We have now to treat of the next subject [i.e. the proper method of establishing constitutions], and we have to do so both in general terms and separately for each constitution. We must first find a proper basis for the treatment of the subject. We may lay it down that there are three elements, or 'powers', in each constitution, and that a good legislator [in establishing a constitution] must consider what is expedient for it under each of these three heads. If all of them are constructed properly, the whole constitution too will be constructed properly; and where they are constructed differently, constitutions will also differ. § 2. The first of the three is the deliberative element concerned with common affairs, and its proper constitution: **1298 a** the second is the element of the magistracies (and here it has to be settled what these magistracies are to be, what matters they are to control, and how their occupants are to be appointed): the third is the judicial element, and the proper constitution of that element.[1]

§ 3. The deliberative element is sovereign (1) on the issues of war and peace, and the making and breaking of alliances; (2) in the enacting of laws; (3) in cases where the penalty of death, exile, and confiscation is involved; and (4) in the appointment of magistrates and the calling of them to account on the expiration of their office.[2] Three different arrangements of this element are possible: first, to give the decision on *all* the issues it covers to *all* the citizens; secondly, to give the decision on *all* the issues to *some* of the citizens (either by referring them all to one magistracy or combination of magistracies, or by referring different issues to different magistracies); and thirdly, to give the decision on *some issues to all* the citizens, and on *other issues to some* of them.

§ 4. The first of these arrangements, which assigns all the issues of deliberation to all the citizens, is characteristic of democracies: the equality which it implies is exactly what the people desire. But there are a number of different ways in which it may be effected. First, all the citizens may meet to deliberate in relays,

[1] See Note NN, p. 193.
[2] Compare Book III, c. XI, §§ 15–16, where 'the election of magistrates, and their examination at the end of their tenure', are stated to be the most important of issues, and to be connected with 'deliberation'.

and not in a single body. This was the scheme in the constitution of Telecles of Miletus. (We may also cite, as a variation of this scheme, the example of some other constitutions, in which the different boards of magistrates meet together for deliberation in a single body, but the citizens join the boards in relays—drawn from the tribes and the smallest units within the tribes—until they have all been included in the cycle.[1]) It is also a part of this scheme, under which all the citizens meet to deliberate in relays, that they assemble only for the purpose of enacting laws, for dealing with constitutional matters, and for hearing the announcements of the magistrates.[2] § 5. A second way in which this first arrangement may be carried out is that all the citizens should meet to deliberate in a single body, but only for the three purposes of appointing and examining the magistrates, enacting laws, and dealing with issues of war and peace. The other matters [i.e. matters which involve the penalties of death, exile, and confiscation] will then be left for the deliberation of the magistracies assigned to deal with each branch; but appointment to such magistracies will be open—whether it is made by election or by lot—to all the citizens. § 6. A third way is that the citizens should meet for the two purposes of appointing and examining the magistrates, and deliberating on issues of war and foreign policy, but other matters [i.e. the enactment of laws, and the infliction of major penalties] should be left to the control of boards of magistrates which, as far as possible, are kept elective[3]—boards to which men of experience and knowledge ought to be appointed. § 7. A fourth way is that all should meet to deliberate on all issues, and boards of magistrates should have no power of giving a decision on any issue, but only that of making preliminary investigations. This is the way in which extreme democracy—a form of democracy analogous, as we have suggested, to the dynastic form of oligarchy and the tyrannical form of monarchy—is nowadays conducted.[4]

[1] These constitutions appear at first sight to confine deliberation to *some* of the citizens (since they vest it primarily in a combination of magistracies); but as they open the magistracies to *all* the citizens (in their turn), they really vest the power of deliberation in *all* the citizens (again in their turn).

[2] Problems arise in regard to this sentence, which limits, and limits greatly, the number of the issues on which all the citizens deliberate. Generally, a scheme which makes the citizens deliberate only in relays, and only on a limited number of issues, can hardly be said to be a way of giving effect to the arrangement which assigns *all* issues of deliberation to *all* the citizens.

[3] See Note OO, p. 193.

[4] This parallel has already been drawn in c. IV, § 27 and c. VI, § 11. It may be added that these four sections (4–7) all offer a logical difficulty. They start from an intention of describing various ways in which all may deliberate on all issues. Actually, they seem more concerned with ways in which not-all may deliberate on not-all issues.

All these ways of arranging the distribution of deliberative power are democratic. A second system of arrangement, which may also be carried into effect in a number of different ways, is that *some* of the citizens should deliberate on *all* matters. This is characteristic of oligarchy. § 8. One way of carrying this second system into effect is that the members of the deliberative body should be eligible on the basis of a moderate property qualification, and should therefore be fairly numerous; that they should not make changes in matters where the law prohibits change, but should obey its rules; and that all who acquire property to the amount of the qualification required should be allowed to share in the right of deliberation. Here we have something which is an oligarchy, but an oligarchy tending to 'polity' by virtue of its moderation. A second way of giving effect to this system is that membership of the deliberative body should belong only to selected persons—and not to all persons [who acquire property to the amount of the qualification required]—but that these persons **1298 b** should act, as before, in obedience to the rules of law. This is a way characteristic of oligarchy. § 9. Another way of carrying this system into effect is that those who possess the power of deliberation should recruit themselves by co-optation, or should simply succeed by heredity, and should have the power of overruling the laws. This is a way of arrangement which inevitably means oligarchy.

§ 10. A third system of arrangement is that *some* of the citizens should deliberate on *some* matters—but not on all. [The effect will be that on other matters *all* the citizens will deliberate.] For instance, all the citizens may exercise the deliberative power in regard to war and peace and the examination of magistrates; but the magistrates only may exercise that power on issues other than these, and these magistrates may be appointed by election.[1] When this is the case, the constitution is an aristocracy. Another alternative is that some issues of deliberation should go to persons appointed by election, and others to persons appointed by lot (with the chance of the lot either open to all or open only to candidates selected in advance), or, again, that all issues should go to a mixed body of elected persons and persons appointed by lot, deliberating together. Such ways of arrangement are partly

---

[1] In the Greek text the words 'or by lot' follow. But the addition of these words would make the form of government described a democracy, and not, as it is said to be, an aristocracy. I therefore follow the editors who have bracketed these words as an interpolation. It may be added that in this section Aristotle appears to be describing (but implicitly rather than explicitly) the third main arrangement described at the end of § 3—that of assigning the power of decision on some issues to all, and on other issues to some. He does not, however, make it clear that this is another main type of arrangement; on the contrary, he seems to add it as an appendix to his description of the second (or oligarchical) type.

characteristic of a 'polity' verging on aristocracy, and partly of a pure 'polity'.[1]

§ 11. These are the different forms of the deliberative body which correspond to the different constitutions. Each constitution is organized on the basis of one or other of the systems we have distinguished. [We may now turn from the actual *practice* to the proper *policy* of states.]

§ 12. The policy which is in the interest of a democracy—a democracy, that is to say, of the type which is nowadays held to be peculiarly and specially democratic (and this is the type where the sovereignty of the people dominates even the laws)—is to improve the quality of the deliberative body by applying to it the plan which oligarchies apply to the meetings of the law courts. They compel the attendance of all whose presence is desired in the courts under sanction of a fine—the converse of the democratic plan of persuading men to attend by pay. A democracy will do well to apply this plan of compulsory attendance to the deliberative assembly. The results of deliberation are better when all deliberate together; when the populace is mixed with the notables and they, in their turn, with the populace. § 13. It is also in the interest of a democracy that the parts of the state should be represented in the deliberative body by an equal number of members, either elected for the purpose or appointed by the use of the lot.[2] It is also in its interest, when the members of the populace largely exceed the notables who have political experience, that payment for attendance at the assembly should not be given to all the citizens, but only to so many as will balance the number of the notables or, alternatively, that the lot should be used to eliminate the excess of ordinary citizens over the notables.

§ 14. The policy which is in the interest of oligarchies is to co-opt to the deliberative body some members drawn from the populace; or, alternatively, to erect an institution of the type which exists in some states, under the name of 'preliminary council' or 'council of legal supervision', and then to allow the citizen-body to deal with any issues which have already been considered, in

---

[1] The second alternative suggested in the latter part of § 10 seems more characteristic of a pure 'polity': the first alternative (especially when the persons appointed by lot are drawn from candidates selected in advance) seems more characteristic of a 'polity' inclining to aristocracy.

[2] It is important to notice that Aristotle here suggests a *representative* organ of deliberation (cf. also Book VI, c. III, § 1). This shows that the idea of representative institutions was not altogether unknown to the Greeks. It may be added that the new Athenian League, instituted in 377 B.C., made provision for a double parliament—part consisting of the Athenian Council and Assembly, and the other part being 'a synod of representatives from all the other states of the league' (*Cambridge Ancient History*, vol. vi, p. 73).

advance, by the members of this institution. (On this latter plan the people at large will share in the right of deliberation, but they will not be able to abrogate any rule of the constitution.) § 15. Another line of policy which is in the interest of oligarchies is that the people should only be free to vote for measures which are identical, or at any rate in agreement, with those submitted by the government; or, alternatively, that the people as a whole should have a consultative voice, but the deliberative organ should be the body of magistrates. If the latter alternative is adopted, it should be applied in a way which is the opposite of the practice followed in 'polities'. The people should be sovereign for the purpose of rejecting proposals, but not for the purpose of passing them; and any proposals which they pass should be referred back to the magistrates. § 16. The practice adopted in 'polities' is the reverse of this. The few [i.e. the magistrates] are sovereign for the purpose of rejecting proposals, but not for the purpose of passing them; and any proposal which they pass is **1299 a** referred back to the many.... These are our conclusions in regard to the deliberative or sovereign[1] element in the constitution.

NOTE NN (p. 189): *The three elements of government*

Prima facie, these three 'elements' seem to be identical with the legislative, executive, and judicial powers of modern theory. Actually, Aristotle's deliberative element was hardly a legislative (though it had legislative functions): it was rather concerned with the executive function, and with some of the higher judicial functions. Similarly his magistracies, though they had executive functions (of different specialized kinds), did not constitute an 'executive government' in the modern sense; the deliberative element had overriding power in that respect. Finally, the judicial element, as we have already noticed, was not a body of judges: it was composed of lay or popular courts. The reader has to think himself back into a Greek framework essentially different from the modern, and to abandon any idea of a differentiation of powers on the model of Montesquieu's theory, or of British (or American) practice.

NOTE OO (p. 190): *The use of the lot at Athens*

Popular feeling in democracies ran in favour of the lot, which was held to give the ordinary man a better chance. Election gave a better chance to those who could plead capacity—or (one may also add) could bring influence to bear.

Appointment to office by means of the lot—the usual procedure at Athens except for the generals and other military officers (Appendix IV. B. 3)—may seem strange to-day. But it was safeguarded at Athens in three ways—first, by a formal test of fitness before entry on office (*dokimasia*); secondly, by a vote in the assembly on the conduct of any officer during his tenure (*epicheirotonia*), a vote to which he was at once

[1] The identification of the deliberative with the sovereign element has already been made in Book III, c. XI, § 15, and, more explicitly, in Book II, c. VI, § 2.

subjected if the assembly held that there was ground for examination; and thirdly, by a scrutiny at the end of the tenure of office (*euthūnai*), which included not only a financial audit, but also examination before a board of scrutiny, or, in the case of the higher officers, before the Council and the popular courts: see Vinogradoff, *Historical Jurisprudence*, vol. ii, pp. 140–2.

CHAPTER XV

The second element is the executive, or the system of magistracies. Differences in the system of magistracies turn on four points—number; functions; tenure; and methods of appointment. Definition of the term 'magistracy'; and a general consideration of the number, functions, and tenure of magistracies, with a discussion of the relation of different magistracies (e.g. the Boulē *and the* Probouloi) *to different constitutions. The methods of appointment: the three main factors to be considered, the choice of alternatives presented by each, and the various modes of handling the choice of alternatives. The arrangements for the appointment of magistrates best suited to different constitutions— democracy, 'polity', oligarchy, and aristocracy.*

§ 1. The next subject for examination is the [executive element, or the] magistracies. This element of the constitution, like the deliberative, admits of a number of different arrangements. These differences arise on a variety of points: (1) the number of the magistracies; (2) the subjects with which they deal; and (3) the length of the tenure of each. ... In some states the tenure is six months; in some it is a less period; in others it is a year; and in others, again, it is a longer period. We have not only to compare these periods; we have also to inquire generally whether magistracies should be held for life, or for a long term of years, or neither for life nor for a long term but only for shorter periods, and whether, in that case, the same person should hold office more than once, or each should be eligible only for a single term. ... There is also (4) a further point to be considered—the method of appointment; and this raises three questions—who should be eligible; who should have the right of election; and how should the election be conducted? § 2. We have first to distinguish the various methods which it is possible to apply to each of these questions, and then, on that basis, we have to determine the particular form of magistracies which will suit a particular form of constitution. We are confronted, however, with an initial difficulty of definition. What is to be included under the term 'magistrate'? A political association needs a large number of different officers. We cannot, therefore, reckon as magistrates all the persons appointed—by election or lot—to any office. We can hardly include, for example, the priests of the public cults, whose office must be reckoned as something different from the political magistracies. § 3. The same is true of the officials concerned with the production of plays:[1] it is true of the heralds; it is true of the persons elected to go on embassies. The general range of official duties may be divided into three classes. The first is the political, where the duty is one of directing, in some particular sphere of action, either the whole body of the citizens (as e.g. a general directs the civic army in the field), or some section of the citizens (as e.g. the inspectors of women and children direct their respective charges). The second is the economic; and here the officers elected to measure the corn for distribution (they are to be found in many states) may be cited as an example. The third class is that of subordinate or menial duties—duties of the sort which, in wealthy states, the public slaves are set to discharge. § 4. Among all these offices the title of magistracy should, on the whole, be reserved for those which are charged with the duty, in some given field, of deliberating, deciding, and giving instructions—and more especially with the duty of giving instructions, which is the special mark of the magistrate. But it is all a matter of style, which can hardly be said to have any importance in practice. No decision has been given about it in courts, the issue being merely a matter of terminology; and it only offers an opportunity for speculative inquiry.

§ 5. In dealing with all constitutions, but especially in dealing with those of small states, it is a matter of more importance to distinguish what sort and number of magistracies are necessary to the state's *existence*, and what sort are of value—even if they are not necessary—in ensuring a *good* constitution. § 6. In large states it is both possible and proper that a separate magistracy should be allotted to each separate function. The number of the citizens makes it convenient for a number of persons to enter on office: it permits some of the offices to be held only once in a lifetime, and others (though held more than once) to be held again only after a long interval; and, apart from convenience, each function gets better attention when it is the only one undertaken, and not one among a number of others.

1299 b   § 7. In small states, on the other hand, a large number of functions have to be accumulated in the hands of but a few persons. The small number of the citizens makes it difficult for many persons to be in office together; and if there were, who would be their successors? It is true that small states sometimes need the same magistracies, and the same laws about their tenure and duties, as large states. But it is also true that large states

---

[1] To equip a chorus for a public dramatic festival was an expensive office for which the Athenian tribes provided men in their turn.

need their magistracies almost continuously, and small states only need theirs at long intervals.   § 8. There is thus no reason why small states should not impose a number of duties simultaneously on their officers. They will not interfere with one another; and anyhow it is necessary, where the population is small, to turn magistrates into jacks-of-all-trades.[1]

But before this question can be settled finally, there are a number of questions to be considered. One thing which will help us to determine how many magistracies can be combined in the hands of a single magistrate is to know beforehand how many magistracies a state *must* have, and how many others it *ought* to have even though they are not absolutely necessary.   § 9. Secondly, we must not omit to consider which matters need the attention of different local magistracies acting in different places, and which ought to be controlled by one central magistracy acting for the whole area.[2] The maintenance of order is an example. It raises the question whether we should have one person to keep order in the market-place and another in another place, or whether we should have a single person to keep order in every place. Thirdly, we have also to consider whether to allocate duties on the basis of the subject to be handled, or on that of the class of persons concerned: e.g. should we have one officer for the whole subject of the maintenance of order, or a separate officer for the class of children and another for that of women?   § 10. Fourthly, we have also to take into account the difference of constitutions. This raises the question whether the scheme of magistracies varies from one constitution to another, or is the same for all constitutions. Are we to say that in all constitutions alike (democracy, oligarchy, aristocracy, and monarchy) the same magistracies form the government—with the one difference that the magistrates personally do not come from the same, or a similar, social class, but are drawn from a different class in each different constitution (in aristocracies, for example, from the cultured class; in oligarchies from the wealthy; and in democracies from the free-born)? Or shall we say that the magistracies too, as well as the magistrates, differ in some respects from one constitution to another; and shall we then add, as a qualification, that in some cases the same magistracies are suitable, but in other cases they are bound to differ? (In some constitutions, for example, it may be appropriate that

---

[1] This is a free translation. Aristotle's word, in the Greek, is one which denotes a spit that can also serve as a lamp-holder—something like 'the Delphic knife' mentioned in Book I, c. II, § 3.

[2] It is often said that the Greek city-state knew no distinction between central and local government. This passage shows the germ of such a distinction, as the previous passage in c. XIV, § 13, shows the germ of the idea of representation.

magistracies should be powerful: in others it may be appropriate that the same magistracies should be weak.)

§ 11. Some magistracies, it is true, are altogether peculiar to one type of constitution. A preliminary council, or body of *probouloi*, is an example. Such a body does not square with democracy, where the ordinary council, or *boulē*, is the appropriate institution. There ought, indeed, to be some sort of body charged with the duty of preliminary deliberation on behalf of the people: otherwise the people will not be able to attend to their ordinary business. But if such a body is small, it becomes an oligarchical institution; and a body of *probouloi* will always be small, and therefore will always be oligarchical. § 12. Where a *boulē* and a body of *probouloi* are both to be found, the latter are a check on the former; they are an oligarchical element, and the *boulē* is democratic. Yet even the authority of the *boulē* itself is subverted in democracies of the extreme type, where the people assembles in person to transact the whole business of the state.[1] **1300 a** § 13. This usually happens when there is a high rate of pay for those who attend the assembly. Men need not then mind their business; and therefore they hold frequent meetings and decide all issues themselves. . . . Officers for the maintenance of order among women and children, and other magistrates charged with similar duties of supervision, are suited more to an aristocracy than to a democracy (it would be impossible to control the comings and goings of the wives of the poor); nor are they congenial to an oligarchy, where the wives of the ruling class live a life of luxury.

§ 14. Enough has been said, for the present, about these matters: and we must now attempt to give a full account of the appointment of magistrates. The differences here are connected with three factors, which produce, in combination, all the possible modes. The three factors are (1) the persons appointing, (2) the persons eligible for appointment, and (3) the machinery of appointment. § 15. Each of these three factors admits of a choice of alternatives, and there are thus three choices of alternatives corresponding to the

---

[1] A Council or *Boulē* with a large membership (at Athens there were 500 members, chosen by lot) is in Aristotle's view consistent with democracy, and forms (we may say) a sort of second chamber by the side of the assembly. A body of *probouloi* with a small membership (probably chosen by election) is, in his view, of a different character. It is not in the nature of a second chamber in a system of democracy, but rather an oligarchical drag or check on the democratic council.

Probouloi (or, as we may call them, 'pre-councillors', or even 'privy councillors') formed a committee for initiating measures. They did not exist at Athens, except on one brief occasion—for about the space of a year, after the end of the Sicilian expedition in 413 B.C. Normally the Council of 500 prepared the business for the assembly: see Appendix IV. B. 2, p. 383.

three factors. (1) The persons appointing may be all the citizens, or only a section. (2) The persons eligible for appointment may be all the citizens, or only a section—a section determined by a property qualification, or birth, or merit, or some similar quality (in Megara, for example, the only persons eligible for appointment were those who had returned from exile together and fought together against the populace). (3) The machinery of appointment may be election, or it may be lot. § 16. In addition we may also have a conjunction of both alternatives, with the result that (1) for some offices the persons appointing may be all the citizens, and for others only a section; (2) for some offices the persons eligible may be all the citizens, and for others only a section; and (3) for some offices the machinery of appointment may be election, and for others it may be lot.

Four modes[1] are possible in handling each of the choices of alternatives. § 17. The alternative which consists in all the citizens appointing may mean (1) that all appoint from all by election; (2) that all appoint from all by lot (the appointment from all, in both these cases, being *either* made successively from sections— such as tribes and wards and clans—until all have eventually been included, *or* continuously from all); (3) that all appoint from a section by election; or (4) that all appoint from a section by lot. (But it is also possible that all the citizens, as the appointing body, may appoint to some offices in one of these ways, and to others in another.) § 18. Similarly, the alternative which consists in a section of the citizens appointing may mean (1) that the section appoints from all by election; (2) that it appoints from all by lot; (3) that it appoints from a section by election; or (4) that it appoints from a section by lot. (But here, again, it is also possible that a section, as the appointing body, may appoint to some offices in one of these ways and to others in another: e.g. it may appoint to some offices, 'from all by election' and to others 'from all by lot', or it may appoint to some offices 'from a section by election' and to others 'from a section by lot'.) There are thus twelve modes[1] in all, if we [take into account the first conjunction mentioned in § 16 and its various modes, and] omit the other two conjunctions.

§ 19. [How do their different arrangements fit different constitutions? We may answer in four propositions.] First, there are two which are democratic—(a) that by which all appoint from all *either* by election *or* lot, and (b) that by which all appoint from all *both* by election *and* lot, using the one method in some and the other in other cases. Secondly, there are various arrangements which fit a 'polity'. (a) One is when all appoint from all (either

[1] See Note PP. p. 199.

by election or lot or both by election and lot), but do so in sections taken successively and not as a continuously active body. (b) Another is when all appoint from all to some of the offices, but appoint from a section to others (either by election or lot or both by election and lot). § 20. (c) Still another arrangement which fits a 'polity'—but a 'polity' inclining more towards oligarchy—is when a section appoints from all, and does so by election for some of the offices and by lot for the others. (d) A last arrangement which fits a 'polity'—but a 'polity' verging on aristocracy—is when a section appoints simultaneously both from all and from a section (i.e. from all to some offices and from a section to others), whether it does so wholly by election, or wholly by lot, or by election for some offices and by lot for others. **1300 b** § 21. Thirdly, an arrangement which fits an oligarchy is when a section appoints from a section—by election, by lot, or by a mixture of both. Finally, an arrangement which fits an aristocracy is one under which a section appoints from all, or all appoint from a section, by the method of election.[1]

§ 22. Such is the number of the different methods which may be used in appointing magistrates, and such is their distribution among different types of constitution. We have still to consider the nature of the functions of the different magistracies, before we can understand which method is expedient for each, and how, in each case, the appointments ought to be made. When we speak of the functions of a magistracy we mean functions such as control of the revenue or control of the defence force. [The functions of different magistrates differ:] there is a difference in kind, for example, between the function of a general and that of an officer charged with the superintendence of contracts made in the market.[2]

NOTE PP (p. 198): *The possible modes in the appointment of magistrates*

This statement would seem to need some modification, in the light of the argument which follows. What Aristotle actually does is this. (1) He takes the first choice of alternatives—that the persons appointing should be all the citizens, or only a section—and he describes four modes by which all may appoint, and another four by which a section may appoint. He thus describes eight modes as possible in handling the first choice of alternatives. In addition, however, as the reader will see, Aristotle includes the two other choices of alternatives—that the persons eligible should be all *or* some, and that the machinery of election should be election

[1] The text here translated, from the beginning of § 17 to the end of § 21, is that proposed by Newman at the foot of vol. iv, p. 30, of his edition.
[2] This suggestion of an investigation into the different functions of different magistracies is not acted upon. We are left with such hints about the number of the different magistracies, and the general scope of their functions, as are contained in the first half of the chapter (§§ 1–13).

or lot—in dealing with the modes which are possible in handling the
first choice of alternatives. He has thus exhausted all the three choices
in his consideration of the modes which are possible in handling the first
choice. (2) But there is also the possibility of a *conjunction* of alternatives
(instead of a *choice* of alternatives)—or rather (to speak more exactly) of
three conjunctions of alternatives, corresponding to the three choices of
alternatives. Aristotle takes the first conjunction—that of all the citizens
appointing with only a section appointing—and he implies that four
modes are possible in handling that conjunction. (He does *not* consider
the two other conjunctions—that of all being eligible with only a section
being eligible, and that of the use of the lot with the use of the election—
but only, as he says, the first, 'omitting the other two'.) These four
modes, along with the eight previously mentioned, form the twelve modes
mentioned at the end of § 18.

It should be added that Aristotle does not make clear in the text the
four modes possible in handling the first conjunction. He only implies
them. But on the same lines which he follows in dealing separately with
'all' and a 'section', we may describe the four modes of a conjunction of
'all' with a 'section' as follows:

(1) The conjunction appoints from all by election.
(2) It appoints from all by lot.
(3) It appoints from a section by election.
(4) It appoints from a section by lot.

It should also be added that the conjunctions described in parentheses
in §§ 17-18 are not conjunctions of 'all' with a 'section' in making appointments, but conjunctions of different sets of persons eligible with different
machineries of appointment (i.e. election and lot).

CHAPTER XVI

The third element is the judicial, or the system of law courts (dikastēria). *An enumeration of eight different types of law courts, and a
consideration of the three main ways in which courts may be constituted.
The types of constitution to which these different ways are best suited.*

§ 1. Of the three powers [the deliberative, the executive, and
the judicial], the last alone remains to be considered. The same
plan [which we followed in regard to the executive] must also be
followed in determining questions connected with courts of law.
Here the three points on which differences arise are (1) the
membership of the courts; (2) their competence; and (3) the machinery for appointing the members. Membership raises the question
whether the courts are to be constituted from all the citizens or
from a section; competence raises the question how many kinds
of courts there are; the machinery of appointment raises the question whether appointment should be by vote or by lot.

§ 2. We must first determine how many kinds of courts there
are. These may be said to be eight. There is one for the review of
the conduct of magistrates; a second for dealing with any offence
against any point of public interest; a third for cases which bear

on the constitution; a fourth (which includes in its scope both officials and private persons) for cases of disputes about the amount of fines; a fifth for contracts between private persons, where a considerable amount is involved; a sixth for cases of homicide; and a seventh for cases of aliens. . . . § 3. It should be noted that the court which deals with homicide has a number of divisions, which may either be combined under one set of judges or come before different sets. One of these divisions is concerned with deliberate homicide; a second with involuntary homicide; a third with homicides where the act is admitted, but its justification is disputed; and a fourth for acts of deliberate homicide committed, upon their return, by persons who have been previously exiled for involuntary homicide. An example of the last division is the court at Athens which is known as 'the Court at Phreatto';[1] but cases of this order happen infrequently, even in large states. § 4. Similarly the court for cases of aliens has two divisions—one for cases between alien and alien, and one for cases between alien and citizen. . . . Finally, there is an eighth court for contracts between private persons which only involve a small sum—a matter of a shilling, or five shillings, or some sum a little larger. Here a decision has to be given, but there is no need for a large court to give it.

§ 5. We need not go further into the last three sorts of courts, and we may confine our attention to the first five. These have all a political character, as they deal with issues which, unless properly handled, create dissension and constitutional disturbance. Here we must have [if all the citizens are eligible for membership of the courts] one or other of the following systems. (1) All the citizens should be eligible to judge on all the matters we have distinguished, and should be chosen for the purpose either (*a*) by vote or (*b*) by lot. (2) All the citizens should be eligible to judge on all these matters; but for some of them the courts should be recruited by vote, and for others by lot. (3) All the citizens should be eligible to judge, but only on part of these matters; and the courts concerned with that part should all be similarly recruited, partly by vote and partly by lot. **1301 a** § 6. This means four different systems [if we count the two alternatives under (1) as separate systems]. There will be an equal number of systems if a sectional method be followed—i.e. if it is only a section of the citizens, and not all, who are eligible to sit in the courts. In that case we may have (1) judges drawn from a section by vote to judge

---

[1] This was a court, with the curious procedure that the accused was on board ship and the judges were on the land, which dealt with persons who had been exiled for a year for involuntary homicide and had then been guilty of homicide or assault before they had been legally allowed to settle again in Athens; cf. the *Constitution of Athens*, c. LVII, § 3.

on all matters; or (2) judges drawn from a section by lot to judge on all matters; or (3) judges drawn from a section by vote for some matters and by lot for others [but, together, judging on *all* matters]; or (4) judges sitting in a limited number of courts, [and thus dealing with some matters only, and not with all], which are similarly recruited partly by vote and partly by lot. It will be seen that these last four systems, as has just been said, correspond exactly to the previous four. § 7. In addition, we may have a conjunction of both sorts of systems; for example we may have some courts with members drawn from the whole civic body, others with members drawn from a section of the civic body, and others, again, with a mixed membership (the same court being, in that case, composed of members drawn from the whole and of members drawn from a section); and again we may have the members appointed either by vote, or by lot, or by a mixture of both.

§ 8. This gives us a complete list of all the possible systems on which courts can be constituted. The first sort of system, in which the membership of the courts is drawn from all, and the courts decide on all matters, is democratic. The second sort, in which the membership is drawn from a section, and the courts decide on all matters, is oligarchical. The third sort, [which is a conjunction of the first two, and] in which the membership of some courts is drawn from all, and that of others from a section, is characteristic of aristocracies and 'polities'.

BOOK V

CAUSES OF REVOLUTION AND CONSTITUTIONAL CHANGE

A

THE GENERAL CAUSES OF REVOLUTION AND CHANGE IN ALL TYPES OF CONSTITUTION (cc. I–IV)

CHAPTER I

Different interpretations of justice and equality lead to the making of different claims by different parties; and the conflict of these claims causes political struggles and changes. The different forms which programmes of political change may take either imply the overthrow of the existing constitution, or involve some sort of modification. Whatever the difference of form may be, the general motive is always a passion for some conception of equality, which is held to be involved in the very idea of justice. There are two main conceptions of equality —the numerical and the proportionate: democracy is based on the one, and oligarchy on the other. Neither conception should be exclusively followed; but, of the two, the democratic is the safer, and the less likely to provoke revolution.

1301 a 19 § 1. We have now practically completed our discussion of the first four subjects stated in our programme; and it only remains to treat, in conclusion, of the last. Under this head we have to consider the general causes which produce changes in constitutions, and to examine their number and nature. We have also to consider the particular way in which each constitution is liable to degenerate—i.e. to explain *from* what a constitution is most likely to change *to* what. In addition we have to suggest the *policies* likely to ensure the stability of constitutions, collectively and individually, and to indicate the *means* which may best be employed to secure each particular constitution.[1]

§ 2. We must first assume, as a basis of our argument, that the reason why there is a variety of different constitutions is the fact— already mentioned[2]—that while men are all agreed in doing

---

[1] Following the programme laid down at the end of Book IV, c. II, and having considered already, in Book IV, four of the five subject s of that programme, Aristotle now considers the fifth and last—the causes of the destruction, and the methods of the preservation, of different constitutions. This subject occupies the whole of the next two books. Book V is concerned with 'destruction', or in other words revolutions; Book VI is concerned with 'preservation'— but only so far as democracies and oligarchies are concerned. (There is, however, an excursus on methods of preservation intercalated in the treatment of revolutions in Book V, cc. VIII–IX.)

[2] In Book III, c. IX, § 1, and c. XII, §§ 1–2.

homage to justice, and to the principle of proportionate equality [in which it issues], they fail to achieve it in practice [i.e. disagree in their actual interpretations].   § 3. Democracy arose in the strength of an opinion that those who were equal in any one respect were equal absolutely, and in all respects. (Men are prone to think that the fact of their all being equally free-born means that they are all absolutely equal.) Oligarchy similarly arose from an opinion that those who were unequal in some one respect were altogether unequal. (Those who are superior in point of wealth readily regard themselves as absolutely superior.)   § 4. Acting on such opinions, the democrats proceed to claim an equal share in everything, on the ground of their equality; the oligarchs proceed to press for more, on the ground that they are unequal—that is to say, more than equal.   § 5. Both democracy and oligarchy are based on a sort of justice; but they both fall short of absolute justice. This is the reason why either side turns to sedition if it does not enjoy the share of constitutional rights which accords with the conception of justice it happens to entertain.   § 6. Those who are pre-eminent in merit would be the most justified in attempting sedition (though they are the last to make the attempt); for they—and they only— can reasonably **1301 b** be regarded as enjoying an absolute superiority.   § 7. There is also some justification for those who, possessing an advantage of birth, regard themselves as entitled to more than an equal share on the ground of this advantage. Good birth is commonly regarded as the attribute of those whose ancestors had merit as well as wealth.

These, in a general sense, are the sources and springs of sedition, and the causes of seditious action.[1]   § 8. These considerations will also explain the two different ways in which constitutional changes may happen. (1) Sometimes sedition is directed against the existing constitution, and is intended to change its nature—to turn democracy into oligarchy, or oligarchy into democracy; or, again, to turn democracy and oligarchy into 'polity' and aristocracy, or, conversely, the latter into the former. (2) Sometimes, however, it is not directed against the existing constitution. The seditious party [may follow a more moderate line, in one or other of three directions. First, it] may decide to maintain the system of government—an oligarchy, for example, or a monarchy—as it stands;

[1] The word here translated 'sedition' is the Greek *stasis*. *Stasis* is the act of forming (and thence, by an easy transference, the body of persons forming) a combination 'for the attainment of some political end by legal and illegal means' (Newman). From this point of view, and because it may include illegal as well as legal means, *stasis* may involve revolutionary action, and thus issue in revolution; though it may sometimes stop short of that issue, and only produce non-revolutionary changes, within the four walls of the constitution. Aristotle accordingly connects two different forms of constitutional change with *stasis*.

but it will desire to get the administration into the hands of its members. § 9. Secondly, a seditious party [while leaving a constitution generally intact] may wish to make it more pronounced or more moderate. It may wish, for example, to make an oligarchy more, or less, oligarchical. It may wish to make a democracy more, or less, democratic. It may similarly seek to tighten, or loosen, the strings in any of the other forms of constitution. § 10. Thirdly, a seditious party may direct its efforts towards changing only one part of the constitution. It may wish, for example, to erect, or to abolish, some particular magistracy. Some writers state that Lysander attempted to abolish the kingship at Sparta, and King Pausanias the ephoralty. At Epidaurus, again, there was a partial change of the constitution; and a Council [of a democratic character] was substituted for the meeting of heads of tribes. § 11. But even at the present time [Epidaurus is so far from being a democracy that] the magistrates are the only members of the civic body who are obliged to attend the public assembly, when the appointment to a magistracy is being put to the vote; and the existence of a single Archon [instead of a college of Archons] continues to present another oligarchical feature.

In all these cases [whether sedition is directed against the constitution, or only towards its modification] the cause of sedition is always to be found in inequality—though there is no inequality [and therefore no justification for sedition] when unequals are treated in proportion to the inequality existing between them (and therefore an hereditary monarchy only involves inequality when it exists among equals). It is the passion for equality which is thus at the root of sedition. § 12. But equality is of two sorts. One sort is numerical equality: the other sort is equality proportionate to desert. 'Numerical equality' means being treated equally, or identically, in the number and volume of things which you get; 'equality proportionate to desert' means being treated on the basis of equality of ratios.[1] To give an example—numerically, the excess of 3 over 2 is equal to the excess of 2 over 1; but proportionally, the excess of 4 over 2 is equal to the excess of 2 over 1—2 being the same fraction of 4 as 1 is of 2.[2] § 13. Now men are ready to agree to the principle that absolute justice [in the division of rights] consists [in their being divided] in proportion to desert; but they

[1] Aristotle always argues, as he has argued in Book III, that true equality is proportionate equality, or in other words an equality of ratios—i.e. equality of the ratio between A's desert and what he gets with the ratio between B's desert and what *he* gets.

[2] As Newman remarks, this illustration touches only the mathematical point, and does not show that equality in proportion to desert is the true form of political equality.

differ, as we noted at the beginning of this chapter, [as soon as it comes to practice]. Some take the line that if men are equal in one respect, they may consider themselves equal in all: others take the line that if they are superior in one respect, they may claim superiority all round.

§ 14. The result of men's taking these two lines is that two types of constitution—democracy and oligarchy—are particularly prevalent. Good birth and merit are found in few persons; but the qualities on which democracy and oligarchy are based are found in a much larger number. In no state would you find as many as a hundred **1302 a** men of good birth and merit: there are many in which you would find that number of wealthy persons. But a constitutional system based absolutely, and at all points, on either the oligarchical or the democratic conception of equality is a poor sort of thing. The facts are evidence enough: constitutions of this sort never endure. § 15. The reason is simple. When one begins with an initial error, it is inevitable that one should end badly. The right course is [not to pursue either conception exclusively, but] to use in some cases the principle of numerical equality, and in others that of equality proportionate to desert. Yet it must be admitted that democracy is a form of government which is safer, and less vexed by sedition, than oligarchy. § 16. Oligarchies are prone to two sorts of sedition—the one within the ranks of the oligarchical party itself, and the other between that party and the party of the people. Democracies are only exposed to sedition between the democratic party and the oligarchical; and there are no internal dissensions—at any rate none worth mentioning—which divide democratic parties against themselves. Democracy, too, has the advantage that it comes nearer than oligarchy does to the form of government—the 'polity' based on the middle classes—which is the most stable of all the forms with which we are here concerned [i.e. the imperfect forms which fall short of the ideal].

Chapter II

In dealing with the general origins and causes of revolution, we may do so under three heads: (1) psychological motives; (2) the objects in view; and (3) the initial occasions, which in turn are of two main kinds.

§ 1. Since we have to consider the various reasons which lead to the rise of seditions and changes in the general run of constitutions, we had better begin with a general view of their origins and causes. They may be said to be three in number; and we must begin by giving a brief outline of each of them separately. The three things we have to investigate are (1) the state of mind which leads to sedition; (2) the objects which are at stake; and (3) the occasions which serve to start political disturbance and mutual dissension.

§ 2. The principal and general cause of an attitude of mind which disposes men towards change is the cause of which we have just spoken. There are some who stir up sedition because their minds are filled by a passion for equality, which arises from their thinking that they have the worst of the bargain in spite of being the equals of those who have got the advantage. There are others who do it because their minds are filled with a passion for inequality (i.e. superiority), which arises from their conceiving that they get no advantage over others (but only an equal amount, or even a smaller amount) although they are really more than equal to others. § 3. (Either of these passions may have some justification; and either may be without any.) Thus inferiors become revolutionaries in order to be equals, and equals in order to be superiors.

This is the state of mind which creates sedition. The objects which are at stake are profit and honour. They are also their opposites—loss and disgrace; for the authors of political sedition may be simply seeking to avert some disgrace, or a fine, from themselves or their friends.

§ 4. The occasions and origins of disturbances—occasions which encourage the attitude of mind, and lead to the pursuit of the objects, which have just been mentioned—may be counted, from one point of view, as seven, but from another as more than that number.[1] § 5. Two of these occasions (profit and honour) are identical with two of the objects which have just been mentioned; but when considered as occasions they act in a different way. As objects, profit and honour provoke dissension because (as we have just noted) men want to get them themselves: as **1302 b** occasions, they lead to dissension because men see other persons getting a larger share—some justly and some unjustly—than they themselves get. § 6. Other occasions, besides profit and honour, are insolence; fear; the presence of some form of superiority; contempt; or a disproportionate increase in some part of the state. Four other occasions leading to dissension—but in a different way [i.e. incidentally, and not in themselves]—are election intrigues; wilful negligence; [the neglect of] trifling changes; and dissimilarity of elements [in the composition of a state].

---

[1] The seven main occasions are those which intrinsically, and in their own nature, lead to seditious feelings and action. There are also, however, four other occasions which leads to sedition incidentally, or, we may even say, accidentally. These are enumerated at the end of the chapter.

CHAPTER III

A study of the way in which initial occasions may operate. (1) *There is the kind of occasion which operates intrinsically, or from reasons inherent in its own nature: of this there are seven varieties—insolence; the desire of profit; the point of honour; the presence of some sort of superiority; fear; contempt; and the disproportionate increase of one or other element in the state.* (2) *There is the kind of occasion which operates accidentally, and not from reasons inherent in its own nature: of this there are four varieties—election intrigues; wilful neglect; the overlooking of trifling changes; and the dissimilarity of elements in the composition of the state.*

§ 1. Among these occasions[1] it is fairly clear what influence *insolence* and *profit-making* [among those who are in authority] may exert, and in what ways they may lead to sedition. When those who are in office show insolence, and seek their personal advantage, the citizens turn seditious—not only attacking other persons, but also attacking the constitution which gives such persons power. Personal advantage, we may note in passing, is sometimes sought at the expense of individuals; sometimes at that of the public. § 2. It is also clear how *honour* may serve as an occasion; what influence it may exert; and how it may lead to sedition. Men turn seditious when they suffer dishonour themselves, and when they see others honoured. Both of these things may be unjustifiable, if the honour given, or the dishonour inflicted, is undeserved: both may be justifiable, if the honour or dishonour is deserved. § 3. The *presence of some form of superiority* becomes an occasion for sedition when a person, or body of persons, is in a position of strength which is too great for the state and more than a match for the strength of the general body of citizens. Such a position usually results in a monarchy, or in a 'dynastic' oligarchy. It is for this reason that, in a number of states, a policy of ostracism comes to be used. Argos and Athens are examples. But it is a better policy to begin by ensuring that there shall be no such persons of outstanding eminence, than first to allow them to arise and then to attempt a remedy afterwards.

§ 4. *Fear* is an occasion which leads to sedition among two classes of persons—wrongdoers, who are afraid of punishment;

---

[1] The order in which the various occasions are treated in this chapter is different from the order in which they are stated in the previous chapter. Here Aristotle takes together, as logically connected, the four occasions of insolence, profit, honour, and the existence of some sort of superiority (§§ 1–3): he then takes together the two occasions of fear and contempt (§§ 4–5); and he then treats at some length the seventh occasion—disproportionate increase (§§ 6–8). The four additional occasions of an incidental order are then treated successively, in the order of their previous statement, in §§ 9–16.

and persons expecting to suffer wrong, who are anxious to antici-
pate what they expect. An instance of the latter class may be cited
from Rhodes, where the notables were moved to conspire against
the people by alarm at the number of law-suits with which they
were being threatened.[1] § 5. *Contempt* is another occasion of sedition and insurrection. We can see this in oligarchies, when those
who are not in enjoyment of political rights are more numerous
and consequently think themselves stronger: we can also see it in
democracies, when the wealthy despise the disorder and anarchy
which they see prevalent. There are several examples of democracies collapsing from contempt—Thebes, where after the battle
of Oenophyta [456 B.C.] democracy was ruined by misgovernment;
Megara, where it perished as the result of a defeat which was
caused by disorder and anarchy; Syracuse, where it began to
collapse before Gelon became tyrant; and Rhodes, in the period
before the rising of the notables just mentioned.

§ 6. The *disproportionate increase of a part* of the state is also an
occasion which leads to constitutional changes. The analogy of the
body is instructive. The body is composed of parts, and it must
grow proportionately if symmetry is to be maintained. Otherwise
it perishes (as it will if the foot be four ells long and the rest of the
body two spans); or again it may sometimes change into the form
of some other animal, as it will if a disproportionate increase means
a change of quality as well as quantity.[2] The same is true of a state.
It, **1303 a** too, is composed of parts; and one of the parts may often
grow imperceptibly out of proportion. The number of the poor,
for example, may become disproportionate in democracies and in
'polities'. § 7. Sometimes this may be the result of accident. At
Tarentum, for example, a 'polity' was turned into a democracy in
consequence of the defeat and death of a number of the notables
at the hands of the neighbouring Iapygian tribe, just after the
Persian Wars [480 B.C.]. At Argos the destruction of 'the men of
the Seventh',[3] by the Spartan king Cleomenes [*circa* 500 B.C.],
made it necessary to admit some of the serfs into the civic body
[and thus changed the constitution in the direction of democracy].
At Athens the reverses suffered on land, during the Peloponnesian
War, depleted the numbers of the notables, under the system of
compulsory service for all registered citizens; [and this fostered

---

[1] This is explained in c. v, § 2 of this Book.

[2] Newman notes that some diseases, such as elephantiasis, were held by the
Greeks to produce qualitative effects which made the human form approach
that of an animal.

[3] It is not clear who the 'men of the Seventh' were. The words may mean
'the men who fell on the seventh day of the month' (and in that case one may
compare the habit, during the French Revolution, of speaking of 14me Juillet
or 19me Brumaire); or they may mean 'the members of the seventh tribe'.

the growth of democracy].   § 8. [These are all cases of change, due to disproportionate increase, in oligarchical or moderate constitutions; but] similar changes may also happen for the same reason in democracies—though this is less likely. If the rich become more numerous, or if properties increase, democracies turn into oligarchies and 'dynasties' [or family cliques].

§ 9. [Turning to the 'incidental' occasions of change], we may first note the effects of *election intrigues*, which may lead to constitutional changes without causing actual sedition. At Heraea, for example, the fact that the results of elections were determined by intrigues led to the use of the lot being substituted for the vote [and was thus the occasion of a constitutional change]. *Wilful negligence*, again, may be an occasion; and persons who are not loyal to the constitution may be allowed to find their way into the highest of the magistracies. Oreus, in Euboea, may serve as an example: its oligarchy was overthrown when Heracleodorus was allowed to become a magistrate, and he proceeded to turn it into a democracy—or rather a 'polity'. § 10. Another occasion is *the neglect of trifling changes*. A great change of the whole system of institutions may come about unperceived if small changes are overlooked. In Ambracia, for example, the property qualification for office—small to begin with—was finally allowed to disappear, under the idea that there was little or no difference between having a small qualification and having none at all. § 11. [The last of the incidental occasions of change is *dissimilarity of elements in the composition of a state*.] Heterogeneity of stocks may lead to sedition— at any rate until they have had time to assimilate. A state cannot be constituted from any chance body of persons, or in any chance period of time. Most of the states which have admitted persons of another stock,[1] either at the time of their foundation or later, have been troubled by sedition. There are many instances. The Achaeans joined with settlers from Troezen in founding Sybaris, but expelled them when their own numbers increased; and this involved their city in a curse. § 12. At Thurii the Sybarites quarrelled with the other settlers who had joined them in its colonization; and demanding special privileges, on the ground that they were the owners of the territory, they were driven out of the colony.[2] At Byzantium the later settlers were detected in a

---

[1] 'Stock' only means, in Aristotle's use, members of a Greek city. In this sense the Athenians were of a different 'stock' from the Thebans.

[2] These two instances of heterogeneity of stock leading to sedition have been instances of the admission of different stocks at the time of the original foundation of a colony (Aristotle is only concerned with colonies, where mixture of stock was natural). The six instances which follow are all instances of the admission of a different stock at a later date in the history of a colony.

conspiracy against the original colonists, and were expelled by force; and a similar expulsion befell the exiles from Chios who were admitted to Antissa by the original colonists. At Zancle, on the other hand, the original colonists were themselves expelled by the Samians whom they admitted. § 13. At Apollonia, on the Black Sea, sedition was caused by the introduction of new settlers: at Syracuse the conferring of civic rights on aliens and mercenaries, at the end of **1303 b** the period of the tyrants, led to sedition and civil war; and at Amphipolis the original citizens, after admitting Chalcidian colonists, were nearly all expelled by the colonists they had admitted.

(§ 14. In oligarchies, as has already been noted, the ground which the masses take in justification of sedition is that they are unjustly treated in being denied equal rights although they are actually equal. In democracies the ground taken by the notables is the injustice of their having only equal rights although they are actually superior.)[1]

§ 15. [Besides heterogeneity of stock] heterogeneity of territory is also an occasion of sedition. This happens in states with a territory not naturally adapted to political unity. At Clazomenae the inhabitants of the suburb of Chytrus [on the mainland] were at discord with the inhabitants of the island; and there was a similar discord between Colophon and its sea-port Notium. At Athens, again, there is a similar difference: the inhabitants of the port of Peiraeus are more democratic than those of the city of Athens. § 16. Taking our analogy from war, where the dividing line of a ditch, however small it may be, makes a regiment scatter in crossing, we may say that every difference is apt to create a division. The greatest division is perhaps that between virtue and vice; then there is the division between wealth and poverty; and there are also other divisions, some greater and some smaller, arising from other differences. Among these last we may count the division caused by difference of territory.

CHAPTER IV

The occasions of revolutions may be small, but the issues are great: small and personal matters may lead to large and general consequences. It may be added that revolutionary changes may also be due (1) to the growth in reputation and power of some office, or some part of the state, and (2) to an even balance of parties, resulting in a deadlock. It may also be added that force and fraud both play their part in the conduct of revolutions.

---

[1] This bracketed section interrupts the argument, and seems to be out of its place. It is a sort of lost or strayed note.

§ 1. But though sedition springs from small occasions, it does not turn on small issues. The issues involved are large. Even petty seditions [i.e. those springing from small occasions] attain great dimensions when they involve the members of the government. There is an example in the history of Syracuse, where a constitutional revolution arose from a quarrel between two young men, who were both in office, about a love affair. § 2. In the absence of one of the two the other (in spite of being his colleague) seduced the affections of his friend;[1] and the injured man, in his anger, retaliated by seducing his colleague's wife. Both of them, in the issue, drew the whole civic body into their quarrel and divided it into factions. § 3. The moral is that precautions ought to be taken at the very beginning of such feuds, and quarrels which involve men of leading and influence ought to be composed at once. The error is made at the start;[2] and since, as the proverb goes, 'The start is half of the job', a small mistake at the start is equal to all the mistakes made in the rest of the business. § 4. Generally speaking, we may lay it down that discords among the notables involve all the state in their consequences. This may be seen from the events at Hestiaea after the Persian Wars. Two brothers quarrelled about the division of an inheritance: the poorer of the two, on the ground that the other refused to declare the estate, or to disclose the amount of a treasure which their father had found, enlisted the popular party in his cause; the other, possessing a large estate, secured the aid of the wealthy. § 5. At Delphi, again, the beginning of all the later discords was a dispute **1304 a** which arose from a marriage. The bridegroom, interpreting as an evil omen some accident that had happened at the bride's home, on his coming to escort her away, departed without her; the bride's relations, considering themselves insulted, retaliated by putting some of the sacred treasures among his offerings during a sacrifice and then killing him for his supposed sacrilege. § 6. Similarly, at Mitylene, a dispute about the marriage of heiresses was the beginning of a host of troubles—including the war with Athens, in the course of which Paches captured the city. Timophanes, one of the wealthier citizens, had left two daughters. Dexander, another citizen, began a suit, in which he failed, to vindicate the right of his sons to marry the heiresses. Thereupon he stirred up sedition, and incited the Athenians, for whom he acted as consul, to interfere. § 7. In Phocis, again, another dispute about the marriage of an heiress, in which Mnaseas the father of

---

[1] The reference is to a homosexual connexion.

[2] There is here a pun, or play on words. The same Greek word (*archē*) means both 'beginning' (or 'start') and 'magistracy'; and thus an 'error made at the start' is also an 'error made in (or by) a magistracy'. See the Introduction, IV. 2.

Mnason and Euthycrates the father of Onomarchus were concerned, was the beginning of the Sacred War in which all Phocis came to be involved. A marriage affair was also the cause of a constitutional revolution at Epidamnus. A man had betrothed his daughter to another man, and was afterwards fined by the father of this man, who had just been made a magistrate; whereupon, regarding himself as insulted, he allied himself with the disfranchised classes [for the overthrow of the constitution].[1]

§ 8. Constitutions may also be changed—in the direction of oligarchy, or democracy, or a 'polity'—as a result of the growth in reputation or power of one of the magistracies, or of some other part of the state. The Council of the Areopagus at Athens, for example, gained in reputation during the Persian War; and the result appeared for a time to be a tightening of the constitution [i.e. a movement in the direction of oligarchy]. Then the tide turned: the common people, who served in the navy, were responsible for the victory of Salamis, and secured for Athens an empire which depended on naval power; and the effect of this was to strengthen the cause of democracy.[2] § 9. The notables of Argos gained in reputation by their conduct in the battle against the Spartans at Mantinea [418 B.C.], and they were encouraged by this to attempt the suppression of democracy: at Syracuse, on the other hand, the people were responsible for the victory won in the war against Athens, and they proceeded to turn the existing 'polity' into a democracy. At Chalcis the people united with the notables to remove the tyrant Phoxus, and by the part they played they immediately got a firm hold on the constitution. At Ambracia too, in much the same way, the people joined with the conspirators against him in expelling the tyrant Periander, and they then changed the constitution into a popular form. § 10. Generally, experience teaches the lesson, which ought always to be remembered, that any person or body which adds new power to the state—an individual, a board of magistrates, a tribe, or generally any section or group,

[1] The petty occasions hitherto treated have all been matters involving some sort of 'insolence', leading to some real or fancied insult (cf. c. III, § 1). Aristotle now turns to occasions connected with a disproportionate increase of some part of the state (cf. c. III, §§ 6 ff.).

[2] The connexion between Athenian sea-power and Athenian democracy is noticed in Aristotle's *Constitution of Athens*, xxvii, § 1 (see Appendix IV, A. 3), and it is mentioned again, by implication, in the *Politics*, Book VII, c. VI, § 7 (see the note). 'Those of the seamen who were citizens were drawn from the class of Thetes, who for the most part were resident in Athens and the Piraeus, and formed the radical element of the community' (Dr. E. M. Walker, in the *Cambridge Ancient History*, vol. v, p. 111). There was thus a logical connexion between (1) the Athenian empire and the Athenian navy; (2) the Athenian navy and the radically minded seamen who, living in Athens and the Piraeus, could attend the assembly and determine its policy.

whatever it may be—will tend to produce sedition; and the sedition will either be started by persons who envy the honours of those who have won success, or be due to the refusal of the latter to remain on a footing of equality when they feel themselves superior.

§ 11. Revolutions also occur when the sections of the state which are usually regarded as antagonists—for example, the rich and the common people—are equally **1304 b** balanced, with little or nothing of a middle class to turn the scale; for where either side has a clear preponderance, the other will be unwilling to risk a struggle with the side which is obviously the stronger. § 12. This is the reason why men of pre-eminent merit do not, as a rule, attempt to stir up sedition: they are only a few against many.

Such, on a general view, are the springs and causes of sedition and change in all constitutions. We may add that political revolutions are sometimes achieved by force, and sometimes by fraud. Force may either be used initially or at a later stage. Fraud, too, may be used at two different stages. § 13. Sometimes it is used in the initial stage. In this way a change may be made at the moment with general assent; but those who have made it then proceed to keep control of affairs in the teeth of all opposition. This was the case with the revolution of the Four Hundred at Athens [in 411 B.C.]: they first defrauded the people by an assurance that the Persian King would provide money for the war against Sparta, and after this act of fraud they attempted to keep the constitution permanently under their control. Sometimes, however, an initial act of persuasion is followed up afterwards by a similar policy, and control is thus kept with general consent. Such, on a summary view, are the causes of change in all constitutions.[1]

B

THE PARTICULAR CAUSES OF REVOLUTION AND CHANGE IN DIFFERENT TYPES OF CONSTITUTION (cc. v–xii)

CHAPTER V

1. Democracies. *Here revolution tends to be caused by the policy of demagogues in attacking the rich, individually or collectively. In early times demagogues often made themselves tyrants: they no longer do so; and indeed tyrannies of every sort are becoming rare, owing—among other causes—to the increased size of the modern state. Democracy is liable to change from the older and more moderate forms to a new and extreme type. This is largely due to the courting of the people by eager candidates for office.*

---

[1] This last paragraph, which interrupts the argument, may be an interpolation —the more as it begins with a general summary which is repeated at the end of the paragraph.

§ 1. We must now take the different constitutions separately, and study successively, in the light of these general propositions, what happens in each of the types.

In democracies changes are chiefly due to the wanton licence of demagogues. This takes two forms. Sometimes they attack the rich individually, by bringing false accusations, and thus force them to combine (for a common danger unites even the bitterest enemies): sometimes they attack them as a class, by egging on the people against them. The result of such action may be seen in a number of instances. § 2. At Cos democracy was overthrown by the rise of discreditable demagogues and the combination of the notables against them. The same thing happened at Rhodes, where the demagogues first introduced a system of payment [for attendance at the assembly and courts], and then [in order to secure the necessary funds] withheld the sums due to the trierarchs for their expenses in fitting out triremes; the result was that the trierarchs, vexed by the suits brought against them [by the ship-builders who had fitted out the triremes for them], were compelled to combine and overthrow the democracy. § 3. At Heraclea [on the Black Sea], democracy was ruined by the behaviour of demagogues soon after the colony was founded. They treated the notables unjustly, and drove them out by their conduct; but the notables gathered their forces, returned, and overthrew the democracy. § 4. At Megara, too [the city on the Greek mainland which had founded Heraclea], democracy was ruined in a similar way. The demagogues, anxious to have an excuse for confiscating their property, drove a number of the notables into exile, with the result that the exiles became so numerous that they effected their return, defeated the people in battle, and established an oligarchy. 1305 a The same fate also befell the democracy at Cyme, which was overthrown by Thrasymachus.[1] § 5. A survey of the changes in most of the other Greek states is sufficient to show that they have generally been of this character [i.e. changes from democracy to oligarchy due to the action of demagogues]. Sometimes the demagogues, anxious to win popular favour, drive the notables to combine by the injuries they inflict in imposing public burdens—burdens which either force them to break up their estates or [at any rate] cripple their revenues. Sometimes they bring false accusations in the courts, in order to be in a position to confiscate the property of the wealthier citizens.

---

[1] As Newman notes, all these instances of the overthrow of democracies owing to the action of demagogues are taken from the history of Dorian colonies in Asia Minor—except for Megara, which seems to be incidentally mentioned as the founder of one of these colonies.

§ 6. In early times, when the same man combined in his person the offices of demagogue and general, democracies changed into tyrannies. Most of the early tyrants were men who had first been demagogues. § 7. The reason why this was once the case, and is no longer so, is a matter of social development. In early times, when oratory was still in its infancy, demagogues were always drawn from the ranks of military commanders. To-day, with the growth of the art of rhetoric, men with the gift of speech are the men who make themselves demagogues; but men of this type, unversed in war, make no attempt at becoming tyrants—though here and there a case or two may have occurred. § 8. Another reason why tyrannies were more frequent in early times is that great offices were then entrusted to individuals, [as they now no longer are]. The tyranny [of Thrasybulus] at Miletus, for example, was due to his holding the office of prytanis, which carried a number of important prerogatives. A further reason is the smaller size of the cities of early times. The people generally lived in the country, occupied with the daily duties of their farms; and their leaders, when they were men of military capacity, had thus the chance of establishing a tyranny. § 9. They generally did so on the strength of popular confidence; and the basis of this confidence was the hostility they showed to the wealthy. Thus at Athens Peisistratus rose to be tyrant by leading a rising against the [wealthy] party of the Plain.[1] Theagenes became the tyrant of Megara after slaughtering the herds of the rich landlords whom he caught pasturing their cattle outside their own lands by the riverside. § 10. At Syracuse Dionysius attained the position of tyrant by denouncing Daphnaeus and the rest of the rich; his enmity to them made the people put their trust in him as a good democrat.

Changes may also take place from the traditional and 'ancestral'[2] form of democracy to the latest and most modern form. Where the offices are filled by vote, without any property qualification, and the whole of the people has the vote, candidates for office begin to play the demagogue, and matters are brought to a pass in which law itself in included in the scope of popular sovereignty. § 11. To prevent this result—or, at any rate, to diminish its full effect—the proper course is to give the vote to the separate tribes,[3]

---

[1] This party was opposed to the poorer party of the Coast.

[2] 'Ancestral democracy' was a catch-word at Athens in the fourth century, and had been so since the end of the Peloponnesian War in 404 B.C. See Appendix IV, p. 380, and n. 2.

[3] This is to act on the motto of *divide et impera*. The tribes, as Newman notes, might vote in turn; or different tribes might elect to different magistracies; or each tribe might elect a member to each board of magistrates. In any case there would be some brake on the power of the people. The system suggested is something like that which is nowadays called 'functional' representation.

and not to the whole of the people. . . . These, in the main, are the causes of all the changes in democracies.

CHAPTER VI

2. Oligarchies. *Here revolutions are due, partly to unjust treatment of the masses, and partly to dissensions within the governing class. Such dissensions may arise* (1) *if a section of that class begins to play the demagogue,* (2) *if some of its members become impoverished and turn revolutionary, and* (3) *if an inner ring is formed inside the governing body. Personal disputes may affect the stability of oligarchies; and accidental causes* (e.g. *a general growth of wealth, increasing the number of persons eligible for office*) *may insensibly alter their character.*

§ 1. There are two particular, and most obvious, methods by which changes are brought about in oligarchies. One is the unjust treatment of the masses by the government. Any leader is then an adequate champion, especially when it so happens that the leader comes from the ranks of the governing class itself. This was the case with Lygdamis of Naxos, who afterwards made himself tyrant of the island. § 2. Sedition which begins in a movement **1305 b** of resistance *outside* the governing class may take several different forms. Sometimes an oligarchy is undermined by persons who themselves are wealthy, but who are excluded from office. This happens when the holders of office are a very limited number; it has happened at Massilia, at Istros, at Heraclea, and in other cities. § 3. In all these oligarchies those who had no share in office continued to cause disturbance till some share was finally given, first to the elder brothers in a family and then to the younger too. (It should be explained that in some states father and son, and in others an elder and a younger brother, are not allowed to hold office together.) The final result was that the oligarchy at Massilia was turned into something more of the nature of a 'polity'; that at Istros ended by becoming a democracy; and the oligarchy at Heraclea, from being in the hands of a narrow ring, was broadened to include as many as 600 members. § 4. At Cnidos, too, there was a change in the oligarchy; [but this was more drastic]. Here sedition began *inside* the ranks of the notables. Few of them were admitted to office; and the rule was enforced (which we have just had occasion to mention) that if a father were admitted, his son should not be eligible, and if there were several brothers in a family, only the eldest was eligible. In the course of this internal sedition, the people took a hand; and finding a leader among the notables, they attacked and won the day—division (as it always does) leading to the fall of their enemies. § 5. Something of the same sort happened at Erythrae. It was governed oligarchically, in old times, by the clan of the Basilidae, and the government managed affairs with prudence; but the people took offence at its exclusive character and altered the constitution.[1]

[We now come to the second method by which changes are made in oligarchies.] Oligarchies are disturbed from *inside* when their members themselves play the demagogue, for reasons of personal rivalry. § 6. They may do so in two different ways. One way is to practise the art of the demagogue on the governing body itself. A demagogue can arise even in a narrow circle: in the days of the Thirty at Athens [404 B.C.] Charicles and his followers gained power by courting the favour of the Thirty, and in the days of the Four Hundred [411 B.C.] Phrynichus and his followers acted on the same lines. The other way in which the members of oligarchies can play the demagogue is by practising on the masses. This was the case at Larisa, where the police magistrates paid their court to the masses because they were elected by them; and it generally happens in all oligarchies where the magistrates—instead of being elected on a franchise limited to those who are eligible for office themselves—are elected on a broad franchise, including all the army or even the whole of the people, but with eligibility limited to the owners of large properties or the members of political clubs.[2] (This used to be the rule at Abydus.) § 7. We may add that similar troubles also arise in oligarchies where the law courts are composed of persons not belonging to the sovereign civic body. When this is the case, men begin to practise the tricks of the demagogue in order to secure a verdict; and this leads to dissensions and constitutional change, as it did at Heraclea on the Black Sea. Troubles also arise when some of its members try to make an oligarchy still more exclusive; and those who champion equality of rights are then compelled to enlist the aid of the people.

§ 8. Another way in which oligarchies may be disturbed from inside is when their members waste their substance in riotous living. Men who have done that want to create a revolution; and they either attempt to be tyrants **1306 a** themselves or set up some other person. Hipparinus set up Dionysius at Syracuse in this way. At Amphipolis a man of the name of Cleotimus [having lost his fortune] introduced Chalcidian settlers, and incited them after their settlement to make an attack on the rich. § 9. At Aegina,

---

[1] The first method by which changes are brought about in oligarchies is the method followed when change starts *outside* the governing circle—either as a movement of opposition among the excluded grandees (§§ 2–3), or as a movement which, beginning among them, then spreads to the people at large (§ 4). The second method, to which Aristotle now turns, is the method followed when changes start *inside* the governing circle.   [2] See Note QQ, p. 220.

again, it was a similar cause [i.e. dissipation] which moved the man who conducted the transaction with Chares to attempt a change of the constitution.[1] Men of this type will sometimes go straight for some attempt at political change: sometimes they stop short at embezzling the public funds; but even that leads to sedition eventually, whether the sedition be started by the culprits themselves or whether (as happened at Apollonia on the Black Sea) it is begun by those who oppose their misconduct.   § 10. An oligarchy at one with itself is not easily overthrown from within. The constitution of Pharsalus may serve as an example: the governing body, restricted as it is, manages to control a large population because its members behave well towards one another.

Still another way in which oligarchies may be undermined from inside is when an inner oligarchy is created within the outer. § 11. Few as are the members of the whole citizen-body, even these few are not all admitted, in such a case, to the highest offices. This is what happened at one time in Elis. The constitution was already in the hands of a small body of senators; but it was only a very small handful of men who were ever appointed to the Senate. Its members, who were ninety in number, all held office for life; and they were elected, much like the Spartan senators, in a way which favoured the interests of a narrow range of families.

§ 12. Changes may happen in oligarchies [owing to internal reasons, and without any attack from outside] alike in war and in peace. They happen in war when the members of an oligarchy are compelled by distrust of the people to employ an army of mercenaries. If a single man is entrusted with the command of these mercenaries, he frequently becomes a tyrant, as Timophanes did at Corinth; and if the command is vested in a number of persons, they make themselves a governing clique [*dynasteia*]. Fear of such consequences sometimes forces an oligarchy to employ a popular force, and thus to give the masses some share in constitutional rights.   § 13. Changes happen in peace when the members of an oligarchy, under the impulse of mutual distrust, entrust the maintenance of internal security to mercenaries and a neutral arbiter—who occasionally ends as the master of both the contending factions. This happened at Larisa during the government of Simias, one of the Aleuad clan, [in the capacity of arbiter]: it also happened at Abydus during the struggles of the clubs, one of which was the club of Iphiades.[2]

[1] Apparently he tried to bargain with the Athenian general Chares for support in an attempt to institute a tyranny.

[2] It would seem, from the logic of the argument, that in the contention of the different clubs the leader of one of them, Iphiades, was appointed to the office of neutral arbiter, and then made himself supreme.

§ 14. Seditions may also arise inside an oligarchy on matters of marriages and lawsuits, which lead to the discomfiture of one of its sections by another, and thus produce dissension. Some examples of dissension arising from matters of marriage have already been cited (c. IV, §§ 5–7); we may also mention the overthrow of the oligarchy of the knights at Eretria by Diagoras, in resentment at an injustice he had suffered in a matter of marriage. § 15. Decisions given in lawsuits led to dissension at Heraclea [on the Black Sea] and at Thebes. In both cases the offence was that of adultery; and in both cases punishment was exacted (at Heraclea from Eurytion, and at Thebes from Archias) by a method which mixed **1306 b** the spirit of party with the spirit of justice—the enemies of the guilty persons carrying their resentment to the point of having them pilloried in public. . . . § 16. It has also frequently happened that oligarchies have been overthrown, because they were too oppressive, by members of the governing class who resented the methods they used. This was the case, for example, with the oligarchies of Cnidus and Chios. . . .

Finally, constitutional change may sometimes be due to accidents. This is the case with the constitutions called 'polities', and with those forms of oligarchy where a property qualification is necessary for membership of the council and law courts and the holding of other offices. § 17. The qualification may have been originally fixed, on the basis of existing conditions, in a way which limited constitutional rights—in oligarchies to the few, and in 'polities' to the middle class. Then, as frequently happens, there may ensue a period of prosperity, due to long peace or some other good fortune; and the result will be that the same estate [which was once assessed at a moderate amount] must now be assessed at a value many times in excess of the old. When this is the case, the whole body of citizens becomes entitled to every right—a change which may sometimes come about gradually, by small degrees and without being noticed, but sometimes may come about rapidly.

§ 18. Such are the causes of change and sedition in oligarchies. A general observation may be added. Both democracies and oligarchies are occasionally transformed, not into the opposite types of constitution, but into some other variety of their own type. Democracies and oligarchies which are limited by law may turn, for example, into forms which are absolutely sovereign; and the converse may equally happen.

NOTE QQ (p. 218): *Why electors and eligible should be identical*

Aristotle here suggests that in a stable oligarchy the electors to office should be identical with the persons eligible for office. If this is not the case, and if the electors to office are a larger body than the persons eligible for office, there will (he implies) be trouble—even though the oligarchical principle of restriction, while sacrificed in the matter of election, is retained in the other matter of eligibility. You must restrict in *both* ways, and not in *one* only; at any rate you must not combine restriction of the circle of eligibility with a wide extension of the circle of the electorate.

Newman's note may be cited. 'The cause of constitutional change here indicated by Aristotle—the rivalry of the holders of great offices in courting those who elect them with a view to their own aggrandisement— is indeed widely traceable in history both ancient and modern.'

Chapter VII

3. Aristocracies. *Here revolutions are due to a policy of narrowing the circle of the government. The collapse of aristocracies—as also of 'polities', which are closely allied—is generally due to a defective balance of the different elements combined in the constitution: this may lead either to change in the direction in which the balance is tilted, or to violent reaction towards the opposite extreme. Aristocracies are particularly liable to be the victims of trifling occasions. All constitutions may be affected and undermined by the influence of powerful neighbouring states.*

§ 1. In aristocracies sedition may arise, among other reasons, from the limitation of office and honours to a narrow circle. This is a cause which, as we have mentioned (c. VI, § 2), produces commotions in oligarchies; and it naturally affects aristocracies, because they too are in some sense oligarchies. In both types of constitutions—though for different reasons—the ruling class is small; and it is this common feature which will explain why an aristocracy may be regarded as a kind of oligarchy. § 2. Sedition due to this cause must particularly tend to arise when the mass of a people consists of men animated by the conviction that they are as good as their masters in quality. This was the case with those who were called the Partheniae at Sparta. They were the [illegitimate] sons of Spartan peers: they conspired together to vindicate their rights; but their conspiracy was detected, and they were sent out to colonize Tarentum.[1] Sedition of the same kind may also arise when persons of great ability, and second to none in their merits, are treated dishonourably by those who themselves enjoy higher honours—as Lysander was by the kings of Sparta. § 3. It may happen, again, when a man of high spirit—like Cinadon, the leader of the conspiracy against the Spartan peers in the reign of king

[1] The Partheniae, who colonized Tarentum at the end of the eighth century B.C., were apparently the descendants of Spartan 'peers' (or full citizens) by some sort of irregular union.

Agesilaus—is debarred from honours and office. It may happen, too, when some of the ruling class become excessively poor, and others excessively rich. This is a change which happens particularly in times of war. It happened, for example, at Sparta in the time of the Messenian War. § 4. The poem of Tyrtaeus, **1307 a** entitled 'The Rule of Law', is sufficient evidence: it tells us of men, impoverished by the war, who demanded a redistribution of landed property. [Pure ambition may also cause sedition in aristocracies]: a man who has a great position, and the capacity for a still greater, will promote sedition in order to make himself the one ruler. Pausanias, the generalissimo during the Persian War, is an example at Sparta; Hanno at Carthage is another.

§ 5. The actual downfall of aristocracies, and also of 'polities', is chiefly due to some deviation from justice in the constitution itself. In either case the origin of the downfall is a failure to combine different elements properly. In 'polities' the elements are democracy and oligarchy: in aristocracies they are both of these and the further element of merit; but even in the latter the real difficulty is that of combining the first two elements, which are the only elements that most of the so-called aristocracies (as well as 'polities') actually attempt to combine. § 6. The only difference between aristocracies and the constitutions called 'polities' consists in their different ways of mixing the same two elements; and this is also the reason why the former are less secure than the latter. Constitutions where the elements are so mixed that the tendency is more towards oligarchy are called aristocracies: those where the mixture is such that the tendency is more in favour of the masses are called 'polities'. This will explain why the latter are more secure than the former. The greater number forms a stronger support: and the masses are ready to acquiesce in a government when they have an equal share of power. § 7. It is different with men of considerable means. When the constitution gives them a position of superiority, they are apt to fall into arrogance and to covet even more. Generally, however, it may be said that if a constitution is not equally balanced, but is inclined in one or another direction, it will tend to change in that direction. The favoured element will proceed to increase its advantage: a 'polity', for instance, will change to democracy; and aristocracy will change into oligarchy.

§ 8. It is possible, however, that change may also go in the opposite direction. Aristocracy may change, for example, into democracy, because the poorer classes, feeling themselves unjustly treated, may divert its natural tendency into the opposite direction; and 'polities' may similarly change into oligarchies, from the growth of a conviction that stability—the aim of every 'polity'—is only to be found under a system of proportionate equality, on the basis of desert, by which each man receives his corresponding due.[1] § 9. It was a change of this nature [i.e. a change in the opposite direction] which happened to the aristocracy at Thurii. The first stage, due to reaction against the high property qualification required from holders of office, was a change to a lower qualification, coupled with an increase in the number of offices. The next stage, due to the fact that the notables had bought up illegally the whole of the land (the oligarchical bias of the constitution enabling them to indulge their greed), was the outbreak of civil war. Here the masses, becoming hardened in the course of hostilities, proved stronger than the civic guard; those who had more land than the law allowed were forced to relinquish their hold; [and the old aristocracy thus became a democracy]. § 10. We may add that the oligarchical bias present in all aristocratic constitutions has a general tendency to make the notables too grasping. In Sparta, for example, we see estates passing steadily into the hands of a narrow circle. Generally, too, the notables have too much power to do what they will, and to marry as they will. This explains the collapse of Locri [in southern Italy], which was due to a marriage between the daughter of one of its citizens and Dionysius of Syracuse [a marriage which eventually led to a Syracusan tyranny in Locri]. This would never have happened in a democracy, or in a properly balanced aristocracy.

§ 11. A general observation which has already been made[2] in regard to all types of constitutions **1307 b**—that even trifles may be the cause of revolutions—is particularly true of aristocracies. They are especially apt to change imperceptibly, through being undermined little by little. Once they have abandoned one of the elements of the constitution, they find it easier afterwards to alter some other feature of a little greater importance; and they end eventually by altering the whole system of the state. § 12. This was what actually befell the constitution of Thurii.[3] There was a law that the office of general should only be held a second time

---

[1] See above, Book III, c. IX, where a distinction is drawn between (1) the democratic idea of absolute equality and (2) the aristocratic–oligarchic idea of proportionate equality based on desert, under which each man gets his due in proportion to his desert, and all are treated equally in the sense that the ratio between recognition and desert in one case is equal to the ratio between them in every other.

[2] See c. III, § 10: 'a great change . . . may come about unperceived if small changes are overlooked.'

[3] Thurii recurs as an example in the course of this Book; cf. c. III, § 12, and § 9 of this chapter. It was an Athenian colony, founded under the supervision of Pericles.

after an interval of five years. Some of the younger men showed
soldierly qualities, and won a reputation with the rank and file of
the guard. Despising the men who were in charge of affairs, and
calculating on an easy triumph, these younger men set out to
abrogate the law, wishing to make it possible for generals to serve
continuously, and knowing that, in that case, the people would
readily elect them for one term after another.   § 13. The magistrates charged with the duty of considering such proposals—they
were called the Board of Councillors—began by making an effort
to resist the repeal of the law; but they were eventually led to agree,
in the idea that when this change had been made the rest of the
constitution would not be touched. [They found themselves
deceived]; other changes were afterwards mooted; when they
sought to oppose them, they failed to make any headway; and the
whole scheme of the constitution was changed into an aristocratic
junto composed of the revolutionaries.

§ 14. Constitutions generally may be undermined from without,
as well as from within. This happens when they are confronted by
a constitution of an opposite type, which is either their close
neighbour or powerful even if distant. It happened in the days of
the Athenian and Spartan empires. The Athenians everywhere put
down oligarchies; the Spartans, in turn, suppressed democracies.

Chapter VIII

4. The methods of ensuring constitutional stability in the three
previous types of constitution. *Precautions should be taken against
lawlessness, and especially against its petty forms. No reliance should
be placed on devices intended to hoodwink the masses. A spirit of
fairness should be cultivated; and something of the temper, and even
some of the institutions, of democracy may therefore be advisable in
oligarchies and aristocracies. To maintain a feeling of emergency may
help to maintain the government. Promotions, and the award or with-
drawal of honours, should be carefully handled. Watch should be kept
both on private extravagance and the sudden rise of a whole social
class to a new degree of prosperity. In particular, steps should be taken
to prevent office from being made a source of profit. Finally, democracies will do well to spare the rich, and oligarchies to encourage and
help the poor.*

§ 1. The causes of revolution and sedition in different constitutions have now been generally described. It remains to treat of the
methods for preserving constitutions generally, and each type
severally.[1] We may begin with a general proposition. To know

[1] See Note RR, p. 229.

the causes which destroy constitutions is also to know the causes which ensure their preservation. Opposite effects are brought about by opposite causes; and destruction and preservation are opposite effects. § 2. On this basis we may draw a number of conclusions. The first is that in constitutions where the elements are well mixed there is one thing as vitally important as any—to keep a look-out against all lawlessness, and, more particularly, to be on guard against any of its petty forms.[1] Lawlessness, when it takes such forms, may creep in unperceived—just as petty expenditures, constantly repeated, will gradually destroy the whole of a fortune. § 3. Because it is not all incurred at once, such expenditure goes unperceived; and our minds are misled by it in the same way as they are misled by the logical fallacy, 'When each is small, all are small too'.[2] This is true in one sense, but it is not true in another. The Whole or All is not little, although it is made up of Littles.

§ 4. This is one precaution which ought to be taken—to prevent the beginning of trouble in petty acts of lawlessness. Secondly, we may lay down the rule that 1308 a confidence should never be placed in devices intended to hoodwink the masses. They are always exploded in actual experience. (We have already explained the nature of the constitutional devices to which we are here referring.)[3]

§ 5. Thirdly, we have to observe (and the observation is true of oligarchies as well as of aristocracies) that some states owe their stability not so much to the solidity of their constitutional systems, as to the good relations in which their officers stand alike with the unenfranchised and the members of the civic body. In such states the unenfranchised are never treated unjustly; on the contrary, their leading members are promoted to share in constitutional rights; and while the ambitious among them are not wronged on points of honour, the rank and file are not maltreated in matters of money and profit. Similarly, in these states, the officers and the other members of the governing class behave towards one another in a democratic spirit of equality. § 6. Democrats seek to widen the principle of equality until it is made to include all the masses. What is certainly just—and expedient as well as just—is that the principle should extend to all who are really 'peers'. In any state, therefore, where the members of the governing class are numerous, a number of democratic institutions will be expedient. It will be expedient, for instance, to restrict the tenure of office to a period of

[1] This is a warning already implied in c. III, § 10 and c. VII, §§ 11–13.
[2] The answer to the fallacy is that, though 'all' separately may be small, 'all' collectively may form a large sum.   [3] Book IV, c. XIII, §§ 1–5.

six months, and thus to enable all who belong to the class of 'peers' to enjoy their turn. A numerous class of 'peers' is already, by its nature, a sort of democracy; and that is why, as has already been noticed (c. VI, § 6), we often find demagogues emerging in such a class. § 7. When such a policy is adopted, oligarchies and aristo-cracies are less prone to fall into the hands of family cliques. Officers with a short tenure can hardly do as much harm as those who have a long tenure; and it is long possession of office which leads to the rise of tyrannies in oligarchies and democracies. The persons who make a bid for tyranny, in both types of constitution, are either the principal men (who in democracies are the dema-gogues, and in oligarchies the heads of great families), or else the holders of the main offices who have held them for a long period.

§ 8. The preservation of a constitution may not only be due to the fact that a state is far removed from the menace of any danger:[1] it may also, on occasion, be due to the very opposite. When danger is imminent, men are alarmed, and they therefore keep a firmer grip on their constitution. All who are concerned for the constitution should therefore (4) foster alarms, which will put men on their guard, and will make them keep an unwearied watch like sentinels on night-duty. They must, in a word, make the remote come near.

§ 9. An endeavour should also be made, by legislation as well as by personal action, (5) to guard against quarrels and seditions among the notables;[2] and watch should also be kept in advance on those who are not yet involved, before they too have caught the spirit of rivalry. Ordinary men cannot see the beginning of troubles ahead; it requires the genuine statesman.

§ 10. Change may arise, in oligarchies and 'polities', through the working of the system of assessment connected with the requirement of a property-qualification.[3] It will tend to arise, for example, when the monetary amount of the property-qualification is left unchanged but the amount of money in circulation shows a large increase. To meet this danger (6) a comparison should regularly be made between the present sum-total of all the assess-

---

[1] Aristotle here refers back to the last section of the previous chapter.
[2] Here the reference back is to c. IV, §§ 1–7.
[3] See c. VI, §§ 16–17. The assessments mentioned are not connected with the methods of taxation, but with the system of requiring a property-qualifica-tion from candidates for office. If the standard of the property-qualification required were left unchanged, when the assessments connected with it began to show that a much larger number of persons were attaining the standard, a constitution would be automatically changed. Far more persons would now be eligible for office: and thus a 'polity' or an oligarchy might be unintentionally turned into a democracy. Hence Aristotle's counsel, 'Watch the movement of the assessments.'

ments and their sum-total in a previous year. Where the assessment is annual, the comparison should be made **1308 b** annually; where—as in the larger states—the assessment is made at intervals of three or four years, the comparison should be made at those intervals. If the sum-total is then found to be many times greater (or many times less) than it was on the previous occasion when the assessments obligatory under the constitution were fixed, a law should be passed to provide for the raising (or lowering) of the qualification required to a corresponding extent. § 11. In oligarchies and 'polities' where this policy is not adopted change will be inevitable. In one event [i.e. when the amount of money in circulation decreases, but the qualification is left unchanged] the change will be from 'polity' to oligarchy, and from oligarchy to a family clique; in the other [i.e. when the amount of money in circulation increases, but the qualification remains unaltered] change will move in the reverse direction—from a 'polity' to a democracy, and from an oligarchy either to a 'polity' or a democracy.

§ 12. A rule (7) which applies both to democracies and oligarchies—indeed it applies to all constitutions—is that no person should be advanced by the state out of all proportion to others.[1] It is a better policy to award small honours over a period of time than to give great honours rapidly. (Men are easily spoiled; and it is not all who can stand prosperity.) If this rule is not followed, and if honours are bestowed on a man promiscuously, the least that can be done is not to revoke them promiscuously, but to do so by degrees. It is also good policy to aim at providing, by means of appropriate legislation, against the risk of any man gaining a position of superiority by the strength of his wealth or connexions. Failing that, men who gain such a position should be removed from it by being sent out of the country.

§ 13. Men tend to become revolutionaries from circumstances connected with their private lives [as well as from causes connected with public life]. This suggests (8) that a magistracy should be instituted to supervise those who live in a way out of harmony with the established constitution—who in a democracy do not live democratically; in an oligarchy do not live oligarchically; and so in each other type.[2] For similar reasons [i.e. for reasons connected with circumstances of private life] watch should be kept over the social section which is particularly flourishing at any moment. § 14. The remedy for the difficulties which the flourishing of such a section may cause is either (a) always to give the

---

[1] Here the reference is to c. III, § 3.
[2] Here the reference is to c. VI, §§ 8–9, and also to c. III, §§ 6–8.

conduct of affairs and the enjoyment of office to the opposite section (it should be explained that the two sections here in question are the quality and the masses, or the wealthy and the poor), and thus to attempt a balance or fusion between the poor and the wealthy section, or (b) to seek to increase the strength of the middle or intervening element.[1] Such a policy will prevent the dissensions which arise from inequality.

§ 15. The most important rule of all, in all types of constitution, is (9) that provision should be made—not only by law, but also by the general system of economy—to prevent the magistrates from being able to use their office for their own gain.[2] In oligarchical constitutions, above all others, this is a matter which demands attention. § 16. The masses are not so greatly offended at being excluded from office (they may even be glad to be given the leisure for attending to their own business); what really annoys them is to think that those who have the enjoyment of office are embezzling public funds. That makes them feel a double annoyance at a double loss—the loss of profit as well as office. § 17. If an arrangement could be made to stop men from using office as a means of private gain, it would provide a way—the only possible way—for combining democracy with aristocracy. Both the notables and **1309 a** the masses could then get what they desire. The right to hold office would be open to all, as befits a democracy: the notables would actually be in office, as befits an aristocracy. § 18. Both results could be achieved simultaneously if the use of office as a means of profit were made impossible. The poor would no longer desire to hold office (because they would derive no advantage from doing so), and they would prefer to attend to their own affairs. The rich would be able to afford to take office, as they would need no subvention from public funds to meet its expenses. The poor would thus have the advantage of becoming wealthy by diligent attention to work; the notables would enjoy the consolation of not being governed by any chance comer. § 19. [To make assurance sure, and] to prevent the embezzling of public funds, the outgoing officers should hand over such funds in the presence of the whole civic body; and inventories of them should be deposited with each clan, ward, and tribe.[3] To ensure that no profit should be made

---

[1] The two forms of policy here suggested are (1) a balance or mixture of two opposite sections, which can be achieved if the social prosperity enjoyed by one is offset by the political power given to the other, or (2) the creation of a *tertium quid*, or strong middle section, which will correct both the arrogance of the socially prosperous and the discontent of the opposite section.

[2] See Note SS, p. 230.

[3] Wards are local subdivisions. Clans and tribes are the smaller and larger kin-groups.

by any magistrate in other ways,[1] the law should provide for the award of honours to those who earn a good reputation.

§ 20. (Lastly (10), two different, but yet corresponding, rules may be suggested—one for democracies, and the other for oligarchies.] In democracies, the rich should be spared. Not only should their estates be safe from the threat of redistribution: the produce of the estates should be equally secure; and the practice of sharing it out, which has insensibly developed under some constitutions, should not be allowed. It is good policy, too, to prevent the rich, even if they are willing, from undertaking expensive, and yet useless, public services, such as the equipping of choruses for dramatic festivals, or the provision of the expenses of torch-races, or other services of that order.[2] In oligarchies, on the other hand, a good deal of attention should be paid to the poor. They should be assigned the offices to which any perquisites are attached; and if a rich man does them violence, the penalties should be heavier than if he had been guilty of violence against members of his own class. Nor should inheritances pass by title of bequest; they should go by right of descent,[3] and not more than one inheritance should ever go to one person. On this system estates would be more evenly distributed, and more of the poor might rise to a position of affluence. § 21. [These suggestions relate to property.] In matters other than property [e.g. honours and ceremonies] a position of equality, or even of precedence, may well be given to those who have fewer constitutional rights—in a democracy to the rich; in an oligarchy to the poor. An exception must, however, be made for the sovereign offices of the constitution.[4] These should be entrusted only, or at any rate entrusted mainly, to those who have full constitutional rights.

NOTE RR (p. 224): *The course of the argument in* cc. VIII–IX

It has already been observed, in the note at the beginning of c. I of this book, that these two chapters on preservation (a theme which generally belongs to Book VI) are here intercalated in the middle of a treatment of revolutions. The reason for the intercalation appears to be that the methods of preservation here suggested are (as Newman points out in volume iv of his edition, pp. 569–70) 'as a rule deduced from the investigations, in the preceding part of the Book, as to the causes of the overthrow of constitutions'. Each remedy thus corresponds to a disease

[1] e.g. by taking bribes, or by making extortions, from individuals.
[2] Compare c. v, §§ 1–5.
[3] If there were a right of bequest, property might be accumulated in the hands of a few legatees. If the transmission of property is based on the title of descent, Aristotle implies (assuming, it would seem, the absence of primogeniture) that there will be a diffusion of property.
[4] According to the argument of Book III, the deliberative organ is the sovereign organ of the constitution. It may thus be argued that the 'offices' to which Aristotle is here referring are the offices of member of the Council and member of the Assembly. But he probably refers to the highest *executive* offices.

which has just been noticed; and it is natural, therefore, that Aristotle should add a list of remedies immediately after his list of diseases. But he recurs again, after these two chapters, to the theme of revolutions—first dealing, in c. X, with the causes of revolution in monarchical states (though here again he proceeds to add, in c. XI, an account of the methods of preservation which correspond to these causes), and then dealing finally, in c. XII, with the inadequacy of Plato's account of revolutions. It will thus be seen that Aristotle gives two accounts of methods of preservation—(1) an *ad hoc* account in cc. VIII–IX, and in c. XI, of Book V, where the methods are adapted to the causes of revolution which have just been mentioned: and (2) a general account, in the course of Book VI, which is not immediately related to the previous account of the causes of revolution.

NOTE SS (p. 228): *Political power and economic advantage*

The reference back here is to c. III, § 1. The danger to which Aristotle draws attention—that political power may be used to secure economic advantage—is one which is also noticed by Thucydides and Plato. Thucydides, speaking of the fierce dissensions which arose at Corcyra, writes (iii. 82, § 8), 'The cause of all these things was the pursuit of office for reasons of greed, and through ambition to rise.' Plato, contrasting his ideal state with the actual states of Greece, writes (*Republic* 521 A), 'All goes wrong when, starved for lack of anything good in their own lives, men turn to public affairs hoping to snatch from them the happiness they hunger for. They set about fighting for power, and this internecine conflict ruins them and their country' (Cornford's translation). Aristotle repeatedly draws attention to the same danger; and we may compare with the present passage that in Book III, c. VI, § 10, 'Moved by the profits to be derived from office and the handling of public property, men want to hold office continuously.'

It is thus a steady theme of Greek political theory that political power tends to be used, and should not be used, to secure economic advantage. That theme was not the invention of Marx—though he varied and amplified it.

CHAPTER IX

*Further consideration of the methods of ensuring constitutional stabi-
lity in the three first types of constitution. In the interest of constitutional stability, three qualities are required in the holders of high office;
their relative importance. It is always wise to ensure that a majority
of the citizen body is in favour of the constitution. The value of the
mean, and of refusing to push political issues to an extreme: not all
democratic or oligarchic measures are calculated to ensure the permanence of democracy or oligarchy. The cardinal importance of
educating citizens to live and act in the spirit of the constitution: this
is too often neglected, especially in extreme democracies, which encourage the idea of 'living as one likes'.*

§ 1. Three qualifications are necessary in those who have to fill the sovereign offices.[1] The first is loyalty to the established con-

[1] Aristotle, taking his cue from the theme of the 'sovereign offices', which has just been mentioned at the end of the previous chapter, proceeds to supplement

stitution. The second is a high degree of capacity for the duties of the office. The third is the quality of goodness and justice, in the particular form which suits the nature of each constitution. (If the *principle* of justice varies from constitution to constitution,[1] the *quality* of justice must also have its corresponding varieties.) § 2. Where these three qualifications are not united in a single person, a problem obviously arises: how is the choice to be made? A may possess, **1309 b** for instance, the second qualification, and have military capacity; but he may lack the other two, and be neither good in character nor loyal to the constitution. B may be just in character and loyal to the constitution, [but deficient in capacity]. How are we to choose? It would seem that we ought to consider two points—which, on the whole, is the commoner qualification, and which of them is the rarer; [and on that basis we ought to choose the man with the rarer qualification.] § 3. Thus, for a military office, we must have regard to military experience rather than character: military capacity is rare, and goodness is more common. For the post of custodian of property, or that of treasurer, we must follow the opposite rule: such posts require a standard of character above the average, but the knowledge which they demand is such as we all possess. § 4. A further problem may also be raised in regard to these three qualifications. If a man possesses the two qualifications of capacity and loyalty to the constitution, is there any need for him to have the third qualification of goodness, and will not the first two, by themselves, secure the public interest? We may answer this question by asking another. May not men who possess these two first qualifications be unable to command their passions? and is it not true that men who have no command of their passions will fail to serve their own interest— even though they possess self-knowledge and self-loyalty—and will equally fail to serve the public interest [even though they possess a knowledge of public affairs and public loyalty]?

§ 5. Generally, we may add, a constitution will tend to be preserved by the observance of all the legal rules already suggested, in the course of our argument, as making for constitutional stability. Here we may note, as of paramount importance, the elementary

the ten specific rules for the preservation of states, which he has stated in that chapter, by a number of more general rules. These general rules are still to some extent based on deduction from the previous study of the causes of revolution. But they raise broader and more fundamental issues of policy; the reference to the previous study of the causes of revolution is slight; and the main reference which they involve is a reference to the general argument of the previous books.

[1] This 'relativity' of the principle of justice, with its corollary of the 'relativity' of the quality of justice, has been previously discussed in Book III: see cc. IV and IX of that book, and the notes at the beginning of those chapters.

principle which has been again and again suggested—the principle
of ensuring that the number of those who wish a constitution to
continue shall be greater than the number of those who do not.[1]

§ 6. In addition to all these things, there is another which ought
to be remembered, but which, in fact, is forgotten in perverted
forms of government. This is the value of the mean.[2] Many of
the measures which are reckoned democratic really undermine
democracies: many which are reckoned oligarchical actually undermine oligarchies. § 7. The partisans of either of these forms of
government, each thinking their own the only right form, push
matters to an extreme. They fail to see that proportion is as
necessary to a constitution as it is (let us say) to a nose. A nose
may deviate in some degree from the ideal of straightness, and
incline towards the hooked or the snub, without ceasing to be
well shaped and agreeable to the eye. But push the deviation still
further towards either of these extremes, and the nose will begin
to be out of proportion with the rest of the face: carry it further
still, and it will cease to look like a nose at all, because it will go
too far towards one, and too far away from the other, of these two
opposite extremes. § 8. What is true of the nose, and of other
parts of the body, is true also of constitutions. Both oligarchy and
democracy may be tolerable forms of government, even though
they deviate from the ideal. But if you push either of them further
still in the direction to which it tends, you will begin by making
it a worse constitution, and you may end by turning it into something which is not a constitution at all.

§ 9. It is thus the duty of legislators and statesmen to know
which democratic measures preserve, and which destroy, a democracy; similarly, it is their duty to know which oligarchical measures
will save, and which will ruin, an oligarchy. Neither of these
constitutions can exist, or continue in existence, unless it includes
both the rich and the poor. If, therefore, a system of equal ownership be introduced into either, the effect will inevitably be a new
and different form of constitution; and the radical legislation which
abolishes riches and poverty will thus **1310 a** abolish along with
them the old constitutions based on their presence.[3] § 10. [For

---

[1] See Note TT, p. 234.

[2] There is a natural transition from the doctrine that a majority should be in
favour of the constitution to the doctrine of moderation. A moderate constitution, which steers between the extremities of the right and the left, will tend to
command a general allegiance. The reference here again (as in the previous
paragraph) is to Book IV, c. xii, especially §§ 4–6.

[3] The modern reader will perhaps doubt whether a democracy ceases to be a
democracy if property is equalized. The doubt is natural enough if the word
'democracy' be understood in a modern sense, as the government of the whole
people by the whole people for the whole people. In Aristotle's sense of the

want of the knowledge they ought to possess][1] errors are made by statesmen alike in democracies and oligarchies. They are made, for instance, by demagogues, in those forms of democracy where the will of the people is superior to the law. Demagogues are always dividing the state into two, and waging war against the rich. Their proper policy is the very reverse: they should always profess to be speaking in defence of the rich. A similar policy should be followed in oligarchies: the oligarchs should profess to speak on behalf of the poor; and the oaths they take should be the opposite of those which they now take. § 11. There are states in which their oath runs, 'I will bear ill will to the people, and I will plan against them all the evil I can.' The opinion which they ought to hold and exhibit is the very opposite; and their oaths should contain the declaration, 'I will not do wrong to the people.'

The greatest, however, of all the means we have mentioned for ensuring the stability of constitutions—but one which is nowadays generally neglected—is the education of citizens in the spirit of their constitution.[2] § 12. There is no profit in the best of laws, even when they are sanctioned by general civic consent, if the citizens themselves have not been attuned, by the force of habit and the influence of teaching, to the right constitutional temper—which will be the temper of democracy where the laws are democratic, and where they are oligarchical will be that of oligarchy. Licentiousness may exist in a state as well as in individual persons, [and training is thus needed for states as well as for individuals]. § 13. The education of a citizen in the spirit of his constitution does not consist in his doing the actions in which the partisans of oligarchy, or the adherents of democracy, delight. It consists in his doing the actions by which an oligarchy, or a democracy, will be enabled to survive. Actual practice, to-day, is on very different lines. In oligarchies the sons of the magistrates live lives of luxury, and this at a time when the sons of the poor are being hardened by exercise, and by their daily work, and are thus acquiring the will and the power to make a clean sweep. § 14. In democracies of the extreme type—the type which is regarded as being peculiarly democratic[3]—the policy followed is the very reverse of their real

word, however, democracy is the government of one of the social sections, as oligarchy is that of another. If all social sections disappear, both of these forms of government will also disappear.

[1] i.e. knowledge of the difference between the measures which will really preserve a constitution and those which (though they are supposed to preserve it) really tend towards its destruction.

[2] This theme has been previously touched upon in Book IV, c. XI, § 6. It recurs, and is developed, later—especially in Book VIII, c. I, §§ 1–2.

[3] See Book IV, c. XIV, § 12, where it appears that these democracies are of the type in which the 'will of the people' is superior to 'the rule of law'.

interest. The reason for this aberration is a false conception of liberty. There are two conceptions which are generally held to be characteristic of democracy. One of them is the conception of the sovereignty of the majority; the other is that of the liberty of individuals.[1] § 15. The democrat starts by assuming that justice consists in equality: he proceeds to identify equality with the sovereignty of the will of the masses; he ends with the view that 'liberty and equality' consist in 'doing what one likes'. The result of such a view is that, in these extreme democracies, each man lives as he likes—or, as Euripides says,

> For any end he chances to desire.

§ 16. This is a mean conception of liberty. To live by the rule of the constitution ought not to be regarded as slavery, but rather as salvation.[2]

Such, in general, are the causes which lead to the change and destruction of constitutions, and such are the means of ensuring their preservation and stability.

NOTE TT (p. 232): *Aristotle on the need of consent and the principle of unanimity*

Aristotle, in the preceding section, has discussed the three qualifications which *magistrates* must possess if the constitution is to be stable. One of these is loyalty to the constitution. He now adds, taking a more general view, that the majority of the citizens *generally* must possess the quality of loyalty to the constitution, in the sense of cherishing a will for its survival. Here he is referring back to the argument of Book IV, c. XII, § 1.

There is a passage in the *Ethics*, Book IX, c. VI, which may be cited in illustration of the argument. Aristotle is there discussing the conception of unanimity, or what may be called, in the sphere of politics, solidarity or *fraternité*. 'States are said to be unanimous when their members have the same conception of their interest; will the same objects; and execute common resolves (§ 1). It is therefore about matters of action that men show unanimity, and especially about matters of action which are of major importance and in which it is possible for both or all parties to get their way: e.g. a state is unanimous when all its members think that offices should be elective, or that an alliance should be made with Sparta. . . . When each of two parties wishes to have a thing for itself . . . they are in a state of faction (*stasis*); for unanimity does not consist in each party just thinking of the same thing, but in each thinking of it as vested in the same hands—which is the case, for example, when the common people and the better sort both wish the best men to rule. It is then, and then only, that all parties get their way' (§ 2).

[1] As Newman justly notes, the two conceptions are not necessarily consistent with one another. The sovereignty of the majority may drastically curtail the liberty of the individual.
[2] How would Aristotle himself have defined liberty? As Newman says (in his note) the passage before us makes it probable that he would have defined it as obedience to rightly constituted law—or as consisting not, as Hobbes wrote, in the things 'which the sovereign hath *pretermitted*', but, as Montesquieu said, in what the laws *permit*.

CHAPTER X

5. Monarchies—including both kingships and tyrannies. *The distinction, especially in origins, between kingship and tyranny. Kingship is allied to aristocracy, and its general function is that of impartial guardianship of society; tyranny is directed to personal interest, and it combines the more selfish side of oligarchy with the more selfish side of democracy. In monarchies generally, revolutions are caused by resentment of insults; by fear; by contempt; or by a desire for fame. Tyrannies are liable to be overthrown by the influence of neighbouring states of an opposite character: they may also be destroyed by internal causes; and the causes which particularly lead to their overthrow are hatred and contempt. Kingships are more durable; but with the general growth of equality they are becoming antiquated, and the form of monarchical government now prevalent is tyranny based on force.*

§ 1. We have still, however, to treat of the causes of destruction, and the means of preservation, when the government is a monarchy.[1] **1310 b** Generally, what has already been said of constitutions proper is almost equally true of kingships and tyrannies.[2] § 2. Kingship is in the nature of an aristocracy. Tyranny is a compound of the extreme forms of oligarchy and democracy, and that is why it is more injurious to its subjects than any other form of government; it is composed of two bad forms, and it combines the perversions and errors of both. § 3. The two forms of monarchical government differ from one another—and differ diametrically—in their very origin. Kingships have grown for the purpose of helping the better classes against the populace; it is from these classes that kings have been drawn; and the basis of their position has been their own pre-eminence, or the pre-eminence of their family, in character and conduct. Tyrants, on the contrary, are drawn from the populace and the masses, to serve as their protectors against the notables, and in order to prevent them from suffering any injustice from that class. § 4. The record of history attests the fact; and it may safely be said that most tyrants have begun their careers as demagogues, who won the popular confidence by calumniating the notables. § 5. But though it is true that a large number of tyrannies arose in this way, in the days when states were becoming much more populous, there were others, of an earlier date, which arose in different ways. Some of them had their origin in the ambition of kings, who transgressed traditional limitations, and aimed at a more despotic authority. Others were founded by persons who had originally been elected to the highest magistracies

---

[1] A 'monarchy' (or one-man government) may be, in Aristotle's usage, either a 'kingship' or a 'tyranny'. 'Monarchy', therefore, is not synonymous with 'kingship'. It is a wider term.   [2] See Note UU, p. 241.

—all the more easily because there was a habit, in ancient times, of giving long tenures to public 'craftsmen' and 'overseers'.[1] Others, again, arose from a practice, followed in oligarchies, of appointing a single person to supervise the chief magistracies. § 6. In all these ways an ambitious person was given the chance, if he so desired, of effecting his purpose with ease; he had already power in his hands for a start—here as king, and there as the holder of some other high office. Pheidon of Argos and a number of others started as kings and ended as tyrants. The tyrants of Ionia and Phalaris of Agrigentum used other offices as stepping-stones. Panaetius at Leontini, Cypselus at Corinth, Pisistratus at Athens, Dionysius at Syracuse, and a number of others elsewhere, began as demagogues.

§ 7. Kingship, as we have already observed, may be classified as being in the nature of aristocracy. Like aristocracy it is based on merit. The merit on which it is based may consist in personal (or family) qualities; it may consist in benefits rendered; it may consist in a combination of both of these with capacity. § 8. The men who have gained the position of king have all been men who had actually benefited, or were capable of benefiting, their city or their country. Some of them, like Codrus of Athens, had saved their state from defeat in war: others, like Cyrus of Persia, had been its liberators; others, again, had settled or acquired the territory of their state, like the kings of Sparta and Macedonia, or the Molossian kings in Epirus. § 9. It is the aim of a king to be in the position of a guardian of society, **1311 a** protecting the owners of property from any unjust treatment, and saving the bulk of the people from arrogance and oppression.[2] Tyranny, as we have often noted, is just the opposite. It has no regard to any public interest which does not also serve the tyrant's own advantage. The aim of a tyrant is his own pleasure: the aim of a king is the Good. § 10. We can see the results which follow. A tyrant covets riches; a king covets what makes for renown. The guard of a king is a civic guard: the guard of a tyrant is a foreign guard of mercenary troops.

---

[1] Aristotle here uses, in the Greek, two peculiar terms for magistrates which were employed in states of the Peloponnese. For the first of these terms see Book III, c. II, § 2, and note.

[2] This conception of the monarch as a neutral guardian or arbitrator, set above the play of society and preventing any social element from oppressing others, has analogies with the Hegelian conception of monarchy.

It may be noted that in the edition of the *Politics* by the Positivist Richard Congreve (second edition, 1874) there is appended an essay on monarchy, in which it is argued that, to meet the difficulties and problems of modern society, 'there will be needed a dictatorial power ("monocratic", but not "monarchical" in the sense of hereditary) sufficiently representing the interests of the classes that are growing, and at the same time strong enough to protect the weaker and decaying—a power able to act as a mediator' (p. 507). There is here a curious conjunction of Aristotle, Hegel, and Comte.

§ 11. Tyranny [being a compound of both][1] has obviously the vices both of oligarchy and democracy. From oligarchy it derives its aim and end of amassing wealth; for it is by his wealth, and by it alone, that a tyrant has to maintain his guard and his luxury. It is also from oligarchy that tyranny derives its habit of distrusting the masses, and the policy, consequent upon it, of depriving them of arms. Tyranny, too, joins hands with oligarchy in oppressing the common people, expelling it from the city, and dispersing it in the country. § 12. From democracy it derives its attitude of hostility to the notables; its policy of ruining them, secretly or openly; its habit of driving them into banishment, as the rivals and hindrances to its power. In fact the notables are more than a hindrance to tyrants: they are also the active cause of conspiracies against them—some because they want to be rulers themselves; others because they do not want to be slaves. § 13. This explains the advice which was offered by Periander to his fellow-tyrant Thrasybulus, when he switched off with his stick the outstanding ears in the corn field. It was a hint that he ought, from time to time, to remove outstanding citizens.

It has already been suggested[2] that the *origins* of revolution in states with a monarchical system must be considered the same as they are in states with regular constitutions. Unjust oppression, fear, and contempt, are often the reasons why subjects rebel against their monarchs. The form of unjust oppression which most frequently leads to rebellion is insult; but the confiscation of property has sometimes the same effect. § 14. The *aims* pursued by revolutionaries, like the origins of revolution, are the same in tyrannies and kingships as they are under regular constitutions. Sovereign rulers enjoy a pre-eminence of wealth and honour; and wealth and honour are objects of general desire. The actual attacks of revolutionaries are sometimes delivered against the person of the sovereign, and sometimes against his office. Attacks provoked by insults are directed against his person.

§ 15. Insults are of many kinds; but anger is the common effect produced by all the kinds.[3] Those who attack a sovereign in anger generally do so for the sake of revenge, and not for reasons of

---

[1] See § 2 of this chapter.

[2] Aristotle is here referring back to § 1 of this chapter, and, by implication to the catalogue of causes of sedition which he has already given in c. 11 of this Book.

[3] The logic of the arrangement followed in the succeeding sections is based on the causes enumerated in § 13. Unjust oppression, especially in the form of *insult*, is treated in §§ 15–20, *fear* is treated in § 21; and *contempt* in §§ 22–5. But in § 26 Aristotle begins to go outside the causes enumerated in § 13; and after first making a natural transition from contempt of the sovereign to personal ambition (§§ 26–8), he goes on—not without some repetition—to a number of other causes.

ambition. The attack on the sons of Peisistratus at Athens, by Harmodius and Aristogiton, was caused by the dishonour offered to the sister of Harmodius and the injury thus done to her brother. Harmodius attacked for his sister's sake; and his friend Aristogiton joined the attack **1311 a 39** for *his* sake. [In the next three sections, §§ 16–18, Aristotle cites other instances of attacks made on ruling sovereigns for sexual or homosexual reasons. The instances cover a wide geographical range: several of them are drawn from the history of Macedonia, one from the history of Cyprus, one from that of Thrace, and one from that of Ambracia. None of them belong to the area or the history of the Greek city-state.][1] **1311 b 23** § 19. Insult may also take the form of physical assault. Men have often been moved to anger by such indignities; and feeling themselves insulted they have either killed, or attempted to kill, even royal officers, and persons connected with the royal circle [let alone actual sovereigns]. [In the rest of this section, and in § 20, Aristotle cites instances at Mytilene and in Macedonia.][1]

1311 b 36 § 21. Fear is also a motive which, as we have previously noted, operates similarly in monarchies and in constitutional states as a cause of rebellion. It was fear that led the Persian captain Artapanes to murder his master Xerxes. He was afraid of being accused of having had Darius hung—without any orders from Xerxes—in the expectation that, unable to remember what he might have said in his cups, Xerxes would pardon the act.

§ 22. Monarchs are sometimes attacked from the motive of contempt. Sardanapalus of Assyria **1312 a** was killed by a man who saw him carding wool among women (at any rate that is the traveller's tale, which may not be true; but if it is not true of him, it may well be true of some other man). § 23. Dionysius the Younger of Syracuse was similarly attacked by Dion in a spirit of contempt: he saw that he was despised even by his own subjects, and was always drunk. The very friends of a single ruler will sometimes attack him because they despise him: the confidence he gives them breeds their contempt, and they are led to believe that he will notice nothing. § 24. Contempt, of a sort, is also the motive of rebels who think that they can seize power: they are ready to strike because they feel themselves strong, and able, in virtue of their strength, to despise any risks. This is the reason why generals attack their sovereigns. Cyrus, for instance, attacked Astyages because he despised both his habit of life, which had sunk into luxury, and his capacity, which had become effete. The Thracian Seuthes, when he was general, attacked King Amadocus for similar reasons. § 25. Attacks are sometimes due not to a single cause,

[1] See Note VV (p. 242).

but to a plurality of causes. Contempt, for instance, may be mingled with avarice, as it was. in the attack which Mithridates made on his father, the Persian satrap Ariobarzanes. But rebellions due to a plurality of causes generally proceed from men who combine a hardy temper with a position of military honour in the service of their sovereign. Courage armed with power turns into hardihood; and it is this combination of courage and power which leads men to rebel, in the confidence of easy victory.

When rebellion is due to desire for fame, we have a cause of a different character from any of those hitherto mentioned. § 26. A man who resolves to risk rebellion out of a desire for fame behaves in a different way from men who attempt the lives of tyrants with an eye to great gain or high honours. Men of that sort are merely moved by greed or ambition; the man who desires true fame will attack a ruler in the same high spirit as if he were offered the chance of some other great adventure likely to win a man name and fame among his fellows—he will want to get glory, and not a kingdom. § 27. It is true that those who are moved by such reasons are only a handful. Their action supposes an utter disregard for their own safety in the event of failure. § 28. They must have in their hearts the resolve of Dion—a resolve to which only a few can rise—when he sailed on his expedition against Dionysius the Younger with his little band of followers: 'I am of this mind—whatever the point I am able to reach, it is enough for me to have got so far in this undertaking; yes, if I die at once, just after getting ashore, it will be well for me to die like that.'

§ 29. One of the ways in which a tyranny may be destroyed—and the same is true, as we have already noted,[1] of all other forms of government—is by external causes. **1312 b** Another state, with an opposite form of constitution, may be stronger than a tyranny. The conflict of opposite principles[2] will obviously lead such a state to will the destruction of the tyranny; and where there is a will, and power behind it, there is always a way. § 30. This opposition of constitutions may take different forms. Democracy, in its extreme form of the tyranny of the masses,[3] quarrels with tyranny in the same sort of way as, says Hesiod, 'potter quarrels with potter'. Kingship and aristocracy quarrel with tyranny for the opposite reason, and because their constitutions are the opposite of its spirit. This was the reason why Sparta, ruled as she was by kings, suppressed most tyrannies, and why Syracuse

---

[1] The reference is to c. VII, § 14.
[2] In modern terminology, there will be 'a conflict of ideologies' between a dictatorial state and a state (or states) based on opposite principles.
[3] See Book IV, c. IV, § 27.

pursued the same policy during the period in which she enjoyed a good constitution.[1]

§ 31. Another way in which tyrannies may be destroyed is by internal causes. The partners in a tyranny may quarrel with one another.[2] This happened at Syracuse in the family of Gelo, and it has happened again in our own days in the family of Dionysius the Younger. The tyranny established by Gelo was destroyed by Thrasybulus. He was the brother of Gelo and of Gelo's successor, Hiero. On Hiero's death he flattered the next heir, Gelo's son, and ambitious to secure power for himself he seduced him into a life of pleasure. The relatives of the heir thereupon formed a party, originally with the idea of overthrowing Thrasybulus and saving the tyranny; but in the event this party, feeling that the opportunity was ripe, expelled the whole of the family. § 32. The overthrow of Dionysius was due to his relative, Dion, who led an expedition against him, succeeded in winning popular support, and expelled him—only to perish himself in the issue.[3]

[We may now proceed to study the causes which are particularly apt to ruin tyrannies.][4] Hate and contempt are the two most frequent causes of attack. Hate is a passion all tyrants are bound to arouse; but contempt is often the cause by which tyrannies are actually overthrown. § 33. It is a proof of this truth that the tyrants who have won the position by their own efforts have generally managed to retain it, while their successors proceed to lose it almost immediately. Living luxurious lives, they make themselves contemptible, and offer their assailants plenty of opportunities. Hate must be reckoned as including anger, which produces much the same sort of effects. § 34. Anger, indeed, is often a more effective stimulus; an angry man will attack with more fury, because his passion prevents him from stopping to calculate. There is nothing which frays men's tempers more than being insulted: this was what caused the collapse of the tyranny of Peisistratus's family, and of many other tyrannies. § 35. Hate can stop to calculate: you can hate your enemy without feeling pain. Anger is inseparable from pain; and pain makes calculation difficult.

In brief, all the causes previously mentioned as tending to over-

[1] Aristotle refers to the period of about fifty years (*circa* 465 to *circa* 413) in which the constitution of Syracuse was an aristocracy or aristocratic 'polity'.

[2] Aristotle, as his instances show, is thinking of family quarrels in the tyrant's own family.

[3] He established himself as tyrant, and was assassinated in consequence.

[4] Aristotle has already dealt with the causes particularly apt to destroy other constitutions (for democracies, see c. v, § 1; for oligarchies, c. vi, § 1; for aristocracies and 'polities', c. vii, § 5). He now follows the same procedure in regard to tyrannies.

throw the unmixed and ultimate form of oligarchy, and the extreme form of democracy, must be counted as equally fatal to tyranny: indeed those forms are themselves no more than collective tyrannies. § 36. Kingship is the constitution least liable to be destroyed by external causes. It therefore tends to be durable; and when it is destroyed, the causes are generally internal. Such causes may take two forms. One is **1313 a** dissension among the members of the royal family: the other consists in attempting to govern like a tyrant rather than a king, and claiming a larger prerogative without any legal restrictions. § 37. Kingship has now gone out of fashion; and any government of that type which emerges to-day is a personal government or tyranny. Kingship is a government by consent, with sovereign authority in matters of major importance; [and such a government is now an anachronism]. Equality is generally diffused; and there is nobody outstanding enough for the grandeur and the dignity of the office of king. There is thus no basis of consent for such a form of government; and when it is imposed, by fraud or by force, it is instantly regarded as a form of tyranny. § 38. Kingships limited to a single family are liable to be overthrown by a further cause which has still to be mentioned. Kings of this type often incur the contempt of their subjects; or—forgetting that they enjoy the dignity of a king, and not the power of a tyrant—they are guilty of insult and injury. Their overthrow is then an easy matter. Kings cease to be kings when their subjects cease to be willing subjects, though tyrants can continue to be tyrants whether their subjects are willing or no.[1]

The destruction of monarchical forms of government is due to these and similar causes: [we may now pass on to the methods of their preservation].

Note UU (p. 235): *Aristotle's interest in tyrannies*

Here Aristotle seems to draw a distinction between 'monarchies' (including kingships and tyrannies) and 'constitutions proper'. He thus appears to imply that a monarchy is not a 'constitution', but merely a personal system—if indeed it can even be called a system. (This contradicts, we may note in passing, the general view of Book III, where

---

[1] The concluding sections of this long chapter (as has already been noticed in the note to § 15) are somewhat desultory. First the idea of 'internal or external causes' occurs to the writer, and this occupies him from § 29 to the beginning of § 32. Next the idea of 'the causes particularly apt to destroy tyrannies' occurs, and this engages his attention to the beginning of § 35. Then the idea occurs that extreme oligarchy and extreme democracy are both really tyrannies, and that the causes which destroy them will also destroy tyrannies; but having stated the idea, the writer lets himself glide away from it into treating of kingships, and of their differences from tyrannies and the causes of their collapse. All this may be Aristotle; but it would seem to be an Aristotle who throws the reins on the neck of the argument.

kingship and tyranny are both classed among constitutions, and kingship is specifically stated, in c. xiv, § 1, to be one of the 'right' or normal constitutions). Why, then, it may be asked, does Aristotle devote two long and detailed chapters to a study of 'monarchy' generally, and more especially of tyranny—particularly when he has already said, in Book IV, c. x, § 1, that 'there is not much to be said about it'? Newman suggests, in his note, that he wished to amend the worst of Greek institutions, and that he may also have desired to keep Macedonian kingship on the right track. Perhaps, however, it is simply the encyclopaedic and analytic nature of Aristotle's mind which leads him to examine any and every material and to generalize from it all as far as he possibly can. The doctor in him (we have always to remember his medical ancestry and interest) was attracted to the diagnosis of symptoms and the suggestion of cures; and the problems of one-man government, especially in its tyrannical form, afforded him curious and abnormal material.

NOTE VV (p. 238): *Revolutions due to sexual offences and physical indignities*

The translator has omitted these passages in the text. They are matters of scandal, or at the best curiosities of history (such as Aristotle, with his encyclopaedic habit, loved to collect), rather than matters of politics and political theory. But they contain some curious particulars, especially about Macedonia (and incidentally about the poet Euripides, who spent his latter days in that country), which would naturally interest Aristotle—coming as he did from Stagira, on its confines, and having lived, as he had done while he was tutor to Alexander, at the Macedonian court.

The following are the two passages omitted in the text:

(1) *Revolutions caused by sexual offences*. § 16. There was also a conspiracy against Periander, a tyrant in Ambracia, because he once asked his favourite, when they were carousing together, 'Aren't you yet with child by me?' **1311 b** The attack made by Pausanias on Philip [of Macedon] was due to the fact that Philip had allowed an outrage to be inflicted on him by Attalus and his circle; the attack of Derdas on Amyntas the Little was due to Amyntas boasting that he had enjoyed his youthful favours; and the attack of the eunuch on Evagoras of Cyprus was due to a similar motive—the son of Evagoras had seduced his wife, and he killed the father in resentment at the outrage. § 17. Many attacks have also been made as the result of insults offered by monarchs to the person of their subjects. The attack of Crataeus on Archelaus [of Macedonia] is an example. Crataeus had always resented his connexion with Archelaus; and even a trifling occasion could thus become a sufficient excuse for revenge. But it may be that his real reason was that Archelaus did not give him either of his daughters in marriage, in spite of having agreed to do so. Instead of keeping his promise, he gave the elder to the king of Elimeia, when he found himself hard pressed in a war with Sirras and Arribaeus; and the younger he gave to Amyntas, his son [by a previous marriage], thinking that the result would be to prevent any likelihood of a quarrel between this son and his son by [a later marriage with] Cleopatra. But, however that may have been, the actual beginning of the estrangement was the chafing of Crataeus at the sexual connexion between Archelaus and himself. § 18. The same sort of reason explains why Hellanocrates of Larissa joined with Crataeus in making the attack on Archelaus. When

he found that Archelaus, though he enjoyed his favours, would not restore
him to his native city, in spite of the promise he had given that he would
do so, Hellanocrates began to think that their connexion had not been due
to any real passion of love, but merely to the insolence of pride. Another
instance is the murder of Cotys, the king of Thrace, by Parrhon and
Heraclides of Aenus, in revenge for the outrage which he had inflicted
on their father. Similarly Adamas revolted against Cotys in resentment
at the outrage which he had suffered in being emasculated, on the king's
orders, during his boyhood.

(2) *Revolutions caused by physical indignities.* **1311 b 26** § 19 (continued).
In Mytilene, for example, Megacles, with the aid of his friends, attacked
and murdered the members of the Penthelid family for going about and
bludgeoning their fellow-citizens with clubs; and some time afterwards
Smerdis, who had been flogged and dragged away from his wife, assassinated [another member of the family who bore the name of] Penthilus.
§ 20. It was for a similar reason that Decamnichus became the leader in
the attack on Archelaus [with Crataeus and Hellanocrates as his associates],
acting as the prime mover in egging on the conspirators. His indignation
against Archelaus was due to the fact that the king had given him up to the
poet Euripides to be scourged—Euripides being angry with him for the
remarks he had passed upon his bad breath.

CHAPTER XI

The methods of ensuring the stability of monarchies. Kingships are
best preserved by a policy of moderation. There are two ways of
preserving tyrannies. One way is the traditional tyrant's policy of
repression, which has its analogy with the policy of extreme democracy:
its three main objects are to break the spirit of subjects, to sow distrust
among them, and to make them incapable of action. The other way is
a policy of assimilating tyranny to kingship, by a good administration
and the exercise of personal restraint; a wise tyrant will adorn his
city, pay heed to public worship, honour the good, keep his own pas-
sions in check, and enlist in his favour as large a measure of social
support as he possibly can. In this way he may prolong his days, and
attain a state of 'half-goodness'.

§ 1. Taking a general view of monarchical forms of government,
we may say that they are all preserved by methods the converse
of those which are apt to cause their destruction. Looking at them
in detail, and taking kingship first, we may say that a king will
preserve his throne by a policy of moderation. The less the area
of his prerogative, the longer will the authority of a king last
unimpaired: he will himself be less of a master and behave more
like an equal, and his subjects, on their side, will envy him less.
§ 2. This is the reason for the long survival of kingship among the
Molossians; and the survival of the Spartan kingship may also be
attributed partly to the original division of power between the two
kings, and partly to the general policy of moderation afterwards

followed by Theopompus,[1] above all in his institution of the office of Ephor. He may be said to have strengthened Spartan kingship, in the long run, by depriving it of some of its original power; and there is a sense in which he increased rather than diminished its importance. § 3. This is the point of the answer which he is said to have given to his wife, when she asked him if he were not ashamed to be leaving his sons less power than he had inherited from his father. 'Certainly not', he replied; 'I am leaving them a power that will last much longer.'

§ 4. Tyrannies can be preserved in two ways, which are utterly opposed to one another. One of them is the traditional way; and it is also the method of government still followed by the majority of tyrants. Many of its characteristics are supposed to have been originally instituted by Periander of Corinth; but many of its features may also be derived from the Persian system of government. § 5. This method includes some measures previously mentioned, in the course of our argument, as tending to the preservation of tyranny (so far as it can be preserved): it includes, for instance, the 'lopping off' of outstanding men, and the removal of men of spirit.[2] But it also includes a number of other and additional measures. One of them is the forbidding of common meals, clubs, **1313 b** education, and anything of a like character—or, in other words, a defensive attitude against everything likely to produce the two qualities of mutual confidence and a high spirit.[3] A second measure is to prohibit societies for cultural purposes, and any gathering of a similar character: in a word, the adoption of every means for making every subject as much of a stranger as is possible to every other. (Mutual acquaintance always tends to create mutual confidence.) § 6. A third line of policy is to require every resident in the city to be constantly appearing in public, and always hanging about the palace gates. (This is meant to give the ruler a peep-hole into the actions of his subjects, and to inure them to humility by a habit of daily slavery.) This line of policy also includes other measures of a similar character, common in Persia and among the barbarians, which have all the same general effect of fostering tyranny.[4] § 7. A fourth line of policy is that of endeavouring to get regular information about every man's sayings and doings. This entails a secret police, like the female spies employed

[1] One of the Spartan kings, in the middle of the eighth century B.C.

[2] This measure (ascribed to Periander) has been previously mentioned in Book III, c. XIII, §§ 16-17, and again in the previous chapter of this Book, § 13.

[3] Common meals and clubs might encourage the second of these qualities: education the first.

[4] Among such other measures, as Newman suggests, Aristotle may have in mind 'proskynēsis', or the adoration of the ruler in the form of prostration at his feet—the form of the Chinese 'kotow'.

at Syracuse, or the eavesdroppers sent by the tyrant Hiero to all social gatherings and public meetings. (Men are not so likely to speak their minds if they go in fear of a secret police; and if they do speak out, they are less likely to go undetected.) § 8. Still another line of policy is to sow mutual distrust and to foster discord between friend and friend; between people and notables; between one section of the rich and another. Finally, a policy pursued by tyrants is that of impoverishing their subjects—partly to prevent them from having the means for maintaining a civic guard; partly to keep them so busy in earning a daily pittance that they have no time for plotting. § 9. One example of this policy is the building of the Egyptian pyramids: another is the lavish offerings to temples made by the family of Cypselus; a third is the erection of the temple to Olympian Zeus by the family of Peisistratus; a fourth is the additions made by Polycrates to the Samian monuments. (All these actions have the same object: to increase the poverty of the tyrant's subjects and to curtail their leisure.) § 10. The imposition of taxes produces a similar result. We may cite the example of Syracuse, where in a period of five years, during the tyranny of Dionysius the Elder, people were made to pay the whole of their property to the state.[1] The same vein of policy also makes tyrants war-mongers, with the object of keeping their subjects constantly occupied and continually in need of a leader.

[It is the sowing of distrust which is the special characteristic of tyrants.] Kings are maintained and secured by their friends; tyrants, going on the principle 'All men want my overthrow, but my friends have most power to effect it', distrust them above all others. § 11. The methods applied in extreme democracies are thus all to be found in tyrannies. They both encourage feminine influence in the family, in the hope that wives will tell tales of their husbands; and for a similar reason they are both indulgent to slaves. Slaves and women are not likely to plot against tyrants: indeed, as they prosper under them, they are bound to favour their rule—as they will also favour democracies, where the people likes to play the sovereign as much as any tyrant. § 12. This is the reason why courtiers attain a position of honour under both these forms of government. Democracies are fond of demagogues, who may be called 'the courtiers of democracy', and tyrants like obsequious associates—1314 a which it is the business of courtiers to be. Tyranny is thus a system which chooses bad men for its friends. Tyrants love to be flattered, and nobody with the soul of a freeman can ever stoop to *that*; a good man may be a friend, but at any rate he will not be a flatterer. § 13. [Bad men are not only ready to

---

[1] This would involve a property-tax of 20 per cent. per annum.

flatter]: they are also good tools for bad objects; 'nail knocks out nail', as the proverb says. It is a habit of tyrants never to like a man with a spirit of dignity and independence. The tyrant claims a monopoly of such qualities for himself; he feels that anybody who asserts a rival dignity, or acts with independence, is trenching on *his* prerogative and the majesty of his sovereign power; and he hates him accordingly as a subverter of his own authority. § 14. It is also a habit of tyrants to prefer the company of aliens to that of citizens at table and in society; citizens, they feel, are enemies, but aliens will offer no opposition.

Such are the arts of the tyrant, and such are the means he uses in order to maintain his authority; but [however astute they may be] they plumb the depth of wrongdoing. We may regard them as all summed up under three main headings, which correspond to the three main ends pursued by tyrants. § 15. Their first end and aim is to break the spirit of their subjects. They know that a poor-spirited man will never plot against anybody. Their second aim is to breed mutual distrust. Tyranny is never overthrown until men can begin to trust one another; and this is the reason why tyrants are always at outs with the good. They feel that good men are doubly dangerous to their authority—dangerous, first, in thinking it shame to be governed as if they were slaves; dangerous, again, in their spirit of mutual and general loyalty, and in their refusal to betray one another or anybody else. § 16. The third and last aim of tyrants is to make their subjects incapable of action. Nobody attempts the impossible. Nobody, therefore, will attempt the overthrow of a tyranny, when all are incapable of action.

We have here three principles to which the ordinary policies of tyrants may be reduced—three ideas to which their measures may all be referred: (1) to breed mutual distrust among their subjects, (2) to make them incapable of action, and (3) to break their spirit. § 17. Here, too, we have one of the two main methods for the preservation of tyrannies. But there is also a second method, where the line of action followed is almost the very reverse.[1] § 18. We shall be able to understand the nature of this method if we go back, for a moment, to the causes which destroy kingships. We saw that one way of their destruction was the turning of kingship into the nature of a tyranny. This suggests that a way of preserving tyrannies may be the turning of tyranny into the nature

[1] Newman's note (vol. iv, p. 448) illustrates the difference of the two methods: 'In the first it is taken for granted that the subjects of a tyrant are necessarily hostile to him, and the aim is to make them *unable* to conspire . . . in the second the aim is to make the subjects of the tyrant *indisposed* to conspire.'

of a kingship—subject to the one safeguard that the reformed
tyrant still retains power, and is still in a position to govern his
subjects with or without their consent. To surrender even power
is to surrender tyranny itself. § 19. Power must thus be retained,
as an essential condition of tyranny; but otherwise the tyrant
should act, or at any rate appear to act, in the role of a good player
of the part of King. He must show himself,[1] in the first place,
concerned for the public funds. **1314 b** Not only must he refrain
from expenditure in lavishing gifts which cause public discontent
(and that will always arise when money is painfully wrung from a
toiling and moiling people, and then lavishly squandered on har-
lots, aliens, and luxury trades); he must also render accounts of his
income and expenditure—a policy which a number of tyrants have
actually practised. This is a method of government which will
make him appear to be more of a steward than a tyrant. § 20. There
is no need to fear that it will involve him in a deficit, so long as he
keeps control of affairs; and if he is compelled to be absent from
home he may even find that it is more to his advantage to have a
deficit than it would be to leave a hoard behind him. The regents
whom he appoints will be less likely, in that case, to make a bid
for power; and a tyrant campaigning abroad has more reason to
fear his regents than he has to fear the citizen body itself. The
regents remain behind: the citizens go abroad with their ruler.
§ 21. Next, and in the second place, he should levy taxes, and
require other contributions, in such a way that they can be seen
to be intended for the proper management of public services, or
to be meant for use, in case of need, on military emergencies; and
generally, he should act in the role of a guardian, or steward, who
is handling public revenues rather than private income.

[In his personal behaviour] a tyrant should appear grave, without being harsh; and his carriage should be such that men who come
into his presence will do so with awe, and not in fear. § 22. This
is an aim which cannot easily be achieved if he fails to inspire
respect. He should therefore cultivate military qualities,[2] even if
he fails to cultivate others, and should give the impression of
military efficiency. He should also avoid all sexual offences: he
should be personally free from any suspicion of violating the
chastity of any of his subjects, boy or girl, and all his associates
should be equally free from suspicion. § 23. The women of his
family should observe the same rule in dealing with other women:

---

[1] In the following sections Aristotle anticipates the character of Machiavelli,
and gives 'politic' advice to a 'new prince' in a realistic way. But his advice is
fundamentally different from that of Machiavelli. He bids the new prince abjure
'reason of State', and play the king—and the man.

[2] Reading '*polemikē*', and not '*politikē*'.

the insolence of women has often been the ruin of tyrannies. In the matter of personal indulgence [in the pleasures of the table] the tyrant should be the opposite of some of the tyrants of our days, who—not content with starting at dawn and going on for days on end—actually want to parade their excesses, in the idea that men will admire their bliss and felicity. § 24. Ideally, a tyrant should be moderate in his pleasures: if he cannot attain that ideal, he should at any rate appear in the eyes of the world as a man who eschews pleasure. It is the drunkards, and not the sober —the drowsy, and not the vigilant—who are easily attacked and readily despised.

Indeed, a tyrant should be the opposite of nearly everything which we have previously described as characteristic of tyrants. He should plan and adorn his city as if he were not a tyrant, but a trustee for its benefit. § 25. He should always show a particular zeal in the cult of the gods. Men are less afraid of being treated unjustly by a ruler, when they think that he is god-fearing **1315 a** and pays some regard to the gods; and they are less ready to conspire against him, if they feel that the gods themselves are his friends. At the same time, the tyrant should show his zeal without falling into folly.[1] § 26. He should also honour good men, in any walk of life; and he should do so in such a way as to make them think that they could not possibly have been honoured more by their own fellow-citizens, if their fellow-citizens had been free to distribute honours themselves. He should distribute such honours personally; but he should leave all punishments to be inflicted by the magistrates or the law courts. § 27. It is a precaution common to all forms of monarchical government [and not peculiar to tyranny] that no single man should be promoted to any great position, and if such promotion has to be made, it should be shared by a number of persons, who will then keep a watch upon one another. But if, after all, a single man must needs be promoted to some great position, he should never be a man of bold spirit: tempers of that sort are the quickest to strike in all fields of action. If, on the other hand, a decision is taken to remove a man from a position of power, the removal should be gradual, and he should not be deprived of all his authority at a single blow. § 28. A tyrant should abstain from every form of outrage, and from two forms above all others—the infliction of physical indignities, and violation

---

[1] It may seem to the modern reader that Aristotle is here treating religion in a Machiavellian way. But he is not dealing with religion, in our sense of the word: he is dealing with the ritual worship of civic deities—with formal sacrifices, and auguries, and the general apparatus of formal civic worship. Aristotle's religious views must be sought in the *Metaphysics*, and they are profound enough. The civic tradition of formal worship was something different from religion.

of the chastity of the young. He should show a particular caution of behaviour when he is dealing with men of sensitive honour. Arrogance in matters of money is resented by men who care about money; but it is arrogance in matters affecting honour which is resented by men of honour and virtue.   § 29. A tyrant should therefore abstain from such acts; or, at the very least, he should make it clear that when he inflicts any punishment, he is doing so not from arrogance but in a spirit of paternal discipline, and when he indulges himself with the young, he is doing so not in the licence of power but because he is genuinely in love. In all such cases, too, he should atone for the dishonours which he appears to inflict by the gift of still greater honours.

§ 30. Attempts at assassination are most dangerous, and need most watching, when they are made by men who are not concerned about escaping with their lives after the deed is done.   § 31. For this reason special precautions ought to be taken against any persons who feel that either they themselves, or others for whom they care, are being subjected to outrage. Men who are acting in hot blood take little heed to themselves: witness the saying of Heraclitus, 'It is hard to fight against heat of the spirit, for it is willing to pay the price of life.'

§ 32. [In matters of social policy] a tyrant should always remember that a state is composed of two sections—the poor and the rich. If it is possible, both of these sections should be induced to think that it is the tyrant's power which secures them in their position, and prevents either from suffering injury at the hands of the other. If, however, one of the sections is stronger than the other, the tyrant should attach that section particularly to his side. There will be no need, if he has its support, to resort to such measures as the emancipation of slaves or the disarming of citizens. The addition of either section to the power which he already possesses will make him strong enough to defeat any attempt against his position.

§ 33. It is unnecessary to treat such matters as these in detail. The general aim is sufficiently evident. A tyrant should appear to his subjects not as a despot, **1315 b** but as a steward and king of his people. He should show himself a trustee for the public interest, not a man intent on his own; he should make moderation, and not excess, the aim and end of his life; he should seek the society of the notables, and yet court the favour of the masses. § 34. The benefit which he is bound to gain by such methods will be twofold. In the first place, his rule will be a nobler and a more enviable rule: his subjects will be men of a better stamp, free from humiliation, and he himself will cease to be an object of hatred and fear. In the second place, his rule will also be more lasting; and he will himself attain a habit of character, if not wholly disposed to goodness, at any rate half-good—half-good and yet half-bad, but at any rate not *wholly* bad.

CHAPTER XII

The first part of this chapter explains that tyrannies, in the past, have been generally short-lived. The rest contains a criticism of Plato's account, in the Republic, *of the causes of revolution and constitutional change. The criticism is partly concerned with Plato's attempt to give a mathematical explanation of change and corruption in the ideal state, and partly with his failure (1) to explain at all the cause of change in tyrannies and (2) to explain satisfactorily the causes of change and revolution in oligarchies.*

[The first six sections of this chapter are bracketed by Newman, and other editors, as an interpolation; and they certainly interrupt the argument. Their gist is that, as a matter of fact and in spite of any suggestion of methods for making them lasting, tyrannies are short-lived, and there are really only four instances of any length of duration. These instances (which stop short about 450 B.C., and from which the durable tyrannies of Aristotle's own century are somewhat curiously omitted) are then recited in detail—with some errors of fact and chronology.][1]

1315 b 40 § 7. We have now treated of all (or almost all) the causes which lead to the destruction and the preservation of constitutions and monarchies.[2] We may note, **1316 a** in conclusion, that the subject of constitutional change is treated by Plato in the *Republic*; but the treatment is defective.[3] In the first place, he fails to mention specifically the cause of the change peculiar to his own first and ideal constitution. § 8. He says that the cause is that nothing abides, and that everything changes in a given period; and he goes on to say that the source [of such general change] is to be found in a system of numbers, 'where the root ratio of 4 to 3, wedded to 5, furnishes two harmonical progressions' (he adds words to

---

[1] See Note WW, p. 253.

[2] Aristotle here, as in other passages of this book, distinguishes between 'constitutions' (where there is an arrangement regulating the holding of offices, which is, in his view, the essence of a constitution) and 'monarchies' or single-man governments (where there is no such arrangement); see above, note UU on p. 241.

[3] It should be noticed that Plato's general treatment of constitutional change was meant to give an account of its inner logic rather than of its historical chronology. Aristotle's historical criticism is therefore hardly relevant: see the translator's *Greek Political Theory* (*Plato and His Predecessors*), pp. 244–6.

the effect that this happens when the arithmetical value of the diagram is cubed).[1] The implication here is that [through a failure to conform to the mathematical principles regulating man, as they also regulate the whole of the universe] the reproduction of the species sometimes issues in men of poor quality, who are beyond the reach of education.[2] This implication, in itself, is perhaps not incorrect: there may be persons who cannot possibly be educated or made into good men.   § 9. But why should this be a cause of change peculiar to the ideal state depicted in the *Republic*, rather than one common to all states, and indeed to all things in existence? There is a further point. Can the efflux of time, which, he says, causes all things to change,[3] explain how things which did not begin simultaneously should simultaneously undergo change? Does a thing which came into existence on the day before the turn of the tide change simultaneously [with things of an earlier origin]?

§ 10. Again, we may ask why the ideal state should turn [as Plato makes it turn] into a state of the Spartan type. Constitutions change, as a rule, more readily into an opposite than into a cognate form. The same argument also applies to the other changes mentioned by Plato, when he depicts the Spartan type as changing into oligarchy, oligarchy into democracy, and democracy into tyranny. § 11. The very reverse may equally happen: democracy, for example, can change into oligarchy, and indeed it can do so more easily than it can change into monarchy.

When it comes to tyrannies Plato stops: he never explains whether they do, or do not, change, nor, if they do, why they do so, or into what constitution they change. The reason of this

[1] Aristotle here first quotes some words of Plato, and then adds his own version of the effect of some other words. The words in Plato are a famous puzzle (the puzzle of 'the nuptial number', as it is called by scholars); and Aristotle does not contribute to the solution of the puzzle. It is sufficient to say that there is a reference to the Pythagorean right-angled triangle (hence Aristotle's use of the word 'diagram'), with its sides in the proportions 3, 4, and 5, and with the square of the hypotenuse equal to the sum of the squares of the two other sides ($5^2 = 3^2 + 4^2$). As Professor Cornford says, in his translation of the *Republic* (p. 263, n. 3), 'the serious idea behind . . . is the affinity and correspondence of macrocosm and microcosm, and the embodiment of mathematical principles in both'. See the Excursus on p. 254.

[2] In explanation of this passage, it should be noted that Plato (inspired by a sort of mathematical mysticism) had argued that the rulers of his ideal state should so arrange marriage, and so control the reproduction of the species, that their times were 'propitious', in the sense of being in accordance with the mathematical principles (common to the macrocosm of the universe and the microcosm of man) to which they ought to conform.

[3] Plato had not argued that time, of itself, changes everything. He had argued that things must change, in the course of time, if the mathematical principles governing man and the universe were not observed. But Aristotle fastens on a sentence in the *Republic* (which should be read in its context), 'all that comes into being must decay' (*Republic* 546 A), and interprets it generally and unconditionally.

omission is that any explanation would have been difficult. The matter cannot be settled along the lines of his argument; for on those lines a tyranny would have to change back into the first and ideal constitution, in order to maintain continuity in the revolving cycle of change.   § 12. Actually, however, a tyranny may change into another form of tyranny, as the tyranny at Sicyon changed from the form under Myro to that under Cleisthenes; it may equally change into oligarchy, like the tyranny of Antileon at Chalcis; it may also turn into democracy, like the tyranny of Gelo at Syracuse; or it may change into aristocracy, as happened to the tyranny of Charilaus at Sparta, and as also happened at Carthage. § 13. Tyranny, again, may succeed to oligarchy [and not, as Plato suggests, to democracy].[1] This was the fate that befell most of the ancient oligarchies in Sicily: for instance, the tyranny of Panaetius succeeded to an oligarchy at Leontini, the tyranny of Cleander to one at Gela, and the tyranny of Anaxilaus to one at Rhegium. The same order of change has also been followed in a number of other states.

§ 14. It is curious that Plato should imagine that the change [of the Spartan type of constitution] into oligarchy is merely due to the fact that the magistrates turn money-lovers and profit-makers, and not to the conviction, **1316 b** natural in men of greatly superior wealth, that it is an offence against justice for men without property to be put on a level in the state with the owners of property. Actually, in a number of oligarchies, profit-making is forbidden, and there are specific laws to the contrary. On the other hand at Carthage, although it is democratically governed [and not an oligarchy], profit-making is common—and yet the constitution has never yet changed its character.   § 15. It is also absurd that Plato should say that an oligarchical state is two states—a state of the rich and a state of the poor.[2] Does it show this character more than the Spartan type of state, or more than any other type where all are not equal in property or on the same level of merit?   § 16. Without a single man having become any poorer than he was previously, an oligarchy may none the less turn into a democracy, for the simple reason that the poor have become the majority. Conversely, a democracy may also change into an oligarchy, for the simple reason that the wealthier classes show themselves stronger than the masses, and are active while these are passive.

§ 17. There are thus a number of causes which may produce

---

[1] Aristotle here passes, by an easy transition, from discussing the question 'what succeeds to tyranny' to discussing the question, 'to what does tyranny succeed'.

[2] Aristotle is here criticizing Plato's contention that oligarchies change into democracies because the poor get poorer and poorer, until they are forced to claim and assume political power.

a change from oligarchy to democracy; but Plato confines himself to one—extravagance, leading to debt, and ending in poverty—a view which assumes that all men, or most, are rich to begin with. This is not the truth of the matter. What *is* true is that when any of the leading men lose their property, they become revolutionaries. But the rest may lose their property without any untoward consequence; and any change that may ensue is no more likely to be a change to democracy than it is to be a change to some other form of constitution. § 18. There is also a further point. To have no share in honours and office, or to suffer injustice or insult, is sufficient to cause dissensions and constitutional changes, even if there has been no squandering of property through that licence to 'do as you like' which is caused, in Plato's view, by an exaggerated sense of liberty.

Though there are many varieties of oligarchy and democracy, Socrates [i.e. Plato] discusses their changes as if there were only one form of either. . . .[1]

Note WW (p. 250): *The duration of tyrannies*

(1) For the convenience of the reader a translation of the six sections is given.

1315 b 11 § 1. Yet no constitutions are so short-lived as oligarchy and tyranny. The tyranny of longest duration was that of Orthagoras and his descendants at Sicyon, which lasted for a century. The reason for its permanence was the moderation of their behaviour towards their subjects, and their general obedience to rules of law: Cleisthenes [one of the later tyrants at Sicyon] was too much of a soldier to be despised, and the dynasty generally courted the favour of its subjects by the attentions it paid them. § 2. It is recorded of Cleisthenes that he awarded a crown to the judge who gave a verdict against him in the games; and there are some who say that the seated figure in the public square at Sicyon is a statue of the judge who gave this verdict. There is a similar story that Peisistratus, the tyrant of Athens, once allowed himself to be summoned as defendant in a case before the Areopagus.

§ 3. The second tyranny in point of length was that of the family of Cypselus at Corinth, which lasted seventy-three years and a half: Cypselus himself was tyrant for thirty years, Periander for forty years and a half, and Psammetichus the son of Gordias for three. § 4. The causes of this long duration were the same as at Sicyon: Cypselus courted the favour of his subjects, and dispensed with a bodyguard during the whole of his reign; Periander proved himself a soldier, if he also proved a despot.

§ 5. The third tyranny in point of length was that of the family of Peisistratus at Athens; but this was not continuous. Peisistratus was

[1] This chapter is in the nature of a digression, and it is a curious mixture of criticism of Plato with chronological and other details about tyranny. 'It seems', as Newman says, 'too characteristic of Aristotle not to be his'; but it also seems to contain a number of jottings rather than a sustained argument. On some points of historical fact (e.g. in regard to the change at Syracuse on Gelo's death, and the general constitutional development of Syracuse) it does not square with statements in other parts of the *Politics*. In any case the abrupt termination of the chapter, almost in the middle of a sentence, suggests that it is unfinished.

expelled twice during the course of his reign, and was only tyrant for seventeen years in a period of thirty-three: his sons between them ruled for eighteen years; and the whole reign of the family was thus confined to a period of thirty-five years.

§ 6. The most durable of the other tyrannies was that of Hiero and Gelo at Syracuse. But it, too, was comparatively brief, and only lasted for eighteen years altogether: Gelo was tyrant for seven years, and died in the eighth year of his reign: Hiero ruled for ten years: Thrasybulus was expelled after ruling for ten months.

1315 b 39 Tyrannies generally have all been quite short-lived.

EXCURSUS (p. 251, n. 1): *A Chinese parallel*

It is curious to note a parallel between Plato's idea and a basic idea of the Confucianism of China. The Chinese Emperor was expected to act as a link, or means of concordance, between 'the Way of Heaven' and the way of man—between the macrocosm and the microcosm. In order to perform that duty, he issued a calendar which set forth the times designated by Heaven as propitious for human activities—marriage, ploughing, litigation, journeys, changes of occupation. If the times were not observed, and 'the Way of Heaven' were neglected, it was believed that the life of the Empire would suffer, and the end would be rebellion and political collapse. (M. Collis, *The Great Within*, p. 151.) There is something in this belief which corresponds to Plato's conception of the cause of political change.

BOOK VI

METHODS OF CONSTRUCTING DEMOCRACIES AND OLIGARCHIES WITH A SPECIAL VIEW TO THEIR GREATER STABILITY

A

THE CONSTRUCTION OF DEMOCRACIES (cc. I–v)

CHAPTER I

The varieties of democracy: they are due to two causes—the different characters of the populace, and the different combinations of democratic institutions, in different democracies.

1316 b 31 § 1. A number of topics have now been treated. We have discussed the number and nature of the varieties to be found (*a*) in the deliberative organ, which is the sovereign organ of the constitution, (*b*) in the structure of the executive offices, and (*c*) in judicial bodies; and we have discussed, in that connexion, the character of the variety appropriate to each form of constitution.[1] We have also dealt with the occasions and the causes of the destruction and preservation of the different constitutions.[2] § 2. [We may now turn to consider the theme of the construction of constitutions.][3] Democracy and the other types of constitution have each a number of varieties; we must therefore consider what still remains to be said about each variety,[4] and—more especially— what is the mode of organization appropriate and advantageous to each. § 3. We must also investigate the possible combinations of the various modes of organizing each of the three powers [i.e. the deliberative, the executive, and the judicial]; **1317 a** for the effect of such combinations is to make constitutions overlap with, or shade off into, each other—to make aristocracy, for instance, overlap with oligarchy, or the 'polity' with a democracy. § 4. The possible combinations—which ought to be considered, but have not hitherto been—may be illustrated by examples. The deliberative organ and the method of electing the executive officers may be arranged on an oligarchical basis, while the judicial bodies are constituted on an aristocratic basis. The judicial bodies and the deliberative organ may be constituted on an oligarchical basis, while the method of electing the executive officers is arranged on an aristocratic basis. Other ways may also be followed for getting

---

[1] These topics have been treated in Book IV, cc. XIV–XVI.
[2] These topics have been treated in Book V.   [3] See Note XX, p. 257.
[4] Over and above what has already been said in Book IV, cc. IV–VI.

at the same result—that the parts or elements of a constitution should not one and all have the same complexion.[1]

§ 5. We have already explained[2] what variety of democracy is appropriate to what type of civic body; what variety of oligarchy agrees with what type of society; and which of the other constitutions suits which sort of population. [But our present purpose demands something more.] § 6. It is not enough to ascertain which variety of constitution is best for each state. We have also to ascertain the proper way of *constructing* these—and other—varieties. We must treat the problem succinctly; but if we begin with democracy, we shall also, in dealing with it, be learning to understand its opposite, which is commonly termed oligarchy. § 7. For the purposes of this inquiry [into the proper way of constructing *all* the varieties of democracy] we have to take into account *all* the attributes of democracy, and every feature generally held to be characteristic of it. The sum of these attributes will explain the origin of different types of democracy. It will explain why there is more than one type, and why the types vary.

§ 8. There are two reasons why there are several types of democracy. One has already been mentioned.[3] This is the difference of character between the peoples of different states. Here you may have a populace of farmers; there you may have one of mechanics and day-labourers. The democracies which they constitute differ; but if you add farmers to mechanics, and then add day-labourers to both, you create a new difference which is not so much one between better and worse sorts of the same thing, as one between totally different things.[4] This first reason, however, does not concern us here, and we have to deal with a second and different reason. § 9. The second reason for the existence of different types of democracy is the different possible combinations of the features which characterize democracy and are supposed to be its attributes. One variety of democracy will have fewer of these attributes; a second will have more; a third will have them all. Now there is a double advantage in studying all the separate attributes of democracy. Such study not only helps in constructing

---

[1] Aristotle's doctrine of 'combination' of powers may be compared with some forms of the eighteenth-century English doctrine of the 'balance' of powers (Aristotle's 'combination' is also of the nature of a 'balance'). Both doctrines connect themselves with the idea of the mixed constitution.

[2] The reference is to Book IV, c. XII.

[3] Book IV, c. IV, §§ 20-1; c. VI, §§ 2-6; c. XII, § 3. See also below, c. IV.

[4] Aristotle appears to imply that a democracy which mixes farmers, mechanics, and day-labourers differs in kind (and not merely in degree) from one of farmers only, or one of mechanics and labourers only. Does he mean that it is too socially divided to possess any stability? This seems to be suggested by the subsequent argument of c. IV, §§ 15-20.

some new variety which one may happen to want: it also helps the reform of existing varieties.[1] § 10. Men who are engaged in building a constitution will often seek to lump together all the attributes connected with the idea on which the constitution is based. But this is an error, as we have already[2] noted in dealing with the subject of the destruction and preservation of constitutions.

Let us now consider the postulates, the moral temper, and the aims, of democratic constitutions.[3]

NOTE XX (p. 255): *The new programme of Book VI*

From problems of the destruction and preservation of constitutions *as they stand*, Aristotle here turns to the problem of the construction of constitutions *in a way that will enable them to stand more securely*. He had already discussed, at the end of Book IV, the proper structure of each of the three powers (deliberative, executive, and judicial); and he now promises to discuss the proper structure of the whole constitution, with reference to each type of constitution and the varieties of each type. Actually he deals only with two types (democracy and oligarchy) and the varieties of those two types—varieties which have already been described in Book IV, cc. IV–VI. We may add that the general programme stated at the end of Book IV, c. II, which has been followed through the whole of Books IV and V, is now left, and a new programme is started. Book VI may thus be regarded as a separate section or 'method'; and in its course, accordingly, Aristotle more than once refers back to Books IV and V as 'the previous section'.

CHAPTER II

The underlying idea of democracies is liberty. Liberty as conceived in democracies is twofold; it is partly political liberty, which means that all have a term of office and the will of all prevails; it is partly civil, and consists in 'living as you like'. The institutions involved by this idea, in the spheres of the executive, the judicature, and the deliberative; the payment of the people for political services, and the democratic objection to any long tenure of office. On the other hand,

[1] Aristotle here, in using the word 'reform', is recurring for the moment to the theme of 'preservation'. But it is construction, and not preservation, which is his real theme.

[2] Book V, c. IX. It may be added, in explanation of the connexion between § 9 and § 10, that in § 9 Aristotle has argued in favour of *studying* all the attributes of democracy, while in § 10 he argues against *using* all the attributes indiscriminately. The point is that, if you study each attribute, you will see that some of the attributes connected with democracy do not advance its cause, and you will realize that 'all is not gold that glitters'. Want of this knowledge makes founders of democracies commit the error of pouring into them every attribute that can be held to be characteristic of democracy, and thus really defeating its cause.

[3] These three things—postulates, moral temper, and aims—may be said to constitute the 'idea' (or hypothesis) of democracy. The 'attributes' (or features, or characteristics), which have been previously mentioned, are the institutions through which democracies seek to realize this 'idea' in practice. In the next chapter Aristotle proceeds to study, in §§ 1–4, the idea or hypothesis of democracy—or, as we might say, 'the democratic cause'—and he then returns to the theme of the attributes or actual practices of democracy.

it is to be noted that a specially typical form of democracy (the agricultural or 'peasant' form?) may be based on an idea of justice which involves a general and all-round system of equality—i.e. a system which does not favour the poorer class.

§ 1. The underlying idea of the democratic type of constitution is liberty. (This, it is commonly said, can only be enjoyed in democracy; and this, it is also **1317 b** said, is the aim of every democracy.) Liberty has more than one form. One of its forms [is the political, which] consists in the interchange of ruling and being ruled. § 2. The democratic conception of justice[1] is the enjoyment of arithmetical equality, and not the enjoyment of proportionate equality on the basis of desert. On this arithmetical conception of justice the masses must necessarily be sovereign; the will of the majority must be ultimate and must be the expression of justice. The argument is that each citizen should be on an equality with the rest; and the result which follows in democracies is that the poor—they being in a majority, and the will of the majority being sovereign—are more sovereign than the rich. § 3. Such is the first form of liberty, which all democrats agree in making the aim of their sort of constitution. The other form [is the civil, which] consists in 'living as you like'. Such a life, the democrats argue, is the function of the free man, just as the function of slaves is *not* to live as they like. § 4. This is the second aim of democracy. Its issue is, ideally, freedom from any interference of government, and, failing that, such freedom as comes from the interchange of ruling and being ruled. It contributes, in this way, to a general system of liberty based on equality.

§ 5. Such being the idea of democracy, and the root from which it develops, we can now proceed to study its attributes or institutions. [Under the head of the executive], there is the election of officers *by* all, and *from* all; there is the system of all ruling over each, and each, in his turn, over all; there is the method of appointing by lot to all offices—or, at any rate, to all which do not require some practical experience and professional skill; there is the rule that there should be no property-qualification for office—or, at any rate, the lowest possible; there is the rule that, apart from the military offices, no office should ever be held twice by the same person—or, at any rate, only on few occasions, and those relating only to a few offices; there is, finally, the rule that the tenure of every office—or, at any rate, of as many as possible—should be brief. [Under the head of the judicature], there is the system of

---

[1] Aristotle assumes that the idea of liberty, on its political side, is ultimately based on the conception of justice (i.e. distributive justice)—see Book III, c. IX, and the note to § 3 of that chapter.

popular courts, composed of all the citizens or of persons selected from all, and competent to decide all cases—or, at any rate, most of them, and those the greatest and most important, such as the audit of official accounts, constitutional issues, and matters of contract. [Under the head of the deliberative] there is the rule that the popular assembly should be sovereign in all matters—or, at any rate, in the most important; and conversely that the executive magistracies should be sovereign in none—or, at any rate, in as few as possible.

§ 6. Among the executive magistracies the one most popular in democracies is the Council,[1] wherever there are not adequate means for paying all the citizens to attend the popular assembly. If there *are* adequate means, the Council itself is deprived of its power; and the people, once it is furnished with pay, begins to take everything into its hands, as has already been noticed in the previous section of our inquiry.[2] § 7. This system of payment is a further attribute of democracy. The ideal is payment in every sphere—popular assembly, courts, and executive magistracies; but if that cannot be had, there will at any rate be payment for attending the courts, the council, and the stated meetings of the popular assembly, and also for serving on any board of magistrates—or, at the least, any board whose members are required to have a common table.[3] (It may be remarked that while oligarchy is characterized by good birth, wealth, and culture, the attributes of democracy would appear to be the very opposite—low birth, poverty, and vulgarity.)[4] § 8. Another attribute of democracy is to dispense with all life offices—or at least to curtail the powers of any such offices, **1318 a** if they have been left surviving from some earlier epoch of change, and to make appointments to any life-office depend on the use of the lot and not on election.

§ 9. These are the attributes common to democracies generally. But if we look at the form of democracy and the sort of populace which is generally held to be specially typical, we have to connect it [not so much with these attributes, as] with the conception of justice which is the recognized democratic conception—that of equality of rights for all on an arithmetical basis.[5] Equality here

[1] It should be noticed that the council is included among the executive magistracies. At Athens it was a body of 500 members (chosen by lot, and paid for attendance) which not only prepared business for the popular assembly, but also managed the revenues and discharged other executive functions.

[2] Book IV, c. xv, §§ 12–13. The word here translated 'section' is the Greek *methodos*: see the Introduction, p. xxxvii.

[3] The system of a common table was intended to keep the members of executive boards in close and constant contact. A 'subsistence allowance' for this purpose would seem to be something different from the payment of a salary.

[4] This sentence is bracketed by Newman and other editors.

[5] Aristotle is here referring back to Book IV, c. iv, §§ 22–3, and repeating

might be taken to mean that the poorer class should exercise no greater authority than the rich, or, in other words, that sovereignty should not be exercised only by it, but equally vested in all the citizens on a numerical basis. If that were the interpretation followed, the upholders of democracy could afford to believe that equality—and liberty—was really achieved by their constitution.

Chapter III

How is equality to be secured in democracies? Should the basis be property, and should equal rights be given to equal amounts of property; or should it be personality? It may be suggested that property and personality should both be taken into account, and that sovereignty should rest with the will of a majority of persons who are also the owners of a majority of property.

§ 1. This raises the question, 'How is such equality actually to be secured?'[1] Should the assessed *properties* of the citizens be divided into two equal blocks, but with one block containing 500 large and the other 1,000 small owners, and should the 1,000 and the 500 have equal voting power? Or, alternatively, should equality of this order [i.e. equality based on property, and not on personality] be calculated on some other system—a system, for example, by which properties are divided into two equal blocks, as before, but equal numbers of representatives are then selected from the 500 owners in the one block and the 1,000 in the other, and the representatives so selected are given control of the elections [of magistrates] and the law courts?[2] § 2. [Either system means, in effect, the basing of the constitution on property.] Now is a constitution so based the one most in accordance with justice, as justice is conceived in democracies? Or is a constitution based on numbers [i.e. on *persons*, rather than property] more truly in accordance with justice? Democrats reply by saying that justice consists in the will of a majority of persons. Oligarchs reply by saying that it consists in the will of a majority of property-owners,

some of the phrases he had before used in that passage. In that passage it is the 'agricultural' form of democracy, and a populace of peasant farmers, which Aristotle describes. It is not clear whether, in the present section, 'the form of democracy and the sort of populace which is generally held to be specially typical' is the same as the agricultural form of democracy and a populace of peasant farmers. The similarity of the phrasing here to that of Book IV, c. iv, would suggest that they are. So, too, would the fact that Aristotle proceeds, in the next chapter of this book, to discuss the social basis of democracy, and then, in the next chapter after that, to describe and praise the agricultural form of democracy.   [1] See Note YY, p. 262.

[2] The difference of this system from the previous system is (1) that it involves the use of representation, and (2) that the representatives form a single body, while in the previous system the group of 1,000 and that of 500 would be two separate bodies. (For the idea of representation see Book IV, c. xiv, § 13, and note.)

and that decisions should be taken on the basis of weight of property. §3. Both of these answers involve inequality and injustice. If justice is made to consist in the will of the few [i.e. the few who own the greatest amount of property], tyranny is the logical result; for if we carry the oligarchical conception of justice to its logical consequence, a single person who owns more than all the other owners of property put together will have a just claim to be the sole ruler. If, on the other hand, justice is made to consist in the will of a majority of persons, that majority will be sure to act unjustly, as we have already noted,[1] and to confiscate the property of the rich minority.

§4. In this position we have to ask, in the light of the definitions of justice propounded by both sides, 'What is the sort of equality to which both sides can agree?' Both sides affirm that the will of the major part of the civic body should be sovereign. We may accept that statement; but we cannot accept it without modification. [We may modify it as follows.] There are two classes which compose the state—the wealthy class, and the poor. We may attribute sovereignty, accordingly, to the will of both these classes, or that of a majority of both. [This assumes that the wills, or the majority-wills, of the two classes are agreed.] Suppose, however, that the two classes are not agreed, and are resolved on conflicting measures. In that case we may attribute sovereignty to the will of a majority of persons *who are also the owners of a majority of property*.[2] §5. We may give an illustration. Suppose that there are 10 in the wealthy class, and 20 in the poor; and suppose that 6 of the 10 have arrived at a decision conflicting with that of 15 of the 20. This means that the minority of 4 in the wealthy class agrees with the majority in the poorer class, and, again, that the minority of 5 in the poorer class agrees with the majority in the wealthy class. In that case sovereignty should rest with the will of that side [be it the side of the 6+5, of that of the 15+4] whose members, on both of its elements being added together, have property in excess of that belonging to the members of the other.[3] §6. The result may, of course, be a deadlock, with both sides

---

[1] Book III, c. x, §1.
[2] This solution, Newman notes, is different from that of the oligarchs, 'because it takes account of the property of the poor, and adds it together [i.e. adds it in with that of the rich to determine who are the owners of a majority of property], whereas oligarchs would claim that the will of those who own property in large amounts should prevail'.
[3] There are thus, to begin with, two *classes*. From these two classes, when a vote is taken, there emerge two *sides*, each composed of *elements* drawn from both classes. You add up the properties of both the elements on one side, and then those of both the elements on the other, to determine the actual decision and the residence of sovereignty.

absolutely equal; but this presents no greater difficulties than those which ordinarily arise to-day when a popular assembly or a law court is equally divided. The remedy is decision by lot, or some other similar method.

1318 b To find theoretically where truth resides, in these matters of equality and justice, is a very difficult task. Difficult as it may be, it is an easier task than that of persuading men to act justly, if they have power enough to secure their own selfish interests. The weaker are always anxious for equality and justice. The strong pay no heed to either.

NOTE YY (p. 260): *Voting on the basis of property*

The question which Aristotle proceeds to raise is whether equality should be calculated on the basis of property, or on that of personality. (In Book IV, c. IV, § 24, he has already suggested that there can be a variety of democracy which is based on property.) If equality is calculated on the basis of property, he proposes a general method of the classification of citizens, under which equal blocks of property carry equal weights, though the number of persons in each block is different. The proposal may remind us of the Prussian three-class system, as applied till the end of the war of 1914–18, under which there were three blocks of citizens, each equal in terms of property and voting power, but with one block containing only about 5 per cent. of the population, another about 15 per cent., and the third the remaining 80 per cent.

The system of equal blocks of assessed property was practised in fourth-century Athens, though not on the lines here suggested by Aristotle. About 377 B.C. the Athenians made a general assessment of property, real and personal, which amounted to some £1,400,000. All tax-payers were then divided into 100 'symmories' or blocks of equal aggregate wealth (as recorded in the assessment); and each block contributed an equal amount of the taxes required for the year, charging each member of the block with his quota (*Cambridge Ancient History*, vol. vi, p. 74).

CHAPTER IV

(a) *The agricultural form of democracy. It needs, in the interest of stability, a balance between the rights of the whole civic body and the rights of the propertied classes; and that balance may be secured* (1) *by giving to the whole civic body the three rights of electing the magistrates, calling them to account, and constituting the law-courts, and* (2) *by giving to the propertied classes the right to hold the more important magistracies. Methods may also be used for encouraging the growth of an agricultural population.* (b) *The pastoral form of democracy.* (c) *The form based on a populace of mechanics, shopkeepers, and day-labourers. This last form is too often connected with the policy of giving rights indiscriminately to all and sundry: it is a wiser policy to stop short at the point at which the strength of the masses just exceeds the combined strength of the upper and middle classes. Other policies which may also be followed in this form of democracy.*

§ 1. Of the four varieties of democracy[1] the best, as has already been noted in the previous section of our inquiry, is the one that comes first in the order of classification. It is also the oldest of all the varieties. But the reason why it comes first is not that: it is a reason connected with the grading of the different kinds of populace. The first and best kind of populace is one of farmers;[2] and there is thus no difficulty in constructing a democracy where the bulk of the people live by arable or pastoral farming. § 2. Such people, not having any great amount of property, are busily occupied; and they have thus no time for attending the assembly. Not possessing the necessities of life, they stick to their work, and do not covet what does not belong to them; indeed they find more pleasure in work than they do in politics and government—unless there are large pickings to be got from having a finger in government. § 3. The masses covet profits more than they covet honours; witness the patience with which they bore the old-time tyrannies, and still continue to tolerate oligarchies if only they are allowed to get on with their work and are not robbed of their earnings. Give them the chance and they soon make their way—either up into riches, or, at any rate, out of poverty. § 4. Any craving which the masses may feel for position and power will be satisfied if they are given the right of electing magistrates and calling them to account. Indeed there are instances which show that the masses will be contented with a still smaller measure of power. We may cite the example of Mantinea, where the people did not enjoy the right of electing the magistrates (it was vested instead in persons selected from the body of the people on a system of rotation), but exercised, at any rate, the power of deliberation. § 5. Such a system [even if it gives only limited power to the people] must still be considered as a system of democracy, and it was such at Mantinea.[3]

On these general grounds we may argue that policy, as well as

[1] The discussion of justice, and equality, which runs from c. II, § 8, to the end of c. III, may seem something of a digression. (It has been bracketed as an interpolation by some editors; but hardly with good reason, for it logically follows on c. II and logically prepares the way for c. IV—see the note at the end of c. II.) Aristotle now returns to his specific theme—the proper method of constructing democracy, in the light of the statement of 'attributes' in c. II, §§ 5–8. But he first proceeds to distinguish again the four varieties of democracy (already distinguished and graded in Book IV, c. IV, §§ 22–31); and he does so because different methods of construction are needed for the different varieties.

[2] The agrarian (we may even say the anti-commercial and anti-industrial) trend of Aristotle's thought has already been expressed in the first book of the *Politics*, cc. IX–XI.

[3] This system of government at Mantinea, which Aristotle refers to the past, may perhaps be dated about 421 B.C. or nearly a century before his time. It

general practice, suggests a system of balance in the first [i.e. the agricultural] variety of democracy. On the one hand all the citizens will enjoy the three rights of electing the magistrates, calling them to account, and sitting in the law courts; on the other hand the most important offices will be filled by election, and confined to those who can satisfy a property qualification. The greater the importance of an office, the greater might be the property qualification required. Alternatively, no property qualification might be required for any office, but only men of capacity would actually be appointed.   § 6. A state which is governed in this way will be sure to be well governed (its offices will always be in the hands of the best of its members, with the people giving its consent and bearing no grudge against persons of quality); and the men of quality and the notables will be sure to be satisfied, under a system which at once preserves them from being governed by other and inferior persons and ensures (by giving others the right to call them to account) that they will themselves govern justly.   § 7. To be kept in such dependence, and to be denied the power of doing just as he pleases, is an advantage to any man. The power of acting at will leaves men with no defence 1319 a against the evil impulses present in all of us. Where there is responsibility, the result must always be an advantage of the first order in any constitution: government will be conducted by men of quality, and they will be saved from misconduct, while the masses will have their just rights.

§ 8. It is evident that this form of democracy [the form based on a farming populace] is the best; and the reason is also evident— that the populace on which it is based possesses a definite quality. In the creation of such a populace some of the laws which were generally current in earlier ages may all be of service—laws, for example, forbidding absolutely the acquisition of property in land beyond a certain amount, or, at any rate, forbidding it within a fixed distance from the city centre or the city boundaries. § 9. There used to be also laws, in a considerable number of states, prohibiting an owner from selling the allotment of land originally made to his family; there is also the law [at Elis], attributed to Oxylus, which prohibits, in effect, the raising of a mortgage on a certain proportion of any landowner's estate. [If there are no such laws, and the damage is already done], a law like that of Aphytis [a town near Salonica] should be adopted as a corrective, and as likely to help in securing the object we have in view.   § 10. The inhabitants of

has sometimes been described as an instance of the idea of representation. That description is incorrect. There was a primary assembly (not a representative body) for purposes of deliberation; and representatives, elected on some plan which Aristotle does not explain, were used only for the purpose of indirect election of the magistrates.

Aphytis, although they combine a large population with a small territory, are all engaged in farming. The reason is that estates are not assessed as single units. Estates are divided, for purposes of assessment, into a number of sections; and the sections are small enough to ensure that even the poorer land-owners will show an assessment exceeding the amount required [as a qualification for political rights].[1]

§ 11. Next to a populace of farmers, the best sort [as a basis for democracy] is a pastoral populace living by its herds and flocks. Many of their characteristics are similar to those of farmers; but with their robust physique, and their capacity for camping out in the open, they are specially trained and hardened into a good condition for war. § 12. The other kinds of populace, which form the basis of the other varieties of democracy, are almost without exception of a much poorer stamp. They lead a poor sort of life: and none of the occupations followed by a populace which consists of mechanics, shop-keepers, and day labourers, leaves any room for excellence. § 13. Revolving round the market-place[2] and the city centre, people of this class generally find it easy to attend the sessions of the popular assembly—unlike the farmers who, scattered through the country-side, neither meet so often nor feel so much the need for society of this sort. § 14. When [in addition to a populace of farmers or pastoralists] there is also the further advantage of a country-side which lies at a considerable distance from the city,[3] it is easy to construct a good democracy or a good 'polity'. The mass of the people are then compelled to fix their abode outside the city, on their lands; and even if there is still a mob left which lives round the market-place, a rule will have to be made, where the constitution is democratic, that there shall be no meetings of the popular assembly which cannot be attended by all the inhabitants of the country-side.

§ 15. It has now been shown how the first and best variety of democracy ought to be constructed. It is also clear, from what has been said, how the other varieties should be constituted. They should deviate [from the norm of the first variety] in successive stages, and by the inclusion,[4] at each, of a progressively poorer class.

[1] Aphytis required a property-qualification, in terms of the assessed value of land, as a condition of the exercise of political rights. It pitched, and kept, this property-qualification low, by means of the system described. The lowness of the qualification encouraged all its inhabitants to cling to the necessary minimum of land, and thus made them all farmers.

[2] 'The mechanics and the shop-keepers came to the market-place to sell what they had to sell, and the day-labourers to be hired' (Newman's note, vol. iv, p. 519).

[3] The city might, for instance, be on the coast, while the arable or pastoral land belonging to it lay at some distance inland.

[4] In the Greek, Aristotle uses the word 'exclusion'—looking at the class

1319 b The last variety, which includes all classes alike, is one that cannot be borne by all states, and can hardly itself endure, unless it is properly constituted in point of laws and customs. The causes which lead to the destruction of this as of other forms of government have already been, in the main, described [in the previous book]. § 16. In attempting its construction the leaders of popular parties usually follow the policy of seeking to strengthen the populace by simply increasing its numbers to the utmost possible extent. Citizenship is given not only to the lawfully born, but also to the illegitimate; it is given to those who have only one citizen parent, whether that parent be father or mother: in fact there is nothing of this order but will serve, in such a state, as so much grist for 'the people'. § 17. But if this is the policy of construction usually followed by demagogues, the policy which ought to be followed is different. Increase of numbers should stop at the point at which the masses just exceed the combined strength of the notables and the middle class. It should never go beyond this point. Any greater proportion will at once disturb the balance of the constitution; and it will also incite the notables to chafe still more against democracy—a state of feeling which led to the revolution in Cyrene. A small evil may be overlooked; but an evil which grows to large dimensions is always before men's eyes. § 18. Other measures which are also useful in constructing this last and most extreme type of democracy are measures like those introduced by Cleisthenes at Athens, when he sought to advance the cause of democracy, or those which were taken by the founders of popular government at Cyrene. § 19. This means that a number of new tribes and clans should be instituted by the side of the old; that private cults should be reduced in number and conducted at common centres;[1] and that every contrivance should be employed to make all the citizens mix, as much as they possibly can, and to break down their old loyalties. § 20. The measures adopted by tyrants may equally be regarded as all congenial to democracy [in its extreme form]. We may cite as an instance the license allowed to slaves (which, up to a point, may be advantageous as well as congenial), and the license permitted to women and children. We may also cite the policy of connivance at the practice of 'living as you like'. Such a policy ensures a large body of support for the

---

excluded from the franchise, and regarding this excluded class as becoming poorer and poorer through the admission of more and more classes to the enjoyment of political rights.

[1] 'The private cults' are those of tribes, clans, and sacrificial unions, some of which were celebrated in the private houses of the more influential members. Aristotle suggests the reduction of their number, and the holding of their celebrations in common centres.

constitution in which it is followed. Most men find more pleasure in living without any discipline than they find in a life of temperance.

CHAPTER V [1]

Besides constructing democracies on a sound basis, it is also necessary to ensure their permanence. The true policy is not one which guarantees the greatest possible amount of democracy, but one which guarantees its longest possible duration. Moderation is therefore advisable. On the one hand, the rich should not be alienated by a policy of confiscating their riches, and the system of payment for political services should be kept within modest bounds; on the other hand, measures should also be taken to improve the lot of the common people by a system of social services, both public and private.

§ 1. Legislators and would-be founders of any constitution of this type [i.e. the type of extreme democracy] will find that the work of construction is not their only or principal business. The maintenance of a constitution is the thing which really matters. A state may last for two or three days under any kind of constitution; [the real test is the test of survival]. § 2. Legislators should therefore direct their attention to the causes which lead to the preservation and the destruction of constitutions—a theme which has already been treated—and on that basis they should devote their effort to the construction of stability.[2] They must be on their guard against all the elements of destruction; they must leave their state with a body of laws, **1320 a** customary as well as enacted, which will include, above everything else, all the elements of preservation; they must believe that the true policy, for democracy and oligarchy alike, is not one which ensures the greatest possible amount of either, but one which will ensure the longest possible life for both. § 3. The demagogues of our own day, zealous to please the peoples of their states, cause a large amount of property to be confiscated to public use by means of the law courts.[3] Those

---

[1] In this chapter Aristotle deserts the general theme of Book VI (which is the theme of construction), and reverts to the theme of preservation already treated in Book V. The reason would appear to be that in Book V, cc. VIII–IX, the theme of preservation had only been handled in general terms, and without specific reference to particular constitutions (except for the treatment of 'monarchies' in c. XI); and thus Aristotle is now led to handle the theme with particular reference to democracy, and especially to extreme democracy—the more, as this form of constitution was now the general and current form.

[2] These words repeat the keyword of Book VI (the word 'construction'); they repeat it, however, not in regard to constitution-making, which in Aristotle's sober thought is the less important matter, but in regard to constitution-keeping.

[3] The Greek word for 'confiscate' (which literally means 'to make public') comes from the same root as the word for 'people'. The popular law-courts could easily be used to transfer property from private hands into the hands of the people.

who care for the well-being of their constitution should labour to
correct such practices. They should have a law passed which
prevents the fines imposed in law courts from becoming public
property or being paid into the treasury, and makes them, instead
of that, temple-property. Wrong-doers would not, in that case,
be any more heedless than they are now (they would still have to
pay the same fine), and the people, having nothing to gain, would
be less inclined to condemn all defendants. § 4. Public prosecutions should also be made as few as possible; and heavy fines
should be used to deter prosecutors from bringing them at random.
Such prosecutions are usually brought against notables only, and
not against those who belong to the popular party; but the proper
policy, wherever it can be pursued, is to keep all citizens alike
attached to the constitution and the government under it, or at any
rate, failing that, to prevent any citizen from regarding the government as his enemy.

§ 5. Extreme democracies are generally to be found in populous
states, where it is difficult to get the citizens to attend the popular
assembly without a system of payment. Such a system bears
hardly on the notables—unless a state has already in hand sufficient
revenues to pay its cost. The necessary funds have to be procured
by a tax on property, by confiscation, and through the agency of
bad law courts; and these are all methods which have led in the
past to the overthrow of many democracies. This suggests that,
unless there are sufficient revenues already in hand, the meetings
of the popular assembly should be infrequent, and the number of
sittings of the popular law courts should be as small as their membership is large. § 6. If the sittings of the courts are thus restricted,
two advantages will ensue. In the first place, the wealthier classes
will cease to fear the expenditure involved—the more if it is only
the poor, and not also the well-to-do, who are allowed to receive
any pay; and secondly, the cases before the courts will be much
better decided, as the rich (who do not care to be absent from their
business for days together, but do not mind a short absence) will
now be willing to attend. § 7. When, on the other hand, a state
has sufficient revenues to defray the cost of a system of payment,
[they should be husbanded for that purpose, and] the policy nowadays followed by demagogues should be avoided. It is their habit
to distribute any surplus among the people; and the people, in the
act of taking, ask for the same again. To help the poor in this way
is to fill a leaky jar. . . . Yet it is the duty of a genuine democrat to see
to it that the masses are not excessively poor. § 8. Poverty is the
cause of the defects of democracy. That is the reason why measures
should be taken to ensure a permanent level of prosperity. This

is in the interest of all classes, including the prosperous themselves; and therefore the proper policy is to accumulate any surplus revenue in a fund, and then to distribute this fund in block grants to the poor. The ideal method of distribution, if a sufficient fund can be accumulated, is to make such grants sufficient for the purchase of a plot of land: failing that, they should be large enough to start men in commerce **1320 b** or agriculture. § 9. If such grants cannot be made to all the poor simultaneously, they should be distributed successively, by tribes or other divisions: and meanwhile the rich should contribute a sum sufficient to provide the poor with payment for their attendance at the obligatory meetings of the assembly, and should be excused, in return, from the rendering of useless public services [such as the equipping of choruses at dramatic festivals].[1] It is by a policy of this general nature that the Carthaginian government has secured the goodwill of the people. It sends persons drawn from the ranks of the people regularly to the provincial towns, and thus enables them to become prosperous.[2] § 10. Notables who are men of feeling and good sense may also undertake the duty of helping the poor to find occupations—each taking charge of a group, and each giving a grant to enable the members of his group to make a start.[3] The example of the citizens of Tarentum may also be commended for imitation: the well-to-do share with the poor the use of their property, and thereby conciliate the goodwill of the masses.[4] § 11. The Tarentines have also divided all magistracies into two classes—one with appointments made by election, and the other with appointments made by lot—in the idea that the latter will give the people a share in office, while the former will help to ensure a better administration. The same result may also be achieved by dividing the members of each board of magistrates into two classes—an elected class, and a class appointed by lot.

---

[1] This scheme of what we should nowadays call 'public social services' is notable. It is a scheme of constructive public assistance, designed less to furnish relief in cases of destitution than to provide a capital sum which will enable men to set themselves up in life. It may be noted that Athens had actually something of a scheme of public assistance, though only for the relief of destitution, as Aristotle notes in his *Constitution of Athens* (c. XLIX, § 4): 'there is a law to the effect that persons with less than 3 minas, who are so crippled in body as to be unable to work, should be examined by the council and then given 2 obols a day from the public funds for their support'. See also Appendix IV, A 2 (p. 377).

[2] Apparently they were given some sort of office, and official emoluments, in the provincial towns (see Book II, c. xi, § 15).

[3] Here Aristotle adds a scheme of 'voluntary social service' to his previous scheme of 'public social services' or constructive public assistance.

[4] This passage may remind us of Aristotle's formula for the proper conception of property—'Private possession, common use' (Book II, c. v, §§ 5–8).

THE CONSTRUCTION OF OLIGARCHIES (oc. vi–viii)

CHAPTER VI

The best sort of oligarchy will answer to the best, or agricultural, sort of democracy: it will require a moderate property qualification for the holding of any office. The last form of oligarchy, answering to the last, or 'extreme', form of democracy, needs the greatest vigilance. Generally, while democracies rely on quantity or numbers, oligarchies ought to rely on the quality of their organization.

§ 1. We have now explained how democracies should be constructed; and in doing so we have virtually shown how oligarchies ought to be constituted. Each variety of oligarchy should be framed on the principle of opposites—that is to say, the structure of each should be calculated by that of the corresponding variety of democracy. The first and best balanced of oligarchies [will thus answer to the first and best of democracies. Indeed, it] is closely akin to the constitution which goes by the name of 'polity'.[1] § 2. In an oligarchy of this type there should be two separate assessment rolls, a higher and a lower. Entry in the lower roll should qualify men for appointment to the lowest offices that have to be filled; but entry in the higher should be required for appointment to the more important. On the other hand any person who acquires sufficient property to be put on an assessment roll should be given constitutional rights; and by this means a sufficient number of the people at large will be admitted to make those who enjoy rights in the state a stronger body than those who do not. § 3. The persons newly admitted to rights should always be drawn from the better sections of the people.

The next succeeding variety of oligarchy should be constructed on lines like the first, but with some little tightening [of the qualifications required for office]. Eventually we shall reach the variety of oligarchy which corresponds to extreme democracy. This is the type of oligarchy which is most in the nature of a ruling clique and most akin to tyranny; and, as it is worst of all, it requires all the greater vigilance. § 4. A man with a healthy

---

[1] Aristotle begins by arguing, logically, that each variety of oligarchy should correspond to, and be the opposite of, the parallel variety of democracy. But the logical argument would appear to be abandoned, and abandoned instantly, when he deals with the first and best form of oligarchy. Actually this variety is *not* opposed to the first and best variety of democracy. We are told that it is near to polity, which in turn is near to the first and best variety of democracy. There is thus similarity, rather than opposition, between the first variety of democracy and the corresponding variety of oligarchy.

physique can afford to run risks: a ship suited for navigation, with a good crew on board, can survive a number of mishaps without being sent to the bottom; but a man of feeble and sickly physique, or a ship badly jointed and poorly manned, cannot face even a slight misadventure. Just the same is true of constitutions: the worst need the greatest **1321 a** vigilance. § 5. In democracies the size of the population is generally the saving factor; and with them numbers serve in lieu of the opposite factor—a system of distributive justice on the basis of merit—[which preserves better constitutions]. Oligarchies, on the other hand, must obviously seek security by a method which is the opposite of that of democracies—the quality of their organization.[1]

CHAPTER VII

Military factors have an important bearing on oligarchies. A cavalry force is favourable to a strict form of oligarchy; on the other hand, light-armed troops and naval forces are favourable to democracy. It is a wise policy for an oligarchy to train its own members to serve as light-armed troops. Oligarchies will also do well to give the masses some share in the government, and to require their more important officials to perform unpaid public services. In a word, they should direct themselves by the idea of public service rather than by that of private profit.

§ 1. Just as there are four chief divisions of the mass of the population—farmers, mechanics, shopkeepers, and day-labourers—so there are also four kinds of military forces—cavalry, heavy infantry, light-armed troops, and the navy. Where a territory is suitable for the use of cavalry, there is a favourable ground for the construction of a strong form of oligarchy:[2] the inhabitants of such a territory need a cavalry force for security, and it is only men of large means who can afford to breed and keep horses. Where a territory is suitable for the use of heavy infantry, the next [and less exclusive] variety of oligarchy is natural; service in the heavy infantry is a matter for the well-to-do rather than for the poor. § 2. Light-armed troops, and the navy, are [drawn from the

---

[1] In other words, they must organize the distribution of office and honours on a system of distributive justice based on the standard of merit.

[2] The connexion between military and constitutional development has already been treated in Book IV, c. III, §§ 1–3. (In that passage, as here, Aristotle begins by connecting social with military divisions, and then proceeds to connect military development with constitutional—his idea being that social, military, and constitutional factors are all interconnected.) On the historical connexion between changes of military methods and the constitutional development of the city states of ancient Greece see the *Cambridge Ancient History*, vol. iii, pp. 695–6.

mass of the people, and are thus] wholly on the side of democracy; and in our days—with light-armed troops and naval forces as large as they are—the oligarchical side is generally worsted in any civil dispute. This situation should be met, and remedied, by following the practice of some military commanders, who combine an appropriate number of light-armed troops with the cavalry and heavy infantry.[1] § 3. The reason why the masses can defeat the wealthier classes, in any civil dissension, is that a light-armed and mobile force finds it easy to cope with a force of cavalry and heavy infantry. An oligarchy which builds up a light-armed force exclusively from the masses is thus only building up a challenge to itself. [The system of recruitment should be altered.] A distinction of age-groups should be made; and while they are in the lower age-group, the sons of oligarchs should also be instructed [along with the sons of the poor] in light-infantry drill and weapons. They will then be able, when they are moved up into the higher age-groups, to perform themselves, in actual practice, the duties of a light infantry.

§ 4. There are various ways in which an oligarchy may give the masses some place in the civic body.[2] One way, which has already been mentioned (c. VI, § 2), is that the right of holding office should be given to any man who acquires sufficient property to put him on the assessment roll. Another way, of which Thebes affords an example, is that the right should be given to those who have not followed any mechanical occupation for a number of years. A third way, which is that followed at Massalia, is to compile a list of all who are worthy of office, whether or no they have at the time a place in the civic body.

§ 5. [There are some other measures which should also be taken to construct a good oligarchy.] The most important offices, which must necessarily be held by full citizens,[3] should involve the duty of performing unpaid public services. This will have the effect of making the people willing to acquiesce in their own

[1] Aristotle does not mean that the practice should be exactly followed. He is using an analogy loosely. What he really means, as he proceeds to explain, is that young men of the upper classes, from which cavalry and heavy infantry are drawn, should be trained as light-armed infantry, in order that they may act with their friends in the event of civil dissension. This will prevent the whole of the light infantry from being composed of the lower classes—though it will not prevent the whole of the cavalry and heavy infantry from being composed of the upper.

[2] The arrangement of this chapter is somewhat composite. It begins as though it were to be exclusively concerned with the military system proper to oligarchies. It ends by going back to the constitutional method which should be followed in constructing a good form of oligarchy—a theme already handled at the beginning of the previous chapter.

[3] In the previous chapter, § 2, Aristotle has suggested that the most important offices should be confined to the citizens who have a higher property qualification.

exclusion from such offices, and it will make them ready to tolerate officials who pay so heavy a price for the privilege. § 6. These higher officials may also be properly expected to offer magnificent sacrifices on their entry into their office, and to erect some public building during its course. The people—sharing in these entertainments, and seeing their city decorated with votive ornaments and edifices—will readily tolerate the survival of oligarchy; and the notables will have their reward in visible memorials of their own outlay. § 7. But it is not this policy which is pursued by the oligarchs of our days. Their policy is the very opposite; they covet profit as well as honour: and from this point of view oligarchy may well be described as democracy 'writ small'.

Chapter VIII

A study of the best modes of organizing the executive offices in states generally. A first list of the six indispensable offices which are required for the performance of the minimum functions of a state. A second list of the four more important offices, which are concerned with more important functions and require a higher capacity—military command, the control of finance, the preparation of business for the deliberative body, and the direction of public worship. A final classification of all offices under a number of heads, according to the general character of their functions.

1321 b § 1. This may suffice as an account of the methods which ought to be followed in constructing democracies and oligarchies. It leads us on naturally to consider the right distribution of the executive offices, and to examine their number, their nature, and the functions proper to each—a subject which has already been treated in a previous passage.[1] No state can exist at all in the absence of those offices which are absolutely indispensable; no properly governed state can exist in the absence of those which ensure good organization and order. § 2. [This is one general rule.] It is another that there should be fewer offices in small and a greater number in large states, as indeed we have already noted;[2] and accordingly we must not omit to consider which offices can be conjoined, and which ought to be kept separate.

§ 3. Among the indispensable offices the first is the office charged with the care of the market-place. This requires a magistrate [the *Agoranomos*] for the supervision of contracts and the maintenance of good order. Buying and selling are needed in all states equally, for the mutual satisfaction of wants; they are also the readiest means for the attainment of self-sufficiency, which is

---

[1] See Note ZZ, p. 278.

[2] In Book IV, c. xv, §§ 6–7.

generally regarded as the chief object of men's coming together under a common constitution.[1]

§ 4. A second function, which follows on this first, and is closely connected with it, is the superintendence of private and public property in the city-centre, with a view to good order; the maintenance and repair of derelict buildings and roads; the superintendence of boundaries, with a view to the prevention of disputes; and other similar matters demanding public attention.   § 5. The officer charged with this function is generally called the City-superintendent [*Astynomos*]; but in more populous states there may be a number of departments, each with its own special province, such as maintenance of the city walls, superintendence of public fountains, and control of the city's harbour.

§ 6. The third indispensable office is closely akin to the second. Its functions are just the same; but they are exercised outside the city, and in the country-side. The holders of this office are sometimes called rural inspectors [*Agronomoi*], and sometimes forest-wardens.

Besides these three first offices, with their respective functions, there is a fourth for receiving and holding the public revenues, and for paying them out in quotas among the several departments. The holders of this office go by the name of receivers of accounts, or treasurers.

§ 7. The fifth office deals with the registration of private contracts and court decisions: indictments have also to be deposited with it, and preliminary proceedings begun before it. In a number of states this office (like that of the city-superintendent) is divided into departments, though a single officer (or board of officers) remains in general control of the whole. The holders of the office go by the name of public recorders, masters, plain recorders, or other similar titles.

§ 8. We now come to an office which follows naturally on the fifth, but which is also, in itself, at once the most indispensable and the most difficult of all offices. This is the office which deals with the execution of sentences on offenders; **1322 a** with the recovery of debts due to the state from persons placarded on the public lists; and with the custody of prisoners.   § 9. It is a difficult office, because it involves a good deal of odium; and unless it affords opportunities for making considerable gains, men either shrink from it or, if they accept it, are loath to discharge its duties with the rigour the law demands. But it is, none the less, an indispensable office. There is nothing to be got by bringing suits for the determination of rights, when they reach no effective conclusion;

[1] See Book I, c. II, § 8.

and if men cannot share a common life without a system for deciding suits, neither can they do so without a system for enforcing such decisions. § 10. In view of its difficulties, the duties of the office should not be vested in a single specialized body of persons. They should be vested in representatives drawn from the different courts, [generally responsible for enforcing the decisions of all the courts]; and an attempt should be made, in the same sort of way, to distribute the duty of placarding names on the list of public debtors. In addition, the various boards of magistrates might give some help in enforcing decisions. More especially, penalties inflicted by an outgoing board of magistrates might be left for enforcement to the incoming board; or if this be impossible, and penalties have to be inflicted and enforced by magistrates of the same tenure of office, the enforcement of a penalty might be left to a different board from that which inflicts it—for instance, the city-superintendents might enforce any penalty inflicted by the market-inspectors, and other officers might, in turn, enforce any penalty *they* had inflicted. § 11. The less the odium which attaches to the enforcement of penalties, the more effective will such enforcement be. When the same body of persons which inflicts a penalty also enforces the penalty, that body is doubly disliked; but when one and the same set of officers has to enforce every penalty, it will be hated by everybody. . . . In a number of states there is a further division between the office charged with the custody of prisoners and the office charged with the execution of sentences. At Athens, for instance, the custody of prisoners is the special duty of The Eleven.[1] § 12. This suggests that it may be best to make it a separate office, and then to apply to that office the same devices of policy as in the enforcement of penalties.[2] The office of the gaoler is as indispensable as that for enforcing penalties; but it is an office which the good particularly shun, and which cannot safely be given to the bad (who are more in need of a gaoler themselves than capable of acting as gaolers to others). § 13. We may therefore conclude that the superintendence of gaols should not be assigned to a board appointed for that one purpose, or left permanently to any one board. It is a duty which should be undertaken by different and successive sections—sections partly drawn (in states where young men are given some training in military and police duties) from the younger citizens, and partly from the boards of magistrates.

These six offices must be ranked first, as being the most indispensable [though not the highest]. Next in order come a

---

[1] Actually, the Eleven were charged with the execution of capital sentences as well as with the custody of prisoners. But there *were* separate officials for the enforcement of many penalties.   [2] i.e. the devices already suggested in § 10.

number of other offices, which are also indispensable, but of a higher order of importance. They are offices which require a large experience and a high degree of fidelity. § 14. We may count among them, first and foremost, the offices charged with the defence of the city, and any others intended for military purposes. In peace as well as in war, there must be persons to superintend the defence of the city's gates and walls, and to inspect and drill its citizens. Some states have a number of different offices to deal with these various duties, others have only a few, and small states may even be content with a single office to deal with them all. § 15. The holders of these offices are commonly called generals or commandants. **1322 b** Where there are separate forces of cavalry, light-armed troops, archers, and marines, each of them is sometimes placed under a separate command; and the officer commanding is then termed admiral, or general of horse, or general of the light forces. Their subordinate officers, in turn, are termed naval captains, captains of horse, and company commanders; and corresponding titles are given to the officers commanding smaller sections. The whole of this organization forms a single depart-ment—that of military command.

§ 16. From the organization of military command, as it has just been described, we may next turn to the organization of finance. Several of the offices of a state, if not all, handle large amounts of public money. There must accordingly be a separate office for finance [i.e. a treasury department] which receives and audits the accounts of other offices, and is only concerned with this one function. The holders of this office go by different names in different places—auditors, accountants, examiners, or advocates of the fisc.

§ 17. Besides the various offices already mentioned, there is another which controls, more than any other office, the whole range of public affairs. The office in question is one which, in a large number of states, possesses the double power of introducing matters [to the assembly] and of bringing them to completion. Short of that, and where the people itself is in control, it presides over the assembly; for there must be a body to act as convener to the controlling authority of the constitution. The holders of this office are in some states called *Probouloi*, or the preliminary council, because they initiate deliberation;[1] but where there is a popular assembly, they are called the *Boulē* or Council.

---

[1] On the nature of *Probouloi* see Book IV, c. xiv, §§ 14–16, and c. xv, §§ 11–12 (with the note on § 12). It would appear to be assumed in this passage that where there is only a council, and not a popular assembly, a preliminary council will be needed to initiate matters for the council: where there is both a council and an assembly, the council will initiate matters for the assembly, and no preliminary council will be needed.

§ 18. Such is the general nature of the main political offices. But there is also another province of affairs, which is concerned with the cult of the civic deities; and this requires officers such as priests and custodians of temples—custodians charged with the maintenance and repair of fabrics and the management of any other property assigned to the service of the gods. § 19. Occasionally (for example, in small states) the whole of this province is assigned to a single office; in other states it may be divided among a number of offices, and apart from priests there may also be the superintendents of sacrifices, the guardians of shrines, and the stewards of religious property. § 20. Closely related to these various offices there may also be a separate office, charged with the management of all public sacrifices which have the distinction of being celebrated on the city's common hearth, and, as such, are not legally assigned to the priests.[1] The holders of this office are in some states called archon, in others king,[2] and in others prytaneis.

§ 21. The offices required in all states may be summarily classified on the basis of their various functions.[3] First, there are the functions connected with public worship, military matters, and revenue and expenditure. Secondly, there are those connected with the market-place, the city-centre, the harbours, and the country-side. Thirdly, there are the functions connected with the law-courts, the registration of contracts, the enforcement of penalties, the custody of prisoners, and the reviewing, scrutiny, and audit of the accounts of magistrates. Finally, there are the functions connected with deliberation on public affairs. § 22. In addition there are offices peculiar to certain states which have a more leisured character and a greater degree of prosperity, and concern themselves with good discipline—offices for the supervision of women; for enforcing obedience to law; for the supervision of **1323 a** children; and for the control of physical training. We may also include the office for the superintendence of athletic contests and dramatic competitions and all other similar spectacles.

[1] The common hearth of a state was in the prytaneum. This was a building consecrated to the goddess of the hearth, in which a perpetual fire was kept burning in her honour; here the magistrates resided and maintained a common table.

[2] The title of king was sometimes kept, even after the disappearance of monarchy, with a religious significance—the early kings having been always priests as well as secular rulers (Book III, c. XIV, § 14).

[3] Aristotle follows in this passage a different order of classification from that followed in the earlier part of the chapter. Previously he had classified offices in an ascending scale of importance. Here he classifies them in four main categories determined by the subject-matter with which they deal—the general category of worship, war, and finance; the category of local affairs; the category of legal business; and the category of public deliberation.

§ 23. Some of these offices—those for the supervision of women and children, for example—are clearly out of place in a democracy: the poor man, not having slaves, is compelled to use his wife and children as followers and attendants.[1]

§ 24. There are three sorts of offices concerned with the conduct of the elections made by the electoral body to the highest magistracies. The first is the Guardians of the Law: the second, the Probouloi; and the third, the Boulē. The first is appropriate to aristocracy: the second to oligarchy: the third to democracy.

We have now given a sketch, in outline, of almost every kind of office; but.[2] . . .

Note ZZ (p. 273)

The previous passage is Book IV, c. xv. It is somewhat puzzling that there should be two different treatments of the same theme; nor can there be said to be any correlation of the two different treatments. Aristotle's first treatment is somewhat dry and analytical: the treatment in the present passage is more concrete, more practical, and more realistic. Here 'he bases his classification of magistracies on the practice of Greek states: he follows this in separating military from civil functions, for this was the general rule, at any rate in democratic states; he follows it also in instituting magistrates for the audit of the accounts of outgoing office-holders, and in reserving the initiative for the Boulē (Council) and its equivalents' (Newman, vol. IV, p. 54). Generally, it may be said that the account of the magistracies given here is closely related to the actual practice of Greek oligarchies and democracies (especially, perhaps, the latter); and in this sense it may be said to follow naturally, as Aristotle remarks, on the account he has previously given of the proper methods of constructing these constitutions.

[1] Newman notes, very justly, that this passage shows the error of the view 'that a Greek democracy was virtually an aristocracy, inasmuch as most, if not all, of the citizens would be the owners of one or more slaves' (vol. iv, p. 567). Aristotle here notes that the poor had no slaves; and the poor, as he states again and again in the *Politics*, were the majority in a democracy.

[2] The chapter ends in an unfinished state. § 24 seems to be a mere jotting; and the last sentence finishes in the middle.

BOOK VII

POLITICAL IDEALS AND EDUCATIONAL PRINCIPLES

A

POLITICAL IDEALS: THE NATURE OF THE HIGHEST GOOD AND OF THE BEST AND HAPPIEST LIFE (cc. I–III)

CHAPTER I

The three 'goods'—external goods; goods of the body; and goods of the soul. The primacy of the goods of the soul is attested by experience and evinced by philosophy: the possession of such goods—courage, wisdom, and the other virtues—'lies not in our stars, but in ourselves'; and it is, for states as well as for individuals, the condition and the cause of the best and happiest life. We thus come to the conclusion that 'the best way of life, both for states and for individuals, is the life of goodness, duly equipped with such a store of requisites—i.e. external goods and goods of the body—as makes it possible to share in the activities of goodness'.

1323 a 14 § 1. Before we can undertake properly the investigation of our next theme—the nature of an ideal constitution—it is necessary for us first to determine the nature of the most desirable way of life.[1] As long as that is obscure, the nature of the ideal constitution must also remain obscure. [The two things are essentially interconnected]; and we may thus expect that—unless something unexpected happens—the best way of life will go together with the best constitution possible in the circumstances of the case.[2] § 2. We must therefore, first of all, find some agreed conception of the way of life which is most desirable for all men and in all cases; and we must then discover whether or no the same way of life is desirable in the case of the community as in that of the individual.

The nature of the best life is a theme which has already been treated by us in works intended for the general public.[3] Much of what has been said there may be considered adequate, and we

[1] These words, as has already been noted, are a repetition of the concluding words of Book III. Their argument may be illustrated from Book IV, c. XI, § 3: 'A constitution is a way of life followed by a citizen-body.' If this be the case, an ideal constitution for a citizen-body involves the most desirable way of life for that body.

[2] It is not quite clear, as Newman notes, why Aristotle adds these words of qualification. The ideal constitution, as he has argued before and argues again in this book, is the absolutely best, and not the best which is 'possible in the circumstances of the case'. It presupposes ideal conditions or circumstances (in other words, an ideal social basis), and it is not adjusted to given conditions or circumstances, such as an imperfect and heterogeneous society.

[3] Literally 'exoteric discourses': see Book III, c. VI, § 5 and note. We may guess that the rest of this chapter is a quotation or summary of these discourses.

must use it here. § 3. There is one classification of the constituent elements of the best life which it is certain that no one
would challenge. This is the classification of these elements into
external goods; goods of the body; and goods of the soul. It
will also be generally agreed that *all* of these different 'goods'
should belong to the happy man.[1] § 4. No one would call a man
happy who had no particle of fortitude, temperance, justice, or
wisdom [i.e. none of the goods of the soul]:[2] who feared the flies
buzzing about his head; who abstained from none of the extremest
forms of extravagance whenever he felt hungry or thirsty; who
would ruin his dearest friends for the sake of a farthing; whose
mind was as senseless, and as much astray, as that of a child or
a madman. § 5. These are all propositions which would be accepted
by nearly everybody as soon as they were stated. But differences
begin to arise when we ask, 'How much of each good should men
have? And what is the relative superiority of one good over
another?' Any modicum of goodness [i.e. of the 'goods of the soul']
is regarded as adequate; but wealth and property, power, reputation, and all such things, are coveted to an excess which knows no
bounds or limits. § 6. There is an answer which can be given to
men who act in this way. 'The facts themselves make it easy for
you to assure yourselves on these issues. You can see for yourselves that the goods of the soul are not gained or maintained by
external goods. It is the other way round. You can see for yourselves **1323 b** that felicity—no matter whether men find it in
pleasure, or goodness, or both of the two—belongs more to those
who have cultivated their character and mind to the uttermost,
and kept acquisition of external goods within moderate limits, than
it does to those who have managed to acquire more external goods
than they can possibly use, and are lacking in the goods of the soul.'
[That is the answer given by actual experience of life.] But the
problem can also be easily solved if we consider it theoretically.

§ 7. External goods, like all other instruments, have a necessary
limit of size.[3] Indeed all things of utility [including the goods of
the body as well as external goods] are of this character; and
any excessive amount of such things must either cause its possessor

---

[1] The word 'happy' fails to give a just idea of the Greek. The word which
Aristotle uses here (*makarios*) is perhaps even stronger than a similar word
which he uses more frequently (*eudaimōn*); but both words signify the supreme
happiness which is of the nature of what we may call 'felicity'—the happiness
springing from a full excellence (*aretē*) of 'mind, body, and estate', without which
it cannot exist (c. IX, § 3, of this book).

[2] These are 'the four virtues', in the current Greek classification. The four
'extremes' that follow are the corresponding extremes of cowardice, intemperance, injustice, and folly.

[3] This is a doctrine which is stated more fully below, c. IV, § 10.

some injury, or, at any rate, bring him no benefit. [It is the opposite with the goods of the soul.] The greater the amount of each of the goods of the soul, the greater is its utility[1]—if indeed it is proper to predicate 'utility' at all here, and we ought not simply to predicate 'value'. § 8. In general terms, we are clearly entitled to lay down this proposition: 'The best state of thing A is to the best state of thing B, as thing A itself is to thing B.'[2] If, therefore, the soul is a thing more precious—intrinsically as well as in relation to us —than either our property or our body, the best state of the soul must necessarily bear the same relation to the best state of either our property or our body. § 9. Let us add that it is for the sake of the soul that these other things [property, and health of the body] are desirable, and should accordingly be desired by every man of good sense—not the soul for the sake of them.

§ 10. We may therefore join in agreeing that the amount of felicity which falls to the lot of each individual man is equal to the amount of his goodness and his wisdom, and of the good and wise acts that he does. The nature of God Himself bears witness to this conclusion. He is happy and blessed; but He is so in and by Himself, by reason of the nature of His being, and not by virtue of any external good. This will explain why there must always be a difference between being happy and being fortunate. Accident. and chance are causes of the goods external to the soul [and therefore of men's being fortunate]; but no man can be just and temperate [and therefore happy] merely by accident or simply through chance.

§ 11. Next in order, and based on the same general train of reasoning, comes the principle that [what is true of the felicity of individuals is also true of that of communities, and that therefore] the state which is morally best is the state which is happy and 'does well'.[3] To 'do well' is impossible unless you also 'do right'; and there can be no doing right for a state, any more than there can be for an individual, in the absence of goodness and wisdom. § 12. The fortitude of a state, and the justice and wisdom of a state, have the same energy, and the same character, as the qualities

---

[1] Shakespeare says of love what Aristotle says of the goods of the soul:

> My bounty is as boundless as the sea,
> My love as deep: the more I give to thee,
> The more I have, for both are infinite.

[2] This is a paraphrase rather than a translation. Newman translates (vol. iii, p. 315): 'the best state of every individual thing, if we match one against another, corresponds, in respect of superiority, to the distance between the things of which we say that these very states are states.'

[3] See Note AAA, p. 282.

which cause individuals who have them to be called brave, just, and wise.[1]

§ 13. These observations may serve, at any rate so far as they go, as a philosophical preface to our argument. They deal with matters on which it is impossible not to touch; but it is equally impossible to develop here the whole of the argument which is involved. That is a matter for another and different branch of study. Here it may be sufficient to lay down this proposition: 'The best way of life, for individuals severally as well as for states collectively, is the life of goodness duly equipped with such a store of requisites [i.e. of external goods and of the goods of the body] as **1324 a** makes it possible to share in the activities of goodness.'[2]   § 14. The proposition may conceivably be challenged; but we must leave the matter there—so far as our present inquiry is concerned—and defer to a later occasion any attempt to answer the arguments of those who refuse to accept our views.

NOTE AAA (p. 281): *The connexion of felicity and goodness*

The phrase in the Greek, translated by the words 'does well', is a phrase used in a double sense—the sense of 'faring well' or 'succeeding', and the sense of 'behaving well' or 'doing right'. The two senses are closely connected; and the connexion implies that 'faring well' is the result of 'behaving well', or that happiness comes from goodness. The connexion between happiness and goodness is the theme of Aristotle's verses on Plato (*Fragmenta*, ed. Rose, no. 673): Plato, he writes, was the only man, or the first, who clearly showed by his own life and the arguments of his writings that man attains goodness and happiness together. The connexion also forms the theme of his verses on Hermias of Atarneus (ibid., no. 675): goodness brings to the mind a harvest undying, better than gold, better than ancestors, better than soft-eyed sleep.

---

[1] The argument of this section, as Newman notes, is that 'the happiness of a state, like that of an individual, cannot exist apart from the moral and intellectual virtues, and action in accordance with them: its happiness is inseparable from the very same virtues with which happiness is associated in the individual'. Aristotle naturally advances from the proposition of § 10, that each individual has as much happiness as he has goodness, to the proposition here stated, that each state also has as much happiness as it has goodness. If the two propositions are put together, they imply (as Aristotle proceeds to state explicitly at the beginning of the next chapter) that the happiness of the state is the same as that of the individual.

[2] It will be noticed that here, as also in § 10, Aristotle lays stress on action. Goodness means good actions as well as a good disposition. . . . It will also be noticed that active goodness requires, in Aristotle's view, a *choregia* or equipment —enough of 'external goods' for active liberality, and even for munificence; enough of 'the goods of the body' (health and general fitness) for active fortitude and temperance. Moral and intellectual virtue, as we are told in the *Ethics* (Book X, c. VIII, § 4), both need an external equipment. (And yet, as we are also told in the *Ethics* (Book I, c. X, § 12), even in the absence of such equipment 'nobility shines through, when a man calmly bears a flood of heavy troubles'.)

CHAPTER II

Assuming that the best way of life, alike for the state and for the individual, is the life of goodness, we may go on to raise the question whether the life of goodness consists more in external action, or more in internal development. So far as states are concerned, we are presented with a choice between (a) *the life of politics and action, which issues in the assumption of authority over other states, and* (b) *the life of the self-contained state, engaged in developing its own resources and culture. The former ideal is illustrated by Sparta, and by other military and imperialist states; but it raises doubts in the mind when one reflects on the ethics of conquest and the claims of liberty. The conclusion which suggests itself is that while a state should put itself in a position to maintain its own independence, military activity is only a means to the highest good, which is partnership in a good life and the felicity of that life.*

§ 1. It remains to discuss whether the felicity of the state is the same as that of the individual, or different.[1] The answer is clear [if only we look at the verdict of general opinion]: *all* are agreed that they are the same.[2] § 2. The men who believe that the well-being of the individual consists in his wealth, will also believe that the state as a whole is happy when it is wealthy. The men who rank the life of a tyrant higher than any other, will also rank the state which possesses the largest empire as being the happiest state. The man who grades [the felicity of] individuals by their goodness, will also regard the felicity of states as proportionate to their goodness.

§ 3. Two questions arise at this point which both need consideration. The first is, 'Which way of life is the more desirable—to join with other citizens and share in the state's activity, or to live in it like an alien, absolved from the ties of political society?' The second is, 'Which is the best constitution and the best disposition of a state—no matter whether we assume that a share in its activity is desirable for all, or regard it as desirable for the majority only?'[3]

---

[1] This, as we have noted above (note on c. 1, § 12), has already been implied by the course of Aristotle's argument. Here he makes the point explicitly—arguing that, as a matter of fact, all schools of opinion are agreed in identifying the happiness of the state with that of the individual. Different schools have different conceptions of the nature of happiness. Some, like Aristotle himself, make it consist in goodness: some make it consist in wealth: some make it consist in power. Whatever the difference between their conceptions, all are agreed in believing that what is happiness for the individual (be it goodness, or wealth, or power) is also happiness for the state.

[2] In matters of ethics Aristotle appeals to the *consensus mundi* as the final court: 'what all hold, *is*' (*Ethics*, Book X, c. 11, § 4). This is in the same vein as his appeal to facts and experience in the previous chapter of this Book.

[3] See Note BBB, p. 287.

§ 4. This second question—unlike the first, which raises the issue of what is good for the individual—is a matter for political thought and political speculation; and as we are now engaged on a discussion which belongs to that field, we may regard it as falling within the scope of our present inquiry[1]—as the other question can hardly be said to do. § 5. There is one thing clear about the best constitution: it must be a political organization which will enable all sorts of men [e.g. the 'contemplative' as well as the 'practical'] to be at their best and live happily. But if that is clear, there is another point on which opinions diverge. Even those who agree in holding that the good life is most desirable are divided upon the issue, 'Which way of life is the more desirable? The way of politics and action? Or the way of detachment from all external things— the way, let us say, of contemplation, which some regard as the only way that is worthy of a philosopher?' § 6. Here, we may say, are the two ways of life—the political and the philosophic—that are evidently chosen by those who have been most eager to win a reputation for goodness, in our own and in previous ages. It is a matter of no small moment on which of the two sides truth lies: for whether individuals[2] or states are in question, it is always the duty of wisdom to aim at the higher mark. § 7. There are some who dislike the exercise of authority over neighbouring states. They regard it as the height of injustice when the authority is despotic: they still regard it as a hindrance to one's own well-being, if not as an injustice to others, when the authority is constitutional. [This is a view which inclines to the idea of a self-contained state, developing its own inner life.] Others again take an opposite view: they hold that the practical and political life is the only life for a man: they believe that a private life gives no more scope for action, **1324 b** in any of the fields of goodness [courage, temperance, justice, and wisdom] than the life of public affairs and political interests. § 8. Some of the advocates of the practical and political life are willing to stop at this point: others go further, and argue that the despotic and tyrannical form of constitution is the only one which gives felicity; and indeed there are states where the exercise of despotic authority over neighbouring

[1] 'Inquiry' (in the Greek *methodos*) denotes the general theme which forms the subject of a book (or books) of the *Politics*. Here the *methodos* is that of Books VII and VIII.

[2] Aristotle here appears to glide back into the question of the more desirable life for the individual—a question which in § 4 he had dismissed as irrelevant. But he only appears to do so. Actually, he is concerned with the more desirable life for the state, and with the form of political constitution which such a life requires; and it is only incidentally that he mentions the individual. The real question throughout this chapter is whether a *state* should devote itself to internal cultivation or to external aggrandisement.

states is made the standard to which both constitution and laws must conform.[1]

§ 9. It is true that, in most states, most of the laws are only a promiscuous heap of legislation; but we have to confess that where they are directed, in any degree, to a single object, that object is always conquest. In Sparta, for instance, and in Crete the system of education and most of the laws are framed with a general view to war. § 10. Similarly all the uncivilized peoples which are strong enough to conquer others pay the highest honours to military prowess; as witness the Scythians, the Persians, the Thracians, and the Celts. Some of these nations even have laws for the definite encouragement of military qualities: Carthage, for instance, is said to decorate its soldiers with a new armlet for every fresh campaign. § 11. Macedonia, again, had once a law condemning men who had never killed an enemy to wear a halter instead of a belt. It was a custom among the Scythians that a man who had never killed an enemy was not entitled to drink from the loving-cup passed round at a certain festival. The Iberians, who are a warlike people, have a similar custom: they place a circle of pointed stones round the tombs of the dead, one for each enemy they have killed.

§ 12. There are many institutions of this kind, which vary from people to people—some of them sanctioned by laws, and some of them matters of custom. Yet it cannot, perhaps, but appear very strange, to a mind which is ready to reflect, that a statesman should be expected to be able to lay his plans for ruling and dominating border states, without any regard for their feelings. § 13. How can a thing which is not even lawful be proper for a statesman or law-maker? And how can it ever be lawful to rule without regard to the right or wrong of what you are doing? Conquerors may be in the wrong. There is no profession in which we can find a parallel for statesmanship of this type. Doctors and pilots are never expected to use coercion or cajolery in handling their patients or crews. § 14. But when it comes to politics most people appear to believe that mastery is the true statesmanship; and men are not ashamed of behaving to others in ways which they would refuse to

---

[1] Aristotle here distinguishes a moderate and an extreme variety of the general school of opinion which favours the practical and political life. The moderate variety is to the effect that the best form of constitution, which will lead to the happiest life of the community, is one which enlists the citizens in internal political activity. The extreme variety is to the effect that the best form, which will secure most happiness for the community, is one under which the citizens live a life of political activity by ruling despotically over neighbouring states. The first variety involves a belief in an active *internal* political life: the second a belief in an active *external* political life, devoted to conquest and empire.

acknowledge as just, or even expedient, among themselves.[1] For their own affairs, and among themselves, they want an authority based on justice; but when other men are in question, their interest in justice stops. § 15. The world would be a curious place if it did not include some elements meant to be free, as well as some that are meant to be subject to control; and if that is its nature any attempt to establish control should be confined to the elements meant for control, and not extended to all. One does not hunt *men* to furnish a banquet or a festival: one hunts what is meant to be hunted for that purpose; and what is meant to be hunted for that purpose is any wild animal meant to be eaten.[2] **1325 a** § 16. It is possible to imagine a solitary state which is happy in itself and in isolation. Assume such a state, living somewhere or other all by itself, and living under a good system of law. It will obviously have a good constitution; but the scheme of its constitution will have no regard to war, or to the conquest of enemies, who, upon our hypothesis, will not exist.

§ 17. It is clear, then, from the course of the argument, that if military pursuits are one and all to be counted good,[3] they are good in a qualified sense. They are not the chief end of man, transcending all other ends: they are means to his chief end. The true end which good law-givers should keep in view, for any state or stock or society with which they may be concerned, is the enjoyment of partnership in a good life and the felicity thereby attainable. § 18. [This end will be invariable; but] some of the laws enacted will vary according to circumstances.[4] If a state has a number of neighbours, it will be the duty of its legislator to provide the modes of military training suited to their different characters, and, generally, to take the proper measures for meeting the challenge offered by each. But the problem here raised—which is that of the end at which an ideal constitution should aim—may well be reserved for consideration at a later stage.[5]

[1] In other words a *community* will practise, in dealing with other *communities*, methods which it would repudiate in its own internal life. Aristotle is thinking, throughout this passage, of communities rather than individuals. It may be added that in repudiating (as he does by implication) the idea that 'mastery' is 'statesmanship', he is returning to an idea enunciated at the very beginning of the *Politics*, where he argues that 'it is a mistake to believe that the statesman is the same as . . . the master of a number of slaves' (Book I, c. 1, § 2).

[2] All this involves a teleological view of creation, according to which each creature has a *telos* or end which it is 'meant' to serve, and the ends of all other creatures are subordinate to that of man.

[3] Because they elicit the virtue of fortitude in the community at large.

[4] The circumstances are, in a word, frontier problems. Where these are in any way pressing, they will affect internal politics and legislation; and each different problem will produce a different effect.

[5] It is considered in c. XIII and c. XIV.

NOTE BBB (p. 283): *The course of the argument in* c. II

The transition made at the beginning of this section needs some slight explanation. In the first two sections the happiness of the individual has been identified with that of the state. This might seem, *prima facie*, to immerse the individual in the state. Aristotle therefore proceeds to inquire whether he will actually be happier if he immerses himself in the state's affairs, or if he leads the quiet life of the recluse. But this raises in turn the question, 'What is the sort of state in which the individual has the chance of immersing himself, and what is its constitution and general disposition?' Obviously the answer to this latter question will tend to affect the answer given to the former. A state which has such a constitution, and has so disposed its life, that it can give its members a chance of the highest possible activities, will obviously tend to draw them away from the quiet life into the life of politics.

CHAPTER III

From discussing the relative claims of external action and internal development in their bearing on states, we may now turn to discuss them in their bearing on the individual. Is it better for him to follow the way of political action, with his life wrapped up in that of the state, or to follow the more solitary way of thought and contemplation? It may be argued that the activity of political management of equals, in a free society, is something higher and finer than the activity of managing slaves; and it may also be argued that true felicity, by its nature, connotes activity. On the other hand the permanent management of others, whatever its basis may be, is not a desirable object; and even if felicity means activity, thought is an activity as much as action itself, and it may even be more of an activity than action is. The self-contained individual—like the self-contained state—may be busily active: the activity of God and the universe is that of a self-contained life.

§ 1. We must now consider the views of those who are agreed in accepting the general principle that a life of goodness is most desirable, but divided in their opinion about the right way of living that life.[1] Two different schools of opinion have thus to be discussed. One is the school which eschews political office, distinguishing the life of the individual freeman from that of the politician, and preferring it to all others. The other is the school which regards the life of the politician as best; they argue that men who do nothing cannot be said to 'do well',[2] and they identify felicity with active 'well-doing'. Both of these schools are right

[1] Aristotle here appears to return to the first of the two questions propounded in c. II, § 3—the question whether the practical and political, or the contemplative and private life, is the more desirable. He had dismissed that question in c. II, § 4, as hardly 'political'. But it does, after all, raise political issues; and it is accordingly raised again in this chapter.
[2] See the note on c. I, § 11.

on some points and wrong on others. § 2. The first school is right
in holding that the life of a free individual is better than that of the
master of any number of slaves. There is nothing very dignified in
managing slaves, when they are acting in that capacity; and the giving of orders about menial duties is an act of no high quality. On
the other hand it is wrong to regard every form of authority as so
much 'mastery'. Authority over freemen differs as much from
authority over slaves as the man who is naturally a freeman does
from the natural slave. But enough has already been said on that
theme in the first book. § 3. It is another error of this first school
that it praises inaction in preference to action. Felicity is a state
of activity; and it is the actions of just and temperate men which
are the fulfilment of a great part of goodness.

The conclusion to which we have just come [i.e. that felicity
is a state of activity] may possibly be interpreted to mean that
sovereign power is the highest of all goods, because it is also the
power of practising the greatest number of the highest and best
activities. § 4. It would follow on this that a man who is able to
wield authority should never surrender it to his neighbour: on the
contrary, he should wrest it from him. A father should pay no
regard to his children, children none to their father, and friends
of any kind none to their friends: no man should think of another
when it comes to this cardinal point: all should act on the principle,
'The best is the most desirable: and to "*do* well" is the best'.
There might be truth in such a view if it were really the case that
those who practised plunder and **1325 b** violence *did* attain a
supremely desirable object. § 5. But it is perhaps impossible that
they should; and to assume that they do is really to make a false
assumption. Actions cannot be good and outstanding unless the
doer himself has a degree of pre-eminence over others as great as
a husband has over his wife, or a parent over his children, or a
master over his slaves.[1] It follows that the transgressor [who sinks
below others by what he does, instead of rising above them] can
never achieve any subsequent gain which will equal the loss of goodness already involved in his transgression. [We may thus dismiss
the idea that the permanent exercise of sovereign power is the
highest of all goods.] In a society of peers it is right and just that
office should go on the principle of rotation, which is demanded
by the ideas of equality and parity. § 6. But that equals should be
given unequal shares, and men on a footing of parity treated on a
basis of disparity, is a thing which is contrary to nature; and nothing
contrary to nature is right. We thus come to the conclusion that

---

[1] i.e. a degree of pre-eminence as great as the head of a family has over its
three constituent parts.

the one conjuncture in which it is right to follow, and just to obey, another is when a person emerges who is superior to others in goodness and (we may add) in capacity for actually *doing* the best. § 7. Goodness by itself is not enough: there must also be a capacity for being active in doing good.[1]

If we are right in our view, and felicity should be held to consist in 'well-*doing*', it follows that the life of action is best, alike for every state as a whole and for each individual in his own conduct.   § 8. But the life of action need not be, as is sometimes thought, a life which involves relations to others. Nor should our thoughts be held to be active only when they are directed to objects which have to be achieved by action. Thoughts with no object beyond themselves, and speculations and trains of reflection followed purely for their own sake, are far more deserving of the name of active. 'Well-doing' is the end we seek: action of some sort or other is therefore our end and aim; but, even in the sphere of outward acts, action can also be predicated—and that in the fullest measure and the true sense of the word—of those who, by their thoughts, are the prime authors of such acts. § 9. [As thought in itself may be activity, so activity may exist without relation to others.][2] States situated by themselves, and resolved to live in isolation, need not be therefore inactive.[3] They can achieve activity by sections: the different sections of such a state will have many mutual connexions; [and the whole will thus be active, in its own internal life]. § 10. This is also, and equally, true of the individual human being. If it were not so, there would be something wrong with God himself and the whole of the universe, who have no activities other than those of their own internal life.

It is therefore clear that the same way of life which is best for the individual must also be best for the state as a whole and for all its members.

B

THE POPULATION, THE TERRITORY, THE NATURAL ENDOW-
MENT OF THE INHABITANTS, THE SOCIAL STRUCTURE, AND
THE PHYSICAL PLANNING OF THE CENTRAL CITY, IN AN IDEAL
STATE (cc. IV–XII)

CHAPTER IV

1. *The* population, *in size and quantity, must be neither too large nor too small for the discharge of its civic function. The size of the popula-*

---

[1] See above, c. I, § 13, and note.
[2] Aristotle here reverts to the first of the two propositions stated at the beginning of § 8.
[3] Aristotle has already argued, in c. II, § 16, that such a state may enjoy happiness. He now adds—logically enough on his own conception of happiness—that it may also enjoy activity.

tion is therefore determined and limited by the nature of the civic function; and a great population is not an index of civic greatness. A very populous state will find it difficult to enforce law and order, but a thinly populated state will find it difficult to achieve self-sufficiency. A state, like a ship, must be neither too large nor too small for the business it has to do. In order to do civic business properly, the citizens of a state should know one another personally; and we may thus define the optimum number of the population as 'the greatest surveyable *number required for achieving a life of self-sufficiency'.*

§ 1. In the light of this general preface, and bearing in mind our previous discussion of other ideal states [in Book II], we may now embark on the rest of our theme. The first question which arises is, 'What are the necessary bases for the construction of an ideal state?' § 2. An ideal constitution is bound to require an equipment appropriate to its nature.[1] We must therefore assume, as its basis, a number of ideal conditions, which must be capable of fulfilment as well as being ideal. These conditions include, among others, a citizen body and a territory. § 3. All producers—weavers, for instance, **1326 a** or shipwrights—must have the materials proper to their particular branch of production; and the better prepared these materials are, the better will be the products of their skill. Like other producers, the statesman and the law-maker must have their proper materials, and they must have them in a condition which is suited to their needs. § 4. The primary factor necessary, in the equipment of a state, is the human material; and this involves us in considering the quality, as well as the quantity, of the population naturally required. The second factor is territory; and here too we have to consider quality as well as quantity. Most men think that the happiness of a state depends on its being great. They may be right; but even if they are, they do not know what it is that makes a state great or small. § 5. They judge greatness in numerical terms, by the size of the population; but it is capacity, rather than size, which should properly be the criterion. States, like other things, have a function to perform; and the state which shows the highest capacity for performing the function of a state is therefore the one which should be counted greatest. In the same way Hippocrates would naturally be described as 'greater' (not as a man, but as a doctor) than somebody who was superior in point of bodily size. § 6. But even if it were

---

[1] Any good way of life (and *a fortiori* the best way of life, which is the way of life under an ideal constitution) requires an equipment or *chorēgia*, or in other words a material basis of social conditions (cf. c. 1, § 13, and note). This being the case, an ideal state living under an ideal constitution requires an ideal social basis. In other words, it must be the best possible *under the best possible conditions* (cf. c. 1, § 1, and note).

right to judge a state by the size of its population, it would still be wrong to judge in the light of some mere chance total. We have to remember that states will very likely contain a large number of slaves, resident aliens, and foreigners. If we judge a state by the standard of its population, we ought to limit the population to those who are members of the state and essential elements in its composition. An outstanding number of these may be evidence of a great state; but a state which sends into the field a large force of mere mechanics, and can only raise a handful of heavy-armed infantry, cannot possibly be great. A great state is not the same as a populous state.

§ 7. There is a further consideration. Experience shows that it is difficult, if not indeed impossible, for a very populous state to secure a general habit of obedience to law. Observation tells us that none of the states which have a reputation for being well governed are without some limit of population. But the point can also be established on the strength of philosophical grounds. § 8. Law is a system of order; and a general habit of obedience to law must therefore involve a general system of orderliness. Order, however, is the one thing which is impossible for an excessive number. The creation of order for an infinite number is a task for the divine power which holds together [and reduces to order] the whole of this universe, where beauty [which goes with order] is usually found attending on number and magnitude. § 9. We may therefore conclude that the state with the greatest beauty will be one which combines magnitude with the standard of order suggested above.[1] But we may also note [apart from this general rule] that states, like all other things (animals, plants, and inanimate instruments), have a definite measure of size. § 10. Any object will lose its power of performing its function if it is either excessively small or of an excessive size. Sometimes it will wholly forfeit its nature; sometimes, short of that, it will merely be defective. We may take the example of a ship. A ship which is only 6 inches in length, or is as much as 1,200 feet long, will not be a ship at all;[2] and even a ship of more moderate size **1326 b** may still cause difficulties of navigation, either because it is not large enough or because it is unwieldily large. § 11. The

---

[1] In simple terms, it is the argument of Aristotle that divine power can order great numbers and large magnitudes, and that beauty may be found in such numbers and magnitudes when they are so ordered. But man is man; he cannot order such numbers and magnitudes: the best he can do, and the furthest he can go in following the example of the divine power, is to go *as far* in number and magnitude as is compatible with *his* power of ordering.

[2] To-day a ship may be nearly 1,000 ft. in length. The same idea which is expressed here recurs in the *Ethics*, Book IX, c. x, § 3: 'a state cannot be made out of ten citizens, and one which is made out of ten times ten thousand is no longer a state'.

same is true of states. A state composed of too few members is a
state without self-sufficiency (and the state, by its definition, is a
self-sufficient society).[1] A state composed of too many will indeed
be self-sufficient in the matter of material necessities (as an uncivilized people may equally be); but it will not be a true state, for
the simple reason that it can hardly have a true constitution.[2] Who
can be the general of a mass so excessively large? And who can
give it orders, unless he has Stentor's voice?

The initial stage of the state may therefore be said to require
such an initial amount of population as will be self-sufficient for
the purpose of achieving a good way of life in the shape and form
of a political association. § 12. A state which exceeds this initial
amount may be a still greater state; but such increase of size, as
has already been noticed, cannot continue indefinitely. What the
limit of increase should be is a question easily answered if we look
at the actual facts. The activities of a state are partly the activities
of its governors, and partly those of the governed. The function of
governors is to issue commands and give decisions: [the function
of the governed is to elect the governors]. § 13. Both in order to
give decisions in matters of disputed rights, and to distribute the
offices of government according to the merit of candidates, the
citizens of a state must know one another's characters.[3] Where
this is not the case, the distribution of offices and the giving of
decisions will suffer. Both are matters in which it is wrong to act
on the spur of the moment; but that is what obviously happens
where the population is overlarge. § 14. Another thing also
happens under these conditions. Foreigners and resident aliens
readily assume a share in the exercise of political rights: it is easy
for them to go undetected among the crowd.

These considerations indicate clearly the optimum standard of
population. It is, in a word, 'the greatest surveyable number
required for achieving a life of self-sufficiency'.[4] Here we may end
our discussion of the proper size of the population.

[1] Book I, c. II, § 8.

[2] It follows that a state must have two attributes in order to be a state—the
attribute of self-sufficiency, and the attribute of a 'way of life' expressed in a
constitution.

[3] It throws a light on Greek jurisprudence that Aristotle should suggest that
judges must know litigants personally in order to judge properly. Greek law-
courts had hardly achieved the stage of impersonal justice. It also throws a light on
Greek politics that he should suggest that electors should know the candidates
personally. The Greek candidate for office did not stand as the representative
of an impersonal programme, but on his own personal merits.

[4] The formula contains two factors. First, the population must be large
enough to provide for itself, and from its own resources, every material and spiritual
requisite of a complete and rounded good life. Secondly, it must not be so large
but that it can be readily surveyed, in the sense that all its members can 'know
one another's characters'.

CHAPTER V

2. *The* territory *should also be of a moderate size—no more, and no less, than will enable the citizens to live a life of leisure which combines temperance and liberality. Like the population, it should be 'surveyable'. This will enable the defence of the state to be properly planned, and will ensure the proper relation of the central city to the surrounding country for economic as well as for military purposes.*

§ 1. Similar considerations apply also to the matter of territory. So far as the *character* of the soil is concerned, everybody would obviously give the preference to a territory which ensured the maximum of self-sufficiency; and as that consists in having everything, and needing nothing, such a territory must be one which produces all kinds of crops. In point of *extent* and size, the territory should be large enough to enable its inhabitants to live a life of leisure which combines liberality with temperance. § 2. Whether this standard is right or wrong is a question we shall have to examine more closely at a later stage of the argument, when we come to consider the general problem of property and the possession of means, and to examine the relation which ought to exist between possession and use.[1] This is a much disputed matter; and men tend to conduct their lives in a way that runs to one or other of two extremes—miserliness or extravagance. § 3. As for the general lie of the land, it is easy to make the suggestion (though here a number of questions arise on which the advice of military experts ought to be taken) that the territory of a state should be difficult of access to enemies, and easy of egress for its **1327 a** inhabitants. What was said above of the population—that it should be such as to be surveyable—is equally true of the territory. A territory which can be easily surveyed is also a territory which can be easily defended. The ideal position for the central city should be determined by considerations of its being easy of access both by land and by sea. § 4. [Two matters are here involved.] The first, which has already been mentioned, is that the city should be a common military centre for the dispatch of aid to all points in the territory. The second is that it should also be a convenient commercial centre, where the transport of food supplies, timber for building, and raw materials for any other similar industry which the territory may possess, can easily be handled.

---

[1] This is a promise which is not fulfilled. But the subject has already been treated, first in Book I, and then in Book II, where the formula of 'private possession, common use' has been suggested.

CHAPTER VI

It is a question much debated whether the territory of a state should have a close connexion with the sea. Some argue that maritime connexions mean the introduction of a crowd of undesirable aliens; but on the other hand there are reasons, both of military security and of economic supply, which make such connexions valuable. A state should not be a mart for the world, but it ought to secure its own market; and a certain amount of naval power is also desirable—though the oarsmen required as the basis of such power should not be citizens, but serfs and labourers.

§ 1. It is a hotly debated question whether connexion with the sea is to the advantage, or the detriment, of a well-ordered state. There are some who maintain that the introduction of strangers, who have been born and bred under other laws, and the consequent increase of population, is prejudicial to good order. They argue that such an increase is inevitable when numbers of merchants use the sea for the export and import of commodities; and they regard it as inimical to good government. § 2. On the other hand, and if only this increase can be avoided, there can be no doubt that it is better, in the interest both of security and of a good supply of material necessities, for the city and territory of a state to be connected with the sea. § 3. In order to enjoy security, and to meet enemy attacks more easily, a state should be capable of being defended by sea as well as by land. It will also be in a better position for taking the offensive, and inflicting losses on its assailants, if it is able to use both elements, and to act on one or the other if not on both simultaneously. § 4. Similarly, in order to procure supplies, it is imperative that a state should be able to import commodities which it does not itself produce, and to export, in return, the surplus of its own products. It should act as a merchant for itself—but not as a merchant for others. States which make themselves marts for the world only do it for the sake of revenue; and if a state ought not to indulge in this sort of profit-making, it follows that it ought not to be an exchange centre of that kind. § 5. We see from the practice of our own times that territories and cities often have ports and harbours which are conveniently placed in relation to the main city—distinct and separate, but not too remote, and thus in a position to be commanded by connecting walls and other and similar fortifications.[1] Any advantage which can

---

[1] The obvious example is Athens. Here the port—the Peiraeus—lay at a distance of about 5 miles from the main city, but was connected with it by the 'Long Walls' which enabled the city to command the port. Athens could thus enjoy the advantages of connexion with the sea, without being greatly affected by the bustling life of the port and its foreign elements: the port was kept at a distance, and yet kept under control.

be derived from connexion with ports and harbours will obviously be secured by these methods; any disadvantage which may threaten can easily be met by legislation which states and defines the persons who may, or may not, have dealings with one another.

§ 6. A certain amount of naval power is obviously a great advantage. This is more than a matter of self-defence. There will also be neighbouring **1327 b** powers which a state must be in a position to intimidate, or to assist, by sea as well as by land. § 7. The actual size and amount of such power depends upon, and must be determined by, the way of life which a state prefers to pursue. If that way is to be one of leadership, and of active relations with other states, naval power must be commensurate with the activities which are involved. The increase of the population by a mass of naval oarsmen is a consequence which need not follow: such men should not be an integral part of the citizen body.[1] § 8. The marines [as distinct from the oarsmen] belong to the class of full freemen: they count as part of the infantry, and are in control and command on shipboard. But [the oarsmen are a different matter, and] if there are masses of serfs and farm-labourers ready to hand, it should always be possible to draw an abundant supply from this source. We may observe that this policy is actually followed, at the present day, in a number of states. It is followed, for instance, at Heraclea [on the Black Sea], which fits out a considerable number of triremes with a citizen body smaller in size than those of other states.

This may suffice by way of conclusions about territory, harbours, towns, the sea, and naval power.

Chapter VII

3. *The* natural endowment *proper to the citizens of an ideal state is suggested by a comparison of three peoples—the people of the colder regions of Europe; the people of Asia; and the Greek people. The first has high spirit, but less skill and intelligence: the second has skill and intelligence, but little spirit: the Greeks combine both sets of qualities. The legislator for an ideal state will naturally prefer the mixed en-*

---

[1] Two observations may be made on this section. First, Aristotle assumes—naturally enough, in the light of previous Greek history—that leadership, or 'hegemony', involves a fleet. Secondly, as Greek fleets were composed of triremes or large galleys propelled by three banks of oars, he assumes that a fleet will involve what he calls 'a mob of oarsmen', who, if they are admitted to citizenship, may swamp the civic body (cf. Book IV, c. IV, § 21 and Book V, c. IV, § 8). He would accordingly disfranchise naval oarsmen, and treat them not as an integral part of the state, but as a mere condition or *sine qua non* of its existence. What he has in mind is the experience of Athens, where 'the mob of oarsmen' had led, in his view, to the growth of extreme democracy. See Appendix IV. p. 378.

dowment; and he will not, as Plato does, attach too great an importance
to the factor of high spirit—valuable as that factor is in its sphere.

§ 1. We have already discussed the proper standard for determining the quantity of the population of a state [c. IV, § 6]. We
have now to consider its quality, and to inquire what sort of natural
endowment its members ought to have. We may get some idea
of what this endowment should be if we take a general view, which
not only embraces the Greek states of standing and reputation, but
also includes the non-Greek peoples in their distribution throughout the whole of the habitable world. § 2. The peoples of cold
countries generally, and particularly those of Europe, are full of
spirit, but deficient in skill and intelligence; and this is why they
continue to remain comparatively free, but attain no political
development and show no capacity for governing others.[1] The
peoples of Asia are endowed with skill and intelligence, but are
deficient in spirit; and this is why they continue to be peoples of
subjects and slaves. § 3. The Greek stock, intermediate in geographical position, unites the qualities of both sets of peoples. It
possesses both spirit and intelligence: the one quality makes it
continue free; the other enables it to attain the highest political
development, and to show a capacity for governing every other
people—if only it could once achieve political unity.[2] § 4. The
same sort of difference as that between Greek and non-Greek
peoples may also be traced among Greek peoples themselves.
Some of them are of a one-sided nature: others show a happy
mixture of spirit and intelligence.

The argument shows that the sort of people which a legislator
can easily guide into the way of goodness is one with a natural
endowment that combines intelligence and spirit. § 5. The attitude which some[3] require in their guardians—to be friendly disposed to all whom they know, and stern to all who are unknown—
is the attitude of a high-spirited temper. Spirit is the faculty

[1] Aristotle's idea of the 'spirit' of the peoples of the colder countries of
Europe may be illustrated from what he says of the Celts in the *Ethics* (III. VII,
§ 7), who 'fear nothing whatever, neither earthquakes nor the waves of the sea'.
[2] Newman remarks that political unity may either mean unity under a
hegemony, such as Macedonia had recently assumed, or unity in a free federation
freely entered into by free states. 'The latter kind of union', he adds, 'would be
more truly a union' of the Greek stock, such as Aristotle has in view (vol. iii,
p. 366). But the reference here would naturally seem to be a reference to the
Macedonian policy, inaugurated by Philip of Macedon at the Congress of
Corinth in 338 B.C., of combining the Greek states in a political and military
alliance. This was the policy continued by Alexander and by Antipater.
[3] Aristotle is here alluding to Plato's division of the soul into the three
faculties of reason, 'spirit' (*thȳmos*), and desire. The 'spirited' man is the man
who is highly sensitive to the claims of honour and keenly alive to the obligations
of friendship.

1328 a of our souls which issues in love and friendship; and it is a proof of this that when we think ourselves slighted our spirit is stirred more deeply against acquaintances and friends than ever it is against strangers. § 6. This explains why Archilochus, when he is complaining of his friends, is naturally led to address his spirit, and to say to it

Verily thou wert wounded in the house of thine own friends.

This faculty of our souls not only issues in love and friendship: it is also the source for us all of any power of commanding and any feeling for freedom. Spirit is a commanding and an unconquerable thing. § 7. But it is wrong to say [as Plato does] that men ought to be harsh to those who are unknown to them. They ought not to be harsh to anybody; and magnanimous men, as a matter of fact, are not of a stern disposition—except when they have to deal with wrongdoers. Even then they are likely to show still greater sternness, as we have just had reason to notice, if the persons by whom they think themselves wronged are their own acquaintances. § 8. This is only what might be expected. We feel, in such a case, that men whom we regard as under an obligation to repay us for our services are adding insult to injury, and ingratitude to wrongdoing.

Stern is the strife between brethren,

as one of our poets says; and as another also says,

Those who have loved exceedingly can hate
As much as they have loved.[1]

§ 9. Such, in general terms (for the degree of precision required in a philosophical argument is not as great as is needed in dealing with the data of sense-perception) are the conclusions which we have reached about the bases necessary for an ideal state—i.e. (1) the right size of the citizen-body, and the proper character of its natural endowment; and (2) the right size of the territory, and the proper character of its soil.

CHAPTER VIII

4. *In considering the* social structure *required in an ideal state, we must begin by making a distinction between 'integral parts' and 'necessary conditions'. The integral parts of a state are the full citizens who share actively in the full good life of the state: the necessary conditions are the ancillary members who make it possible for the*

---

[1] The first of these passages is ascribed by Plutarch to Euripides. The author of the other is unknown.

*full citizens to share in that life. Including together both 'parts' and
'conditions', we may enumerate six services which must be supplied by
the social structure of the state—the service of agriculture; the service
of arts and crafts; the service of defence; the service of land-ownership;
the service of public worship; and the service of political deliberation
and civil jurisdiction.*

§ 1. In the state, as in other natural compounds, [there is a
distinction to be drawn between 'conditions' and 'parts':] the
conditions which are necessary for the existence of the whole are
not organic parts of the whole system which they serve. The
conclusion which clearly follows is that we cannot regard the
elements which are necessary for the existence of the state, or of
any other association forming a single whole, as being 'parts' of
the state or of any such association.[1]

§ 2. [We have spoken of associations forming a single whole.]
This means that there must be some one thing which is common
to all the members, and identical for them all. Their shares in the
thing may be equal or unequal. The thing itself may be various—
food, for instance, or a stretch of territory, or anything else of the
kind. [But there must be some one thing which is common and
identical.] § 3. Now there is nothing joint or common to the
means which serve an end and the end which is served by those
means—except that the means produce and the end takes over the
product. Take, for example, the relation in which building tools,
and the workmen who use them, stand to the result produced by
their action. There is nothing in common between the builder
and the dwelling-house he builds: the builder's skill is simply a
means, and the dwelling-house is the end.[2] § 4. On this it follows
that, if states need property, [as a dwelling-house needs building
tools and workmen to use them], property nevertheless is not a
part of the state. It is true that property includes a number of
animate beings [i.e. slaves], as well as inanimate objects. But [two
other things are also true:] the state is an association of equals, and
only of equals; and its object is the best and highest life possible,

---

[1] In this passage Aristotle uses a number of technical terms and conceptions.
First, he uses the term 'whole' (*holon*), and 'compound' (*syntheton*), on which see
Book III, c. 1, § 2 and note. Secondly, he uses the distinction between the
integral part sharing actively in the life of the whole (the *meros* or *morion*), and
the necessary 'condition', or rather conditions (the *hōn ouk aneu*), without which
that life is impossible, but which none the less stand outside it and do not themselves participate in it (see c. VI above, § 7 and note).

[2] Aristotle's argument may well be criticized by a generation far later in time.
To-day we should hardly lump together the builder and his tools as 'means'.
We should be more apt to consider the house as a means and the builder as an
end in himself, in virtue of being a man. There is logic in Aristotle's argument;
but its moral implications may be challenged.

[in which the slave cannot share].   § 5. The highest good is felicity; and that consists in the energy and perfect practice of goodness. But in actual life this is not for all; some may share in it fully, but others can only share in it partially or cannot even share at all. The consequence is obvious. These different capacities will issue in different kinds and varieties of states, and in a number of different constitutions.   **1328 b** Pursuing felicity in various ways and by various means, different peoples create for themselves different ways of life and different constitutions.[1]

§ 6. It remains for us now to enumerate *all* the elements necessary for the existence of the state. Our list of these elements will include what we have called the 'parts' of the state as well as what we have termed its 'conditions'. To make such a list we must first determine how many services a state performs; and then we shall easily see how many elements it must contain.   § 7. The first thing to be provided is food. The next is arts and crafts; for life is a business which needs many tools. The third is arms: the members of a state must bear arms in person, partly in order to maintain authority and repress disobedience, and partly in order to meet any threat of external aggression. The fourth thing which has to be provided is a certain supply of property, alike for domestic use and for military purposes. The fifth (but, in order of merit, the first) is an establishment for the service of the gods, or, as it is called, public worship. The sixth thing, and the most vitally necessary, is a method of deciding what is demanded by the public interest and what is just in men's private dealings [i.e. some system of deliberation and jurisdiction].   § 8. These are the services which every state may be said to need. A state is not a mere casual group. It is a group which, as we have said, must be self-sufficient for the purposes of life; and if any of these services is missing it cannot be totally self-sufficient.   § 9. A state should accordingly be so constituted as to be competent for all these services. It must therefore contain a body of farmers to produce the necessary food; craftsmen; a military force; a propertied class; priests; and a body for deciding necessary issues and determining what is the public interest.[2]

---

[1] See Note CCC, p. 300.

[2] This account of functions, and of corresponding classes, may be compared with the account given before in Book IV, c. IV. The two accounts are different: they come in different contexts—the one in connexion with democracy, the other in connexion with the ideal state; and though they can be compared, they can hardly be co-ordinated. It adds to our difficulties that Aristotle also gives another account of the functions and classes of the state in Book IV, c. III, and that this account, as already noted (see the note to the first section of that chapter), does not square with the account which immediately follows in c. IV.

This section is puzzling, because the consequence drawn, at the end, from the premiss stated in the beginning, is not the conclusion we should expect. The conclusion we should expect, from the premiss that all men cannot share in happiness, is that all men cannot share in, or be 'parts' of, the best and happiest state. (This would explain the exclusion of slaves and others who are merely means.) The conclusion actually drawn is different. Arguing that different men share differently in happiness or felicity, Aristotle concludes that different peoples must develop different ways of life, and must therefore (as a constitution is 'a way of life') have different constitutions.

It would seem to follow from this conclusion that there may, after all, be states in which men who are merely means are none the less 'parts' of the state. But as the whole argument of Book VII is concerned only with the ideal state, this admission—if it is made or implied—would hardly seem to be necessary.

CHAPTER IX

The question arises whether each of the necessary services should be discharged by a separate social class, or whether some of them may be combined—and, if so, which. We may answer that (1) the first two services—agriculture, and the arts and crafts—cannot be rendered by the full citizens, because their life needs leisure, and (2) three of the other services—defence, public worship, and the service of deliberation and jurisdiction—should, from one point of view, be combined in the hands of the same body of persons, but, from another, be discharged by different bodies of persons. This last result can be achieved if (a) all full citizens are concerned with all these three services at some time or other of their lives, but (b) the younger citizens are set to render the service of defence, the middle-aged to render the service of deliberation and jurisdiction, and the aged to render the service of public worship. The effect will be that each citizen will be concerned with each of these three services, but will be concerned with each at a different period of his life. The remaining service—that of land-ownership—should be assigned to the whole body of full citizens (which is the contrary of Plato's view in the Republic, *where the full citizens are debarred from the ownership of land).*

§ 1. These points determined, a further point is still left for consideration. Should all the members share in the performance of all these services? (That is a possibility: the same persons may all be engaged simultaneously in farming, the practice of arts and crafts, and the work of deliberation and jurisdiction.) Or should we assume a separate body of persons for each of the different services? Or, again, should some of the services be assigned to different sets of persons, and others be shared by all? The same system need not be followed in every constitution. § 2. Different systems, as we have noted,¹ are possible: all may share in all functions, or different persons may undertake different functions. The existence of these alternatives explains why constitutions differ: in democracies all men share in all functions, while the opposite practice is followed in oligarchies. § 3. Here we are only concerned with the best or ideal constitution. Now the best constitution is that under which the state can attain the greatest felicity (c. II, § 5); and that, as we have already stated (c. I, §§ 11–12), cannot exist without goodness. Upon these principles it clearly follows² that a state with an ideal constitution—a state which has for its members men who are absolutely just, and not men who are merely just in relation to some particular standard³—cannot have its citizens living the life of mechanics or shopkeepers, which is ignoble and inimical to goodness. § 4. Nor can it have them **1329 a** engaged in farming: leisure is a necessity, both for growth in goodness and for the pursuit of political activities.⁴

On the other hand a military force, and a body to deliberate on matters of public interest and to give decisions in matters of justice, are both essential, and are evidently 'parts' of the state in a particular and special sense. Should they be kept separate? or should both functions be given to one and the same set of persons? § 5. The obvious answer is that in one sense, and from one point of view, they should be given to the same set of persons, but in another sense, and from another point of view, they ought to be kept separate. On the one hand either function requires a different prime of life: deliberation needs the wisdom of maturity, and war the vigour of youth; and from this point of view they ought to go to different bodies of persons.⁵ On the other hand, men who have vigour enough to use force (or to prevent it from being used)

¹ Aristotle may be referring here, as Newman suggests, to what he has just said in the previous section of this chapter. But he may be also referring back to Book IV, c. IV, § 18, where the same point is made.

² i.e. if goodness is necessary to felicity, and felicity is necessary to the best (or ideal) constitution, then it follows that the persons who can share in such a constitution must be good—and good with that active goodness (of fortitude, temperance, justice, and wisdom) which is denied to mechanics and farmers.

³ i.e. the particular standard of an oligarchy, or a democracy, which has its own—and lower—conception of justice.

⁴ 'The wisdom of the scribe cometh by opportunity of leisure; and he that hath little business shall become wise. How then shall he become wise that holdeth the plough . . . whose discourse is of the stock of bulls?' Ecclesiasticus xxxviii. 24–5. The 'scribe' of Ecclesiasticus is the guardian and interpreter of the law of the Jewish community. The book, written about 200 B.C., 'exhibits unmistakably some of the permanent effects of Greek influence' (G. H. Box, *Judaism in the Greek Period*, p. 162).

⁵ There is a passage in the *Rhetoric* (Book II, cc. XII–XIV) which throws light on the views expressed by Aristotle here about the three ages of man and their different characteristics. In that passage Aristotle successively examines the characteristics of growth (c. XII), those of old age (c. XIII), and those of middle

cannot possibly be expected to remain in permanent subjection; and from this point of view the two functions should go to the same set of persons [the members of the military force thus joining in deliberation]. We have to reflect that control of military power is also control of the future destiny of a constitution. § 6. The only course thus left to us is to vest these constitutional powers [i.e. the military and the deliberative] in one set of the persons—that is, in *both* age-groups—but to do so successively, and not simultaneously. The order of nature gives vigour to youth and wisdom to years; and it is policy to follow that order in distributing powers among the two age-groups of the state. It is justice as well as policy; for distribution on such a basis is the award of rights in proportion to desert.[1]

§ 7. The persons who exercise these powers must also be the owners of property; [and they will thus form the propertied class].[2] ... The *citizens* of our state must have a supply of property [in order to have leisure for goodness and political activities]; and it is these persons who are citizens—they, and they only. The class of mechanics has no share in the state; nor has any other class which is not a 'producer' of goodness.[3] ... This conclusion clearly follows from the principle of the ideal state. That principle requires that felicity, or happiness, should go hand in hand with goodness. Now happiness can only be ascribed to a state if we extend our view to embrace the whole body of its citizens, and do not confine ourselves to a single one of its elements.[4] § 8. A further argument is provided for the view that property ought to belong to citizens,

age (c. XIV). Regarding middle age as the mean, and following his general view that the mean is the best, he says of the middle-aged (1) that they possess the merits both of youth and old age, and (2) that they reduce the defects both of youth and old age (e.g. the temerity of the one and the caution of the other) to moderate and proper proportions. He places the physical prime at the age of 30 to 35, and the mental at about the age of 49.

[1] The simple gist is that the same persons who have been soldiers in youth should be councillors and judges in age (say after the age of 50). This is policy, because it will give the state a more efficient (because younger) army, and a more efficient (because older) government; it is also justice of the true order, which means the proportion of rights to desert—because it gives to each age-group exactly the rights it deserves.

[2] Aristotle has dealt with two of the six factors of the state—farming, and the arts and crafts—at the beginning of the chapter, and has decided that they are *not* the concern of the citizens of the ideal state. He has dealt with two others—arms, and government—in §§ 4–6, and has decided that they *are* the concern of the citizens. He now turns to the fifth factor ('a supply of property'), and decides that it too is a concern of the citizens—of *all* of them, but only of them.

[3] To understand this passage, we must remember that Plato in the *Republic* had deprived his guardians of property, and had vested property in the farming class. Aristotle would reverse this: he would vest property in the class which corresponds to Plato's guardians (the class concerned with arms and government); and he would make the farming class consist of landless and propertyless labourers.

[4] The argument here used in regard to happiness is also a reference to, and a criticism of, Plato (*Republic*, 419–21): see Book II, c. v, § 27 of the *Politics*,

if we consider that the farming population ought by rights to be one of slaves or barbarian serfs.

Of the six elements or classes which we enumerated, only the priesthood is left. § 9. The plan on which it ought to be based is clear. Nobody belonging to the farming or the mechanic class should be made a priest. The cult of the gods should be a matter for citizens. Citizens, on the plan just proposed, are divided into two groups—the military or junior, and the deliberative or senior. It is the older members of the senior group—men who are already weary with years—who ought to conduct the worship of the gods and to find rest in their service; and they are therefore the class to which the priestly offices should be assigned. § 10. This completes our survey of the 'conditions' necessary to constitute a state, and of its integral 'parts'. Farmers, craftsmen, and the general body of day-labourers, belong to the first of these categories: the second includes the military force and the deliberative and judicial body. Each of these is a separate element—the separation being for life in some cases, and for a period of life in others, with one element succeeding to another at the end of that period.[1]

CHAPTER X

A system of classes, we may note in passing, appeared at an early date in Egypt and Crete. The system of common tables (suggested later in Chapter XII) may also be found in ancient Crete; and it appeared even earlier in south Italy. This leads us to note that institutions generally have been invented again and again, in the course of time, in a number of different places. Returning to the subject of land-ownership, we have to consider the problem of the distribution of such ownership. The land should not be entirely owned in common—though some of it may be, in order to provide for a system of common tables and for the needs of public worship. On this basis we may suggest (1) that some of the land should be publicly owned, for the purpose of such provision, but (2) that the rest should be privately owned, and each owner should have two plots—one near the central city, and one on the frontier. The cultivation of all the land should be assigned to slaves or serfs.

§ 1. It does not appear to be a new or even a recent discovery in

where Aristotle argues that Plato has deprived the governors (i.e. the citizens proper) of happiness in depriving them of property. Generally Plato, in Aristotle's view, had gone the wrong way to work in the matter of making his state happy. He had confined himself to the one element of the farming class, to which alone he had given property and the happiness it brings (cf. II, c. v, §§ 8–9); and he had not extended his view to embrace the real 'parts' of the state (the military and governing classes), which he had deprived of property and thereby of happiness.

[1] The elements in the first category are fixed in their position for life. Each of the elements in the second occupies its position for a period determined by the age of its members, and is then succeeded by the new age-group which has grown up to take its place.

the theory of the state that states ought to be divided into classes, **1329 b** and the military class and the farming class should be separate. Even to-day this is still the case in Egypt, as it is also in Crete: the practice began in Egypt, so it is said, with the legislation of Sesostris, and it began in Crete with that of Minos. . . . § 2. The institution of common tables also appears to be ancient. It started in Crete with the reign of Minos; but it goes back farther still in southern Italy. § 3. The chroniclers of those parts tell of a legendary King of Oenotria, by the name of Italus, from whom the Oenotrians (changing their previous name) came to be known as 'Italians', and who gave the name of 'Italy' to the projection of Europe[1] which lies to the south of a line drawn from the bay of Scylacium to that of Lametus—two bays which are only half a day's journey from one another. § 4. According to the chroniclers, this Italus turned the Oenotrians from a pastoral into an agricultural people; and besides enacting other laws he instituted, for the first time, a system of common tables. That system, and some of his laws, still survive to-day among some of his descendants. § 5. To the north-west of the line just mentioned, as far as Campania, there lived the Opici, who were formerly (and indeed still are) surnamed Ausonians; to the north-east, and towards Iapygia and the Ionian gulf, in the territory known as Siritis, there lived the Chonians, who were also of Oenotrian origin. § 6. It was thus in southern Italy that the system of common tables originated. . . . The other institution mentioned above—the division of the body politic into classes—originated in Egypt [*not* in Crete]: the reign of Sesostris is long anterior to that of Minos. § 7. [Just as these two institutions were invented independently in different places and at different times] so, we must also believe, were most other institutions. They have been invented in the course of the years on a number of different occasions—indeed an indefinite number. Necessity itself, we may reasonably suppose, will steadily be the mother of indispensable inventions: on that basis, and with *these* once provided, we may fairly expect that inventions which make for the adornment and graces of life will also steadily develop; and this general rule must be held to be true in matters of politics as well as in other spheres. § 8. The history of Egypt attests the antiquity of all political institutions. The Egyptians are generally accounted the oldest people on earth; and they have always had a body of law and a system of politics. [This may teach us a lesson.] We ought to take over and use what has already been adequately expressed before us, and confine ourselves to attempting to discover what has hitherto been omitted.[2]

---

[1] i.e. the 'toe' of modern Italy.   [2] See Note DDD, p. 306.

§ 9. It has already been stated that the land should be owned, in our ideal state, by the class which bears arms and the class which shares in the conduct of government. It has also been explained why the farming class should be separate from these two classes; what the extent of the territory should be; and what kind of soil it should have. We have now to discuss the distribution of the land; to decide how it should be farmed; and to determine the character of the farming class. On our view of the problem of distribution, two things should be combined. On the one hand, property ought not to be owned in common, as some writers have maintained— **1330 a** though it ought to be used in common and as friends treat their belongings.[1] On the other hand, none of the citizens should go in need of subsistence. § 10. The institution of common tables is generally agreed to be for the advantage of all well-ordered states; and we shall have reason to explain, at a later point, why we share this view.[2] The right of dining at the common tables should be equally open to every citizen; but poor men will always find it difficult to contribute their quota of the cost from their own resources, when they have also to provide simultaneously for the rest of the family expenditure. [This is an argument for meeting the cost of the system of common tables from public funds]; and expenditure on public worship should also be a charge on the state in general.

§ 11. We may accordingly suggest that the territory of our state should be divided into two parts, one of which will be public property, while the other will belong to private owners. Each of these parts should again be divided into two sections. One section of the public property should be allocated to the service of the gods, and the other to the expenses of the system of common tables. The land which belongs to private owners should be so divided that one section lies on the frontiers, and the other is near the city—each individual receiving a plot in either section, and all alike thus having an interest in both. This arrangement[3] has two advantages: it satisfies the claims of equality and justice; and it produces more solidarity in the face of border wars. § 12. In the

---

[1] This is a reference back to Book II, c. v, §§ 6–7.

[2] Aristotle turns aside for the moment to this matter of common tables, partly because they are an example of the common use of property, which he has just been commending, and partly because the mention of them prepares the way for the general scheme of distribution which he proceeds to suggest in the next section. The promise to explain why he favours a system of common tables is not fulfilled; but the simple fact that it is of the nature of common use of property is sufficient to explain his approval.

[3] It is an arrangement which Plato had already proposed in the *Laws*. Aristotle borrows his proposal here (though he had criticized it in Book II, c. VI, §§ 15–16); and in the course of Books VII and VIII he borrows many other proposals from the *Laws*. See the translator's *Greek Political Theory*, pp. 380–2.

absence of such an arrangement, some of the citizens [i.e. those with estates remote from the frontiers] will think little of provoking the enmity of a neighbouring state, while others [i.e. those in the opposite position] will think of it only too much, and more than honour can justify. This will explain why some states have laws which prohibit citizens on the frontier from joining in deliberations about hostilities with neighbouring states; the reason is that their personal interest would affect their judgement adversely.

§ 13. This is the way in which we suggest that the territory of our state should be distributed, and these are the reasons for our suggestions. The class which farms it should ideally, and if we can choose at will, be slaves—but slaves not drawn from a single stock, or from stocks of a spirited temper. This will at once secure the advantage of a good supply of labour and eliminate any danger of revolutionary designs. Failing slaves, the next best class will be one of serfs who are not of Greek origin and whose character is like what has just been described. § 14. The farm hands employed on private estates should belong to the owners of those estates: those who are employed on public property should belong to the public. How the slaves who till the soil should be treated, and why it is wise to offer all slaves the eventual reward of emancipation, is a matter which we shall discuss later.[1]

NOTE DDD (p. 304): *The argument of* c. x, §§ 1–8

The whole of this passage, down to § 8, may be an antiquarian interpolation. If that view be accepted, the recapitulation in § 10 of the previous chapter, which prepares the way for it, must also be held to be an interpolation—the more as its substance is repeated again in § 9 of this chapter. But though the passage may be an interpolation, the argument of its last two sections (§§ 7–8) is none the less striking, and it has certainly an Aristotelian flavour. (One may compare with it a similar passage in Book II, c. v, § 16: one may also compare the passage from the *Metaphysics* quoted in the last footnote to Appendix V.) The effect of the argument goes counter to the theory of the 'diffusion' of each invention from a single centre (a theory held by some modern anthropologists), and in favour of the view that an invention may be repeated independently in different places and at different times.

CHAPTER XI

5. *The* planning of the central city *should be determined mainly by* (a) *considerations of health (which require a good exposure and a good water-supply), and* (b) *considerations of defence (which affect the internal layout of the city and raise the vexed question of fortifications). Other considerations which affect the planning of the city are*

---

[1] This promise, again, is not fulfilled. (But it may be noted that Aristotle provided in his own will for the emancipation of his slaves; see the Introduction, pp. xxiii–xxiv.)

(c) convenience for political activities (§ 2), and (d) beauty of appearance (§ 7, end).

§ 1. The city of our state, as we have already noticed, should be, so far as circumstances permit, a common centre, linked to the sea as well as the land, and equally linked to the whole of the territory. Internally, and in its own layout, we ought to plan the ideal of our city with an eye to four considerations.[1] The first, as being the most indispensable, is health. § 2. Cities which slope towards the east, and are exposed to the winds which blow from that quarter, are the healthiest: the next best aspect, which is healthy in the winter season, is one sheltered from the north wind [and therefore facing south]. **1330 b** Two other considerations to be borne in mind are matters of the city's convenience for political and military activities. § 3. For the purpose of military activities it should be easy of egress for its inhabitants, but difficult to approach or blockade for any enemies. It should also have, if possible, a natural supply of waters and streams; but if there is no such supply, a substitute has now been found in the construction of large and bountiful reservoirs of rain-water, which will not fail even when the inhabitants are cut off by the pressure of war from the territory round their city. § 4. Due regard for the health of the inhabitants not only means that their place of abode should be in a healthy locality and should have a healthy exposure: it also means that they should have the use of good water. This is a matter which ought not to be treated lightly. The elements we use most and oftenest for the support of our bodies contribute most to their health; and water and air have both an effect of this nature.[2] § 5. It should therefore be laid down, in all prudently conducted states, that if all the streams are not equally wholesome, and the supply of wholesome streams is inadequate, the drinking-water ought to be separated from the water used for other purposes.[3]

In the planning of strongholds there is no one policy which is equally good for all constitutions. A citadel (or *acropolis*) is suitable

[1] 'The four things seem to be health, adaptation to the needs of political life, adaptation to those of war, and beauty (see the end of § 7), though Aristotle in his haste omits to mention the last' (Newman, vol. iii, p. 396).

[2] In his observations on the 'siting' and planning of cities with a view to health, Aristotle may be remembering his own medical training. The subject was one which had been handled by writers of the school of Hippocrates, and especially by the author of the remarkable little treatise *On Airs, Waters, and Places*. It will be noticed in the text that the three subjects of its title are all handled by Aristotle.

[3] Aristotle's concern for public health deserves notice. In the Greek cities of the Hellenistic age elaborate provision was made for water-supply; and on the site of one city as many as 11 metal water-pipes have been discovered by excavators, crossing a single street, side by side, under the pavement (Breasted, *Ancient Times*, c. xxi).

to oligarchies and monarchies; a level plain suits the character of democracy; neither suits an aristocracy, for which a number of different strong places is preferable. § 6. The arrangement of private houses is generally considered to be more sightly, and more convenient for peace-time activities, when it is regularly planned [i.e. with straight streets] in the modern style introduced by Hippodamus.[1] For reasons of military security, however, the very reverse is preferable; and from this point of view there is much to be said for the haphazard arrangement of ancient times, which made it difficult for a foreign garrison to make its way out and for any assailants to find their way in. § 7. The two methods of arrangement should accordingly be combined; and this may be done by adopting the system which vine-growers follow in planting their 'clumps' of vines.[2] Alternatively, regular planning might be confined to certain sections and districts, and not made to cover the whole of the city. This would conduce at once to security and to beauty.

§ 8. The fortification of cities by walls is a matter of dispute. It is sometimes argued that states which lay claim to military excellence ought to dispense with any such aids. This is a singularly antiquated notion—all the more as it is plain to the eye that states which prided themselves on this point are being refuted by the logic of fact.[3] § 9. When the question at issue is one of coping with an enemy state of a similar character, which is only slightly superior in numbers, there is little honour to be got from an attempt to attain security by the erection of a barrier of walls. But it sometimes happens—and it is always possible—that the superiority of an assailant may be more than a match for mere courage, human or superhuman; and then, if a state is to avoid destruction, and to escape from suffering and humiliation, the securest possible barrier of walls should be deemed the best of military **1331 a** methods—especially to-day, when the invention of catapults and other engines for the siege of cities has attained

[1] Hippodamus, the town-planner, who also proposed what may be called 'an engineer's system of political planning', has already been mentioned in Book II, c. VIII.

[2] The vines were grown in the form of a quincunx i.e. the five spots on dice,
× ×

×   , so that the lines ran obliquely, and not straight. This was held to look
× ×
better, and to make the vines more productive.

[3] Sparta (which had always prided itself on being defended by men, not walls) had been humiliated by Epaminondas in 369 B.C. and afterwards, and this is the fact of which Aristotle is thinking. The Greek dispute about 'walls' is much the same as the modern dispute about 'Maginot lines'. Aristotle may have been moved to discuss the theme in consequence of the repair and strengthening of the walls of Athens by the contemporary statesman Lycurgus: see the Introduction, p. xxi.

such a high degree of precision.   § 10. To demand that a city should be left undefended by walls is much the same as to want to have the territory of a state left open to invasion, and to lay every elevation level with the ground. It is like refusing to have walls for the exterior of a private house, for fear they will make its inhabitants cowards. § 11. We have also to remember that a people with a city defended by walls has a choice of alternatives— to treat its city as walled [and therefore to act on the defensive], or to treat it as if it were unwalled [and therefore to take the offensive] —but a people without any walls is a people without any choice. If this argument be accepted, the conclusion will not only be that a city ought to be surrounded by walls; it will also be that the walls should always be kept in good order, and be made to satisfy both the claims of beauty and the needs of military utility—especially the needs revealed by recent military inventions. § 12. It is always the concern of the offensive to discover new methods by which it may seize an advantage; but it is equally the concern of the defensive, which has already made some inventions, to search and think out others. An assailant will not even attempt to make an attack on men who are well prepared.

CHAPTER XII

The common tables maintained in the city should be placed in the temples; and the temples should be placed on a commanding site, with the 'Free Square' at its foot for the recreations of the older citizens. There should also be a separate 'Market Square', with the courts of law for business matters adjacent to it. In the countryside the common tables should be connected with the guard-houses of the militia, and there should be a number of country temples.

§ 1. If we assume that the citizens should be distributed at common tables, and the walls should be dotted with guard-houses and towers at convenient intervals, the idea will naturally occur that some of the common tables should be established in these guard-houses. § 2. This will be one combination. [It will also be well to make another.] The principal common tables of the magistrates may be associated with the buildings devoted to public worship, on some convenient and common site—except for such temples as are required by law, or by a rule of the Delphic oracle, to be kept distinct and separate.[1] § 3. This site should be on an eminence, conspicuous enough for men to look up and see good-

---

[1] The effect would be that the younger citizens, under the age of 50, would mainly have their common tables in the guard-houses, while the older citizens who conducted the government, along with the aged priests, would have their common tables in temple buildings.

ness enthroned, and strong enough to command the adjacent quarters of the city. Below this site provision should be made for a public square, of the sort which is called in Thessaly by the name of the Free Square. § 4. This should be clear of all merchandise; and no mechanic, or farmer, or other such person, should be permitted to enter, except on the summons of the magistrates. The place would be all the more pleasant if recreation grounds for the older men were included in its plan. § 5. The arrangements for recreation (like those for the common tables) should be different for different age-groups; and if this plan be followed some of the magistrates should stay with the younger men [near their guard-houses], while the older men should remain [in the public square] with the other magistrates. To be under the eyes of the magistrates will serve, above anything else, to create a true feeling of modesty and the fear of shame which should animate freemen.[1] 1331 b § 6. The market-square for buying and selling should be separate from the public square, and at a distance from it: it should occupy a site which forms a good depot, alike for commodities imported by sea and those which come from the state's own territory.

The directors of the state[2] include priests as well as magistrates. [We have already settled where the magistrates should have their common tables]; and it is fitting that those of the priests should be associated, in the same way as theirs, with the temple buildings. § 7. The proper place in which to establish the magistrates who deal with contracts, indictments in lawsuits, summonses into court, and other business of that order—and, we may also add, those concerned with the superintendence of the market square and the duties of 'city-superintendence'[3]—will be near some square or general centre of public resort. The place which suits this requirement best is the site of the market square. The public square, on its higher ground, is assigned on our plan to leisure: the market square belongs to the business activities of life. § 8. The general system we have described should also be applied to the country-side. There, too, the various magistrates—who are sometimes termed forest-wardens, and sometimes rural inspectors[4]—

[1] Aristotle has here in mind, as in other passages of the *Politics*, the tendency to homosexual passion, which might be encouraged by unregulated games and recreations.
[2] Reading, with Newman, *to proestos* (the directing element) instead of *to plēthos* (the general body).
[3] On these magistrates see Book VI, c. VIII, §§ 3–4. It will be noticed that Aristotle fixes these 'business magistrates' in or near the market-square—leaving the public or 'free' square for the higher magistrates.
[4] On these magistrates, too, see Book VI, c. VIII, § 6. It is an argument in favour of keeping the existing order of the books of the *Politics* that Aristotle

should have guard-houses and common tables in connexion with
their duties; and the country should be studded with temples,
some of them dedicated to the gods and others to heroes.

§ 9. But it would be a waste of time to linger here over details
and explanations. It is easy enough to theorize about such matters:
it is far less easy to realize one's theories. We talk about them in
terms of our wants; what actually happens depends upon chance.[1]
We may therefore dismiss, for the present, any further study of
these issues.

C

THE GENERAL PRINCIPLES OF EDUCATION (cc. xiii–xv)

CHAPTER XIII

1. The End and the Means. *For the attainment of well-being, or
felicity, it is necessary to know the right end as well as to choose the
right means.* (a) *So far as the* end *is concerned, felicity has been
defined in the* Ethics *as 'the energy and practice of goodness, to a
degree of perfection, and in an absolute mode'. The point of the words
'in an absolute mode' is that goodness must not be handicapped (in
which case the mode of its energy will only be 'relative'), but must
go into action furnished with the proper advantages of health, wealth,
and general equipment. In order, therefore, to be in a position to attain
the end of felicity, a state must start with the proper advantages—
which is a matter of good fortune rather than of man's art; in order
actually to attain it, a state (i.e. its members) must achieve 'the
energy and practice of goodness'—and this belongs to the realm
of human knowledge and purpose, where the art of the legislator can
operate. We thus turn to consider means.* (b) *There are three* means
*by which the members of a state may achieve goodness—natural
endowment; habit; and rational principle. Natural endowment has
already been considered in Chapter VII: we have now to discuss habit
and rational principle; and here we enter the domain of education and
legislative art.*

§ 1. We have now to speak of the constitution itself;[2] and here

seems to refer back here to Book VI as if it had immediately preceded the
present book. The reference made to guard-houses in the country-side also
suggests that Aristotle may be referring to the system of military training for the
Athenian youth introduced after 338 B.C.: see Appendix IV. B. 5.

[1] As Newman points out, there is a jingle in both pairs of antitheses in the
original Greek (*noēsai* and *poiēsai, euchē* and *tuchē*). The translator has tried to
preserve the jingle—perhaps awkwardly—in the English.

[2] Hitherto Aristotle has been discussing the territory and the population
required for an ideal state. He now comes to the essential thing—the constitution (or 'way of life') which should be built on that basis.

we have to explain the nature and character of the elements required if a state is to enjoy a happy life and possess a good constitution. § 2. There are two things in which well-being always and everywhere consists. The first is to determine aright the aim and end of your actions. The second is to find out the actions which will best conduce to that end. These two things—ends and means —may be concordant or discordant. Sometimes the aim is determined aright, but there is a failure to attain it in action. Sometimes the means to the end are all successfully attained, but the end originally fixed is only a poor sort of end. Sometimes there is failure is both respects: a doctor, for example, may not only misjudge the proper nature of physical health, but he may also fail to discover the means that produce the object which he actually has in view. The proper course, in all arts and sciences, is to get a grasp of both equally—alike of the end itself, and of the actions which conduce to the end. § 3. The good life, or felicity, is obviously the end at which all men aim. Some men have the power of attaining that end. Others are stopped from attaining it by something in their own endowment, or by some lack of opportunity. (We have to remember that a certain amount of equipment [which depends upon opportunity] is necessary for the good life, and while this amount need not be so great for those whose endowment **1332 a** is good, more is required for those whose endowment is poor.) § 4. Others, again, start wrong from the outset; and though they have the power of attaining felicity they seek it along wrong lines. Here, and for the purposes of our inquiry, it is obviously necessary to be clear about the nature of felicity. The object we have in view is to discover the best constitution. The best constitution is that under which the state is best constituted. The best constituted state is the state which possesses the greatest possibility of achieving felicity.[1]

§ 5. It has been argued in the *Ethics* (if the argument there used is of any value) that felicity is 'the energy and practice of goodness, to a degree of perfection, and in a mode which is absolute and not relative'.[2] § 6. [We must explain the concluding words of this definition.] By 'relative' we mean a mode of action which is necessary and enforced; by 'absolute' we mean a mode of action which possesses intrinsic value. Consider, for example, the case of just

---

[1] There are two equations which must be borne in mind in following Aristotle's thought. First, constitution = way of life; and therefore the best or ideal constitution = the best or ideal way of life. Secondly, goodness = felicity; and therefore the constitution which is the most good or ideal constitution (and, as such, is the most good or ideal way of life) = the happiest way of life.

[2] The phrase does not occur, *totidem verbis*, in the *Nicomachean Ethics*. But the same thing is implied in more than one passage.

actions [i.e. actions in which the particular virtue of justice is practised]. To inflict a just penalty or punishment is indeed an act of goodness; but it is also an act which is forced on the agent, and it has value only as being a necessity. (It would be better if neither individuals nor states ever needed recourse to any such action.) Acts done with a view to bestowing honours and wealth on others [i.e. acts of distributive, as distinct from criminal justice] are in a different category: they are acts of the highest value.[1] § 7. An act of punishment is a choice of something which, in a sense, is an evil [i.e. the infliction of pain]: acts of the order first mentioned have an opposite character—they are foundations and creations of something good. We may argue, along the same line, that while a good man would handle well the evils of poverty, sickness, and the other mishaps of life, the fact remains that felicity consists in the opposites of these evils.[2] The truly good and happy man, as we have stated elsewhere in our arguments on ethics,[3] is one who by the nature of his goodness [which is *absolute*] has advantages at hand which are *absolute* advantages.   § 8. It is plain that his use of such advantages must also show an absolute goodness, and possess an absolute value. But the fact [that the good and happy man has absolute advantages ready to hand] leads men to think that external advantages are the *causes* of felicity. One might as well say that a well-executed piece of fine harp-playing was due to the instrument, and not to the skill of the artist.

It follows from what has been said that some elements of the state should be 'given', or ready to hand, and the rest should be provided by the art of the legislator. § 9. We may therefore pray that our state should be ideally equipped at all points where fortune is sovereign—as we assume her to be in the sphere of the 'given'. The goodness of the state is a different matter: here we leave the realm of fortune, and we enter the realm of human knowledge and purpose [where the art of the legislator can act]. A state is good in virtue of the goodness of the citizens who share in its government. In our state all the citizens have a share in the government [and all must therefore be good]. § 10. We have therefore to con-

[1] When you punish wrongdoing, you may be engaged in 'the energy and practice of goodness to a degree of perfection', but the mode of your action is *forced* upon you by the existence of wrong-doing, and it is relative to wrong-doing. When you do good to others (by bestowing honours or wealth according to their desert), you are acting freely; and from that point of view your mode of action may be called absolute.

[2] In other words you can only attain absolute goodness, and with it absolute felicity, if you have the requisite wealth, the requisite health, and the general requisite 'equipment' of life.

[3] The reference here would appear to be not so much to the *Nicomachean Ethics*, as to two other ethical treatises also ascribed to Aristotle.

sider how a man can become a good man. [This is a matter of *each* individual.] True, it is possible for all to be good collectively, without each being good individually. But the better thing is that each individual citizen should be good. The goodness of all is necessarily involved in the goodness of each.

There are three means by which individuals become good and virtuous. § 11. These three means are the natural endowment we have at birth; the habits we form; and the rational principle within us. In the matter of endowment we must start by being men—and not some other species of animal—and men too who have certain qualities both of body and soul. **1332 b** There are, indeed, some qualities which it is no help to have had at the start. Habits cause them to change: implanted by nature in a neutral form, they can be modified by the force of habit either for better or worse. § 12. Animate beings other than men live mostly by natural impulse, though some are also guided to a slight extent by habit. Man lives by rational principle too [as well as natural impulse and habit]; and he is unique in having this gift. It follows that all the three powers of man must be tuned to agree. [The power of rational principle will play a great part in this tuning]: men are often led by that principle not to follow habit and natural impulse, once they have been persuaded that some other course is better. § 13. We have already determined, in an earlier chapter (VII), the character of the natural endowment which is needed for our citizens, if they are to be easily moulded by the art of the legislator. When they have that endowment, the rest is entirely a matter of the education which he provides; and they will partly learn it from a training in habits, partly from a system of instruction [which makes an appeal to their reason].

CHAPTER XIV

2. Education and citizenship: education for leisure, and education of character. *Should there be two different systems of education—one for the governors (as in Plato's* Republic), *and one for the governed? Fundamentally, in the ideal state, all the citizens will belong to a single society of freemen and peers; but, as has been already suggested in Chapter IX, there is a distinction (which is one of age-groups passing on into one another, and not one of classes kept permanently separate) between the young who are still under government and the older citizens who conduct the government. The young must learn to obey a free government of which they will eventually be members; and in doing so they will also be learning to govern when their turn comes. In thus learning generally 'the virtue of the good citizen', they will also be learning 'the virtue of the good man'; for the two virtues, as*

has been argued before (in Book III, c. iv), are here fundamentally the same.

In planning the system of education which will produce the good man and citizen, we must make two distinctions. (1) We must distinguish the different parts of the soul—the part which has rational principle (in its turn divided into a practical and a speculative part), and the part which has simply the capacity for obeying such a principle. (2) We must also distinguish the different parts or aspects of life (which are implied in the previous distinction)—action and leisure; war and peace. Education must regard all the different parts of the soul and the different parts or aspects of life. States in the past, e.g. Sparta, have tended to concentrate on only one part of the soul and one aspect of life: they have forgotten the part of the soul which has rational principle, and the aspect of life which is concerned with peace and leisure, and they have devoted themselves to war and empire. States, however, like individuals, should devote themselves in the main to the aspect of life which is concerned with peace and leisure.

§ 1. As all political associations are composed of governors and governed, we have to consider whether the two should be distinguished for life, or merged together in a single body. The system of education will necessarily vary according to the answer we give. § 2. We may imagine one set of circumstances in which it would be obviously better that a lasting distinction should once and for all be established between governors and governed. This would be if there were one class in the state surpassing all others as much as gods and heroes are supposed to surpass mankind—a class of men so outstanding, physically as well as mentally, that the superiority of the ruling stock was indisputably clear to their subjects. § 3. But that is a difficult assumption to make; and we have nothing in actual life like the gulf between kings and subjects which the writer Scylax describes as existing in India. We may therefore draw the conclusion, which can be defended on many grounds, that all should share alike in a system of government under which they rule and are ruled by turns. In a society of peers equality means that all should have the same rights: and a constitution can hardly survive if it is founded on injustice [i.e. if it gives *different* rights to men who are of the same quality]. § 4. The subject citizens will then be joined by all [the serfs] of the country-side in a common policy of revolution; and the civic body will be too small to cope successfully with all its enemies. On the other hand, it cannot be denied that there should be a difference between governors and governed. How they can differ, and yet share alike, is a dilemma which legislators

have to solve. § 5. We have already touched on a possible solution
in a previous chapter.[1]

Nature, we have suggested, has provided us with the distinction
we need. She has divided a body of citizens who are all generically
the same into two different age-groups, a younger and an older,
one of them meant to be governed and the other to act as the
government. Youth never resents being governed, or thinks itself
better than its governors; and it is all the less likely to do so if it
knows that it will take over the government on reaching a proper
maturity. § 6. In one sense, therefore, it has to be said that
governors and governed are the same sort of persons; in another,
that they are different. The same will be true of their education:
1333 a from one point of view it must be the same; from another
it has to be different, and, as the saying goes, 'If you would
learn to govern well, you must first learn how to obey.' [We may
first treat of learning how to obey.] Government, as has already
been said in our first part,[2] may be conducted in two different
ways. One way is to govern in the interest of the governors: the
other, to govern in the interest of the governed. The former way
is what we call 'despotic' [i.e. a government of slaves]; the latter is
what we call 'the government of freemen'.[3] § 7. [This is the sort
of government which the young must begin by learning to obey;
but they must also learn to obey some orders which may seem
more appropriate to a government of slaves.] Some of the duties
imposed [on the free] differ [from those of slaves] not in the work
they involve, but in the object for which they are to be done. This
means that a good deal of the work which is generally accounted
menial may none the less be the sort of work which young freemen
can honourably do. It is not the inherent nature of actions, but
the end or object for which they are done, which make one action
differ from another in the way of honour or dishonour.

§ 8. [We may now treat of learning how to govern.] We have
laid it down that the excellence of the full citizen who shares in
the government is the same as that of the good man.[4] We have also
assumed that the man who begins by being a subject must ultimately share in the government [and will therefore require the

---

[1] c. IX, §§ 4–6.

[2] The reference is to Book III, c. IV, §§ 10–13 and c. VI, § 6; but cf. also this
book, c. III, §§ 1–2.

[3] Aristotle, in the course of this section, begins to discuss education as something different for the governed from what it is for the governor. The governed,
he argues, must be taught to obey, but to obey with the obedience of freemen.
But this proviso, he proceeds to add (§ 7), will not preclude the governed from
being taught to do menial duties which are usually done by slaves—if only they
are taught to do them in the spirit of freemen.

[4] This has been argued in Book III, c. IV.

same sort of excellence as the good man]. It follows on this that the legislator must labour to ensure that his citizens become good men. He must therefore know what institutions will produce this result, and what is the end or aim to which a good life is directed.

§ 9. There are two different parts of the soul. One of these parts has a rational principle intrinsically and in its own nature. The other has not; but it has the capacity for obeying such a principle. When we speak of a man as being 'good', we mean that he has the goodnesses of these two parts of the soul. But in which of the parts is the end of man's life *more particularly* to be found? The answer is one which admits of no doubt to those who accept the division just made. § 10. In the world of nature as well as of art the lower always exists for the sake of the higher.[1] The part of the soul which has rational principle is the higher part. [It is therefore the part in which the end of man's life is more particularly to be found.] But this part may in turn be divided, on the scheme which we generally follow, into two parts of its own. Rational principle, according to that scheme, is partly practical, partly speculative. § 11. It is obvious, therefore, that the part of the soul which has this principle must fall into two corresponding parts. We may add that as the parts of the soul have their hierarchy, so, too, have the activities of those parts. It follows on this that those who can attain *all* the activities possible [i.e. rational activity of the speculative order, rational activity of the practical order, and the activity of obedience to rational principle], or *two* of those activities, will be bound to prefer the activity of the part which is in its nature the higher. All of us always prefer the highest we can attain.[2]

§ 12. Life as a whole is also divided into its different parts— action and leisure, war and peace; and in the sphere of action we may further distinguish acts which are merely necessary, or merely and simply useful, from acts which are good in themselves. § 13. The preferences which we give to the parts of life and their different activities will inevitably follow the same general line as those which we give to the parts of the soul and their different activities. War must therefore be regarded as only a means to peace; action as a means to leisure; and acts which are merely necessary, or merely and simply useful, as means to acts which are good in themselves. The legislation of the true statesman must be framed with a view to all of these factors. In the first place, it must cover the different parts of the soul and their different activities; and in this field it should be directed more to the higher than

[1] Man, in his art, creates the lower in order to achieve the higher: nature, in her process of genesis, produces the lower as a stage in a development tending to the higher.   [2] See Note EEE, p. 320.

the lower, and rather to ends than means.   § 14. In the second place it must also cover, and it must place in the same perspective, the different parts or ways of life and the different categories of acts.[1] It is true that the citizens of our state must be able to lead a life of action and war; **1333 b** but they must be even more able to lead a life of leisure and peace. It is true, again, that they must be able to do necessary or useful acts; but they must be even more able to do good acts. These are the general aims which ought to be followed in the education of childhood and of the stages of adolescence which still require education.[2]

§ 15. The Greek states of our day which are counted as having the best constitutions [and therefore the best 'ways of life'], and the legislators who framed their constitutional systems, have fallen short of this ideal. It is plain that their constitutions have not been made with a view to the higher ends of life, or their laws and systems of education directed to all the virtues. On the contrary, there has been a vulgar decline into the cultivation of qualities supposed to be useful and of a more profitable character. § 16. A similar spirit appears in some of our recent writers who have adopted this point of view. They laud the constitution of Sparta, and they admire the aim of the Spartan legislator in directing the whole of his legislation to the goal of conquest and war. This is a view which can be easily refuted by argument, and it has now been also refuted by the evidence of fact.[3]   § 17. Most men are believers in the cause of empire, on the ground that empire leads to a large accession of material prosperity.[4] It is evidently in this spirit that Thibron, like all the other writers on the constitution of Sparta, lauds its legislator for having trained men to meet danger and so created an empire. § 18. To-day the Spartans have lost their empire; and we can all see for ourselves that they were not a happy community and their legislator was not right. It is indeed a strange result of

[1] See Note FFF, p. 320.

[2] To what age would Aristotle continue the education of the young? Apparently beyond the first stage of adolescence (and possibly to the age of 21): otherwise he would not speak of different stages—in the plural.

[3] Aristotle is here alluding to the collapse of Sparta before Epaminondas. See above, c. XI, § 8.

[4] It is possible that Aristotle, in this general discussion of the merits of a peace policy and a war policy, had in mind the politics of Athens, though it is to Sparta that he actually refers. Down to 336 B.C. there had been a peace party at Athens, which had been in favour of using the 'theoric fund' liberally to give the citizens the benefits of leisure—a policy which precluded expenditure on preparation for war; and there had been what may be called a war-party, represented by Demosthenes, which was in favour of maintaining the old traditions of Athenian policy and championing the cause of liberty against the growth of tyranny. The antinomy is modern as well as ancient. It is an antinomy between the cause of internal development and social progress, and the cause of foreign affairs and the assumption of political responsibilities.

his labours: here is a people which has stuck to his laws and never been hindered in carrying them out, and yet it has lost all that makes life worth living. § 19. In any case the partisans of Sparta are in error about the type of government for which the legislator should show a preference. [It is not, as they think, the 'despotic' type]: the government of freemen is a finer government, and a government more connected with goodness, than any form of despotism. . . . We may add a further reflection. There is another reason why a state should not be considered happy, or its legislator praised, when its citizens are trained for victory in war and the subjugation of neighbouring states. Such a policy involves a great risk of injury [to the internal life of the state]. § 20. It obviously implies that any citizen who can do so should make it his object to capture the government of his own state.[1] This is exactly what the Spartans accuse their King Pausanias of having attempted to do—and this although he already held an office of such great dignity.

We may justly conclude that none of these arguments [in favour of a training directed to the acquisition of empire] and none of the policies advocated is statesmanlike, or useful, or right. § 21. The Good is one and the same for individuals and communities; and it is the Good which the legislator ought to instil into the minds of his citizens.[2] Training for war should not be pursued with a view to enslaving men who do not deserve such a fate. Its objects should be these—first, to prevent men from ever becoming enslaved themselves; secondly, to put men in a position to exercise leadership—but **1334 a** leadership directed to the interest of the led, and not to the establishment of a general system of slavery; and thirdly, to enable men to make themselves masters of those who naturally deserve to be slaves.[3] § 22. In support of the view that the legislator should make leisure and peace the cardinal aims of all legislation bearing on war—or indeed, for that matter, on anything else—we may cite the evidence

[1] This suggestion—that *imperium* is not only prejudicial to the *libertas* of dependencies, but also to that of the imperial state itself—is, as Newman remarks, both original and shrewd. It was the argument urged by the Whigs of 1770 against the American policy of George III.

[2] Aristotle thus suggests that the morality of the Athenian state—i.e. of the 40,000 citizens who formed the political association called Athens—is identical with the morality of each individual Athenian. It was less easy to hold a doctrine of *raison d'état* when the state was thus a body of citizens, and not a sovereign prince. But the Melian dialogue recorded by Thucydides shows that even the body of Athenian citizens could speak the language and hold the doctrine of Machiavelli.

[3] A Greek state, Aristotle implies, should exercise only a leadership (*hēgemonia*) over other Greek states, and it should exercise it in their interest; but it may also exercise the despotic control of a master over uncivilized peoples naturally intended for slavery.

of actual fact. Most of the states which make war their aim are safe only while they are fighting. They collapse as soon as they have established an empire, and lose the edge of their temper, like an unused sword, in time of peace. The legislator is to blame for having provided no training for the proper use of leisure.

NOTE EEE (p. 317): *The soul and its parts*

Aristotle begins by dividing the soul into two parts—the part which has a rational principle intrinsically, and the part which has the capacity for obeying such a principle. He then subdivides the first part into two divisions—a practical and a speculative. We may therefore say that there are, in all, *three* divisions or parts of the soul. These three divisions have three corresponding activities; and both the divisions and their activities can be graded in an order of value. Beginning at the bottom, and proceeding upwards, we may say (1) that the part of the soul with a capacity for obeying rational principle issues in the activity of temperance; (2) that the practical division of the purely rational part of the soul issues in the activity of moral prudence (or *phronēsis*); and (3) that the speculative division of the purely rational part issues in the activity of wisdom. A man who can attain all the three activities will prefer the third to the other two: a man who can attain the first two only will prefer the second to the first: the man who can only attain the first will have to be content with the first.

On the general analysis of the nature of the soul here suggested see also the *Ethics*, Book I, c. XIII. 'The genuine statesman (*politikos*)', it is there stated, 'is regarded as one who has spent his labours on goodness above everything else, for his object is to make his fellow-citizens good and obedient to the laws (§ 2). . . . The statesman must therefore study the soul [goodness being a state and activity of the soul]; but he must study it [only] with this object in view, and just so far as this object requires' (§ 8). The rest of the chapter deals mainly with the 'desiderative' part of the soul which has the capacity for obeying rational principle. Later in the *Ethics*, in the course of Book VI, Aristotle proceeds to deal with the part of the soul which has a rational principle inherently and in its own nature; and, as in the *Politics*, he divides this part into two divisions—the speculative or contemplative, and the calculative or practical (c. 1, §§ 5-6).

NOTE FFF (p. 318): *The different parts or ways of life*

The different 'parts or ways of life' are the life of action as contrasted with the life of leisure, and the life of war as contrasted with the life of peace. The different 'categories of acts' are acts which are merely necessary or useful, as contrasted with acts which are good in themselves.

The antithesis of the two 'ways of life'—action and war)(leisure and peace—appears also in the last book of the *Ethics* (Book X, c. VII, §§ 6-7). Here Aristotle, speaking in praise of the contemplative life, puts politics generally, as well as the politics of war, on a lower plane. 'We occupy ourselves with action in order that we may have leisure, and we make war in order to enjoy peace. The activity of the practical virtues is shown in political or military affairs, but our action in such affairs must be held to be unleisured action. Military action is entirely so . . . but the action of the statesman too is unleisured action.'

CHAPTER XV

If leisure is thus of major importance, we may go on to notice that its enjoyment demands certain conditions, or, in other words, requires certain virtues—especially the virtues of wisdom and temperance. This will explain why a training such as the Spartan, which encourages only the virtue of courage, is defective and breaks down in practice. . . . Reverting now to the means of education—training in habits and the training of rational principle—we must inquire, 'which of them should first be employed'? The answer is that the training of rational principle should, from the very first, be kept in view as the ultimate aim; but the training which ought to be given first is that of the part of the soul which has the capacity for obeying rational principle, and we must therefore begin by providing for the training of this part in habits. But even prior to the training of this part of the soul, there is a physical problem to be considered—the problem of ensuring a good physique which will be a good servant of the soul.

§ 1. The final end of men is the same whether they are acting individually or acting collectively; and the standard followed by the best individual is thus the same as the standard followed by the best political constitution. It is therefore evident that the qualities required for the use of leisure must belong to the state as well as the individual; for [these are the qualities which particularly matter, and], as we have repeatedly argued, peace is the final end of war, and leisure the final end of occupation. § 2. The qualities required for the use of leisure and the cultivation of the mind are twofold. Some of them are operative in and during leisure itself: some are operative in and during the activity of occupation.[1] [To understand why qualities of the latter sort are required, we must note that] a number of necessary conditions must be present, before the use of leisure is possible. This is why a state must possess the quality of temperance, and why, again, it must possess the quality of courage and endurance. 'There's no leisure for slaves', as the proverb goes, and men who cannot face danger courageously become the slaves of the first to assail them. § 3. The quality of courage and endurance is required for the activities of occupation: wisdom is required for those of leisure: temperance and justice are qualities required at both times and under both heads—though they are particularly required in times of peace and leisure.[2] A time of war automatically enforces

[1] See Note GGG, p. 323.
[2] It is interesting to note the distribution of the four virtues—fortitude, temperance, justice, and wisdom—in the thought of this passage. Fortitude is regarded as operative only in and during occupation, though it also provides a necessary condition for leisure; the virtues of temperance and justice are

temperance and justice: a time of the enjoyment of prosperity, and leisure accompanied by peace, is more apt to make men over-bearing. § 4. A special degree of justice and temperance is there-fore required in those who appear to be faring exceptionally well and enjoying all that the world accounts to be happiness, like the denizens of 'the happy isles' of which poets sing; and the greater the leisure which these men are able to use, when they are set among an abundance of blessings, the greater too will be their need of wisdom, as well as of temperance and justice. § 5. We can now understand why a state which seeks to achieve felicity, and to be good, must partake of all these three virtues. If some shame must always attach to *any* failure to use aright the goods of life, a special measure of shame must attach to a failure to use them aright in times of leisure; and people who show themselves good in times of occupation and war, but sink to the level of slaves in times of peace and leisure, will be bound to incur particular censure. § 6. Excellence must not be sought by a training such as the Spartan. The Spartans are like the rest of the world in their view of the **1334 b** nature of life's highest goods [which they identify, like everybody else, with the external goods of fortune]: they only differ from others in thinking that the right way of getting them is to cultivate a single excellence [i.e. military courage]. Regarding external goods as higher than any others, and the enjoyment they give as greater than that derived from the general cultivation of excellence, [they cultivate only the single excellence which they consider useful as a means to securing those goods. But it is the *whole* of excellence which ought to be cultivated],[1] and cultivated *for its own sake*, as our argument has already shown. That still leaves us, however, with the problem, 'How, and by what means, is a general excellence to be achieved?'

§ 7. Using the distinction already made in a previous chapter,[2] we may say that the means required for achieving general excellence are natural endowment, habit, and rational principle. So far as the first of these is concerned, we have already determined [in c. VII] the character of the endowment with which our citizens should start. It remains to consider the other two means, and to deter-mine whether training in habit or training in rational principle ought to come first. The two modes of training must be adjusted to one another as harmoniously as possible [which not only means starting first with the mode that ought to come first, but also

assigned the higher position of being operative in and during both occupation and leisure; and the virtue of wisdom is given the still higher position of being purely operative in and during leisure.

[1] The passage in brackets represents Newman's conjecture of a passage which has dropped out in the Greek text as it has come down to us.　　[2] c. XIII, § 11.

directing both modes alike to the same sort of high purpose]; otherwise rational principle may fail to attain the highest ideal, and the
training given through habit may show a similar defect. § 8. With
a view to this result, we may assume two things as evident.[1]
§ 8. First, in the sphere of man's life (as in all life generally), birth
has a first beginning [i.e. the union of parents], but the end
attained from such a beginning is only a step to some further end.
The exercise of rational principle and thought is the ultimate end
of man's nature. It is therefore with a view to the exercise of these
faculties that we should regulate, from the first, the birth and the
training in habits of our citizens.[2] § 9. Secondly, as soul and body
are two, so there are also two parts of the soul, the irrational and
the rational; and there are also two corresponding states of these
parts—the state of appetite, and the state of pure thought. In
order of time and in date of birth, the body is prior to the soul,
and the irrational part of the soul is prior to the rational. § 10. This
is proved by the fact that all the signs of appetite—such as anger,
self-will, and desire—are visible in children from their very birth;
while reasoning and thought are faculties which only appear, as
a rule, when they grow older. The conclusion which follows is
obvious. Children's bodies should be given attention before their
souls; and their appetites should be the next part of them to be
regulated. But the regulation of their appetites should be intended
for the benefit of their minds—just as the attention given to their
bodies should be intended for the benefit of their souls.

NOTE GGG (p. 321): *Aristotle's conception of leisure*

Some words should be said about the general conception of leisure
(*scholē*). In the first place we must note that leisure is not contrasted with
activity. It is itself activity, and the highest form of activity—the activity
of the part of the soul which possesses rational principle, and especially
of the speculative division of that part. It is therefore contrasted not with
activity, but with 'occupation' (*ascholia*)—in other words with the sort of
activity which is pursued not for its own sake (as the activity of leisure is),
but for the sake of something else. Secondly, we must note that leisure
is not only contrasted with, or distinguished from, 'occupation': it is also
contrasted with, or distinguished from, 'recreation' (*anapausis*) and 'amusement' (*paidia*—'the sort of thing children do'). Amusement and recreation

---

[1] Newman's note (vol. iii, p. 454) will elucidate the argument: 'Aristotle is
about to decide that training through habit must precede training through reason,
but that training through habit must be adjusted to and pursued for the sake of
reason, which is the end; and he proves the second proposition first (in § 8), and
then the first (in §§ 9–10).'

[2] The argument is that there is a *scala naturae*. On the first rung of the ladder
parents unite to secure the end of the birth of a child. But that end is not final:
it leads to the next rung of the ladder (the training of the child in habits); and
that in turn leads to a further rung (the training of the child in the use of rational
principle and thought). It is the final rung of the ladder which controls the
previous and lower rungs: cf. *supra*, c. XIV, § 11.

mean rest after occupation, and preparation for new occupation: they are thus both essentially connected with the idea of occupation. Leisure stands by itself, in its own independent right. Aristotle thus operates with three different notions—the notion of leisure; the notion of occupation; and the notion (in one sense intermediate between the two, but in another sense closer to the latter) of amusement and recreation.

If it be asked, 'What is the activity of leisure', we may answer in one word, '*diagōgē*', or the cultivation of the mind. *Scholē* is spent in *diagōgē* (Book VIII, c. III, § 6), and conversely *diagōgē* is pursued in and during *scholē* (Book VIII, c. III, § 8). Newman's words may also be quoted (vol. iii, p. 442): *scholē* 'is employment in work desirable for its own sake—the hearing of noble music and no doubt of noble poetry; intercourse with friends chosen for their worth; and above all the exercise, in company or otherwise, of the speculative faculty.'

On Aristotle's general conception of leisure, and its significance in his philosophy, see the article on *scholē* by J. L. Stocks in the *Classical Quarterly* for 1936, pp. 177–87.

D

THE EARLY STAGES OF EDUCATION (cc. xvi–xvii)

Chapter XVI

1. *The regulation of* marriage *is the first necessity, if we are to ensure a good physique for our future citizens. The age at which husband and wife marry affects the physique of their offspring; and on physical grounds it may be suggested that the husband should be older than the wife, and the man of 37 should marry the woman of 18. The husband's physique should not be spoiled by over-exercise or the reverse; the wife should take regular exercise during pregnancy. If the size of the family has to be limited, it will be necessary to consider means such as the exposure of infants and the procuring of miscarriages. The age at which procreation should cease, and the treatment of adultery.*

§ 1. If we assume that the legislator ought, for a start, to see to the provision of a stock of the healthiest possible bodies in the nurseries of our state, it follows that his first attention must be devoted to marriage; and here he will have to consider what the ages of the partners should be, and what qualities they ought to possess. § 2. The first thing to be taken into account, in legislating about matrimony, is the length of time that husband and wife are likely to live together. The right thing is that they should arrive simultaneously at the same epoch of sexual life. There should be no divergence of physical power, with the husband still able to beget but the wife unable to conceive, or the wife still able to conceive and the husband unable to beget. Such a position is apt to cause discord and difference between married persons. The second thing to be taken into account is the difference of age between children and their parents. § 3. On the one hand, there should not be too much of a gap (elderly fathers cannot give their children the benefit of parental guidance, or receive from them in return the benefit of filial piety); and yet, on the other hand, there should not be too little **1335 a** of a gap. § 4. That, too, leads to considerable difficulties: it makes children treat parents with less respect, feeling that they are almost contemporaries, and it readily leads to quarrels about the management of the household. The third thing the legislator has to take into account—and here we return to the point from which we have just digressed—is the provision of a stock of healthy children answerable to his purposes.

Now all these objects may be secured at once by a single policy. § 5. The period of procreation finally ends, as a rule, at the age of 70 for men, and the age of 50 for women; and the beginning of marital intercourse should therefore be fixed for both parties with a corresponding interval. [The husband will thus be 20 years older than his wife at the time of marriage.] § 6. The union of young parents is bad for the procreation of issue. In the whole of the animal world the descendants of young parents have imperfections. They tend to be of the female sex, and they are diminutive in figure. We are bound to expect the same sort of result among human beings. There is evidence to warrant that expectation. In all the states[1] where it is the custom for men and women to marry young, the inhabitants are imperfectly developed and small of stature. § 7. We may add that young mothers have harder labours and die more often in childbirth. This was the reason, according to some accounts, for the response once given by the oracle to the people of Troezen ['Plough not the young fallow']. It had no relation to the cultivation of crops, but referred to the large mortality caused by the marriage of girls at too early an age. § 8. It also conduces to sexual restraint if the daughters of a family are not married early: young women are supposed to be more intemperate when once they have had experience of sexual intercourse. The physique of men is also supposed to be stunted in its growth, when intercourse is begun before the seed has finished *its* growth.[2]

---

[1] Aristotle may have in mind here the Cretans of his time, as well as the people of Troezen.

[2] In considering this physical approach to the subject of marriage, we must remember that Aristotle was the son of a doctor, and that he had received a medical training. In his reference to seed (*sperma*, which is the reading of the better manuscripts, though the word *soma* is found in some), Aristotle seems to suggest that the male seed grows; that its growth is not finished till a given date; and that if sexual intercourse begins before its growth is finished, the whole physique of the person indulging in intercourse will be adversely affected.

It may be added, in regard to the suggestion that men should marry at 37 or thereabouts, that he places the period of physical prime at the age of 30 to 35 in the *Rhetoric* (Book II, c. xiv, § 4).

(The seed, too, has its own period of growth—a period which it observes exactly, or with only a slight variation, in the course of its development.) § 9. Women should therefore marry about the age of 18, and men at 37 or thereabouts. If these ages are observed, union will begin while the bodies of both the partners are still in their prime, and it will end for both simultaneously with the simultaneous ending of their power of procreation. The succession of children to parents will also be as it should be. § 10. If reproduction, as we may reasonably expect, begins immediately after marriage, children will be ready to take over in the beginning of their own prime, and just at the time when the period of the father's vigour has come to an end with the attainment of the age of 70.

We have now discussed the proper ages for marriage. In regard to the proper season of the year, it is best to follow the sensible practice, which is observed by the majority of people to-day, of fixing winter as the time for men and women to set up house together. § 11. Married couples should also study for themselves the lessons to be learned from doctors and natural philosophers about the bringing of children into the world. Doctors can tell them all they need to know about **1335 b** the times of good physical condition: natural philosophers can tell them about favourable winds (for instance, they hold that the north wind is better than the south).

§ 12. What habit of body in the parents is likely to be of most benefit to the future physique of their children? That is a theme to which closer attention will have to be paid when we come to treat of the management of children;[1] but some general indication may be given here. The athlete's habit of body neither produces a good condition for the general purposes of civic life, nor does it encourage ordinary health and the procreation of children. The habit of valetudinarians and persons unfit for any exertion is equally unfavourable. The best habit is one which comes midway between the athletic and the valetudinarian. § 13. Some amount of exertion must therefore go to its making. But the exertion must not be violent or specialized, as is the case with the athlete; it should rather be a general exertion, directed to all the activities of a freeman.

Wives, as well as husbands, need the physical qualities of which we have just been speaking. § 14. Pregnant mothers should pay attention to their bodies: they should take regular exercise,

---

It is not clear why the proper physique of parents should be a matter to be treated in connexion with the management of children. In any case, no treatment of that subject follows.

and follow a nourishing diet. The legislator can easily lead them
to a habit of regular exercise if he requires them to make some
daily pilgrimage for the purpose of worshipping at the shrines of
the goddesses who preside over childbirth.[1] Their minds, unlike
their bodies, should be kept free from exertion; for children
evidently draw on the mother who carries them in her womb, just
as plants draw on the soil.[2]

§ 15. The question arises whether children should always be
reared or may sometimes be exposed to die.[3] There should certainly be a law to prevent the rearing of deformed children. On
the other hand, there should also be a law, in all states where the
system of social habits is opposed to unrestricted increase, to
prevent the exposure of children to death *merely* in order to keep
the population down. The proper thing to do is to limit the size of
each family, and if children are then conceived in excess of the
limit so fixed, to have miscarriage induced before sense and life
have begun in the embryo. (Whether it is right or wrong to
induce a miscarriage will thus depend on whether sense and life
are still to come, or have already begun.)

§ 16. We have now determined the ages at which men and
women should begin their married life. It remains to determine
the length of time for which they should render service to the state
by bringing children into the world. The offspring of elderly men,
like that of very young men, tends to be physically and mentally
imperfect; and the children of old age are weakly. We may therefore fix the length of time for which procreation lasts by reference
to the mental prime.[4] § 17. This comes for most men—as some
of the poets, who measure life in seven-year periods, have suggested
—about the age of 50. Men may therefore be released from the
service of bringing children into the world when they are four or
five years above this age; and from that time forward we must
regard them as indulging in intercourse for reasons of health, or

[1] Artemis was one of these goddesses; but the Greeks had also a special deity
of childbirth (Eileithuia—the Latin Lucina).

[2] Here, as in § 8 above, Aristotle seems to take a purely physical view of
woman (the Greek world was a masculine world). It seems curious, if children
draw on the mother who carries them, that they should not draw on the whole of
her—mind as well as body. But Aristotle apparently desires the mother to be
like the patient unthinking earth in which the seed is germinating.

[3] The exposure of children (sometimes in the hills that rose above the city)
was not uncommon among the Greeks; and the heroine of a Greek play or
romance (it was especially daughters who were thus 'exposed') is sometimes a
foundling of this character. The very word 'foundling' shows the survival of
the practice in modern times; but modern charity has provided the foundling
hospital in lieu of the bare hillside.

[4] 'Aristotle is here speaking of the mental prime of the husband, not the wife'
(Newman, vol. iii, p. 476).

for some similar cause. § 18. For husband or wife to be detected
in the commission of adultery—at whatever time it may happen,
and in whatever shape or form, during all the period of their being
married and being called husband and wife—must be made a
matter of disgrace. But to be detected in adultery **1336 a** during
the very period of bringing children into the world is a thing to be
punished by a stigma of infamy proportionate to such an offence.

<h2 style="text-align:center">Chapter XVII</h2>

2. The nursery and the infant school. *The first stage: the diet of the
infant; the proper use of its limbs; the enuring of children to cold.
The second stage, to the age of 5: games and stories: young children
should be protected from bad company, and safeguarded from hearing
indecent language or seeing indecent pictures: generally, they should
be saved from an early familiarity with anything low, since early
impressions go deep. The third stage, from the age of 5 to that of 7:
children of this age should watch other children doing the work they
will have to do later themselves.*

*After the age of 7 education will fall into two periods—the first
from the age of 7 to that of puberty: the second from the age of
puberty to the age of 21. Should there be a code of regulations, and
should education be managed by the state or privately managed?*

§ 1. When children are born, their physical powers will be
seriously affected, during their growth, by the nature of the
nourishment which they are given. On any consideration of the
matter, and whether we look to the animal world or to the example
of those uncivilized peoples who make it their aim to produce a
martial habit of body, it is evident that a diet abounding in milk
is best suited to the physical development of children; and the
less wine they are given the better, if they are to escape diseases.
§ 2. It is also good to encourage every sort of physical movement
which their little bodies can make; but in order to prevent any
distortion of their soft limbs, some uncivilized peoples still use
mechanical appliances which keep their bodies straight.[1] It is
good to habituate children to the endurance of cold from their
earliest infancy; and this is a practice which greatly conduces to
their general health, as well as hardening them in advance for
military service. § 3. This will explain why some uncivilized
peoples[2] have the habit of plunging their children at birth into a

[1] Aristotle does not explain what these 'instruments' were; but we may
remember the back-boards in which girls used to be pent.
[2] The various references made here, and in other passages of the *Politics*, to
the practices of uncivilized peoples (the *ethnē*, or 'gentiles', outside the Greek
pale), are probably drawn from the collection of the customs of such peoples
which Aristotle made: see below, Appendix V. iii. 2.

cold river, or (like the Celts) of making them go lightly clad. Wherever it is possible to implant a habit in children, it is best to begin the process of habituation in their earliest years, and then to increase it gradually. The physical constitution of children, owing to their natural warmth, is well adapted for training in the endurance of cold.

§ 4. The earliest years will best be handled in the ways we have just described, and in other similar ways. The next stage of the child's life, which lasts to the age of five, is one which cannot be set any lessons, or put to any compulsory tasks, for fear of hindering its growth. But it is a stage which needs some practice in movement, to prevent the body from becoming limp; and this should be provided by games, as well as in other ways. § 5. The games should be neither laborious nor effeminate, but such as become a freeman. Care should also be taken by the officers in charge (who are generally termed the superintendents of education) to determine the sort of tales and stories which children of this age ought to be told. All these things should prepare the way for the occupations of later years; and even the games of children should be for the most part mimicries of what will later be earnest. § 6. Plato, in his *Laws*, would like to stop children from straining their lungs and sobbing; but thinkers of his sort are wrong in the view they take of the matter. It helps the growth of children: it is, in its way, a sort of physical exercise; and just as holding the breath gives adults strength for exertion, so straining the lungs will equally strengthen children.

§ 7. The superintendents of education must exercise a general control over the way in which children pass their time. In particular, they must be careful that very little of their time is passed in the company of slaves. The stage of life through **1336 b** which children pass down to the age of seven is bound to be one of home training; and young as they are they will be likely to contract vulgar habits from anything vulgar they hear or see. § 8. It should therefore be a primary duty of the legislator to exorcize the use of bad language everywhere in our state. To use bad language of any sort lightly is next door to acting badly. The young, especially, should be kept free from hearing, or using, any such language. § 9. Those who are guilty, in spite of all prohibitions, of talking or acting indecently must be punished accordingly. The younger freemen, who are not yet allowed to recline at the common tables,[1] should be subjected to corporal punishment and other indignities;

---

[1] Reclining was the usual posture of the Greeks and Romans at the dinner-table: hence the Latin word *triclinium* for a dining-room. The younger freemen, however, sat on chairs, instead of reclining on couches.

and men of an older age should pay the penalty for behaving like slaves by undergoing indignities of a degrading character.

If the use of indecent language is thus to be proscribed, it is obvious that we must also prevent the exhibition of indecent pictures and the performance of indecent plays. § 10. It should therefore be the duty of the government to prohibit all statuary and painting which portrays any sort of indecent action.[1] An exception may, however, be made for the festivals of deities where even the use of scurrility is licensed by the law.[2] (But here, we may note, the law also allows men who have reached a proper maturity to acquit their wives and children from attendance by attending in person themselves.) § 11. The seeing of mimes or comedies should be forbidden to young persons by the legislator, until they have reached the age when they are allowed to share with the older men in the right of reclining and taking wine at the common tables. By that time their education will have made them all immune from the evil effects of such performances.

§ 12. We have now given a cursory account of this question. We must give it our attention, and settle it in more detail, at a later stage, when we have gone into the arguments for and against such legal control, and discussed the form which it ought to take. Here we have only touched on the issue so far as the occasion immediately requires. § 13. Perhaps there is point in the remark of Theodorus, the tragic actor, that he had never yet allowed any other actor, however poor he might be, to make his entrance before he did, because (as he put it) 'spectators get fond of those they hear first'. This is a fate which is apt to befall us not only in our associations with persons, but also in our contacts with things: we always prefer what we come across first.[3] § 14. The young must therefore be kept from an early familiarity with anything that is low, and especially anything that may suggest depravity or malice. When the first five years are safely over, children should then spend the next two years, down to the age of seven, in watching others at work on the lessons which they will afterwards have to learn themselves.

§ 15. [This brings us to the stage of regular education.] There

---

[1] Aristotle, beginning with the idea of protecting children from hearing bad language, allows himself to digress into the general problem of censorship, for old as well as for young. He takes censorship in his stride (as Plato had done before him), with little or no regard to our modern ideas of the artist's 'freedom' or to general 'freedom of thought'.

[2] We may remember that mock ceremonies might be conducted even in medieval churches, with 'boy-bishops' and 'abbots of unreason'.

[3] Horace said the same thing later:

> Quo semel est imbuta recens servabit odorem
> Testa diu.

should be two different periods of education—the first from the age of seven to that of puberty; the second from puberty to the age of twenty-one. Those who divide man's life into seven-year periods are on the whole right. But the divisions which we ought to follow [when we are planning the course of education] **1337 a** are the divisions made by nature herself. The purpose of education, like that of art generally, is simply to copy nature by making her deficiencies good.[1] § 16. Three subjects here suggest themselves for our consideration. The first is whether there ought to be some code of regulations governing the education of children. The second is whether the education of children should be a matter for the state, or should be conducted on a private basis, as it still is, even to-day, in the great majority of cases. The third question which we have to consider is the proper nature of a code of regulations.

> [1] This is an art
> Which doth mend Nature—change it rather; but
> The art itself is Nature.   (*The Winter's Tale*, Act IV, sc. iv, 95–7.)

BOOK VIII
THE TRAINING OF YOUTH
A
THE GENERAL SCHEME OF TRAINING (cc. I–III)
CHAPTER I

Legislation is needed to regulate education, both for political and for moral reasons. There should be a uniform system for all, and it should be a system of state education.

1337 a 11 § 1. All would agree that the legislator should make the education of the young his chief and foremost concern.[1] [There are two reasons for taking this view.] In the first place, the constitution of a state will suffer if education is neglected. § 2. The citizens of a state should always be educated to suit the constitution of their state.[2] The type of character appropriate to a constitution is the power which continues to sustain it, as it is also the force which originally creates it. The democratic type of character creates and sustains democracy; the oligarchical type creates and sustains oligarchy; and as the progression ascends each higher type of character will always tend to produce a higher form of constitution. In the second place every capacity, and every form of art, requires as a condition of its exercise some measure of previous training and some amount of preliminary habituation. Men must therefore be trained and habituated before they can do acts of goodness, as members of a state should do. [There is thus a moral, as well as a political reason, for making education the chief concern of the legislator.]

§ 3. The whole of a state [i.e. the whole body of its members] has one common End. Evidently, therefore, the system of education in a state must also be one and the same for all, and the provision of this system must be a matter of public action.[3] It cannot be left, as it is at present, to private enterprise, with each parent making provision privately for his own children, and having

---

[1] This is Aristotle's answer to the first question raised at the end of the previous book—'Should there be a code of regulations governing the education of children?' He answers, 'Yes—and that code should be of the foremost importance.'

[2] We have to remember, as always, that the constitution, in Aristotle's view, is not only 'an arrangement of offices', but also 'a way of life'.

[3] This is Aristotle's answer to the second question raised at the end of the previous book—'Should education be managed by the state, or conducted on a private basis?' The answer is that there ought to be a state system of education. Here, as in his answer to the first question, he gives two reasons for the view which he adopts. The first reason is connected with his doctrine of Ends: the second with his doctrine of Wholes and the relation between the Whole and its parts.

them privately instructed as he himself thinks fit. Training for an end which is common should also itself be common. § 4. [There is another reason for taking this view.] We must not regard a citizen as belonging just to himself: we must rather regard every citizen as belonging to the state.[1] Each is a part of the state; and the provision made for each part will naturally be adjusted to the provision made for the Whole. Here, as in some other respects, the Spartans are to be praised. They pay the greatest attention to the training of the young; and they pay that attention collectively, and not in their private capacity.

CHAPTER II

The absence of any clear view about the proper subjects of instruction: the conflicting claims of utility, moral discipline, and the advancement of knowledge. Some subjects should be taught because of their utility; but the teaching of such subjects should never go so far as to produce a mechanical bias, and even the more liberal subjects should not be studied too professionally.

Two things are now evident. The first is that there ought to be laws to regulate education. The second is that education ought to be conducted by the state. § 1. We have now to consider the nature of the education to be given, and the methods by which it ought to be given.[2] At present opinion is divided about the subjects of education. All do not take the same view about what should be learned by the young, either with a view to plain goodness or with a view to the best life possible;[3] nor is opinion clear whether education should be directed mainly to the understanding, or mainly to moral character.[4] § 2. If we look at actual practice, the

[1] This is almost an echo of a passage in Plato's *Laws* (923 A): 'I, as your legislator, do not count either your persons or your property as your own: I count them as belonging to your family, past and future; and still more do I count the whole of your family and your property as belonging to the state.' From the same point of view, in the *Ethics*, Book V, c. XI, §§ 2-3, Aristotle regards the suicide as acting unjustly towards the state; 'and this', he notes, 'is the reason why the state punishes him, and some loss of civic rights is inflicted on the man who destroys himself, as a wrongdoer against the state.'

[2] This is the third of the questions propounded at the end of the previous book—What should be the nature of the code of regulations governing education? The answer to this question—so far as it is actually given—occupies the rest of this Book.

[3] The distinction here implied is somewhat obscure. Perhaps 'plain goodness' is a matter of the virtues belonging to the practical division of the rational part of the soul; while 'the best possible life' goes further, and includes also (and more particularly) the virtues of the speculative and higher division of that part of the soul (see Book VII, c. XIV, § 11, and note).

[4] This sentence may be interpreted to mean, first, that there is no agreement

result is sadly confusing; it throws no light on the problem whether the proper studies to be followed are those which are useful in life, or those which make for goodness, or those which advance the bounds of knowledge. Each sort of study receives some votes in its **1337 b** favour; [none of them has a clear case]. If one looks, for example, at the studies which make for goodness, one finds a total absence of agreement. Goodness itself, to begin with, has not the same meaning for all the different people who honour it; and when that is the case, it is hardly surprising that there should also be difference about the right methods of practising goodness.

§ 3. There can be no doubt that such useful subjects as are really necessary ought to be part of the instruction of children. But this does not mean the inclusion of every useful subject.[1] Occupations are divided into those which are fit for freemen and those which are unfit for them; and it follows from this that the total amount of useful knowledge imparted to children should never be large enough to make them mechanically minded. § 4. The term 'mechanical' (*banausos*) should properly be applied to any occupation, art, or instruction, which is calculated to make the body, or soul, or mind, of a freeman unfit for the pursuit and practice of goodness. § 5. We may accordingly apply the word 'mechanical' to any art or craft which adversely affects men's physical fitness, and to any employment which is pursued for the sake of gain and keeps men's minds too much, and too meanly, occupied. Much the same may also be said of the liberal branches of knowledge. Some of these branches can be studied, up to a point, without any illiberality; but too much concentration upon them, with a view to attaining perfection, is liable to cause the same evil effects that have just been mentioned. § 6. A good deal depends on the purpose for which acts are done or subjects are studied. Anything done to satisfy a personal need, or to help a friend, or to attain goodness, will not be illiberal; but the very same act, when done repeatedly at the instance of other persons, may be counted menial and servile.[2]

---

about the subjects which ought to be taught, whichever part of the human spirit be regarded as the more important; secondly, that there is no clear answer to the question, 'which is the more important part of the human spirit?'

[1] The useful subjects which are necessary may include reading, writing, some arithmetic, and some geometry. Domestic science may be an example of a useful subject which is not necessary. (Newman, vol. iii, p. 506.)

[2] In something of an English fashion—at any rate as that fashion went in the eighteenth century—Aristotle feels that the freeman or 'gentleman' ought to preserve an amateur character. Even in the liberal arts—such as music, painting,

CHAPTER III

There are four subjects of instruction to be considered—reading and writing; drawing; gymnastic; and music. The first two have an element of utility: the third promotes the moral virtue of courage: the purpose of the fourth is not so clear, but it may be argued that it serves to promote the proper use of leisure. This leads us to note the distinction between (1) occupation, (2) play or relaxation, and (3) the use of leisure. The real purpose of music is to be found in the cultivation of leisure; and drawing too, while it has its utility, may also serve to give the young an observant eye for beauty of form and figure.

§ 1. The studies now generally established as parts of the curriculum may be regarded, as has already been said, from two different points of view.[1] There are some four subjects which are usually made the basis of education. They include reading and writing, physical training, and music; and some would also add drawing. The first and the last of these subjects are generally regarded as useful for the practical purposes of life in a number of different ways. Physical training is commonly thought to foster the virtue of courage. The object of training in music is a matter of doubt and dispute. § 2. At present, indeed, it is mainly studied as if its object were pleasure; but the real reason which originally led to its being made a subject of education is something higher. Our very nature has a tendency (on which we have often remarked) to seek of itself for ways and means which will enable us to use leisure rightly, as well as to find some right occupation; indeed it is the power to use leisure rightly, as we would once more repeat, which is the basis of all our life.[2] § 3. It is true that both occupation and leisure are necessary; but it is also true that leisure is higher than occupation, and is the end to which occupation is directed. Our problem, therefore, is to find modes of activity which will fill our leisure. We can hardly fill our leisure with play. To do so would be to make play the be-all and end-all of life.

and literature—he must be a dilettante, with a fine edge of appreciation, but with an edge of execution which is not too precious or virtuose. Something of the same circle of ideas already inspires Castiglione's *Il Cortegiano*, at the beginning of the sixteenth century. The courtier must have a sort of magnanimity, or *sprezzatura*, about all the knowledge which he professes, 'employing in everything a certain disdain which conceals art'. On the idea of 'the mechanical', or 'banausic', see the Introduction, p. lxxiv.

[1] 'i.e. they may be used in support of the view that useful subjects should be studied, or in support of the view that subjects tending to promote virtue should be studied' (Newman, vol. iii, p. 510).

[2] The fact has already been insisted upon, in Book VII c. XIV, § 22, and c. XV, §§ 1-2.

§ 4. That is an impossibility. Play is a thing to be chiefly used in connexion with one side of life—the side of occupation. (A simple argument shows that this is the case. Occupation is the companion of work and exertion: the worker needs relaxation: play is intended to provide relaxation.) We may therefore conclude that play and games should only be admitted into our state at the proper times and seasons, and should be applied as restoratives. The feelings which play produces in the mind are feelings of relief from **1338 a** exertion; and the pleasure it gives provides relaxation. Leisure is a different matter: we think of it as having in itself intrinsic pleasure, intrinsic happiness, intrinsic felicity.[1] § 5. Happiness of that order does not belong to those who are engaged in occupation: it belongs to those who have leisure. Those who are engaged in occupation are so engaged with a view to some end which they regard as still unattained. But felicity is a present end; and all men think of it as accompanied by pleasure and not by pain. It is true that all are not equally agreed about the nature of the pleasure which accompanies felicity. Different persons estimate its nature differently, according to their own personality and disposition. But the highest pleasure, derived from the noblest sources, will be that of the man of greatest goodness.

§ 6. It is clear, therefore, that there are some branches of learning and education which ought to be studied with a view to the proper use of leisure in the cultivation of the mind. It is clear, too, that these studies should be regarded as ends in themselves, while studies pursued with a view to an occupation should be regarded merely as means and matters of necessity. § 7. This will explain why our forefathers made music a part of education. They did not do so because it was necessary: it is nothing of the sort. Nor did they do so because it is useful, as some other subjects are. Reading and writing, for example, are useful in various ways—for money-making; for house-keeping; for the acquisition of knowledge; and for a number of political activities. Drawing may be held to be useful in helping men to judge more correctly [and therefore to purchase more wisely] the works of different artists. [Music serves none of these uses.] Nor is it, like physical training, useful in improving health and military prowess: it has no visible effect upon either. § 8. We are thus left with its value for the cultivation of the mind in leisure. This is evidently the reason of its being introduced into education: it ranks as a part of the

---

[1] The argument here is that occupation has no intrinsic pleasure, but has to be supplemented by an extrinsic pleasure derived from subsequent play. Leisure, on the contrary, has an intrinsic pleasure, which is felt in the very act and moment of its use.

cultivation which men think proper to freemen. This is the meaning of the lines in Homer, beginning,

> Such are they who alone should be called to the bountiful
> banquet,

and continuing (after a mention of various guests) with the words,

§ 9. With them call they a minstrel, to pleasure all men with
his music.

Again, in another passage, Odysseus is made to say that music is
the best of pastimes when men are all merry, and

> They who feast in the hall lend their ears to the minstrel
> in silence,
> Sitting in order due.

§ 10. We may take it as evident, from what has been said, that
there is a kind of education in which parents should have their
sons trained not because it is necessary, or because it is useful, but
simply because it is liberal and something good in itself. Whether
this kind of education is confined to a single subject, or includes
a number of subjects; what the subjects are (if they are several),
and how they should be studied—all this must be left for further
discussion.   § 11. But we have already reached a point at which
we are entitled to say that the evidence of tradition supports our
general view. This is shown by the old-established subjects of
study; and the example of music is sufficient to make it clear. We
are also entitled to say that the reason why some of the useful
subjects ought to be taught to children—for example, reading and
writing—is not only the fact of their being useful: it is also the
fact that they make it possible to acquire many other branches
of knowledge.   § 12. Similarly the object of instruction in drawing
is not so much to save people from making mistakes in their
private purchases, or from being deceived in the buying and selling
1338 b of articles; it is rather to give them an observant eye for
beauty of form and figure. To aim at utility everywhere is utterly
unbecoming to high-minded and liberal spirits.

§ 13. In educating children we must use the instrument of
habits before we use that of reason, and we must deal with the
body before we deal with the mind. We must therefore begin by
putting them into the hands of physical instructors and games-
masters. The former will give them a proper habit of body: the
latter will teach them all the necessary accomplishments.

B

PHYSICAL TRAINING, OR GYMNASTIC (c. iv)

CHAPTER IV

There are dangers in over-athleticism, and defects in the Spartan
system of education: courage is not the only virtue, and a training
meant to produce toughness is one-sided and ineffective, even in the
matter of fostering true courage. The right policy in regard to physical
training is to avoid an excessive early training, which stunts the proper
development of the body. Light exercises till the age of puberty,
followed by a period of three years spent in study, which should be
followed in turn by a period of hard exercise and strict diet—this is
the best system. The young should not be made to work hard with
body and mind simultaneously.

§ 1. Among the states which are generally regarded as paying
the greatest attention to the training of youth, there are some which
seek to create an athletic habit of body, but do so at the cost of
serious injury both to the figure and the growth of the body. The
Spartans have not been guilty of this particular error; but they
turn the young into savages by imposing rigorous exercises, in the
idea that this is the best way of fostering the virtue of courage.
§ 2. It is, however, a mistake, as we have repeatedly said, to direct
the training of youth exclusively, or mainly, to this one virtue; and
even if courage were the main object, the Spartans are wrong in
their way of encouraging it. Both in the animal world, and among
uncivilized peoples, courage is always found, as observation will
show us, not in association with the greatest ferocity, but in
connexion with a gentler and more lion-like temper. § 3. There
are, it is true, many uncivilized peoples which are ready enough
to indulge in murder and cannibalism. Among the peoples on the
coast of the Black Sea, the Achaeans and Heniochi are of this
sort, and some of the inland peoples are equally or even more
savage; they are peoples of bandits—but they have no real courage.
§ 4. Even the Spartans themselves, as we know from experience,
were superior to others only so long as they were the only people
which assiduously practised the rigours of discipline; and nowadays
they are beaten both in athletic contests and in actual war. Their
previous superiority was not due to the particular training which
they gave to their youth: it was simply and solely due to their
having some sort of discipline when their antagonists had none at
all. § 5. The noble heart—not the ferocious temper—should bear
the palm. It is not wolves, or other savage animals, that will fight
a good fight in the presence of a noble danger: it is the man who is

of a good courage. § 6. To let youth run wild in savage pursuits, and to leave them untrained in the disciplines they really need, is really to degrade them into vulgarity. It is to make them serve the statesman's purposes in one respect, and one only; and even there, as our argument shows,[1] it is to make them of less service than those who have been differently trained. § 7. We must not judge the Spartans on the grounds of their former achievement, but on the grounds of their present position. The Spartan training has now to face rivals. Formerly it had none.

There is now general agreement about the necessity of physical training, and about the way in which it ought to be given. Till the age of puberty the exercises used should be light, and there should be no rigorous dieting or violent exertion, such as may hinder the proper growth of the body. § 8. The bad effects of excessive early training **1339 a** are strikingly evident. In the lists of Olympic victors there are only two or three cases of the same person having won in the men's events who had previously won in the boys'; and the reason is that early training, and the compulsory exercises which it involved, had resulted in loss of energy. § 9. [There will thus be light exercises in the years before puberty.] After that age is reached, the next three years may be spent in other studies [such as reading and writing, music, and drawing]; and then the next period of development may properly be given to hard exercise and strict diet. It is not right to do work with the mind and the body at the same time. The two different sorts of work tend naturally to produce different, and indeed opposite, effects. Physical work clogs the mind; and mental work hampers the body.

C

THE AIMS AND METHODS OF EDUCATION IN MUSIC (cc. v–vii)

CHAPTER V

There are three possible views about the purpose of education in music—(1) that it serves for amusement and relaxation; (2) that it serves as a means of moral training; (3) that it serves as a means to the cultivation of the mind. Amusement cannot be the aim: if it were, we should not want to have children taught to play music themselves; we should be content to let them get amusement by listening to the playing of others. But this argument cuts several ways at once. If moral training be regarded as the purpose of music, we may equally ask whether children should be taught to play themselves for that purpose; and even if the cultivation of the mind be regarded as its aim, we may still raise the same question. We may therefore dismiss for

---

[1] This argument has shown, in § 4, that the Spartans are beaten by others even on their own chosen field.

the present the question whether children should play themselves, and turn back to consider the aim of education in music independently of that question.

In a sense education in music has more than one aim. Music produces pleasure, and the pleasure which it produces may serve the purpose of amusement as well as that of cultivation of the mind and the right use of leisure. (The fact that music and its pleasure can serve both purposes explains how easy it is to fall into the idea that amusement is the one end of life: we look at the simpler and more obvious of the two purposes served, and forget the other.) But may not music also serve the purpose of moral training, as well as those of amusement and cultivation of the mind? It would appear that it can. Music can supply 'images' of the virtues, and by inducing us to take pleasure in the 'images' it can induce us to take pleasure in the virtues themselves. All artistic representations (e.g. paintings as well as musical compositions) have this quality; but music has it in a special degree. Both the modes and the times of music have obvious ethical effects, especially upon the young; and indeed harmony, in the view of many thinkers, is the essence—or at any rate an attribute—of the soul.

§ 1. Some questions concerning music have already been raised at an earlier stage of our argument; but it will be well to pick up the thread again here, and to pursue the matter further. We may thus provide something in the nature of a preface to the considerations which would naturally be advanced in any full view of the subject. § 2. It is difficult to define the exact effects of music; and it is equally difficult to define the exact purpose for which it ought to be studied. Some would hold that the purpose of music, like that of sleeping or drinking, is simply amusement and relaxation. Sleep and drink are not in themselves good things; but they are at any rate pleasurable things, and, as Euripides says, they 'bid dull cares avaunt'. § 3. It is on this ground that music is sometimes ranked with them both, and that sleep and drink and music (to which dancing may also be added) are all treated in just the same way. Another possible view is that music should be regarded as something of an influence making for goodness, inasmuch as it has the power of giving a tone to our character (just as physical training can give a tone to our bodies) by habituating us to feel pleasure in the right sort of way.[1] § 4. There is still a third possible view— that music has some contribution to make to the cultivation of our minds and to the growth of moral wisdom.[2]

---

[1] A piece of music, e.g. the *Marseillaise*, may affect our character, and give it a tone, by habituating us to take pleasure in the message of courage which it conveys.

[2] These three views may be compared with the threefold classification of the soul in Book VII, c. XIV, §§ 11-12 (see the note *ad locum*). The view that music,

It is clear that amusement is *not* the object with a view to which the young should be educated. Learning is not a matter of amusement. It is attended by effort and pain. On the other hand it is also true that cultivation of the mind is not a thing which is proper for children or the young of a tender age. Those who are themselves still short of their own end cannot yet cope with the ultimate end. § 5. [A case may indeed be made out for amusement, and] we may argue that the serious studies of children [including music] are ways and means to the amusement which they will be able to enjoy when they reach their full growth as adults. But if that ground be taken, why (we may ask) should children be taught to play music them*selves*? Why should they not follow the example of the Persian and Median kings, and get their pleasure and instruction through listening to others who make a business of music? § 6. Those who make it an occupation and a profession are bound to attain a better result than those who only practise it long enough just to learn. We may add that if children are to be made to work away at musical performances, they ought equally to be made to work at the business of cooking—which is absurd.

§ 7. The problem whether children should learn to play themselves equally arises if we look at music as a power which can improve character. Here, too, we may ask, 'Why should children learn to perform themselves, and why should not listening to the music of others be enough to give them the **1339 b** power of enjoying and appreciating music in the right sort of way?' The Spartans act on that principle: they do not learn to play; but report says that they are able to appreciate properly the difference between good and bad tunes. § 8. Much the same may be said if we take the third view about music, and hold that it ought to be used to promote our felicity and to give us a liberal cultivation. Why, for this purpose, should we learn ourselves, instead of drawing on the services of others? Here we shall do well to remember the conception we hold of the gods. The Zeus of our poets does not sing, or play on the harp; [he simply listens]. We are apt to regard as vulgar those who do otherwise, and we think of them as behaving in a way in which a man would not behave unless he were drunk or jesting.

§ 9. This, however, is perhaps a matter for later consideration. We must first inquire whether music should, or should not, be included in education; and that leads us to ask, 'In which of the

like sleep and drink, is a form of amusement and relaxation, connects it with the irrational part of the soul. The view that music makes for goodness connects it with the practical division of the rational part of the soul. The third and last view connects it with the speculative division of that part.

three ways previously distinguished does it act—the way of education [or the giving of tone to the character], or that of amusement,
or that of cultivation of the mind?' There are reasons for connecting it with all three; for it evidently embraces elements common to
all. § 10. [Let us take, for example, as one of these elements, the
element of pleasure.] Amusement is intended to produce relaxation; and relaxation, which is in its nature a remedy for the pain
produced by exertion, must necessarily contain the element of
pleasure. Similarly, again, cultivation of the mind is generally
agreed to have an element of pleasure, as well as an element of
nobility; and the spirit of true felicity is a spirit composed of *both*
of these elements. [Pleasure, therefore, is an element common
both to amusement and to cultivation.] § 11. Now we all agree
that music, whether instrumental or accompanied by the voice, is
one of the greatest of pleasures.[1] At any rate we can cite the
testimony of the poet Musaeus:

> Song is to mortals the sweetest;

and here we may see the reason why men very naturally enlist the
aid of music for their social parties and pastimes—it has the power
of gladdening their hearts. We may therefore conclude that the
pleasure it gives them is one of the reasons why children ought to
be educated in music. § 12. All innocent pleasures have a double
use: they not only help us to achieve our end [i.e. felicity], but
they also serve us as means of relaxation. It is seldom we enjoy
the fruition of our end. But we can often enjoy relaxation, and
indulge ourselves in amusements (not so much with a view to
something beyond, but just for the pleasure they give us); and it
may therefore be well to let the young rest and relax for a while in
the pleasures which come from music.

§ 13. Men fall, it is true, into a way of making amusements the
end of their life. The reason for their doing so is that the end of
life would seem to involve a kind of pleasure. This kind of pleasure
is not the ordinary, but in their search for it men are apt to mistake
ordinary pleasure for it; and they do so because pleasure generally
has some sort of likeness to the ultimate end of human activity.
This end is desirable just for itself, and not for the sake of any
future result; and the pleasures of amusement are similar—they
are not desired for the sake of some result in the future, but rather
because of something which has happened in the past, that is to
say, the exertion and pain which have already been undergone.

---

[1] The argument is that music is a great pleasure; that pleasure is an element
common both to amusement and to cultivation; and that music, therefore, is
intended both for amusement and cultivation—and not for one object only.

§ 14. This, it may reasonably be held, is the cause which induces men to seek happiness from pleasures of this order.

Pleasure is not the only reason why men have recourse to music. Another reason is its *utility* in furnishing relaxation.[1] This is how the case for it seems to stand. § 15. But we have to inquire whether it does not possess, over and above these *accidents* [of pleasure and utility], **1340 a** an *essence* which is of higher value than the uses hitherto mentioned. Perhaps there is more in question than our sharing in the common pleasure which all men derive from music— a pleasure, indeed, which is natural and instinctive, and which explains why the use of music appeals to all ages and all types of character—and perhaps we ought to consider whether music has not also some sort of bearing on our characters and our souls. § 16. It will clearly have such a bearing if our characters are actually affected by music. That they are so affected is evident from the influence exercised by a number of different tunes, but especially by those of Olympus. His tunes, by general consent, have an inspiring effect on the soul; and a feeling of inspiration is an affection of the soul's character.[2] § 17. We may add that, in listening to mere imitative sounds, where there is no question of time or tune, all men are moved to feelings of sympathy.

Since music belongs to the category of pleasures, and since goodness consists in *feeling delight* where one should, and loving and hating aright, we may clearly draw some conclusions.[3] First, there is no lesson which we are so much concerned to learn, and no habit which we are so much concerned to acquire, as that of forming right judgements on, and feeling delight in, fine characters and good actions. § 18. Next, musical times and tunes provide us with images of states of character—images of anger, and of calm; images of fortitude and temperance, and of all the forms of their opposites; images of the other states—which come closer to their

---

[1] The distinction here drawn is somewhat subtle. Aristotle has previously said that there are three headings under which music may be discussed—amusement, moral instruction, and the cultivation of the mind. Here he appears to draw a distinction within the first heading—the distinction between amusement which is just pure pleasure, and amusement which has utility because it brings recreation and refreshes the mind.

[2] Newman notes (vol. iii, p. 536), 'Aristotle has to prove that music affects the character of the soul; therefore he has to prove that the inspiration which it admittedly produces is an affection of the character of the soul. Some may have regarded it as a *bodily* affection, . . . and others as a special condition of the *mind*, . . . but Aristotle regards it as connected with an impulse to action, . . . and this is perhaps the reason why he here traces it to the *character of the soul*.'

[3] The general argument is that, since (1) music can give pleasure, and (2) goodness consists in feeling pleasure aright (i.e. in connexion with the right sort of acts and the right sort of characters), music of the right character can help in producing goodness, because it can help in producing a feeling of pleasure in acts and characters of the right sort.

actual nature than anything else can do. This is a fact which is clear from our own experience; to listen to these images is to undergo a real change of the soul. § 19. Now to acquire a habit of feeling pain or taking delight in an image is something closely allied to feeling pain or taking delight in the actual reality. The man, for example, who finds delight in looking at the sculptured image of some object—purely on the ground of its intrinsic form [and not on the ground of its material, or the beauty and cost of that material]—will also be bound to find pleasure in looking at the actual object itself. § 20. It is true that the objects of some of the senses, such as touch and taste, cannot furnish any resemblance to states of character. Objects of sight may do so, but only to a slight extent. There are indeed shapes and figures which bear a resemblance to states of character, but the resemblance is not great; and we have to remember that all sorts of persons have the sense of sight.[1] Moreover, the shapes and colours presented by visual art are not *representations* of states of character: they are merely *indications*. § 21. And they are indications which can only be given by depicting the body when under the influence of some emotion.[2] But in so far as there *is* any difference between the effects of looking at different works of art, the young should be discouraged from looking at the works of Pauso, and encouraged to study the works of Polygnotus and any other painter or sculptor who depicts moral character.

With musical compositions, however, the case is different. They are, in their very nature, representations of states of character. § 22. This is an evident fact. In the first place, the nature of the modes varies; and listeners will be differently affected according as they listen to different modes. The effect of some will be to produce a sadder and graver temper **1340 b**—this is the case, for example, with the mode called the Mixolydian. The effect of others (such as the soft modes)[3] is to relax the tone of the mind. Another mode is specially calculated to produce a moderate and collected temper; this is held to be the peculiar power of the Dorian mode, while the Phrygian mode is held to give inspiration and fire. § 23. We may well approve of the views thus advanced by those who have studied the subject of musical education; for

[1] The argument would appear to be (1) that objects of sight can only resemble states of character to a small extent, and (2) that—as all sorts of persons have the sense of sight—this small resemblance will tend to pass unregarded among the mass.

[2] Statuary, therefore, cannot *represent* courage: it can only *indicate* it—and that only by depicting a human body when under the influence of the emotions aroused by the presence of danger. Music, on the other hand, can get to the soul of courage.

[3] The softer varieties, Newman suggests, of the Ionian and Lydian modes.

the evidence by which they support their theories is derived from actual facts.

What has just been said about musical modes is equally applicable to the varieties of musical time. Some of these varieties have a more steady character: others have a lively quality; and these last may again be divided, according as they move with a more vulgar rhythm or move in a manner more suited to freemen. § 24. What we have said makes it clear that music possesses the power of producing an effect on the character of the soul.[1] If it can produce this effect, it must clearly be made a subject of study and taught to the young. § 25. We may add that the teaching of music is congenial to the natural endowment of youth. Owing to their tender years, the young will not willingly tolerate any unsweetened fare; and music, by its nature, has a quality of sweetness. Nor is that all. The modes and rhythms of music have an affinity with the soul, as well as a natural sweetness. This explains why many thinkers connect the soul with harmony—some saying that it *is* a harmony, and others that it possesses the attribute of harmony.[2]

CHAPTER VI

We return to the question, 'Should children be taught to play themselves?' To judge any performance well, you ought to be able to perform yourself; and the answer to the question is therefore 'Yes'—provided that the performance of music is not carried to professional lengths. Three inquiries thus suggest themselves—(1) what is the length to which the performance of music should be carried; (2) what sorts of melodies and rhythms should children learn to play; and (3) what instruments should they use? In regard to the first of these questions, we may say that difficult compositions should not be attempted, and the point to which children should go in learning to play themselves is the point at which they begin to be able to appreciate good melodies and rhythms. In regard to the last of the three ques-

---

[1] Aristotle never gets to the highest of the topics previously suggested—that of the effect of music on the *speculative* division of the rational part of the soul, or, in other words, on 'the cultivation of the mind'. But cf. c. v, § 4.

[2]   From harmony, from heavenly harmony
This universal frame began:
From harmony to harmony
Through all the compass of the notes it ran,
The diapason closing full in man.
          (Dryden, *Song for Saint Cecilia's Day*.)

Jaeger, in his *Aristoteles* (p. 43), remarks that Aristotle's own doctrine of the soul in the *De Anima* 'stands midway between the materialistic conception that the soul is a harmony of the body and the Platonic conception . . . that it is itself a substance'.

tions, we may deprecate the use of the flute or similar instruments.
We may also deprecate any attempt at professional skill and any
entering for competitions, which tends to have a vulgarizing effect.

§ 1. It remains to answer the question, which has already been
tentatively raised, whether children ought to learn music by actually
singing and playing. It is clear that it makes a great difference to
the acquisition of an aptitude whether one has, or has not, joined
in an actual performance. It is difficult, if not impossible, for those
who have never joined in a performance to become good judges
of others. § 2. Children, too, should always have something to
keep them occupied; and the rattle of Archytas (which parents
give to children in order to divert their attention and stop them
from breaking things in the house) must be counted an admirable
invention. Young things can never keep quiet: a real rattle suits
children in infancy: and a training in music will serve as a rattle
for children of an older growth.

§ 3. These considerations make it plain that a training in music
should include some share in its actual performance. There is no
difficulty in determining what is suitable or unsuitable for the
different ages of growth; and we can easily answer the objection
that a study of music which includes execution is professional and
mechanical. § 4. We must begin by noting that the purpose for
which the young should join in the actual performance of music
is only that they should be able to judge [the performances of
others]. This means that they ought to practise execution in their
earlier years; but it also means that they ought to be released from
it at a later age, when the education they have received in their youth
should have made them able to judge what is good and to appreciate music properly. § 5. The censure which is sometimes passed
on music—that it produces a professional or mechanical turn of
mind—may be easily answered if we pause to make a few inquiries.
What, in the first place, is the point up to which those who are
being trained with a view to civic excellence should continue to
join in actual performances? Secondly, what is the quality **1341 a**
of the melodies and rhythms in which they ought to be instructed?
Thirdly, what is the nature of the instruments (for that, too, is
likely to make a difference) in the use of which they ought to be
trained? § 6. If we answer these questions we shall also be able to
answer the censure. There may well be *some* kinds of music which
have a mechanical effect; [but we must begin by distinguishing
the different effects of different kinds before we can really judge].

We may take it for granted that the study of music should be
pursued in such a way that it will neither impede the activities of

later and riper years, nor produce a mechanical habit of body which
is ineffective for the purposes of the period of military and civic
training—ineffective, initially, in bodily exercise, and afterwards
in the pursuit of knowledge. § 7. The study of music might
follow these lines if two conditions were observed—first, that
pupils were not set to work on the sort of performances which
belong to professional competitions; secondly, that they were not
made to attempt the extraordinary and extravagant feats of execution which have recently been introduced into competitions, and
have thence passed on into education. § 8. Even so [i.e. when such
excesses have been excluded], performances should only be carried
to the point at which students begin to be able to appreciate good
melodies and rhythms, and are not content merely to enjoy that common element in music [i.e. the element of mere pleasure] which is
felt by some of the animals and by nearly all slaves and children.

The nature of the instruments which should be used may also
be inferred from what has just been said. § 9. Flutes should not
be used in musical education; and we ought to avoid any other
instrument which requires professional skill, such as the harp and
all other such instruments. The instruments which ought to be
used are those that will make students intelligent, whether in the
field of music itself or in other fields of study. A further argument
against the flute [besides the technique which it requires] is the
fact that it does not express a state of character, but rather a mood
of religious excitement; and it should therefore be used on those
occasions when the effect to be produced on the audience is the
release of emotion (*katharsis*), and not instruction. § 10. Another
reason against the use of the flute in education is the fact that
flute-playing prevents the player from using his voice. Our
ancestors were therefore right in debarring the use of the flute
to youths and freemen—although they had in earlier days encouraged it. § 11. In those earlier days wealth had given them
increased leisure and a higher appetite for general excellence:
their achievements, in the period of the Persian wars and afterwards, had elated their pride; and anxious only to explore fresh
fields they took all studies indiscriminately for their province. It
was in this spirit that they introduced flute-playing into education.
§ 12. Even in Sparta the leader of a chorus is reported to have
played the flute for his dancers personally [instead of leaving it to
a hired player]; but at Athens flute-playing attained such vogue
that most freemen joined in the fashion—witness the tablet erected
by Thrasippus, who had equipped a chorus of dancers, in honour
of Ecphantides [the fluteplayer of the chorus]. At a later date,
when men were better able to judge what really conduced to

excellence, and what had the opposite effect, a larger experience of flute-playing led to its final rejection. § 13. Many of the older instruments were also included in the rejection—zithers, lutes, and similar instruments calculated merely to please the audience; and, along with them, heptagons, triangles, sackbuts, and all other instruments merely **1341 b** requiring manual dexterity. There is wisdom in the myth of the ancients about the flute. Athene, it tells us, invented the flute—and then threw it away. § 14. There is some point, too, in the rest of the story—that she threw it away in disgust at the ugly look of her face when she was playing upon it. But Athene is the goddess to whom we ascribe the gift of knowledge and skill in the arts; and it seems more likely that she threw it away because the study of flute-playing has nothing to do with the mind.

§ 15. Both in regard to the instruments used, and the degree of proficiency sought, we may accordingly reject any professional system of instruction. By that we mean any system intended to prepare pupils for competitions. On such a system the player, instead of treating music as a means to his own improvement, makes it serve the pleasure—and that a vulgar pleasure—of the audience to which he is playing. That is why we regard his performance as something improper in a freeman, and more befitting a hireling. § 16. The players themselves may also become vulgar in the process. The standard by which they fix their aim [i.e. the pleasure of their audience] is a bad standard: the commonness of the audience tends to debase the quality of the music; and the artists themselves, with their eyes on the audience, are affected by it—affected not only in mind, but also even in body, as they move and swing to suit the taste of their hearers.

CHAPTER VII

In regard to the second question—what sort of melodies and rhythms should children learn to play?—there is this to be said. Melodies can be divided into (1) those which are expressive of character, (2) those which stimulate to action, and (3) those which produce inspiration. The benefits which may be derived from music can also be stated under three heads—(1) education, (2) release of emotion, and (3) cultivation of the mind, with which we may also link relaxation and recreation. The relation of the different sorts of melodies to the different benefits: the melodies suitable for producing the benefit of release of emotion. The adaptation of melodies to different sorts of audiences—the educated and the uneducated. The character of the different modes, especially the Dorian and Phrygian, and the different effects which they produce. The different ages of life best suited by different sorts of music.

§ 1. It remains to consider the different modes and times;[1] to determine whether they should all be used, or a choice should be made among them; and to decide whether those who are practising music with a view to education should observe the same rule [as all others who practise it] or a special rule of their own. There is also a further subject to be considered. Music is produced, as we may easily observe, by the two means of melody and time; and we ought therefore to know the influence exercised on education by either of these means, and to ask ourselves whether we ought to prefer music with good melody to music in good time.[2] § 2. But we believe that there is a good deal of truth in the observations made on these matters by some of the musicians of our day, and also by some of our thinkers, on the more philosophic side, who are versed in the general subject of musical education. We therefore propose to refer any student who desires a precise treatment of each subject to these authorities; and we confine ourselves here to sketching general outlines and laying down, much as a law does, the broad rules to be followed.

§ 3. We accept the classification of melodies, which is made by some of our philosophic thinkers, into those which are expressive of character, those which stimulate to action, and those which produce inspiration; and we note that these thinkers would also make the nature of the musical modes correlative to that of these classes, with each different mode corresponding to each different class of melody. On the other hand we hold, as has already been stated,[3] that music should not be pursued for any single benefit which it can give, but for the sake of several. There are three benefits which it can give. One is education: a second is release of emotion (the sense of that term will be explained more clearly in our lectures on poetics, but may be left to speak for itself at the moment): a third is the benefit of cultivation, with which may be linked that of recreation and relaxation of strain.[4] It is clear from **1342 a** the view we have stated that all the modes should be used,

---

[1] Aristotle has treated two of the subjects mentioned in § 5 of the previous chapter—the first and the third: he now discusses, in conclusion, the remaining subject—the second in the original order of enumeration.

[2] The translation follows an emendation of the text suggested by Newman.

[3] See c. v, §§ 9–10.

[4] See c. III, § 4, of this Book, where Aristotle also mentions together—but mentions as different—the two ideas of (1) leisure and cultivation and (2) recreation and relaxation. It should be added that the three 'benefits' of music here mentioned are different from the three effects ascribed to music in the beginning of chapter v. There the three effects of music are explained as (a) amusement and relaxation, (b) moral training, and (c) cultivation of the mind. Here Aristotle adds release of emotion as a new effect, but combines (a) and (c) together—retaining (b) as it stands, though with the new style of 'education . . . through the modes which express character best'.

but not in the same sort of way. When education is the object in view, the modes which ought to be used are those which express character best: when it is a question of listening to the performance of others, we may also admit the modes which stimulate men to action or provide them with inspiration. § 4. Any affection which strongly moves the souls of several persons will move the souls of all, and will only differ from person to person with a difference of degree. Pity, fear, and inspiration are such affections. The feeling of being possessed by some sort of inspiration is one to which a number of persons are particularly liable. These persons, as we can observe for ourselves, are affected by religious melodies; and when they come under the influence of melodies which fill the soul with religious excitement they are calmed and restored as if they had undergone a medical treatment and purging.[1] § 5. The same sort of effect will also be produced [i.e. by appropriate music] on those who are specially subject to feelings of fear and pity, or to feelings of any kind; indeed it will also be produced on the rest of us, in proportion as each is liable to some degree of feeling; and the result will be that all alike will experience some sort of purging, and some release of emotion accompanied by pleasure. We may add that melodies which are specially designed to purge the emotions are likewise also a source of innocent delight to us all.

§ 6. We may go on to argue that these are the modes and melodies which competitors in musical contests ought to be required to use. But there are two different kinds of audiences. One is an audience composed of the free and educated; the other is the common audience composed of mechanics, hired labourers, and the like. There should therefore be contests and festivals not only for the first kind of audience, but also for the second, to give it the relaxation of which it stands in need. § 7. [The music for this second kind of audience will correspond to its state of mind]; just as the souls of its members are distorted from their natural state, so there are musical modes which are correspondingly perverted, and melodies which are similarly strained and overcoloured. A man derives pleasure from what suits him best; and we must therefore permit musicians who are competing before an audience of the baser sort to use a baser sort of music which corresponds to their audience.

[1] Aristotle uses the same word (*Katharsis*) for what has before been translated as 'release of emotion' and for what is here translated as 'purging'. The release of the bowels by purging is analogous, in his view, to the release of the feelings by listening to some forms of music—or by listening to tragedy (*Poetics*, c. VI). Newman quotes Milton's lines about music in *Paradise Lost*, Book I,

Not wanting power to *mitigate and suage*
With solemn touches troubled thoughts.

§ 8. For education, as we have already noted, the melodies and modes which ought to be used are those expressive of character. The Dorian, as we have already observed, is one of these modes; but we must also adopt any of the other modes which we find recommended by those who have been concerned in philosophical studies and musical education. § 9. Plato, in the *Republic*, makes the error of selecting the Phrygian mode as the only one to be kept along with the Dorian; and his error is the more striking, as he has previously rejected the use of the flute. Actually the Phrygian mode **1342 b** is related to the others, in the effect which it produces, as the flute is to other instruments: the effect of both is religious excitement and general emotion. § 10. We can see from poetry that this is so. Dionysiac frenzy, and all such agitations of the mind, are more naturally expressed [when depicted in poetry] by an accompaniment on the flute than by one on any other instrument. Similarly, in the matter of modes, we find that melodies which are in the Phrygian mode are the vehicle suitable for such states of mind. The dithyramb,[1] which is generally agreed to be Phrygian in character, will serve as an example. § 11. Many instances attesting the character of the dithyramb are cited by experts in the art of music. The case of Philoxenus is one. He attempted, but failed, to compose a dithyramb, entitled 'The Mysians', in the Dorian mode; and he was driven by the very nature of his theme to fall back on the Phrygian mode as the more appropriate. § 12. The Dorian mode is generally agreed to be the gravest and the most expressive of a temper of fortitude. It has also another merit. On our general view the mean, which lies midway between extremes, is preferable and ought to be followed. Now the Dorian mode stands to other modes in the position of the mean. It is therefore Dorian melodies which suit the young best as an instrument of education.[2]

§ 13. There are two aims which men pursue—the possible, and the proper; and each man, in his pursuit of these aims, should concern himself particularly with what is possible and proper *in his own case*. This is determined for him by his age. Those who are old and exhausted find it difficult to sing in high-pitched modes; and nature herself prompts the use of the lower and softer modes for that age. § 14. There is therefore justice in the censure which some musicians pass upon Plato for rejecting the lower and

[1] A song, with music and dancing, originally concerned with the birth and fortunes of the god Dionysus, but afterwards taking a wider range; it was in a lofty but often inflated style, and was always in the Phrygian mode and therefore accompanied by the flute.

[2] Here, as in c. v (see the note on § 24 of that chapter), Aristotle omits to consider the melodies and modes which are suited to the cultivation of the mind during leisure.

softer modes as instruments of education, on the ground that they are connected with drinking—an argument which is not founded on the immediate effect of drink (which is mainly one of inspiring a frenzy of intoxication), but on its after-effect in producing exhaustion. We must remember [as Plato failed to do] the years to come and the days of old age; and with a view to their needs the lower and softer modes and melodies must also be used [i.e. in youth, and as a part of the education of youth].   § 15. We must also include any mode which is proper to the age of youth by virtue of combining the attraction of beauty with some instructive power. This is a combination which the Lydian mode would seem particularly to present. There are thus three standards to which education in music should conform—the mean, the possible, and the proper.[1]

NOTE HHH: *The Conclusion of the Politics*

The mean is a standard which suggests the Dorian mode. The possible is a standard which suggests that age should avoid the high-pitched modes, and content itself with the lower (e.g. the Phrygian)—though (as is suggested in § 14) the lower modes may also be studied in youth, with a view to the needs of age, along with the high-pitched modes which are possible for the young. The proper is a standard which suggests the Lydian mode, as being, by its combination of beauty and instruction, particularly proper for the young.

At this point the sketch of the ideal state ends—apparently in the middle of an unfinished discussion of education, and with the later life and activities of the citizen (after his education is finished) still to be described. There is more to be said about the *subjects* of education ('gymnastic', for example, and intellectual studies): Aristotle has, on the whole, confined himself to 'music'. There is more to be said about the different *stages* of education: Aristotle has dealt, in the main, only with the early years. There are also a number of promises of 'future discussions' which are not fulfilled. All that one can say is simple. Aristotle's notes stopped at this point. That is just what happens to a set of notes or a course of lectures, as many lecturers can testify; and there is no more to be said. We cannot apply the standards of a printed book to the manuscript of a set of notes. . . . Almost every 'method' or section of the *Politics* stops abruptly. It is not surprising that the last of the 'methods' should have a similar ending.

[1] See Note HHH.

APPENDIXES

THE subject of politics was treated by Aristotle not only in the treatise which bears that name, but also in some of his other treatises and some of his general writings.

Foremost in importance among the other treatises is the *Ethics*.[1] In the life of the Greek city-state, which drew little distinction between what was private and what was public, and included in its scope the area of social life and moral conduct as well as that of political action, ethics could be regarded as a part or branch of politics. This is the view which Aristotle adopts in many parts of the *Politics*. But his general view of the relation in which ethics stands to politics can hardly be said to be constant; and the very fact that he wrote a separate work on ethics would suggest that he assigned to it a relative independence. In any case, however, the two subjects are closely connected; and the student of the *Politics* who wishes to grasp the whole of Aristotle's political theory is bound to consider the references to politics which are also to be found in the *Ethics*.

Next in importance to the *Ethics*, in its bearing on Aristotle's theory of politics, is the *Rhetoric*. Something is said about the general nature of this treatise in a later passage (p. 359). Here it is sufficient to say that rhetoric, or the art of oratory, was the training-ground for a political career in the practice of ancient Greece—and, later, of ancient Rome—and that Aristotle's treatise on rhetoric is therefore concerned, by the nature of its subject, with questions of politics.

In the first three of the following appendixes a translation is accordingly given of some of the most important passages in the *Ethics* and the *Rhetoric* which bear on matters of politics. The method which is followed is that of selecting three main themes (Aristotle's conception of politics; his conception of justice, law, and equity; and his classification of constitutions), and of translating separately the passages of the *Ethics* and the *Rhetoric* which bear on each of these themes. The reader will, it is hoped, profit more from the use of this method than if the translator had arranged all the passages from the *Ethics* and the *Rhetoric* according to the order in which they appear in Aristotle's text.

The two last appendixes explain themselves. In the first of them a translation is given of some passages from the *Constitution of Athens*, a compilation in which Aristotle describes the constitutional history of Athens and gives an account of the actual working of the Athenian constitution of his time. The reader will see for himself, from these passages, how much Athenian democracy formed the background of Aristotle's theory of politics.

The fifth and last appendix contains a brief account (with a few incidental translations) of the surviving fragments of lost Aristotelian writings—dialogues, pamphlets, compilations, and letters—which touched on political themes. The reader may perhaps find a particular interest in the recorded fragments of Aristotle's letters to his pupil Alexander and his friend Antipater, the Macedonian regent who dealt with Greek affairs during Alexander's absence in Asia.

[1] By the *Ethics* the reader is asked to understand the *Nicomachean Ethics*. The translator has not considered the other treatise (probably also Aristotelian) which is called the *Eudemian Ethics*.

APPENDIX I

ARISTOTLE'S CONCEPTION OF POLITICS IN THE *ETHICS* AND THE *RHETORIC*

A. THE CONCEPTION IN THE *ETHICS*

1. *The conception at the beginning of the* Ethics

BOOK I. CHAPTER I

1094 a § 1. Every art we follow and every inquiry we make—and similarly each of our actions and pursuits—may be held to aim at some good or end. . . . § 3. Actions, arts, and sciences are manifold; and their ends must therefore be equally manifold. Medicine, for instance, will have health for its end: shipbuilding will have boats; the art of war will have victory; and the art of household management wealth. § 4. [Not only is there a plurality of arts and their ends: there is also a hierarchy.] There are a number of arts which come under some single controlling capacity. The art of bridle-making for instance—and, with it, all other arts concerned with the instruments for riding—comes under the art of riding. The art of riding in turn—and, with it, all forms of actions which are connected with war—comes under the art of war. Similarly [and on a still further progression] each art will come under yet others; [and thus the art of war may come under an even higher art—the art of politics]. Now in all these cases the ends of the master-arts are preferable to all the subordinate ends [which are served by the lower arts coming under the master-arts]. It is for the sake of the former [ends] that the latter ends are pursued. . . . [We have therefore to inquire, 'what is the master-art, and what is its master-end?']

CHAPTER II

§ 1. If there is some end of the things done by us which we desire *for its own sake*, and which is the cause of our desiring other ends—if, in other words, we do not choose everything for the sake of something other than itself (which would mean an unending series of choices, and would make desire an empty and idle thing)—it clearly follows that this master-end is the Good, or rather the Highest Good. § 2. We may ask ourselves, therefore, the question, 'Has not the knowledge of this end a large influence on our actual life? Shall we not, if we possess it, be more likely to hit the mark of duty, like archers who have a mark to aim at?' § 3. If we answer 'Yes' to the question, then we must attempt to comprehend, at any rate in outline, the nature of this master-end, and to discover which is the science, or capacity, that has it for its object. § 4. That science would naturally seem to be the most sovereign of the sciences—the science which is most of a master-science. § 5. Now politics appears to be of this nature.[1] **1094 b** § 6. In the first place, it

---

[1] 'Politics' in the Greek is an adjectival form—as if we should say 'the political'. What is the noun which it implies? Strictly, it is the noun 'science'

is politics that determines what other sciences should be studied in states; which of them should be learned by each group of citizens; and to what extent they should be learned.[1] In the second place, observation shows that even the forms of capacity which are most highly esteemed—the art of war; the art of household management; the art of oratory—come under the control of politics. § 7. If politics thus makes use of the other sciences, and if, in addition to that, it lays down rules determining what we should do and what we should leave undone, the end of politics will embrace the ends of the other arts and sciences; and that end will therefore be the Good of man. § 8. True, the end of the individual is the same [in *kind*] as that of the political community, [and from that point of view we might also say that the end of the individual is the Good of man]; but, even so, the end of the political community is [in *degree*] a greater thing to attain and maintain, and a thing more ultimate,[2] than the end of the individual. In a word, the [human] end is something well worth while even for the individual considered by himself; but it is a finer thing, and a thing of diviner quality, for a people and for civic communities.

These, then, are the aims to which our inquiry into ethics is addressed —being, as it is, of the nature of a *political* inquiry.

[It would thus seem, from the beginning of the *Ethics*, that ethics is in a sense subordinate to politics—which does not mean for a moment that political *raison d'état* can overbear ethics, but only that 'community ethics' (the ethics of a political community living under a constitution which enshrines 'a way of life') is a higher stage in the march of human development than 'individual ethics'. We may now turn from the beginning of the *Ethics* to the end, and consider the point of view at which Aristotle has arrived after conducting his inquiry into ethics through the ten books of his treatise.]

2. *The conception at the end of the* Ethics

BOOK X, CHAPTER IX

1179 a 33 § 1. If these subjects—the nature of happiness (or felicity), the various forms of goodness, and, in addition, friendship and pleasure[3]

(*epistēmē*). But since sciences may be, in Aristotle's view, practical as well as theoretical, and since the science of politics is largely practical, we may say that 'the political' implies the noun 'art' or 'capacity' (*technē* or *dynamis*) no less than it implies the noun 'science'. In a word, it implies both. 'Politics' is the scientific study of the *polis*, and of all things political, *with a view to political action* or the proper exercise of the political 'art'.

[1] Accordingly, in Book VIII of the *Politics*, it prescribes that music should be studied, and studied by the younger age-groups, but not to an extent which involves professional skill.

[2] The Greek noun for 'end' is *telos*. The adjective of that noun is *teleios*; and that adjective indicates the state of having reached the end. The word which is here translated as 'more ultimate' thus means 'more in the state of having reached the end'. The end of the political community is the furthest reach of the whole progression of human ends, and in it and by it the whole progression is 'more in the state having reached the end'.

[3] These are the main subjects of the *Ethics*. The *various forms of goodness*, moral

—have been treated sufficiently in outline, may we conclude that our programme of inquiry has attained its end? [Hardly: there is something more to be added.] In the sphere of doing, it is generally said that the end we seek does not consist in studying or knowing the different things to be done; it consists in actually doing them. § 2. Where the issue which confronts us is [not only that of doing things, but also that of doing them *well*, and is thus an issue of] goodness, knowledge is certainly not enough. We must also endeavour to possess and practise goodness, or we must try any other means there may be for becoming actually good.

[In succeeding sections Aristotle argues—much as he argues afterwards in the last two books of the *Politics*—that the great and sovereign means for becoming actually good is a right training in habits during the years of youth. He then raises the question, 'By what means, and in what institution, should this training be given?' The answer he gives to that question is, 'Through a system of law, and in the state'. In order that it may turn from knowledge to act, ethics thus becomes a matter of legislation, and thereby a concern of politics. The same note which is struck at the beginning of the *Ethics* accordingly recurs again at the end. But there is now less speech of politics as the 'master-science', and emphasis is now mainly laid on legislative science (or 'nomothetics') as being a propaedeutic—one may almost say, an ancillary—study which prepares the soul, 'like earth which is to nourish the seed', for an eventual understanding of the lessons of moral philosophy. Ethics and politics are still closely connected; but there is a shifting of values which seems to result in an enthroning of ethics or moral philosophy, with 'nomothetics' or political philosophy serving as its chief minister. This shifting of values gradually appears in the further course of the argument.]

1180 a 14 § 11. We assume that the man who is to become good must first be trained and habituated properly, and then go on to spend his time, in the spirit thus engendered, on worthy occupations—doing nothing base or mean either willingly or unwillingly. We also assume that this object can be attained if men live their lives in obedience to some sort of wisdom and under some form of right order—provided this order has sufficient force. § 12. [Where, then, are such wisdom and order to be found?] Paternal discipline has not enough force, and cannot exert sufficient compulsion. The same is generally true of any sort of discipline exerted by a single *person*—unless such a person has the position of king or some other similar position. Law, on the other hand, possesses compulsive power, while it is at the same time a rule (or order) proceeding from a sort of moral prudence and from understanding. [But there is also a further advantage in an impersonal law.] We hate all *persons* who oppose our impulses, even when their opposition

and intellectual, have occupied Books II–VI: *friendship* has been treated in Books VIII–IX; there has been a discussion of *pleasure* (following on a consideration of continence and incontinence) in Book VII; and Aristotle has just finished, in the previous chapters of Book X, a further discussion of pleasure which has led to a discussion of *happiness* or felicity (*eudaimonia*).

is right; we do not feel that law is a burden when it imposes rules of right conduct. § 13. Sparta is the only state—or at any rate one of the few states—in which the legislator can be held to have made any provision by law for the training and the occupations of citizens. In most states these matters have been neglected: each man lives as he likes, 'ruling over his children and wife' in the fashion of the Cyclopes. § 14. The conclusion to which we thus come is that the best course is to have a system of public and proper provision for these matters; though, failing that, and in the event of public neglect, it would seem to be the duty of each private person to help his children and friends towards the attainment of goodness, and to show some capacity, or at least some desire, for doing so.

[Aristotle proceeds to argue that whether the attempt is made publicly or privately—but he is clear that it should be made publicly—those who make the attempt should have a 'nomothetic' equipment: in other words, they should themselves have the knowledge which a good legislator (or *nomothetēs*) needs before he can lay down rules for the training men should have and the occupations they should pursue. This leads him to ask how such knowledge can be acquired.]

1180 b 28 § 18. Ought we not therefore to ask, 'From what source, and in what way, can a man learn how to legislate?'[1] Shall we say, in reply, that here as elsewhere the people to learn from are those who are engaged in practice—in this case the practice of politics? It is an argument in favour of this reply that legislation has already been counted by us[2] as part of the art of politics. Or ought we rather to say that there is obviously a difference between the art of politics and the method of the other sciences and arts? There, the persons who actually practise an art are also the transmitters of the art. Doctors and painters, for example, are practitioners and teachers in one. Politics, however, is different. Here the sophists offer to teach,[3] but none of them practises the science he teaches. **1181 a** That is reserved for politicians; and they would appear to act by dint of some technique, and in the strength of experience, rather than by reflection. At any rate we never find them writing or lecturing on political matters (though that might well have been a better occupation than the composition of speeches for the law courts and the assembly); and we do not find that they have ever succeeded in turning their sons or any of any of their friends into statesmen. § 19. Yet we

---

[1] The conception of the legislator here implied is like that of Jeremy Bentham —and yet unlike. Like Bentham, Aristotle wants a legislator who has apprehended the 'grand principle' of life and will express it in a corresponding code. Unlike Bentham, he thinks that the legislator should primarily seek to institute a state system of education which supplies a moral discipline.

[2] Aristotle is referring back to Book VI, c. VIII, of the *Ethics*—where, however, 'nomothetics' is said to be the master-science in matters concerning the state, and 'politics' (though it has the more general title) to be related to 'nomothetics' as particulars are to the universal. Here the relation seems to be reversed.

[3] This is a Platonic passage, which recalls the argument of the *Meno*. It is not clear whether Aristotle is here referring to the sophists of the fifth century, such as Gorgias and Protagoras, who offered to train men in oratory and politics, or to contemporary teachers of rhetoric such as Isocrates.

might reasonably expect them to have done so, if only they had had the power. There is no better legacy which they could have left to their state, and no greater distinction which they could have desired for themselves, or for their dearest friends. ... At the same time we have to confess that experience does seem to contribute largely to success. If it were not so, men could not have become politicians simply by virtue of being familiar with politics. There is thus some reason for saying that those who aim at mastering the art of politics need experience as well [as study].

§ 20. [If politicians are of little avail, the sophists are hardly better.] Those of the sophists who profess [to impart a knowledge of legislation] seem to be very far from teaching what they profess. In general, they do not even know what legislation is, or what are the subjects with which it deals. If they did, they would never have classed it as on a level with rhetoric, or even as something inferior; and they would never have cherished the idea that legislation is an easy matter for anybody who will take the trouble to collect all reputable laws.[1] 'It is always possible', they say, 'to pick out the best laws', as though the picking itself did not require intelligence, and as though good judgement were not here too— just as it is in music—the very greatest of all things. Experience is always needed, in every sphere of activity, for judging rightly the results attained; for understanding intelligently the means and methods by which they are attained; and for seeing which of them harmonizes with which. (Inexperience must be content if it gets as far as just distinguishing between work which has been well done and work which has been done badly—this is the case, for example, in painting.) Laws are, as it were, 'results' produced by the art of politics. We are thus confronted by the question, 'How can these "results" [simply in themselves, and without the factor of experience] **1181 b** enable men to become legislators or to judge which laws are the best?' § 21. [Let us take an analogy.] We do not find that treatises[2] are able to make men doctors; and yet their authors not only attempt to state the [general] treatments— they also try to distinguish different types of physical condition, and to explain how particular sorts of patients may be cured and ought to be treated.[3] [Even so, and in spite of this detail], medical treatises are regarded as helpful only to experienced doctors and useless for the inexperienced. [What is the lesson of this analogy?] It would appear to be this. Collections of different laws—and of different constitutions—

---

[1] This is a direct reference to Isocrates. There is a passage in his *De Antidosi* in which it is maintained that the task of the legislator is simply to study the mass of existing laws, and to bring together those which have found a general acceptance, 'which any man might easily do at will'.

[2] The Greek word here used can mean indifferently a 'treatise' (and sometimes a 'prescription'), or an 'ordinance' (and sometimes a 'clause of a law'). It thus readily enables Aristotle to compare 'treatises' with 'laws'.

[3] This, Aristotle implies, goes beyond the generality of law, which treats all sorts of persons as equal and like for its purposes, and thus stops at 'general treatments'. The conclusion thus suggested is that if medical treatises, in spite of all their detail, cannot make doctors, laws, with their bare generality, cannot possibly make legislators.

are useful to those who are able to speculate, and to form a judgement on the questions, 'Which of these different results has been properly attained, and which not?', and 'Which of these results is in harmony with which?';[1] but those who peruse such collections without that ability and habit of mind will not be in a position to form a good judgement (except fortuitously)—though they may possibly become in the process more intelligent in such matters.[2]

§ 22. Previous thinkers have left this subject of legislation unexplored; and it may therefore be proper that we should examine it—along with the general subject of 'polity'[3]—in order that our philosophy of things human may be completed to the best of our power. We may therefore attempt (1) to review any contributions of value made by our predecessors, on any particular point, and (2) to determine, in the light of the descriptions of polities which we have collected, the factors which preserve or destroy states generally, the factors which preserve or destroy each several type of polity, and the reasons why some states are well governed and others not. When we have studied these subjects, we may perhaps be in a better position (3) to decide what type of polity is the best or ideal, how each type must be constructed in order to attain its best, and what laws and customs it must employ to that end.

With that we may begin [our discourses on Politics].[4]

B. The Conception of Politics in the *Rhetoric*

[The *Rhetoric* is a treatise generally studied, like the *Poetics*, in connexion with literature and literary criticism. But it is, by its nature, a treatise on political and forensic oratory; and it must therefore be also studied in connexion with politics—the more so because, as the last chapter

---

[1] The Greek original in the last clause (as in the similar clause in § 20) may mean either 'Which result suits which other result?', or 'Which result suits which sort of people?'. The former version, *in this context*, seems the more probable; but it must be admitted that the latter version is more appropriate to the general argument of the *Politics*, where Aristotle discusses the suitability of laws and constitutions to particular sorts of peoples.

[2] The general result of this argument is that the method of the school of Isocrates is not enough, and that something more is needed. The 'something more' is experience; but it is also something more than experience. It is experience enriched by a philosophic study of the values behind politics and 'nomothetics'—the study which Aristotle seeks to provide in the *Politics*.

[3] Polity (*politeia*) is the title of the Platonic dialogue generally termed 'the *Republic*'. The word would seem to be used here in the same large sense by Aristotle.

[4] The programme here stated is generally followed in the *Politics*. (1) The review of the contributions of predecessors is attempted in Book II (after a preliminary Book I which starts from a reference to Aristotle's greatest predecessor, Plato). (2) The factors which destroy or preserve states and polities, and the causes of their being well governed or the reverse, are discussed in Books IV–VI (after a preliminary Book III which classifies states and lays down the general principles of politics). (3) The best state is discussed in Books VII–VIII (after a previous discussion in Book VI of the methods of so constructing other types—especially democracy and oligarchy—that *they* may attain their best).

The 'descriptions of polities which we have collected' are the 158 'polities' which Aristotle is recorded to have had compiled, of which 'The Polity of the Athenians' alone survives (see p. 386).

of the *Ethics* shows, schools of rhetoric professed to train men not only in oratory, but also in the science of politics and legislation. Hobbes, who had otherwise a contempt for Aristotle ('the worst teacher that ever was') confessed that 'his rhetorique . . . was rare'. The *Rhetoric* has a large store of psychological insight,[1] on which Hobbes drew: it has also some notable passages on the study of politics, the nature of law, and the different forms of constitutions. The passage translated below is that concerned with the study of politics.]

Book I, c. II, part of § 7 (**1356 a 25–30**). Rhetoric is of the nature of an offshoot—on the one hand of logic,[2] and on the other of the study of ethics.[3] The study of ethics may not improperly be termed a study of politics.[4] [Being an offshoot of ethics, which is thus connected with politics], rhetoric is accordingly led to assume the mantle of politics; and those who profess the subject pose as professors of politics—a claim partly due to pure ignorance, partly to self-conceit, and partly to other human defects. [Actually the claim is unfounded]; for rhetoric is essentially a branch or expression of the logic of probabilities [even if it is also connected with ethics, and thereby with politics]. Neither rhetoric nor the logic of probabilities is a scientific study, dealing with a definite subject and explaining the nature of that subject; both of them are simply forms of technique for providing arguments.

[In the passage just translated, Aristotle seeks to put in their proper place the claims of teachers of rhetoric such as Isocrates. In a later passage (Book I, c. IV) he proceeds to develop his own views of the kind of equipment which the orator-statesman needs, and which a school of rhetoric should provide. It is an equipment not unlike the equipment suggested in the *Politics* for the statesman proper (the *politikos*): indeed the orator-statesman and the statesman proper obviously overlap. We have always to remember that in the system of the Greek city-state, with its assembly and its popular law-courts, oratory was a great force— as it still is in the system of the modern British state, with its parliament and its body of barristers pleading in the courts.

In order to determine the equipment of the orator-statesman, Aristotle begins by stating the subjects on which he will have to speak and advise. They are five in number—finance, foreign policy, military defence, trade, and legislation. He must be versed in the knowledge required for

---

[1] The first part of Book II (cc. I–XVII) is full of suggestions—particularly, perhaps, the study of the psychological characteristics of the different *ages* of man (cc. XII–XIV), and that of the characteristics produced by different *conditions* —birth, wealth, and power (cc. XV–XVII).

[2] More exactly, 'the logic of probabilities', to which Aristotle applies the particular designation of 'dialectic'—as contrasted with the logic of certainties, or 'apodeictic'.

[3] The connexion of rhetoric with ethics and politics is well illustrated in a later passage on constitutions, translated in Appendix III B, which explains why the orator must understand (1) the ends, (2) the moral qualities, and (3) the manners, institutions, and interests, of different forms of constitution.

[4] Ethics may be so termed, because politics is the art or science of producing a *good* community, and ethics is the art or science of producing a *good* man. The two thus blend. See the *Ethics*, I. c. II, § 8, translated at the beginning of this Appendix.

each of the five—but particularly and especially in the knowledge required for legislation.]

Book I, c. IV, § 12 (**1360 a 18–37**). For the security of the state, the orator ought to be able to take *all* these matters into his view; but he must understand more especially the subject of legislation. It is on the laws of a state that its whole well-being depends. It is therefore necessary, [since laws are based upon, and vary with, the form of constitution], that an orator should know how many different forms of constitution there are; what are the measures suited to the maintenance of each; and what are the causes, whether domestic or hostile [i.e. internal or external], by which each form is liable to be destroyed.[1] When I speak of domestic or internal causes of destruction, I mean that (with the one exception of the best or ideal constitution) all forms are liable to be destroyed if the principle proper to each is either relaxed or exaggerated. Democracy, for example, will be more and more weakened, until it finally turns into oligarchy, alike by the relaxation and by the exaggeration of its principle of liberty. [It is with constitutions as it is with noses]; a hooked or snub nose may, it is true, be reduced to a happy mean by some diminution of its excess; but if it becomes excessively hooked, or excessively snub, it gets into a condition in which it does not even look like a nose.[2]

§ 13. It is a useful thing, for the purpose of [oratory on] matters of legislation, not only to seek to understand what constitution is expedient for a state through a study of its past history [the historical method], but also to seek to know the constitutions of other countries and to understand what kinds of constitution are appropriate to what kinds of people [the comparative method].[3] This explains why books of travel are useful aids to legislation, enabling one, as they do, to comprehend the laws of non-Greek peoples.[4] It also explains why the researches of those who write accounts of events are useful aids in political debates.[5] But all this is, strictly speaking, the province of politics, and not of rhetoric. . . .

[1] Compare *Politics*, Book V, c. VII, § 14, where the same distinction of internal and external causes of destruction is made.

[2] The same simile is used in the *Politics*, Book V, c. IX, § 7. But the reader will observe that the parallel between noses and constitutions is not drawn so logically in this passage as it is in the corresponding passage of the *Politics*.

[3] This is a fundamental point which Aristotle also makes in the *Politics* (e.g. Book IV, c. I, §§ 1–3). Aristotle thoroughly understood a point often made by modern thinkers—that a particular type of democracy (e.g. the Swiss or the British) works well for a particular type of people, and cannot be applied elsewhere with success unless it is applied to a similar type of people.

[4] Hence Aristotle, in addition to having descriptions of 158 Greek constitutions compiled in his school, also produced an account of the institutions (*nomima*) of the non-Greek peoples.

[5] Hence Aristotle, in the description of the Athenian constitution (the one surviving description from his general compilation), devotes the first and larger half to a description of Athenian history from 600 to 400 B.C.

APPENDIX II

ARISTOTLE'S CONCEPTION OF JUSTICE, LAW, AND EQUITY IN THE *ETHICS* AND THE *RHETORIC*

A. THE CONCEPTION IN THE *ETHICS*

[In the account here given of the argument of the *Ethics*, the translator has mainly given an *analysis* of Aristotle's thought: but he has illustrated it, from time to time, by passages of *translation*, which are marked by inverted commas.]

In treating of justice, in the *Ethics*, Aristotle makes a number of distinctions, which may be briefly stated. But we must first note that the Greek word for justice (*dikaiosynē*) has a broader sweep than our word 'justice'; is something more than legal; and includes the ethical notions (or some of the ethical notions) which belong to our word 'righteousness'. In this connexion it should be observed that the Greek title of Plato's *Republic* is *politeia ē peri dikaiosynēs*—'polity, or concerning righteousness' (the word 'justice' would fail to convey Plato's meaning); and it should also be observed that in the Greek of St. Paul the word which is translated 'righteousness' in our English version is *dikaiosynē*. It may also be observed that St. Augustine uses the word *iustitia* in his *De Civitate Dei* with the same broad sweep and in the same general sense as our word 'righteousness'.[1]

(1) This will enable us to understand the first distinction which Aristotle makes. It is a distinction between 'general' and 'particular' justice.

(a) *General* justice is the same as goodness: it is our 'righteousness': it is, in Aristotle's words, 'the justice which answers to *the whole of goodness* . . . being the exercise of goodness *as a whole* . . . towards one's neighbour' (*Ethics*, Book V, c. II, § 10).[2]

(b) *Particular* justice is one part of general justice: it is the part which is concerned with the specific form of goodness which consists in behaving 'fairly', or, as Aristotle calls it, 'equally', to other men: it is, we may say in the phrase of Justinian, *constans et perpetua voluntas suum cuique tribuendi*.

Particular justice, as we shall presently notice, has its own divisions or distinctions. But before we come to these distinctions, we must first examine the notion of the 'fair' or the 'equal' (*to ison*), with which the whole idea of particular justice is connected. Aristotle always assumes

---

[1] See the Introduction, pp. lxix–lxx.

[2] See also c. I, §§ 15–20 of the same book: 'General justice is complete goodness—not absolutely [for it does not include contemplative goodness], but so far as regards our neighbours. . . . It is complete goodness in the fullest sense, because it is the *exercise* of complete goodness: it is complete because he who has it can exercise his goodness *not only in himself but also towards his neighbours*.'

a political association which is composed of men who are free and equal. The essence of all particular justice, whatever its divisions or distinctions, consists in the behaviour appropriate to an association so composed— the 'fair' behaviour which ensures the 'fair' working of an association of the free and equal.

(2) Particular justice, so conceived, is distinguished into two different kinds. (*a*) The first kind is *distributive* justice, which is the justice shown by the whole state in distributing offices, honours, and other benefits among its members.[1] In Aristotle's words, **1130 b 31** 'one kind of particular justice... is that operative in distributions of honour, or of moneys, or of other divisible things, among all who share in constitutional rights; for in such matters it is possible for one man to have a share which is either unequal or equal to that of another man [and thus problems of justice, or "fairness", arise]'. (Book V, c. II, § 12.) (*b*) The other kind is *rectificatory* justice, or the justice which the state seeks to maintain not so much between itself and its members, as between one member and another. In Aristotle's words, **1131 a 1** 'another kind of particular justice is that concerned with the rectification of transactions between individuals; and this has two subdivisions, according as the transactions are voluntary or involuntary' (ibidem, § 13). These two subdivisions are (1) transactions based on a contract between the parties, which one or the other has broken, (2) transactions independent of any consent, in which one party has wronged the other; and the problem in both cases is to correct what is amiss by an award which restores to the one party what he has lost, deprives the other of what he has gained, and thus restores a position of fairness or equality which has been disturbed.

Of the two different kinds of particular justice, the distributive and the rectificatory, it is obviously the first, and only the first, which is important for political theory. Here it is important to notice that while Aristotle may speak, abstractly, of a political association in which the members are equal integers, each of equal merit, and each therefore receiving an equal award, he none the less regards any actual association as consisting of unequal integers, which receive unequal awards because they are of unequal merit. On this view justice *seems* to lose its connexion with fairness or equality: indeed it seems to turn into injustice, because it turns into inequality. Aristotle, however, insists that this is only a matter of seeming. Distributive justice which gives unequal awards to unequal degrees of merit, *in exact proportion to the inequality of the degrees*, is still connected with equality or fairness, because the proportion of award to merit is kept unswervingly equal. From this point of view we have to revise the formula that a political association is composed of men who are free and equal. We have to say, as Aristotle says (*Ethics*, Book V, c. VI, § 4), that it is composed of men who are 'free and either proportionately or arithmetically equal'. Men *may* be arithmetically equal, if each has the same merit as others, and accord-

[1] Greek city-states, such as Athens, distributed among their citizens not only political offices and honours, but also 'payment' (*misthos*) for attending the assembly and law-courts, and, occasionally, gifts in kind or in money.

ingly receives the same award as others; but normally men will be proportionately equal, in the sense that, while they are of unequal merit, each still gets an award which is proportionate to his merit, and all are therefore equally treated in virtue of receiving an award proportionate to their merits.[1]

(3) In one passage of the *Ethics* (Book V, c. VI) Aristotle draws a distinction between 'absolute' and 'political' justice. (*a*) *Absolute* justice is not further defined; but we may conjecture that it is absolute in the sense that it is not relative to any particular community. Absolute justice will thus be justice as between man and man *sub specie humanitatis*; and it will, as such, be distinguishable from justice as between citizen and citizen *sub specie civitatis*. (*b*) *Political* justice is justice of the latter order. It is justice as it exists in a political association; and we shall be warranted in holding that, as such, it includes not only both of the subdivisions of particular justice (the distributive and the rectificatory), but also general justice (as defined in 1 *a* above), or in other words the general system of righteousness expressed in a state's constitution, in its laws, and in its scheme of education.[2]

This political justice is defined by Aristotle (Book V, c. VI, § 4) as being **1134 a 26** 'what is found among men who share in a common life, with a view to the attainment of self-sufficiency, as freemen and as equals either proportionately or arithmetically [in a word men living in a *polis*, and under its system of law]. It follows that where men are not in this position, there is no political justice to govern their relations: there is only justice of a sort, or something analogous to justice. Justice exists only as between men whose relations to one another are governed by a system of law.'

This passage is explained by a later passage in the same chapter (§§ 8–9). **1134 b 8** 'Justice between a master and his slaves, or between a parent and his children, is not the same as justice between citizens, although it is similar. A man cannot act unjustly, in the strict sense of that term, towards objects which belong to him. § 9. Chattel-slaves, and children under a certain age before they are separate persons, are like parts of the master's or parent's self; and nobody intends to injure himself, or can therefore be guilty of injustice towards himself. It follows that there is here no question of political justice or injustice [i.e. of the sort of justice or injustice which exists as between citizen

---

[1] In Aristotle's view men's sense of equality is not offended by this conception of proportionate equality. All men will accept the conception that award should be proportionate to merit; and disagreement only begins when the question has to be answered, 'Proportionate to which sort of merit?' In other words, they accept the formal principle of proportion: they quarrel about its application. 'All men agree that just distribution consists in distribution according to merit; but all men do not mean the same thing when they speak of merit. Democrats mean free birth; oligarchs mean wealth, or sometimes good birth: aristocrats mean goodness.' (*Ethics*, Book V, c. III, § 7.)

[2] A *constitution*, we learn from the *Politics*, is 'a way of life': *laws* are 'intended to make the citizens good'; *education* is a process of moral habituation, which prepares the ground for conscious goodness. In all these ways every *polis* is a system of general justice, and each particular *polis* is a variety of such justice.

and citizen]. Justice of that sort, as we have seen, is based upon law: it exists between persons who are naturally connected by law [in virtue of being members of a state]; and these, as we have also seen, are persons who share equally in a system of ruling and being ruled by turns. We may therefore say that justice exists between husband and wife more than it does between parent and child, or between master and slave. Justice as between husband and wife may be termed "house-justice"; but even this differs from political justice.'

(4) Political justice, or justice as it exists in the state, is further distinguished by Aristotle, in another distinction which he makes, into two different kinds—the 'natural' and the 'legal'. We have seen, under (3) above, that political justice is a total or comprehensive term, which includes both general and particular justice, and therefore also includes both the rectificatory and the distributive branch of the latter. The distinction which Aristotle now proceeds to make within this comprehensive term is not a distinction between different *provinces* or *scopes*, as were the distinctions made under (1) and (2) above: it is a distinction between different *origins*. Whatever the provinces which it covers— whether the general or the particular: whether the distributive aspect of the particular, or the rectificatory aspect—political justice draws some of its rules from a 'natural' or universal origin, and others from a 'legal' or local origin. This is the argument of chapter VII, §§ 1–5.

1134 b 18 § 1. 'One part of political justice is natural: another is legal. The natural part is that which has everywhere the same force, and which is not brought into existence by our thinking in this way or that. The legal part is that which originally is a matter of indifference, but which ceases to be indifferent as soon as it is fixed by enactment. That a prisoner's ransom should be a sum of four pounds, or that a sacrifice should consist of a goat and not of two sheep, are examples of legal justice: so, again, are all laws which are passed to cover particular cases—a law, for instance, that sacrifices shall be offered in honour of Brasidas; and so, too, are orders and regulations. § 2. Some hold that the whole of justice is of this character. What exists by nature (they feel) is immutable, and has everywhere the same force: fire burns both in Greece and in Persia; but conceptions of justice shift and change. § 3. It is not strictly true that *all* justice is legal, though it may be true in a sense. Or rather there is perhaps no sense in which it is true for the gods [with whom *all* justice is natural]; and among us men there is also *some* natural justice. True, all our human justice is mutable; but that does not prevent some of it from having a natural origin, side by side with some which has not. § 4. [If we are asked to say which is which]—if, [in other words], we have to divide a generally mutable whole into two sorts of parts, both alike liable to change, but one of them existing by nature and the other by law and convention—the answer is plain enough. [The problem is not peculiar to the sphere of justice]: the same distinction of natural and conventional may be properly applied in other spheres; the right hand, for example, is stronger by nature, but it is possible for all men to make themselves ambidextrous. § 5. The part of justice which depends on convention and convenience may be said to be like weights and measures. **1135 a** The weights and measures for corn and wine are not equal in every market: larger weights and measures are used in wholesale and smaller in retail markets. In just the same way, the elements of justice which exist by human institution, and not by nature, are not the same everywhere—the reason being that constitutions too [on which laws depend] are not the same everywhere. And yet there is but one constitution which is naturally the best everywhere.'[1]

(5) There is a final distinction made by Aristotle in the course of the *Ethics*—the distinction between law (*nomos*) and equity (*epieikeia*)—which has still to be mentioned. This is not a distinction between different kinds of *justice*: it is something of a different order.

It may seem indeed, prima facie, that the distinction between law and equity is the same as that between legal and natural justice. No doubt it is a similar distinction; but it can hardly be said to be the same. Justice, in Aristotle's view, is generally connected with law. The 'just' is the same as the 'lawful'; and whether (in point of *scope*) we look at 'general' or 'particular' justice, or whether again (in point of *origin*) we look at 'natural' or 'legal' justice, the identity of the 'just' and the 'lawful' still remains. (Natural justice itself has its origin in natural *law*.) But equity is, in its nature, something distinct from law—something which 'corrects' law; and *so far as justice is connected with law*,[2] equity must also be separate from justice. We must beware of importing into Aristotle's conception of equity any legal or juridical notions such as go with our English conception of the 'law of equity'. Equity is, in his view, something outside the area of law, and something, therefore, which lies outside the conterminous area of justice.

Before we translate the passage of the *Ethics* in which Aristotle states and defines his conception of equity, it will be well to give some account of the passages which show his conception of law. This will at once complete the account of his conception of justice (so closely connected with that of law) and prepare the way for an account of his conception of equity.

We may summarize Aristotle's conception of law under some three main heads: (*a*) There are some passages in the *Ethics* which connect the idea of law with that of 'convention', and oppose it to the idea of 'nature'. But this is a turn of language (due to the fact that the same Greek word serves to designate both 'law' and 'convention'), rather than the expression of Aristotle's own view; and indeed, since part of justice is natural, part of law must also be natural. It cannot, therefore, be the essence of law that it is conventional, or enacted. The essence of law consists in the fact that it is an impersonal rule, 'proceeding from

---

[1] In a later passage of the *Ethics* (Book VIII, c. XIII, § 5) Aristotle distinguishes two species of justice—the unwritten and the legal. This seems different from the distinction between the natural and the legal: the unwritten may here be the *customary* (which is something different from the natural), as opposed to *enacted* law. Thus 'the legal', in the narrower sense of 'the enacted', will go with 'the unwritten' or customary to constitute 'the legal' in the broader sense, in which it is contrasted with 'the natural'. But see also p. 370.

[2] The qualification is important. Justice, as we shall see later, is not (after all) totally and wholly connected with law. See below, p. 368, n. 1.

moral prudence and understanding', which is accepted, and regarded as not being burdensome, because it has this impersonal origin (X, c. IX, § 12). The rule of law is the rule of rational principle (*logos*), and not of a person or persons (V, c. VI, § 5). (*b*) The legislator has indeed the function of discovering and declaring this impersonal rule; but he declares it rather than enacts it.[1] He must himself possess the gifts of moral prudence and understanding in order to declare the impersonal rule in which they issue; and that is why the *Ethics* ends by raising the question, 'How can the capacity for acting as a legislator be acquired?' (X, c. IX, § 18.) This high duty of the legislator also explains why Aristotle, in another passage of the *Ethics*, sets 'legislative' wisdom higher than 'political' wisdom. Legislative wisdom, we are told, is concerned with universal rules: political wisdom only with particular acts. **1141 b 24** 'The wisdom which deals with the state is twofold: it is partly legislative wisdom, acting as the master-wisdom; it is partly a wisdom related to this as particulars are to their universal, and this latter wisdom bears the general name of "political wisdom". This political wisdom is concerned with doing and deliberation; it issues in the decree, which is something that has to be done as an individual act. This is the reason why only those who promote and execute decrees are said "to take an active part in politics"; it is only they who "do" things, in the same sense as manual labourers' (Book VI, c. VIII, § 2). (*c*) If the lawgiver stands at this height of legislative wisdom, laws must also stand on a similar height. Their rules, proceeding from moral prudence and understanding, mean something more for Aristotle than rules of law mean for us. They are the *ultimate* sovereign of the state: it is their impersonal system, and not a ruling person or body of ruling persons, that is *ultimately* sovereign in any society of freemen. The purpose of their sovereignty is a moral purpose; they are 'intended to make men good and righteous'. They serve and ensure 'general' justice —the justice which is righteousness—as well as the 'particular' justice of distribution and rectification; and they are thus an education as well as a system of regulation. **1103 b 2** 'Legislators make the citizens good by forming their habits. This is what all legislators wish to do; and those who do not do it effectively miss their mark. Indeed, this is what makes a good constitution differ from a poor one.' (*Ethics*, Book II, c. I, § 5.)

But high as law thus stands, its very height involves a certain defect, or, at any rate, involves the need of a certain corrective or supplement, which is provided by equity.[2] Law by its very nature, as a system of rules, is general, or universal; it cannot 'condescend upon particulars'. Equity has that grace of condescension; and this is explained in a famous chapter of the *Ethics* (V, c. x).

1137 a 31 § 1. 'The next subject for consideration is equity and the equitable, and their relation to the conceptions of justice and the just. These two sets of terms, when we proceed to examine their

[1] The element of 'convention' thus turns out to be only 'declaration.

[2] The Aristotelian term 'equity', as has been noticed, has a meaning different in kind from that of Equity in English law. See also below, p. 371, n. 3.

meanings, appear to be neither absolutely identical nor yet generically different. On the one hand, we sometimes praise the equitable and the equitable man; and **1137 b** along this line we are led to transfer the term, as a term of praise, to the sphere of the other virtues, substituting it for the term "good", and really meaning that an act is "better" when we actually speak of it as "more equitable". [Here we assume that the two sets of terms are not generically different.] On the other hand, we sometimes find it strange—when we reason the matter out [and find that we cannot assume the identity of the two sets of terms]—that "the "equitable" should differ from "the just" and yet be a term of praise. [This seems to involve us in a dilemma.] If the just and the equitable are different, they cannot both be good. If they are both good, they cannot at the same time be different.

§ 2. These are the conflicting considerations which make the nature of "the equitable" something of a problem. The considerations are all, in one sense, justified, and not contradictory of one another. The equitable, while it is something better than one sort of the just, is none the less still just; and if it is better than the just, it is not so in the sense of being a different class of thing. The just and the equitable belong to one class; both are good, but the equitable is the better. § 3. What creates the problem is the fact that the equitable, though it is just, is not *legally* just. On the contrary, it is by its nature a corrective of the legally just.[1] § 4. The reason [for the existence of such a corrective] is that every law is a universal rule, but there are some things about which a universal proposition cannot be made correctly. Where it is at once necessary to make such a proposition and impossible to make it correctly, the law takes for its province the general average of cases. The law is aware that there is a possibility of error [i.e. in the exceptional case]; but the law [as a general rule] is none the less correct. The error which is possible is not in the law, nor, again, in the legislator, but in the nature of the act to be dealt with. It is the stuff of action itself which has from the start this variable quality. § 5. When the law states a universal proposition, and the facts in a given case do not square with the proposition, the right course to pursue is therefore the following. The legislator having left a gap, and committed an error, by making an unqualified proposition, we must correct his omission; we must say for him what he would have said himself if he had been present, and what he would have put into his law if only he had known. § 6. So considered, the corrective action of equity is just, and an improvement upon one sort of justice; but the justice upon which it is an improvement is not absolute justice—it is [legal justice—or rather] the error that arises from the absolute statements of law. The nature of the equitable may accordingly be defined as "a correction of law where law is defective owing to its universality". This possible defect of law will also explain why not all matters are determined by law: there are matters on which it is impos-

---

[1] Here Aristotle divorces justice, to some extent, from law. Identified with law through most of its range, justice parts company from it on the ground of equity. Equity is justice, but it is not law; and so far as equity is concerned, the equation 'law = justice' ceases to be true.

sible to lay down a law, and for which the use of a decree is thus necessary. § 7. What is itself indeterminate must also have an indeterminate rule, like the flexible rule of lead used in the Lesbian style of building, which bends and alters to suit the shape of the stone much as a decree adapts itself to suit the facts of the case. § 8. We can now understand the nature of the equitable; we can see that it is just, and an improvement upon one sort of the just. We can also understand, from what has been said, the nature of the equitable man. He is a man who chooses and does acts such as we have described: a man who is not a martinet for justice in a bad sense, but ready to yield a point **1138 a** even when he has the law on his side. This is the state of character which constitutes a spirit of equity; and the spirit of equity is thus a sort of justice [i.e. a sort of righteousness, or "general" justice], and not a separate state of character.'

These are the main lessons of the *Ethics* in the matter of justice, and in the connected matters of law and equity. We may now turn to see how these matters are handled in the *Rhetoric*.

B. The Conception of Justice, Law, and Equity in the *Rhetoric*
BOOK I. CHAPTERS XIII *and part of* XV

[In this section the text consists only of passages of translation, except for two brief intercalated notes.]

1373 b 1   XIII. § 1. . . . We define acts of justice and injustice partly by the two sorts of law with which they may be connected, and partly by the two classes of persons with which they may be concerned.

§ 2. The two sorts of law in question are the particular and the universal. *Particular* law is the law defined and declared by each community for its own members: it falls into two parts—the written [or enacted], and the unwritten. *Universal* law is the law of nature. [We are entitled to speak of such a law of nature]; for there really exists, as all of us in some measure divine, a natural form of the just and unjust which is common to all men, even when there is no community or covenant to bind them to one another. It is this form which the Antigone of Sophocles' play evidently has in her mind, when she says that it was a just act to bury her brother Polynices in spite of Creon's decree to the contrary—just, she means, in the sense of being *naturally* just.

> Not of to-day or yesterday its force:
> It springs eternal: no man knows its birth.

Empedocles has the same idea when he speaks of our not killing anything that has life: he regards this not as a matter which some have a right to do and others are wrong in doing,

> No, but a rule for all, unbroken spread
> Through Heaven's wide realm and all the range of earth.

Alcidamas, too, had this idea in the passage in his Messenian oration ['God has left all men free, and nature has made no man a slave'].[1]

---

[1] See Introduction, p. lvii. On the general conception of natural law see also the translator's introduction to Gierke, *Natural Law and the Theory of Society*, pp. xxxiv–l.

§ 3. The acts which we ought or ought not to do [i.e. acts of justice and injustice] are also divided into two classes in relation to the persons who are concerned, and according as they affect either the general community or some one particular member. From this point of view we can commit acts of injustice, or perform acts of justice, in one or other of two ways—either in relation to a single determinate person, or in relation to the community. The man who commits adultery or an assault is guilty of an injustice to one of a number of determinate persons: the man who fails to do military service is guilty of an injustice to the community.

[Aristotle proceeds to discuss, in §§ 4–10, the character of the offences —whether against individuals or against the community—which are contraventions of the written part of 'particular law'. He then examines offences which are contraventions of the unwritten part; and this leads him to consider the nature of unwritten law—a term here used in a broader sense than in the *Ethics* (supra p. 366, n. 1).]

1374 a 18 § 11. There are, as we have already noticed, two sorts of just and unjust acts [corresponding to the two parts of 'particular' law] —one sort for which provision is made by written enactments, and another for which it is made by unwritten rules. We have already discussed the sort about which law explicitly speaks. The other sort (i.e. the acts covered by unwritten rules) falls again into two divisions. § 12. First, there are the acts which spring from an exceptional degree of goodness or badness, and are accordingly attended by censure or by praise—by the infliction of dishonour or by honours and rewards. This category of acts includes the showing of gratitude to benefactors, the repayment of their benefactions, the helping of friends, and other acts of a similar nature.[1] Secondly, there are the acts which belong to a gap that is left uncovered by law proper or, in other words, written law.[2] § 13. This gap is covered by equity. Equity is regarded by general opinion as a form of justice; and in fact it *is* a form of justice which goes beyond written law. It comes into existence in two different ways —sometimes without any intention on the part of the legislator, and sometimes by his intention. It comes into existence without intention, when the legislator simply fails to notice the gap which he is leaving. It comes into existence by his intention, when he finds himself unable to make a rule [which fits all the cases] exactly, but is none the less com-

[1] Aristotle, though he illustrates this category of acts, does not illustrate or explain the nature of the unwritten law by which provision is made for encouraging or discouraging such acts. We may conjecture that it takes the form of 'social opinion', and that such 'social opinion' is therefore one of the two forms of unwritten law—the other being, as Aristotle explains, 'equity'.

[2] Here Aristotle does the converse of what is mentioned in the previous note: he does not illustrate (at any rate to begin with) the category of acts which he has in mind, but turns at once to the form of unwritten law by which provision is made for dealing with the acts. But the order which he follows in both cases is natural. When we are thinking of the *moral* sphere, we think first of moral (or non-moral) action, and then of the social opinion which is its 'atmosphere'. When we are thinking of the sphere of *equity*, we think first of the 'atmosphere' of equity, and then of the acts which come under its purview.

pelled to state a universal rule—which is not, however, universally
applicable, but only applicable in a majority of cases. It may also come
into existence by the legislator's intention when the infinite number of
possible cases makes it difficult for him to lay down a definite rule. He
can hardly, for instance, make a definite rule for each size, and each
sort, of weapon that may possibly be used for causing a wound: a
lifetime would be too short to enumerate the possible cases. § 14. If,
then, an exact rule is impossible, but legislation is none the less needed,
the legislator will have to express himself in unqualified terms,[1] and
the result will be that a man who is simply wearing a ring when he
lifts his hand against another man, or actually strikes him, will present
the judge with a dilemma. According to the letter of the law, he is a
wrongdoer liable to punishment; but really he has done no wrong.
Equity is the way of dealing with **1374 b** this dilemma.

§ 15. If the equitable is what we have just described it as being, there
is no difficulty in understanding what sort of acts, and what sort of persons, should be regarded as equitable or the reverse. § 16. Equitable acts
are those which [may be contrary to the law, but] ought to be condoned;
and equity thus means our not putting errors or misfortunes on a level
with acts of wrongdoing. ('Misfortunes' are acts leading to unexpected
consequences, but not proceeding from vice; 'errors' are acts leading
to consequences that might have been expected, but still not proceeding
from any vice; 'acts of wrong-doing' are acts which not only lead to
consequences that might have been expected, but *do* proceed from
vice—as is bound to be the case with all acts done under the impulse
of appetite.) § 17. It is equitable to show sympathy for the weaknesses
of human nature; to look to the legislator and not the law, and to the
legislator's meaning rather than his language; to consider a man's
intention and not his act;[2] § 18. to consider the whole of an occurrence
and not a part; to ask what a man is now, and not what he has always,
or usually, been. It is equitable to think of benefits received rather than
injuries suffered, and, when we think of benefits, to remember those
we have received rather than those we have conferred; to be patient
under wrongdoing; to agree to a settlement by the balance of argument
rather than by the balance of force; § 19. to be willing to go before an
arbitrator rather than to go to law. The arbitrator has the equitable
in view, while the judge has only the law; and the very purpose for
which arbitration was introduced was to give due weight to equity.[3]

---

[1] i.e. he will speak of '*any* instrument'.

[2] A modern lawyer might criticize, with some justice, the suggestion that a
judge should consider the meaning intended by the legislator, rather than the
expression which he actually used, or that he should consider a man's subjective
intention more than his objective act.

[3] The position of 'equity' (*epieikeia*) in Greek jurisprudence is discussed in
Vinogradoff's *Historical Jurisprudence*, vol. ii, c. iii, § 5. Greek 'equity' was based
on an idea of fairness and humanity in some ways analogous to the idea underlying English Equity or the Roman *Ius Naturae*; but it was in no sense (as they
were) a formulated body of law. On the whole, Greek equity was an Athenian
conception; and to understand its nature we must take into account the nature
of Athenian law and the Athenian popular courts. (1) Athenian law was largely

[There is also another passage in the *Rhetoric*, where Aristotle is discussing effective modes of pleading in the courts, which recurs to the subject of law and equity. It comes in Book I, c. xv, §§ 3–8.]

1375 a 25 § 3. We may first take the topic of law, and consider how it should be used by the pleader in persuasion and dissuasion, accusation and defence. § 4. It is evident that, if the written law tells against his case, he must take the ground of 'universal law' and 'equity', and plead that they are more consonant with justice.[1] § 5. He must plead that the oath taken by the members of the court, 'to make true deliverance to the best of our judgement', means that they will not exclusively apply the written law, [but will actually use their own judgement]. § 6. He must plead that equity is always constant, and never changes, and that universal law, in virtue of being the law of nature, is equally unchanging; while written laws often change. (This is the meaning of the lines in Sophocles' play, where Antigone pleads that the burial of her brother offended against Creon's law, but not against the unwritten:

> Not of to-day or yesterday its force;
> It springs eternal . . .
> I would not for the fear of any man. . . .)[2]

§ 7. He must plead that the just is something real and of actual utility, and not merely a matter of what seems good to the authorities; and that it cannot, therefore, be simply identified with written law—the more as written law may fail to fulfil the true purpose of law. He must plead that the judge is like an assay-master of the mint, with the duty of separating what is dross from the sterling ore. § 8. He must plead that, the better a man is, the more he must use and stand fast by unwritten laws, in preference to the written.

an archaic law, because Athenian procedure made new legislation difficult: this archaic law had to be interpreted liberally, or fairly, or 'equitably'; and the oath of the members of the popular courts accordingly obliged them, in cases where the application of the law was dubious, to give 'the justest decision possible' (cf. Book III, c. xvi, § 5, and note). (2). The Athenian popular courts were large bodies containing hundreds of persons, who might readily feel, and were encouraged by the pleadings of advocates to feel, a general sentiment of what was a fair and humane decision in a given case. It was in them that the exercise of 'equity' was vested: it was they who used a 'discretionary power' which 'constituted an appeal to what is termed residuary justice' (op. cit., p. 69); and on the whole their exercise of equity was a 'guarantee that the legal process would follow the line of public opinion', and afforded 'good reason to trust the jurors in their general estimates of the rights and wrongs of a case' (ibid., p. 144).

[1] It should be noticed that 'natural law' and 'equity' are distinct in the argument of the *Rhetoric*. Natural law is the *universal* law: equity is one of the two subdivisions of the unwritten part of *particular* law.

[2] Aristotle finishes the quotation in the middle of a sentence, content with giving the cue. The sentence continues

> Brave Heaven's vengeance by defying *that*.

APPENDIX III

ARISTOTLE'S CLASSIFICATION OF CONSTITUTIONS IN THE *ETHICS* AND THE *RHETORIC*

A. The Classification in the *Ethics*

BOOK VIII. CHAPTER X

[The general theme of Book VIII is friendship. In dealing with that theme, Aristotle is led to treat of associations which enjoy a common life, and therefore possess a social cohesion, or 'friendship', arising from that common life. The state is such an association, enjoying a common life and possessing the quality of 'friendship': indeed it is the general and comprehensive association, of which all others may be regarded as parts. But there are different kinds of states; and there must therefore be different types of common life, and different qualities of 'friendship', in these different kinds. Aristotle accordingly proceeds to classify states, or political associations, from this general point of view—i.e. according to the type of their common life and the quality of their social cohesion or 'friendship'.[1]]

1160 a 31 § 1. There are three kinds of constitution, and an equal number of deviations, or, as it were, corruptions, of these three kinds. The three kinds of constitution are kingship, aristocracy, and the kind in which membership of the governing body depends on a property qualification—a kind which it seems appropriate to call 'timocratic',[2] but which is generally called, in actual usage, the 'polity'. § 2. Monarchy is the best of these three kinds: 'timocracy' is the worst. The deviation, or corruption, of kingship is tyranny. Both kingship and tyranny are forms of government by a single person, **1160 b** but they differ greatly from one another: the tyrant studies his own advantage, but the king looks to that of his subjects. A king must have two attributes—he must be sufficient to himself, and he must excel his subjects in every quality. If he has these attributes, he needs nothing further; and therefore he will not seek to compass his own advantage, but will only look to that of his subjects. If he does not possess these attributes, he will only be a king by mere chance.[3] Tyranny is the very opposite of kingship of the true sort; the tyrant pursues only his own good. It is even clearer that tyranny is the worst of the deviations [than it is that 'timocracy' is the worst of the true forms]: the opposite of the best is obviously the worst.

---

[1] 'While the structure of society depends primarily on justice, the . . . internal creative force of society depends on civic friendship. Friendship brings about the agreement of wills, required by nature but freely undertaken, which lies at the origin of the social community. . . . This was well known to Aristotle, who distinguished types of communities according to types of friendship' (Jacques Maritain, *The Rights of Man*, pp. 22–3).

[2] The Greek word for 'property qualification' is *timēma*.

[3] The Greek is 'a sort of king appointed by lot'—i.e., no better, in his office of king, than a magistrate appointed by the chance of the lot in his office of magistrate.

§ 3. [Each of the three kinds of constitution is liable to change.] (*a*) Kingship may turn into tyranny; tyranny is the deterioration of the government of a single person, and a bad king turns into a tyrant. (*b*) Aristocracy may turn into oligarchy when the governing class misbehave, and distribute the honours and offices of the state on another standard than that of merit—keeping all, or most, of the good things themselves: giving offices perpetually to the same persons; and, generally, making wealth the chief object of their endeavour. The result is the rule of a few [i.e. an oligarchy], and the substitution of bad men for the worthiest. (*c*) Finally, 'timocracy' [or 'polity'] may turn into democracy. They are close neighbours of one another; for 'timocracy', too, tends to mean the rule of the majority, and it, too, counts the possessors of the property qualification as all equal to one another. Democracy is the least bad of all the three deviations; for here the form of the constitution is only a slight deviation [from 'timocracy' or 'polity']. . . . These are the ways in which the three kinds of constitution mostly change; for the transformation which they involve is the least and the most easily made.

§ 4. Parallels and, as it were, patterns for the three kinds of constitution may be found in the life of the family. (*a*) The association between father and sons has a character like that of monarchy. The father takes care of his children as a king does of his subjects; and this is why Homer calls Zeus, the king of the gods, by the name of 'Father'—kingship always tending to mean a paternal form of rule. In Persia, however, the rule of the father has a tyrannical character, and parents treat their children as if they were so many slaves. The government of slaves by their masters has also a tyrannical character: the object to which it is directed is the interest of the master. To govern slaves in this way would appear to be right and proper. But to govern children in the Persian way is wrong: persons who differ [as children and slaves do] should be governed in different ways. § 5. (*b*) The association of husband and wife appears to be of the nature of an aristocracy. The husband rules by virtue of merit, in matters where a husband should; and he leaves to his wife all other matters which suit her gifts. If the husband, however, takes control of all matters, he turns the association into an oligarchy: his action ceases to be based on merit, or to be justified by his superiority. **1161 a** Sometimes [the deviation takes an opposite form, and] women rule the family by virtue of being heiresses; and here their position is based, not on superior excellence, but only on greater riches and power, as is also the case in oligarchies. § 6. (*c*) The association of brothers is parallel to 'timocracy'. They are equal to one another, except in so far as they differ in age; and we may accordingly say that if their difference in age is considerable, the bond which connects them ceases to be a fraternal bond [and becomes more like the bond between parents and children]. The parallel to democracy is chiefly found in households which have no head (here all the members are on a footing of equality), or in which authority is weak and each member is a law to himself.

[In drawing these parallels between the state and the family Aristotle is running somewhat counter to the line which he takes at the beginning of the first book of the *Politics*. There he is concerned to show that there is a *difference* between the political association and all other forms of association, and that there is therefore also a difference between the government or constitution of the state and that of all other associations. . . . But Aristotle might reply that there may still be something of a parallel, even if there is a difference.]

B. THE CLASSIFICATION OF CONSTITUTIONS IN THE *RHETORIC*

BOOK I. CHAPTER VIII

1365 b 22 § 1. The greatest and the most sovereign of all the qualifications which an orator can possess for persuading an assembly, and giving it good advice, is an understanding of all forms of constitution and an ability to distinguish their different manners,[1] institutions, and interests. [There are two reasons for so saying.] § 2. In the first place, all men are persuaded by considerations of interest; and whatever maintains a form of constitution is the interest of those who live under that form. In the second place, sovereignty always resides in the decision of the sovereign body; and sovereign bodies vary with forms of constitution—for there are as many different sovereign bodies as there are different forms of constitution. [An orator must therefore understand forms of constitution in order to understand (1) the interest to which he must appeal, and (2) the nature of the sovereign body which he has to persuade.]

§ 3. There are four forms of constitution—democracy, oligarchy, aristocracy, and monarchy. It follows that the sovereign and deciding body, in these four forms, is always either a section of the civic body [as in the three last] or the whole of that body [as in the first]. § 4. Democracy is a form of constitution in which all the members of the civic body distribute the magistracies among themselves, and do so by lot; oligarchy a form in which persons determined by a property qualification distribute the magistracies among themselves; and aristocracy a form in which persons who satisfy a standard of education distribute magistracies among themselves. . . . The education of which we are speaking here is that prescribed by the law [or, in other words, *public* education, as distinct from education which is conducted *privately*]. The magistrates of an aristocracy are accordingly those who have been true to the institutions of their state [i.e. its system of public education]. Such men must necessarily be looked upon as the best [*aristoi*]; and this is the origin of the name of this form of constitution. . . . **1366 a** Monarchy, as its name indicates, is a form of constitution in which a single person (*monos*) is sovereign in all matters. It has two forms—kingship, where it conforms to some sort of constitutional system; tyranny, where there are no limits to the sovereignty it exercises.

---

[1] If a constitution is a 'way of life', different constitutions will have different sets of manners, as well as different institutions and interests.

§ 5. The end[1] pursued by each form of constitution should also be remembered by every orator. The end of each form determines the means which the people choose [who are living under the form]. The end of democracy is freedom: of oligarchy, wealth: of aristocracy, the maintenance of a system of education and institutions; that of tyranny, the protection of the tyrant. [As the ends pursued are thus different, and] as men choose their means by reference to their ends, an orator must always discriminate the particular manners, institutions, and interests which are appropriate to the particular end pursued by each form of constitution. § 6. [There is a further thing which he must also do.] An orator persuades his audience not only by his logical argument, but also by his moral appeal. Men put their trust in a speaker when he shows, by what he says, that he has certain moral qualities—qualities such as goodness, or a good will towards them, or both of these qualities. An orator should therefore be able to evince the moral qualities peculiar to each form of constitution; for the quality which is peculiar to a particular form must always be the most effective means of persuasion in addressing those who live under that form. These qualities can be learned by the same means as those previously mentioned [i.e. by understanding the end pursued by each form of constitution]: moral qualities are shown by the choice men make, and the choice they make is determined by the end which they have in view.

[1] Aristotle appears to be using the term 'end' in much the same sense in which the term 'interest' has been previously used. Having explained, in §§ 3–4, the nature of the sovereign body which an orator has to persuade under each form of constitution, he now explains the nature of the interest, or end, to which he has to appeal.

APPENDIX IV

ARISTOTLE ON THE CONSTITUTION OF ATHENS

[Aristotle's treatise on the Constitution of Athens is the one surviving example of a number of constitutional hand-books (see below, Appendix V. III. 1). The first forty chapters give a sketch of the constitutional history of Athens down to the end of the fifth century B.C.: the next thirty sketch the constitution of Athens in Aristotle's own day (about 330 B.C.).[1] Some passages are here translated, from both parts, which bear more particularly on the argument of the *Politics*.]

A. CONSTITUTIONAL HISTORY OF ATHENS

1. *The Solonian reforms* (594 B.C.): c. VIII, § 5; c. IX, § 1.

VIII, § 5. Solon—observing that the state was often plunged in dissensions, while a number of its citizens acquiesced in any turn of events, because they were too indolent to do otherwise—enacted a law expressly intended to deal with such persons. This law disfranchised, and deprived of civic rights, all who failed, in a time of civic dissension, to take up arms on either of the two sides. . . .

IX, § 1. Of the . . . features in the Solonian constitution which may be regarded as the most democratic . . . the one which is generally said to have given most power to the masses was the institution of a system of appeal to popular law-courts. When the people at large is the sovereign of the voting-urn,[2] it is the sovereign of the constitution.

2. *The policy of Peisistratus* (560–527 B.C.): c. XVI, §§ 2–4 (cf. *Politics*, Book VI, c. v, §§ 7–11).

XVI, § 2. The government of Peisistratus was moderate, and more consonant with the character of a constitutional statesman than with that of a tyrant. He was generally humane and mild, and ready to pardon offenders; and, more especially, he pursued a policy of advancing money to the poor to give them employment and to enable them to make a living by farming. § 3. There were two reasons for this policy. The first was to stop the poor from spending their time in the central city, and to spread them out over the country-side: the second was to ensure (by giving them a moderate competence and some business to engage their attention) that they should have neither the desire nor the leisure to concern themselves with public affairs. § 4. It was an additional advantage of this policy that the revenues of the state were increased by the more efficient cultivation of the land; for a tax of 10 per cent. was imposed on all the produce.

3. *The growth of Athenian democracy, and the extension of the system of state-pay* (480–431 B.C.): c. XXIV, c. XXVII, c. XLI, § 3.

XXIV, § 1. After the Persian Wars, with the state growing in confi-

---

[1] From internal references the date of the description may be fixed between 329 B.C. and 325 B.C.
[2] More exactly, 'of the pebble', or ballot ball, which each member of a popular court deposited in the urn to record his vote.

dence, and with its resources greatly increased, Aristides [as 'leader of the people'¹] counselled the people to fix their grasp on the leadership of the league [i.e. the Delian league, which united Athens and its allies in the islands and round the coasts of the Aegaean sea], and to that end to leave the country and make their home in the city. They would all find a living there, some by serving in the army, some by doing garrison duty, and others by taking part in public affairs; and they would then be able to attain a position of leadership. § 2. The people followed this advice. Assuming the control of affairs, they acted towards their allies more in the style of masters. . . . § 3. They also provided an ample subsistence for the bulk of the population by the methods which Aristides had suggested. In fact, there were at one time more than 20,000 persons who were maintained from the proceeds of the tributes, the taxes, and the contributions of the allies.² There were 6,000 members of the popular courts; 1,600 archers; 1,200 in the cavalry; 500 members of the Council; 500 on garrison in the dock-yards [i.e. in the Peiraeus], and 50 in the City [i.e. on the Acropolis]: with upwards of 700 magistrates at home, and the same number abroad. [This accounted for over 11,000 persons who were all in receipt of public pay]: in addition, when Athens was afterwards engaged in the [Peloponnesian] war, there were 2,500 in the infantry; there were 20 guard-ships [each with a crew of 200 men]; there were the ships which collected the tributes, with crews amounting to 2,000 men selected by lot for this duty; and finally there were the persons maintained at the common tables in the city-hall, the public orphans, and the gaolers, for all of whom provision was made from public funds.³

[In a later chapter the treatise adds some observations on the policy of Pericles, in the days when he was leader of the people.]

XXVII, § 1. When Pericles . . . rose to the position of popular leader . . . the constitution was carried still further in the direction of democracy. . . . Above all, he pushed the policy of the state towards the acquisition of sea-power, which had the effect of giving new confidence to the masses⁴ and making them incline the balance of the constitution in their own favour. § 2. Then . . . came the Peloponnesian War, during which the populace were shut up in the city and grew accustomed to drawing pay for their military services; and the result was that—half

¹ The leader of the people (*prostatēs tou dēmou*) was the leader of the popular party who had established a *de facto* ascendancy in the counsels of the Athenian democracy.

² Dr. E. M. Walker, in the *Cambridge Ancient History*, vol. v, p. 105, suggests that it would be uncritical to accept this figure for the fifth century—unless [as indeed Aristotle seems to do] we make it include soldiers and sailors on active service and thus relate only to times of war. Generally, he argues, the system of the fifth century was not 'a means of maintaining in idleness any class of the citizens, but . . . the means, and the sole means, of enabling all classes of the citizens alike to take their full share in the work of government'.

³ The total citizen population of Athens in the fifth century B.C., including women and children, has been reckoned at 150,000–170,000 (*Cambridge Ancient History*, vol. v, p. 11). The total number of male adult citizens would thus be about 40,000.

⁴ Cf. *Politics*, Book V, c. IV, § 8, on the 'maritime masses' and their effects.

consciously and half unconsciously—they determined to take over themselves the running of the constitution. § 3. Pericles was also the first to introduce payment for service in the popular courts, as a bid for popular support to match the wealth [and the private generosity] of his rival Cimon. § 4. . . . Inferior in private resources, it was his policy to use public funds for making gifts to the public; and he accordingly instituted a system of payment for members of the popular courts.[1] His action is sometimes criticized as a cause of the deterioration of these courts; for the attraction of pay had the steady effect of making the common people more anxious to get themselves appointed than were men of a better position. . . .

[The system of pay for judicial service was subsequently extended in two directions, to both of which the treatise refers. One was the institution of the spectators' fund (*theōrika*)—a fund intended to enable all applicants to purchase a seat in the theatre at the time of the theatrical competitions; and this is ascribed in the treatise to Cleophon, the 'leader of the people' who had succeeded Cleon (*circa* 420 B.C.), as Cleon had previously succeeded Pericles (after 429 B.C.). The other and more important direction was the institution of payment for attendance at the assembly. This came late in the day, and after the end of the Peloponnesian War—perhaps about the beginning of the fourth century. It is described as follows in a later passage in the treatise.]

XLI, § 3. Payment for attendance at the assembly was, at first, a step which they [i.e. the restored democrats, once more in control after the perturbations at the end of the Peloponnesian War] refused to take. The citizens, however, failed to attend; and the presidents of the assembly were driven to one device after another in order to induce the populace to present themselves for the purpose of ratifying measures. In these circumstances Agyrrhius began by providing an obol a day for attendance: Heraclides . . . increased it to two obols; and Agyrrhius afterwards advanced it to three.[2]

4. *The perturbations during the latter years of the Peloponnesian War* (411–403 B.C.): *the 'polity' of* 411 B.C., *and the restored democracy after* 403 B.C.: C. XXXIII, §§ 1–2 and C. XXXIV, § 1; C. XXXIV, § 3; C. XXXVI; C. XLI.

[In a constitutional crisis of the year 411, which followed a series of Athenian reverses, a plan emerged for a new Council of Four Hundred (in place of the old Council of Five Hundred) acting with a new and limited assembly of only five thousand members. At first, and for a brief period of four months, the Four Hundred took power into their

---

[1] Dr. E. M. Walker, in the *Cambridge Ancient History*, vol. v, pp. 103–4, suggests that Pericles probably also introduced (1) payment for the members of the Council and all the magistrates (other than the military), and (2) payment for soldiers and sailors on active service, over and above their allowance for rations.

[2] For a general statement of the various forms of payment see the second part of the appendix, B. 3, c. LXXII, § 2.

own hands, as a *de facto* oligarchy, and the system of moderate democracy represented by the Five Thousand existed only on paper. A new reverse shattered the power of the Four Hundred; and the moderate democracy of the Five Thousand was called into active play. The treatise describes this system—which commended itself to Thucydides, as it commended itself afterwards to Aristotle[1]—in the following terms.]

XXXIII, § 1. . . . The Four Hundred were deposed, and the management of affairs was committed to the Five Thousand, who consisted of persons possessing a military equipment. It was also voted that pay should not be given to any of the magistrates. § 2. The persons who were most responsible for the deposition of the Four Hundred were Aristocrates and Theramenes: they disagreed with their policy of keeping the management of everything in their own hands and referring nothing to the Five Thousand. The Athenians may be regarded as having had a good constitution for these times: they were engaged in war, and constitutional rights were vested in those who possessed a military equipment. XXXIV, § 1. The people, however, soon deprived the Five Thousand of their control of the constitution [probably in the next year, 410, when the fleet—the peculiar prop of democracy—won a naval victory and returned to Athens].

[Another constitutional crisis ensued, in 404–403 B.C., on the final defeat of Athens at the end of the Peloponnesian War. The following passages from the account of this crisis given in the treatise have a particular bearing on the argument of the *Politics*.]

XXXIV, § 3. It was a condition of the terms of peace [in 404 B.C.] that Athens should be governed by 'the ancestral constitution'. [Different interpretations of this term were advocated.][2] The democrats attempted to preserve [the sovereignty of] the Athenian people. Of the notables [there were two parties:] one party, composed of the members of the [oligarchical] clubs and of the *émigrés* who had returned after the peace, desired an oligarchical régime; another party, whose members did not belong to any club but otherwise enjoyed as high a repute as any of their fellow-citizens, [steered a middle course and] sought to institute

---

[1] Thucydides praises the 'good constitution' of this short period for its spirit of moderation in the mixing of oligarchical and democratic elements (VIII, 97). The short-lived constitution of 411–410 may have been the basis of Aristotle's advocacy of the 'polity' in the *Politics* (especially Book IV, cc. VIII–IX and c. XI). It may be noted that he associates the 'polity' (in Book IV, c. XIII, §§ 10–11, and elsewhere) with the limitation of constitutional rights to those who possess military equipment—the qualification which had been required for membership of the Five Thousand. It may also be noticed that commentators have detected a reference to Theramenes (the politician prominent in 411–410) in the *Politics* (Book IV, c. XI, § 19), and have suggested that Aristotle drew on his principles and policy. (But see the translator's note on that passage.)

[2] It was possible to urge that 'the ancestral constitution' was the democratic constitution which had existed (and developed) since 480. It was also possible to urge that it was the pre-democratic constitution, as it had stood in the days of Solon, just after 600 B.C. It may be noted that Aristotle refers to the 'ancestral' democracy in two passages of the *Politics*—connecting it with Solon in the first (Book II, c. XII, § 2), and contrasting it with the 'most modern' form in the second (Book V, c. V, § 10).

'the ancestral constitution' [i.e. a constitution of the Solonian type]. The last party had ... many members; but its most conspicuous leader was Theramenes. Lysander, the Spartan representative, supported the oligarchical section; and the people were intimidated by force into voting for the establishment of oligarchy.

[The oligarchy of the Thirty, which was thus established, proceeded to extreme measures, and was criticized by Theramenes.]

XXXVI, § 1. Theramenes, chafing at the ruin which the Thirty were bringing on the state, advised them to stop their violent measures, and to give the better classes a share in the conduct of affairs. The Thirty at first resisted his counsels; but when his proposals were bruited abroad among the masses, and the majority showed themselves inclined to take his side, they became afraid that he would make himself 'leader of the people' and overthrow the oligarchical clique. They accordingly made a roll of 3,000 citizens, on whom they made it appear that they intended to confer constitutional rights. § 2. Theramenes criticized this action, as he had criticized their former proceedings. He urged, in the first place, that though they proposed to confer constitutional rights on every reputable citizen, they were actually conferring them only on a body of 3,000 persons—as though all merit were confined to that body. He urged, in the second place, that they were doing two things which were as inconsistent as any two things could be: they were instituting a government based on force, and yet making it weaker [in numbers and therefore in strength] than its subjects.[1]

[Theramenes was defeated, and executed; but the Thirty were soon afterwards defeated by the democrats. The democrats instituted the régime which still existed, over 70 years later, at the time when Aristotle was writing and lecturing on politics. The account of the constitutional history of Athens given in the first part of the treatise ends with the following passage.]

XLI, § 1. ... The people, having gained the control of affairs [403 B.C.], established the constitution which is still in force [circa 329 B.C.]. ... The people may be regarded as justified in taking over control of the constitution, because it had itself effected, by its own efforts, the restoration of its power.[2] ... § 2. Henceforward, down to our own day, this system has continued, with more and more power accruing to the masses. The people has made itself sovereign in all matters, and determines all

[1] They were thus contradicting a principle which Aristotle enunciates more than once in the Politics—that those who support a constitution should be a stronger body than its opponents (see p. 80, n. L).

[2] In the previous chapter (XL, § 3) the treatise pays a striking tribute to the restored democracy. 'The way in which the Athenians handled, alike in private and in public life, the difficulties left them by their previous troubles, may be regarded as the finest and most statesmanlike on record. Not only did they cover the offences of the past by a policy of indemnity: they also repaid to Sparta, from the public funds of the state, the war-debt incurred by the Thirty [when they were in control of affairs].' This policy of acknowledging and honouring the debts incurred by a different authority, under a different constitutional system, perhaps suggested to Aristotle the question discussed in Book III of the Politics (c. III, §§ 1–2).

issues by the decrees of the assembly and the decisions of the courts, in which it has the predominant voice. Even the jurisdiction of the Council has now passed into the hands of the people, and this change may be regarded as proper. A small body is more liable to be corrupted, by bribes and by favours, than a large body.

B. The Constitution of Athens in the Fourth Century

c. XLI, § 1; c. XLIII, §§ 2–6; c. XLV, § 4; c. LXII, §§ 1–3; c. LXVIII, § 1; c. XLIX, § 3; c. XLII, §§ 3–5

[A few passages are translated which bear on the argument of the *Politics*, more especially on that of Book IV, cc. xiv–xvi, and of the first part of Book VI.]

1. *The citizen body.*

XLI, § 1. Constitutional rights are shared by all who are of citizen birth by both parents, and the enrolment of citizens in their demes[1] takes place at the age of 18.

2. *The deliberative.*

XLIII, § 2. The Council, of five hundred members, is elected by lot, fifty from each tribe. The representatives of each tribe form a presiding committee [for one tenth of the year], in an order determined by lot. . . . § 3. The members of this presiding committee (*a*) maintain a common table in their official residence, for which funds are provided by the state, and (*b*) summon the meetings both of the Council and the Assembly. The Council is summoned daily (except for holidays): the Assembly four times during the tenure of each presiding committee [i.e. about once a week]. The presiding committee prepares the agenda for the Council. . . . § 4. The committee also prepares the agenda for the four meetings of the Assembly held during [the period of] its office. One of these meetings is called the 'sovereign' meeting: in it the Assembly must confirm the magistrates in their offices, . . . handle problems of food supply and defence, . . . and deal with any impeachments which a citizen may wish to bring forward. . . . § 5. The 'sovereign' meeting held during the tenure of the sixth presiding committee of the year further considers and decides (*a*) the question whether or no any citizen should be ostracized and (*b*) any complaints against common informers. . . . § 6. Besides a 'sovereign' meeting of the Assembly there are also held, during the tenure of each presiding committee, (*a*) a meeting for petitions, at which any citizen who wishes to do so is at liberty to address the people, after depositing the olive branch of petition, on any issue he wishes to raise, whether public or private, and (*b*) two other meetings for all other subjects. At these two meetings the laws require the Assembly to handle three subjects connected with religion, three connected with heralds and embassies, and three of a secular character.

[1] Each citizen since about 500 B.C. had been enrolled in a deme or parish (in Aristotle's time there were about 150), and every citizen had to be described by the name of the deme to which he belonged. The demes were grouped together in tribes, of which there were 10. Enrolment in a deme corresponded to inscription in the voting registers in a modern state.

Sometimes subjects are handled without a preliminary vote of the Assembly that they should be taken into consideration.

XLV, § 4. The Council considers in advance any matters brought before the people, and the people cannot vote on any matter which has not been so considered and then placed on the agenda by the presiding committee. A citizen who carries a motion in the Assembly [not previously considered by the Council and placed on the agenda by the presiding committee] is liable to be prosecuted, for an unconstitutional proposal.[1]

3. *The executive.*

[The treatise gives an account of the many officers who were appointed by lot, and of the few—the generals and other military officers—who were elected by vote. The account takes the form of a long and detailed catalogue of each office. At the end of the catalogue, the treatise adds some general remarks.]

LXII, § 1. Of the magistrates appointed by lot, some . . . used formerly to be appointed from each tribe as a whole, while others . . . were apportioned among [and appointed from] the different demes. The demes, however, were in the habit of selling appointments;[2] and accordingly all the magistrates who are appointed by lot are now appointed from each tribe as a whole—with the two exceptions of the members of the Council and the guards of the dockyards, who are still assigned to [and appointed from] the different demes.   § 2. Payment is made by the state (*a*) to the members of the Assembly, at the rate of six obols for each ordinary meeting of the assembly and nine for each 'sovereign' meeting; (*b*) to the members of the popular law-courts, at the rate of three obols for each session; (*c*) to the members of the Council, at the rate of five for each session; (*d*) to the members of the presiding committee drawn from the Council, who receive a further obol a day [in addition to what they get as members of the Council] for maintenance; and (*e*) [to a number of magistrates]. § 3. The military offices may be held repeatedly: none of the others may be held more than once, with the one exception that membership of the Council may be held twice.

4. *The judicature.*

LXVIII, § 1. Most of the law courts contain 500 members. . . . When public cases have to be brought before a body of 1,000 members, two courts combine to form that body. [The most important cases] come before a body of 1,500, or three courts combined.

XLIX, § 3. Formerly the Council used to judge the designs for public buildings and the designs for Athena's robe [annually carried in procession at her festival]; but this is now done by one of the popular law-

---

[1] It may be added, in explanation of the powers of the Council, that it was (1) partly a 'second chamber', which besides preparing business for the Assembly had also the right of concurring in decrees (so that the formula ran 'Resolved by the Council and the People'), and (2) partly an administrative body, charged with the supervision of administration (and in that sense acting as part of the executive), but liable in its administrative capacity to encroachment by the Assembly.

[2] The passage in c. XLI, § 2 (see the end of Part A of this Appendix), on the corruptibility of small bodies, is illustrated by this example; see also c. XLIX, § 3 below.

courts, determined by lot, as the Council was thought to show favouritism in its judgements.[1]

5. *The military training of Athenian youth from 18 to 20.*

[The system here described was introduced after the victory of
Philip of Macedon at Chaeronea, in 338 B.C. It would seem to be the
system assumed in Book VII, c. XII, of the *Politics*. If that is the case,
Aristotle had these Athenian arrangements in his mind when he
sketched his ideal state.]

XLII, § 3. These officers [a marshal, or *kosmētēs*, in chief command
of the whole, and a master of discipline, or *sophronistēs*, at the head of
the youth of each tribe] take the youth in charge; and under them they
first make the circuit of the temples in Athens, and then proceed to the
port of the Peiraeus [5 miles away], where some of them garrison
Munychia [on the north side of the port] and others the southern side.
The Assembly also appoints two trainers for the youth, with a staff of
instructors, who teach them infantry drill, the use of the bow and javelin,
and the handling of catapults. The Assembly pays a subsistence allowance of six obols [daily] for each master of discipline and four for each
of the youth. Each master of discipline draws the allowance for the youth
of his tribe, buys the proper provisions for the common mess (each tribe
has a common table), and controls the arrangements generally. § 4. This
is the way in which the first year of training is spent. In the second year,
on the occasion when the Assembly is held in the theatre [at the Dionysiac
festival], the young men give a display of their drill before the people;
shields and spears are then issued to them by the state, and they are set
to patrol the country and to live in the guard-houses.[2] § 5. They are
thus two years on garrison duty, during which they wear the military
cloak and are exempt from all taxes. During this time they cannot sue or
be sued, in order that there may be no excuse for any leave of absence....
At the end of this period they pass on to join the general body of citizens.[3]

[It may be added, to complete the picture, that liability to military
service, in the Athenian democracy of Aristotle's time, lasted from the
age of 18 to that of 60. The citizens were arranged in 'classes' or years
(as they are in modern states with a system of universal service); and the
treatise describes, in c. LIII, the system by which the 'classes' were
called up for service in the event of war.]

[1] The interest of this passage, which shows the popular law-courts judging
on aesthetic issues, is that it may be connected with Aristotle's defence of popular
judgement in matters of art (*Politics*, Book III, c. XI, § 3).
[2] The same word, *phylaktērion*, recurs in the *Politics*, Book VII, c. XII, § 8,
in the same connexion with the country-side.
[3] 'The garrison and patrol duties had always devolved upon the young men
of Attica, but they were now organized into a new and thorough scheme of
discipline—a mild Attic approach to the stern system of Sparta. It almost
strikes one as a conscious effort to arrest the decline of the citizen army in the
face of the encroachments of the mercenary system. The ephebi in their
characteristic dress, the dark mantle and the broad-brimmed hat, are a graceful
feature of Athenian life and art from this time forward' (J. B. Bury, *History
of Greece*, pp. 827–8). Athenian democracy, we may note, even in Aristotle's
time, was a democracy of military service.

APPENDIX V

POLITICAL MISCELLANIES OF ARISTOTLE

The Aristotelian corpus contains a treatise called the *Oeconomica*, in two books. Neither of the two books is the work of Aristotle; but the first book (which consists only of six brief chapters) has some affinities with the first book of the *Politics*, and may have been written by a pupil of Aristotle, or by a pupil of one of his pupils. It is concerned with the art of household management (or 'economics' in the original sense of that word); and it deals summarily with the relations of husband and wife, the treatment of slaves, the proper building of a house, and the proper handling of household property. The second book is a curious cento belonging to a later date. Neither of the two books of the *Oeconomica* can be used to throw light on the argument of the *Politics*.

But ancient writers have left us some description, and have occasionally quoted fragments, of some genuine Aristotelian writings, now lost, which bear on the theme of politics. It will serve to illustrate the width of Aristotle's interest in that theme, and the fertility of his pen, if some account is given of these lost writings.[1] We may arrange the account in the following order:

   I. Early Political Dialogues (in the Platonic form).
  II. Political pamphlets.
 III. Political compilations, of the later period after 336 B.C.
 IV. Political correspondence.

I. EARLY POLITICAL DIALOGUES

1. A dialogue (possibly in two books) 'Concerning the Statesman' (*politikos*), in which, according to Cicero, Aristotle set out *qualem in republica principem esse conveniret*. The recorded references to its contents show that Aristotle dealt (*a*) with the sense of honour, or 'spirit', as a spur to virtue and 'the sinews of the soul' (cf. *Politics*, Book VII, c. VII), and (*b*) with the necessity for that 'release of emotion' which is mentioned, in connexion with music, in Book VIII of the *Politics*, c. VII, §§ 3–5.

2. A dialogue (according to Cicero in four books) 'Concerning Justice'.[2] The recorded references to its contents show little, except that Aristotle made a slighting reference to Sardanapalus, as he also does in the *Politics*, Book V, c. X, § 22.

3. A dialogue 'Concerning Nobility of Birth', from which some passages are quoted, in dialogue form, in a *Florilegium*, or anthology of selected pieces, made many centuries later. This may have been used in passages of the *Politics* such as Book IV, c. VIII, § 9.

---

[1] The account is based on V. Rose's collection, *Aristotelis qui ferebantur librorum fragmenta* (Leipzig 1886).

[2] The same title, as has already been noted, is also used by Plato as an alternative title for his *Republic*.

4. A dialogue 'Concerning Education', which may be the source of Plutarch's quotation from Aristotle, 'Much learning makes many troubles'. This may have been used in the latter part of Book VII and in Book VIII of the *Politics*.

5. A dialogue (or, more probably, an 'Epistle') called the *Protreptikos*, addressed to a prince of Cyprus, and exhorting him to the 'philosophic' or speculative life. This was the most famous, and perhaps the most important, of Aristotle's early writings; and its argument may perhaps be traced in the passages of the *Politics* (Book VII, cc. II–III, cc. XIV–XV) which deal with the relation of speculative to practical activity.

II. POLITICAL PAMPHLETS

1. An epistle or exhortation to Alexander 'Concerning Kingship'. The late accounts given of this pamphlet suggest (*a*) that it was written in answer to a request from Alexander; (*b*) that it so wrought upon Alexander that he was accustomed to say, on days when he had done nobody a good turn, 'To-day I was not a king: I did not help anybody'; and (*c*) that it inverted the famous dictum of Plato (that states would never prosper until kings became philosophers, or philosophers became kings), by arguing that 'for kings to be philosophers was so far from being a necessity, that it was rather a hindrance: what was really necessary was that they should be willing to hear, and ready to accept, the advice of genuine philosophers'.

2. Another epistle, or exhortation, to Alexander 'Concerning Colonies'. This is also said, in a late account, to have been written at Alexander's request, and to have dealt with the proper methods of founding colonies, on which Alexander was engaged during his conquest of the Persian Empire. The nature of the advice given by Aristotle may perhaps be guessed from the records of his letters to Alexander (see below, under IV).

III. POLITICAL COMPILATIONS, OF THE LATER PERIOD
AFTER 336 B.C.

1. The great and main compilation recorded the 'Polities', or Constitutions, of 158 Greek states, of which the *Constitution of Athens* (discovered, in a papyrus in Egypt, as recently as 1890) is the one surviving example. Most of these must have been compiled by disciples or colleagues: some may have been compiled by Aristotle himself; a later Greek commentator certainly refers to the clarity of his exposition in 'his genuine Polities'. In any case it is clear that these 'Polities' were before him, and served as his basis, in several parts of the *Politics*— e.g. in the latter half of Book II, and, more especially, in Books IV–VI, where references are repeatedly made to different constitutions.

The references in ancient authorities give us the names of some 70 or more of the states described in the compilation of 'Polities'. They range from Sinope, on the Black Sea, to Cyrene in north Africa: they extend from Marseilles (a Greek colony going back to 600 B.C.), in the western

Mediterranean, to Crete, Rhodes, and Cyprus in the East. Aristotle thus included colonial constitutions as well as those of metropolitan states; and his descriptions, covering the whole sweep of the Greek 'Dispersion', embraced states on the Aegean, Ionian, and Tyrrhenian Seas, and in the three continents of Europe, Asia, and Africa.

2. A description of the institutions (*nomima*) of the 'barbarian' or non-Greek states. The surviving fragments refer to Caria, Libya, Etruria, and Rome. The institutions described are social rather than political (e.g. the hired women-mourners of Caria, who sing the praises of the dead in front of the house, or the dissolute habits of the Etruscans); but there is also a story of the founding of Rome by Greeks returning from the siege of Troy, with captive Trojan women in their train, who were driven by a storm to the coast of Latium. If the evidence of Cicero be accepted, the description of *nomima* included *mores, instituta, disciplinas*; and under the head of Rome it may thus have contained not only the reference to the origin of the city which has just been cited, but also some account of Roman social and constitutional life about 350 B.C.

3. The claims, or pleas (*dikaiōmata*), of the Greek states. The title appears to indicate a collection of cases of international law, or, more exactly, of the rival claims of cities in inter-city disputes about boundaries. A late Byzantine writer speaks of Philip of Macedon as having used the collection in determining boundaries; but one of the surviving fragments relates to an event which may be dated some four or five years after Philip's death. If the collection is thus posterior to Philip, it may have been used by Alexander—or rather by his deputy in Greece (Antipater, who was certainly active in the Peloponnese[1] in 331 B.C.).

[Besides these three compilations of a specifically political character, other compilations, of what may be called an antiquarian kind, are also mentioned in ancient authorities. There was, for instance, a list of the victors in the national games of Greece, and a catalogue of the different dramas produced for dramatic compositions, with some account of their writers, their dates, and the success they attained. The list of victors in the games may be the basis of a reference in Book VIII, c. IV, § 8, of the *Politics*: the catalogue of dramas appears to be the basis of a reference in the same book, c. VI, § 12.[2]]

---

[1] The late Byzantine authority mentioned in the text makes Philip of Macedon say, in dramatic style (after he had settled inter-city disputes on the basis of Aristotle's compilation), 'I have laid out the land of Pelops'—i.e. determined the boundaries in the Peloponnese.

[2] The importance of these references to the list of victors in the games, and to the catalogue of dramas, is that they help to date the last two books of the *Politics*. They suggest that those books were written when such compilations had already been made—i.e. in the later period of Aristotle's life. We may be sure that Books IV–VI of the *Politics*, which presuppose the existence of the compilation of 'polities', belong to this period; and Book II of the *Politics*, which (with its accounts of Sparta, Crete, and Carthage) seems based not only on that compilation, but also on the description of the institutions of non-Greek states, may also be argued to belong to this period. Since so much of the *Politics* thus depends on the researches contained in the compilations of the later period, it seems reasonable to ascribe the whole of it to that period.

IV. POLITICAL CORRESPONDENCE

A number of Platonic Epistles survive, and they are now generally accepted as, in the main, genuine. The Epistles of Aristotle have disappeared; and we are dependent on scattered references in ancient writers for any knowledge we have of their style and their contents. In style they are reported as having shown the proper epistolary qualities—brevity, clarity, and an avoidance of complicated arguments or phrases; and one writer speaks of them as couched in a better prose than Aristotle's other writings. The two chief correspondents mentioned in the scattered references are Alexander and Antipater. Some of the passages quoted or summarized by ancient writers from Aristotle's correspondence with them deserve to be recorded.

He advised Alexander, in one of his letters, to distribute his benefits equally between the larger and smaller cities. 'The gods', he wrote, 'are equal in both; and as gratitude is a goddess, she will come to you equally from both.' He advised him also (so we are told by Plutarch) to distinguish between Greeks and non-Greeks (or 'barbarians')—dealing with the former as 'leader', and with the latter as 'master'.[1] A more personal note occurs in two other reports of Aristotle's correspondence with Alexander. One report tells us that he sought to dissuade Alexander from his fits of temper, saying, 'High spirit and anger should be shown not to inferiors but only to superiors; and *you* have not even an equal'. Another report (which comes from Aulus Gellius) tells us that Alexander wrote to him once to complain of the publication of the esoteric discourses, or lectures, which he had himself attended, and that Aristotle replied to Alexander, 'They have been published—and yet not published: they can be understood only by those who have actually heard us lecture.'

The correspondence with Antipater—with whom Aristotle had an old and close connexion, and whom he appointed his executor—has a peculiar interest; and whatever we may think of the passages quoted from his letters to Alexander, those which are quoted from his letters to Antipater seem to ring true. He explains to him (as an old friend, and in answer to current criticisms) the reasons for his marriage to the adopted daughter of the ex-slave, Hermias, who had risen to be the tyrant of Atarneus. He tells him (in a passage which is three times mentioned by Plutarch) that 'though Alexander may well be proud of being a ruler over many peoples, those who hold true views of the gods have no less reason for being proud'. When, towards the end of his life, during the popular commotions which followed on the death of Alexander, he had to leave Athens and take refuge in Euboea (saying, as he went, 'I will not let the Athenians offend twice against philo-

[1] Here Aristotle draws a distinction, and makes a gulf, which was being obliterated by the conquests and policy of Alexander, who was uniting the peoples of the eastern Mediterranean and western Asia in a Hellenistic amalgam. Eratosthenes (as reported by Strabo) was more true to the spirit of the age, when, 'refusing to agree with those who divided all mankind into Greeks and barbarians, he declared that it was better to divide men simply into the good and the bad'. See Introduction, Section III, p. lix.

sophy'),[1] he wrote to explain his action to Antipater: 'To continue to stay in Athens would only have been to court trouble:

> Pears upon pears grow old . . . and figs on figs.'[2]

One of the most remarkable passages, however, is a personal confession, which sets thought busy.[3] 'The more I am by myself, and alone, the fonder I have become of myths.' Perhaps the man who had always set so much store by received opinion in his thought about ethics and politics was beginning in his old age to look more and more to the opinion crystallized in myths as a way to those 'true views of the gods' which were a just reason for being proud.[4]

---

[1] A reference to the condemnation and death of Socrates in 399 B.C.

[2] The quotation is from the *Odyssey* (vii. 120–1), where Homer is describing the garden of Alcinous. The sting—and a pun—comes in the words 'figs on figs'. The Attic word for what we call 'a common informer' was a word connected with figs; and by 'figs on figs' Aristotle indicates the mass of 'common informers' at Athens.

[3] There is a striking comment on the passage in Jaeger's *Aristoteles*, p. 342.

[4] There are a number of references to myths in the *Metaphysics*, which are sometimes joined with references to those who have 'spoken' about the Gods, i.e. the *theologoi* or writers of theogonies (e.g. Hesiod) and of cosmogonies (e.g. Empedocles). One of these references may be quoted (Book *Λ*. c. 8). 1074 b 1 'Traditions have been handed down to posterity, from old times and the remotest ages, in the form of myth, to the effect that the heavenly bodies are gods and divinity encompasses the whole of nature. [This is the core]: the rest has been added at a later date, in mythical style, in order to persuade the masses and to serve the practical purposes of legislation and policy. [In these additions] it is said that gods are in the image of men, or in the likeness of other animate beings; and other ideas are added which are consequent or similar in character. But if we abstract the original element from these accretions, and consider that element by itself—the element, that is to say, which consisted in a belief that the 'first substances' were gods—we may well consider that *this* belief was divinely inspired; and we may go on to reflect that—while it is probably true that there has been a series of cycles, in the course of which each art and science has been repeatedly invented and carried to its height, and then has perished again—it may also be true that *these* opinions have survived [throughout] to our own day, like relics of the prime. So far, and only so far, can we see into the nature of the opinion which was held by our forefathers and ultimately derived from the originals of our kind.' (In an earlier passage of the *Metaphysics*, *A*, c. 2, Aristotle remarks that philosophy begins in wonder, and proceeds to say, **982 b 17** 'A man who is puzzled and wonders thinks himself ignorant [and tries to escape from his ignorance into wisdom], and therefore the man who is a lover of myth is also in a sense a philosopher or lover of wisdom—for myth is composed of wonders.')

With this passage we may end. It will be noticed by the reader that the idea of things having been repeatedly invented in the course of the ages recurs in the *Politics* (Book VII, c. x, § 7, and, in a slightly different form, Book II, c. V, § 16). But what he will notice even more will be Aristotle's respect for 'opinion' (*doxa*); and he may guess that this respect may explain why Aristotle, when he retired into himself, and away from the arguments of the Schools, became still fonder of myths and the old 'opinion' which they enshrined.

INDEX

The index is not exhaustive. It does not, for instance, contain all the names of persons and places mentioned in the text, but only those which seemed to the translator to be of some more particular importance. In a word, it is simply intended as a general working guide to readers and students of the type described by the translator in his preface, p. iv. (For a fuller index the reader is referred to the Oxford translation of the works of Aristotle, volume X. For a full and most useful index of the Greek text the classical scholar is referred to Richard Congreve's edition (2nd), 1874, pp. 409–91; but Congreve's references suppose a different order of the Books of the *Politics*—in which Books VII–VIII come after Book III, and Book VI is intercalated between Book IV and Book V—and this makes the use of his index difficult.) The main references are indicated in a heavier type.